0 162440 C00 17
AF841584
I

4.000

New Approaches to Modeling, Specification Selection and Econometric Inference brings together presentations of some of the new and innovative methodological research now being done in econometrics.

The contents of this volume comprise the proceedings of the first conference in the series which began as *The Austin Symposia in Econometrics* and is now known as *The International Symposia in Economic Theory and Economics*. It was held at the IC^2 Institute (Innovation, Creativity and Capital) at the University of Texas at Austin on May 10-11, 1984. The symposia in this series are sponsored by the IC^2 Institute and the RGK Foundation. This first conference was also sponsored by the Economics Department and the Center for Statistical Sciences at the University of Texas at Austin.

This volume was edited by William A. Barnett and A. Ronald Gallant. It originally appeared as Volume 30 of the *Journal of Econometrics*.

New approaches to modeling, specification selection and econometric inference

International Symposia in Economic Theory and Econometrics

Editor
William A. Barnett, *University of Texas at Austin*

Other books in the series
William A. Barnett and Kenneth J. Singleton
New approaches to monetary economics
William A. Barnett, Ernst R. Berndt, and Halbert White
Dynamic econometric modeling
William A. Barnett, John Geweke, and Karl Shell
Economic complexity

New approaches to modeling, specification selection and econometric inference

Proceedings of the First International Symposium
in Economic Theory and Econometrics

edited by

WILLIAM A. BARNETT
University of Texas at Austin
and

A. RONALD GALLANT
North Carolina State University

CAMBRIDGE UNIVERSITY PRESS

Cambridge
New York Port Chester Melbourne Sydney

Published by the Press Syndicate of the University of Cambridge
The Pitt Building, Trumpington Street, Cambridge CB2 1RP
40 West 20th Street, New York, NY 10011, USA
10 Stamford Road, Oakleigh, Melbourne 3166, Australia

© Elsevier Sequoia S.A. 1989

First published by Elsevier Sequoia S.A. 1985 as
Volume 30 of the *Journal of Econometrics*
This edition published by Cambridge University Press 1989

Printed in the United States of America

Library of Congress Cataloging-in-Publication Data

International Symposium in Economic Theory and Econometrics (1st: 1984: Austin, Tex.)
New approaches to modeling, specification selection, and econometric inference: proceedings of the First International Symposium in Economic Theory and Econometrics/edited by William A. Barnett, A. Ronald Gallant.
p. cm. – (International symposia in economic theory and econometrics)
Includes bibliographical references.
ISBN 0-521-38465-6
1. Econometric models – Congresses. I. Barnett, William A. II. Gallant, A. Ronald, 1942- . III. Title. IV. Series.
HB141.157 1984
330′.01′5195 – dc20 89-25460
CIP

DUNDEE INSTITUTE
OF TECHNOLOGY
LIBRARY
-4 DEC 1990

Contents

EDITORS' INTRODUCTION

The contents of this volume comprise the proceedings of a conference held at the IC^2 Institute at the University of Texas at Austin on May 10–11, 1984.[1] The conference title was 'New Approaches to Modeling, Specification Selection, and Econometric Inference' and was organized to bring together presentations of some of the particularly innovative new methodological research which recently has been under way in the field of econometrics. Much of this research merges statistical theory and economic theory in new ways to address problems of model specification and econometric inference. We believe that this conference included pathbreaking research and revealed some fundamental trends in the directions in which econometric research is beginning to move.

The conference that produced this proceedings volume is the first in a new conference series, called the Austin Symposia in Economics. The symposia in the series are sponsored by the IC^2 Institute at the University of Texas at Austin and are cosponsored by the RGK Foundation. The first conference was also cosponsored by the Economics Department and the Center for Statistical Sciences at the University of Texas at Austin.

Beginning with the second symposium, the proceedings of the symposia will appear as volumes in a new Cambridge University Press monograph series, entitled *The Austin Symposia in Economics*. The series is under the general editorship of William Barnett. Individual volumes in the series will often have co-editors, and the series has a permanent Board of Advisory Editors. The co-organizer of the first symposium and co-editor of its proceedings volume, which appears in this journal edition, is Ronald Gallant. The co-organizer of the second symposium and co-editor of its proceedings volume, which will appear as the first volume in the Cambridge monograph series, is Kenneth Singleton.[2] The intention of the volumes in the proceedings series is to provide refereed journal-quality collections of research papers of unusual importance in areas of currently highly visible activity within the economics profession. Because of the refereeing requirements associated with the editing of the proceedings, the volumes in the series will not necessarily contain all of the papers presented at the corresponding symposia.

May 1985

WILLIAM A. BARNETT
University of Texas at Austin

A. RONALD GALLANT
North Carolina State University

[1] IC^2 stands for Innovation, Creativity, and Capital.

[2] The title of the second symposium, to appear as the first volume of the new Cambridge monograph series, is 'New Approaches to Monetary Economics'.

Contributors

William A. Barnett
Department of Economics
University of Texas at Austin

R. L. Basmann
Department of Economics
Texas A & M University

J. B. Carlin
Department of Economics
Harvard University

A. Charnes
Department of Economics
The University of Texas at Austin

W. W. Cooper
Department of Economics
The University of Texas at Austin

Angus Deaton
Woodrow Wilson School
Princeton University

A. P. Dempster
Department of Economics
Harvard University

C. A. Diamond
Department of Economics
Utah State University

W. E. Diewert
Department of Economics
University of British Columbia

Larry Epstein
Department of Economics
University of Toronto

J. C. Frentrup
Department of Economics
University of Texas at Arlington

A. Ronald Gallant
Department of Economics
North Carolina State University

B. Golany
Department of Economics
The University of Texas at Austin

Lars Peter Hansen
Department of Economics
University of Chicago

James J. Heckman
Department of Economics
University of Chicago

Melvin J. Hinich
Department of Economics
University of Texas at Austin

David Hinkley
Department of Economics
University of Texas at Austin

A. B. Jonas
Department of Economics
Harvard University

Dale W. Jorgenson
Department of Economics
Harvard University

Terry A. Marsh
Sloan School of Management
Massachusetts Institute of Technology

John F. Monahan
Department of Economics
North Carolina State University

Yul W. Lee
Department of Economics
University of Texas at Austin

C. Parkan
Department of Economics
University of Calgary

Douglas M. Patterson
Department of Economics
Virginia Polytechnic Institute and State University

James L. Powell
Department of Economics
Massachusetts Institute of Technology

Richard Robb, Jr.
Department of Economics
University of Chicago

Peter E. Rossi
Department of Economics
Northwestern University

Ryuzo Sato
Department of Economics
New York University
and Department of Economics
Harvard University

L. Seiford
Department of Economics
The University of Texas at Austin

Daniel Slesnick
Department of Economics
University of Texas at Austin

Thomas M. Stoker
Department of Economics
Massachusetts Institute of Technology

Kenneth J. Singleton
Department of Economics
Carnegie-Mellon University and NBER

J. Sturtz
Department of Economics
University of Miami at Coral Gables

George Tauchen
Department of Economics
Duke University

Hal R. Varian
Department of Economics
University of Michigan

William Veloce
Department of Economics
Brock University

S. N. White
Department of Economics
Texas A & M University

Michael D. Wolfe
Department of Economics
University of Texas at Austin

Adonis J. Yatchew
Department of Economics
University of Toronto

Arnold Zellner
Department of Economics
University of Chicago

New approaches to modeling, specification selection and econometric inference

THE THREE-DIMENSIONAL GLOBAL PROPERTIES OF THE MINFLEX LAURENT, GENERALIZED LEONTIEF, AND TRANSLOG FLEXIBLE FUNCTIONAL FORMS

William A. BARNETT, Yul W. LEE and Michael D. WOLFE*

University of Texas at Austin, Austin, TX 78712, USA

We use the Caves and Christensen procedure to produce the regular regions of three flexible functional forms: generalized Leontief, translog, and Barnett's new minflex Laurent model. We display the regular regions in six cases with three goods using both three-dimensional color graphics and two-dimensional sections. We find that minflex Laurent generally has the largest regular region. In addition, the regular regions of that model are the most stable in shape across the six cases and always expand as real income increases. Consequently that model is especially well suited for use with income-trended time series data.

1. Introduction

Many important hypotheses in consumption theory are equivalent to restrictions on Allen–Uzawa elasticities of substitution (AUES). Hence the ability of a functional form to attain arbitrary AUES's, subject only to the restrictions of maintained economic theory, is needed in testing such hypotheses. However, Uzawa (1962) proved that it is impossible for any function to attain an arbitrary set of constant AUES's. As a result, a literature has arisen on utility function specifications having the more modest capability of being able to attain arbitrary elasticities of substitution at a single point. Such specifications are called 'flexible functional forms'.

Recently much concern has arisen about the behavior of those functional forms over finite regions (rather than at a single point). When originally proposed, those models were intended to be used only in those cases in which the specified utility function was found to be monotonically increasing and strictly quasi-concave at *each* data point. However, experience soon indicated that the available flexible functional forms tended to violate the maintained

*William A. Barnett is the Stuart Centennial Professor of Economics and the Briscoe Centennial fellow of the IC^2 Institute at the University of Texas at Austin. Yul W. Lee is a Ph.D. candidate in Finance at the University of Texas at Austin. Michael Wolfe is a Research Associate at the Center for Cybernetic Studies at the University of Texas at Austin. We are grateful to Sang Yong Han for his expert computing assistance and to Robert Basmann and Raymond Byron for their helpful comments. This research was partially supported by NSF grant SOC 8305162.

regularity conditions at many points of most data sets.[1] Since that fact became evident, information about the frequency of violation of regularity conditions nearly ceased appearing in the applied literature using flexible functional forms.[2]

However, published concern about the regional (as opposed to local) properties of flexible functional forms reappeared when those models were found to behave poorly in a number of Monte Carlo studies.[3] Since statistical inferences in econometrics depend upon the behavior of the model at every data point, it is now widely believed that those erroneous inferences in Monte Carlo studies resulted from deficiencies in the models' regional properties. The most conspicuous of those deficiencies is the models' tendency to violate maintained regularity conditions within the region of the data.

A particularly constructive approach to this problem was provided by Caves and Christensen (1980). They produced a procedure for deriving and graphically displaying the regular regions of flexible functional forms. Caves and Christensen then applied their procedure to displaying the regular regions of both the translog and generalized Leontief flexible functional forms in the two- and three-good homothetic cases and in the two-good non-homothetic case. The intent was to provide a means of determining the best available flexible functional form, or at least to determine conditions under which each flexible functional form should be preferred.

While the Caves and Christensen approach is valuable, the results of their comparisons between the generalized Leontief and translog models were disappointing. The most systematically evident results in their study were the following. The generalized Leontief model has good regional properties when preferences are near homothetic and substitutability is very low, and the translog model has good regional properties when preferences are near homothetic and all elasticities of substitution between goods are near one. These results are not surprising, since the generalized Leontief model is known to satisfy theoretical regularity conditions everywhere in the Leontief special case, which is characterized by homothetic preferences and zero substitutability; and the translog model is known to satisfy theoretical regularity conditions everywhere if and only if preferences are Cobb–Douglas.

Caves and Christensen found that the regularity properties for each model deteriorated rapidly as elasticities were moved away from those at each model's globally well-behaved special case. As a result, neither model is attractive when little prior knowledge exists about the relevant elasticities, and the selection

[1] See, e.g., Manser (1974) and Humphrey and Moroney (1975).

[2] A noteworthy exception is Moroney and Trapani (1981), who confirmed the earlier findings of frequent violations of maintained regularity conditions.

[3] See, e.g., Wales (1977), Gallant (1981), Guilkey and Lovell (1980), and Guilkey, Lovell and Sickles (1983). Other critiques of the global properties of flexible functional forms can be found in Barnett (1977, 1979, 1981), Blackorby, Primont and Russell (1977), and Flood, Finke and Theil (1983).

between models requires very strong prior knowledge about elasticities. Furthermore, throughout most of the space of relevant elasticities, neither model has attractive regional properties. Since the intent of flexible functional forms is to permit testing of arbitrary hypotheses about those elasticities, the Caves and Christensen results tend to reinforce the Monte Carlo results in suggesting that the available flexible functional forms cannot serve the purposes for which flexible functional forms originally were produced.

However, Caves and Christensen applied their procedure to exploring the properties of only the translog and generalized Leontief models, because those have been the most popular flexible functional forms. Their procedure remains applicable to selecting between newer flexible functional forms. In addition, Caves and Christensen did not consider the non-homothetic three-good case, despite the fact that that case is the one relevant to nearly all applications of those models. In the homothetic case, all models violate Engel's law and hence are generally viewed as inadmissible in the empirical literature.[4] In the two-good case, with or without homotheticity, no need exists for flexible functional forms, since Uzawa's (1962) result is irrelevant with only two goods. Hence in the two-good case, the CES model, which satisfies all regularity conditions everywhere, can be used to test arbitrary hypotheses about elasticities.[5]

We extend the Caves and Christensen results to the three-good non-homothetic cases of the translog and generalized Leontief models. We then apply the extended comparison procedure to the new minflex Laurent flexible functional form, and we display the regular regions in three-dimensional plots and in two-dimensional sections of the three-dimensional solids. Tables of relative volumes of those regular regions, using the logarithmic metric and both symmetric and non-symmetric domains, are available in Barnett and Lee (1985), who also provide the corresponding results and plots in the two-good cases. We find that the regional properties of the minflex Laurent model are preferable to those of the other two flexible functional forms, especially when used with income trended time series data. Among the three models considered, only the minflex Laurent model has the potential to serve the purposes originally contemplated for flexible functional forms.[6]

[4] For a discussion of that issue, see Barnett (1983c).

[5] In the non-homothetic case, an affine translation of the origin is required, as in Barnett (1977, 1980) and Brown and Heien (1972).

[6] Another possibility is Barnett and Jonas's (1983) Müntz–Szatz series model. Although the model is *globally* well-behaved at *all* orders of approximation, the model has a large number of parameters and has not yet been applied with either real or simulated data. As a result, that model's capabilities presently are not fully known. However, Diewert and Wales's (1984) Generalized Barnett production model seems to be promising. Although not fully flexible, the model is quasi-flexible in a sense that permits only slight compromise in the model's flexibility properties. Yet the Generalized Barnett model simultaneously is globally well-behaved. In contrast, minflex Laurent is fully flexible, but permits slight compromise in regularity at early data points in very large data regions.

2. The flexibility criterion

In this section, we define the local flexibility property that is possessed by the class of 'flexible functional forms'.

The earliest definitions of local flexibility appear to have been Diewert's (1971, 1973a, 1974). Let $f(\boldsymbol{v})$ be a function defining a consumer's preferences. The function could, for example, be a utility, indirect utility, or reciprocal indirect utility function.[7] Let $f_{\boldsymbol{\theta}}^*(\boldsymbol{v})$ be a parameterized approximation with parameter vector $\boldsymbol{\theta}$. Then $f_{\boldsymbol{\theta}}^*$ is the specification to be used in estimating f. We seek to define the flexibility of $f_{\boldsymbol{\theta}}^*$ in approximating f at an arbitrary single point, $\boldsymbol{v}_0$.

The following definition was originated by Diewert (1971, 1973a, 1974).

Definition 1. The function $f_{\boldsymbol{\theta}}^*$ is a flexible functional form if, at any point $\boldsymbol{v}_0$ and for any f, there exists $\boldsymbol{\theta}_0 = \boldsymbol{\theta}(\boldsymbol{v}_0)$ such that

$$f^*(\boldsymbol{v}_0) = f(\boldsymbol{v}_0), \quad \left.\frac{\partial f^*}{\partial \boldsymbol{v}}\right|_{\boldsymbol{v}=\boldsymbol{v}_0} = \left.\frac{\partial f}{\partial \boldsymbol{v}}\right|_{\boldsymbol{v}=\boldsymbol{v}_0}, \quad \left.\frac{\partial^2 f^*}{\partial \boldsymbol{v}\,\partial \boldsymbol{v}'}\right|_{\boldsymbol{v}=\boldsymbol{v}_0} = \left.\frac{\partial^2 f}{\partial \boldsymbol{v}\,\partial \boldsymbol{v}'}\right|_{\boldsymbol{v}=\boldsymbol{v}_0}.$$

In other words, $f_{\boldsymbol{\theta}}^*$ is a flexible functional form if it can attain arbitrary level and first- and second-order derivatives at a predetermined single point.

Flexible functional forms also frequently have been equated with second-order approximations. To render that concept rigorous, the following definition was originated by Barnett (1983a, b).

Definition 2. The function f^* can provide a second-order local approximation to f at the point $\boldsymbol{v}_0$, if there exists $\boldsymbol{\theta}_0 = \boldsymbol{\theta}(\boldsymbol{v}_0)$ such that

$$\frac{f_{\boldsymbol{\theta}_0}^*(\boldsymbol{v}) - f(\boldsymbol{v})}{\|\boldsymbol{v} - \boldsymbol{v}_0\|^2} \to 0 \quad \text{as} \quad \boldsymbol{v} \to \boldsymbol{v}_0,$$

where $\|\cdot\|$ designates the Euclidean norm.

Barnett (1983b) proved that flexibility in the Definition 1 sense is necessary and sufficient for Definition 2 to hold for any f. In fact, it can be shown that flexibility in the Definition 1 sense is sufficient for all of the other common definitions of local functional flexibility. See Barnett (1984).

[7]If f is a direct utility function, then $\boldsymbol{v}$ is a vector of goods quantities. If f is an indirect or reciprocal indirect utility function, then $\boldsymbol{v} = \boldsymbol{p}/m$ is a vector of income-normalized prices. We assume that prices and income do not appear in the direct utility function. The case of price-dependent preferences has been considered by Basmann, Molina and Slottje (1983).

The translog and generalized Leontief models both satisfy Definition 1. In addition Barnett (1983a) proved that the new minflex Laurent demand system also satisfies Definition 1. Hence the translog, generalized Leontief, and minflex Laurent demand models are locally flexible functional forms by all of the common definitions. Furthermore, the translog and generalized Leontief models both satisfy the additional property, first defined by Diewert (1971, p. 506), of possessing just enough parametric freedom to satisfy Definition 1. We shall refer to that property as the *minimality property*. Any restrictions on the parameters of either model results in the model's losing its flexibility property, according to any of its four definitions. The minflex Laurent model possesses the minimality property.[8]

As a result, the local flexibility capabilities of the three models are essentially the same. In addition, since each model satisfies the same minimality property, we should not expect any one of the three models to fit systematically better than the others. Although the minflex Laurent model possesses more parameters than the translog or generalized Leontief models, most of the minflex Laurent's coefficients are subject to imposed inequality constraints, while none of the coefficients of the other two models are subject to any inequality constraints. The translog and generalized Leontief models each possess more unconstrained free coefficients than the minflex Laurent model. With all three models satisfying the same minimality property, all three models possess *precisely the same* degree of parametric freedom.

Since no reason exists to expect systematic differences in the local flexibility of these models, relevant comparisons between the models should be based upon their greatly different regional and global properties. We explore those properties below.

3. The models

In this section, we define the three models. Let $\boldsymbol{q} = (q_1, \ldots, q_n)'$ be the vector of goods quantities, and let $\boldsymbol{p} = (p_1, \ldots, p_n)'$ be the vector of corresponding goods prices. Let $m = \boldsymbol{p}'\boldsymbol{q}$ be 'income' (or, more precisely, total expenditure), and let $\boldsymbol{v} = (v_1, \ldots, v_n)'$, where $v_i = p_i/m$. Also let $\boldsymbol{w} = (w_1, \ldots, w_n)'$, where $w_i = v_i^{1/2}$, and let the expenditure shares be $\boldsymbol{s} = (s_1, \ldots, s_n)'$, where $s_i = p_i q_i/m$.

The generalized Leontief demand model is defined such that the reciprocal indirect utility function is

$$\bar{V}(\boldsymbol{v}) = a_0 + 2\boldsymbol{a}'\boldsymbol{w} + \boldsymbol{w}'A\boldsymbol{w}, \tag{3.1}$$

[8] The minflex special case of the Laurent model was acquired by imposing as many restrictions on the full Laurent model as was possible without losing the Definition 1 flexibility property. See Barnett (1983a). Hence the minimality property holds by construction, as was formally proved in Barnett (1985, theorem 2).

where a_0 is a scalar parameter, $\boldsymbol{a}$ is a vector of parameters, and $A=[a_{ij}]$ is a symmetric matrix of parameters. Applying the modified Roy's identity, the following share equations result.[9]

$$s_i = \frac{a_i w_i + \sum_{j=1}^{n} a_{ij} w_j w_i}{\boldsymbol{a}'\boldsymbol{w} + \boldsymbol{w}'A\boldsymbol{w}}. \tag{3.2}$$

Let $\bar{\boldsymbol{w}}=(\bar{w}_1,\ldots,\bar{w}_n)'$, where $\bar{w}_i = w_i^{-1}$, and let $S=\{(i,j)\colon\ i\neq j;\ i,j=1,\ldots,n\}$. The minflex Laurent demand system is defined such that the reciprocal indirect utility function is

$$\bar{V}(\boldsymbol{v}) = a_0 + 2\boldsymbol{a}'\boldsymbol{w} + \sum a_{ii} v_i + \sum\sum_{(i,j)\in S} a_{ij}^2 w_i w_j - \sum\sum_{(i,j)\in S} b_{ij}^2 \bar{w}_i \bar{w}_j, \tag{3.3}$$

where a_0 is a scalar parameter, $\boldsymbol{a}$ is a vector of parameters, and $A=[a_{ij}]$ and $B=[b_{ij}]$ are symmetric matrices of parameters, and $a_{ij}b_{ij}=0$ for all $(i,j)\in S$.[10] Equivalently the exponents could be removed from the squared parameters, if they were estimated subject to non-negativity inequality constraints. Observe from the form of (3.3) that *all of the diagonal elements* of B are zero. Applying the modified Roy's identity, the following share equations result:

$$s_i = \frac{a_i w_i + a_{ii} v_i + \sum_{j:\, j\neq i} a_{ij}^2 w_i w_j + \sum_{j:\, j\neq i} b_{ij}^2 \bar{w}_j \bar{w}_i}{\boldsymbol{a}'\boldsymbol{w} + \sum_k a_{kk} v_k + \sum\sum_{(j,k)\in S} a_{jk}^2 w_j w_k + \sum\sum_{(j,k)\in S} b_{jk}^2 \bar{w}_j \bar{w}_k}. \tag{3.4}$$

The translog demand system is defined such that the indirect utility function is

$$\ln V(\boldsymbol{v}) = \sum_i \alpha_i \ln v_i + \tfrac{1}{2}\sum_i\sum_j \beta_{ij} \ln v_i \ln v_j, \tag{3.5}$$

where $\boldsymbol{\alpha}=(\alpha_1,\ldots,\alpha_n)'$ is a vector of parameters and $[\beta_{ij}]$ is a symmetric index

[9] See, e.g., Barnett (1983a, eq. 4.3) for the modified Roy's identity.

[10] The parametric minimality property proved in Barnett (1985, theorem 2) required imposition of the additional restrictions $a_{ij}b_{ij}=0$ for all $(i,j)\in S$. Although those restrictions need not be imposed in applications, those restrictions nevertheless always have been satisfied by our point estimates without having been imposed in advance, as a result of corner solutions acquired from the necessary non-negativity of a_{ij}^2 and b_{ij}^2. Evidently a form of complementary slackness exists. A similar phenomenon was acquired by Diewert and Wales (1984). See footnote 13 below for a relevant observation.

of parameters. Applying Roy's identity, the following share equations result:

$$s_i = \frac{\alpha_i + \sum_j \beta_{ij} \ln v_j}{\sum_j \alpha_j + \sum_i \sum_j \beta_{ij} \ln v_j}. \tag{3.6}$$

While Definition 1 captures the local properties of these three models, the models can behave very differently regionally and globally as $\boldsymbol{v}$ moves away from $\boldsymbol{v}_0$. While the 'regular regions' displayed below in section 7 best capture the regional properties, the source of the differences between the regional properties of the three models can be seen from inspecting the functional forms. In particular, the translog and generalized Leontief models are second-order Taylor expansions, while the minflex Laurent model is a special case of a second-order Laurent series expansion; the minflex special case is acquired by imposing the minimality condition discussed in section 2 to a full second-order Laurent series expansion.

The global properties of Taylor series and Laurent expansions are very different. In particular, the remainder term of a Laurent expansion varies more gradually than that of a Taylor series. The reason is that the Laurent remainder term is the sum of two terms which always move in opposite directions. The remainder term of a Taylor series expansion is that of an inherently local approximation, since the remainder rapidly varies from zero, at the center of approximation, to large values outside of the radius of convergence.

To see the source of this difference in global properties, let $\Gamma_1 = \{z^m: m = 0, 1, \dots\}$, and let $\Gamma_2 = \{z^{-m}: m = 0, 1, \dots\}$. A Taylor series seeks to use Γ_1 as the basis to span a function space. The Laurent series uses $\Gamma = \Gamma_1 \cup \Gamma_2$ as the basis. If $|z| < 1$, then z^m decreases and m increases. Hence increasing m results in increasing refinement of the approximation. So Γ_1 appears to be a reasonable basis, when $|z| < 1$. This result is consistent with the fact that the Taylor series is inherently a local approximation. Similarly if $|z| > 1$, then x^{-m} decreases as m increases, so that Γ_2 appears to be a reasonable basis when $|z| > 1$. To acquire a basis applicable over a larger region, we need the Laurent basis, $\Gamma = \Gamma_1 \cup \Gamma_2$.[11]

The three models also differ in the extent to which the parameters must be restricted to acquire global monotonicity and strict quasi-concavity of prefer-

[11] This spanning property, which motivated the use of the Laurent series in producing the minflex Laurent model, is not the property that accounts for most other applications of the Laurent series in mathematics. In those applications, the objective is to deal with singularities. See Barnett (1983a, app. B, C). That capability could be used if the model were treated as an expansion about the origin, which typically is a singular point of functions in economics. However, that capability is irrelevant to the properties of the minflex Laurent, since we maintain it as a model. We do not treat it as an expansion approximating an unknown form.

ences. The translog is everywhere well-behaved only in the Cobb–Douglas special case. The generalized Leontief is everywhere well-behaved if all of the coefficients are non-negative. The minflex Laurent model is everywhere well-behaved if all of the coefficients are non-negative; however, many of the coefficients already are restricted to be non-negative in the specification of the model. As a result, the subset of the parameter space within which the minflex Laurent is everywhere well-behaved is generally larger than that for each of the other two models.

The discussion above is suggestive of the possibility that the behavioral regularity properties of the minflex Laurent model may be the best of those of the three models. However, the discussion provides no proof, since we maintain the minflex Laurent as a model, rather than treat it as a series expansion, and since we need to know which model is most likely to be well-behaved throughout the region of the data, regardless of whether or not the model is well-behaved everywhere. To explore that matter systematically and rigorously, we use the Caves and Christensen approach to map each model's regular regions.

Each of the three models requires a parameter normalization, since the share equations are homogeneous of degree zero in the parameters. With the generalized Leontief model, we use the normalization

$$2\sum_i a_i + \sum_i \sum_j a_{ij} = 1. \tag{3.7}$$

With the minflex Laurent model, we use the normalization

$$\sum_i a_{ii} + 2\sum_i a_i + \sum\sum_{(i,j)\in S} a_{ij}^2 - \sum\sum_{(i,j)\in S} b_{ij}^2 = 1. \tag{3.8}$$

With the translog model, we use the usual normalization

$$\sum_i \alpha_i = -1. \tag{3.9}$$

4. Elasticities of the models

To derive and display the regular regions of the three models, we need the formulas for the models' elasticities. We provide those formulas in this section. A number of functions appear repeatedly as factors or terms in the elasticity formulas. In order to permit concise expression of the elasticity formulas, we therefore supply those subfunctions in the appendix and use them in the following expressions.

The following results apply to the minflex Laurent model for each good $i = 1, \ldots, n$. The share equation of good i is

$$s_i = A_i / D.$$

The income elasticity of good i is

$$\eta_{i0} = \left(\bar{A}_i'/\bar{A}_i - D'/D\right)m.$$

The rate of change of that income elasticity is

$$\frac{\partial \eta_{i0}}{\partial m} = \left(\frac{\bar{A}_i''\bar{A}_i - \bar{A}_i'^2}{\bar{A}_i^2} - \frac{D''D - D'^2}{D^2}\right)m + \frac{\eta_{i0}}{m}.$$

The 'own' AUES for good i is

$$\begin{aligned}\sigma_{ii} = \Bigg\{ &- \sum_{j:\, j\neq i} a_j w_j - a_i w_i s_i^{-2}\Bigg(\sum_{j:\, j\neq 1} A_j\Bigg)^2\Bigg(\sum_j A_j\Bigg)^{-2} - w_i s_i^{-2}\sum_{j:\, j\neq i} a_{ij}^2 w_j \\ &- \Bigg[3s_i^{-2}\Bigg(\sum_j A_j^2\Bigg)\Bigg(\sum_j A_j\Bigg)^{-2} - 2s_i^{-1}\Bigg(\sum_{j:\, j\neq i} A_j\Bigg)\Bigg(\sum_j A_j\Bigg)^{-1} \\ &+ 3s_i^{-2}\Bigg(\sum\sum_{(j,k)\in\Delta_i} A_j A_k\Bigg)\Bigg(\sum_j A_j\Bigg)^{-2}\Bigg]\bar{w}_i \sum_{j:\, j\neq i} b_{ij}^2 \bar{w}_j \\ &- 4\sum\sum_{(j,k)\in\Delta_i} b_{jk}^2 \bar{w}_j \bar{w}_k \Bigg\} \Bigg/ 2D,\end{aligned}$$

where $\Delta_i = \{(j,k)\colon\ j\neq k,\ j\neq i,\ k\neq i\}$. The AUES between goods i and j is

$$\begin{aligned}\sigma_{ij} = \Bigg\{ & s_i^{-1}s_j a_i w_i + s_i s_j^{-1} a_j w_j + s_i^{-1}s_j^{-1}\left(a_i w_i A_i + a_j w_j A_j\right) \\ &\times\Bigg(\sum_{k\in\Lambda_{ij}} A_k\Bigg)\Bigg(\sum_k A_k\Bigg)^{-2} - \sum_{k\in\Lambda_{ij}} a_k w_k + s_i^{-1}s_j^{-1}a_{ij}^2 w_i w_j \\ &- \Bigg[2 - 3\left(s_i s_j^{-1} + s_j s_i^{-1}\right) + s_i^{-1}s_j^{-1}\Bigg(\sum_{k\in\Lambda_{ij}} A_k^2\Bigg)\Bigg(\sum_k A_k\Bigg)^{-2} \\ &- 2\left(s_i^{-1} + s_j^{-1}\right)\Bigg(\sum_{k\in\Lambda_{ij}} A_k\Bigg)\Bigg(\sum_k A_k\Bigg)^{-1}\Bigg] b_{ij}^2 \bar{w}_i \bar{w}_j \\ &- 4s_i^{-1}\Bigg(A_i - \sum_{k:\, k\neq i} A_k\Bigg)\Bigg(\sum_k A_k\Bigg)^{-1}\sum_{k\in\Lambda_{ij}} b_{ik}^2 \bar{w}_i \bar{w}_k \\ &- 4s_j^{-1}\Bigg(A_j - \sum_{k:\, k\neq j} A_k\Bigg)\Bigg(\sum_k A_k\Bigg)^{-1}\sum_{k\in\Lambda_{ij}} b_{jk}^2 \bar{w}_j \bar{w}_k \Bigg\} \Bigg/ 2D,\end{aligned}$$

where $\Lambda_{ij} = \{k\colon\ k\neq i,\ k\neq j\}$.

The following results apply to the translog model for each good $i=1,\ldots,n$. The share equation of good i is

$$s_i = B_i/E.$$

The income elasticity of good i is

$$\eta_{i0} = 1 + (B_i'/B_i - E'/E)m.$$

The rate of change of that income elasticity is

$$\frac{\partial \eta_{i0}}{\partial m} = \left(\frac{B_i''B_i - B_i'^2}{B_i^2} - \frac{E''E - E'^2}{E^2} \right) m + \frac{\eta_{i0} - 1}{m}.$$

The 'own' AUES for good i is

$$\sigma_{ii} = 1 + (a_{ii}B_i^{-1} - 1)s_i^{-1} + \left(\sum_j \sum_k a_{jk} - 2s_i^{-1} \sum_j a_{ij} \right) \Big/ E,$$

and the AUES between goods i and j is

$$\sigma_{ij} = 1 + \left[a_{ij}s_i^{-1} - s_i^{-1} \sum_k a_{ik} - s_j^{-1} \sum_k a_{jk} + \sum_h \sum_k a_{hk} \right] \Big/ E.$$

The following results apply to the generalized Leontief model for each good $i=1,\ldots,n$. The share equation of good i is

$$s_i = C_i/F.$$

The income elasticity of good i is

$$\eta_{i0} = (\bar{C}_i'/\bar{C}_i - F'/F)m.$$

The rate of change of that income elasticity is

$$\frac{\partial \eta_{i0}}{\partial m} = \left(\frac{\bar{C}_i''\bar{C}_i - \bar{C}_i'^2}{\bar{C}_i^2} - \frac{F''F - F'^2}{F^2} \right) m + \frac{\eta_{i0}}{m}.$$

The 'own' AUES for good i is

$$\sigma_{ii} = \left[- \sum_{j:\, j \neq i} a_j w_j - 2a_i w_i s_i^{-2} \left(\sum_{j:\, j \neq i} C_j \right)^2 F^{-2} - w_i s_i^{-2} \sum_{j:\, j \neq i} a_{ij} w_j \right] \Big/ 2F,$$

and the AUES between goods i and j is

$$\sigma_{ij} = \left[s_i^{-1} s_j a_i w_i + s_i s_j^{-1} a_j w_j + s_i^{-1} s_j^{-1} (a_i w_i + a_j w_j) \left(\sum_{k \in \Lambda_{ij}} C_k \right) F^{-2} \right.$$

$$\left. - \left(\sum_{k \in \Lambda_{ij}} a_k w_k \right) + s_i^{-1} s_j^{-1} a_{ij} w_i w_j \right] \Big/ 2F.$$

With any of these models, the Cournot (uncompensated) price elasticity of demand for good i with respect to the price of good j, η_{ij}, can be computed from the income elasticities and the AUES's by using the following formula:

$$\eta_{ij} = s_j(\sigma_{ij} - \eta_{i0}). \tag{4.1}$$

5. Solution for the coefficients

For each model, we shall solve for the set of incomes and prices such that the (direct) utility function is monotonically increasing and strictly quasi-concave within that set. However that set, called the regular region by Caves and Christensen (1980), depends upon the parameters of the model. As a result, we need a means of selecting the parameter values at which the regular region is to be displayed. We follow the Caves and Christensen procedure of selecting various values for certain properties of demand, often stated in terms of elasticities, and then solving for the parameter values that produce those properties at the point $(m, \boldsymbol{p}) = \mathbf{1}$. At each such resulting vector of parameter values, we shall display the regular region for the corresponding model. This procedure is consistent with the usual data normalization convention, by which $\boldsymbol{v}$ is set equal to $\mathbf{1}$ at a median observation.

We now consider the number of properties of demand that must be restricted at $(m, \boldsymbol{p}) = \mathbf{1}$ to permit unique solution for the parameter values for each model. In general with systems of non-linear equations, equality of the number of equations and the number of unknowns is neither necessary nor sufficient for existence of a unique solution for the unknowns. This fact becomes especially relevant when inequality constraints are imposed upon some of the unknowns.[12] Hence we cannot immediately be certain that we need as many restrictions on the properties of demand as there are parameters in the model.

[12] For example, in the minflex Laurent model the squared parameters could be replaced by unsquared coefficients subject to non-negativity restrictions. For a convenient estimation procedure with that model, see Barnett (1983a, sec. 9.1).

However, this matter is resolved immediately by Definition 1 and the minimality condition, both of which are satisfied by all three models. The first equation in Definition 1 is needed only to acquire the intercept of each (reciprocal) indirect utility function, $V(\boldsymbol{v})$ or $\bar{V}(\boldsymbol{v})$. However, the intercept produces only a monotonic transformation of utility and therefore is arbitrary. As a result, we can drop the intercept of the (reciprocal) indirect utility function and also the first equation in Definition 1. We then find that we need as many equations as there are first- and second-order derivatives. Hence in the two-good case, we need five equations, and in the three-good case, we need nine equations. Of course we could use more restrictions on elasticities than actually necessary, so long as the resulting set of restrictions does not violate theory, and so long as at least five of the equations are functionally independent in the two-good case, and at least nine of the equations are functionally independent in the three-good case.

Since restrictions will be used on both income elasticities and their income derivatives, redundancies between restrictions can result from either of the following identities:[13]

$$\sum_i s_i \eta_{i0} = -1, \tag{5.1}$$

$$\sum_i s_i \left[\frac{\partial \eta_{i0}}{\partial m} + \frac{\eta_{i0}}{m} (\eta_{i0} - 1) \right] = 0. \tag{5.2}$$

Eq. (5.2) is acquired by differentiating the well-known eq. (5.1) with respect to m.[14] From eq. (5.1), we see that no more than $n-1$ income elasticities can be set independently. From eq. (5.2), we see that once $n-1$ income elasticities have been set, no more than $n-1$ of the derivatives $\partial \eta_{i0}/\partial m$ $(i = 1, \ldots, n)$ can be set independently.

5.1. Three-good case

In the three-good cases, we fix the values of $(\theta_1, \theta_2, \theta_3, \theta_4, \theta_5)$ and solve the following system of nine equations for each model's coefficients at $p_1/p_2 = m/p_2 = m/p_3 = 1$:

[13] In the minflex Laurent case, we use such redundant restrictions to equate the number of equations with the number of parameters, since the computer program used to solve the system requires the system to possess that completeness property. The number of parameters in the minflex Laurent model exceeds the number of functionally independent restrictions needed to assure uniqueness of the solution for the parameters. In applications, this fact usually is reflected by corner solutions at zero for some of the squared coefficients. See Barnett (1983a, sec. 9.1).

[14] Eq. (5.1) is acquired by differentiating the budget constraint with respect to m.

Normalization equation, (3.7), (3.8), or (3.9), (5.3)

$$s_1 = \tfrac{1}{3}, \tag{5.4}$$

$$s_2 = \tfrac{1}{3}, \tag{5.5}$$

$$\eta_{10} = \theta_1, \tag{5.6}$$

$$\eta_{20} = \theta_2, \tag{5.7}$$

$$\partial\eta_{10}/\partial m = 0, \tag{5.8}$$

$$\sigma_{12} = \theta_3, \tag{5.9}$$

$$\sigma_{23} = \theta_4, \tag{5.10}$$

$$\sigma_{31} = \theta_5. \tag{5.11}$$

For each of the three models, the result is a vector of values for the model's parameters.[15] The regular region then is produced for those parameter values, as discussed in section 6. This process is repeated six times, for each of six different choices of the quintuple $(\theta_1, \theta_2, \theta_3, \theta_4, \theta_5)$.[16] The result is six vectors of parameters for each model and six corresponding regular regions.

6. Determination of the regular regions

6.1. *Three-good case*

Let $x = (p_1/p_2)^{1/2}$, $y = (m/p_2)^{1/2}$, and $z = (m/p_3)^{1/2}$. Then the regular region is defined to be the set of (x, y, z) points at which the reciprocal indirect utility function is monotonically increasing and strictly quasi-concave; or, with the translog, the set of (x, y, z) points at which the indirect utility function is monotonically decreasing and strictly quasi-convex.

With the generalized Leontief and minflex Laurent models, the monotonicity condition is $\partial\bar{V}/\partial v > 0$ or equivalently $A_i(x, y, z) > 0$ for $i = 1, 2, 3$. With the

[15] To permit use of a standard system solver computer program, we added three redundant equations in the minflex Laurent case, in order to equate the number of equations with the number of unknowns.

[16] The six cases, to be designated as cases 1–6 respectively, are $(\theta_1, \theta_2, \theta_3, \theta_4, \theta_5) =$ (1.05, 0.95, 1.5, 1.5, 1.5), (1.2, 0.8, 0, 1.5, 1.5), (1.7, 0.3, −0.5, 1.5, 1.5), (1.05, 0.95, 0.5, 0.5, 0.5), (1.2, 0.8, 0, 0.5, 0.5), (1.7, 0.3, −0.1, 0.5, 0.5). We do not restrict any of the own elasticities of substitution, σ_{ii}, at the base point, since we restrict all of the off-diagonal elements of the matrix $[\sigma_{ij}]$. As a result, the σ_{ii}'s are fixed at the base point by the identity $\Sigma_i s_i \eta_{ij} = -s_j$ and eq. (4.1).

translog, the monotonicity condition is $\partial V/\partial v < 0$ or equivalently $A_i(x, y, z) < 0$ for $i = 1, 2, 3$. The quasi-concavity or quasi-convexity condition is satisfied if $\sigma_{11}(x, y, z) < 0$ and $\sigma_{11}(x, y, z)\sigma_{22}(x, y, z) - (\sigma_{12}(x, y, z))^2 > 0$. As a result, the regular regions for the generalized Leontief and minflex Laurent models are

$$r_k = \{(x, y, z) \colon \sigma_{11}(x, y, z) < 0, \sigma_{11}(x, y, z)\sigma_{22}(x, y, z) - (\sigma_{12}(x, y, z))^2 > 0, A_i(x, y, z) > 0, i = 1,2,3\},$$

for $k = 1, \ldots, 6$. The regular regions for the translog model for $k = 1, \ldots, 6$ are

$$R_k = \{(x, y, z) \colon \sigma_{11}(x, y, z) < 0, \sigma_{11}(x, y, z)\sigma_{22}(x, y, z) - (\sigma_{12}(x, y, z))^2 > 0, A_i(x, y, z) < 0, i = 1,2,3\}.$$

However, in the three-good case, the regular regions cannot be fully displayed in two dimensions. As a result, in addition to displaying the regions as three-dimensional solids in color, we also display sections of the regular regions at three different fixed values of z.

7. The results

In applications of flexible functional forms, the three-good case tends to be particularly important. Three-dimensional plots of the models' regular regions are displayed in the three-good case in figs. 1, 2 and 3. The displayed solids are the intersections of the regular regions with the hexahedron $\{(x, y, z) \in R^3\colon 0 \leq x \leq 10,\ 0 \leq y \leq 10,\ 0 \leq z \leq 100\}$, which defines the range of the variables over which we solved for the regular regions' boundaries.

In the six cases that we consider, fig. 1 displays the regular regions of the generalized Leontief and minflex Laurent models. The large light blue or light green solids are the regular regions of the minflex Laurent model. The red or brownish-red region is the regular region of the generalized Leontief model. The shades of color are not necessarily the same between cases. Observe that the regular region of the generalized Leontief model is much smaller than that of the minflex Laurent model and is usually almost entirely contained within that of the minflex Laurent model.

In fig. 2, we superimposed the corresponding regular regions of the translog model onto fig. 1. Hence the regular regions of all three models are displayed in fig. 2 simultaneously. The regular region of the translog model is displayed in dark-blue or medium-blue. The regular regions of the translog are much smaller than those of the minflex Laurent in all six cases. The translog model's regular regions are especially small in cases 3, 5 and 6.

Case 1 $\sigma=(1.5, 1.5, 1.5)$, $\eta=(1.05, 0.95, 1.0)$.

Case 2 $\sigma=(0.0, 1.5, 1.5)$, $\eta=(1.2, 0.8, 1.0)$.

Case 3 $\sigma=(-0.5, 1.5, 1.5)$, $\eta=(1.7, 0.3, 1.0)$.

Case 5 $\sigma=(0.0, 0.5, 0.5)$, $\eta=(1.2, 0.8, 1.0)$.

Case 6 $\sigma=(-0.1, 0.5, 0.5)$, $\eta=(1.7, 0.3, 1.0)$.

Fig. 1. Three-dimensional regular regions in the three-good cases for the generalized Leontief and minflex Laurent models. The regular regions are brownish red and light greenish-blue for the generalized Leontief and minflex Laurent models, respectively. The models' parameters are chosen in each case such that $\boldsymbol{\sigma}=(\sigma_{12}, \sigma_{23}, \sigma_{31})$ and $\boldsymbol{\eta}=(\eta_{10}, \eta_{20}, \eta_{30})$ are as labeled above, when $p_1/p_2=m/p_2=m/p_3=1$ and $s_1=s_2=s_3=\frac{1}{3}$. For case **4**, see fig. 3.

Case 1 $\sigma=(1.5, 1.5, 1.5)$, $\eta=(1.05, 0.95, 1.0)$.

Case 2 $\sigma=(0.0, 1.5, 1.5)$, $\eta=(1.2, 0.8, 1.0)$.

Case 3 $\sigma=(-0.5, 1.5, 1.5)$, $\eta=(1.7, 0.3, 1.0)$.

Case 5 $\sigma=(0.0, 0.5, 0.5)$, $\eta=(1.2, 0.8, 1.0)$.

Case 6 $\sigma=(-0.1, 0.5, 0.5)$, $\eta=(1.7, 0.3, 1.0)$.

Fig. 2. Three-dimensional regular regions in the three-good cases for all three models. The regular regions are brownish red, light greenish-blue, and medium-dark blue for the generalized Leontief, minflex Laurent, and translog models, respectively. The models' parameters are chosen in each case such that $\boldsymbol{\sigma}=(\sigma_{12}, \sigma_{23}, \sigma_{31})$ and $\boldsymbol{\eta}=(\eta_{10}, \eta_{20}, \eta_{30})$ are as labeled above, when $p_1/p_2 = m/p_2 = m/p_3 = 1$ and $s_1 = s_2 = s_3 = \frac{1}{3}$. For case 4, see fig. 3.

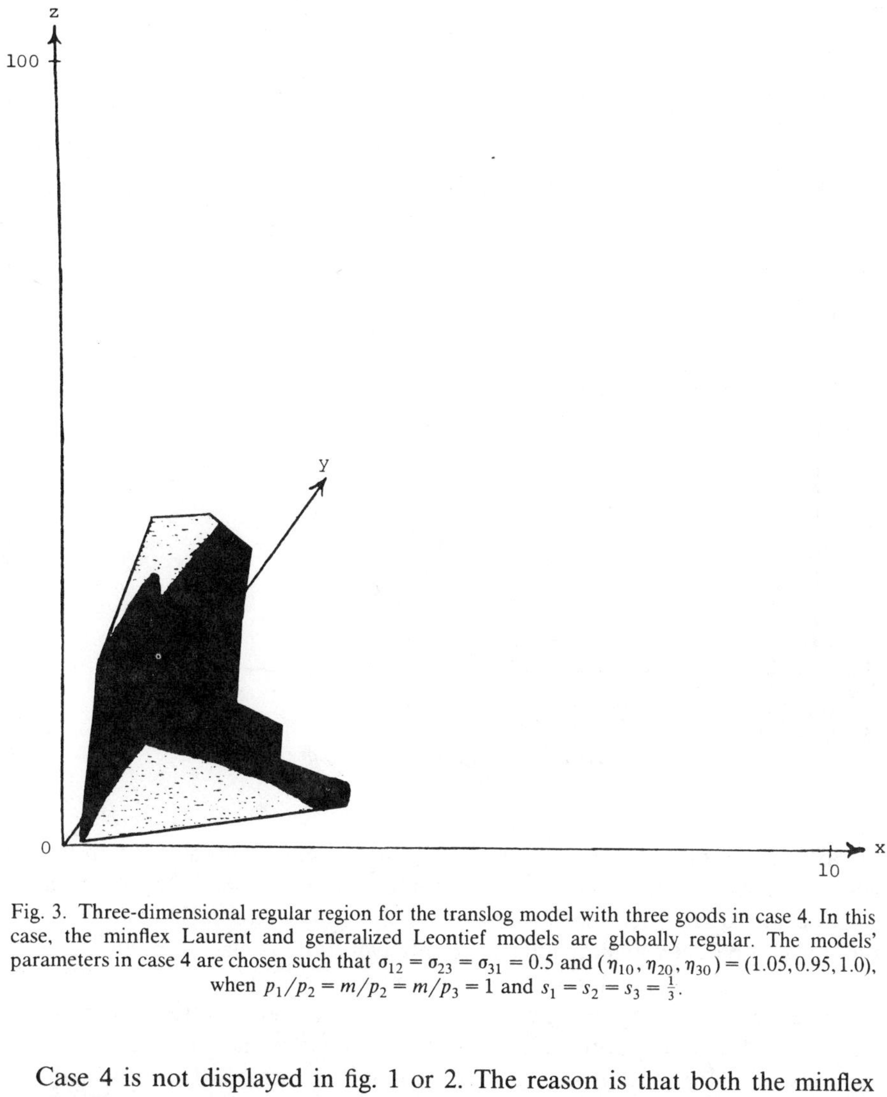

Fig. 3. Three-dimensional regular region for the translog model with three goods in case 4. In this case, the minflex Laurent and generalized Leontief models are globally regular. The models' parameters in case 4 are chosen such that $\sigma_{12} = \sigma_{23} = \sigma_{31} = 0.5$ and $(\eta_{10}, \eta_{20}, \eta_{30}) = (1.05, 0.95, 1.0)$, when $p_1/p_2 = m/p_2 = m/p_3 = 1$ and $s_1 = s_2 = s_3 = \frac{1}{3}$.

Case 4 is not displayed in fig. 1 or 2. The reason is that both the minflex Laurent and generalized Leontief models are globally regular in that case throughout the entire non-negative orthant. The regular region of the translog model in case 4 is displayed in fig. 3.[17]

Figs. 4 and 5 exhibit the labeling and orientation of the axes used in figs. 1–3. Fig. 4 displays the orientation usually used in figs. 1–3. However, that orientation cannot reveal the discontinuity in the minflex Laurent model's regular region in case 6. In addition, that orientation cannot adequately display the regular region of the translog model in case 6. Therefore, the axes were rotated twice (with the z axis remaining vertical). The resulting orientations of

[17]Color was not needed in fig. 3, since only one three-dimensional solid appears in that figure.

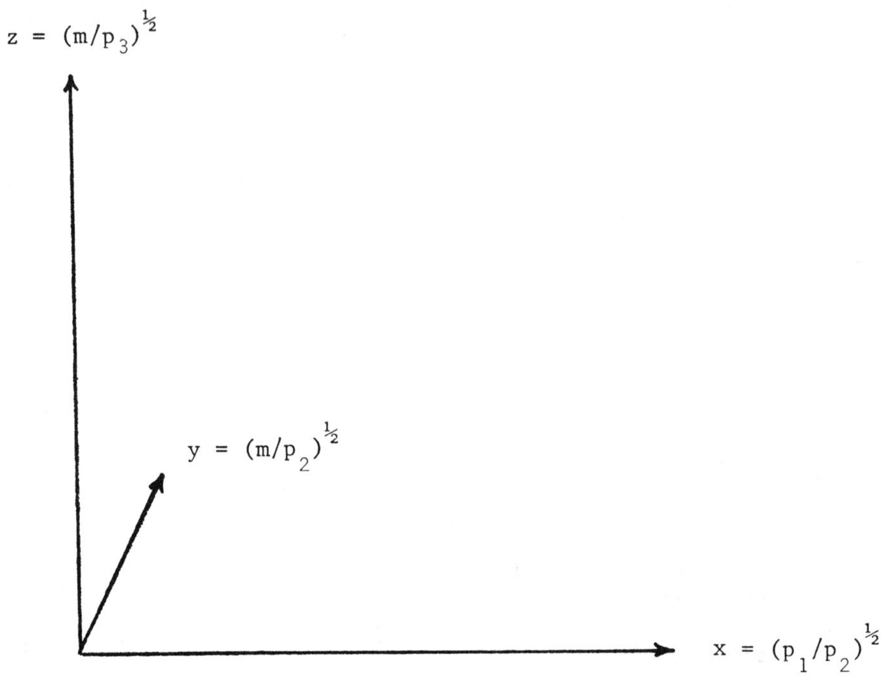

Fig. 4. Orientation and labeling of axes in figs. 1–3 for cases 1–5. The axis labeled y is normal to the page plane and points down into the page.

the axes are displayed in fig. 5. The first 90° rotation produced case 6 in fig. 1, which reveals the discontinuity in the minflex Laurent model's regular region. The second 90° rotation produced case 6 in fig. 2, which reveals the location of the translog model's small regular region. Recall from its elasticities that case 6 was intentionally selected to be very asymmetric.

The effect of growing real income can be seen by moving vertically up the z axis. Barnett (1985) has proved that the minflex Laurent model's regular region expands as real income grows, so that the model is particularly well-suited for use with income-trended time series data. As a result, it is particularly important to compare the size of the three models' regular regions as real income grows. To pursue that comparison further, we cut three horizontal sections through each of the three-dimensional solids of figs. 1–3. The sections are at three successively higher levels of $z=(m/p_3)^{1/2}$, namely at $z=1$, 5 and 10.

We do not display sections at levels of z below $z=1$, since with time series data the behavior of the model is most relevant at recent observations. With the data normalized such that $z=1$ at the median observation and with z

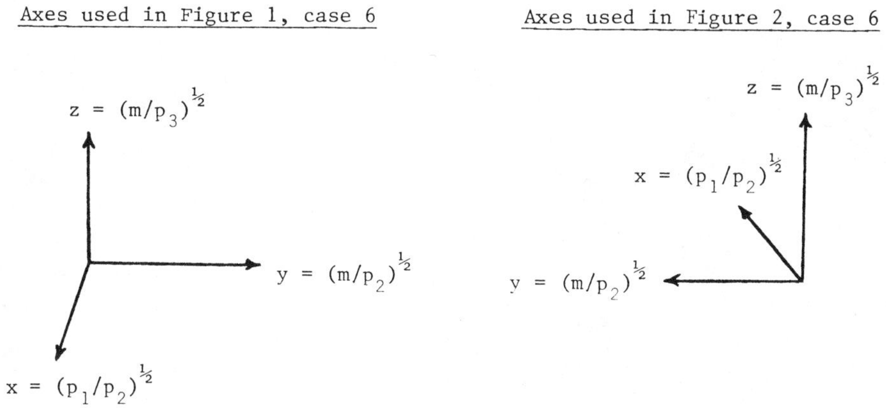

Fig. 5. Orientation and labeling of axes in figs. 1 and 2 for case 6. The axis labeled x is normal to the page plane. In fig. 1, the x axis for case 6 points up out of the page. In fig. 2, the x axis for case 6 points down into the page.

trending upwards over time, the observations with $z < 1$ would be from the oldest data. The resulting sections are displayed in figs. 6–11 and are labeled A, B and C, corresponding to $z = 1$, 5 and 10, respectively. On the figures, the names of the three models are abbreviated as follows: translog (TL), generalized Leontief (GL), and minflex Laurent (ML). The sections plot the boundaries of the regular regions of each model in the y versus x plane at fixed values of z. An arrow indicates the side of the boundary on which the regular region lies. The boundaries of the regular region for the minflex Laurent model are designated by solid lines. The boundaries of the translog regular region are designated by a dotted line. The boundaries of the generalized Leontief regular region are designated by alternate dashes and dots.

The following conclusions follow from the sections in the three-good cases and are consistent with the two-good figures in Barnett and Lee (1985). With the translog model, the only points of the data space that are always in the regular region are points in the immediate neighborhood of the unit vector. Recall that the parameters were selected such that regularity was imposed at the point **1**. In the majority of cases, the translog's regular region is very small in each displayed section with three goods. The exception is case 1, which is the closest case to the Cobb–Douglas, at which the translog is known to be globally well-behaved. In three of the sections, the translog model possesses no regular region at all.

With the generalized Leontief model, again the only points of the data space that are always in the regular region are those very close to the unit vector. In four of the figures, the regular region for the generalized Leontief model was the entire non-negative orthant. However, in all of those same four cases plus

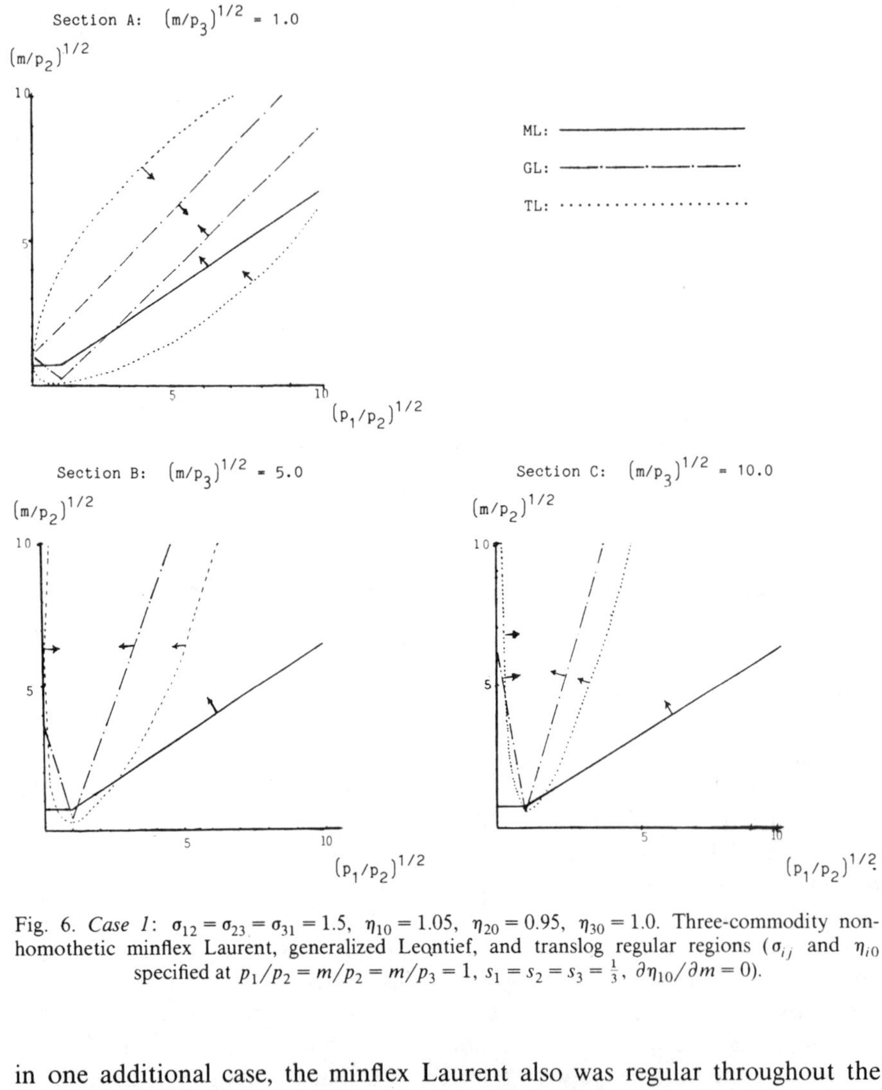

Fig. 6. *Case 1*: $\sigma_{12}=\sigma_{23}=\sigma_{31}=1.5$, $\eta_{10}=1.05$, $\eta_{20}=0.95$, $\eta_{30}=1.0$. Three-commodity non-homothetic minflex Laurent, generalized Leontief, and translog regular regions (σ_{ij} and η_{i0} specified at $p_1/p_2=m/p_2=m/p_3=1$, $s_1=s_2=s_3=\frac{1}{3}$, $\partial\eta_{10}/\partial m=0$).

in one additional case, the minflex Laurent also was regular throughout the entire non-negative orthant. The regular region of the generalized Leontief is never empty in any of the figures. Without extremely strong prior information about elasticities and very little data dispersion, there appears to be very little chance that a data field could reasonably be expected to fall within the translog or generalized Leontief models' regular regions.

As expected, the width of each regular region of the minflex Laurent model, when not infinite, expands as 'real income', $(m/p_2)^{1/2}$, grows. In addition, that model's regular regions are usually considerably larger than the corresponding regular regions of the other two models and usually contain most, if not all, of

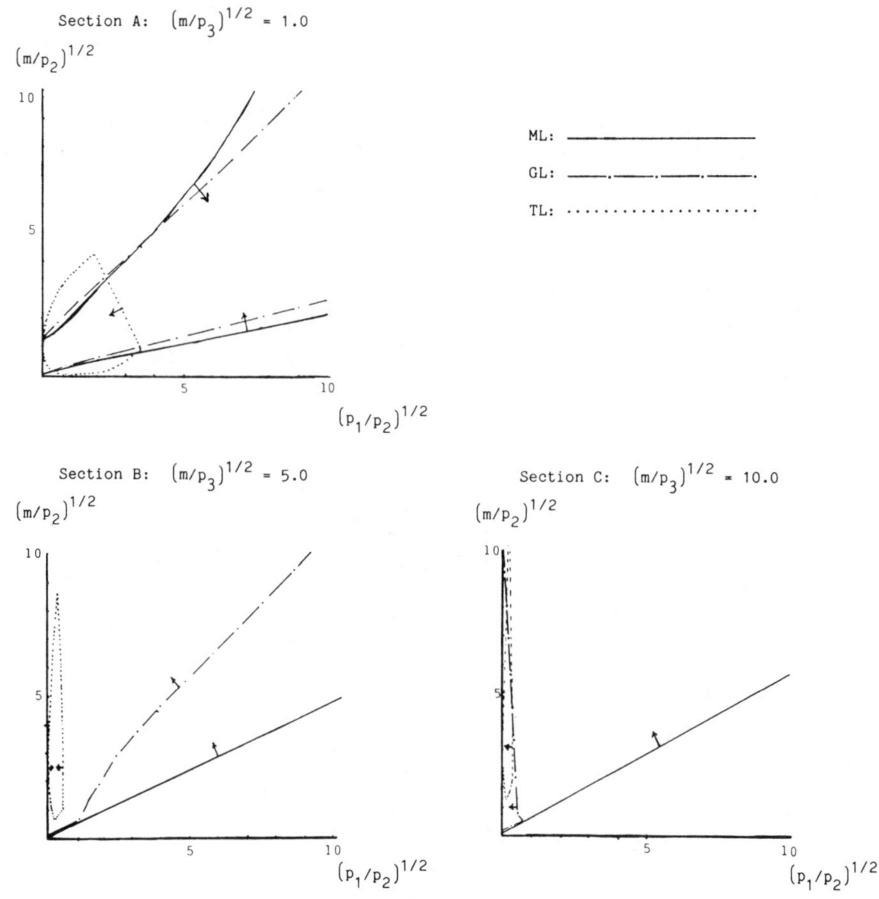

Fig. 7. *Case 2*: $\sigma_{12} = 0.0$, $\sigma_{23} = \sigma_{31} = 1.5$, $\eta_{10} = 1.2$, $\eta_{20} = 0.8$, $\eta_{30} = 1.0$. Three-commodity non-homothetic minflex Laurent, generalized Leontief, and translog regular regions (σ_{ij} and η_{i0} specified at $p_1/p_2 = m/p_2 = m/p_3 = 1$, $s_1 = s_2 = s_3 = \frac{1}{3}$, $\partial\eta_{10}/\partial m = 0$).

the points in the corresponding regular regions of the other two models. The superior regularity of the minflex Laurent model is particularly dramatic at high real income, as was easily anticipated from inspection of figs. 1 and 2.

The square root transformation used in defining the axes and the ranges of values used along each axis were selected to agree with the selections made by Caves and Christensen (1980). In addition the values of z at which the sections were produced were selected to span the Caves and Christensen search range. We exceeded their search range only along the vertical axis in the three-dimensional plots displayed in figs. 1, 2 and 3. Nevertheless, a case could be made for using the logarithmic transformation, rather than the square root transforma-

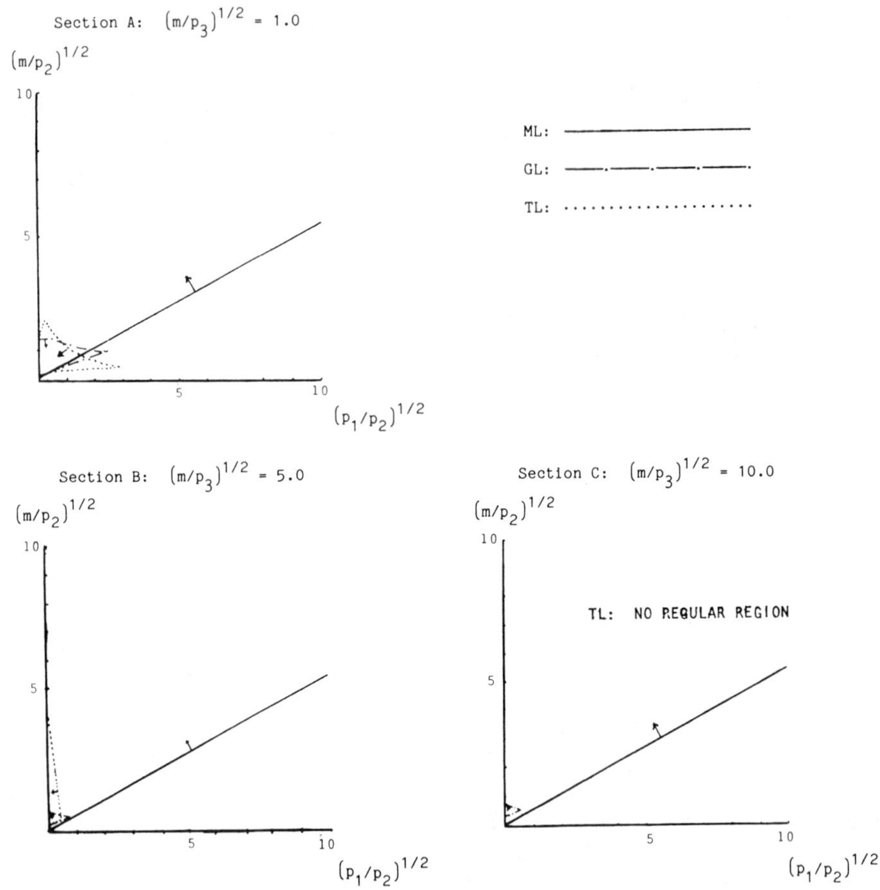

Fig. 8. *Case 3*: $\sigma_{12} = -0.5$, $\sigma_{23} = \sigma_{31} = 1.5$, $\eta_{10} = 1.7$, $\eta_{20} = 0.3$, $\eta_{30} = 1.0$. Three-commodity non-homothetic minflex Laurent, generalized Leontief, and translog regular regions (σ_{ij} and η_{i0} specified at $p_1/p_2 = m/p_2 = m/p_3 = 1$, $s_1 = s_2 = s_3 = \frac{1}{3}$, $\partial\eta_{10}/\partial m = 0$).

tion, along the axes in order to preserve the size of constant percent changes. The tabulated regular region volumes in Barnett and Lee (1985) use the logarithmic transformation. In the current paper we concentrate on providing direct comparability with Caves and Christensen's seminal results.

8. Conclusions

The purpose of flexible functional forms is to permit inferences without prior constraints about elasticities. No currently available model satisfying

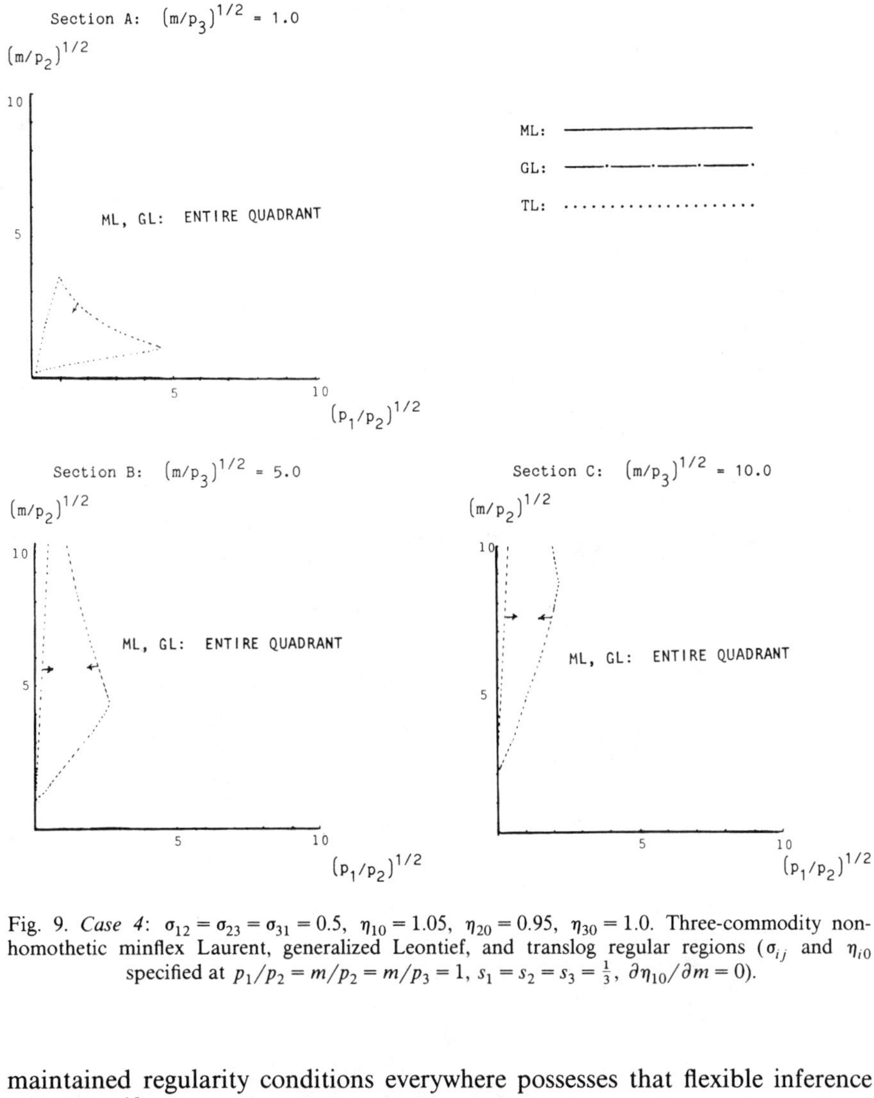

Fig. 9. *Case 4*: $\sigma_{12} = \sigma_{23} = \sigma_{31} = 0.5$, $\eta_{10} = 1.05$, $\eta_{20} = 0.95$, $\eta_{30} = 1.0$. Three-commodity nonhomothetic minflex Laurent, generalized Leontief, and translog regular regions (σ_{ij} and η_{i0} specified at $p_1/p_2 = m/p_2 = m/p_3 = 1$, $s_1 = s_2 = s_3 = \frac{1}{3}$, $\partial\eta_{10}/\partial m = 0$).

maintained regularity conditions everywhere possesses that flexible inference capability.[18] However, the hope with available flexible functional forms is that the maintained regularity conditions reasonably can be expected to hold within the convex closure of the actual data. In a time series context, regularity of the model tends to be particularly important within the region of the most recent observations.

[18] Barnett and Jonas's (1983) Müntz–Szatz model may be an exception. However, that new model's capabilities are not yet fully known. Diewert and Wales' (1985) Generalized Barnett model does possess that capability, but requires some (perhaps small) compromise in flexibility.

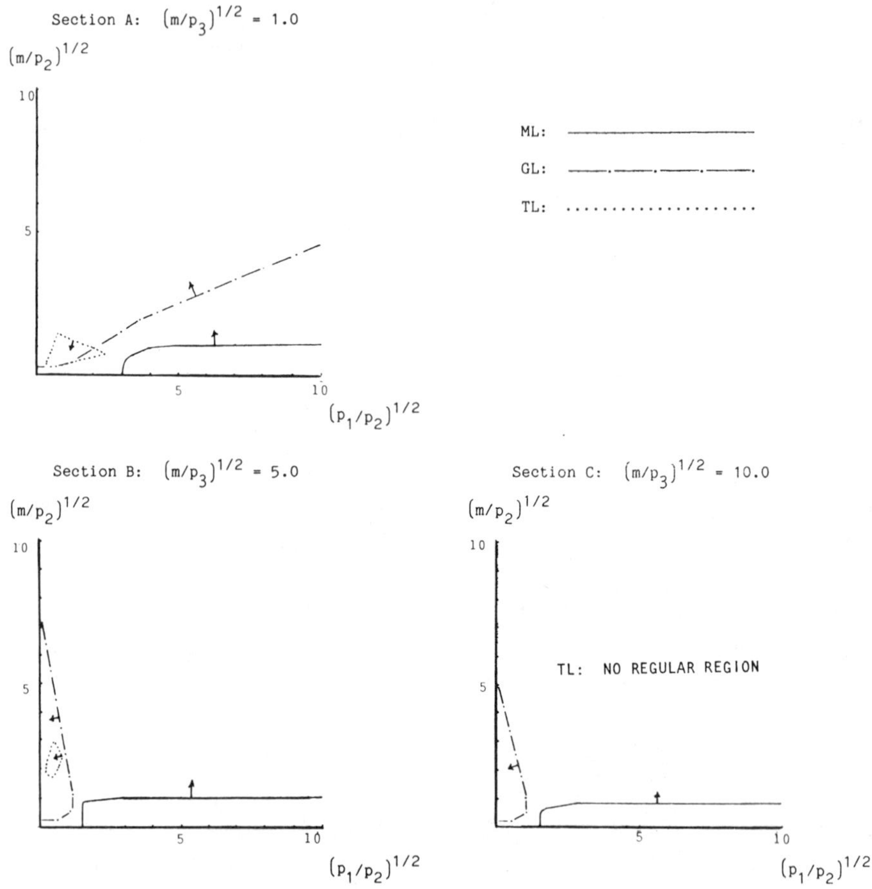

Fig. 10. *Case 5*: $\sigma_{12} = 0.0$, $\sigma_{23} = \sigma_{31} = 0.5$, $\eta_{10} = 1.2$, $\eta_{20} = 0.8$, $\eta_{30} = 1.0$. Three-commodity non-homothetic minflex Laurent, generalized Leontief, and translog regular regions (σ_{ij} and η_{i0} specified at $p_1/p_2 = m/p_2 = m/p_3 = 1$, $s_1 = s_2 = s_3 = \frac{1}{3}$, $\partial\eta_{10}/\partial m = 0$).

We find that that capability is not possessed by the generalized Leontief or translog model. Their regular regions usually are small and tend to move to different areas of the data space as the model's parameters are changed. Hence without strong prior knowledge about the models' parameters, we cannot know where to expect to find their regular regions. The most that we can reasonably expect is that those two models will be well-behaved in the immediate neighborhood of the unit vector, if regularity is imposed at that one point. Since that point conventionally is selected to be at the median observation, regularity typically will not be encountered in the vicinity of the recent-periods boundary of the data set. With any given data set, neither model therefore is satisfactory without strong prior restrictions on elasticities. As a result, neither model is capable of serving the objectives originally contemplated for flexible functional forms.

The regular region of the minflex Laurent model *always* expands as real income grows.[19] As a result, with time series data characterized by growing real income, the probability that a data point will lie within the regular region tends to rise as we move from the earliest to the most recent observations.[20] In addition, the overall regular region of the minflex Laurent model usually is larger than the regular regions of the other two models and has a shape and location that is more stable than those of the other two models. Hence the regional behavior of the minflex Laurent model is better than that of the other two models and is particularly attractive for use with time series data. However, some of the flexible forms not considered by Caves and Christensen, such as Deaton and Muellbauer's (1980) AIDS model, Berndt and Khaled's (1979) generalized Box–Cox model, and Diewert's (1973b) generalized Cobb–Douglas model, still possess unknown regional properties.[21]

The Caves and Christensen approach to mapping out a model's regular regions provides a means of systematically searching over the model's parameter space and producing the model's regular region at each point selected within the parameter space. We used the Caves and Christensen procedure, since flexible functional forms virtually always have been estimated without prior parameter constraints, and hence we need to know a model's behavior within all regions of its parameter space. However, new estimation procedures recently have been proposed by Lau (1978) and Gallant (1982). Their procedures permit estimation of a model subject to the constraint of regularity at a single point.[22] When that estimation approach is used, the regular region must contain the unit vector. However, that local regularity condition was satisfied by all three models in all of the cases displayed in the figures.[23] Hence our conclusions are equally as applicable when the models are estimated subject to local regularity at a point.

[19] For a proof that applies *in general*, see Barnett (1985).

[20] In addition, it appears that the rate of expansion of the regular region can be increased by applying an affine transformation which subtracts preselected constants from all variables, in order to produce transformed variables that approach zero more closely at their minimum. For a discussion of that capability in a related context, see Barnett (1985).

[21] We do not discuss Gallant's (1981) important Fourier series model, since it is based upon a non-parametric approach that has properties not easily compared with those of the 'flexible functional form' approach. For example, the Fourier model's 'regular region' depends upon sample size.

[22] Imposing regularity at more than one point destroys the flexibility of flexible functional forms, when flexibility is defined by any of the definitions in section 2.

[23] The point $(1,1)$ is clearly in the regular region in all of our two-good cases with all three models. Although the translog contains no regular region in some of the sections displayed with three goods, the point $(1,1,1)$ appears only in section A, since $m/p_3 = 1$ only in section A. The point $(1,1,1)$ is in the regular regions of all three models in every section A in the figures.

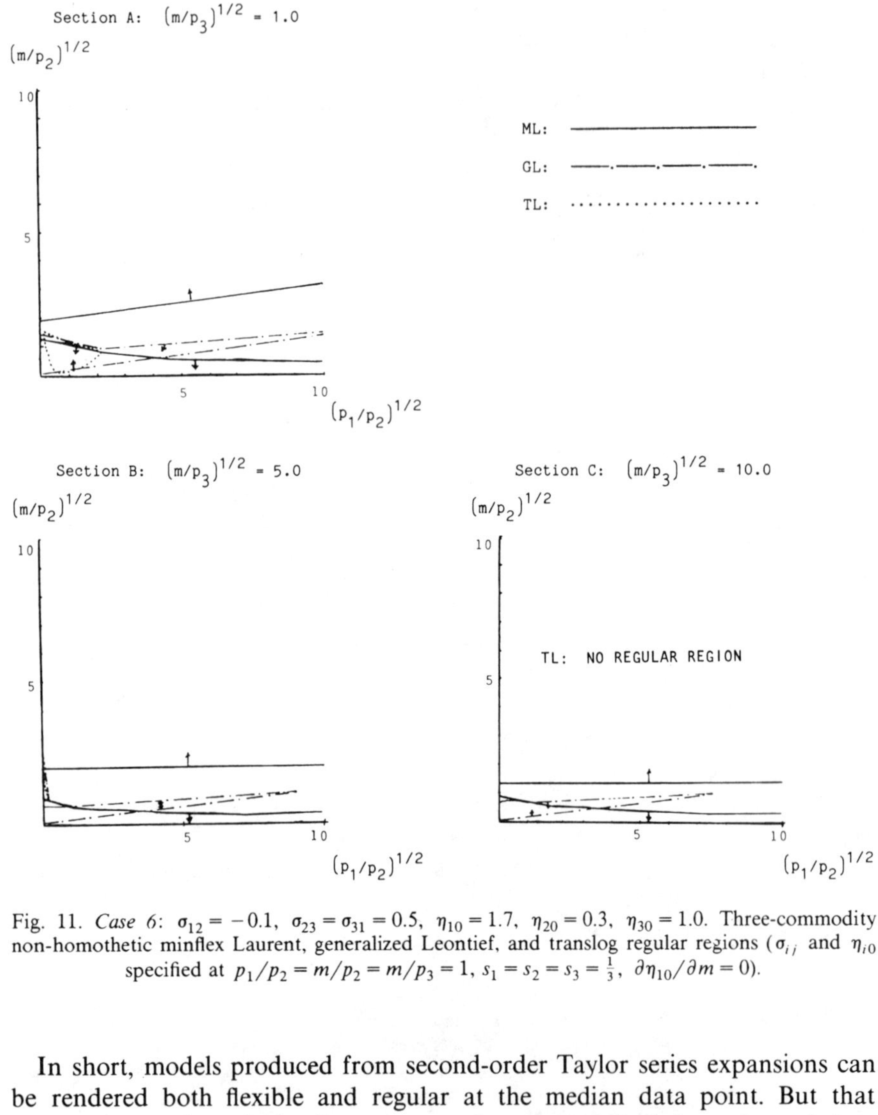

Fig. 11. *Case 6*: $\sigma_{12} = -0.1$, $\sigma_{23} = \sigma_{31} = 0.5$, $\eta_{10} = 1.7$, $\eta_{20} = 0.3$, $\eta_{30} = 1.0$. Three-commodity non-homothetic minflex Laurent, generalized Leontief, and translog regular regions (σ_{ij} and η_{i0} specified at $p_1/p_2 = m/p_2 = m/p_3 = 1$, $s_1 = s_2 = s_3 = \frac{1}{3}$, $\partial\eta_{10}/\partial m = 0$).

In short, models produced from second-order Taylor series expansions can be rendered both flexible and regular at the median data point. But that regularity usually quickly disappears as the recent-periods boundary of time series data sets is approached. The minflex Laurent model also can be rendered both flexible and regular at the median data point. However, doing so with that model assures simultaneously that the model's region of regular behavior actually *expands* as the recent-periods boundary is approached. As a result, the minflex Laurent model should be preferred for conventional modeling purposes to the Taylor series specifications. Such purposes include forecasting, simulation, and construction of inferences imputed to the current period.

Those modeling objectives require the ability to maintain good function behavior, especially within the region of recent observations. The results produced graphically in this paper are further confirmed by the regular regions volumes tabulated in Barnett and Lee (1985) and by their results in the corresponding two-good case, as well as by the dramatically large three-dimensional regular regions displayed by Barnett, Lee and Wolfe (1986) for the related minflex Laurent translog model.

Appendix

The following functions are used in section 4 to simplify the expressions for the elasticities of the three models. In the minflex Laurent case, the following functions appear repeatedly in the elasticity formulas:

$$A_i = a_i w_i + a_{ii} v_i + \sum_{j:\ j\neq i} a_{ij}^2 w_i w_j + \sum_{j:\ j\neq i} b_{ij}^2 \bar{w}_i \bar{w}_j,$$

$$\bar{A}_i = A_i / v_i,$$

$$\bar{A}_i' = \partial \bar{A}_i / \partial m = \left(0.5 a_i \bar{w}_i + 2 \sum_{j:\ j\neq i} b_{ij}^2 \bar{w}_i^3 \bar{w}_j\right) \Big/ m,$$

$$\bar{A}_i'' = \partial^2 \bar{A}_i / \partial m^2 = \left(-0.25 a_i \bar{w}_i + 2 \sum_{j:\ j\neq i} b_{ij}^2 \bar{w}_i^3 \bar{w}_j\right) \Big/ m^2,$$

$$D = \sum_i A_i,$$

$$D' = \partial D / \partial m = \left(-0.5 \sum_i a_i w_i - \sum_i a_{ii} v_i - \sum\sum_{(i,j)\in S} a_{ij}^2 w_i w_j + \sum\sum_{(i,j)\in S} b_{ij}^2 \bar{w}_i \bar{w}_j\right) \Big/ m^2,$$

$$D'' = \partial^2 D / \partial m^2 = \left(0.75 \sum_i a_i w_i + 2 \sum_i a_{ii} v_i + 4 \sum\sum_{(i,j)\in S} a_{ij}^2 w_i w_j\right) \Big/ m^2.$$

With the translog model, the following functions appear in the elasticity formulas:

$$B_i = a_i + \sum_j a_{ij} \ln v_i,$$

$$B_i' = \partial B_i / \partial_m = -\left(\sum_j a_{ij}\right) \Big/ m,$$

$$B_i'' = \partial^2 B_i / \partial m^2 = -B_i' / m,$$

$$E = \sum_i B_i,$$

$$E' = \partial E/\partial m = \sum_i B_i',$$

$$E'' = \sum B_i'',$$

With the generalized Leontief model, the following functions appear in the elasticity formulas:

$$C_i = a_i w_i + a_{ii} v_i + \sum_{j:\, j \neq i} a_{ij} w_i w_j,$$

$$\bar{C}_i = C_i / v_i,$$

$$\bar{C}_i' = \partial \bar{C}_i / \partial m = 0.5 a_i \bar{w}_i / m,$$

$$\bar{C}_i'' = \partial^2 \bar{C}_i / \partial m^2 = -0.25 a_i \bar{w}_i / m^2,$$

$$F = \sum_i C_i,$$

$$F' = \partial F/\partial m = \left(-0.5 \sum_i a_i w_i - \sum_i a_{ii} v_i - \sum\sum_{(i,j) \in S} a_{ij} w_i w_j \right) \Big/ m,$$

$$F'' = \partial^2 F/\partial m^2 = \left(0.75 \sum_i a_i w_i + 2 \sum_i a_{ii} v_i + 4 \sum\sum_{(i,j) \in S} a_{ij} w_i w_j \right) \Big/ m^2.$$

References

Barnett, William A., 1977, Recursive subaggregation and a generalized hypocycloidal demand model, Econometrica 45, 1117–1136.
Barnett, William A., 1979, Theoretical foundations for the Rotterdam model, Review of Economic Studies 46, 109–130.
Barnett, William A., 1980, Economic monetary aggregates: An application of index number and aggregation theory, Journal of Econometrics 14, 11–48.
Barnett, William A., 1981, Consumer demand and labor supply: Goods, monetary assets, and time (North-Holland, Amsterdam).
Barnett, William A., 1982, The flexible Laurent demand system, Proceedings of the 1982 American Statistical Association Meetings, Business and Economic Statistics Section, 82–89.
Barnett, William A., 1983a, New indices of money supply and the flexible Laurent demand system, Journal of Business and Economic Statistics 1, 7–23.
Barnett, William A., 1983b, Definitions of 'second order approximation' and of 'flexible functional form', Economics Letters 12, 31–35.
Barnett, William A., 1983c, The reappearance of the homotheticity restriction on preferences, Journal of Business and Economic Statistics 1, 215–218.
Barnett, William A., 1985, The minflex Laurent translog flexible functional form, Journal of Econometrics, this issue.

Barnett, William A. and Andrew Jonas, 1983, The Müntz–Szatz demand system: An application of a globally well behaved series expansion, Economics Letters 11, 337–342.

Barnett, William A. and Yul W. Lee, 1985, The global properties of the minflex Laurent, generalized Leontief, and translog flexible functional forms, Econometrica, forthcoming.

Barnett, William A., Yul W. Lee and Michael D. Wolfe, 1986, The three-dimensional global properties of the ML translog and ML generalized Leontief flexible functional forms, Journal of Business and Economic Statistics, forthcoming.

Basmann, R.L., D.J. Molina and D.J. Slottje, 1983, Budget constraint prices as preference changing parameters of generalized Fechner–Thurstone direct utility functions, American Economic Review 73, 411–413.

Berndt, E.R. and M.S. Khaled, 1979, Parametric productivity measurement and choice among flexible functional forms, Journal of Political Economy 87, 1220–1246.

Blackorby, Charles, Daniel Primont and R. Robert Russell, 1978, Duality, separability, and functional structure: Theory and economic applications (North-Holland, Amsterdam).

Brown, Murray and Dale H. Heien, 1972, The S-branch utility tree: A generalization of the linear expenditure system, Econometrica 40, 737–747.

Caves, D.W. and L.R. Christensen, 1980, Global properties of flexible functional forms, American Economic Review 70, 422–432.

Deaton, Angus and John Muellbauer, 1980, An almost ideal demand system, American Economic Review 70, 312–326.

Diewert, W.E., 1971, An application of the Shephard duality theorem: A generalized Leontief production function, Journal of Political Economy 79, 461–507.

Diewert, W.E., 1973a, Functional forms for profit and transformation functions, Journal of Economic Theory 6, 284–316.

Diewert, W.E., 1973b, Separability and a generalization of the Cobb–Douglas cost, production, and indirect utility functions (Research Branch, Department of Manpower and Immigration, Ottawa).

Diewert, W.E., 1974, Applications of duality theory, in: M. Intriligator and D. Kendrick, eds., Frontiers in quantitative economics, Vol. 2 (North-Holland, Amsterdam) 106–171.

Diewert, W.E. and T.J. Wales, 1984, Flexible functional forms and global curvature conditions, Technical working paper no. 40 (National Bureau of Economic Research, Cambridge, MA).

Flood, Lennart R., Renate Finke and Henri Theil, 1983, An evaluation of alternative demand systems by means of implied income elasticities, Economics Letters, forthcoming.

Gallant, R.A., 1981, On the bias in flexible functional forms and an essentially unbiased form: The Fourier functional form, Journal of Econometrics 15, 211–245.

Gallant, R.A. and E.H. Golub, 1984, Imposing curvature restrictions on flexible functional forms, Center for Mathematical Studies in Economics and Management Science discussion paper no. 538 (Northwestern University, Evanston, IL).

Guilkey, David K. and C.A. Knox Lovell, 1980, On the flexibility of the translog approximation, International Economic Review 21, 137–147.

Guilkey, David K., C.A. Knox Lovell and Robin C. Sickles, 1983, A comparison of the performance of three flexible functional forms, International Economic Review 24, 591–616.

Humphrey, David and J.R. Moroney, 1975, Substitution among capital, labor, and natural resource products in American manufacturing, Journal of Political Economy 83, 57–82.

Lau, Lawrence, 1978, Testing and imposing monotonicity, convexity, and quasiconcavity, in: M. Fuss and D. McFadden, eds., Production economics: A dual approach to theory and applications, Vol. 1 (North-Holland, Amsterdam) 409–453.

Manser, Marilyn E., 1974, Estimating consumer preferences and cost of living indexes for U.S. meat and produce, 1947–1971, Doctoral dissertation (University of Wisconsin, Madison, WI).

Moroney, John R. and John M. Trapani, 1981, Alternative models of substitution and technical change in natural resource intensive industries, in: Ernst Berndt and Barry Field, eds., Modeling and measuring natural resource substitution (MIT Press, Cambridge, MA) 48–69.

Theil, Henri, 1971, Principles of econometrics (Wiley, New York).

Uzawa, H., 1962, Production functions with constant elasticities of substitution, Review of Economic Studies 29, 291–299.

Wales, T.J., 1977, On the flexibility of flexible functional forms: an empirical approach, Journal of Econometrics 5, 183–193.

THE MINFLEX-LAURENT TRANSLOG FLEXIBLE FUNCTIONAL FORM

William A. BARNETT*

University of Texas at Austin, Austin, TX 78712, USA

Barnett's minflex-Laurent generalized Leontief model was produced from a special case of a second-order Laurent series expansion in the square roots. In this paper we produce a minflex-Laurent translog flexible functional form by the analogous expansion in the logarithms. We prove that the model's regular region always grows monotonically as real income increases. As a result, the model is especially well-suited for use with income-trended time series data. We also prove that the model satisfies Diewert's definition of a flexible functional form and is no more deeply parameterized than is necessary to satisfy the flexibility criterion.

1. Introduction

Many flexible functional forms and many globally well-behaved specifications now exist in the consumer demand modeling literature. However, the flexible functional forms are commonly poorly behaved, and the globally well-behaved specifications are not flexible.[1] An exception is Barnett's (1982, 1983a) minflex Laurent flexible functional form, which Barnett and Lee (1985) and Barnett, Lee and Wolfe (1985, 1986) have shown is regionally well-behaved, especially when used with time series data within the region of the latest observations.[2] The reason is that the model's regular region grows as real income increases, and real income typically trends upwards with time series data.

In this regard, the regular region of a consumer demand system is defined to be the subset of the data space within which the demand system is integrable to a utility function that is monotonically increasing and strictly quasi-concave. Equivalently a model is defined to be regular at each point in the data space at which the model's indirect utility function is monotonically decreasing and strictly quasi-convex.

*William A. Barnett is the Stuart Centennial Professor of Economics and the Briscoe Centennial Fellow of the IC^2 Institute at the University of Texas at Austin. This research was partially supported by NSF grant SOC 8305162.

[1]See Barnett (1977; 1981, app. B4).

[2]Another exception is Barnett and Jonas's (1983) Müntz–Szatz series model. Although that model is *globally* well-behaved at *all* orders of approximation, the model has a large number of parameters and has not yet been applied with either real or simulated data. As a result, little is presently known about that model's capabilities.

The minflex Laurent reciprocal indirect utility function is a flexible functional form and is a special case of a second-order Laurent series expansion in the square roots of the variables. The minflex special case is acquired by imposing a parametric minimality condition on the Laurent series expansion such that no more parametric freedom remains than is needed for the model to be a flexible functional form. The resulting functional form is then treated as a maintained model, rather than as a Laurent series expansion.[3] The term 'flexible functional form' is defined in section 2 below.

Because of the use of the square root transformation and of the relationship between Laurent series and Taylor series expansions, the minflex Laurent model could more fully be called the minflex-Laurent generalized Leontief (ML generalized Leontief) model. By analogy, a minflex-Laurent translog (ML translog) model could be constructed by replacing the square roots with logarithms and by using the functional form to specify the indirect utility function rather than its reciprocal. In this paper, the resulting ML translog flexible functional form is produced and some of its regional properties are derived.

The dominant regional property of the ML generalized Leontief model can be expected to the retained by the ML translog model, as will be proved below. The regular regions of both models grow as real income grows, since that property results from the structure of the Laurent series specification rather than from the initial (square root or logarithmic) data transformation. However, differences in regional behavior also can be expected to exist between the two models. As shown by Barnett and Lee (1985), Barnett, Lee and Wolfe (1985) and Christensen and Caves (1980), substantial differences in behavior exist between the usual Taylor series versions of the translog and generalized Leontief models. Similarly differences in regional behavior exist between the ML translog and ML generalized Leontief models, as shown by Barnett, Lee and Wolfe (1986).

In addition, the capabilities of the ML translog model can be altered by exploiting the fact that logarithms become negative for arguments below 1.0, while square roots can take on only positive values for positive arguments. As shown below, prior affine data translations can keep all data above or below (or evenly distributed about) 1.0, so that the distribution of signs of logarithms can be controlled throughout the data. By thereby selecting the location of the data field relative to the point 1.0, both the direction and rate of increase of the regular region of the ML translog model can be chosen. For example, the size of the regular region can be made to increase as real income decreases. By contrast, the size of the regular region of the ML generalized Leontief model

[3] Nevertheless, the properties of Laurent series expansions motivated the selection of the Laurent basis in the design of the minflex Laurent specification. Of particular relevance are the spanning properties of the Laurent basis and the smooth behavior of the Laurent remainder term. On these subjects, see Barnett (1983, sec. 7) and Barnett, Lee and Wolfe (1985, sec. 3).

In other words, f_{θ}^{*} is a flexible functional form if it can attain arbitrary level and first- and second-order derivatives at a predetermined single point. Flexible functional forms also frequently have been equated with second-order approximations. To render that concept rigorous, the following definition was originated by Barnett (1983a, b).

Definition 3. The function f^{*} can provide a second-order local approximation to f at the point $\boldsymbol{v}_0$ if there exists $\boldsymbol{\theta}_0 = \boldsymbol{\theta}(\boldsymbol{v}_0)$ such that

$$\left(f_{\theta_0}^{*}(\boldsymbol{v}) - f(\boldsymbol{v})\right)/\left(\|\boldsymbol{v} - \boldsymbol{v}_0\|^2\right) \to 0 \quad \text{as} \quad \boldsymbol{v} \to \boldsymbol{v}_0,$$

where $\|\cdot\|$ designates the Euclidean norm.

Caves and Christensen used the following definition of flexibility, which resembles Definition 1.

Definition 4. The function f_{θ}^{*} is a flexible functional form if, at any point $\boldsymbol{v}_0$ and for any f, there exists $\boldsymbol{\theta}_0 = \boldsymbol{\theta}(\boldsymbol{v}_0)$ such that all income elasticities and all own- and cross-price elasticities of demand derived from $f_{\theta_0}^{*}$ at $\boldsymbol{v}_0$ are the same as those derived from f.

In other words, f_{θ}^{*} can generate a demand system with arbitrary income and price elasticities at any single predetermined point.

Barnett (1983b) proved that flexibility in the Definition 2 sense is necessary and sufficient for Definition 3 to hold for any f. Diewert (1971, p. 506) has shown that if f_{θ}^{*} satisfies Definition 2, then f_{θ}^{*} also satisfies Definition 1. By a similar argument to Diewert's it also follows that if f_{θ}^{*} satisfies Definition 2, then f_{θ}^{*} also satisfies Definition 4.[5] Hence if f_{θ}^{*} is flexible in the Definition 2 sense, then f_{θ}^{*} is flexible according to all of the other definitions.

The translog and generalized Leontief models both satisfy Definition 2. In addition, Barnett (1983a) proved that the new minflex Laurent (ML generalized Leontief) demand system also satisfies Definition 2. Hence the translog, generalized Leontief, and ML generalized Leontief demand models are locally flexible functional forms by all of the definitions. Furthermore, the translog and generalized Leontief models both satisfy the additional property, first defined by Diewert (1971, p. 506), of possessing just enough parametric freedom to satisfy Definition 2. We shall refer to that property as the *minimality property*. Any restrictions on the parameters of either model result

[5] In particular, Barten's Fundamental Theorem of Demand [see, e.g., Theil (1971, eq. A10)] shows that all income and price elasticities can be written solely in terms of data on income and prices and first- and second-order derivatives of utility. If f_{θ}^{*} satisfies Definition 2, then all of those derivatives are obtainable, regardless of their values.

necessarily always increases as real income increases. However, that particul[ar] direction of expansion of the regular region is likely usually to be the mos[t] useful one, especially with time series data. Hence the particular affine dat[a] translation which produces that property for the ML translog will be emphasized in the results provided in this paper.

Section 2 explores the relationship between the various definitions of functional flexibility that have appeared in the economics literature. Section 3 contains the definition of the ML translog indirect utility function and the derivation of the resulting system of expenditure share equations. Section 4 contains the proof of the flexibility of the ML translog functional form and the proof of the model's minimality property. Section 5 proves that the model's regular region expands as real income grows.

2. The flexibility criterion

In this section, we define the local flexibility property that is possessed by the class of 'flexible functional forms'. The earliest definitions of functional flexibility appear to have been Diewert's (1971, 1973, 1974). Let $f(\mathbf{v})$ be a function defining a consumer's preferences. The function could, for example, be a utility, indirect utility, or reciprocal indirect utility function.[4] Let $f_{\boldsymbol{\theta}}^*(\mathbf{v})$ be a parameterized approximation with parameter vector $\boldsymbol{\theta}$. Then $f_{\boldsymbol{\theta}}^*$ is the specification to be used in estimating f. We seek to define the flexibility of $f_{\boldsymbol{\theta}}^*$ in approximating f at an arbitrary single point, $\mathbf{v}_0$.

Diewert appears to have originated the following two definitions.

Definition 1. The function $f_{\boldsymbol{\theta}}^*$ is a flexible functional form if, at any point $\mathbf{v}_0$ and for any f, there exists $\boldsymbol{\theta}_0 = \boldsymbol{\theta}(\mathbf{v}_0)$ such that the elasticities of substitution derived from $f_{\boldsymbol{\theta}_0}^*$ at $\mathbf{v}_0$ are the same as those derived from f at $\mathbf{v}_0$.

In other words, $f_{\boldsymbol{\theta}}^*$ can define preferences with arbitrary elasticities of substitution at any single predetermined point. The following definition also was originated by Diewert (1971, 1973, 1974).

Definition 2. The function $f_{\boldsymbol{\theta}}^*$ is a flexible functional form if, at any point $\mathbf{v}_0$ and for any f, there exists $\boldsymbol{\theta}_0 = \boldsymbol{\theta}(\mathbf{v}_0)$ such that

$$f_{\boldsymbol{\theta}_0}^*(\mathbf{v}_0) = f(\mathbf{v}_0),$$

$$\partial f_{\boldsymbol{\theta}_0}^* / \partial \mathbf{v}|_{\mathbf{v}=\mathbf{v}_0} = \partial f / \partial \mathbf{v}|_{\mathbf{v}=\mathbf{v}_0},$$

$$\partial^2 f_{\boldsymbol{\theta}_0}^* / \partial \mathbf{v}\, \partial \mathbf{v}'|_{\mathbf{v}=\mathbf{v}_0} = \partial^2 f / \partial \mathbf{v}\, \partial \mathbf{v}'|_{\mathbf{v}=\mathbf{v}_0}.$$

[4]If f is a direct utility function, then $\mathbf{v}$ is a vector of goods quantities. If f is an indirect [or] reciprocal indirect utility function, then $\mathbf{v} = \mathbf{p}/m$ is a vector of income-normalized prices.

in the loss of the model's flexibility property, according to any of its four definitions. The ML generalized Leontief model possesses the minimality property.[6]

As a result, the local flexibility capabilities of the three models are essentially the same. In addition, since each model satisfies the same minimality property, we should not expect any one of the three models to fit systematically better than the others. Although the two minflex Laurent models (ML generalized Leontief and ML translog) each possess more parameters than the translog or generalized Leontief models, most of the minflex Laurent models' coefficients are subject to imposed inequality constraints, while none of the coefficients of the other two models are subject to any inequality constraints. The translog and generalized Leontief models each possess *more* unconstrained free coefficients than either of the minflex Laurent models. Since all four models satisfy the same minimality property, all three models possess *precisely the same* degree of parametric freedom.

Since no reason exists to expect systematic differences in the local flexibility of these models, relevant comparisons between the models should be based upon their greatly different regional and global properties. In this paper, we define the ML translog model and explore its properties. Analogous proofs would apply to the ML generalized Leontief model.

3. The models

In this section, we define the minflex-Laurent translog model. Let $\boldsymbol{q} = (q_1, \dots, q_n)'$ be the vector of goods quantities, and let $\boldsymbol{p} = (p_1, \dots, p_n)'$ be the vector of corresponding goods prices. Let $m = \boldsymbol{p}'\boldsymbol{q}$ be 'income' (or, more precisely, total expenditure), and let $\boldsymbol{v} = (v_1, \dots, v_n)'$, where $v_i = p_i/m$. Also let the expenditure shares be $\boldsymbol{s} = (s_1, \dots, s_n)'$, where $s_i = p_i q_i/m$.

Let v_{it} designate observation t on v_i, where $t = 1, \dots, T_0$; and let $T = \{1, \dots, T_0\}$, so that $t \in T$. Let $\boldsymbol{\theta} = (\theta_1, \dots, \theta_n)'$ be a vector of constants. Also let $\bar{v}_i = v_i + \theta_i$, and let $w_i = \log \bar{v}_i$. Define the set of pairs of unequal subscripts $S = \{(i, j)\colon\ i \neq j,\ i, j = 1, \dots, n\}$. In accordance with usual conventions, the vectors $\boldsymbol{v}_1, \dots, \boldsymbol{v}_{T_0}$, where $\boldsymbol{v}_t = (v_{1t}, v_{2t}, \dots, v_{nt})'$, could be normalized such that $\boldsymbol{v}_t$ becomes the unit vector at a median observation t_m.[7]

[6] The minflex special case of the Laurent model was acquired by imposing as many restrictions on the full Laurent model as was possible without losing the Definition 2 flexibility property. See Barnett (1983a). Hence the minimality property holds by construction. A formal proof of minimality is provided below for the ML translog. The analogous proof would also apply for the ML generalized Leontief.

[7] The normalization results in the multiplication of each q_i by v_{it_m} and the division of each p_i by v_{it_m}. The normalization is harmless, since it has no effect on $p_i q_i$ and therefore on the shares, $\boldsymbol{s}$.

The indirect utility function $V(\boldsymbol{v})$ of the ML translog model then is defined such that $V^*(\boldsymbol{v}) = \log V(\boldsymbol{v})$, where

$$V^*(\boldsymbol{v}) = a_0 + 2\sum_i a_i w_i + \sum_i a_{ii} w_i^2 - \sum\sum_{(i,j)\in S} \left(a_{ij}^2 w_i w_j - b_{ij}^2 w_i^{-1} w_j^{-1} \right). \tag{3.1}$$

The parameters a_0, a_i $(i = 1, \ldots, n)$, a_{ii} $(i = 1, \ldots, n)$, a_{ij} $((i, j) \in S)$, and b_{ij} $((i, j) \in S)$ are restricted to satisfy

$$b_{ij} a_{ij} = 0, \tag{3.2}$$

$$\left(a_{ij}, b_{ij}\right) = \left(a_{ji}, b_{ji}\right), \tag{3.3}$$

for all $(i, j) \in S$. A slight generalization is easily acquired by not imposing restrictions (3.2), which we impose solely for the purpose of acquiring the minimality result in Theorem 2 below.

The constants $\boldsymbol{\theta} = (\theta_1, \ldots, \theta_n)'$ are not estimated parameters, but rather are preselected constants used to impose prior control on the shape of the model's regular region. In cases in which the regular region is desired to grow with increasing real income, an effective choice would be

$$\theta_i = 1 - \min_{t \in T} v_{it} + \delta_i, \tag{3.4}$$

for $i = 1, \ldots, n$ with $\delta_i > 0$ being small. In most time series studies with growing real income, it would be desirable for the regular region to expand with increasing real income, since recent data points and forecasts then could be expected to lie within the model's regular region.

The selection (3.4) results in $\bar{v}_i > 1$, so that $w_i > 0$ for all $i = 1, \ldots, n$. Since that selection of $\boldsymbol{\theta}$ will be used throughout this paper, $\boldsymbol{w} = (w_1, \ldots, w_n)'$ will be strictly positive. The simplest choice of $\boldsymbol{\delta}$ would be $\delta_i = \min_{t \in T} v_{it}$, in which case $\boldsymbol{\theta} = \mathbf{1}$. However, as we shall see below, decreasing $\boldsymbol{\delta} = (\delta_1, \ldots, \delta_n)'$ towards zero can be expected to result in increasingly rapid growth of the model's regular region as real income increases.[8]

Since V^* is a monotonic transformation of V, either can be used in Roy's identity. Hence Roy's identity can take the form

$$s_i = \left(v_i \partial V^*(\boldsymbol{v}) / \partial v_i\right) / \left(\boldsymbol{v}' \partial V^*(\boldsymbol{v}) / \partial \boldsymbol{v}\right). \tag{3.5}$$

[8] Choices of $\boldsymbol{\theta}$ other than (3.4) could be appropriate in some cross section applications or during periods of declining real income. In such cases, negative values of $\boldsymbol{w}$ could be desirable to obtain a large regular region at low real income.

By (3.1) and (3.5), we get the ML translog model's share equations

$$s_i = A_i/D, \tag{3.6}$$

for $i = 1, \ldots, n$, where

$$A_i = a_i v_i \bar{v}_i^{-1} + a_{ii} v_i \bar{v}_i^{-1} w_i - \sum_{j:\, j \neq i} a_{ij}^2 v_i \bar{v}_i^{-1} w_j$$

$$- \sum_{j:\, j \neq i} b_{ij}^2 v_i w_i^{-2} \bar{v}_i^{-1} w_j^{-1}, \tag{3.7}$$

$$D = \sum_k a_k v_k \bar{v}_k^{-1} + \sum_k a_{kk} v_k \bar{v}_k^{-1} w_k - \sum\sum_{(k,j) \in S} a_{kj}^2 v_k \bar{v}_k^{-1} w_j$$

$$- \sum\sum_{(k,j) \in S} b_{kj}^2 v_k w_k^{-2} \bar{v}_k^{-1} w_j^{-1}. \tag{3.8}$$

Observe that

$$D = \sum_i A_i.$$

The forms of (3.7) and (3.8) are considerably simplified if $\boldsymbol{\theta} = \mathbf{0}$, but our results in section 5 below on the shape of the regular region assume that $\boldsymbol{\theta}$ is selected such that (3.4) holds. Since (3.6) is homogeneous of degree zero in the coefficients of (3.7) and (3.8), an arbitrary parameter normalization is needed.[9] The conventional choice with the usual translog model is $\Sigma_k a_k = -1$, which also could be used with the ML translog.

4. The flexibility of the minflex-Laurent translog functional form

As discussed in section 2, flexibility in the sense of Definition 2 is sufficient for flexibility in all of the other senses defined in section 2. We now prove that $V^*(\boldsymbol{v})$ for the ML translog model is flexible in the sense of Definition 2. That result is stated as Theorem 1.

Theorem 1. *Let $V^*(\boldsymbol{v})$ be as in (3.1). Let c be an arbitrary scalar; let **d** be an arbitrary n-dimensional vector; and let $E = [e_{ij}]$ be an arbitrary symmetric $n \times n$ matrix. Then for any value $\boldsymbol{v}_0 \geq \mathbf{0}$ of the vector $\boldsymbol{v}$ there exist values of the parameters of $V(\boldsymbol{v}_0)$ such that the following conditions, as well as conditions*

[9] In addition, the squared parameters could be replaced by unsquared coefficients subject to imposed non-negativity restrictions. For a convenient estimation procedure using squared parameters, see Barnett (1983a, sec. 9.1).

(3.2) and (3.3), are satisfied:

$$V^*(\boldsymbol{v}_0) = c, \tag{4.1}$$

$$\partial V^*/\partial \boldsymbol{v}|_{\boldsymbol{v}=\boldsymbol{v}_0} = \boldsymbol{d}, \tag{4.2}$$

$$\partial^2 V^*/\partial \boldsymbol{v}\, \partial \boldsymbol{v}'|_{\boldsymbol{v}=\boldsymbol{v}_0} = E. \tag{4.3}$$

In addition, for any choice of $(c, \boldsymbol{d}, E)$ *the resulting values of* a_0, $\boldsymbol{a}$, $\bar{\boldsymbol{a}}$, *and* (a_{ij}^2, b_{ij}^2) *for* $(i, j) \in S$ *are unique.*

Proof. Differentiating V^* twice, we get the following first and second partial derivatives for $k, m = 1, \ldots, n$:

$$\partial V^*/\partial v_k = 2a_k \bar{v}_k^{-1} + 2a_{kk}\bar{v}_k^{-1} w_k - 2 \sum_{j:\ j \neq k} a_{kj}^2 \bar{v}_k^{-1} w_j$$

$$-2 \sum_{j:\ j \neq k} b_{kj}^2 w_k^{-2} \bar{v}_k^{-1} w_j^{-1}, \tag{4.4}$$

$$\partial^2 V^*/\partial v_k^2 = -2a_k \bar{v}_k^{-2} - 2a_{kk}\bar{v}_k^{-2}(w_k - 1) + 2 \sum_{j:\ j \neq k} a_{kj}^2 \bar{v}_k^{-2} w_j$$

$$+2 \sum_{j:\ j \neq k} b_{kj}^2 \bar{v}_k^{-2} w_j^{-1} w_k^{-2}(2w_k^{-1} + 1), \tag{4.5}$$

$$\partial^2 V^*/\partial v_k\, \partial v_m = -2a_{km}^2 \bar{v}_k^{-1} \bar{v}_m^{-1} + 2b_{km}^2 w_k^{-2} \bar{v}_k^{-1} w_m^{-2} \bar{v}_m^{-1}. \tag{4.6}$$

Let $\boldsymbol{v} = \boldsymbol{v}_0$ in (3.1), (4.4), (4.5), and (4.6), and substitute them into (4.1), (4.2), and (4.3) to replace their left-hand sides. We now solve the resulting system of equations for the parameters.

For each $(k, m) \in S$, set $a_{km} = 0$ if e_{km} $(k \neq m)$ is non-negative. Otherwise set $b_{km} = 0$. Then solve the off-diagonal equations of (4.3) for the rest of the off-diagonal elements of the matrices $[a_{km}]$ and $[b_{km}]$. The signs selected for those parameters are arbitrary, since each of them is always squared. Observe that these selections satisfy all restrictions in (3.2) and (3.3) because of the symmetry of E.

For each k, solve the two equations $(\partial^2 V^*/\partial v_k^2)|_{\boldsymbol{v}=\boldsymbol{v}_0} = e_{kk}$ and $(\partial V^*/\partial v_k)|_{\boldsymbol{v}=\boldsymbol{v}_0} = d_k$ simultaneously for the two parameters a_{kk} and a_k. Finally solve (4.1) for a_0.

All selections above are unique except for the signs of a_{km} and b_{km} for $(k, m) \in S$. However, the values of a_{km}^2 and b_{km}^2 are unaffected by the signs of a_{km} and b_{km}. Hence the uniqueness result follows. ■

Theorem 1 produces the unique selection, subject to (3.2) and (3.3), of the coefficients in (3.1). Of those coefficients, $2n+1$ can take any sign. The remaining n^2-n coefficients must be non-negative, since they equal squared parameters. Let the correspondingly partitioned vector of coefficients be $\boldsymbol{\beta} = (\boldsymbol{\beta}_1', \boldsymbol{\beta}_2')'$, where the signs of $\boldsymbol{\beta}_1$ are unconstrained, and the signs of $\boldsymbol{\beta}_2$ are non-negative. Then $\boldsymbol{\beta}_1 \in \boldsymbol{R}^{2n+1}$ and $\boldsymbol{\beta}_2 \in \boldsymbol{R}_+^{n^2-n}$, where $\boldsymbol{R}_+^{n^2-n}$ is the non-negative orthant of $\boldsymbol{R}^{n^2-n}$. Let $\Omega = \{\boldsymbol{\beta}\colon \boldsymbol{\beta}_1 \in \boldsymbol{R}^{2n+1},\ \boldsymbol{\beta}_2 \in \boldsymbol{R}_+^{n^2-n}$, and $\boldsymbol{\beta}$ satisfies (3.2) and (3.3)$\}$. Then G is the feasible set of possible coefficient values used in Theorem 1. The minimality result in Theorem 2 demonstrates that no prior restrictions, other than (3.2) and (3.3), can be imposed upon the coefficients without the loss of the flexibility conditions defined in section 2. Hence the model's degree of parametric freedom is the minimum needed to attain the functional flexibility properties.

Theorem 2. *Let $V^*(\boldsymbol{v})$ be as in (3.1). Let G be a strict subset of Ω. If $\boldsymbol{\beta}$ is restricted to lie within G for every $(c, \boldsymbol{d}, E)$, then the existence result in Theorem 1 fails.*

Proof. Suppose that Theorem 1 holds even if $\boldsymbol{\beta}$ is restricted always to lie within G. Let $\boldsymbol{\beta}_0 \in \Omega - G$, and let $\boldsymbol{v}_0 > 0$. Substitute $\boldsymbol{\beta}_0$ and $\boldsymbol{v}_0$ into (4.1), (4.2), and (4.3), and let $(c_0, \boldsymbol{d}_0, E_0)$ be the resulting values of $(c, \boldsymbol{d}, E)$. By the uniqueness result in Theorem 1, a unique vector of coefficients $\boldsymbol{\beta} \in \Omega$ can produce $(c_0, \boldsymbol{d}_0, E_0)$. By our assumption about Theorem 1, that $\boldsymbol{\beta}$ will lie in G. The assumption $\boldsymbol{\beta}_0 \in \Omega - G$ is thereby contradicted. ■

5. The regional properties of the model

The regional properties of the model can most easily be understood by rewriting $V^*(\boldsymbol{v})$ as

$$V^*(\boldsymbol{v}) = f(\boldsymbol{v}) + g(\boldsymbol{v}),$$

where

$$f(\boldsymbol{v}) = a_0 + 2\sum_i a_i w_i + \sum_i a_{ii} w_i^2 - \sum\sum_{(i,j)\in S} a_{ij}^2 w_i w_j, \tag{5.1}$$

$$g(\boldsymbol{v}) = \sum\sum_{(i,j)\in S} b_{ij}^2 w_i^{-1} w_j^{-1}. \tag{5.2}$$

We then have the following result, which demonstrates globally that g has the same regularity properties as an indirect utility function.

Theorem 3. *Let $\boldsymbol{\theta}$ satisfy (3.4) for $\boldsymbol{\delta} > \mathbf{0}$. Then $(\partial g/\partial \boldsymbol{v}_t)|_{\boldsymbol{v}=\boldsymbol{v}_0} < 0$ for all $t \in T$, and $g(\boldsymbol{v}_t)$ is strictly convex for all $t \in T$.*

Proof. Since w_i^{-1} is monotonically decreasing in v_i, $g(\boldsymbol{v})$ is monotonically decreasing in v_i. Hence $(\partial g/\partial \boldsymbol{v}_t)|_{\boldsymbol{v}=\boldsymbol{v}_0} < 0$ for all $t \in T$.

Consider the Hessian matrix H_h of $h(v_i, v_j) = w_i^{-1} w_j^{-1}$. The determinant of H_h is

$$|H_h| = \bar{v}_i^{-2} \bar{v}_j^{-2} w_i^{-3} w_j^{-3} \left[\left(1 + 2w_i^{-1}\right)\left(1 + 2w_j^{-1}\right) - w_i^{-1} w_j^{-1} \right].$$

So $|H_h| > 0$ if and only if

$$\left(1 + 2w_i^{-1}\right)\left(1 + 2w_j^{-1}\right) > w_i^{-1} w_j^{-1},$$

which is true, since $w_i, w_j > 0$ by (3.4). In addition $\partial^2 h/\partial v_i^2 > 0$, since

$$\partial^2 h/\partial v_i^2 = \bar{v}_i^{-2} w_j^{-1} w_i^{-2}\left(1 + 2w_i^{-1}\right),$$

and since $w_i, w_j, \bar{v}_i > 0$ by (3.4). Hence h is strictly convex by the positive definiteness of H_h. As a result, $g(\boldsymbol{v})$, which is a non-negative linear combination of strictly convex functions, is strictly convex. ■

We can see from Theorem 3 that $V^*(\boldsymbol{v})$ will be regular at $\boldsymbol{v}$ if $g(\boldsymbol{v})$ is large relative to $f(\boldsymbol{v})$, so that the behavior of the sign-unconstrained terms in $f(\boldsymbol{v})$ cannot swamp the properties of the well-behaved terms in $g(\boldsymbol{v})$. Since V is a monotonic transformation of V^*, the same conclusion follows for V. To explore this matter further, suppose we select $\delta_i = \min_{t \in T} v_{it}$ for all i, so that $\boldsymbol{\theta} = \mathbf{1}$. Under that simplifying assumption, the following theorem shows that the behavior of $V^*(\boldsymbol{v})$ will be dominated by that of $g(\boldsymbol{v})$ for sufficiently small values of $\boldsymbol{v}$.

Theorem 4. *Let $\boldsymbol{\theta} = \mathbf{1}$. Then $g(\boldsymbol{v})/f(\boldsymbol{v}) \to \infty$ as $\boldsymbol{v} \to \mathbf{0}$.*

Proof. As $v_i \to 0$, we see that $\log(v_i + \theta_i) \to 0$ and therefore $(\log(v_i + \theta_i))^{-1} \to \infty$. Hence $g(\boldsymbol{v}) \to \infty$ and $f(\boldsymbol{v}) \to a_0$ as $\boldsymbol{v} \to 0$. It follows immediately that $g(\boldsymbol{v})/f(\boldsymbol{v}) \to \infty$ as $\boldsymbol{v} \to \mathbf{0}$. ■

With time series data characterized by rising per-capita real income, we can expect v_{it} to tend to trend down over time for all i. As a result, with such time series data, Theorem 4 tells us that the properties of the well-behaved (globally regular) term $g(\boldsymbol{v})$ will tend increasingly to become dominant at the most recent actual data points or at forecasted future points.

The implications of Theorem 4 for the size of the regular region of $V^*(\boldsymbol{v})$ are suggested by the following corollary.

Corollary 1. *Let* $\boldsymbol{\theta}=\mathbf{1}$, *and let* $\Gamma>0$. *Then for every* $\bar{p}>0$, *no matter how large, there exists* v_1^* *such that if* $v_1<v_1^*$ *then* $g(\boldsymbol{v})/f(\boldsymbol{v})>\Gamma$ *for every* $p_2/p_1, p_3/p_1, \ldots, p_n/p_1 \in (0, \bar{p}]$.

Proof. Let $\bar{p}>0$, $\Gamma>0$, $\boldsymbol{\theta}=\mathbf{1}$, and let $0<p_i/p_1\leq\bar{p}$ for every $i=2,\ldots,n$. Since $v_i=v_1(p_i/p_1)$, it follows that $\boldsymbol{v}\to 0$ as $v_1\to 0$. Hence from Theorem 4, $g(\boldsymbol{v})/f(\boldsymbol{v})\to\infty$ as $v_1\to 0$. The corollary follows immediately. ∎

In other words, no matter how great the variability in relative prices, $g(\boldsymbol{v})/f(\boldsymbol{v})$ can be kept arbitrarily large for sufficiently large 'real' income, $v_1^{-1}=m/p_1$ (nominal income deflated by the numeraire price, p_1). Hence the range over which relative prices can be permitted to vary without losing regularity of $V^*(\boldsymbol{v})$ can be expected to increase as v_1^{-1} increases. This conjecture was verified by Barnett and Lee (1984) and Barnett, Lee and Wolfe (1985, 1986) in the two-good and three-good non-homothetic cases with both the ML generalized Leontief and ML translog models. In every case, they found that the width of the regular region (in terms of the admissible range of relative prices) expands as real income grows.

It should be observed that all of the theorems and corollaries in the present paper are equally applicable to the ML generalized Leontief model, if logarithms are replaced by square roots and if (3.4) is replaced by $\theta_i=-\min_{t\in T}v_{it}+\delta_i$. Correspondingly, the selection $\boldsymbol{\theta}=\mathbf{1}$ in Theorem 4 and its Corollary 1 would be replaced by $\boldsymbol{\theta}=\mathbf{0}$.

6. Concluding remarks

We have proved that the minflex-Laurent translog model is a flexible functional form in all of the senses defined in section 2, and that the model has no more parametric freedom than is necessary to achieve that flexibility. With the model's parameters fixed at any arbitrary values, we have shown that the model's regular region always expands as real income increases.

The results also tend to suggest that the regular region, at any fixed value of real income, would expand if $\boldsymbol{\delta}$ were decreased toward zero. The primary effect of decreasing $\boldsymbol{\delta}$ appears to be to increase the rate at which the regular region expands as real income grows. This observation follows from the fact that as $\boldsymbol{\delta}$ decreases, $g(\boldsymbol{v})/f(\boldsymbol{v})$ tends to increase for the same reasons that produced Theorem 4 above. However, in Theorem 4 all parameters are assumed fixed. By now permitting $\boldsymbol{\delta}$ to decrease, we may encounter shifting parameter estimates. As a result, these conjectures regarding the potentially beneficial effects of selecting low $\boldsymbol{\delta}$'s merit further study. More generally, the ability to select $\boldsymbol{\theta}$, whether or not through (3.4), provides the user of the model with the capability to *design* the shape of the model's regular region. In this paper we have only scratched the surface of that design capability.

References

Barnett, William A., 1977, Recursive subaggregation and a generalized hypocycloidal demand model, Econometrica 45, 1117–1136.

Barnett, William A., 1981, Consumer demand and labor supply: Goods, monetary assets, and time (North-Holland, Amsterdam).

Barnett, William A., 1982, The flexible Laurent demand system, Proceedings of the 1982 American Economic Association Meetings, Business and Economics Statistics Section, 82–89.

Barnett, William A., 1983a, New indices of money supply and the flexible Laurent demand system, Journal of Business and Economic Statistics 1, 7–23.

Barnett, William A., 1983b, Definitions of 'second order approximation' and of 'flexible functional form,' Economics Letters 12, 31–35.

Barnett, William A. and Andrew Jonas, 1983, The Müntz–Szatz demand system: An application of a globally well behaved series expansion, Economics Letters 11, 337–342.

Barnett, William A. and Yul W. Lee, 1985, The global properties of the minflex Laurent, generalized Leontief, and translog flexible functional forms, Econometrica, forthcoming.

Barnett, William A., Yul W. Lee and Michael D. Wolfe, 1985, The three-dimensional global properties of the minflex Laurent, generalized Leontief, and translog flexible functional forms, Journal of Econometrics, this issue.

Barnett, William A., Yul W. Lee and Michael D. Wolfe, 1986, The three-dimensional global properties of the ML translog and ML generalized Leontief flexible functional forms, Journal of Business and Economic Statistics, forthcoming.

Caves, D.W. and L.R. Christensen, 1980, Global properties of flexible functional forms, American Economic Review 70, 422–432.

Diewert, W. E., 1971, An application of the Shephard duality theorem: A generalized Leontief production function, Journal of Political Economy 79, 461–507.

Diewert, W.E., 1973, Functional forms for profit and transformation functions, Journal of Economic Theory 6, 284–316.

Diewert, W.E., 1974, Applications of duality theory, in: M. Intriligator and D. Kendrick, eds., Frontiers in quantitative economics, Vol. 2 (North-Holland, Amsterdam), 106–171.

Theil, Henri, 1971, Principles of econometrics (Wiley, New York).

ON DEVIATIONS BETWEEN NEOCLASSICAL AND GFT-BASED TRUE COST-OF-LIVING INDEXES DERIVED FROM THE SAME DEMAND FUNCTION SYSTEM*

R.L. BASMANN

Texas A&M University, College Station, TX 77843, USA

C.A. DIAMOND

Utah State University, Logan, UT 84321, USA

J.C. FRENTRUP

University of Texas at Arlington, TX 76019, USA

S.N. WHITE

Texas A&M University, College Station, TX 77843, USA

Given that a generalized Fechner–Thurstone (GFT) direct utility function and a neoclassical direct utility function yield exactly the same system of demand functions, then for which combinations of (a) regions of the domain of neoclassical parameters and (b) price and total expenditure regimes, do the alternative true cost-of-living indexes (TCLI's) and their sensitivities to changes in causal factors differ significantly? Practical neoclassical alternatives to the GFT-based non-parametric TCLI's are limited to parametric TCLI's based on the class of implicit utility models discussed by Barnett. This paper describes the design and results of a simulation experiment which generated alternative TCLI's under different parameter specifications. Focus of appraisal is on specifications which produced realistic demand elasticities and large deviations between TCLI's.

1. Introduction

The definition of 'true cost-of-living' presupposes the existence of an indifference 'map' or direct utility function [Konyus (1924, 1936), Fisher and Shell (1968)]. Given an indifference surface, $\boldsymbol{S}$, and two price regimes, $\boldsymbol{p}^e$ and $\boldsymbol{p}^d$,[1] the ratio of the minimum total expenditure required to reach $\boldsymbol{S}$ under $\boldsymbol{p}^e$

*A part of this research was supported by National Science Foundation Grant SOC 77-27068 and by a research grant from the College of Liberal Arts, Texas A&M University. We are also indebted to David Hill, Director, Public Policy Research Laboratory, College of Liberal Arts, Texas A&M University, and Associate Dean Arnold Vedlitz for much valuable assistance. Helpful comments and criticisms have been received from W. A. Barnett, W.E. Diewert, D.W. Jorgenson, D.J. Molina, D.J. Slottje, T.M. Stoker, A. Yatchew, and the two referees of this article. Authors bear sole responsibility for errors and omissions.

[1] $\boldsymbol{p}$ is a vector of n positive prices.

to the minimum total expenditure required to reach $\boldsymbol{S}$ under $\boldsymbol{p}^d$ determines the relative cost-of-living under $\boldsymbol{p}^e$, when $\boldsymbol{S}$ and $\boldsymbol{p}^d$ are taken as standards. The neoclassical definition of 'true cost-of-living index' presupposes the *strict* neoclassical assumption that the taste-descriptive parameters of utility functions ascribed to groups of one or more consumers are absolutely independent of budget constraint prices and total expenditure. The strict neoclassical assumption is sufficient (not necessary) for the derived system of aggregate demand functions to be *regular*.[2] The pitfalls of this extrapolation from neoclassical micro demand theory to aggregate demand theory have been stressed from Schultz (1938, pp. 628–633) to Muellbauer (1975, p. 525). Neoclassical utility functions cannot rationalize the construction of TCLI's when demand function systems are non-regular.

A primary use of the *generalized Fechner–Thurstone* (GFT) form of direct utility function [see (2a)–(2d) below] is to rationalize the construction of Konyus–Fisher–Shell true cost-of-living indexes (TCLI's) from *non-regular* systems of aggregate demand or expenditure functions attributed to groups of consumers. Since the GFT form of direct utility rationalizes any regular or non-regular system of demand functions that satisfy the ordinary linear budget constraint [Basmann et al. (1983a; 1984a, b; 1985, esp. sec. I.C)], it provides the indifference surface $\boldsymbol{S}$ presupposed by the Konyus–Fisher–Shell definition of 'true cost-of-living' in the case of non-regular market demand functions. The GFT form of direct utility function rationalizes the use of *non-parametric* TCLI's. This means that only two observations are required. The calculation requires only base-period and current-period price and total expenditure data. Since no parameter estimation is involved, commodities need not be aggregated into groups. Use of the GFT form of direct utility function specifically rationalizes the *Fisher formulas* 29 and 23 as TCLI's [Fisher (1922; 1927, pp. 468–473)].[3] These non-parametric TCLI's can be computed directly from survey data routinely prepared for computation of the BLS CPI-U and CPI-W at little additional expense.

Obviously the GFT direct utility function can be used as an hypothesis in its own right. In that use it is assumed that tastes are slightly dependent on budget constraint prices and total expenditure. However, it is not assumed that the slight dependence is negligible in all possible applications [Basmann et al. (1985, sec. I.C–D, app. D), Basmann and White (1985)]. As an hypothesis in its own right, it is not an 'approximation' to an imagined 'true' hypothesis.

[2] I.e., the demand system possesses all of the following properties: (1) homogeneity of degree zero in prices and total expenditure; (2) partial derivatives of demand functions form a matrix of *apparent substitution terms* [Basmann et al. (1984b, p. 25)] that is (a) negative definite and (b) symmetric.

[3] Samuelson and Swamy (1974) and Diewert (1981, p. 183) pointed out that these formulas afford TCLI's for the Cobb–Douglas direct utility function with fixed exponents.

On the other hand the GFT form of direct utility function may be used as a 'flexible form'. When the GFT direct utility function is used as a flexible form to approximate an assumed strictly neoclassical direct utility function, it rationalizes the use of *Fisher formula* 123 as a TCLI.[4]

One important use of the non-parametric TCLI formulas based on the GFT direct utility function is the assessment of their sensitivity to changes in prices, total expenditures, changes in (measures of) the riskiness of monetary assets held by consumers and other systematic variables producing changes in consumers' tastes, and stochastic taste changers [Basmann et al. (1985, app. B) and Basmann and Slottje (1985)].

The capability of the GFT direct utility function to rationalize all systems of demand functions, regular or non-regular, puts a considerable premium on estimating regular forms of aggregate demand systems and using the inferred neoclassical utility functions to construct *parametric* TCLI's. It is important to compare them[5] with the GFT-based *non-parametric* TCLI's whenever it is found that the regular demand systems agree well with the aggregate data. Even if the alternative direct utility functions yield exactly the same system of demand functions, their respective TCLI's are different. [This is well illustrated in sections 3 and 4 of this paper.] Other things being equal, the larger the difference, the more interesting the alternatives, at least from the point of view of policy-making. Moreover the GFT TCLI's and the neoclassical TCLI's have different degrees of sensitivity to changes in prices, total expenditure, systematic and stochastic taste changers. It might be that the GFT-based TCLI is much less sensitive to increases in (say) housing prices than the neoclassical TCLI. Considered as alternatives for pegging COLA programs, for instance, the GFT and neoclassical TCLI's would yield different timings and amounts of cost-of-living increases as well as and forecasts of future COLA program costs.

This article presents research on one aspect of the subject. It considers the following question: Given that a GFT direct utility function and a neoclassical direct utility function yield exactly the same system of demand functions, for which combinations of (a) regions of the domain of neoclassical parameters and (b) price and total expenditure regimes do the alternative TCLI's and their sensitivities to changes in causal factors differ 'significantly'?[6] At the present time it appears that practical neoclassical alternatives to the GFT-based TCLI's are limited to TCLI's based on direct utility functions in the class of *implicit utility models* [Barnett (1981, ch. 9) and Hanoch (1971, 1975)]. More-

[4] *Fisher formula* 123 is the simple geometric mean of *formulas* 23 and 29. *Formula* 123 is also known as the Tornqvist index.

[5] No question of an empirical test, or statistical test of hypothesis (a logical impossibility) is involved here.

[6] What is, and what is not, a 'significant' deviation between the alternative TCLI's is dependent on the exigencies of diverse applications. No attempt is made to assign the term a definitive meaning in the present article.

over, the present paper focuses on direct utility functions having the CRES[7] form introduced by Mukerji (1963) and extended by others, e.g., Gorman (1965), Hanoch (1971, 1975) and Barnett (1981, pp. 261–262)].

Section 2.1 describes the GFT direct utility function only very briefly. For a comprehensive treatment, the reader may consult Basmann et al. (1985, esp. app. A, C). Section 2.B, which describes the CRES form of direct utility function, is equally brief. For more details, the reader may consult the papers cited just above. It is important to emphasize that the only GFT direct utility function specifications used in this paper are those that yield exactly the same globally regular demand function systems as the neoclassical specifications of (7a)–(7d) in section 2.B.

Section 3 describes the design of the simulation experiment. Section 4 compares the alternative GFT and neoclassical TCLI's under the different specifications of parameters of (7a)–(7d). Appraisal focuses on parameter specifications that produce (a) 'realistic' demand elasticities and (b) the greatest deviations between alternative TCLI's. Concluding remarks appear in section 5.

2. The alternative TCLI's in this study

2.1. TCLI's based on the GFT direct utility function

Let $\boldsymbol{p}=(p_1,\ldots,p_n)$ be a vector of positive prices and let M be a positive quantity of nominal money. Assume that a collection of one or more consumers allocates M to the purchase of commodities in accordance with the usual linear budget constraint

$$\sum_{k=1}^{n} p_k X_k = M. \tag{1}$$

This allocative behavior necessarily results in maximization of a direct utility function having the form

$$U(\boldsymbol{X};\theta)=\prod_{i=1}^{n}(X_i-\gamma_i)^{\theta_i}, \tag{2a}$$

where

$$X_i > \max\{0,\gamma_i\}, \tag{2b}$$

$$\theta_i=\theta_i^*(p,M,\Psi)\mathrm{e}^{u_i},\quad \theta_i>0,\quad i=1,2,\ldots,n, \tag{2c}$$

$$\theta=\sum_{i=1}^{n}\theta_i. \tag{2d}$$

[7]Constant ratio of elasticity of substitution. This name is due to Hanoch.

In general, the exponents θ_i are dependent on $\boldsymbol{p}$ and M. At each point $\boldsymbol{X}$ of the domain of (2a)–(2d) the marginal rate of substitution of commodity k for i is directly proportional to the ratio θ_i/θ_k, $i, k = 1, \ldots, n$. Consequently at each fixed point $\boldsymbol{X}$, variations of the budget constraint prices $\boldsymbol{p}$ and total expenditure M produce changes in marginal rates of substitution and convexity-preserving deformations of the indifference surface through $\boldsymbol{X}$. [The fixed point $\boldsymbol{X}$ is not necessarily in the budget plane.]

In empirical applications of the GFT direct utility function Ψ is a taste-descriptive parameter vector that depends on a specified observable non-stochastic vector, z. In the present article no loss of generality is caused by assuming that the taste-descriptive parameter $\gamma = 0$.

$\boldsymbol{u} = (u_1, \ldots, u_n)$ is a latent taste-descriptive random vector with zero mean vector and finite positive definite variance matrix, $\boldsymbol{W}_0$. An economic theory of the vector stochastic process $\{\boldsymbol{u}_t\}$, applicable to all forms of direct utility function, is presented in Basmann (1985) and Basmann et al. (1985, app. A).

The systematic parts of the exponent functions (2c) can be specified and estimated by a variety of methods. Non-parametric methods are the least restrictive on the form of demand function systems ascribed to groups of one or more consumers. We consider them first, postponing mention of parametric methods to the end of the discussion of non-parametric TCLI's. Given a sample of observations $(\boldsymbol{p}, M, z)$, let demand elasticities E_{i0}, E_{ij} and E_{iz} with respect to M, to p_j and to z_q be assigned to each observation. Various computer algorithms are available for this. Let the systematic parts of the exponent parameters θ_i be specified by

$$\theta_i^* = p_i \left(\beta_i M^{E_{i0}} \prod_{j=1}^{n} p_j^{E_{ij}} \right) \left(\prod_{q=1}^{n} z_q^{E_{iz_q}} \right), \quad i = 1, \ldots, n. \tag{3}$$

The method just described is not the only method of determining the exponent functions θ_i from non-parametrically estimated demand elasticities [Basmann et al. (1985, sec. I.C), Basmann and Slottje (1985) and Basmann and White (1985)]. However, it is the procedure used in section 3 of this paper.

Use of (3) and non-parametrically estimated demand elasticities is not essential to the non-parametric character of TCLI's based on the GFT direct utility function (2a)–(2d). Given the base-period expenditures and prices, the current-period expenditures and prices, the GFT TCLI's are uniquely determined for a broad class of alternative parameter specifications. We explain briefly.

Let a magnitude U^0 of (2a) be given. The minimum expenditure required to reach the indifference surface $U(\boldsymbol{X}, \theta) = U^0$ at $\boldsymbol{p}$ is given by the formula

$$M(U^0) = (U^0)^{1/\theta} \left[\prod_{i=1}^{n} p_i^{\theta_i/\theta} \right] \Big/ \prod_{i=1}^{n} (\theta_i/\theta)^{\theta_i/\theta}. \tag{4}$$

The base-period and current-period expenditures on commodities are assumed to be equilibrium expenditures. At equilibrium, first-order conditions imply that each expenditure share, M_i/M, is equal to the corresponding exponent ratio, θ_i/θ. Consequently, for the GFT form (2a)–(2d) the true cost-of-living indexes TCLI(0) and TCLI(1) are expressed by the following formulas:

$$\text{GFT TCLI}(0)=\prod_{i=1}^{n}\left(p_i^1/p_i^0\right)^{M_i^0/M^0}, \tag{5a}$$

$$\text{GFT TCLI}(1)=\prod_{i=1}^{n}\left(p_i^1/p_i^0\right)^{M_i^1/M^1}, \tag{5b}$$

where M_i denotes expenditure on the ith commodity. Superscripts indicate the period in which the expenditure is made. '0' denotes the *base period*, '1' denotes the *current period*.

Formula (5a) is the GFT version of one valid kind of relative cost-of-living index,[8] a kind that ignores the changes of taste between base period and current period [Samuelson and Swamy (1974, p. 586)]. Formula (5b) is the GFT version of another kind of relative cost-of-living index; this kind takes into account the changes in taste between base period and current period. Fisher and Shell (1968, p. 100) define another kind of TCLI that takes account of changes in taste. The GFT version of the Fisher–Shell TCLI, however, coincides in value with GFT TCLI(1). Yet another kind of TCLI that takes account of changes in taste between periods is mentioned in Basmann et al. (1985, sec. II.B) along with the Fisher–Shell definition. However, its GFT version coincides in value with the GFT-based Fisher–Shell TCLI and the GFT TCLI(1).

The sensitivities of GFT TCLI(1) with respect to changes of current-period prices, total expenditure, M, systematic taste changers in z, and random taste changers in $\boldsymbol{u}$ are expressed as elasticities. The formulas for those elasticities of (5b) can be expressed directly in terms of the demand elasticities, namely, E_{i0} and E_{ij}, $i, j=1,\ldots,n$, etc. However, there is one caution to be exercised in this procedure: positive estimates of own-price elasticities E_{ii} should not be substituted in the sensitivity formulas [Basmann et al. (1985, sec. II.B)] without consideration of their 'realism' and the possible need of corrective action, e.g., respecification of the elements of z.

When the GFT direct utility function is used as a flexible form approximation for a neoclassical direct utility function, the ordinary geometric mean of

[8] It is essential to notice that simultaneous existence of two or more valid kinds of TCLI is not unique to the GFT form of direct utility function [Fisher and Shell (1968, p. 97) and Basmann et al. (1985, sec. II.B)].

GFT TCLI(0) and GFT TCLI(1),

$$\text{GFT TCLI}(*) = \{[\text{GFT TCLI}(0)] * [\text{GFT TCLI}(1)]\}^{1/2}, \tag{6}$$

is used as an approximation of the neoclassical-based TCLI. We shall use (6) in section 3.

Other specifications of the systematic parts of the exponents θ_i, $i = 1, \ldots, n$, in (2a)–(d) are available. They leave the TCLI's invariant, but yield alternative assessments of sensitivities of TCLI's to changes in prices, total expenditure, etc. Flexible forms, such as the translog form [Christensen et al. (1975)], the generalized Leontief form [Caves and Christensen (1980)], the Fourier flexible form [Gallant (1981)], and the minflex Laurent flexible form [Barnett (1985) and Barnett and Lee (1985)] can be used for the purpose. Regions of regularity of the demand function systems derived from the GFT direct utility function in such cases necessarily coincide with those of the flexible form used [Basmann et al. (1985, sec. I.C)].

Another method of determining the systematic parts of θ_i in (2a)–(2d) is mentioned here because (a variant of) it is used in the simulation experiment. Given parametric estimates or specifications of the parameters of a neoclassical direct utility function, e.g., (7a)–(7d) below, use the derived parametric expressions for the demand elasticities in (3) to substitute in (3). The resulting parametric specification of the GFT direct utility function rationalizes the same regular demand function system but yields different TCLI's.

2.2. *Neoclassical-based TCLI's considered in this study*

The set of strictly *neoclassical* direct utility functions we have simulated thus far has the CRES form (7a)–(7d). With stochastic taste changers omitted, i.e., with $\boldsymbol{u} = 0$, (7a)–(7d) becomes Mukerji's extension of the CES form of production function [Mukerji (1963, p. 233)]. Formal properties of (7a)–(7d) have been comprehensively analyzed by Gorman (1965), Hanoch (1971, pp. 708–711; 1975, pp. 416–418) and Barnett (1981, pp. 265–266).

$$V(\boldsymbol{X}; \Psi, \boldsymbol{u}) = \left[\sum_{i=1}^{n} e^{u_i} \beta_i^{1-c_i} X_i^{c_i}\right]^{\delta}, \qquad X_i > 0, \tag{7a}$$

$$\delta \neq 0, \qquad c_i \neq 0, \qquad c_i < 1; \tag{7b}$$

$$c_i < 0 \quad \text{for every } i \quad \text{if} \quad c_i < 0, \tag{7c}$$

$$\delta \text{ has the same sign as } c_i, \qquad i, k = 1, \ldots, n. \tag{7d}$$

The subset of CES direct utility functions is defined by identity of the c_i parameters, *viz*,

$$c_i = c, \qquad i = 1, \ldots, n: \tag{8}$$

All of the CES direct utility functions used in the study reported here belong to the subset that satisfies

$$\delta = (1 - c)/c. \tag{9}$$

In addition to TCLI's based on the strict neoclassical direct utility functions having the CRES form, we shall also consider TCLI's based on a form of direct utility functions that can be obtained from the CRES form (7a)–(7d) with the specifications (8)–(9) by allowing the parameters β_i to depend on p_i and M according to

$$\beta_i = K\mu_i (M/p_i)^{1+b_i} p_i^{c/(c-1)} \tag{10a}$$

$$b_i > -1, \tag{10b}$$

$$\mu_i > 0, \tag{10c}$$

$$\sum_{i=1}^{n} \mu_i = 1, \tag{10d}$$

where K is a positive constant.

Except in the special cases just defined, analytic expressions for the system of demand functions rationalized by (7a)–(7d) are not available. However, the magnitudes of the demand functions can be determined by means of an algorithm. Such an algorithm is used in section 3. Systems of demand functions rationalized by the CES direct utility function (7a)–(7d) under specification (8)–(9) have the *generalized Klein–Rubin* form [Klein and Rubin (1947), Basmann (1968, pp. 154–165) and Christensen and Manser (1975)]. Systems of demand functions derived under (8), (9) and (10a)–(10d) rationalize the *addilog* system of demand functions [Leser (1941-2), Houthakker (1960), Arrow (1961) and Gorman (1963)].

3. Design of the simulation

A brief look at the computer-generated graphics in figs. 1 and 2 shows how the simulation results help to find significant neoclassical alternatives to the non-parametric cost-of-living indexes based on the GFT form. For (7a)–(7d) with $n = 2$, figs. 1 and 2 show deviations between the TCLI based on (7a)–(7d)

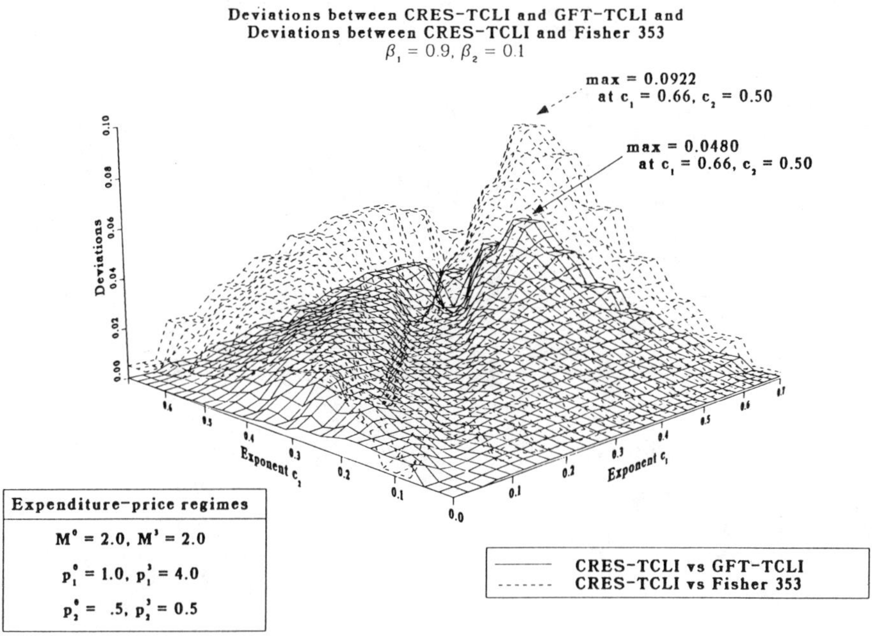

Fig. 1

and the GFT TCLI based on (2a)–(2d) when the two direct utility functions rationalize the same system of demand functions exactly. The deviations are shown plotted (solid lines)[9] against parameter specifications (c_1, c_2).[10] The base- and current-period price data simulate a considerable degree of price inflation (as measured by a Laspeyres price index)[11] that is due to an increase of the price ratio p_1/p_2 to 400 percent of its base-period magnitude. Higher levels of price inflation favor the finding of neoclassical-based TCLI's that are significant alternatives to their GFT-based counterparts. Figs. 1 and 2 depict the 'valley of homotheticity' running along the line $c_1 = c_2$ in both regions of the domain. The CES special cases of (7a)–(7d) are located in the 'streambed' of that 'valley'. The graphics make clear where to look for parameters (c_1, c_2) for which – when $\beta_1 = 0.9$ – the neoclassical-based TCLI is likely to differ significantly from the non-parametric GFT-based TCLI.

[9] The surface described by dashed lines show the deviations between the neoclassical TCLI and *Fisher formula* 353. The special use of this price index in the experiment will be explained later.

[10] Notice in fig. 1 that the part of the domain for which $c_i > 0.7$, $i = 1, 2$, is not shown. This will be explained later.

[11] From 160.0 to about 300. Details later.

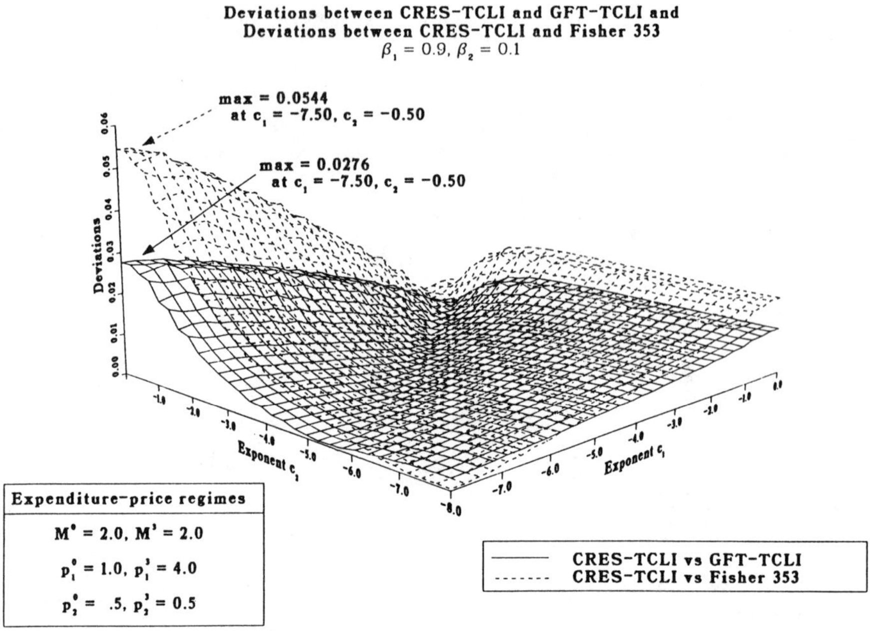

Fig. 2

A few remarks about the design of the experiment are needed. Of course, the major thing was to ensure that the globally regular direct utility functions (7a)–(7d) and (10a)–(10d) and the GFT direct utility functions generated the same system of demand functions exactly. This has been accomplished as follows: In this initial phase we specify that the stochastic taste changer, $\boldsymbol{u}$, appearing in (2a)–(2d) and (7a)–(7d), is constant and equal to 0. This loss of verisimilitude was unavoidable.[12] Then, given one of the $(\boldsymbol{p}, M)$ regimes shown in table 1 (lower left), we compute the equilibrium demand magnitudes for various parameter specifications (β_1, c_1, c_2). Using this data we proceed directly to compute the non-parametric TCLI's based on the GFT direct utility function. The neoclassical TCLI's for the general CRES direct utility function (7a)–(7d) are computed by an algorithm. Neoclassical TCLI's under the CES specification (8)–(9), and the globally regular non-neoclassical TCLI's under (10a)–(10d) are computed by means of an algorithm.

For each specification of parameters of the CRES direct utility function the standard indifference surface S^0 is determined by calculating the base-period

[12]A very limited budget would have dictated this specification anyway. A *Monte Carlo* simulation with statistical estimates of parameters of (7a)–(7d) and the stochastic process $\{\boldsymbol{u}_t\}$ described in Basmann (1985, app. A) would be needed.

equilibrium demand X^0. This base-period X^0 is also used to construct a *measure of inflation* to correspond to the TCLI's [Basmann et al. (1985, sec. III.A)]. We use the *Fisher formula* 53, or Laspeyres price index, for this purpose. X^0 and p^0 determine the weights. For each different current-period price regime, the Laspeyres price index varies from specification to specification of parameters β_1, c_1, c_2. See tables 1–4. For each parameter specification the current-period equilibrium demand vector is used to construct weights for the Paasche price index.[13]

'Verisimilitude' of demand elasticities has to do for us what statistical tests of the globally regular direct utility functions would do in application to actual price and expenditure data. In actual practice, serious consideration of TCLI's based on neoclassical and globally regular direct utility functions as alternatives to the non-parametric GFT-based TCLI's has value only under very special circumstances.

In that region of the (c_1, c_2) domain for which at least one c_i exceeds 0.7, the CRES direct utility function (7a)–(7d) generates very large own-price elasticities. For instance, with the price regime of period 3, the CRES specified by $\beta_1 = 0.5$, $c_1 = c_2 = 0.95$, the own-price elasticity $E_{11} = -20$. Even with $c_1 = c_2 = 0.8$, the own-price elasticity $E_{11} = -5.000$. Such magnitudes of own-price elasticites lack verisimilitude. In other words, demand functions derived from a parametric specification of the neoclassical (7a)–(7d) that implied such large elasticities, simply would not fit actual time-series data very well; at least not actual data like that which is available. Yet it is just in this region, where at least one $c_i > 0.7$, that the TCLI's based on (7a)–(7d) begin to deviate considerably from the non-parametric TCLI's based on (2a)–(2d). Other things being equal, the greater such deviations, the more warrant for considering the neoclassical TCLI's as alternatives to the non-parametric GFT TCLI's. In fact, with $c_1 = 0.95$ and $c_2 = 0.4$ (approximately) or 0.65 (approximately) the deviation reaches almost 20 percent of the mean value of the alternative TCLI's.[14]

Consider a designer of COLA's who has a strong belief in the empirical truth of the extrapolation of the strict neoclassical assumption to aggregate con-

[13] The Laspeyres and Paasche price indexes that appear in the tables below are based on equilibrium demands, X^0 in the base period and X^1 in the current period, where total expenditure is the same in both periods. The Paasche index is computed routinely in our simulation experiments and its use in maintaining verisimilitude is the same as that of the simulated Laspeyres price index. See tables 1 and 2. [See Basmann et al. (1985, sec. III.A).]

[14] We tried specifications of (c_1, c_2) with c_1 or c_2 smaller than -7.50, but encountered computational difficulties. The objective function (associated with at least one minimum expenditure bundle for which we attempted to find a solution) required the evaluation of a small number raised to a (relatively) large negative power. We succeeded in running the experiment under c_1, c_2 values as large as -11.0, but were unable to maintain a uniform distribution over the subdomain for values less than -7.50. Some of these deviations are in fact slightly larger than those reported here, the absolute largest being the deviation between the CRES TCLI and the *Fisher formula* 353 at 0.1265 for $\beta_1 = 0.5$, period 3, $c_1 = -11.0$, $c_2 = -1.0$. The largest deviation between the CRES TCLI and the GFT TCLI is 0.0910 for $\beta_1 = 0.5$, $c_1 = -11.0$, $c_2 = -1.0$, for period 3.

Table 1

Dedicated cost-of-living indexes and selected largest deviations for the constant ratios of elasticities of substitution (CRES) utility function; specification (13a)–(13e); $\beta_1 = 0.5$, $\beta_2 = 0.5$.

$c_1/$ c_2	Period	CRES TCLI[a]	GFT TCLI[b]	Deviation[c] CRES TCLI and GFT TCLI	F(353)	Deviation[c] CRES TCLI and F(353)	Fisher 53 (Laspeyres)	Fisher 54 (Paasche)
−9.00/	1	1.323	1.323	0.0003	1.323	0.0000	1.325	1.321
−9.00	2	1.644	1.640	0.0014	1.643	0.0002	1.651	1.635
	3	2.911	2.863	0.0083	2.905	0.0011	2.953	2.857
−7.50/	1	1.203	1.220	0.0112	1.220	0.0111	1.208	1.232
−0.50	2	1.400	1.466	0.0324	1.469	0.0338	1.416	1.523
	3	2.149	2.562	0.0882	2.766	0.1266	2.248	3.403
−7.00/	1	1.207	1.224	0.0112	1.224	0.0112	1.212	1.236
−0.50	2	1.407	1.473	0.0320	1.476	0.0337	1.425	1.529
	3	2.168	2.572	0.0857	2.771	0.1231	2.274	3.378
−6.00/	1	1.217	1.233	0.0111	1.233	0.0112	1.222	1.245
−0.50	2	1.425	1.489	0.0311	1.493	0.0330	1.445	1.543
	3	2.212	2.596	0.0800	2.783	0.1150	2.334	3.318
0.30/	1	1.427	1.424	0.0018	1.422	0.0029	1.440	1.405
0.06	2	1.835	1.823	0.0047	1.811	0.0096	1.880	1.744
	3	3.350	3.253	0.0148	3.080	0.0420	3.639	2.607
0.30/	1	1.054	1.055	0.0004	1.057	0.0017	1.071	1.042
0.54	2	1.089	1.091	0.0012	1.099	0.0065	1.142	1.057
	3	1.160	1.168	0.0035	1.233	0.0305	1.427	1.066
0.58/	1	1.308	1.301	0.0047	1.299	0.0062	1.348	1.251
0.34	2	1.556	1.528	0.0129	1.518	0.0177	1.695	1.359
	3	2.209	2.053	0.0366	2.038	0.0403	3.085	1.346
0.66/	1	1.399	1.389	0.0056	1.386	0.0077	1.421	1.352
0.26	2	1.762	1.722	0.0164	1.700	0.0253	1.842	1.570
	3	2.977	2.627	0.0626	2.452	0.0971	3.525	1.705
0.66/	1	1.350	1.339	0.0064	1.336	0.0085	1.384	1.289
0.34	2	1.644	1.602	0.0184	1.584	0.0261	1.767	1.421
	3	2.475	2.191	0.0610	2.132	0.0748	3.301	1.376
0.66/	1	1.202	1.198	0.0030	1.199	0.0022	1.262	1.139
0.50	2	1.323	1.313	0.0053	1.324	0.0007	1.525	1.150
	3	1.507	1.534	0.0088	1.663	0.0493	2.575	1.074
0.66/	1	1.122	1.122	0.0003	1.126	0.0031	1.179	1.076
0.58	2	1.180	1.187	0.0039	1.207	0.0160	1.359	1.072
	3	1.250	1.318	0.0268	1.463	0.0790	2.076	1.031
0.67/	1	1.061	1.063	0.0015	1.067	0.0047	1.100	1.035
0.67	2	1.085	1.094	0.0059	1.112	0.0176	1.200	1.030
	3	1.109	1.161	0.0227	1.272	0.0685	1.600	1.012

Expenditure–price regimes

Period	M	p_1	p_2
0	2	1.0	0.5
1	2	1.5	0.5
2	2	2.0	0.5
3	2	4.0	0.5

[a] CRES TCLI computed according to (10a)–(10d).
[b] GFT TCLI computed according to (6).
[c] Deviations computed according to (11a)–(11b).

Table 2

Dedicated cost-of-living indexes and selected largest deviations for the constant ratios of elasticities of substitution (CRES) utility function; specification (13a)–(13e); $\beta_1 = 0.9$, $\beta_2 = 0.1$.

$c_1/$ c_2	Period	CRES TCLI[a]	GFT TCLI[b]	Deviation[c] CRES TCLI and GFT TCLI	F(353)	Deviation[c] CRES TCLI and F(353)	Fisher 53 (Laspeyres)	Fisher 54 (Paasche)
−9.00/	1	1.471	1.471	0.0003	1.471	0.0000	1.472	1.471
−9.00	2	1.942	1.941	0.0006	1.942	0.0001	1.944	1.940
	3	3.822	3.803	0.0026	3.820	0.0004	3.831	3.808
−7.50/	1	1.401	1.428	0.0154	1.432	0.0180	1.407	1.459
−0.50	2	1.794	1.864	0.0269	1.888	0.0362	1.813	1.966
	3	3.324	3.513	0.0276	3.706	0.0544	3.440	3.993
−7.00/	1	1.407	1.432	0.0143	1.437	0.0168	1.413	1.460
−0.50	2	1.807	1.872	0.0250	1.895	0.0337	1.826	1.966
	3	3.361	3.543	0.0264	3.725	0.0514	3.478	3.991
−6.00/	1	1.420	1.441	0.0120	1.445	0.0140	1.426	1.464
−0.50	2	1.832	1.888	0.0211	1.907	0.0283	1.852	1.965
	3	3.439	3.606	0.0236	3.764	0.0451	3.555	3.985
0.30/	1	1.490	1.489	0.0003	1.489	0.0005	1.492	1.486
0.06	2	1.976	1.974	0.0008	1.971	0.0019	1.983	1.959
	3	3.903	3.883	0.0026	3.828	0.0098	3.949	3.710
0.30/	1	1.212	1.217	0.0034	1.217	0.0035	1.255	1.180
0.54	2	1.366	1.381	0.0081	1.384	0.0092	1.510	1.268
	3	1.731	1.805	0.0208	1.845	0.0317	2.530	1.345
0.58/	1	1.466	1.463	0.0016	1.461	0.0026	1.474	1.448
0.34	2	1.917	1.904	0.0048	1.890	0.0100	1.949	1.832
	3	3.607	3.455	0.0214	3.224	0.0561	3.847	2.703
0.66/	1	1.483	1.481	0.0012	1.480	0.0018	1.487	1.473
0.26	2	1.960	1.950	0.0036	1.942	0.0066	1.974	1.909
	3	3.818	3.701	0.0156	3.530	0.0392	3.923	3.177
0.66/	1	1.474	1.471	0.0016	1.469	0.0026	1.481	1.458
0.34	2	1.936	1.922	0.0052	1.910	0.0099	1.961	1.859
	3	3.697	3.520	0.0244	3.288	0.0585	3.884	2.784
0.66/	1	1.433	1.428	0.0029	1.424	0.0051	1.454	1.395
0.50	2	1.827	1.801	0.0100	1.776	0.0200	1.908	1.653
	3	3.079	2.797	0.0480	2.561	0.0922	3.723	1.762
0.66/	1	1.381	1.376	0.0031	1.371	0.0060	1.421	1.323
0.58	2	1.689	1.664	0.0106	1.638	0.0216	1.841	1.457
	3	2.419	2.259	0.0342	2.169	0.0546	3.523	1.335
0.67/	1	1.275	1.273	0.0008	1.271	0.0024	1.346	1.200
0.67	2	1.442	1.440	0.0010	1.437	0.0028	1.692	1.219
	3	1.668	1.760	0.0209	1.841	0.0435	3.077	1.102

Expenditure–price regimes

Period	M	p_1	p_2
0	2	1.0	0.5
1	2	1.5	0.5
2	2	2.0	0.5
3	2	4.0	0.5

[a] CRES TCLI computed according to (10a)–(10d).
[b] GFT TCLI computed according to (6).
[c] Deviations computed according to (11a)–(11b).

sumer preferences. He could validly interpret the GFT-based TCLI's in tables 1 and 2 as potentially useful 'proxies' for the neoclassical TCLI. There is precedent for that kind of interpretation. A statistical price index often proposed as a 'proxy' for the unique TCLI based on an *unspecified* neoclassical direct utility function is the *Fisher formula* 353 [Fisher (1922; 1927, pp. 227–230)]. Under the assumption that the indifference map remains approximately constant, it is a reasonable expectation that the *Fisher formula* 353 would afford a good approximation for the Konyus true cost-of-living index. This expectation has received considerable support in the comprehensive investigations by Diewert (1973, 1976, 1978), Diewert and Parkan (1978, 1979) and Diewert (1981). We compute this index routinely. Deviations between the neoclassical TCLI and the *Fisher formula* 353 are shown in tables 1 and 2.[15] Those combinations of neoclassical indifference 'map' parameters and price and expenditure data for which they are not good 'proxies', where they differ significantly, remain the cases of practical interest under this interpretation.

In assessing the 'closeness' of approximation of one true cost-of-living index by another, the deviation between them it appears appropriate to be weight deviations inversely by a measure of the deviation of ratios of current-period to base-period prices,

$$p_i^1/p_i^0, \qquad i=1,2,\ldots,n.$$

The smaller the deviation of these prices ratios, the greater the weight of a 'unit' of deviation. We use a weighted measure, D, of 'closeness' or 'deviation' between two cost-of-living indexes, I_1 and I_2, which is defined by the following formula:

$$D=\left[e^{-\omega}|I_1-I_2|\right]/\sqrt{(I_1\times I_2)}, \tag{11a}$$

where ω is the standard deviation of logarithms of ratios

$$\omega=\sqrt{\left[(1/n)\sum_{i=1}^{n}\left\{\ln(p_i^1/p_i^0)-\left[\frac{\sum_{i=1}^{n}\ln(p_i^1/p_i^0)}{n}\right]\right\}\right]^2}. \tag{11b}$$

The weight, $e^{-\omega}$, measures the extent to which the current budget constraint is parallel to the base-period budget constraint. This weighting scheme is in-

[15]The non-parametric index numbers, developed by Afriat (1967, 1981) [also cf. Diewert (1981, pp. 198–199)], would afford appropriate alternatives to the non-parametric cost-of-living indexes based on the GFT direct utility function, at least in those cases where the neoclassical or regular direct utility function is approximately homothetic and the parameter Ψ is independent of the budget constraint and other parameters affecting the indifference 'map'. More interesting, however, would be a comparison of the GFT-based cost-of-living indexes and the Afriat and Diewert non-parametric indexes on data batches generated by direct utility functions with markedly non-homothetic indifference 'maps'.

tended to compensate for the differential effects of ceteris paribus changes in total expenditure on the cost-of-living indexes being compared.

4. Deviations between GFT TCLI's and neoclassical TCLI's

4.1. Deviations between CES TCLI and GFT TCLI

The two CES cases for which the deviations between the CES TCLI and the GFT TCLI are largest are shown in tables 1 and 2, *viz*, $c = -9.0$ and $c = 0.67$. The only difference between table 1 and table 2 is in the specification of the parameter β_1 of the CRES direct utility function (7a)–(7d).

In both tables the maximum deviation between CES TCLI and GFT TCLI occurs for the specification $c = 0.67$ with the price regime of period 3. In table 1 the *maximum* CES deviation is 0.0227 (2.3 percent); in table 2 the *maximum* CES deviation is 0.0209 (2.1 percent). In each table the equilibrium demand associated with the maximum deviation occurs very near the X_2 axis of the indifference map. In table 1, the period 3 equilibrium demand vector is $(0.00769, 3.938)$; in table 2, the period 3 equilibrium demand vector is $(0.0616, 3.507)$. In table 1 the own-price elasticities of demand associated with the maximum deviation (period 3) are $E_{11} = -2.97$, $E_{22} = -1.031$; in table 2 the corresponding own-price elasticities are $E_{11} = -2.75$, $E_{22} = -1.25$.

In table 1, for each specification of $c_1 = c_2 = c$ the largest deviation between CES TCLI and GFT TCLI occurs for period 3; the next-to-largest occurs for period 2; the smallest deviation for the specification occurs for period 1. The level of price inflation as measured by the Laspeyres price index is greatest when the deviation is greatest (for a given specification) and least when the deviation is least.

Moving along the $c_1 = c_2$ line, the deviations between CES TCLI and GFT TCLI for a given period steadily decrease as the parameter specification of c decreases towards zero, then increase as c decreases through negative specifications. This pattern is seen to hold for both $\beta_1 = 0.5$ and $\beta_2 = 0.9$ specifications.

Deviations between the CES TCLI and the GFT TCLI remain smaller than the corresponding deviations between the CES TCLI and the *Fisher formula* 353 until the magnitude of parameter c decreases to -2. After that the *Fisher formula* 353 index remains closer to CES TCLI as both indexes converge to their limiting value as $c \to \infty$ [Basmann et al. (1985, sec. III.B)].

Comparison of table 1 and table 2 indicates that variation in the relative 'importance' of commodity 1, as reflected by the magnitude of β_1, has little effect on deviations between the CES TCLI and the GFT TCLI.

4.2. Comparison of GFT TCLI(1) and VAL TCLI(1)

No system of demand functions $\boldsymbol{X}(\boldsymbol{p}, M; \Psi, \boldsymbol{u})$ determines a unique direct utility function. However, every system determines a unique family of *Engel functions*. Just as the demand function system might be rationalized by at least one direct utility function besides the GFT form, so, too, might the system of Engel functions. In the present case the demand functions and Engel functions are rationalized by the budget constraint dependent direct utility function specified by (7a)–(7d), (8), and (10a)–(10d), $\delta = 2.0$. For convenience we refer to the TCLI(1) derived from this specification as VAL TCLI(1). It is to be compared with the GFT TCLI(1) derived from the GFT direct utility function that rationalizes the same demand functions.

We simulate these systems here because the addilog Engel functions sometimes exhibit pronounced non-linearity. The 'non-inferiority' of commodities is capable of 'catastrophic' reversals [Basmann et al. (1985, sec. III.C)]. This feature contrasts markedly with the neoclassical versions of (7a)–(7d). The element of chief interest to us in the addilog simulations is the effect on the ability of VAL TCLI(1) to deviate significantly from its GFT TCLI(1) counterpart. Consequently emphasis is placed on the variation of total expenditure M rather than on variation of prices. In addition to the base-period price vector $\boldsymbol{p}^0$, only two alternative current-period price vectors $\boldsymbol{p}^1$ are used, namely, $(2, 0.5)$ and $(4, 0.5)$. Base-period data and fifteen alternative current periods (not necessarily a temporal succession of periods) for 442 alternative parameter specifications of b_i, $i = 1, 2$, $\mu_1 = 0.9$.

Of the 6613 deviations observed in the simulation under the specification $p_1/p_2 = 4.0$ and distributed uniformly over parameter space $b_1, b_2 \in [-5, +5]$, the *maximum* deviation observed between VAL TCLI(1) and GFT TCLI(1) was 0.02120, less than three percent. It occurs under the parameter specifications ($b_1 = 0.9$, $b_2 = 0.4$, $M_5 = 1.5$) and ($b_1 = 1.4$, $b_2 = 0.9$, $M_{10} = 6.0$).

6613 deviations were observed under the price regime where $p_1/p_2 = 8$, with specifications distributed uniformly over the parameter space $(b_1, b_2) \in [-5, +5]$. The maximum deviation observed between VAL TCLI(1) and GFT TCLI(1) was 0.05969. It occurs under the parameter specification ($b_1 = 4.40$, $b_2 = 1.40$, $M_{15} = 11.0$). For this parameter specification commodity 1 is a gross substitute for commodity 2, and commodity 2 is a gross substitute for commodity 1. Both relations are 'strong'.

Under some specifications of (b_1, b_2), the increase of total expenditure M produces a steady decrease in VAL TCLI(1) and GFT TCLI(1), while in others it produces a steady increase. Notice that the simulation experiment *respecifies* the standard indifference surface with each change of M [section 2.2]. Actually the same respecification takes place with the simulation of the CES TCLI; due to homotheticity, however, the respecification has no effect on CES TCLI or GFT TCLI. In the present case things are different.

Consider the specification ($b_1 = -5, b_2 = -1.5$). With current-period price ratio $p_1/p_2 = 4.0$ both cost-of-living indexes decrease with increasing M from 200.0 to 130.0 approximately. What this means is this (and only this): given two consumer groups whose *systems* of tastes are described by (7a)–(7d), (8), and (10a)–(10d) but with different total expenditures, the specific tastes differ between the groups by reason of the difference in total expenditure. For the expenditure strata able to spend $M_9 = 5.00$ or more, tastes have changed to the extent that the more expensive commodity 1 has turned 'inferior' relative to commodity 2. The relative cost-of-living between base period and current period is different for the two groups. Thus the relative cost-of-living due to the increase of p_1 from the base period (in this example) is less for the group of consumers that makes the larger expenditure.

The opposite of this occurs for the specification ($b_1 = 5$, $b_2 = 1.5$). Both VAL TCLI(1) and GFT TCLI(1) steadily increase with total expenditure M.

The phenomenon of relative cost-of-living *increasing* from lower to higher expenditure strata is related to the parameter specifications in the following way: We are simulating a case in which the price of the 'more important' good ($\mu_1 = 0.9$) increases relative to the price p_2. Both VAL TCLI(1) and GFT TCLI(1) increase with increasing M under those specifications for which the 'more important' good is a strong gross substitute for the other, or the 'less important' good (and smaller price increase) is a gross complement of the 'more important'. On the other hand, the phenomenon of relative cost *decreasing* from lower to higher expenditure strata occurs when the 'more important' good is only a weak gross substitute for the 'less important', or it is gross complement for the latter.

4.3. Comparison of CRES TCLI and GFT TCLI

The deviations graphically displayed in figs. 1 and 2 are those between CRES TCLI, derived from (7a)–(7d) with parameters satisfying the neoclassical paradigm, and the non-parametric GFT TCLI, the geometric mean of GFT TCLI(0) and GFT TCLI(1), derived the (2a)–(2d). The two alternative utility functions rationalize exactly the same system of demand functions in this simulation. The deviations shown in figs. 1 and 2 are for the price regime of period 3 and are the largest (generally).[16] As in the comparisons of CES TCLI and GFT TCLI we show corresponding deviations between CRES TCLI and *Fisher formula* 353. The latter are represented by the dashed lines in figs. 1 and 2.

Maximum deviations between CRES TCLI and GFT TCLI are located on each figure. So, too, are maximum deviations between CRES TCLI and *Fisher formula* 353.

For both specifications of parameter β_1, two-hundred forty-four evenly distributed (c_1, c_2) combinations in the positive quadrant are computed for each price and expenditure regime. In the negative quadrant, four-hundred

[16] In the sense that the surfaces depicted in figs. 1 and 2 lie above the corresponding surfaces for the other price regimes.

Table 3

Fisher 53 (Laspeyres) indexes associated with the variable taste addilog direct utility function; specification (18a)–(18c) under (13a)–(13e); $\beta_1 = 0.9$, $\beta_2 = 0.1$.

b_1	b_2	Fisher 53 (Laspeyres)
−5.00	−1.50	1.927
−5.00	1.50	1.614
−2.00	−0.50	1.864
−2.00	0.50	1.761
−0.50	−2.00	1.947
−0.50	2.00	1.529
0.50	−2.00	1.947
0.50	2.00	1.529
2.00	−0.50	1.864
2.00	0.50	1.761
5.00	−1.50	1.927
5.00	1.50	1.614

	Price regimes	
	p_1	p_2
Base period	1.0	0.5
Current periods	2.0	0.5

eighteen evenly distributed (c_2, c_2) combinations are computed for each regime. The largest deviation between the GFT TCLI and the CRES TCLI observed in the experiment is 0.0882 for $\beta_1 = 0.5$, period 3, $c_1 = -7.50$ and $c_2 = -0.50$.[17] Table 1 displays selected *large* deviations between CRES TCLI and GFT TCLI when $\beta_1 = 0.5$ in (7a)–(7d). Each deviation shown there is among the 5 percent *largest* deviations for that specification. Table 2 shows the same information for the parameter specification $\beta_1 = 0.9$.

The deviations reported in tables 1 and 2 are a typical, therefore of practical interest. However, we shall summarize information about the typical deviations first. For $\beta_1 = 0.5$, with (c_1, c_2) in the positive quadrant, period 1, about half of the deviations between CRES TCLI and GFT TCLI are less than 0.0006; 75 percent are less than 0.0019; 95 percent are less than 0.0047. For period 2, half are less than 0.0017; 75 percent are less than 0.0053; 95 percent are less than 0.0129. For period 3, half are less than 0.0059; 75 percent are less than 0.0171; 95 percent are less than 0.0428.

For $\beta_1 = 0.5$, with (c_1, c_2) in the negative quadrant, period 1, about half of the deviations between the CRES TCLI and the GFT TCLI are less than 0.0042; 75 percent are less than 0.0065; 95 percent are less than 0.0091. For period 2, half are less than 0.0102; 75 percent are less than 0.0158; 95 percent are less than 0.0251. For period 3, half are less than 0.0236; 75 percent are less than 0.0375; 95 percent are less than 0.06.

[17] The largest deviation between the *Fisher formula* 353 and the CRES TCLI observed in the experiment is 0.1266 for $\beta_1 = 0.5$, period 3, $c_1 = -7.50$ and $c_2 = -0.50$.

Table 4

Fisher 53 (Laspeyres) indexes associated with the variable taste addilog direct utility function; specification (18a)–(18c) under (13a)–(13e); $\beta_1 = 0.9$, $\beta_2 = 0.1$.

b_1	b_2	Fisher 53 (Laspeyres)
−5.00	−1.50	3.781
−5.00	1.50	2.842
−2.00	−0.50	3.593
−2.00	0.50	3.283
−0.50	−2.00	3.842
−0.50	2.00	2.588
0.50	−2.00	3.842
0.50	2.00	2.588
2.00	−0.50	3.593
2.00	0.50	3.283
5.00	−1.50	3.781
5.00	1.50	2.842

	Price regimes	
	p_1	p_2
Base period	1.0	0.5
Current periods	4.0	0.5

For $\beta_1 = 0.9$, with (c_1, c_2) in the positive quadrant, period 1, about half of the deviations between the CRES TCLI and the GFT TCLI are less than 0.0009; 75 percent are less than 0.0018; 95 percent are less than 0.0030. For period 2, half the deviations between the CRES TCLI and the GFT TCLI are less than 0.0024; 75 percent are less than 0.0050; 95 percent are less than 0.0077. For period 3, half are less than 0.0021; 75 percent are less than 0.0054; 95 percent are less than 0.0084.

For $\beta_1 = 0.9$, with (c_1, c_2) in the negative quadrant, period 1, about half of the deviations between the CRES TCLI and the GFT TCLI are less than 0.0012; 75 percent are less than 0.0020; 95 percent are less than 0.0079. For period 2, half are less than 0.0026; 75 percent are less than 0.0044; 95 percent are less than 0.0145. For period 3, half are less than 0.0051; 75 percent are less than 0.0084; 95 percent are less than 0.0170.[18]

[18] The size distribution of the deviations between the CRES TCLI and the *Fisher formula* 353 is quite similar to that between the CRES TCLI and the GFT TCLI, although the deviations associated with the *Fisher formula* 353 tend to be larger over *most* of the parameter subdomain. Figs. 1 and 2 illustrate this for specification $\beta_1 = 0.9$, period 3. Both the CRES TCLI and GFT TCLI surface and the CRES TCLI and *Fisher* 353 surface have approximately the same shape in both figures except the values of the respective deviations at particular c_1, c_2 combinations. A more comprehensive description these deviations is given in Basmann et al. (1985, sec. III.D).

5. Conclusion

The argument for pegging wage escalation and COLA's to dedicated cost-of-living indexes rather than to dedicated inflation measures is primarily that the former is less distorting of efficient economic behavior than the latter. On the other hand the argument for pegging COLA's to a dedicated inflation measure like a Laspeyres price index is essentially pragmatic. It rests on the fact that their determination is *non-parametric* and involves no speculative assumptions about the form of direct utility function from which a TCLI could be derived. Moreover limitations on the numbers of commodities that can separately enter the index are not stringent. Where there are no unknown parameters to estimate hundreds of commodities can be separately included in the index formula, yet only two observations are needed: one for a base period and one for a current period. In such respects, however, use of inflation measures, such as a Laspeyres or a modified Laspeyres price index, e.g., the CPI W and CPI U, enjoys no advantage over the non-parametric GFT TCLI's.

Neoclassical TCLI's are relatively expensive to produce. Estimation of the neoclassical direct utility function parameters requires (in practice) that the hundreds of commodities be aggregated into a very few. Rational argument for incurring much greater cost to estimate and test neoclassical direct utility functions empirically cannot invoke the regularity properties of the demand function system. Rational argument for the use of strictly neoclassical TCLI's cannot be that they are in better agreement with empirical data than the corresponding GFT-based TCLI. However, when a neoclassical direct utility function does fit empirical data very well (a situation simulated in our experiments) there is a rational argument for considering it as an alternative basis for TCLI's. That argument is that it yields significantly different relative cost of living from that of the GFT TCLI on the same data. In such a circumstance – other things (cost of use) being equal – it would be highly desirable that negotiators of escalator clauses and designers of COLA's (members of Congress) be aware of the differences of the two indexes and of the projected consequences of each.

'Significant' deviations between CRES-based TCLI's and their GFT-based alternatives are found to occur at CRES parameter specifications near the boundaries of the admissible domain. However, demand elasticities for such parameter specifications have tended to lack 'verisimilitude'. However, no attempt to draw any definitive conclusions from this result should be made at this time. Results do indicate that searches of the broader class of implicit utility models [Barnett (1981, ch. 9)] would offer great promise of finding (a) 'significant' deviations between GFT TCLI's and neoclassical TCLI's coupled with (b) simulated data producing more realistic demand elasticities.

References

Afriat, S.N., 1967, The construction of utility functions from expenditure data, International Economic Review 8, 67–77.

Afriat, S.N., 1981, On the constructability of consistent price indices between several periods simultaneously, in: Angus Deaton, ed., Essays in the theory and measurement of consumer behavior (Cambridge University Press, Cambridge) 133–161.

Arrow, K.J., 1981, Additive logarithmic demand functions and the Slutsky relations, Review of Economic Studies 28, 176–181.

Barnett, W.A., 1981, Consumer demand and labor supply (North-Holland, Amsterdam).

Barnett, W.A., 1985, The minflex-Laurent translog flexible functional form, Journal of Econometrics, this issue.

Barnett, W.A., Y.W. Lee and M. Wolfe, The three-dimensional global properties of the minflex Laurent, generalized Leontief, and translog flexible functional forms, Journal of Econometrics, this issue.

Basmann, R.L., 1968, Hypothesis formulation in quantitative economics: A contribution to demand analysis, in: James P. Quirk and Arvid M. Zarley, eds., Papers in quantitative economics (University Press of Kansas, Lawrence, KS).

Basmann, R.L., 1985, On the serial correlation of stochastic taste changers in direct utility functions, Econometric Theory 1, forthcoming.

Basmann, R.L., D.J. Molina and D.J. Slottje, 1983, Budget constraint prices as preference changing parameters of generalized Fechner–Thurstone direct utility functions, American Economic Review 73, 411–413.

Basmann, R.L., D.J. Molina and D.J. Slottje, 1984a, A note on aggregation of Fechner–Thurstone direct utility functions, Economics Letters 14, 117–122.

Basmann, R.L., D.J. Molina and D.J. Slottje, 1984b, Variable consumer preferences, economic inequality, and the cost-of-living concept: Part one, in: R.L. Basmann and G.F. Rhodes, Jr., eds., Advances in econometrics, Vol. III (JAI Press, Greenwich, NJ).

Basmann, R.L., C.A. Diamond, J.C. Frentrup and S. White, 1985, Variable consumer preferences, economic inequality, and the cost-of-living concept: Part two, in: R.L. Basmann and G.F. Rhodes, eds., Advances in econometrics, Vol. IV (JAI Press, Greenwich, NJ) forthcoming.

Basmann, R.L. and D.J. Slottje, 1985, Sensitivity of true cost-of-living indexes to price- and income-induced changes of secondary utility, Unpublished manuscript.

Basmann, R.L. and S.N. White, 1984, Stigler's challenge and a terse derivation of the law of demand, Public policy paper no. 10 (College of Liberal Arts, Texas A&M University, College Station, TX).

Caves, D.W. and L.R. Christensen, 1980, Global properties of flexible functional forms, American Economic Review 70, 422–432.

Christensen, L.R., D.W. Jorgenson and L.J. Lau, 1975, Transcendental logarithmic utility functions, American Economic Review 655, 367–383.

Christensen, L.R. and M.E. Manser, 1975, Cost of living indexes for U.S. meat and produce, 1947–1971, in: Nestor Terlecky, ed., Household production and consumption (National Bureau of Economic Research, New York).

Diewert, W.E., 1973, Afriat and revealed preference theory, Review of Economic Studies 40, 419–425.

Diewert, W.E., 1976, Exact and superlative index numbers, Journal of Econometrics 4, 115–145.

Diewert, W.E., 1978, Superlative index numbers and consistency in aggregation, Econometrica 46, 883–900.

Diewert, W.E. and C. Parkan, 1978, Tests for the consistency of consumer data and nonparametric index numbers, Discussion paper no. 78-27 (Department of Economics, University of British Columbia, Vancouver).

Diewert, W.E. and C. Parkan, 1979, Linear programming tests of regularity conditions for production functions, Discussion paper no. 79-01 (Department of Economics, University of British Columbia, Vancouver).

Diewert, W.E., 1981, The economic theory of index numbers, in: Angus Deaton, ed., Theory and measurement of consumer behavior (Cambridge University Press, Cambridge).
Fisher, Franklin M. and Karl Shell, 1968, Taste and quality change in the pure theory of the true cost-of-living index, in: J.N. Wolfe, ed., Value, capital, and growth: Papers in honour of Sir John Hicks (University of Edinburgh Press, Edinburgh).
Fisher, Irving, 1927, The making of index numbers, 3rd ed. (Houghton Mifflin Co., Boston, MA).
Gallant, R.A., 1981, On the bias in flexible functional forms and an essentially unbiased form: The Fourier functional form, Journal of Econometrics 15, 211–245.
Gorman, W.M., 1963, Additive logarithmic preferences: A further note, Review of Economic Studies 30, 56–62.
Gorman, W.M., 1965, Production functions in which the elasticities of substitution stand in fixed proportion to each other, Review of Economic Studies 32, 217–224.
Hanoch, Giora, 1971, CRESH production functions, Econometrica 39, 695–712.
Hanoch, Giora, 1975, Production and demand models with direct or indirect implicit additivity, Econometrica 43, 395–419.
Houthakker, H.S., 1960, Additive preferences, Econometrica 28, 244–257.
Klein, L.R. and H. Rubin, 1947, A constant utility index of the cost of living, Review of Economic Studies 15, 84–87.
Konyus, A.A., 1924, The problem of the true index of the cost-of-living, Economic Bulletin of the Institute of Economic Conjecture no. 9-10; 1936, English translation, Econometrica 7, 110–129.
Leser, C.E.V., 1941-2, Family budget data and price elasticities of demand, Review of Economic Studies 9, 40–57.
Mukerji, V., 1963, Generalized SMAC function with constant ratios of elasticities of substitution, Review of Economic Studies 30, 233–236.
Muellbauer, J., 1975, Aggregation, income distribution, and consumer demand, Review of Economic Studies 42, 525–543.
Samuelson, P.A. and S. Swamy, 1974, Invariant economic index numbers and canonical duality: Survey and synthesis, American Economic Review 64, 566–593.
Schultz, H., 1938, The theory and measurement of demand (University of Chicago Press, Chicago, IL).
Scitovsky, Tibor, Some consequences of judging quality by price, Review of Economic Studies 11, 100–105.

ON MODELS AND METHODS FOR BAYESIAN TIME SERIES ANALYSIS*

J.B. CARLIN, A.P. DEMPSTER and A.B. JONAS

Harvard University, Cambridge, MA 02138, USA

A new approach to the applied econometric problems of adjusting and forecasting univariate time series with component models is described. The models used differ from the familiar ARIMA class by having components derived from fractionally differenced Gaussian processes and by allowing for simultaneous estimation of deterministic along with random components. Methodology proposed for fitting these models is based on Bayesian principles, with particular emphasis placed on assessing sensitivity of conclusions to model assumptions. The methods require extensive likelihood-related computations, using frequency domain representations to produce a range of new graphical diagnostic displays. They are illustrated with an extended example.

1. Introduction

Familiar tasks of applied econometric analysis are to examine an individual time series and then apply statistical techniques which attempt to adjust the series, or forecast the series, or both. The goal of adjustment is to remove effects which are obscuring other quantities of immediate interest, while forecasts, for example, of a seasonally adjusted series, may be used to assess the direction and size of trends in underlying economic processes. We approach these tasks through modelling and Bayesian inference, drawing upon models, statistical techniques and computing strategies which innovate in several ways.

The recent paper by Bell and Hillmer (1984), together with its accompanying printed discussion, gives an important review of methods of seasonal adjustment, including arguments for a model-based approach. All approaches share an assumption that the time series is composed of a sum of meaningful components representing trends, seasonal patterns, and random components of various kinds. Bell and Hillmer distinguish three classes of methods (1984, p. 314). In the first class are methods which solve the problems of definition and choice of technique by simply adopting a rule for what computations to apply to the data to produce the desired estimated decomposition or forecast. These methods raise difficult questions of evaluation and justification, which in turn lead to a need to formulate assumptions and models. Bell and Hillmer prefer

*This work was facilitated in part by National Science Foundation Grant SES-82-00086.

overtly model-based methods, as we do, and divide these into two classes, namely, 'methods that choose models for the components' and 'methods that model the observed data and deduce models for the components'. Although Bell and Hillmer place an early version of our work in the first of these classes, and put their own approach in the second, we are unable to see a convincing distinction along the lines suggested, since both approaches are restricted to models which are effectively component models, and both seek to model the data within their restricted classes of models.

We adopt a class of models which differ in a particular way from the seasonal ARIMA models of the Wisconsin school. Basic references for ARIMA are Box and Jenkins (1976), Cleveland and Tiao (1976), Box, Hillmer and Tiao (1978), and Pierce (1978). See also Burman (1980), Pierce (1980), and the above-mentioned Bell and Hillmer (1984). Our models in effect replace the AR of ARIMA by adopting a power law feature for the spectral density, while retaining the I feature (for integral differencing to obtain stationarity) and the MA feature (for shaping the spectral density away from zero frequency). As explained in section 2, the power law formulation is interpretable as allowing for fractional differencing on top of the usual integral differencing to obtain a spectral density which is finite and nonzero at zero frequency. In other words, these models provide for differencing by an integer plus d for $-\frac{1}{2} < d < \frac{1}{2}$, in place of simply an integer as in ARIMA modelling. An analogous power law feature at the seasonal frequencies is used to model the random seasonal component. As implemented, we assume monthly data with stationary first differences in the non-seasonal component of the model, so that the fractional differencing is $1 + d$ for $-\frac{1}{2} < d < \frac{1}{2}$, and correspondingly we assume stationary annual differences in the random seasonal component.

Our Bayesian perspective suggests that the primary goal of analysis is the assessment of posterior distributions for quantities of substantive interest, including, for example, forecasts and adjusted current values. In this view, a given model provides a joint probability distribution to represent prior uncertainty about the observable series and its unobservable components. From this it is conceptually straightforward, although often computationally demanding, to obtain the required posterior distributions. As a byproduct of the calculations, several diagnostic measures of the fit between model and data are available and these may be used to suggest improved models. The overall data analysis is an iterative process which passes many models over the given data set, assessing both the relative support from the data for various models and the sensitivity of substantive inferences (forecasts, adjustments, etc.) to the assumed model.

Through extensive software development we have a system which handles complex models whose components include both fixed and random effects. The facility to include fixed effects (or regression terms) in our models is important, not only for the traditional purpose of representing exogenous influences, but also to represent an initial monthly pattern which provides a base level from which the stationary random increments depart. Here we differ again from the standard ARIMA approach, which does not explicitly model an initial seasonal pattern but instead discusses assumptions and procedures for handling end effects [cf. Bell (1984)]. In Bayesian terms, fixed effect generally means a linear term assigned effectively infinite prior variance. The resulting computational linear algebra is standard, and is common to both Bayesian and non-Bayesian theories, and so has required only extensions of familiar algorithms to handle the special complexities of our models.

Our model-fitting procedures are outlined in section 3, but most computing details are omitted from this paper. Instead, we emphasize defining and illustrating several new diagnostic procedures which we have used to aid model-fitting. These procedures are derived from frequency domain rather than time domain representations of time series behavior.

This paper leaves many questions for further research. We describe and illustrate proposed models and methods, but we do not provide any deep analysis of them. It is evident, both from mathematical understanding and from the empirical example presented in section 4, that the choice of the parameter d (or, as we prefer, $h = d + \frac{1}{2}$) in the non-seasonal component, together with the scale factor representing the amount of power or variance associated with the spectral dip or peak near zero frequency, affects both the trajectory of forecasts and the error variance associated with forecasts. We are not yet expert at describing or measuring these effects in terms useful to practicing time series analysts. Similarly, we need detailed investigations of how accurately the parameters representing fractional differencing and variance close to zero frequency can be estimated from the finite, indeed relatively short, data records typical of economic time series. These two sorts of studies will tell the tale concerning how model-dependent, or in Bayesian terms how dependent on external information sources, the desired forecasts necessarily are. Parallel studies need to be carried out for seasonal adjustment. We anticipate that much of this work will be numerical, making use of the software developed to fit and use the models.

2. Models

We begin by specifying a reasonably broad class of Gaussian time series models. All of our discussion is in the context of monthly time series, with a seasonal period of 12. The basic linear structure may be described as a variance components model including both fixed and random effects. The random effects are generated by stationary Gaussian processes which we represent in both time and frequency domains, the former because time series come that way, and the latter because frequency domain representations are conceptually illuminating and offer new statistical and computational tools.

Suppose that an observed economic time series, possibly after transformation, is written $Y_0, Y_1, \ldots, Y_{n-1}$, where 0 is an artificial time origin specified to coincide with the first observation, and n denotes the number of successive months observed. We postulate a linear structure of the form

$$Y_t = \mu_{t*} + \boldsymbol{\phi F}_t + N_t + S_t + E_t, \tag{2.1}$$

where $t^* = t \bmod 12$ is an index which cycles through $0, 1, 2, \ldots, 11$. Thus, $\mu_0, \mu_1, \ldots, \mu_{11}$ denote fixed effects which model the initial level of the series in the 12 calendar months. The next term,

$$\boldsymbol{\phi F}_t = \phi_1 F_{1t} + \phi_2 F_{2t} + \cdots \phi_m F_{mt}, \tag{2.2}$$

denotes a further set of general user-specified fixed effects or regression terms. For example, F_{1t} might denote the number of business days in month t, while $F_{2t} = 1$ for $t = 99$ and $F_{2t} = 0$ for $t \neq 99$ would serve as an indicator for the 100th observation. This general formulation allows flexible specification of adjustments for outliers and missing observations. The estimation of fixed effects is carried out jointly with that of random effects in a manner outlined in section 3.

The N_t and S_t terms in (2.1) denote, respectively, non-seasonal and seasonal random components. Setting $N_0 = 0$ implies that an initial level for the non-seasonal random component is incorporated into μ_0. The focus of attention is on the sequence of month-to-month changes

$$N_t' = N_t - N_{t-1}, \qquad t = 1, 2, \ldots, n-1, \tag{2.3}$$

which we model as a zero mean stationary process. Similarly, setting $S_0 = S_1 = \cdots = S_{11} = 0$ implies that the initial random seasonal levels are absorbed in the seasonal fixed effects $\mu_0, \mu_1, \ldots, \mu_{11}$. We proceed analogously to (2.3) and model

$$S_t'' = S_t - S_{t-12}, \qquad t = 12, 13, \ldots, n-1, \tag{2.4}$$

as a zero mean stationary process of annual changes in the seasonal component. Finally, random survey error is represented by a stationary process in undifferenced form. In the modelling reported below we represent survey error by Gaussian white noise, but a correlation structure could easily be specified in our program as a reflection of prior knowledge of the data collection mechanism, e.g., to reflect serial correlation implied by a rotating panel survey design.

For modelling the stationary process N_t' of month-to-month changes in the non-seasonal component we select one of two closely related processes which exhibit power law behavior in the spectral density function near the origin. A summary of the mathematical properties of these so-called persistent memory random processes may be found in Jonas (1983). The processes are characterized by covariance functions which decay as a power of the separation between correlated observations, rather than exponentially as in the case of ARMA models. At zero frequency, the corresponding spectral densities have a singularity of fractional order that is either a zero or a pole. The two processes have somewhat different forms in their spectral densities f away from zero frequency, and correspondingly differ in the short-range dependence expressed by their covariance functions γ. More importantly, however, they share the asymptotic behavior of the Fourier pair (f, γ) given by

$$f(\lambda) \propto |\lambda|^{-2d} \quad \text{as} \quad |\lambda| \to 0,$$
$$\gamma(t) \propto |t|^{2d-1} \quad \text{as} \quad |t| \to \infty, \tag{2.5}$$

where d is a parameter in the interval $(-\frac{1}{2}, \frac{1}{2})$.

The first of these models was introduced by Kolmogorov (1940), but its recognition as a useful statistical tool is largely due to a series of publications by Mandelbrot and several collaborators, e.g., Mandelbrot and Van Ness (1968). The motion process, continuous in time, is commonly called fractional Brownian motion (fBm), while its stationary increments are called fractional Gaussian noise (fGn). The term fractional enters because fBm and fGn can formally be represented through fractional integrals of, respectively, ordinary Brownian motion and Gaussian white noise. The Fourier pair (f, γ) for fGn, whose derivation we omit, is

$$f(\lambda) = \sigma^2 (2\pi)^{-1-2h} \Gamma(1+2h) \sin \pi h \, |e^{2\pi i \lambda} - 1|^2 \sum_{n=-\infty}^{+\infty} |n + \lambda|^{-1-2h},$$

$$\gamma(t) = \tfrac{1}{2}\sigma^2 \left[|t+1|^{2h} - 2|t|^{2h} + |t-1|^{2h} \right] = \sigma^2 \sum_{k=1}^{\infty} \binom{2h}{2k} |t|^{2h-2k}. \tag{2.6}$$

Here the fractional parameter d has been replaced, as is usual, by $h = d + \frac{1}{2}$, which takes values on $0 < h < 1$. Varying the fractional parameter gives direct control over the low-frequency shape of the spectral density, as may be appreciated from inspection of fig. 1.

The second model is obtained by fractionally differencing discrete white noise, as proposed independently by Granger and Joyeux (1980) and Hosking (1981). The fractional differencing is accomplished by raising the differencing operator $\Delta = (I - B)$ to a fractional power d, and formally evaluating the expression Δ^d through a binomial expansion. Geweke and Porter-Hudak

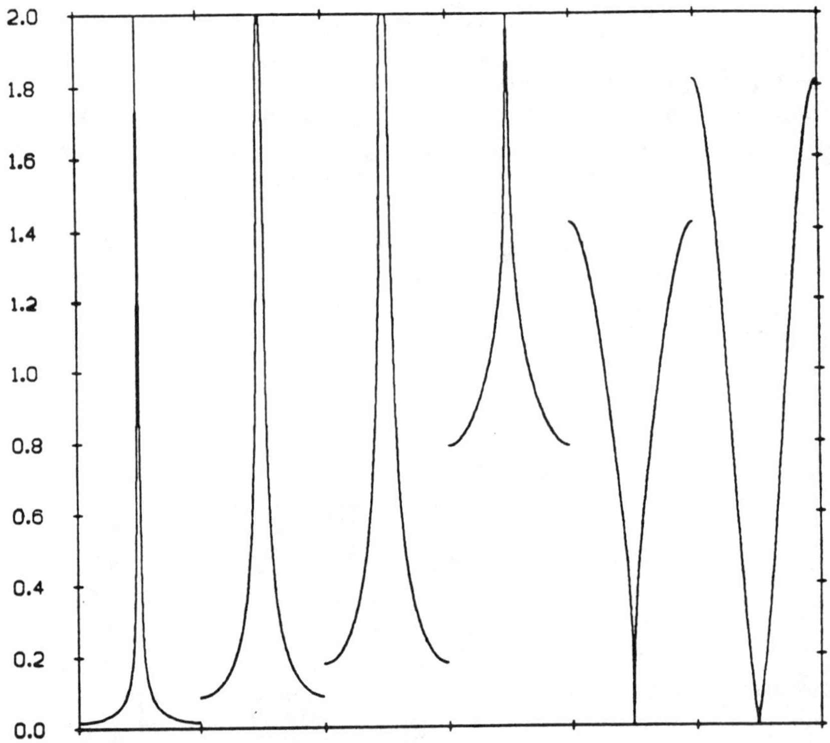

Fig. 1. The spectral density of fractional Gaussian noise given by eq. (2.6) is plotted side by side for $h = 0.99$, 0.95, 0.9, 0.6, 0.3, 0.1 and $\sigma^2 = 1$. The interval between successive tick marks corresponds to the fundamental interval $[-\frac{1}{2}, \frac{1}{2}]$, and the area under each density function is identically 1. As $h \to 1$, the spectral density approaches a delta function. The apparently narrow peak for $h = 0.99$ is evidently more massive than that for $h = 0.9$.

(1983) show the close mathematical connection between continuous fractional Gaussian noise, derived by applying continuous differentiation, and discrete fractional differenced noise (fdn), derived by applying discrete differencing.

Both fractional models permit us to control continuously the degree of differencing that is applied to an observed series to achieve stationarity. Within standard ARIMA technology, an analyst is required to make a discrete choice, e.g., among differencing a series once, or twice, or maybe not at all. And yet the consequences of the chosen degree of differencing for inferences made from the data may be far reaching. The fractional models expand the analyst's tool kit by replacing the somewhat drastic $0, 1, 2, \ldots$ choice with the alternative to move continuously between successive degrees of differencing. Our particular implementation permits us to move within an interval of 0.5 on either side of unit differencing.

Although our observed series and corresponding models are discrete in time, we may sometimes think of our observations as periodically recorded values of an underlying continuous phenomenon. This attitude suggests simplifying the complexities of the real world by hypothesizing that the distribution of an observed economic phenomenon should not depend in an essential way on the chosen time scale. The probability law describing the statistical behavior of, for example, weekly quotations of stock prices might also describe the behavior of properly rescaled daily or monthly quotations. Fractional Brownian motion captures this idea in the mathematical property of self-similarity, which is a property of invariance in distribution under a scale renormalization transformation, expressible as

$$\mathscr{L}(X_t) = \mathscr{L}(\alpha^{-h} X_{\alpha t}) \quad \text{for} \quad \alpha > 0. \tag{2.7}$$

The assumption of self-similarity is a natural one for the statistical modelling of phenomena which proceed continuously through time but are only discretely sampled.

Our current modelling techniques are based on the fractional Brownian process, but with two important elaborations. First, the low-frequency behavior of these processes needs to be complemented by an ability to reshape their high-frequency properties. We accomplish this by adopting a spectral density function of the following form for the non-seasonal stationary component N_t':

$$f_N(\lambda) = f(\lambda)\left[\psi_0 + \psi_1(\sin^2\pi\lambda)/s_1 + \cdots + \psi_M(\sin^2 M\pi\lambda)/s_M\right], \tag{2.8}$$

where f is the spectral density of the basic fBm process with unit variance, and $s_1, \ldots, s_M$ are normalizing constants

$$s_j = \int_{-1/2}^{1/2} f(\lambda)\sin^2 j\pi\lambda \, d\lambda, \tag{2.9}$$

chosen so that the parameters $\psi_0, \psi_1, \ldots, \psi_M$ are each commensurate in the sense of measuring a contribution to the total variance of N_t'. The number of terms M may be varied to provide flexible shaping of the spectral density. In practice we have used $M \leq 3$. Note that $\psi_0, \psi_1, \ldots, \psi_M$ must be chosen so that f_N is positive on the range $0 < \lambda < \frac{1}{2}$, but that not all of these parameters need to be positive.

The modification of fBm achieved by (2.8) is equivalent to applying a moving average operator of degree M to the basic process. Since $\sin^2 j\pi\lambda$ is essentially the transfer function of the lag j difference operator $\Delta_j = (I - B^j)$, another interpretation of (2.8) is that the parameters ψ_j give the relative power of each of M *independent* lag j differenced versions of fBm which together compose N_t'.

A second important elaboration of fBm for modelling applications provides a means of constructing a *seasonal* stochastic process from the basic non-seasonal spectral density f. By translating the fractional singularity at 0 to the seasonal frequencies, we model the seasonal spectral density with spikes or dips at $\lambda_s = s/12$ for $s = 1, 2, \ldots, 6$. In the time domain this leads to stochastic processes with large systematic correlations at lags that span repeating seasonal patterns. There are several ways to achieve such a modification, one of which is detailed in appendix I. Fig. 2 shows an example of a seasonal spectral density obtained in this way.

The spectral density of the seasonal component could also be shaped through the inclusion of moving average terms in a manner analogous to (2.8). Such an approach would lead to better models for series with uneven evolution in the seasonal component, where for example pronounced changes were

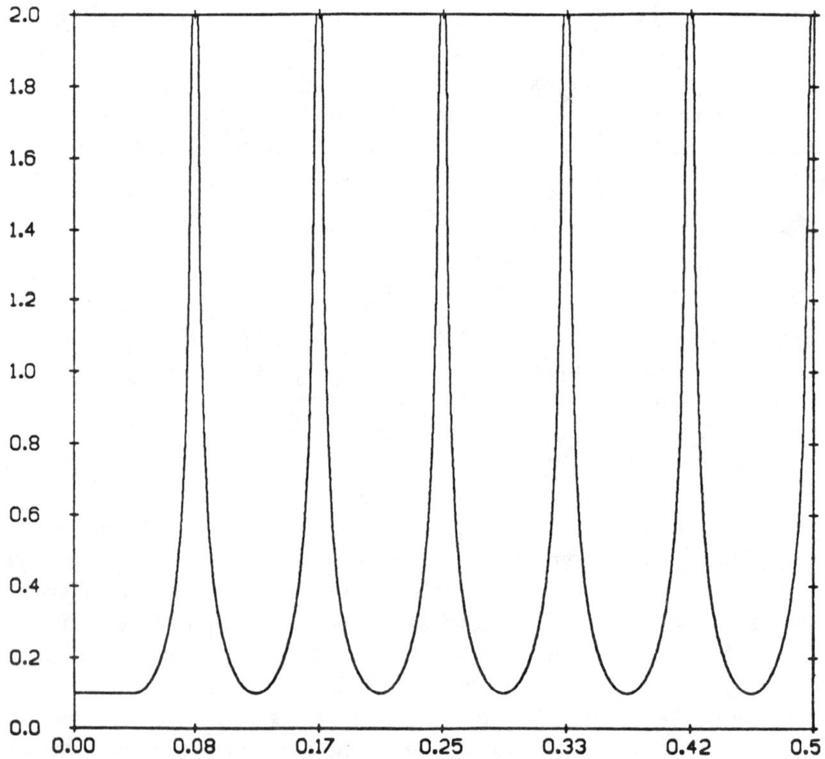

Fig. 2a. The seasonal spectral density derived from fractional Gaussian noise according to eq. (I.1) with $h = 0.9$ and $\alpha = 0.1$ plotted on the interval $[0, \frac{1}{2}]$.

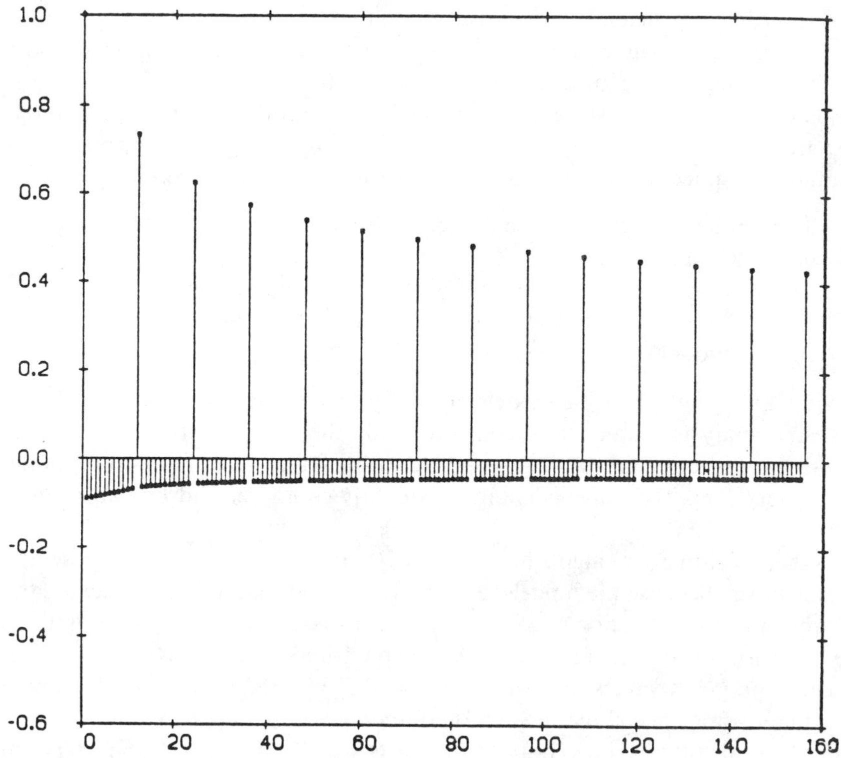

Fig. 2b. The seasonal autocorrelation function derived from fractional Gaussian noise according to eq. (I.2) with $h = 0.9$ and $\alpha = 0.1$, shown through lag 156.

exhibited at the quarterly, but not at the semi-annual, frequency. We have not yet introduced this refinement in our computer implementation.

3. Modelling and inference

Bayesian inference about unobserved components of an observed time series, or about forecasts or backcasts of such components, can be tackled at several levels of sophistication. The simplest level assumes that a judicious combination of prior knowledge and information extracted from data analysis of the observed time series permits a unique choice of model from the class defined by (2.1)–(2.4). At this level, the required posteriors are simply conditional distributions deduced from the assumed Gaussian time series model. The second level formally specifies a prior distribution across the parameters of the model, which leads to averaging the conditional Gaussian posterior across the posterior of the parameters. We emphasize here starting at the simplest level in order to provide the analyst with a quantitative sense of the most basic level of posterior uncertainty, namely, uncertainty about components and forecasts given precise knowledge of the parameters of the model.

Since we would almost never be satisfied with a single choice of model, our current strategy is to follow a process of trial and error, moving interactively through the space of models, computing at each stopping place:

(i) log likelihood of the selected model and its first derivatives with respect to scale parameters,
(ii) various diagnostic measures of possible model inadequacy, and
(iii) if fit is deemed plausible, a selection of posterior inferences given the current model.

Having a range of plausible models, it is easy to simulate the second level (i.e., Bayesian analysis) numerically, thus providing the analyst with a sense of the additional posterior uncertainty associated with Bayesian estimation of model parameters. This style of modelling is evidently computer and operator intensive.

Details of numerical algorithms and computing strategies are not presented in this paper. Because the models (2.1)–(2.4) are linear models, and because the assumed prior distribution of all the linear terms is Gaussian, the computations are all variants of the familiar task of conditioning a multivariate normal distribution given values of a subset of the variables. It is necessary, however, to explain some special features and terminology of our approach.

First, recall that we have both fixed effects such as μ_{t*} or $\phi_j F_{jt}$ and random effects such as E_t, N_t' or S_t''. In our Bayesian approach, fixed and random effects are logically indistinguishable, since both have Gaussian priors and hence Gaussian posteriors. The difference is simply that the Gaussian priors for the fixed effects have infinite variances. There are implications of the infinite variances in terms of algorithms for computing normal posteriors, cf. Dempster (1982), but mathematically the results are ordinary limits of finite variance posteriors. An important advantage of treating fixed and random effects together is that the posterior variances and covariances take account of any effects of confounding, for example, between fixed and random seasonal effects. In contrast, it appears that the approximate posterior variances suggested by Hillmer (1985) do not adjust for the fact that fixed and random effects must be simultaneously estimated.

Second, we find it convenient to classify variables in the linear space defined by the model as *observables*, *generators*, and *targets*. The observables are the Y_t appearing in (2.1), the generators are any basis of fixed and random effects which span the set of observables and targets, and the targets are the immediate objects of inference such as decompositions or forecasts. Thinking this way allows us to define software which provides alternative tracks to the desired inferences. For example, if a basis of generators is included in the framework of variables for which posteriors are computed, then posterior means for targets can be deduced as needed. Alternatively, if current interest focuses on a few targets only, then we can drop the generators and compute more cheaply with a smaller set of targets.

Third, instead of using the given time domain representations of the random effects generators E_t, N_t' and S_t'', we prefer to use a basis of frequency domain generators. Since the random effects in the models are all driven by stationary processes, it is mathematically natural to use the Cramér representation. The basic idea is to compute posterior means, variances, and covariances for the frequency domain generators, and to rely on these for modelling and inference. The required theory is developed in Dempster (1985) and is summarized in appendix II. In particular, the appendix describes some new diagnostic displays which are illustrated with the example in section 4. Frequency domain methods are desirable because the computed statistics relate directly to the spectral densities of model components and these are easily visualized and plotted. For example, if a diagnostic display suggests that more random seasonal variance is needed, then the component of spectral density for random seasonal can be increased under the direct control of the analyst. Frequency domain methods simplify the inference process, as well as the modelling process, because the decomposition of the posterior means of frequency domain generators into posteriors of components is a simple matter of multiplying by the proportion of the spectral density associated with each component.

4. Example

We present here the summary results of an extended analysis of one specific time series. The purpose of the worked example is to illustrate the capabilities of our modelling system and to convey the flavor of our approach to the applied modelling task. An essential feature of the approach is a detailed examination of the individual data set and the interaction between it and various possible models. No attempt has been made to produce automatic model fitting techniques.

Our data is a time series of length 204 months from 1963 to 1979, as shown in fig. 3a. The code name INSXXVS signifies a series of the aggregate value of shipments in an undisclosed industry, collected by the U.S. Bureau of the Census. The data may be an automotive manufacturing series, since before 1973 the prominent slowdown in July and August suggests the traditional period of retooling for a new model year.

The modelling effort begins with an exploratory phase directed at discovering obvious features of the data which should be captured by the constructed model. Fig. 3a exhibits a sequential plot, while fig. 3b redisplays the observations grouped by month and shown as deviations from the monthly averages.

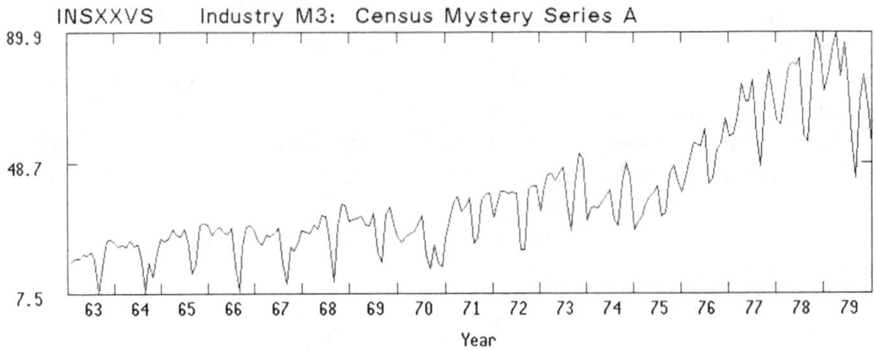

Fig. 3a. Time series INSXXVS of aggregate value of shipments in an industry, 1963–79.

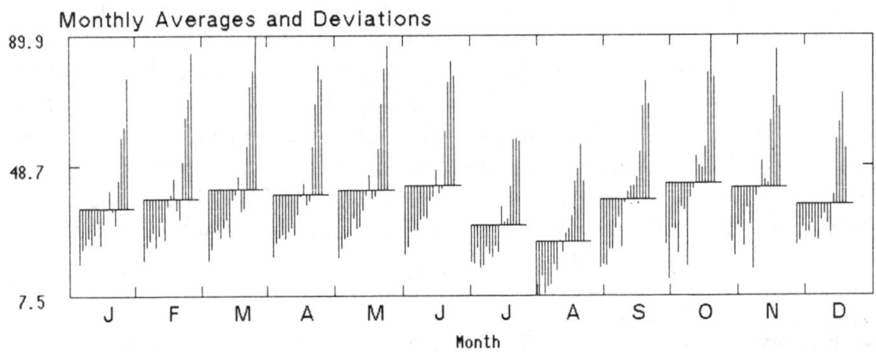

Fig. 3b. Series INSXXVS plotted by month: monthly means and year-to-year deviations from the means.

Examination of exploratory plots may suggest the presence of outliers in the observed series, the need to adjust for various calendar effects, or the possible desirability of transforming the series to stabilize variance through time. This particular series appears to be rather typical of aggregate economic data, exhibiting a positive trend on which is superimposed an irregular, changing seasonal pattern. There is no indication of outliers, although variability appears to increase slightly in the final two to three years.

We proceed to fitting models of the form described in section 2 to the untransformed series, omitting any general fixed effects (regression terms). Model specification thus involves determining the parameter values which specify the stationary covariance structure of the three random components. As already stated, the covariance of E_t, representing survey error, is assumed to be known from external sources. In the present example we assume a white noise error term with a nominal unit variance, since we have no reason to believe the series is affected by substantial sampling error.

The random non-seasonal component, N_t, is characterized by the fractional parameter, h_N, and the scale parameters $\psi_0, \psi_1, \ldots, \psi_M$. Similarly, S_t is characterized by h_S and the variance σ_S^2. Experience has shown that the likelihood surface tends to be flat as a function of the parameters h_N and h_S, reflecting the inability of a relatively short data series to provide strong information about low frequency properties. For this reason we fit models for a range of values of these parameters.

For each choice of h_N and h_S, the likelihood is approximately maximized as a function of the scale parameters, after a choice of M has been made. This is accomplished by an iterative, trial and error process using essentially the first derivatives of log likelihood. As with h_N and h_S, there is often insufficient information in the data to sharply determine the variances, especially if M is 2 or more. This lack of precision is a fact of life rarely discussed by users of linear models, but is less important than it might seem because it is targets rather than the parameters themselves that are of immediate interest. In effect, our procedure directly fits component spectral density functions. If markedly different models cannot be clearly distinguished in terms of likelihood support, and if there is little external, scientific evidence for preferring one model over another, then attention must turn to comparing the implications of the models as tools for forecasting, decomposition, or whatever task is at hand. We illustrate this kind of sensitivity analysis for the data set INSXXVS.

Table 1 shows a range of 10 models fitted to the series; each approximately maximum likelihood for the given choice of h_N, h_S and M, except that, for model J, σ_S^2 is constrained to be zero. The first five models (A–E) have $h_N = h_S$ and they illustrate the difficulty of estimating the fractional parameter. The likelihood is almost equal for models B and C, while support for model D

Table 1

Ten models fitted to time series INSXXVS.

	Parameter values							
Model	h_N	h_S	ψ_0	ψ_1	ψ_2	ψ_3	σ_S^2	$-2\log L$
A	0.95	0.95	0.70	7.5	5.5	−0.4	0.28	763.7
B	0.8	0.8	0.83	5.0	4.0	2.0	0.58	761.2
C	0.6	0.6	2.5	1.0	4.5	2.6	1.25	761.1
D	0.5	0.5	4.7	−1.2	4.2	2.3	1.9	762.3
E	0.3	0.3	12.0	−8.0	3.0	1.0	4.5	772.2
F	0.6	0.8	2.5	2.1	4.6	2.6	0.55	760.4
G	0.6	0.8	3.1	3.2	5.8	0.0	0.55	762.2
H	0.6	0.8	6.1	6.2	0.0	0.0	0.62	771.0
I	0.6	0.8	11.1	0.0	0.0	0.0	0.77	777.0
J	0.6	—	2.1	3.0	10.5	3.8	0.0	792.0

($h_N = h_S = 0.5$, the case of no fractional differencing) and model A ($h_N = h_S = 0.95$, the case of very strong persistence) is substantially weaker. Model E, which has $h_N = h_S = 0.3$, giving anti-persistent component processes, may rather clearly be ruled out. An improved fit over models B and C is obtained by model F, where the h parameters have been uncoupled ($h_N = 0.6$, $h_S = 0.8$). Models G, H and I demonstrate the importance of incorporating moving average terms to shape the middle- and high-frequency range of the spectral density function. In terms of likelihood model G ($M = 2$) is close to the best model F where $M = 3$, but models H and I ($M = 1$ and 0, respectively) lack sufficient flexibility to represent the spectral characteristics of the series. Finally, model J is included to emphasize the need for the random seasonal component in the model.

Fig. 4 shows a plot of the spectral density functions of the random components of the best-fitting model F. Note that the singularities of the

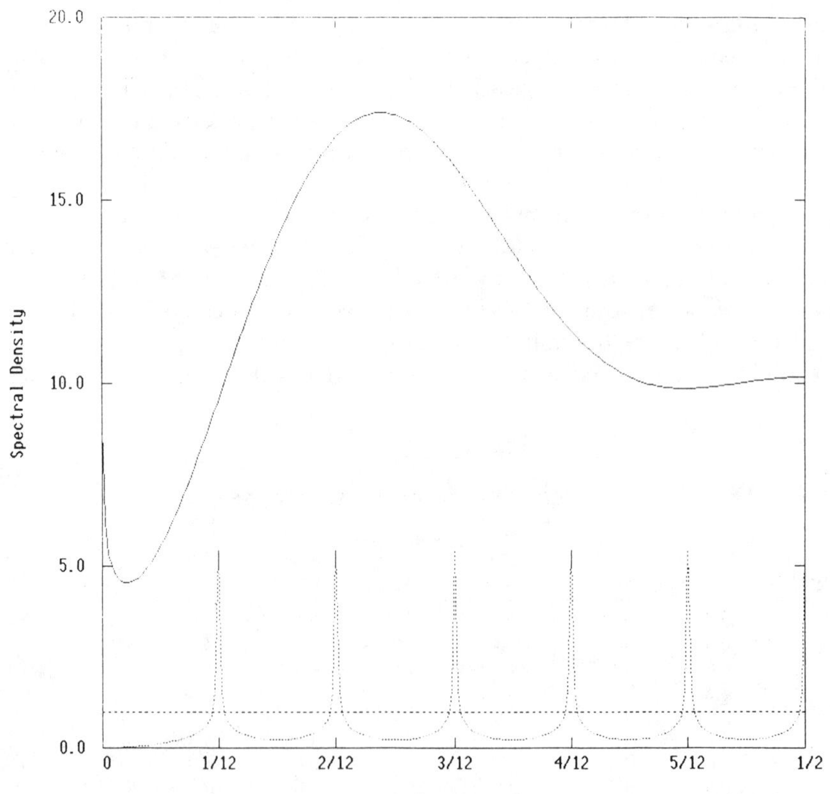

Fig. 4. Spectral density functions of the stationary model components N_t' (solid line), S_t'' (dotted line) and E_t (dashed line) defining model F of table 1.

fractionally differenced processes do not extend to infinity because we compute with a discrete version of the spectral density function, obtained by applying a Fourier transform to a finite length of the corresponding autocovariance function. This plot enables ready visual appreciation of the frequency domain characteristics of the model. Each of the six most reasonable models, A–D, F and G, have the same general shape for the non-seasonal spectral density, and differ principally in the strength of the fractional singularities induced by h_N and h_S.

In figs. 5 and 6, we use selected models from table 1 to illustrate the diagnostic plots mentioned in section 3 and further detailed in appendix II. Fig. 5 gives two examples of a frequency domain residual plot: in fig. 5a for the well-fitting model F and in fig. 5b for the poor model J, which omits the

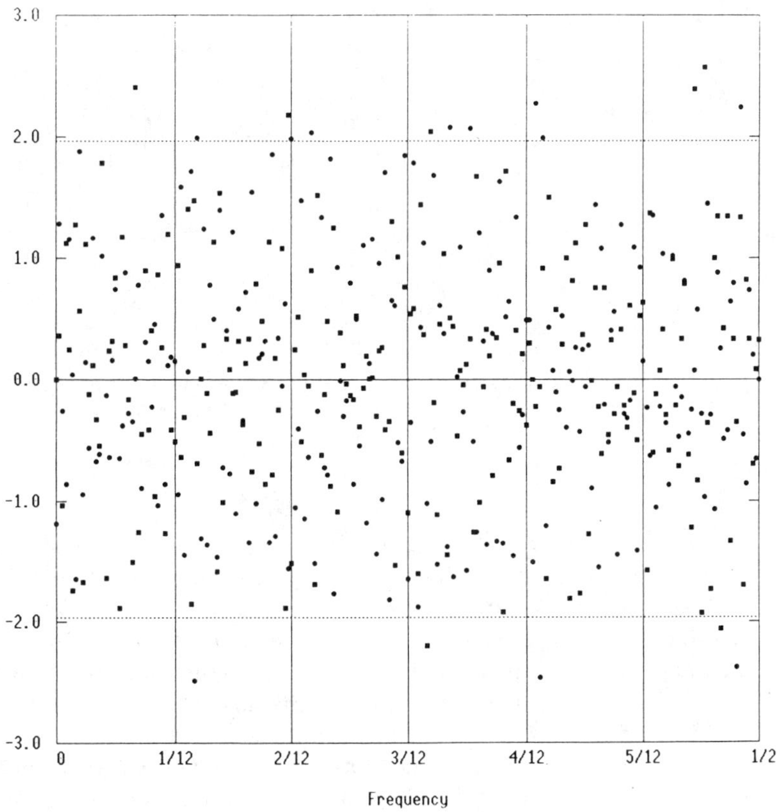

Fig. 5a. *Model F:* Frequency domain 'residual plot', showing the standardized posterior means of the frequency domain generators (cosine component plotted with circles, sine component with squares).

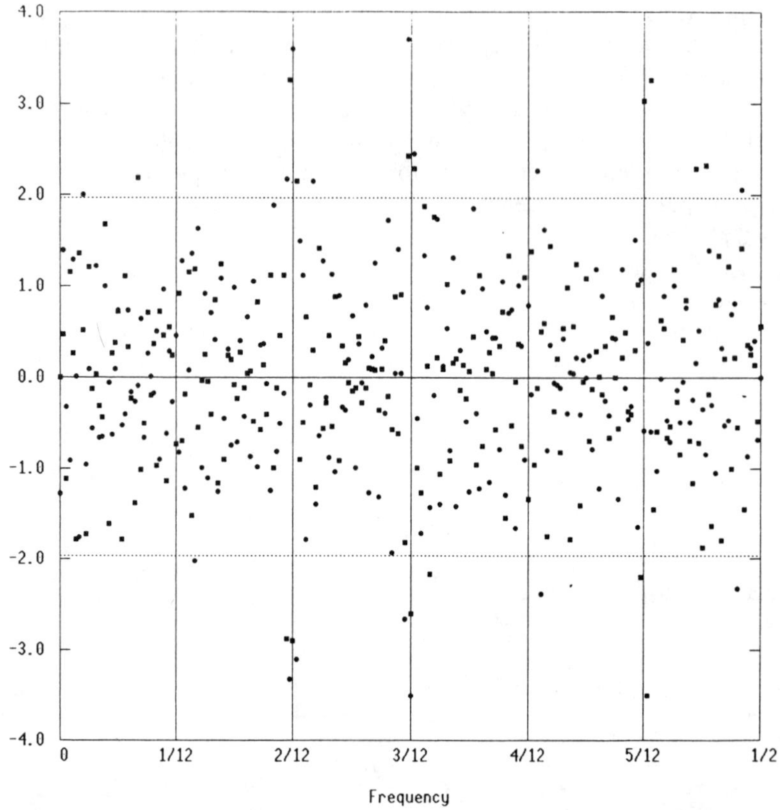

Fig. 5b. *Model J* ($\sigma_S^2 = 0$): Frequency domain 'residual plot', showing the standardized posterior means of the frequency domain generators (cosine component plotted with circles, sine component with squares).

random seasonal component. The plots show the cosine and sine components of the posterior means of the frequency domain generators, standardized by their sampling standard deviations. If the model fits well, we see a random scatter of standard normal deviates, as in fig. 5a. In contrast, in fig. 5b we see significantly extreme values at two and three cycles per year, indicating that the model does not adequately capture the seasonal characteristics of the data.

A second type of diagnostic plot is illustrated in fig. 6: in fig. 6a for model F and in fig. 6b for model D. In the second case, the pronounced spikes in the integrand of the derivative of log likelihood (the difference between the squared posterior mean frequency domain generator and its sampling variance) at the second and third seasonal frequencies suggest that a change in model spectral density which increases power at these frequencies will improve the likelihood. This is confirmed by the improved fit of models F, B and C, which use a higher value of h_S. In fig. 6a it is hard to see how a plausible change in model spectral density could combine with the integrand to improve the likelihood substantially.

Finally, we turn to a brief sensitivity analysis, comparing the implications of the better fitting models of table 1. We concentrate on models A–D and F. For each model we compute posterior distributions for three target quantities over a time span of 24 months, covering the last year of observations and one year of the future. The targets are:

(i) the non-seasonal or 'trend' component of the series, defined as $\bar{\mu} + N_t$, where $\bar{\mu} = \sum_{i=0}^{11} \mu_i / 12$,

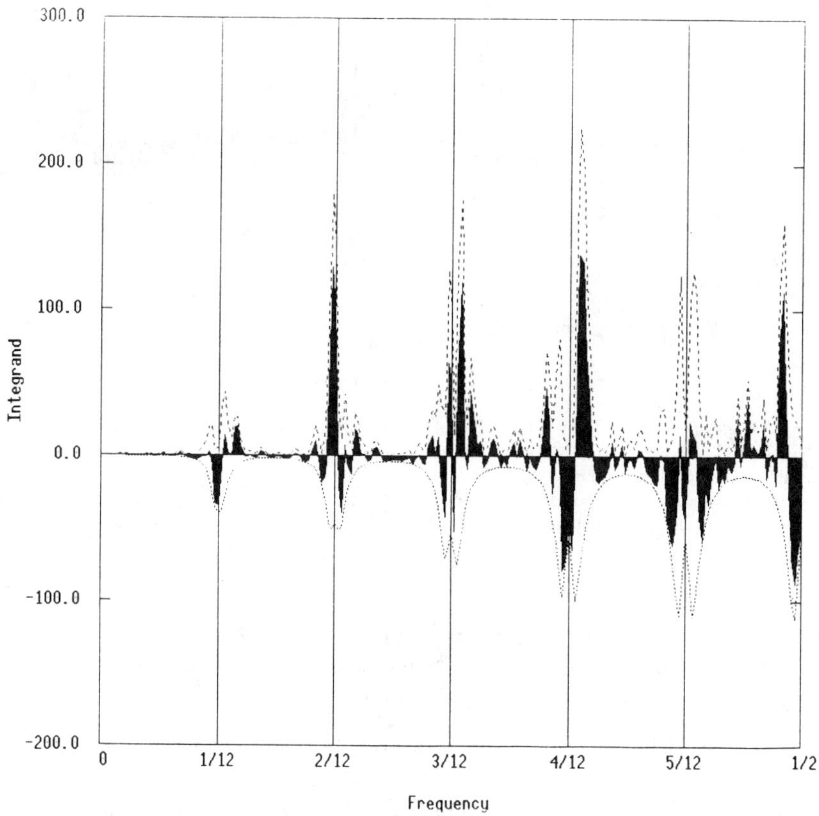

Fig. 6a. *Model F* ($h_N = 0.6$, $h_S = 0.8$): Plot of the integrand used in computing the derivatives of log likelihood. Shown are the squared amplitudes of the posterior mean frequency domain generators (dashed line), their sampling variances (plotted in the negative, dotted line), and the difference between the two (solid). The latter gives the integrand of (II.5) upon multiplying by the appropriate small change in the model spectral density function.

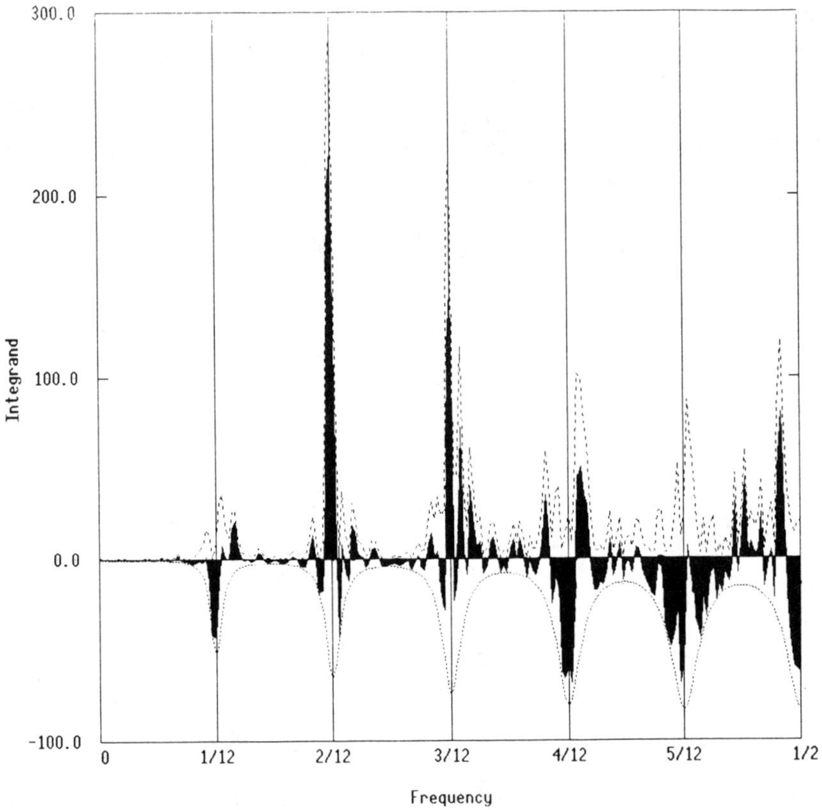

Fig. 6b. *Model D* ($h_N = 0.5$, $h_S = 0.5$): Plot of the integrand used in computing the derivatives of log likelihood. Shown are the squared amplitudes of the posterior mean frequency domain generators (dashed line), their sampling variances (plotted in the negative, dotted line), and the difference between the two (solid). The latter gives the integrand of (II.5) upon multiplying by the appropriate small change in the model spectral density function.

(ii) the seasonal component, defined as $\mu_{t*} - \bar{\mu} + S_t$, and

(iii) the observable series adjusted for measurement error, defined as $Y_t - E_t = \mu_{t*} + N_t + S_t$ [the sum of targets (i) and (ii)].

For the best-fitting model, F, figs. 7a and 7b display posterior means, with uncertainty bounds given by twice the posterior standard deviations, for targets (i) and (iii) respectively. (On each plot the actual observations of the last year are superimposed.) Thus fig. 7a shows an estimate of the seasonally (and error-) adjusted last 12 months of the series, with a forecast of the same component 12 months into the future. We see that, under the model, seasonal effects account for a large part but not all of the rather large fluctuations observed in the last 12 months of data. The non-seasonal forecast function levels out after 3 months of modest increase and uncertainty in the forecasts increases rapidly. The first half of fig. 7b reflects the assumption that measurement error comprises only a small component of this series ($\sigma_E^2 = 1$): the error-adjusted series is practically indistinguishable from the observed data. The forecast function repeats the seasonal pattern of the current year, with some shrinkage toward a less pronounced annual fluctuation.

In fig. 8 we display the posterior means of the non-seasonal component [target (i)] for each of the five models A–D and F. In terms of seasonal adjustment for the last year of data, the models provide broadly similar conclusions, although differences of 1% to 2% are common between the more extreme models, model A ($h_N = h_S = 0.95$) and model D ($h_N = h_S = 0.5$). In terms of forecasts, the models differ more substantially, with those models having higher values for h_N and h_S predicting stronger persistence in upward trend. Examination of fig. 3a suggests a rather strong trend in the years 1975 through 1978, with a noticeable faltering in the final year, 1979. This explains the fact that it is the models with the longest 'memory' which forecast the strongest continuing trend.

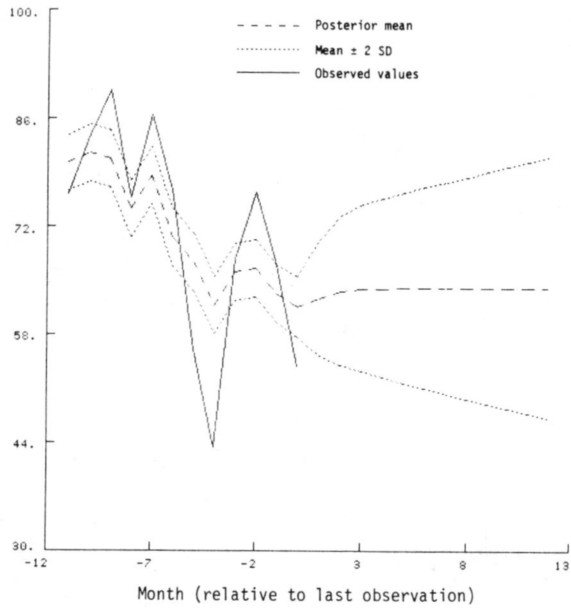

Fig. 7a. *Non-seasonal component*, $\bar{\mu} + N_t$: Posterior means with two standard-deviation limits for target quantities for the last 12 months of observations and forecast 12 months ahead, under the assumption of model F.

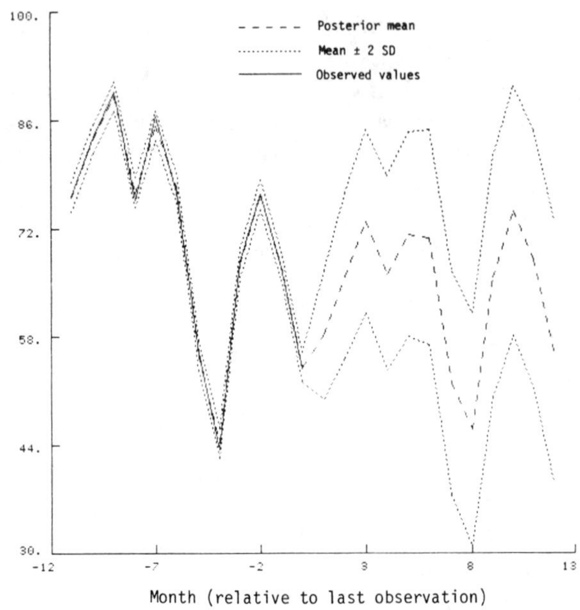

Fig. 7b. *Series minus error*, $Y_t - E_t$: Posterior means with two standard-deviation limits for target quantities for the last 12 months of observations and forecast 12 months ahead, under the assumption of model F.

From the likelihood analysis there is little to choose between models F, B and C, yet we see that rather different forecasts do result from each model. However, comparison with fig. 7a shows that posterior uncertainty given a model considerably outweighs the differences between models. Of course, combining the latter source of uncertainty (assuming that prior information is not available to strongly assist the choice of model) with the former would lead to even wider posterior probability intervals than those of fig. 7a.

Appendix I: Details of the random seasonal model

Given a non-seasonal stochastic process defined by the Fourier pair (f, γ), we derive a *seasonal* process with the following definition:

$$\begin{aligned} f_S(\lambda) &= f(12\lambda) - m + \alpha, \qquad \tfrac{1}{24} \le |\lambda| \le \tfrac{1}{2}, \\ &= f(\tfrac{1}{2}) - m + \alpha, \qquad |\lambda| < \tfrac{1}{24}, \end{aligned} \tag{I.1}$$

where $m = \min f(\lambda)$ $(\lambda \in [0, \frac{1}{2}])$, $\alpha > 0$ is an arbitrary small constant ensuring

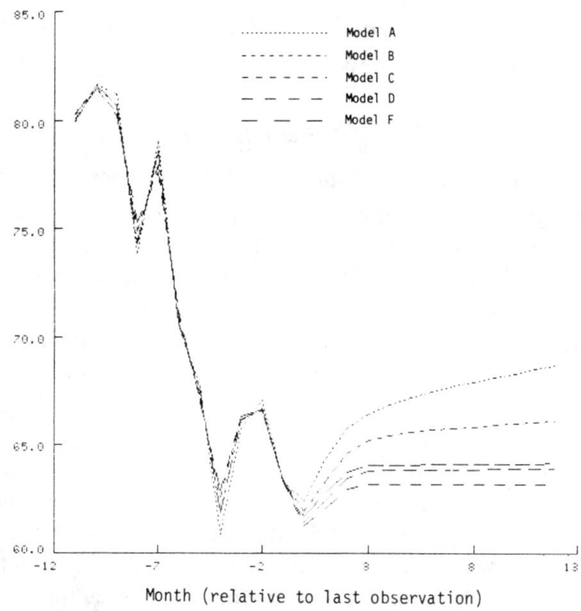

Fig. 8. Comparison of posterior means for the non-seasonal component, $\bar{\mu} + N_t$, under 5 alternative models (A–D and F).

that the constructed seasonal process remains non-deterministic, and $f(\cdot)$ has been extended periodically in the obvious way.

Essentially this definition just translates the fundamental shape of f from the interval $[-\frac{1}{2}, \frac{1}{2}]$ into each of the 12 intervals, $[(k-1)/12, k/12]$ for $k = -5, \ldots, 6$, with an obvious modification close to zero frequency (since seasonality is only to be identified with the fundamental frequency $\frac{1}{12}$ and its harmonics), and a further adjustment (subtracting m) to remove white noise characteristics from the seasonal process. In practice we take α to be effectively zero since we compute with a discrete approximation to (I.1) (corresponding to a finite sequence of covariances) where singularity problems do not arise.

The seasonal covariance function γ_S, obtained by Fourier transformation of (I.1), may be expressed in terms of (f, γ) as follows:

$$\begin{aligned} \gamma_S(t) &= -\tfrac{1}{12}\gamma(t/12), && t \neq 0 \bmod 12, \\ &= \tfrac{11}{12}\gamma(t/12), && t = \pm 12, \pm 24, \ldots, \\ &= \tfrac{11}{12}\gamma(0) + \tfrac{1}{12}f\left(\tfrac{1}{2}\right) - m + \alpha, && t = 0, \end{aligned} \qquad \text{(I.2)}$$

where the definition of $\gamma(t)$ has been extended formally to cover non-integral values of t. We note from (I.2) that $\gamma_S(0) \neq \gamma(0)$, so that a rescaling is required to achieve a seasonal process with variance equal to $\gamma(0)$.

Appendix II: Details of frequency domain diagnostics

The model (2.1) specifies that the observed series $Y_0, Y_1, \ldots, Y_{n-1}$ is composed of three types of random component (non-seasonal, seasonal, and error) and two types of fixed component (initial seasonal pattern, and general fixed effects). Until near the end of this appendix, we suppose no general fixed effects. Consequently, when we represent the data using $Y_0, Y_1, \ldots, Y_{11}, Y_{12}'', Y_{13}'', \ldots, Y_{n-1}''$, with $Y_t'' = Y_t - Y_{t-12}$, it turns out that the annual difference series $Y_{12}'', Y_{13}'', \ldots, Y_{n-1}''$ is modelled as a stationary Gaussian process with zero mean, while the initial $Y_0, Y_1, \ldots, Y_{11}$ contain random effects which are totally confounded with the initial fixed seasonal effects $\mu_0, \mu_1, \ldots, \mu_{11}$. Because $\mu_0, \mu_1, \ldots, \mu_{11}$ have an infinite variance prior, there is no information in $Y_0, Y_1, \ldots, Y_{11}$ about the parameters of the random component models, so that the modelling proceeds as though the data were a stationary zero mean process $Y_{12}'', \ldots, Y_{n-1}''$ with specified covariance and spectral density functions.

To eliminate awkward notation, we now present theory for $X_0, X_1, \ldots, X_{n-1}$ assumed to be a zero mean stationary Gaussian process with spectral density $f(\lambda)$, remembering that the intended application is to $Y_{12}'', \ldots, Y_{n-1}''$. In Dempster (1985), the familiar Cramér (1942) frequency domain representation of the series is written

$$X_t = \int_0^{1/2} \sqrt{f(\lambda)} \begin{bmatrix} \cos 2\pi\lambda t \\ \sin 2\pi\lambda t \end{bmatrix}^T \begin{bmatrix} d\mu_1(\lambda) \\ d\mu_2(\lambda) \end{bmatrix}, \tag{II.1}$$

where $d\mu_1(\lambda)$ and $d\mu_2(\lambda)$ are independent Brownian motion processes of independent increments with variance $d\lambda$ on $0 < \lambda < \frac{1}{2}$. It is easily deduced that the posterior means of $d\mu_1(\lambda)$ and $d\mu_2(\lambda)$ given observed $X_0, \ldots, X_{n-1}$ are $\sqrt{f(\lambda)}\, U_1(\lambda)\, d\lambda$, $\sqrt{f(\lambda)}\, U_2(\lambda)\, d\lambda$ where

$$\begin{bmatrix} U_1(\lambda) \\ U_2(\lambda) \end{bmatrix} = \boldsymbol{C}(\lambda)\boldsymbol{Q}^{-1}\boldsymbol{X}. \tag{II.2}$$

In (II.2), $\boldsymbol{X}$ is the $n \times 1$ vector of the observed time series, $\boldsymbol{Q}$ is the $n \times n$ Toeplitz matrix of stationary covariances of $\boldsymbol{X}$, and $\boldsymbol{C}(\lambda)$ is the finite Fourier transform

$$\boldsymbol{C}(\lambda) = \begin{bmatrix} 1 & \cos 2\pi\lambda & \cos 4\pi\lambda & \cdots & \cos 2\pi(n-1)\lambda \\ 0 & \sin 2\pi\lambda & \sin 4\pi\lambda & \cdots & \sin 2\pi(n-1)\lambda \end{bmatrix}. \tag{II.3}$$

Similarly, it is easily seen that the sampling covariance between $[U_1(\lambda), U_2(\lambda)]$ and $[U_1(\omega), U_2(\omega)]$ is given by

$$\begin{bmatrix} \tau_{11}(\lambda,\omega) & \tau_{12}(\lambda,\omega) \\ \tau_{21}(\lambda,\omega) & \tau_{22}(\lambda,\omega) \end{bmatrix} = \boldsymbol{C}(\lambda)\boldsymbol{Q}^{-1}\boldsymbol{C}(\omega)^T. \tag{II.4}$$

In particular, the sampling variances of $U_1(\lambda)$ and $U_2(\lambda)$ are $\tau_{11}(\lambda,\lambda)$ and $\tau_{22}(\lambda,\lambda)$.

The proposed frequency domain diagnostics which are illustrated in section 4 are based on the quantities just defined. The plots shown in figs. 5a and 5b plot $U_1(\lambda)/\sqrt{\tau_{11}(\lambda,\lambda)}$ and $U_2(\lambda)/\sqrt{\tau_{22}(\lambda,\lambda)}$ for a discrete set of frequency values.[1] The number of frequencies used is a computationally convenient integer slightly greater than the length of the series. These plots are natural model diagnostics from our Bayesian standpoint because they are posterior means. Of course, no specific value carries much weight, but a collection of adjacent values being too large (or too small) indicates that the time series model needs more (or less) power at nearby frequencies.

The quantities $U_1(\lambda)$, $U_2(\lambda)$, $\tau_{11}(\lambda,\lambda)$, and $\tau_{22}(\lambda,\lambda)$ have a precise relationship with derivatives of log likelihood, and this relationship suggests the alternative diagnostic shown in fig. 6. In Dempster (1985) it is shown that if the spectral density function $f(\lambda)$ is perturbed to $f(\lambda)+\delta g(\lambda)$, then for small δ the change in 2 log likelihood is given by

$$\delta\int_0^{1/2} g(\lambda)\left[U_1(\lambda)^2 + U_2(\lambda)^2 - \tau_{11}(\lambda,\lambda) - \tau_{22}(\lambda,\lambda)\right] \mathrm{d}\lambda. \tag{II.5}$$

In the fig. 6 diagnostic plot, we show $U_1(\lambda)^2 + U_2(\lambda)^2$ plotted above the axis and $\tau_{11}(\lambda,\lambda)+\tau_{22}(\lambda,\lambda)$ plotted below the axis, with the difference shown by the solid area. It thus becomes possible to gauge roughly how much change in log likelihood can be obtained by raising or lowering $f(\lambda)$ in the neighborhood of any λ.

Finally, we note that the formulas presented in this appendix are applicable only for models without general fixed effects. Fixed effects are in general confounded with estimates of frequency components of random effects, whence the correct calculation of posterior means of $\mathrm{d}\mu_1(\lambda)$ and $\mathrm{d}\mu_2(\lambda)$ and their sampling variances requires additional computations. These are not difficult, and form a small part of the overall computation, but the details are omitted here.

[1]Actually, the plots represent phase shifted $U_1(\lambda)$ and $U_2(\lambda)$ derived by shifting zero time to the midpoint of the data. The effect is to make $U_1(\lambda)$ more nearly uncorrelated with $U_2(\omega)$ for all λ, ω pairs.

References

Bell, W.R., 1984, Signal extraction for nonstationary time series, Annals of Statistics 12, 646–664.

Bell, W.R. and S.C. Hillmer, 1984, Issues involved with the seasonal adjustment of economic time series, Journal of Business and Economic Statistics 2, 291–320.

Box, G.E.P., S.C. Hillmer and G.C. Tiao, 1978, Analysis and modelling of seasonal time series, in: A. Zellner, ed., Seasonal analysis of economic time series (U.S. Department of Commerce, Bureau of the Census, Washington, DC) 309–334.

Box, G.E.P. and G.M. Jenkins, 1976, Time series analysis: Forecasting and control, Rev. ed. (Holden Day, San Francisco, CA).

Burman, J.P., 1980, Seasonal adjustment by signal extraction, Journal of the Royal Statistical Society A 143, 321–337.

Cleveland, W.P. and G.C. Tiao, 1976, Decomposition of seasonal time series: A model for the X-11 program, Journal of the American Statistical Association 71, 581–587.

Cramér, H., 1942, On harmonic analysis in certain functional spaces, Arkiv Mat. Astr. Fysik 28B, no. 12, 17 pp.

Dempster, A.P., 1982, Some formulas useful for covariance estimation with Gaussian linear component models, in: G. Kallianpur, P.R. Krishnaiah and J.K. Ghosh, eds., Statistics and probability: Essays in honor of C.R. Rao (North-Holland, Amsterdam) 213–220.

Dempster, A.P., 1985, Derivative and related computations for Gaussian time series analysis, in: P.R. Krishnaiah, ed., Multivariate analysis – VI: Proceedings of the sixth international symposium on multivariate analysis (North-Holland, Amsterdam) 165–176.

Geweke, J. and S. Porter-Hudak, 1983, The estimation and application of long-memory time series models, Journal of Time Series Analysis 4, 221–238.

Granger, C. and R. Joyeux, 1980, An introduction to long-memory time series models and fractional differencing, Journal of Time Series Analysis 1, 15–29.

Hillmer, S.C., 1985, Measures of variability for model-based seasonal adjustment procedures, Journal of Business and Economic Statistics 3, 60–68.

Hosking, J., 1981, Fractional differencing, Biometrika 68, 165–176.

Jonas, A.B., 1983, Persistent memory random processes, Unpublished Ph.D. thesis (Department of Statistics, Harvard University, Cambridge, MA).

Kolmogorov, A.N., 1940, Wienersche Spiralen und einige andere interessante Kurven im Hilbertschen Raum, Comptes Rendus (Doklady) de l'Academie des Sciences de l'URSS 26, no. 2 (in German).

Pierce, D.A., 1978, Seasonal adjustment when both deterministic and stochastic seasonality are present, in: A. Zellner, ed., Seasonal analysis of economic time series (U.S. Department of Commerce, Bureau of the Census, Washington, DC) 242–269.

Pierce, D.A., 1980, A survey of recent developments in seasonal adjustment, The American Statistician 34, 125–134.

FOUNDATIONS OF DATA ENVELOPMENT ANALYSIS FOR PARETO–KOOPMANS EFFICIENT EMPIRICAL PRODUCTION FUNCTIONS*

A. CHARNES, W.W. COOPER, B. GOLANY and L. SEIFORD

The University of Texas, Austin, TX 78712, USA

J. STUTZ

University of Miami, Coral Gables, FL 00000, USA

The construction and analysis of Pareto-efficient frontier production functions by a new Data Envelopment Analysis method is presented in the context of new theoretical characterizations of the inherent structure and capabilities of such empirical production functions. Contrasts and connections with other developments, including solutions of some remaining problems, are made re aspects such as informatics, economies of scale, isotonicity and non-concavity, discretionary and non-discretionary inputs, piecewise linearity, partial derivatives and Cobb–Douglas properties of the functions. Non-Archimedean constructs are *not* required.

1. Introduction

Classically, the economic theory of production is heavily based on the conceptual use of the Pareto-efficiency (or Pareto-optimal) frontier of production possibility sets to define *the* production function. The work of Shephard (1953, 1970), under restrictions on the mathematical structure of production possibility sets and cost relations, developed an elegant 'transform' theory between production aspects and cost aspects as in Charnes, Cooper and Schinnar (1982). This was applied to various classes of explicitly given parametric functional forms, and problems of statistical estimation of parameters from data were considered in classical statistical contexts especially by successors like Afriat (1972), Aigner, Lovell and Schmidt (1977), and Försund and Hjalmarsson (1979).[1] These efforts were almost exclusively for single-output functions.

Farrell (1957), partly responding to the inadequacies of separate indices of labor productivity, capital productivity, etc., undertook what he referred to as

*This research was partly supported by NSF Grant SES-8408134 and USARI Contract MDA903-83-K-0312 with the Center for Cybernetic Studies, The University of Texas at Austin. Reproduction in whole or in part is permitted for any purpose of the Unisted States Government.

[1] The need for some method of estimating frontier functions had been pointed out as early as 1935 by R. Frisch (1935) in his statistical study of chocolate production in France.

an 'activity analysis' approach[2] that could deal more adequately with the problem. Possibly because of the limitations of the elaborate matrix inversion routines he was employing, Farrell confined his numerical examples and discussion to single-output situations, although he did formulate the multiple-output case. If anything, the need for being able to deal directly with multiple outputs has grown ever more urgent with the continuing growth of the not-for-profit and service sectors in the United States and other 'western type' economies. As we have elsewhere observed,[3] one can otherwise do almost nothing with important parts of not-for-profit and governmental activities without becoming involved in arbitrary weighting schemes. Even attempts at measuring and evaluating 'total factor productivity' will fall short of what is required since this is inherently a single-output concept. Farrell was right, therefore, in re-orienting the direction of development toward the various types of efficiencies that he referred to as 'technical', 'scale', and 'allocative efficiencies'.

Building on the individual firm or country (= Decision Making Unit)[4] evaluations of Farrell and the engineering ratio idea of efficiency measure for a single-input, single-output efficiency analysis in its managerial aspects and its constructible extensions to multi-input, multi-output situations was initiated by Charnes, Cooper and Rhodes (1978, 1981). Subsequent extensions and elaborations by the former pair with other students and colleagues [Charnes, Cooper, Lewin, Morey and Rousseau (forthcoming), Charnes, Cooper, Seiford and Stutz (1982, 1983), and Charnes, Cooper and Sherman (forthcoming)] were made with more detailed attention to classical economic aspects and deeper analysis of the production function side of the mathematical duality structure and Data Envelopment Analysis first presented in the original CCR work. The CCR ratio measures and the variants of Farrell, Shephard, Färe et al. on the dual linear programming side require, however, non-Archimedean constructs for rigorous theory and usage. Their solution methods also do not easily provide important needed properties of their associated empirical production functions.

Thus, in this paper we introduce as basic the idea of Pareto-optimality with respect to an empirically defined production possibility set. We characterize the mathematical structures permitted under our minimal assumptions and contrast these with work by others. Properties such as isotonicity, non-concavity, economies of scale, piece-wise linearity, Cobb–Douglas forms, discretionary and non-discretionary inputs are treated through a new Data Envelopment

[2] In the sense of the original work by T.C. Koopmans that is described in Chapter IX of Charnes and Cooper (1980) where it was also accorded an explicit linear programming formulation and interpretation.

[3] See Banker, Bowlin, Charnes and Cooper (in process).

[4] This term was introduced in Charnes, Cooper and Rhodes (1978) and contracted to DMU because it was recognized that something like it was needed to refer to public sector organizations.

Analysis method and informatics which permit a constructive development of an empirical production function and its partial derivatives without loss of efficiency analysis or use of non-Archimedean field extensions.

2. Empirical function setting and generation

By an 'empirical' function we shall mean a vector function whose values are known at a finite number of points and whose values at other points in its domain are given by linear (usually convex) combinations of values at known points. The points in the domain are 'inputs', the component values of the vector function 'output'. We shall assume that inputs are so chosen that convex combinations of input values for each input are meaningful input values. We assume this for output values as well.

In efficiency analysis, observations are generated by a finite number of 'DMUs', or 'productive', or 'response' units, all of which have the same inputs and outputs. A relative efficiency rating is to be obtained for each unit. Typically, observations over time will be made of each unit and the results of efficiency analyses will be employed to assist in managing each of the units. We assume n units, s outputs and m inputs. The observed values are to be non-negative (sometimes positive) numbers.

We shall employ the notation X_j, Y_j for respectively the observed vectors of the inputs and outputs of the jth DMU. By X and Y we shall mean the *matrices* whose n column vectors are respectively those of the n DMUs. We use x, y, λ and s to denote column vectors, also with e the column vector of ones. We use 'T' as a superscript to denote the transpose, e.g. e^{T} is the *row* vector of ones. Point sets are denoted by (capital) script letters. The inequality symbol between vectors means that inequality holds for each component.

3. A hypograph empirical production possibility set

Given the (empirical) points (X_j, Y_j), $j = 1, \dots, n$, with $(m \times 1)$ 'input' vectors $X_j \geq 0$ and $(s \times 1)$ 'output' vectors $Y_j \geq 0$, we define the 'empirical production set' $\mathcal{P}_E$ to be the convex hull of these points, i.e.,

$$\mathcal{P}_E \triangleq \left\{ (x, y) : x = \sum_{j=1}^{n} X_j \mu_j,\ y = \sum_{j=1}^{n} Y_j \mu_j, \forall \mu_j \geq 0, \sum_j \mu_m = 1 \right\}. \tag{3.1}$$

We extend it to our 'empirical production possibility set' $\mathcal{Q}_E$ by adding to $\mathcal{P}_E$ all points with inputs in $\mathcal{P}_E$ and outputs not greater than some output in $\mathcal{P}_E$, i.e.,

$$\mathcal{Q}_E \triangleq \{ (x, y) : x = \bar{x},\ y \leq \bar{y} \text{ for some } (\bar{x}, \bar{y}) \in \mathcal{P}_E \}. \tag{3.2}$$

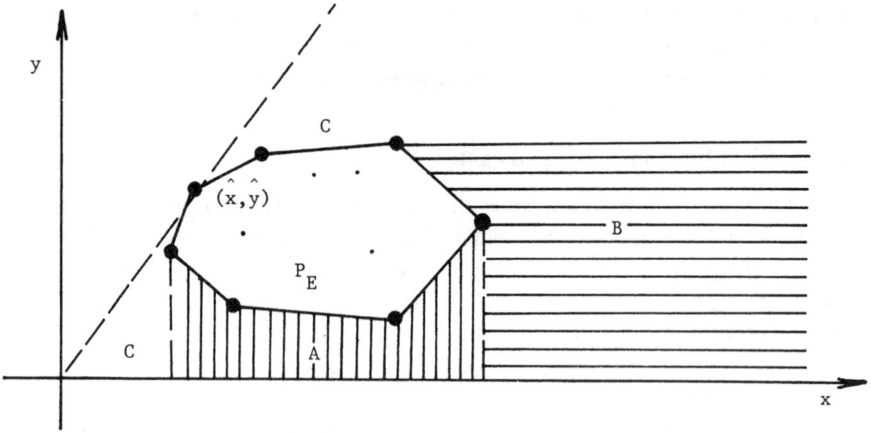

Fig. 1

Note that $\mathcal{Q}_E$ is contained in (e.g., is smaller than) *every* production possibility set heretofore employed, i.e., those studies by Farrell (1957), Shephard (1970), Banker, Charnes and Cooper (1984), Fare and Lovell (1978), etc. We also use fewer axioms than the others, including even Banker (1984) who, up to this point in *journal* publication, had used the most parsimonious axiom system to characterize the production possibility set of DEA.[5] The Farrell, Shephard, Färe sets are (truncated) cones; the BCC set (when not also a cone) adds to $\mathcal{Q}_E$ the set

$$\{(x, y): x \geq \bar{x},\ y = \bar{y} \text{ for some } (\bar{x}, \bar{y}) \in \mathcal{Q}_E\}.$$

These relations may be visualized in the schematic plot of fig. 1, where $\mathcal{Q}_E = \mathcal{P}_E \cup \mathcal{A}$, the BCC set is $\mathcal{Q}_E \cup \mathcal{B}$, and the Farrell, Shephard, Färe set is $\mathcal{Q}_E \cup \mathcal{B} \cup \mathcal{C}$.

Let $\mathcal{P}_E^\imath$, $\mathcal{Q}_E^\imath$ denote the sets corresponding to $\mathcal{P}_E$ and $\mathcal{Q}_E$ when only the output $y_\imath$ is the ordinate. Evidently a frontier function $f_\imath(x)$ is determined by

$$f_\imath(x) = \max y_\imath \quad \text{for} \quad (x, y_\imath) \in \mathcal{Q}_E^\imath. \tag{3.3}$$

Then:

Theorem 1. $\mathcal{Q}_E^\imath$ *is the hypograph of* $f_\imath(x)$ *over* $\{x: (x, y) \in \mathcal{Q}_E\}$.

[5] Our usage antedates his since we used this in the Ph.D. and other work with Rhodes (the 'R' of CCR).

Proof. The hypograph $H_\imath$ of $f_\imath(x)$ is the set

$$H_\imath \triangleq \{(x, y_\imath): y_\imath \leq f_\imath(x), (x, y) \in \mathcal{Q}_E\}. \quad \blacksquare$$

Let $\mathcal{D}_E$ denote $\{x: (x, y) \in \mathcal{Q}_E\}$. It is the domain (the input set) of our empirical frontier functions.

Theorem 2. $f_\imath(x)$ *is a concave, piecewise linear function on* $\mathcal{P}_E$.

Proof. A necessary and sufficient condition for $f_\imath(x)$ to be concave is that its hypograph is a convex set [cf. Rockafellar (1970) or Fenchel (1953)]. The piecewise linearity also follows from the construction of $\mathcal{Q}_E$ by all convex combinations of the empirical points (X_j, Y_j), $j = 1, \ldots, n$. $\blacksquare$

We further observe explicitly that *no use* whatever has been made of *non-negativity* of input and output values in the sets, functions or proof of Theorems 1 and 2. Therefore, they hold without this restriction – a fact we shall employ elsewhere.

Also, *no* assumptions have been made about the properties of *any* underlying function, or function hypograph, from which the (X_j, Y_j) of our empirical construct may be considered samples. Theorem 2 shows, therefore, that any *empirical* (maximum) frontier function is the 'concave cap' function of its graph.

4. The empirical Pareto-efficient production function

A Pareto-efficient (minimum) point for a finite set of functions $g_1(x), \ldots, g_K(x)$ is a point x^* such that there is no other point x in the domain of these functions such that

$$g_k(x) \leq g_k(x^*), \qquad k = 1, \ldots, K, \tag{4.1}$$

with at least one strict inequality. Charnes and Cooper (1962, ch. IX) showed that x^* is Pareto-efficient iff x^* is an optimal solution to the mathematical (goal) program[6]

$$\min_x \sum_{k=1}^{K} g_k(x) \quad \text{subject to} \quad g_k(x) \leq g_k(x^*), \qquad k = 1, \ldots, K. \tag{4.2}$$

This was employed by Ben-Israel, Ben-Tal and Charnes (1977) to develop the

[6] For a formal definition of goal programming and some of its history, see Charnes and Cooper (1977).

currently strongest necessary and sufficient conditions for a Pareto-minimum in convex programming.

Utilizing (4.2) we can now define and construct, im(or ex-)plicitly, the Pareto-efficient empirical (frontier) production function. Because of Koopmans' work in this area [see Charnes and Cooper (1961)], we shall use interchangeably the designations 'Pareto-efficient' and 'Pareto–Koopmans efficient', etc. in this paper. Other usages of (4.2) to generalizations such as the 'functional efficiency' of Charnes and Cooper (1961) will not be developed here.

First, by (4.2), the Pareto-efficient points among our n empirical points can be determined. The empirical Pareto-efficient function is then defined on the convex hull of their inputs by convex combinations of the 'output' values. Note that the convex hull of the Pareto-efficient points might not include all of $\mathscr{P}_E$ since only the doubled line portion of the frontier corresponds to Pareto-efficient points.

Since for efficient production we wish to maximize on outputs while minimizing on inputs, our relevant $g_k(x)$ include both outputs and inputs, e.g.,

$$\begin{aligned} -g_k(x) &\triangleq y_k, \qquad 1 \le k \le s, \\ &\triangleq -x_i, \quad k = s+i, \quad i = 1,\dots,m, \quad \text{for } (x, y) \in \mathscr{Q}_E, \end{aligned} \tag{4.3}$$

For the optimization in (4.2) we clearly need only consider $(x, y) \in \mathscr{P}_E$ rather than $\mathscr{Q}_E$. Thus the constraint inequalities in (4.2) are for a test point (x^*, y^*):

$$y \ge y^*, \qquad x \le x^*, \tag{4.4}$$

and we have, since these are the envelopment constraints of Data Envelopment Analysis for an observed input vector x^* and corresponding output vector y^*:

Theorem 3. The envelopment constraints of Data Envelopment Analysis in production analysis are the Charnes–Cooper constraints of (4.2) for testing Pareto–Koopmans efficiency of an empirical production point.

In no way is what we call 'Data Envelopment Analysis' restricted to linear constant returns to scale functions or to truncated cone domains. Evidently via (4.2), Data Envelopment Analysis applies to much more general convex functions, function domains and other situations than the current *empirical* production function one.

To test an empirical 'input–output' point (X_0, Y_0) for Pareto–Koopmans efficiency, the Charnes–Cooper test of (4.2) becomes

$$\min_{\lambda, s^+, s^-} \; -e^{\mathrm{T}} Y\lambda + e^{\mathrm{T}} X\lambda,$$

subject to

$$Y\lambda - s^{+} = Y_0, \quad -X\lambda - s^{-} = -X_0, \quad e^{\mathrm{T}}\lambda = 1, \tag{4.5}$$

$$\lambda, s^{+}, s^{-} \geq 0,$$

where

$$X \triangleq [X_1, \ldots, X_n], \qquad Y \triangleq [Y_1, \ldots, Y_n].$$

Since $-e^{\mathrm{T}}(Y\lambda - Y_0) + e^{\mathrm{T}}(X\lambda - X_0)$ is an equivalent functional (it differs from the above one only by a constant), we can rewrite the problem for convenience in later comparisons as

$$\min_{\lambda, s^{+}, s^{-}} \; -e^{\mathrm{T}}s^{+} - e^{\mathrm{T}}s^{-},$$

subject to

$$Y\lambda - s^{+} = Y_0, \quad -X\lambda - s^{-} = -X_0, \quad e^{\mathrm{T}}\lambda = 1, \tag{4.6}$$

$$\lambda, s^{+}, s^{-} \geq 0.$$

Here, $\min -e^{\mathrm{T}}s^{+} - e^{\mathrm{T}}s^{-} = -e^{\mathrm{T}}s^{+*} - e^{\mathrm{T}}s^{-*} = 0$ if and only if Y_0, X_0 is Pareto–Koopmans efficient.[7] This is the new DEA form for obtaining and characterizing the production possibility set $\mathscr{Q}_E$ via $\mathscr{P}_E$. The linear program (4.6) maximizes the l_1-distance of a point in $\mathscr{P}_E$ to (X_0, Y_0). We solve (4.6) for all n DMUs considered as (X_0, Y_0). From these we get the efficient and non-efficient points and can construct as desired the points of $\mathscr{P}_E$ by convex combinations. As we shall see later, other variations of $\mathscr{Q}_E$ can be accommodated easily by simple modifications of or additions to the constraints on λ. Its informatics and software, as developed by Ali and Stutz of the Center for Cybernetic Studies of The University of Texas at Austin, involve only minor modification from that of Charnes, Cooper, Seiford and Stutz (1983).

5. Efficiency analysis

As mentioned, managerial and program comparison aspects of efficiency analysis were initiated in Charnes, Cooper and Rhodes (1978, 1981) and Charnes and Cooper (1980), through a generalization of the single-input, single-output absolute efficiency determination of classical engineering and science to multi-input, multi-output relative efficiencies of a finite number of decision-making units 'DMUs' (sometimes called 'productive' units or 'response' units). The multi-input, multi-output situations were reduced to 'virtual' single-input, single-output ones through use of virtual multipliers and

[7] See Charnes and Cooper (1961, ch. IX).

sums. Explicitly, the CCR ratio measure of efficiency of the DMU designated '0' is given by the non-linear, non-convex, non-Archimedean fractional program [see Charnes, Cooper, Lewin, Morey and Rousseau (forthcoming)]

$$\max_{\eta,\xi} \eta^{\mathrm{T}} Y_0/\xi^{\mathrm{T}} X_0,$$

subject to

$$\eta^{\mathrm{T}} Y_j/\xi^{\mathrm{T}} X_j \leq 1, \quad -\eta^{\mathrm{T}}/\xi^{\mathrm{T}} X_0 \leq -\varepsilon e^{\mathrm{T}}, \quad -\xi^{\mathrm{T}}/\xi^{\mathrm{T}} X_0 \leq -\varepsilon e^{\mathrm{T}}, \tag{5.1}$$

for $j = 1, \ldots, n$, where the entries of the X_j and Y_j are assumed positive, ε is a non-Archimedean infinitesimal, e^{T} is a row vector of ones, and, by abuse of notation, has s entries for η^{T}, m entries for ξ^{T}. (X_0, Y_0) is one of the n input–output pairs.

Employing the Charnes–Cooper transformation of fractional programming[8]

$$\mu^{\mathrm{T}} \triangleq \eta^{\mathrm{T}}/\xi^{\mathrm{T}} X_0, \quad \nu^{\mathrm{T}} \triangleq \xi^{\mathrm{T}}/\xi^{\mathrm{T}} X_0, \quad \nu^{\mathrm{T}} X_0 = 1, \tag{5.2}$$

we obtain the dual non-Archimedean linear programs

$$\max_{\eta,\nu} \mu^{\mathrm{T}} Y_0,$$

subject to

$$\nu^{\mathrm{T}} X_0 = 1, \quad \mu^{\mathrm{T}} Y - \nu^{\mathrm{T}} X \leq 0, \quad -\mu^{\mathrm{T}} \leq -\varepsilon e^{\mathrm{T}}, \quad -\nu^{\mathrm{T}} \leq -\varepsilon e^{\mathrm{T}}, \tag{5.3}$$

and

$$\min_{\theta,\lambda,s^+,s^-} \theta - \varepsilon e^{\mathrm{T}} s^+ - \varepsilon e^{\mathrm{T}} s^-,$$

subject to

$$Y\lambda - s^+ = Y_0, \quad \theta X_0 - X\lambda - s^- = 0,$$

$$\lambda, s^+, s^- \geq 0,$$

where

$$X \triangleq [X_1, \ldots, X_n], \qquad Y \triangleq [Y_1, \ldots, Y_n].$$

The first problem is associated with the origin of the term 'Data Envelopment Analysis' since the minimization (a) envelops the output vector Y_0 from above and (b) envelops the input vector X_0 from below via the minimizing choice of the scalar value of the intensity $\theta^* = \min \theta$. The second problem is said to be in efficiency analysis form with the maximization oriented toward the choice of μ^{T} and ν^{T} (called *virtual* multipliers or transformation rates)

[8]See Charnes and Cooper (1962) and Schaible (1974).

which produces the greatest rate of virtual output per unit virtual input allowed by the first constraint together with the requirements (a) virtual output cannot exceed virtual input and (b) all virtual transformation rates must be positive.

Although, clearly, *no* assumptions have been made concerning the type of functional relations for the input–output pairs (X_j, Y_j), the minimization program may be recognized as having the Data Envelopment Analysis constraints for an empirical production possibility set of Farrell, Shephard, etc. cone type $\mathcal{Q}_E \cup \mathcal{B} \cup \mathcal{C}$, and, since

$$\theta - \varepsilon[e^{\mathrm{T}}Y\lambda - e^{\mathrm{T}}X\lambda] \tag{5.4}$$

is an equivalent form for the functional, as being a Charnes–Cooper Pareto-optimality test for $(\theta X_0, Y_0)$ over the cone on the (X_j, Y_j), $j = 1, \ldots, n$, with pre-emption on the intensity θ of input X_0. As mentioned above, DMU_0 is efficient iff $\theta^* = 1$, $s^{*+} = 0$, $s^* = 0$.

Re informatics, which are particularly important since *all n* efficiency evaluations must be made (i.e., n linear programs must be solved), the dual problem can be computed exactly (in the base field) as shown in Charnes and Cooper (1961), e.g., with the code NONARC of Dr. I. Ali (Center for Cybernetic Studies, The University of Texas at Austin), or approximately by using a sufficiently small numerical value for ε. A typical efficient point is designated by $(\hat{x}, \hat{y})$ in fig. 1.

If a DMU is inefficient, the optimal $\lambda_j^* > 0$ in its DEA problem (= Charnes–Cooper test) designate *efficient* DMUs, as do alternate optima. Thus, a 'proper' subset of the efficient DMUs determines the efficiency value of an inefficient DMU. The convex combinations of this subset are also efficient. Thereby to each inefficient DMU a 'facet' of efficient DMU is associated. The transformation,

$$X_0 \to \theta^* X_0 - s^{*-}, \qquad Y_0 \to Y_0 + s^{*+}, \tag{5.5}$$

where the asterisk designates optimality, projects DMU_0, i.e., (X_0, Y_0), onto its efficiency facet.

This projection was introduced by Charnes, Cooper and Rhodes (1981) to correct for differences in managerial ability in order to distinguish between 'program' and 'managerial efficiency' in their analysis of programs Follow-Through and non-Follow-Through. It also shows quantitatively what improvements in inputs and outputs will (*ceteris paribus*) bring a DMU to efficient operation.[9] Thus, although the relative efficiency *measure* of an inefficient

[9]The analysis by Bessent, Bessent, Charnes, Cooper and Thorogood (1983) shows how one might take account of the possible effects on other DMUs when one or more of the efficient DMUs is altered.

DMU will involve the infinitesimal ε, *non*-infinitesimal changes for improvement *are* suggested.

Both Farrell and Shephard knew that ratio measures required adjustments to correctly exhibit inefficiency of the second DMU in examples like the following two-input, one-output, two-DMU case:

DMU	x_1	x_2	y
1	1	2	1
2	1	4	1

Farrell added geometric points at infinity; Shephard simply excluded such cases without giving a method for their exclusion. The non-Archimedean extension in the CCR formulation was introduced to have an algebraically closed system of linear programming type. Linear programming theory holds for non-Archimedean as well as Archimedean entries in the vector and matrix problem data.[10]

Our new Pareto-efficient DEA method like in Charnes, Cooper, Seiford and Stutz (1983) associates facets with non-optimal (= non-Pareto-efficient) DMUs. Clearly, by the Charnes–Cooper test, DMU_0 is Pareto-efficient (Pareto-efficient) DMUs. Clearly, by the Charnes–Cooper test, DMU_0 is Pareto-efficient (Pareto-optimal) iff $-e^{\mathrm{T}}s^{*+} - e^{\mathrm{T}}s^{*-} = 0$, i.e., iff the l_1-distance from (X_0, Y_0) to the farthest 'northwesterly' $\mathcal{Q}_e$ point is zero. The CCR efficient DMUs are also among the new Pareto-efficient DMUs. Projection of a non-optimal DMU onto its Pareto-efficient facet is rendered by

$$X_0 \to X_0 - s^{*-}, \qquad Y_0 \to Y_0 + s^{*+}. \tag{5.6}$$

To achieve a convenient efficiency measure, we modify the functional by multiplying it by a $\delta > 0$ and dividing the s^+ and s^- by respectively the entries in Y_0 and X_0, e.g.,

$$-\delta e^{\mathrm{T}} D^{-1}(Y_0) s^{+} - \delta e^{\mathrm{T}} D^{-1}(X_0) s^{-}, \tag{5.7}$$

where $D^{-1}(Y_0)$ and $D^{-1}(X_0)$ are diagonal matrices whose diagonals are the reciprocals of the entries in Y_0 and X_0 respectively. This achieves a units-invariant measure which may be thought of as the *logarithm* of the efficiency measure. A $\delta = 10/(m+s)$ will yield a logarithm between 0 and -10. This measure might then be called the 'efficiency pH' analogy with the pH of chemistry.

Our new measure relates to the units-invariant multiplicative measure of Charnes, Cooper, Seiford and Stutz (1983) which is necessary and sufficient

[10] See the discussion in Charnes and Cooper (1961, p. 756).

that the DEA envelopments be piecewise Cobb–Douglas, by considering the entries in the X_j, Y_j to be logarithms of the entries in X_j, Y_j which we employ in the multiplicative formulation.

6. Informatics and function properties

6.1. Partial derivatives

The guidance provided by the Charnes–Cooper–Rhodes, Banker–Charnes–Cooper, Charnes–Cooper–Seiford–Stutz formulations does not include convenient access to the rates of change of the outputs with change in the inputs. The optimal dual variables in the DEA side linear programming problems give rates of change of the *efficiency* measure with changes in inputs or outputs. The non-Archimedean formulations further may give infinitesimal rates, which are not easily employed. And, for most of the efficient points one has *non*-differentiability because they are extreme points rather than (relative) interior points. Nevertheless, because of the informatics, e.g., computational tactics, we employ in testing via Charnes–Cooper for Pareto-efficiency, the following constructive method can be employed.

On reaching a non-Pareto-efficient point, our software discovers all the optimal observed points in its facet, hence, implicitly, all the convex combinations which form the facet. Since the Pareto-efficient facet is a linear surface it is not only differentiable everywhere in its relative interior but all its partial derivatives are *constant* throughout the facet. Thus, we need only obtain these for *any* relative interior point of the facet to have them for the whole facet.

Let

$$F(x_1,\dots,x_m,y_1,\dots,y_s)=0 \tag{6.1}$$

be the linear equation of the facet. Since we have sufficient differentiability in the neighborhood of an interior point $(\bar{x},\bar{y})$, we know

$$\partial y_r/\partial x_i'|_{\bar{x},\bar{y}} = -(\partial F/\partial x_i)/(\partial F/\partial y_r), \tag{6.2}$$

where the right-side partial derivatives are also evaluated at $(\bar{x},\bar{y})$. Suppose we run the Charnes–Cooper test with $(\bar{x},\bar{y})$ as the point being tested. Then the optimal dual variables corresponding to the input $\bar{x}_i$ and output $\bar{y}_r$ are respectively $(\partial F/\partial x_i)|_{\bar{x},\bar{y}}$ and $(\partial F/\partial y_r)|_{\bar{x},\bar{y}}$. Thus, the rate of change of output y_r with respect to input x_i is simply the negative of the ratio of the optimal dual x_i constraint variable to the optimal dual y_r constraint variable![11]

[11] See also Charnes, Cooper and Rhodes (1978, p. 439) for a discussion which can *now* relate this development to the ordinary conditions of economic theory for equality between ratios of marginal productivities and marginal rates of substitution.

More specifically, all Pareto-efficient (X_j, Y_j) of the facet for the point $(\bar{x}, \bar{y})$ satisfy

$$\mu^{*T}y - \nu^{*T}x - \varphi^* = 0, \tag{6.3}$$

where (μ^{*T}, ν^{*T}) are the dual evaluators at an optimal basic solution, *since they do not depend on the Charnes–Cooper test right-hand sides.* Thereby,

$$F(x, y) = \mu^{*T}y - \nu^{*T}x - \varphi^* = 0. \tag{6.4}$$

Clearly, $\mu_i^* = \partial F/\partial y_i$ and $-\nu_i^* = \partial F/\partial x_i$ as already stated.

It should be borne in mind, of course, that these rates of change are valid only for changes which keep one within the facet.

6.2. Isotonicity and economies of scale

To date the structure, or 'geometry', of *empirical* Pareto-efficient production functions has received little attention. The structure depends on and varies with the 'production possibility' or 'reference' set chosen. Here we make a beginning for our new set Q_E and leave to later research more in-depth and broader explorations including those for other reference sets.

In many practical situations we try to choose inputs and outputs with the thought that the underlying empirical Pareto-efficient function should be 'isotone' (which means 'order-preserving'). By definition a (vector) function $f(x)$ is isotone if $x^a \leq x^b$ implies $(f(x^a) \leq f(x^b)$.[12] What in fact can be the case? We show here that in the single-output situation the empirical Pareto-efficient function is *always* isotone. The multiple-output situation, however, may only satisfy a weaker function property which we shall call 'c-d-isotone' or 'cone-directional-isotone', i.e., there is a cone of directions in output space on which the outputs projection is isotone.

Consider first the 'facets' of an empirical Pareto-efficient function for our reference set. These consist of convex combinations of the Pareto-efficient sample input–output points with respect to this reference set.

Theorem 3. Every facet of the empirical Pareto-efficient function relation consists of Pareto-efficient input–output points.

Proof. Each facet corresponds to a basic optimal solution to the following linear program (Charnes–Cooper test) for some sample input–output point

[12] The mathematical term 'isotone' is synonymous with the expression 'monotonically increasing'.

(X_0, Y_0):

$$\min_{\lambda, s^+, s^-} \; -e^{\mathrm{T}}s^+ - e^{\mathrm{T}}s^-,$$

subject to

$$Y\lambda - s^+ = Y_0, \quad -X\lambda - s^- = -X_0, \quad e^+\lambda = 1,$$

$$\lambda, s^+, s^- \geq 0,$$

where $Y \triangleq (Y_1, \ldots, Y_n)$, $X \triangleq (X_1, \ldots, X_n)$, with optimal $s^{*+} = 0$, $s^{*-} = 0$. Every (X_j, Y_j) in the optimal basis is Pareto-efficient since (1) the optimal dual evaluators determined by the basic solution do not depend on the right-hand-side vector $(-X_0, Y_0)$, and (2), replacing $(-X_0, Y_0)$ by any $(-X_j, Y_j)$ in the basis preserves the feasibility of the basis for solution with the new right-hand side.

Next, if we Charnes–Cooper test any convex combination of the basic $(-X_j, Y_j)$, e.g., $(-X_B, Y_B)^{\mathrm{T}}\theta_B$ with $\theta_B \geq 0$, $e_B^{\mathrm{T}}\theta_B = 1$ for Pareto-efficiency and this reference set, i.e., insert it in place of $(-X_0, Y_0)^{\mathrm{T}}$, an optimal λ^* is then simply θ_B (plus $s^{*+}, s^{*-} = 0$) with this same basis. Thus the whole facet is Pareto-efficient. ∎

Now we prove:

Theorem 4. If a Pareto-efficient empirical production function has only a single output, then it is an isotone function.

Proof. Suppose $x^a \leq x^b$ for Pareto-efficient (x^a, y^a) and (x^b, y^b). By definition of Pareto-efficiency for (x^b, y^b), some component output y_j^a can exceed y_j^b only if some other output $y_k^a < y_k^b$. Since there is only one output, then $y^a \triangleq f(x^a) \leq y^b \triangleq f(x^b)$. Thus $x^a \leq x^b$ implies $f(x^a) \leq f(x^b)$ for Pareto-efficient points, i.e., the isotone property. ∎

To show that a multiple–output Pareto-efficient production function need not be isotone, consider the following one-input, two-output example with three sample points a, b, c:

	a	b	c
x_1	1	2	3
y_1	5	2	1
y_2	5	7	4

Input–output points a and b are Pareto-efficient, c is not. We do *not* have isotonicity since $x^a < x^b$, but $f_1(x^a) \triangleq y_1^a > f_1(x^b) \triangleq y_1^b$.

If now we 'project' the outputs of a and b along the direction given by w_1 and w_2 for y_1 and y_2 we obtain the *single* output $5w_1 + 5w_2$ for a and $2w_1 + 7w_2$ for b. Requiring

$$7w_2 + 2w_1 \geq 5w_2 + 5w_1$$

implies $w_2 \geq \frac{3}{2}w_1$ as the cone of directions (w_1, w_2) which yields an isotonic relation.

In general when $x^c \geq x^d$, if $y_r^c \geq y_r^d$ for $r \in R^+$, where $R^+ \cup R^- = \{1, 2, \ldots, s\}$, then the cone of isotonic directions $(w_1, \ldots, w_s)$ is specified by

$$\sum_{r \in R^+} (y_r^c - y_r^d) \geq \sum_{r \in R^-} w_r (y_r^d - y_r^c). \tag{6.5}$$

Homogeneous production functions play an important role in the economics literature. Thereby, whether or not a function for which $f(\rho x) = \rho^\alpha f(x)$, with $\rho \geq 0$, had economies of scale would be decided by the value of the exponent α. More generally, increasing or decreasing 'returns to scale' would be present respectively, at $\bar{x}$ if $f(\rho\bar{x}) > \rho f(\bar{x})$ or $f(\rho\bar{x}) < \rho f(\bar{x})$ for $\rho > 1$ at points $\rho\bar{x}$ in a small neighborhood of $\bar{x}$. Banker, Charnes and Cooper (1984) give a criterion for deciding this (with production possibility set $\mathcal{Q}_E \cup \mathcal{B} \cup \mathcal{C}$ or $\mathcal{Q}_E \cup \mathcal{B}$), but does not give us the rates of change.

Because of our preceding theorems, however, we know that empirical Pareto-efficient functions are c-d-isotonic on facets and concave in each component function regardless of the nature of the underlying production possibility set. Thereby, we automatically anticipate lower and lower returns to scale in going from facet to facet with increasing $e^{\mathrm{T}}x$. And our partial derivatives can give us explicitly the rates of change in each observed facet.

Practically, our choices of inputs are generally made with the expectation that the underlying Pareto-optimal function is isotonic, i.e., we choose the form of the inputs so that an increase in an input should not decrease the outputs. But even here we need still more to determine the non-concave portions of an isotonic function. For example, in fig. 2 an isotonic function is plotted together with the resulting concave cap (large dashed lines) obtained as the empirical function.

As suggested in our original paper,[13] non-concavity can be explored by applying (output) component by component strictly concave transformations g_r to obtain $g_r(y_r)$ instead of y_r so that $g_r(y_r(x))$ would be concave and out plot might look like fig. 3.

[13]'An Empirical DEA Production Function' by Charnes, Cooper and Seiford, April 1981, CCS 396, Center for Cybernetic Studies, The University of Texas, Austin, TX.

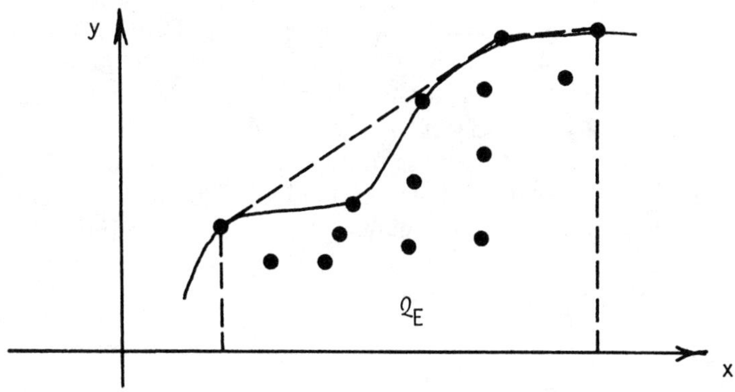

Fig. 2

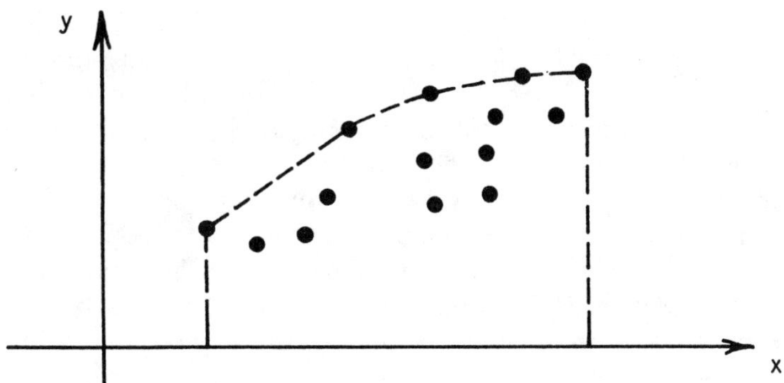

Fig. 3

Informatically, we can do this by applying transformations of form $g_i(y_i) = \bar{y}_i + (y_i - \bar{y}_i)^{1/\beta}$ with $\beta \approx 20$ to obtain possible new facets in the $g_i(y_i)$ (where $\bar{y}_i = \min_j y_{ij}$).

Problems do arise, of course, on whether one gets spurious empirical frontier portions in this manner for empirical points which should 'really' be inefficient. Evidently such non-concave portions are portions of increasing returns to scale if they are truly on the frontier.

6.3. Discretionary and non-discretionary inputs

In a number of practical applications, certain relevant inputs (e.g., unemployment rate, population, median income) are not subject to 'discretionary' change by the decision-makers of decision-making units. These are called 'non-discretionary' inputs.[14] They are important in influencing the outputs and in furnishing the *reference* background in terms of which units' efficiency is rated. Not infrequently the facet associated with an inefficient unit has the same values for the non-discretionary inputs, in which case there is no problem with the rating assigned. If not, however, to obtain more meaningful ratings we can add constraints on λ to those in (4.5) which require the non-discretionary inputs to be the same as that of the unit being evaluated. Thereby, a more meaningful rating will be attained.

7. Conclusions

We have shown how direct application of the Charnes–Cooper test for Pareto-optimality leads to a simpler and more robust method, efficiency pH, encompassing all previous ones for ascertaining 'efficiency'. Further, Pareto-efficiency characterizations and constructions of empirical production functions restrict us methodologically to exploration of such functions by means of concave caps. Economies of scale from these thereby expectedly decrease with increase in the magnitude of the input vectors. Use of transformations of outputs, as we suggest, can uncover non-concave regions of the underlying production function where substantial economies of scale may prevail. Our new informatics device and theory of the use of the facet average (or bary-center) also constructively furnishes quantitative estimates of the rates of change of outputs with respect to inputs which have not been available previously. These new devices, as with other usages of empirical functions, suggest important new areas for development of statistical theory to distinguish between true properties and sampling 'accidents'. The vital importance of further development of the informatics of solution of systems of adaptively developed linear programming problems for Pareto-efficient constructions should also be clear.

References

Afriat, S., 1972, Efficiency estimation of production functions, International Economic Review 13, 568–598.

Aigner, D.J., C.A.K. Lovell and P.J. Schmidt, 1977, Formulation and estimation of stochastic frontier production function models, Journal of Econometrics 6, 21–37.

Banker, R., 1984, Estimating most productive scale size using data envelopment analysis, European Journal of Operational Research 17, 35–44.

Banker, R., A. Charnes and W.W. Cooper, 1984, Models for estimating technical and scale efficiencies in data envelopment analysis, Management Science 30, 1078–1092.

[14] See Charnes and Cooper (forthcoming).

Banker, R., W. Bowlin, A. Charnes and W.W. Cooper, in process, Mix inefficiencies and synergies in data envelopment analysis, CCS report (Center for Cybernetic Studies, The University of Texas, Austin, TX).
Ben-Israel, A., A. Ben-Tal and A. Charnes, 1977, Necessary and sufficient conditions for a Pareto optimum in convex programming, Econometrica 45, 811–820.
Bessent, A., W. Bessent, A. Charnes, W.W. Cooper and N. Thorogood, 1983, Evaluation of educational program proposals by means of DEA, Educational Administration Quarterly 19, 82–107.
Charnes, A. and W.W. Cooper, 1962, Programming with linear fractional functionals, Naval Research Logistics Quarterly 9, nos. 3, 4.
Charnes, A. and W.W. Cooper, 1977, Goal programming and multiple objective optimizations, European Journal of Operational Research 1, no. 1.
Charnes, A. and W.W. Cooper, 1961, Management models and industrial applications of linear programming (Wiley, New York).
Charnes, A. and W.W. Cooper, 1980, Auditing and accounting for program efficiency in not-for-profit entities, Accounting, Organizations and Society 5, 87–107.
Charnes, A. and W.W. Cooper, forthcoming, Preface to topics in data envelopment analysis, Annals of Operations Research.
Charnes, A., W.W. Cooper and E. Rhodes, 1978, Measuring the efficiency of decision-making units, European Journal of Operations Research 2, 429–444.
Charnes, A., W.W. Cooper and E. Rhodes, 1981, Evaluating program and managerial efficiency: An application of data envelopment analysis to program follow through, Management Science 27, 668–687.
Charnes, A., W.W. Cooper and A. Schinnar, 1982, Transforms and approximations in cost and production function relations, Omega 10, 207–211.
Charnes, A., W.W. Cooper and D. Sherman, in process, A comparative study of DEA with ratio and regression approaches to efficiency evaluations, CCS report (Center for Cybernetic Studies, The University of Texas, Austin, TX).
Charnes, A., W.W. Cooper, L. Seiford and J. Stutz, 1982, A multiplicative model for efficiency analysis, Socio-Economic Planning Sciences 6, 223–224.
Charnes, A., W.W. Cooper, L. Seiford and J. Stutz, 1983, A units invariant multiplicative measure, Operations Research Letters.
Charnes, A., W.W. Cooper, A. Lewin, R. Morey and J. Rousseau, forthcoming, An approach to positivity and stability analysis in DEA, Annals of Operations Research.
Färe, R. and C.A.K. Lovell, 1978, Measuring the technical efficiency of production, Journal of Economic Theory 19, 150–162.
Farrell, M.J., 1957, The measurement of productive efficiency, Journal of Royal Statistical Society A 120, 253–281.
Fenchel, W., 1953, Convex sets, cones and functions (Princeton University Press, Princeton, NJ).
Försund, F. and L. Hjalmarsson, 1979, Generalized Farrell measures of efficiency: An application to milk processing in Swedish dairy plants, Economic Journal 89, 294–315.
Frisch, R., 1935, The principles of substitution: An example of its application in the chocolate industry, Nordisk Tidsskrift for Teknisk Ekonomi 1, 12–27.
Rockfellar, T., 1970, Convex analysis (Princeton University Press, Princeton, NJ).
Shephard, R.W., 1953, Cost and production functions (Princeton University Press, Princeton, NJ).
Shephard, R.W., 1970, Theory of cost and production functions (Princeton University Press, Princeton, NJ).
Schaible, S, 1974, Parameter-free convex equivalent and dual programs of fractional programming problems, Zeitschift für Operations Research 18, 187–196.

PANEL DATA FROM TIME SERIES OF CROSS-SECTIONS

Angus DEATON*

Woodrow Wilson School, Princeton University, Princeton, NJ 08544, USA

In many countries, there are few or no panel data, but there exists a series of independent cross-sections. For example, in the United Kingdom, there are no panel data on consumers' expenditure or on household labor supply, but there are several large household surveys carried out every year. Samples for these surveys are drawn anew each year, so that it is impossible to track individual households over time. This paper considers the possibility of tracking 'cohorts' through such data. A 'cohort' is defined as a group with fixed membership, individuals of which can be identified as they show up in the surveys. The most obvious example is an age cohort, e.g. all males born between 1945 and 1950, but there are other possibilities (Korean war veterans or founding members of the Econometric Society). Consider any economic relationship of interest that is linear in parameters (but not necessarily in variables). Corresponding to individual behavior, there will exist a cohort version of the relationship of the same form, but with cohort means replacing individual observations. If there are additive individual fixed effects, there will be corresponding additive cohort fixed effects. Further, the sample cohort means from the surveys are consistent but error-ridden estimates of the true cohort means. Hence, provided errors-in-variables techniques are used (and error variances and covariances can be estimated from the surveys), the sample cohort means can be used as panel data for estimating the relationship. Such data are immune to attrition bias and can be extended for long time periods. There is also evidence to suggest that the errors in variables problems may be just as severe for genuine panel data; in the created panels considered here, the problem is controllable. The paper discusses appropriate errors in variables estimators, with and without fixed effects.

1. Introduction

In many countries, there are few or no panel data, but there exists a series of independent cross-sections. For example, in the United Kingdom, there are no panel data on consumers' expenditure or on household labor supply, but there are several large household surveys that are carried out every year. Samples for these surveys are drawn anew each year, so that *individual* households cannot be traced over time. This paper is concerned with the possibility of tracking 'cohorts' through such data. A 'cohort' is defined as a group with fixed membership, individuals of which can be identified as they show up in the surveys. The most obvious example is an age cohort, for example, all males born between 1945 and 1950, but there are many other possibilities; consider Korean war veterans, or founder members of the Econometric Society. For

*I am grateful to Badi Baltagi, Bill Barnett, Martin Browning, Margaret Irish, Whitney Newey, and an anonymous referee for help and comments.

large enough cohorts, or large enough samples, successive surveys will generate successive random samples of individuals from each of the cohorts. Summary statistics from these random samples generate a time series that can be used to infer behavioral relationships for the cohort as a whole just as if panel data were available. Procedures for constructing such cohorts and for estimation using the resulting data are discussed in this paper.

I consider economic relationships that are linear in parameters, though not necessarily in data, and that may or may not contain individual fixed effects. Corresponding to these individual relationships, there will exist averaged versions of the same form for the cohort population, but with unobservable data points. If there are additive individual fixed effects, there will be corresponding additive cohort fixed effects for the cohort population. Furthermore, the *sample* cohort means from the surveys are consistent but error-ridden estimates of the unobservable cohort populations means. Since the micro data are used to construct the means, they can also be used to construct estimates of the variances and covariances of the sample means. It is therefore possible to use errors-in-variable estimators to estimate consistently the population relationships. Sections 3 and 4 of this paper derive appropriate estimators in the absence and in the presence of individual fixed effects.

Section 2, below, presents some of the models for which the technique is designed with particular emphasis on models of consumption and labor supply. I suggest that the estimation procedures discussed here may shed light on some long-standing puzzles in empirical demand analysis, and that they are likely to be useful for the estimation of life-cycle models in the absence of panel data.

Although the methods discussed here are primarily formulated as a response to the absence of panel data, it is not necessarily the case that they will give inferior results. The attrition problem that effectively curtails the useful length of much panel data is absent here. Because new samples are drawn each year, representativeness is constantly maintained. Indeed, to the extent that long-running panels replace respondents that drop out by 'look alikes', the resulting data will have many of the features discussed here. Of course, the errors-in-variables nature of the current methodology is absent in genuine panel studies, but I suspect that the difference is more apparent than real. Survey statisticians who collect panel data are in little doubt as to the magnitude of response error, particularly in the differenced data for individual respondents. And as Ashenfelter (1983) has shown, it is extremely difficult to interpret the diversity of labor supply elasticities obtainable from the Michigan PSID data (certainly the most heavily used panel data set among American economists), without assigning a central role to large and persistent errors of measurement. The technique discussed here has the advantage of recognizing measurement error from the outset and explicitly controlling for it.

2. Model formation

The models discussed in this section are of substantive interest in their own right and form the basis for current research using the methods discussed below. The main purpose in presenting them here, however, is to motivate the methodological discussion in the following sections. Further, the provision of concrete economic examples will justify some of the specific issues of estimation that are dealt with later.

In all of this work, my ultimate aim has been to bring to bear the methodology of panel data on problems of consumer demand analysis. Even in the United States, there is little panel information on the details of consumer expenditure, and a few isolated examples apart, the same is true of the rest of the world. For cross-sectional consumer expenditure surveys, however, most countries of the world are better supplied than is the United States. For example, the British Family Expenditure Survey is in continuous operation and surveys some 7000 households annually; questions on income, labor supply, and a very detailed disaggregation of consumers' expenditure provide a mass of high-quality data. There are also many excellent series of household surveys from LDC's; India's National Sample Survey Office has run some twenty nationwide household expenditure surveys since independence, and both Indonesia and Sri Lanka have closely comparable household surveys for two or more separate years. There is therefore a large potential for any method that can 'convert' these data sets into panel data.

To illustrate some of the more important issues, consider the Engel curve model,

$$q_{iht} = f_{ih}(x_{ht}, \boldsymbol{a}_{ht}), \tag{1}$$

for quantity purchased of good (or leisure) i by household h in period t, household total outlay x_{ht}, and vector of socio-economic or demographic characteristics $\boldsymbol{a}_{ht}$. A convenient functional form is provided by taking the budget share $w_{iht} = p_{it}q_{iht}/x_{ht}$ as dependent variable and writing

$$w_{iht} = \alpha_i + \beta_i \log x_{ht} + \sum^{J} \gamma_{ij} a_{jht} + \varepsilon_{iht}, \tag{2}$$

where there are J socio-economic characteristics, α, β and γ are parameters, and ε_{iht} represents an error term. Eq. (2) is typically estimated in one of two derived forms. In the first, using a single cross-section, the t subscript is dropped, and systems of Engel curves are estimated. In the second, the equation is aggregated over h to give, for example,

$$\tilde{w}_{it} = \alpha_i + \beta_i \log \tilde{x}_t + \sum \gamma_{ij} \tilde{a}_{jt} + \tilde{\varepsilon}_{it}, \tag{3}$$

where $\tilde{w}_{it}$, $\tilde{a}_{jt}$ and $\tilde{\varepsilon}_{it}$ are weighted averages using $x_h/\sum x_h$ as weights, and $\tilde{x}_t$ is a representative budget level defined by the aggregation procedure [see Deaton and Muellbauer (1980) for a full discussion of the model]. The weighting procedure guarantees that $\tilde{w}_{it}$ is the share of good i in the total of consumers expenditures, and, provided the distribution over households of x does not change over time (as measured by Theil's entropy measure of inequality), $\tilde{x}_t$ can be replaced by $\bar{x}_t$. Consequently, apart from the substitution of demographics for prices, neither of which explains very much in aggregate, (3) is a conventional aggregate demand system.

The point I want to emphasize is that the values of β_i estimated from cross-sections tend to differ substantially from those estimated using time series. Such contradictions were first extensively documented by Kuznets (1962), not only for aggregate consumption, but also for the components of consumption. It is widely known that savings ratios rise more in cross-sections that in aggregate time series. It is less well-known that it is generally true that total expenditure elasticities for many commodities and groups of commodities are further dispersed from unity when estimated on cross-sections than when estimated on time series. For example, the food share in England in 1955 was almost identical to its value a century earlier in spite of a manyfold increase in real income and in spite of the repeated confirmation of Engel's law in every household survey during that century; see Deaton (1975), Stone and Rowe (1966) and Clark (1957) for further details. The presence of such phenomena also poses problems for *forecasting* demands in those situations where only cross-sectional data are available.

In terms of the foregoing model, goods are necessities if $\beta_i < 0$, luxuries if $\beta_i > 0$, and neither if $\beta_i = 0$. The Kuznets' finding, so stylized, is that β_i is closer to zero in time series than in cross-sections. Presumably, the problem lies in inadequate statistical control. Expenditure differences between poor and rich consumers are not likely to be replicated by making a poor man rich unless the poor and rich consumers are otherwise identical. Controlling for even a long list of socio-economic characteristics is not satisfactory compared with the opportunity yielded only by panel data to use individuals as their own controls. Recognizing this, write (2) as

$$w_{iht} = \alpha_i + \beta_i \log x_{ht} + \sum \gamma_{ij} a_{jht} + \theta_{ih} + \varepsilon_{iht}, \tag{4}$$

for individual fixed effect θ_{ih}. Since, in general, θ_{ih} will be correlated with the other explanatory variables, such an equation can only be consistently estimated from panel data. Consider, however, the case where h is a member of a well-defined cohort group that can be tracked via its (randomly chosen) representatives through successive surveys. Let h belong to a cohort c, and take simple *population* averages of (4) over all h belonging to c to obtain

$$w_{ict}^{*} = \alpha_i + \beta_i (\log x_{ct})^{*} + \sum \gamma_{ij} a_{jct}^{*} + \theta_{ic}^{*} + \varepsilon_{ict}^{*}, \tag{5}$$

where asterisks denote population (i.e., cohort population) means. If it were possible to observe the true cohort means, eq. (5) would hold for each cohort in each time period rather than for each household in each time period, and could be directly estimated using cohort dummy variables for the cohort fixed effects θ_{ic}^{*}. This would be feasible since each cohort appears in each time period; it is of course *in*feasible on the individual model (4) since each individual household appears only once. In practice, the other starred variables can only be proxied by cohort means from the *sample*; these will contain sampling errors and if used without appropriate correction will generally lead to inconsistent estimates since the model is effectively one of errors in variables with *all* variables (except dummies) subject to error. However, the sample can be used in the standard way to derive estimates of sampling variances and covariances and these estimates can be used to derive consistent estimators using more or less standard errors in variables procedures; see sections 3 and 4 below.

Two other features of eq. (5) should be noted. First, the total outlay variable is the mean of the logarithms, not the logarithm of the means. There is no need in this context to fudge the issue since the sample can be used just as easily to estimate the mean of a non-linear function as to estimate the non-linear function of the mean. Second, it is usually possible to select cohorts that are more or less broadly defined. Ultimately, the cohort that is all inclusive is the total population and (5) becomes a macroeconomic aggregate time-series model. In consequence, selection of cohort size allows us to move by degrees from micro to macro data; this is ideal for detecting the roots of a contradiction between micro and macro results.

In the foregoing example, the formation of cohorts can be thought of as an instrumentation procedure that removes the inconsistencies associated with the fixed effects. In my second example, the cohort structure arises naturally out of the formulation of the problem. Consider an individual household choosing consumption and labor supply in an intertemporal setting to maximize the expectation

$$\mathrm{E}_t \left\{ \sum_{\tau=t}^{L} u_\tau(q_\tau) \right\}, \tag{6}$$

subject to an evolving and uncertain budget constraint

$$W_{t+1} = (1 + i_{t+1}) \{ W_t + y_t - p_t \cdot q_t \}, \tag{7}$$

where, as before, q_τ includes leisure demands, u_τ is period τ's utility function, W_t is assets at t, y_t is income, and i_{t+1} is the money interest rate from t to $t+1$.

In Browning, Deaton and Irish (1985), it is shown that the solution to this problem can be straightforwardly characterized in terms of Frisch demand/supply functions

$$q_{it} = f_{it}(r_t, p_t), \tag{8}$$

the vector of which is the gradient with respect to p_{it} of a period t 'profit function' $\pi_t(r_t, p_t)$, a convex linearly homogeneous function. The quantity r_t, the period t price of utility, evolves stochastically according to

$$\mathrm{E}_t\{(1 + i_{t+1})/r_{t+1}\} = 1/r_t. \tag{9}$$

Once again, the discussion is more useful given a specific functional form. Browning, Deaton and Irish show that the following is consistent with the theory:

$$q_{it} = \alpha_{it} + \beta_i \log p_{it} + \sum_{j \neq i} \theta_{ij}\{ p_{jt}/p_{it}\}^{1/2} - \beta_i \log r_t. \tag{10}$$

This model is correct both under certainty and under uncertainty. In the former case, (9) holds without the expectation operator so that r_t is simply proportional to a discount factor $\Pi(1 + i_\tau)$ relative to some arbitrary date. Re-introducing the household subscript h, the certainty version of (10) is therefore

$$q_{iht} = \alpha_{iht} + \beta_i \log \tilde{p}_{it} + \sum_{j \neq i} \theta_{ij}(p_{jt}/p_{it})^{1/2} - \beta_i \log r_{0h}, \tag{11}$$

where r_{0h} is independent both of time and the commodity under consideration and $\tilde{p}_{it}$ is p_{it} discounted back to the arbitrary data 0. It is therefore an individual fixed effect which is essentially a sufficient statistic for the influence of current and future values of assets, prices, interest rates, and wages; see MaCurdy (1981). Since r_{0h} is the price of life-time utility to h, it is an increasing function of life-time real wealth given concavity of (6). Consequently r_{0h} will vary with h and thus with cohorts in the cohort version of (11). Moreover, since younger cohorts are on average wealthier than older ones, we should expect the cohort dummy variables to be monotonically related to cohort age. The cohort structure here not only has the advantage of linking micro with macro, but also explicitly recognizes the life-cycle nature of consumption and labor supply. Indeed cohort methods have been widely used in work with life-cycle models; see e.g. Ghez and Becker (1975) and Smith (1977), though these authors work with single cross-sections which lack the panel element introduced here.

Under uncertainty, (9) can be written approximately as

$$\Delta \log r_{t+1} = \log(1 + i_{t+1}) + v_{t+1}, \tag{12}$$

where $\mathrm{E}_t(v_{t+1}) = 0$. Taking differences of (10) and substituting

$$\Delta q_{iht} = \Delta\alpha_{iht} - \beta_i \log(1 + \rho_{it}) + \sum \theta_{ij} \Delta (p_{jt}/p_{it})^{1/2} + v_{th}, \tag{13}$$

where ρ_{it} is the real commodity i rate of interest. Note that in this case, even if the shocks to the system, v_t, are stationary, $\log r_t$ will be non-stationary, so that differencing is required to obtain consistent estimates. In general, the v_t can only be guaranteed to be mean stationary, and further assumptions will be required for the consistency of techniques applied to (13). Even so, the differenced version is likely to be a better starting point for estimation than the original version in levels once uncertainty is taken into account. Once again, the aggregation to cohorts provides the repeated observations necessary for differencing, while the microdata provide the estimates of cohort means together with their sampling errors. The differenced versions will have a different measurement error structure than the levels models, and this is discussed below in sections 3 and 4. Note also that in (13), to the extent that the current prices and interest rates contain relevant new information, the innovation v_{th} will be correlated with the explanatory variables necessitating an estimator than can deal with both errors of measurement and simultaneity.

3. Estimation of models in levels

Before presenting the estimator to be discussed, consider an alternative, and perhaps more obvious approach to the estimation of an equation like (4) of section 2. To unify notation, rewrite this in standard form as

$$y_{ht} = \boldsymbol{x}_{ht} \cdot \boldsymbol{\beta} + \theta_h + \varepsilon_{ht}, \tag{14}$$

where the i subscript is no longer required, y_{ht} is the dependent variable for individual h at t, $\boldsymbol{x}_{ht}$ is a vector of explanatory variables, and θ_h is the fixed effect. Aggregate first over those h belonging to cohort c that happen to be observed in the survey taken at t. We then get *observed sample* cohort means which satisfy the relationship

$$\bar{y}_{ct} = \bar{\boldsymbol{x}}_{ct} \cdot \boldsymbol{\beta} + \bar{\theta}_{ct} + \bar{\varepsilon}_{ct}. \tag{15}$$

Note that $\bar{\theta}_{ct}$ is the average of the fixed effects for those members of c that show up in the survey; unlike the unobserved fixed effect for the cohort population mean, θ_c, say, $\bar{\theta}_{ct}$ is *not* constant over time. Furthermore, $\bar{\theta}_{ct}$ is unobserved and, in general, is correlated with the $\bar{x}_{ct}$. Hence, although (15) may be useful for 'signing' the bias in regressing $\bar{y}_{ct}$ on $\bar{x}_{ct}$, it is not an appropriate basis for consistent estimation any more than is (14), unless the cohort sample sizes are so large that $\bar{\theta}_{ct}$ is a very good approximation for θ_c. In this case, (15) can be estimated by replacing $\bar{\theta}_{ct}$ by dummy variables, one for each cohort.

Consider, instead of (15), the cohort *population* version of (14). I write this

$$y^*_{ct} = \boldsymbol{x}^*_{ct} \cdot \boldsymbol{\beta} + \theta_c + \varepsilon_{ct}, \tag{16}$$

where y^*_{ct} and $\boldsymbol{x}^*_{ct}$ are the unobservable cohort population means, and θ_c is the cohort fixed effect. Since the population belonging to the cohort is assumed to be fixed through time, θ_c is a constant for each c and can be replaced in (16) by cohort dummies. The y^*_{ct} and $\boldsymbol{x}^*_{ct}$ cannot be observed, but the cohort sample means $\bar{y}_{ct}$ and $\bar{\boldsymbol{x}}_{ct}$ are error-ridden estimators, with variances that can also be estimated from the micro survey data. Eq. (16) can then be estimated by errors in variables techniques where *all* variables, except the dummies, are measured subject to error.

Eq. (16) can now be written in convenient standard form

$$y^*_t = \boldsymbol{x}^*_t \cdot \boldsymbol{\beta} + \varepsilon_t, \tag{17}$$

where the cohorts and surveys have been 'stacked' into a single index t, running from 1 to T where T is the product of the number of surveys and the number of cohorts. The cohort dummies θ_c have been absorbed into the $\boldsymbol{x}^*_t$'s; there is no loss of generality since the dummies can be thought of as being measured with an error that has zero mean and variance. To fix ideas, take the British Family Expenditure Survey as an illustration. Currently, there are about ten years of data available, with about 7000 observations per year. In Browning, Deaton and Irish's (1985) work on consumption and labor supply, various selection criteria (which are always likely to be present in one form or another) reduce this to between 2500 and 3000 observations, which were formed into sixteen cohorts of five-year age bands. Hence, $T = 80$, but the cohorts, with a maximum size of 300, are not large enough for us to ignore the sampling errors in estimating y^*_t and $\boldsymbol{x}^*_t$ by $\bar{y}_t$ and $\bar{\boldsymbol{x}}_t$. Since, in this context (and in many others) there is a new survey every year, it is sensible to construct estimators that are consistent as T tends to infinity; with sixteen cohorts $T \to \infty$ sixteen times faster than annual, and four times as fast as quarterly time series data. The cohort size, however, is held fixed as T becomes large.

The error ε_t in (17) is assumed to be normal, independent over t, and homoskedastic; if the cohorts are very different in size, this will require that each observation be weighted by the square root of the cohort size. I shall assume this has been done as necessary. The model is completed by adding to (17) the assumed measurement structure. The cohort means, $\bar{y}_t$ and $\bar{\boldsymbol{x}}_t$ are observed; dropping the overbars – from now on these are the basic data – I assume

$$\begin{pmatrix} \bar{y}_t \\ \bar{\boldsymbol{x}}_t \end{pmatrix} \sim \mathrm{N}\begin{pmatrix} y_t^* & \sigma_{00} & \boldsymbol{\sigma}' \\ ; & & \\ \boldsymbol{x}_t^* & \boldsymbol{\sigma} & \Sigma \end{pmatrix}. \tag{18}$$

Given the sampling structure, the normality does not seem to be an implausible assumption. However, the error variances σ_{ij} will in general have to be estimated by their sample counterparts s_{ij} based on the micro survey data. Note that, in estimating the σ_{ij}'s, all T observations can be pooled, so that, if there are n_c observations in each cohort, the sampling variance of s_{ij} diminishes in proportion to $(Tn_c)^{-1}$ and that of $\bar{y}_t$ and $\bar{x}_t$ as $(n_c)^{-1}$. The former is (a) smaller, and (b) tends to zero as $T \to \infty$ instead of remaining fixed, so that it may be reasonable to assume that the σ's are known in carrying out the estimation. Nevertheless, I shall derive formulae for both cases, when σ_{00}, $\boldsymbol{\sigma}$ and Σ are known, and when they are estimated by s_{00}, $\boldsymbol{s}$ and S.

The model is now in the form in which I can apply the results of Fuller (1975, 1981); indeed, in the rest of this section, I essentially repeat Fuller's (1975) formulae in the current context and notation. The interested reader is referred to that paper for further details.

Assume that means have been removed from all data and let the sample moments and cross-product matrices of X and y be M_{xx}, $\boldsymbol{m}_{xy}$ and m_{yy} in an obvious notation. Write σ_ε^2 for the variance of ε_t and Ω for the moment matrix of the unobservable x_t^*'s. Hence

$$\mathrm{E}(M_{xx}) = \Omega + \Sigma = \Sigma_{xx}, \quad \text{say,} \tag{19}$$

$$\mathrm{E}(\boldsymbol{m}_{xy}) = \Omega\boldsymbol{\beta} + \boldsymbol{\sigma} = \boldsymbol{\sigma}_{xy}, \quad \text{say,} \tag{20}$$

$$\mathrm{E}(m_{yy}) = \boldsymbol{\beta}'\Omega\boldsymbol{\beta} + \sigma_{00} + \sigma_\varepsilon^2 = \sigma_{yy}, \quad \text{say.} \tag{21}$$

The estimator $\tilde{\boldsymbol{\beta}}$ is then clearly consistent as $T \to \infty$, where

$$\tilde{\boldsymbol{\beta}} = (M_{xx} - \Sigma)^{-1}(\boldsymbol{m}_{xy} - \boldsymbol{\sigma}) \tag{22}$$

$$= (X'X - T\Sigma)^{-1}(X'\boldsymbol{y} - T\boldsymbol{\sigma}), \tag{23}$$

and, provided $(X'X - T\Sigma)$ is positive definite, will be a MLE under the normality assumptions on $\boldsymbol{x}_t^*$ that are sometimes made in errors in variables models. I shall not assume normality of $\boldsymbol{x}_t^*$ here. Note that if Σ and $\boldsymbol{\sigma}$ are replaced by estimators S and $\boldsymbol{s}$, $\tilde{\boldsymbol{\beta}}$ is replaced by

$$\boldsymbol{\beta}^* = (M_{xx} - S)^{-1}(\boldsymbol{m}_{xy} - \boldsymbol{s}) = (X'X - TS)^{-1}(X'y - T\boldsymbol{s}). \tag{24}$$

The formula for the variances are derived first for the case where Σ, $\boldsymbol{\sigma}$ and σ_{00} are known, i.e., for $\tilde{\boldsymbol{\beta}}$. Expanding (22) yields

$$\tilde{\boldsymbol{\beta}} - \boldsymbol{\beta} = \Omega^{-1}(\boldsymbol{m}_{xy} - \boldsymbol{\sigma}_{xy}) - \Omega^{-1}(M_{xx} - \Sigma_{xx})\Omega^{-1}(\boldsymbol{\sigma}_{xy} - \boldsymbol{\sigma}) + \mathrm{O}_p(T^{-1}), \tag{25}$$

But, from (20), $\Omega^{-1}(\boldsymbol{\sigma}_{xy} - \boldsymbol{\sigma}) = \boldsymbol{\beta}$, so that

$$\tilde{\boldsymbol{\beta}} - \boldsymbol{\beta} = \Omega^{-1}\left[(\boldsymbol{m}_{xy} - M_{xx}\boldsymbol{\beta}) - (\boldsymbol{\sigma}_{xy} - \Sigma_{xx}\boldsymbol{\beta})\right] + \mathrm{O}_p(T^{-1}). \tag{26}$$

The variance of $\tilde{\boldsymbol{\beta}}$ thus depends asymptotically on the variance–covariance matrix of $\boldsymbol{m}_{xy} - M_{xx}\boldsymbol{\beta}$. But

$$\{\boldsymbol{m}_{xy} - M_{xx}\boldsymbol{\beta}\}_i = \frac{1}{T}\sum_t x_{ti}\left(y_t - \sum_k x_{tk}\beta_k\right) \tag{27}$$

$$= \frac{1}{T}\sum_t (x_{ti}^* + u_{ti})\left(\varepsilon_t + u_{t0} - \sum_k u_{tk}\beta_k\right), \tag{28}$$

where

$$u_{t0} = y_{t0} - y_{t0}^* \quad \text{and} \quad u_{ti} = x_{ti} - x_{ti}^*.$$

Treating the x_{ti}^* as fixed but unknown constants, and using the standard properties of the normal distribution yields

$$TV\{\boldsymbol{m}_{xy} - M_{xx}\boldsymbol{\beta}\} = \Sigma_{xx}(\sigma_\varepsilon^2 + \sigma_{00} + \boldsymbol{\beta}'\Sigma\boldsymbol{\beta} - 2\boldsymbol{\sigma}'\boldsymbol{\beta}) + (\boldsymbol{\sigma} - \Sigma\boldsymbol{\beta})(\boldsymbol{\sigma} - \Sigma\boldsymbol{\beta})'. \tag{29}$$

Hence the asymptotic variance–covariance matrix of $\tilde{\boldsymbol{\beta}}$ is given by

$$TV(\tilde{\boldsymbol{\beta}}) = \Omega^{-1}\left[\Sigma_{xx}\omega^2 + (\boldsymbol{\sigma} - \Sigma\boldsymbol{\beta})(\boldsymbol{\sigma} - \Sigma\boldsymbol{\beta})'\right]\Omega^{-1}, \tag{30}$$

where

$$\omega^2 = \sigma_\varepsilon^2 + \sigma_{00} + \boldsymbol{\beta}'\Sigma\boldsymbol{\beta} - 2\boldsymbol{\sigma}'\boldsymbol{\beta}. \tag{31}$$

An estimate of (30) is straightforwardly derived from the observable moment matrices. From (19) to (21)

$$\tilde{\Omega} = M_{xx} - \Sigma, \tag{32}$$

$$\tilde{\sigma}_\varepsilon^2 = m_{yy} - \sigma_{00} - \tilde{\boldsymbol{\beta}}'\tilde{\Omega}\tilde{\boldsymbol{\beta}}. \tag{33}$$

Substitution in (31) yields an estimate of ω^2, i.e.,

$$\tilde{\omega}^2 = \frac{1}{T}(y - X\tilde{\boldsymbol{\beta}})'(y - X\tilde{\boldsymbol{\beta}}) = \frac{1}{T}\boldsymbol{e}'\boldsymbol{e}, \tag{34}$$

where

$$\boldsymbol{e} = y - X\tilde{\boldsymbol{\beta}}. \tag{35}$$

But

$$\Sigma\tilde{\boldsymbol{\beta}} - \boldsymbol{\sigma} = (\Sigma\tilde{\boldsymbol{\beta}} + \Omega\tilde{\boldsymbol{\beta}}) - (\boldsymbol{\sigma} + \Omega\tilde{\boldsymbol{\beta}}) \tag{36}$$

$$= M_{xx}\tilde{\boldsymbol{\beta}} - \boldsymbol{\sigma}_{xy} = \frac{1}{T}X'\boldsymbol{e}. \tag{37}$$

Hence, the estimated variance–covariance matrix is given by

$$T\tilde{V}(\tilde{\boldsymbol{\beta}}) = \tilde{\Omega}^{-1}\left[T^{-1}M_{xx}\boldsymbol{e}'\boldsymbol{e} + T^{-2}X'\boldsymbol{e}\boldsymbol{e}'X\right]\tilde{\Omega}^{-1}, \tag{38}$$

which is straightforwardly evaluated in practice.

The derivation of the variance–covariance matrix of $\boldsymbol{\beta}^*$, the estimator using the *estimated* error variances, requires only minor modification of the above. I assume that the estimates s_{ij} of σ_{ij}, $i, j = 0, 1, \ldots, K$, the dimension of $\boldsymbol{x}$, are based on νT degrees of freedom. If all cohorts are pooled in estimating the s_{ij}'s, $\nu = n_c$, the number of observations per cohort, but clearly other schemes are possible. Some estimate of the variances and covariances of the s_{ij} is also required; to focus attention I shall use that derived from sampling under normality. Hence, I assume that s_{ij} is consistent for σ_{ij}, and that asymptotically,

$$(\nu T)\mathrm{E}\{(s_{ij} - \sigma_{ij})(s_{kl} - \sigma_{kl})\} = \sigma_{ik}\sigma_{jl} + \sigma_{il}\sigma_{jk}. \tag{39}$$

The derivation proceeds as before except that the expansion (25) has an additional term corresponding to the stochastic variation in S and $\boldsymbol{s}$. Hence,

(26) becomes

$$\boldsymbol{\beta}^* - \boldsymbol{\beta} = \Omega^{-1}\left[(\boldsymbol{m}_{xy} - M_{xx}\boldsymbol{\beta}) - (\boldsymbol{\sigma}_{xy} - \Sigma_{xx}\boldsymbol{\beta})\right]$$

$$-\Omega^{-1}[(\boldsymbol{s} - S\boldsymbol{\beta}) - (\boldsymbol{\sigma} - \Sigma\boldsymbol{\beta})] + \mathrm{O}_p(T^{-1}). \tag{40}$$

By the properties of sampling under normality, the first and second terms are independent, so that, asymptotically

$$TV(\boldsymbol{\beta}^*) = \Omega^{-1}\left[\Sigma_{xx}\omega^2 + (\boldsymbol{\sigma} - \Sigma\boldsymbol{\beta})(\boldsymbol{\sigma} - \Sigma\boldsymbol{\beta})'\right]\Omega^{-1}$$

$$+\nu^{-1}\Omega^{-1}V(\boldsymbol{s} - S\boldsymbol{\beta})\Omega^{-1}. \tag{41}$$

Elementary manipulation yields

$$V(\boldsymbol{s} - S\boldsymbol{\beta}) = \Sigma(\sigma_{00} - 2\boldsymbol{\sigma}'\boldsymbol{\beta} + \boldsymbol{\beta}'\Sigma\boldsymbol{\beta}) + (\boldsymbol{\sigma} - \Sigma\boldsymbol{\beta})(\boldsymbol{\sigma} - \Sigma\boldsymbol{\beta})'. \tag{42}$$

Note that if ν is large, (41) reduces to (30), the case of known variances; this latter is likely to be a formula that would normally be adequate in practice.

Eqs. (23), (24), (38) and (41) are the basic results of this section. I conclude with four issues of practical importance. First, the error variances σ_{00}, $\boldsymbol{\sigma}$ and Σ will generally vary from survey to survey and cohort to cohort. Write σ_{00}^t, $\boldsymbol{\sigma}^t$ and Σ^t for the values at observation t, so that (19) and (20) become

$$\mathrm{E}(M_{xx}) = \Omega + \bar{\Sigma}, \tag{19'}$$

$$\mathrm{E}(\boldsymbol{m}_{xy}) = \Omega\boldsymbol{\beta} + \bar{\boldsymbol{\sigma}}, \tag{20'}$$

where $\bar{\Sigma}, \bar{\boldsymbol{\sigma}}$ are the mean values over the t observations. The analysis then goes through with σ_{00}, $\boldsymbol{\sigma}$ and Σ (or s_{00}, $\boldsymbol{s}$ and S in the case of estimated variances) replaced by their means. Given the nature of the variation with t, an appropriate variance–covariance matrix for the $\bar{S}_{ij}$'s can be derived and substituted for $V(\boldsymbol{s} - S\boldsymbol{\beta})$ in (41). Second, it is necessary to allow for the presence of some x variables that are measured without errors. For example, relationships like (5) of section 2 contain cohort dummies that are clearly error-free. Other variables may not be drawn from the surveys but from other data sources; macroeconomic variables that are the same for all cohorts but vary with time (prices) are the obvious examples, and, exceptionally, there may be other relevant data on the cohorts themselves. One way to proceed is to introduce additional error-free variables to the right-hand side of (14) and to track them through the analysis. This turns out to be equivalent to the simpler (and intuitive) procedure of setting the appropriate elements of $\boldsymbol{\sigma}$ and rows and columns of Σ to zero; the formulae for $\tilde{\boldsymbol{\beta}}, \boldsymbol{\beta}^*$ and their asymptotic variances then remain unchanged. Third, for the reasons discussed in section 2, it may be necessary to recognize contemporaneous correlations between some of the x_t^*'s and ε_t. Instrumental variables will typically be available; in the example of section 2, in the form of lagged cohort wages or prices. On the assumption that the instrument vector w_t is constructed from a survey prior to that used for x_t so that their errors of measurement are uncorrelated, the appropriate instrumental variable estimator is

$$\tilde{\beta}_{\mathrm{IV}} = \left[W'X(W'W - T\Sigma_w)^{-1}X'W\right]^{-1}\left[W'X(W'W - T\Sigma_w)^{-1}W'y\right], \tag{43}$$

with a variance matrix calculable by the methods given above. If measurement errors in W and X are correlated, the obvious additional corrections can be made. Fourth, and finally, note that there will typically be some flexibility in constructing cohorts. If cohorts are constructed by age, the age bands can be taken broad or narrow (e.g., a five-year window versus a one-year window), and other qualifying characteristics can be left unspecified or tightly defined. Clearly, the construction of cohorts with members that are distinct from one another and internally homogeneous will minimize the errors in variable problem and enhance precision. Beyond that, it is possible to use trial cohorts to estimate $\tilde{\beta}$ and its variance, and to use these consistent estimates to gauge the consequences of combining or separating cohorts.

4. Estimation of models in differences

In this section, I develop the estimators appropriate for the case where the model, like the second model of section 2, requires differencing prior to estimation. The previous results do not go through directly because the measurement errors induced by the sampling scheme now have a MA(1) structure relative to the unobservable true first differences.

I now write the model in the form

$$\Delta y_t^* = \Delta x_t^* \cdot \beta + \varepsilon_t, \tag{44}$$

for the true unobservable first differences. Corresponding to (18), the measurement structure is

$$\Delta y_t = \Delta y_t^* + v_{t0}, \tag{45}$$

$$\Delta x_t = \Delta x_t^* + v_t, \tag{46}$$

and

$$y_{t0} = u_{t0} - u_{t-10}, \tag{47}$$

$$v_{ti} = u_{ti} - u_{t-1i}, \tag{48}$$

with u_{t0} and u_{ti} the original measurement errors on the y_t and x_{ti} variables respectively. The relationship between Δy_t and $\Delta \boldsymbol{x}_t$ is therefore given by

$$\Delta y_t = \boldsymbol{\beta} \cdot \Delta \boldsymbol{x}_t + (\varepsilon_t + v_{t0} - \boldsymbol{\beta} \cdot \boldsymbol{v}_t). \tag{49}$$

In passing note a tempting but ineffective possible route to estimation. Consider $Nx_t = x_t + x_{t-1}$, the moving average, as a possible instrument for Δx_t, the first-difference, and for simplicity, assume x_t is scalar. Since $Nx_t = Nx_t^* + u_t + u_{t-1}$, and since $u_t + u_{t-1}$ is independent of $v_t = u_t - u_{t-1}$, Nx_t is orthogonal to the compound error in (49). However, in large samples Nx_t is also orthogonal to the regressor Δx_t; $\mathrm{E}(Nx_t \cdot \Delta x_t) = x_t^{*2} - x_{t-1}^{*2}$, so that $\mathrm{E}(T^{-1} \Sigma Nx_t \cdot \Delta x_t) = T^{-1}(x_T^{*2} - x_0^{*2})$ with a limit as $T \to \infty$ of zero. In consequence, instrumental variables estimation of this type will not work. It is therefore necessary to follow through a scheme similar to that of section 3.

To ease notation, write $n_t \equiv \Delta y_t$ and $z_t \equiv \Delta \boldsymbol{x}_t$ so that, corresponding to (19) to (21) the moment matrices are now

$$\mathrm{E}(M_{zz}) = W + 2\Sigma = \Sigma_{zz}, \quad \text{say}, \tag{50}$$

$$\mathrm{E}(\boldsymbol{m}_{zn}) = W\boldsymbol{\beta} + 2\boldsymbol{\sigma} = \boldsymbol{\sigma}_{zn}, \quad \text{say}, \tag{51}$$

$$\mathrm{E}(\boldsymbol{m}_{nn}) = \boldsymbol{\beta}' W \boldsymbol{\beta} + \sigma_\varepsilon^2 + 2\sigma_{00} = \sigma_{nn}, \quad \text{say}, \tag{52}$$

where W is the sample moment matrix of the $\Delta \boldsymbol{x}_t^* \equiv z_t^*$ variables. The doubled role of measurement error comes from the moving average errors in (47) and (48). The first-difference estimator, $\tilde{\boldsymbol{\beta}}_\Delta$, is immediately given as

$$\tilde{\boldsymbol{\beta}}_\Delta = (M_{zz} - 2\Sigma)^{-1}(\boldsymbol{m}_{zn} - 2\boldsymbol{\sigma}), \tag{53}$$

or equivalently

$$\tilde{\boldsymbol{\beta}}_\Delta = (Z'Z - 2T\Sigma)^{-1}(Z'\boldsymbol{n} - 2T\boldsymbol{\sigma}). \tag{54}$$

Expansion, as in section 3, yields

$$\tilde{\boldsymbol{\beta}}_\Delta - \boldsymbol{\beta} = (\Sigma_{zz} - 2\Sigma)^{-1}\{(m_{zn} - M_{zz}\boldsymbol{\beta}) - (\sigma_{zn} - \Sigma_{zz}\boldsymbol{\beta})\} + \mathrm{O}_p(T^{-1}), \tag{55}$$

so that if C is the variance–covariance matrix of $\boldsymbol{m}_{zn} - M_{zz}\boldsymbol{\beta}$, the asymptotic variance of $\tilde{\boldsymbol{\beta}}_\Delta$ is given by

$$TV(\tilde{\boldsymbol{\beta}}_\Delta) = (\Sigma_{zz} - 2\Sigma)^{-1} C (\Sigma_{zz} - 2\Sigma)^{-1}. \tag{56}$$

Now

$$(\boldsymbol{m}_{zn} - M_{zz}\boldsymbol{\beta})_i = \frac{1}{T}\sum z_{ti}(n_t - \boldsymbol{\beta}\cdot z_t),$$

so that

$$(\boldsymbol{m}_{zn} - M_{zz}\boldsymbol{\beta})_i = \frac{1}{T}\sum (z_{ti}^* + v_{ti})\Big(\varepsilon_t + v_{t0} - \sum_k \beta_k v_{tk}\Big). \tag{57}$$

The variance of this is tedious to calculate, particularly given the MA structure (47) and (48). In the appendix it is shown that

$$C = (W + 2\Sigma)(\sigma_\varepsilon^2 + 2\sigma_A^2) - \sigma_A^2(W^+ + W^- - \Sigma)$$
$$+ 14(\boldsymbol{\sigma} - \Sigma\beta)(\boldsymbol{\sigma} - \Sigma\beta)', \tag{58}$$

where

$$\sigma_A^2 = \sigma_{00}^2 - 2\boldsymbol{\sigma}\cdot\boldsymbol{\beta} + \boldsymbol{\beta}'\Sigma\boldsymbol{\beta}, \tag{59}$$

and

$$W^+ = \frac{1}{T}\sum z_t^* z_{t-1}^{*\prime}, \tag{60}$$

$$W^- = \frac{1}{T}\sum z_{t-1}^* z_t^{*\prime}. \tag{61}$$

The presence of W^+ and W^- reflects the autocorrelation in the measurement error. Comparing with (29), and taking the case where $W^+ = W^- = 0$, the measurement errors now play a much larger role in determining the variance. Put differently, given the same amount of variance in the true unobservables under levels and differences, estimation precision will be lower in the latter case. This result, which is not surprising, can be enhanced or modified by positive or negative autocorrelation in the true z_t^* series.

The asymptotic variance covariance matrix of $\tilde{\boldsymbol{\beta}}_\Delta$ is obtained by substituting (58) into (56). In practice, an estimation formula can be obtained by noting that, from (52),

$$\tilde{\sigma}_{\varepsilon}^{2} = m_{nn} - 2\sigma_{00} - \tilde{\boldsymbol{\beta}}_{\Delta}'\tilde{W}\tilde{\boldsymbol{\beta}}_{\Delta}. \tag{62}$$

Hence, from (59),

$$\tilde{\sigma}_{\varepsilon}^{2} + 2\sigma_{A}^{2} = m_{nn} - 2\tilde{\boldsymbol{\beta}}_{\Delta}'(2\boldsymbol{\sigma} + \tilde{W}\tilde{\boldsymbol{\beta}}_{\Delta}) + \tilde{\boldsymbol{\beta}}_{\Delta}'(\tilde{W} + 2\Sigma)\tilde{\boldsymbol{\beta}}_{\Delta} \tag{63}$$

$$= m_{nn} - 2\tilde{\boldsymbol{\beta}}_{\Delta}'\boldsymbol{m}_{zn} + \tilde{\boldsymbol{\beta}}_{\Delta}'M_{zz}\tilde{\boldsymbol{\beta}}_{\Delta} \tag{64}$$

$$= T^{-1}\boldsymbol{e}'\boldsymbol{e}, \tag{65}$$

where

$$\boldsymbol{e} = \boldsymbol{n} - Z\cdot\tilde{\boldsymbol{\beta}}_{\Delta} = \Delta y - \Delta X\cdot\tilde{\boldsymbol{\beta}}_{\Delta}. \tag{66}$$

Similarly,

$$\begin{aligned} 2\Sigma\tilde{\boldsymbol{\beta}}_{\Delta} - 2\boldsymbol{\sigma} &= 2\Sigma\tilde{\boldsymbol{\beta}}_{\Delta} + \tilde{W}\tilde{\boldsymbol{\beta}}_{\Delta} - \tilde{W}\tilde{\boldsymbol{\beta}}_{\Delta} - 2\boldsymbol{\sigma} \\ &= M_{zz}\tilde{\boldsymbol{\beta}}_{\Delta} - \boldsymbol{m}_{zn} = T^{-1}Z'\boldsymbol{e}. \end{aligned} \tag{67}$$

Finally, therefore, writing M_{zz}^{+} for $T^{-1}\Sigma z_t z_{t-1}$ and M_{zz}^{-} similarly, the estimated variance matrix of $\tilde{\boldsymbol{\beta}}_{\Delta}$ is given by

$$T\hat{V}(\tilde{\boldsymbol{\beta}}_{\Delta}) = \tilde{W}^{-1}\left[M_{zz}\frac{1}{T}\boldsymbol{e}'\boldsymbol{e} - \tilde{\sigma}_{A}^{2}(M_{zz}^{+} + M_{zz}^{-}) + \frac{7}{2T^{2}}Z'\boldsymbol{ee}'Z\right]\tilde{W}^{-1}, \tag{68}$$

$$\tilde{\sigma}_{A}^{2} = \sigma_{00}^{2} - 2\boldsymbol{\sigma}\cdot\tilde{\boldsymbol{\beta}}_{\Delta} + \tilde{\boldsymbol{\beta}}_{\Delta}'\Sigma\tilde{\boldsymbol{\beta}}_{\Delta}. \tag{69}$$

The modification of these formulae for the case where σ_{00}, $\boldsymbol{\sigma}$ and Σ are replaced by estimates is straightforward and is left to the reader.

Appendix: Derivation of the variance for the differenced case

Starting from eq. (57), define

$$\theta_i = (\boldsymbol{m}_{zn} - M_{zz}\boldsymbol{\beta})_i, \tag{A.1}$$

$$\xi_t = \varepsilon_t + v_{t0} - \sum_k \beta_k v_{tk}, \tag{A.2}$$

so that

$$\theta_i = \frac{1}{T}\sum\left(z_{ti}^* + v_{ti}\right)\xi_t. \tag{A.3}$$

To obtain the variance–covariance matrix of θ_i, start from

$$\mathrm{E}(\theta_i\theta_j) = \mathrm{E}\left\{T^{-2}\sum_t\sum_s\left(z_{ti}^* + v_{ti}\right)\xi_t\left(z_{sj}^* + v_{sj}\right)\xi_s\right\} \tag{A.4}$$

$$= \mathrm{E}\left\{T^{-2}\sum_t\sum_s\left(z_{ti}^* z_{sj}^*\xi_t\xi_s + v_{ti}\xi_t v_{sj}\xi_s\right)\right\}, \tag{A.5}$$

since ξ_t and v_t are jointly normal with zero third moments. By the MA(1) structure of the v's,

$$\begin{aligned}\mathrm{E}(\theta_i\theta_j) = T^{-1}\{&\mathrm{E}\left(z_{ti}^* z_{tj}^*\xi_t^2\right) + \mathrm{E}\left(z_{ti}^* z_{t+1j}^*\xi_t\xi_{t+1}\right)\\ &+ \mathrm{E}\left(z_{t+1i}^* z_{tj}^*\xi_{t+1}\xi_t\right) + \mathrm{E}\left(v_{ti}\xi_t v_{tj}\xi_t\right)\\ &+ 2\mathrm{E}\left(v_{ti}\xi_t v_{t+1j}\xi_{t+1}\right)\},\end{aligned} \tag{A.6}$$

Now

$$\mathrm{E}\left(\xi_t^2\right) = \sigma_\varepsilon^2 + 2\sigma_{00}^2 + 2\boldsymbol{\beta}'\Sigma\boldsymbol{\beta} - 4\boldsymbol{\beta}'\boldsymbol{\sigma} = \sigma_\varepsilon^2 + 2\sigma_A^2, \quad \text{say}, \tag{A.7}$$

$$\mathrm{E}(\xi_t\xi_{t+1}) = -\sigma_{00} + 2\boldsymbol{\beta}'\boldsymbol{\sigma} - \boldsymbol{\beta}'\Sigma\boldsymbol{\beta} = -\sigma_A^2. \tag{A.8}$$

Hence, evaluating (A.6) term by term using, where necessary, the standard formulae for fourth movements of normals, gives

$$\mathrm{E}\left(z_{ti}^* z_{tj}^*\xi_t^2\right) = w_{ij}\left(\sigma_\varepsilon^2 + 2\sigma_A^2\right), \tag{A.9}$$

$$\mathrm{E}\left(z_{ti}^* z_{t+1j}^*\xi_t\xi_{t+1}\right) = -w_{ij}^+\sigma_A^2, \tag{A.10}$$

with a similar expression for its transpose,

$$\begin{aligned}\mathrm{E}\left(v_{ti}v_{tj}\xi_t^2\right) &= 2\sigma_{ij}\left(\sigma_\varepsilon^2 + 2\sigma_A^2\right) + 2\left\{2\sigma_i - 2\sum_k\beta_k\sigma_{ik}\right\}\left\{2\sigma_j - 2\sum_k\beta_k\sigma_{jk}\right\}\\ &= 2\sigma_{ij}\left(\sigma_\varepsilon^2 + 2\sigma_A^2\right) + 8(\boldsymbol{\sigma} - \Sigma\boldsymbol{\beta})_i(\boldsymbol{\sigma} - \Sigma\boldsymbol{\beta})_j.\end{aligned} \tag{A.11}$$

$$\mathrm{E}\left(v_{ti}\xi_t v_{t+1j}\xi_{t+1}\right) = \sigma_{ij}\sigma_A^2 + 5(\boldsymbol{\sigma} - \Sigma\boldsymbol{\beta})_i(\boldsymbol{\sigma} - \Sigma\boldsymbol{\beta})_j. \tag{A.12}$$

Hence, collecting terms and subtracting $E(\theta_i)E(\theta_j) = 4(\sigma - \Sigma\beta)_i(\sigma - \Sigma\beta)_j$ yields

$$V(\theta) = (W + 2\Sigma)(\sigma_\varepsilon^2 + 2\sigma_A^2) - \sigma_A^2(W^+ + W^- - \Sigma) + 14(\sigma - \Sigma\beta)(\sigma - \Sigma\beta), \quad \text{(A.13)}$$

which is eq. (58) of the main text.

References

Ashenfelter, O., 1983, Macroeconomic analyses of labor supply and microeconomic analyses of labor supply, Presented to Carnegie–Rochester Conference, Bal Harbor, FL, Nov. 1983.

Browning, M., A. Deaton and M. Irish, 1985, A profitable approach to labor supply and commodity demands over the life-cycle, Econometrica 53, 503–543.

Clark, C., 1957, The conditions of economic progress (Macmillan, London).

Deaton, A., 1975, The structure of demand 1920–1970, in: C.M. Cipolla, ed., The Fontana economic history of Europe (Collins-Fontana, London).

Deaton, A. and J. Muellbauer, 1980, An almost ideal demand system, American Economic Review 70, 312–326.

Fuller, W.A., 1975, Regression analysis for sample survey, Sankhya: The Indian Journal of Statistics C37, 117–132.

Fuller, W.A., 1981, Measurement error models (Department of Statistics, Iowa State University, Ames, IA).

Ghez, G.R. and G.S. Becker, 1975, The allocation of time and goods over the life-cycle (NBER, New York).

Kuznets, S., 1962, Quantitative aspects of the economic growth of nations: VII, The share and structure of consumption, Economic Development and Cultural Change 10, 1–92.

MaCurdy, T.E., 1981, An empirical model of labor supply in a life-cycle setting, Journal of Political Economy 89, 1059–1085.

Smith, J., 1977, Family labor supply over the life-cycle, Explorations in Research 4, 205–276.

Stone, R. and D.A. Rowe, 1966, The measurement of consumers' expenditures and behavior in the United Kingdom 1920–1938, Vol. II (Cambridge University Press, Cambridge).

TESTS FOR THE CONSISTENCY OF CONSUMER DATA*

W.E. DIEWERT

University of British Columbia, Vancouver, Canada

C. PARKAN

University of Calgary, Calgary, Canada

The paper develops non-parametric tests for the weak separability or the additive separability of a decision-maker's utility function, given a finite body of price and quantity data. The tests generalize some earlier tests proposed by Afriat and Varian. Blackorby, Primont and Russell have pointed out that the econometric literature on testing separability hypotheses is seriously deficient since the econometric tests tend to impose unwanted restrictions on the parametric functional form in addition to the particular separability hypothesis being tested. Hence, the non-parametric tests in the present paper should serve as useful supplements to the usual econometric tests for separability.

1. Introduction

Our basic purpose in writing this paper is twofold: (i) we would like to make Afriat's (1967, 1970, 1972, 1973, 1976) non-parametric method for testing whether a finite body of price and quantity data is consistent with utility maximizing behaviour more accessible, and (ii) we derive some new tests for separability which generalize the earlier work of Afriat (1970) and Varian (1983).

In section 2, we deal with point (i) above. It turns out that the necessity of the Afriat conditions can be established in a very intuitive manner if we make stronger than necessary assumptions on the utility function – namely, concavity and differentiability. We make these restrictive assumptions in section 2 and derive the Afriat conditions.[1] In an appendix, we indicate how the differentiability assumptions can be dropped.[2]

*The research for this paper has been supported by the SSHRC of Canada and by grant SES79-12380 from the National Science Foundation to the University of California at Berkeley. Our thanks to W. Barnett and a referee for helpful comments and to Gerard Debreu for his inspiration and generosity to the first author.

[1] Our exposition is based on Diewert and Parkan (1978). Similar expositions are available in Varian (1982, 1983). However, the basic idea may be traced back to Afriat (1970).

[2] All of our proofs involving the non-differentiable case are relegated to the appendix.

In sections 3 and 4, we utilize the techniques developed in section 2 in order to derive some tests for the utility function to be weakly separable and additively separable respectively. Our tests generalize similar tests developed by Afriat (1970) and Varian (1983) in various directions.

Section 5 concludes.

2. The derivation of the Afriat consistency conditions in the concave case

We wish to determine whether a finite body of price and quantity data is consistent with utility maximizing behaviour.

Suppose that we are given T positive price and quantity vectors, $p^t \gg 0_N$ and $x^t \gg 0_N$ for $t = 1, 2, \ldots, T$.[3] Suppose that a decision-maker has the objective or utility function f and that x^t is a solution to his period t utility maximization problem; i.e., suppose

$$x^t \text{ solves } \max_x \{ f(x) \colon p^t \cdot x \leq p^t \cdot x^t,\ x \geq 0_N \} \quad \text{for} \quad t = 1, \ldots, T. \tag{1}$$

Suppose further that the utility function f is: (i) concave,[4] (ii) once differentiable, and (iii) weakly increasing.[5]

Since by assumption, $x^t \gg 0_N$ and so the non-negativity constraints in (1) are not binding, the Kuhn–Tucker necessary conditions for the non-linear programming problems in (1) reduce to:[6] there exist λ^t such that

$$\nabla f(x^t) = \lambda^t p^t, \qquad \lambda^t \geq 0, \qquad t = 1, \ldots, T. \tag{2}$$

The weakly increasing property of f and our assumption that p^t is strictly positive imply that the Lagrange multipliers λ^t appearing in conditions (2) are

[3] Notation: $p \gg 0_N$ means that each component p_n of the N-dimensional vector p is positive; $p \geq 0_N$ means each component of p_n is non-negative; $p > 0_N$ means $p \geq 0_N$ but $p \neq 0_N$; $p \cdot x \equiv \sum_{n=1}^N p_n x_n$ denotes the inner product of the vectors p and x and $\nabla_x f(x, y) \equiv [\partial f(x, y)/\partial x_1, \ldots, \partial f(x, y)/\partial x_N]$ denotes the vector of partial derivatives of f with respect to its x components.

[4] f is concave iff $x' \geq 0_N$, $x'' \geq 0_N$, $0 \leq \lambda \leq 1$ implies $f(\lambda x' + (1 - \lambda) x'') \geq \lambda f(x') + (1 - \lambda) f(x'')$. Throughout this paper we shall assume that concave functions are also continuous over their domain of definition.

[5] In the case of differentiable functions, we say that f is *increasing* if $x > 0_N$ implies $\nabla f(x) \gg 0_N$, *weakly increasing* if $\nabla f(x) > 0_N$, and *non-decreasing* if $\nabla f(x) \geq 0_N$. In the non-differentiable concave case, replace $\nabla f(x)$ in the previous definitions by every $z \in \partial f(x)$ where $\partial f(x)$ denotes the set of supergradients to f at x. z is a supergradient to f at x^0 iff $f(x) \leq f(x^0) + z \cdot (x - x^0)$ for every $x \geq 0_N$; see Rockafellar (1970, p. 214).

[6] See Karlin (1959, p. 204) for a convenient exposition of the Kuhn–Tucker Theorem. The positivity of x^t enables us to conclude that the Slater constraint qualification condition [see problem 12 in Karlin (1959, p. 239)] is satisfied for problem t in (1) since $\frac{1}{2} x^t$ satisfies all constraints strictly.

all positive:

$$\lambda^t > 0, \qquad t = 1, \ldots, T. \tag{3}$$

We require one additional fact about concave functions and then we shall have the Afriat conditions at hand. A differentiable concave function has the property [see, for example, Karlin (1959, p. 405)] that any tangent hyperplane to f (i.e., any first-order Taylor series expansion of f) lies above the function. Thus for each t, the following inequality is valid for all $x \geq 0_N$:

$$f(x) \leq f(x^t) + \nabla f(x^t) \cdot (x - x^t), \qquad t = 1, \ldots, T. \tag{4}$$

Now define $u^t \equiv f(x^t)$ for $t = 1, \ldots, T$, and replace x in (4) by x^s, $s = 1, \ldots, T$. The inequalities (4) then become the following T^2 inequalities:

$$u^s \leq u^t + \lambda^t p^t \cdot (x^s - x^t), \qquad s, t = 1, \ldots, T. \tag{5}$$

Thus we have proven the following theorem, which is a special case of a much stronger theorem due to Afriat (1967, 1973, 1976):

Theorem 1. In order for a body of positive *data*, $\{(p^t, x^t)\colon t = 1, \ldots, T\}$, *to be consistent with utility maximizing behaviour [so that (1) is true] where the utility function f is restricted to be concave, differentiable and weakly increasing, it is* necessary *that there exist 2T numbers* $u^1, \ldots, u^T$ *(which can be interpreted as utility levels) and* $\lambda^1, \ldots, \lambda^T$ *(which can be interpreted as marginal utilities of income) such that* Afriat revealed preference inequalities *(3) and (5) are satisfied.*

In the appendix, we indicate how the same technique of proof may be modified in order to prove a version of Theorem 1 without assuming that f be differentiable.

Conditions (3) and (5) are also *sufficient* for the given data p^t, x^t to be consistent with utility maximizing behaviour. We have the following result:

Theorem 2 [Afriat (1967)]. Suppose $\{(p^t, x^t)\colon t = 1, \ldots, T\}$ *are given price and quantity vectors with* $p^t \gg 0_N$ *and* $x^t \geq 0_N$,[7] *and there exist* u^t, λ^t *such that conditions (3) and (5) are satisfied. Then there exists a concave, increasing utility function f which rationalizes the data; i.e., conditions (1) are satisfied for this f.*

Proof. Define the increasing linear functions f^t by

$$f^t(x) \equiv u^t + \lambda^t p^t \cdot (x - x^t), \qquad t = 1, \ldots, T. \tag{6}$$

[7] Note that we no longer require that $x^t \gg 0_N$ as in Theorem 1.

Define the increasing, concave function f by

$$f(x) \equiv \min_t \{ f^t(x) : t = 1, \ldots, T \}. \tag{7}$$

Since f defined by (7) is the minimum of the f^s, for each s, we must have $f(x) \leq f^s(x)$ and thus, for $s = 1, \ldots, T$,

$$\begin{aligned} &\max_x \{ f(x) : p^s \cdot x \leq p^s \cdot x^s, \ x \geq 0_N \} \\ &\leq \max_x \{ f^s(x) : p^s \cdot x \leq p^s \cdot x^s, \ x \geq 0_N \} \\ &\equiv \max_x \{ u^s + \lambda^s p^s \cdot (x - x^s) : p^s \cdot x \leq p^s \cdot x^s, \ x \geq 0_N \} \\ &= u^s, \end{aligned} \tag{8}$$

since $\lambda^s > 0$. Also, for $s = 1, \ldots, T$,

$$\begin{aligned} f(x^s) &\equiv \min_t \{ f^t(x^s) : t = 1, \ldots, T \} \\ &\equiv \min_t \{ u^t + \lambda^t p^t \cdot (x^s - x^t) : t = 1, \ldots, T \} \\ &= u^s, \end{aligned} \tag{9}$$

using (5). Thus (8) and (9) show that x^s is a solution to the period s utility maximization problem for $s = 1, \ldots, T$ when f is defined in (7). Q.E.D.

To summarize: the existence of numbers u^t and λ^t such that the inequalities (3) and (5) are true is necessary and sufficient for a given body of data $\{ p^t, x^t \}$ to be consistent with utility maximizing behaviour given our regularity conditions on the underlying utility function f.

The Afriat conditions (3) and (5) may be put into several alternative sets of conditions that are easier to check numerically.

For example, a necessary and sufficient condition for the existence of numbers u^t and λ^t such that (3) and (5) are true for a given body of data $\{ (p^t, x^t);\ t = 1, \ldots, T \}$ is that the objective function of the following linear programming problem attain its lower bound of zero:

$$\min \sum_{r=1}^{T} \sum_{t=1}^{T} s^{rt}, \tag{10}$$

subject to

$$s^{rt} = u^t - u^r - \lambda^r p^r \cdot (x^t - x^r) + S^{rt}, \qquad r, t = 1, \ldots, T, \tag{11}$$

$$\lambda^r \geq 1, \qquad r = 1, \ldots, T, \tag{12}$$

$$s^{rt} \geq 0, \quad S^{rt} \geq 0, \qquad r, t = 1, \ldots, T, \tag{13}$$

where the u^r, λ^r, s^{rt} and S^{rt} are variables. The s^{rt} and S^{rt} are non-negative slack variables that are used to convert the inequalities (5) into equalities.[8] If the objective function (10) attains its lower bound of zero, then all of the optimal $s^{rt} = 0$, and it is obvious that (11) and the non-negativity restrictions $S^{rt} \geq 0$ imply (5). Obviously, (12) implies (3). On the other hand, if the inequalities (5) are satisfied with $\lambda^r > 0$ for all r, then all of the numbers u^r and λ^r can be scaled so that the same inequalities (5) are satisfied with $\lambda^r \geq 1$ for $r = 1, \ldots, T$. Hence the linear programming problem (10)–(13) will attain its lower bound of zero in this case.

Another necessary and sufficient condition for the existence of numbers u^t and λ^t such that (3) and (5) are true for a given body of data $\{(p^t, x^t): t = 1, \ldots, T\}$ is that the objective function for the following unconstrained minimization problem attain its lower bound of zero:

$$\min_{u^1, \ldots, u^T, \alpha_1, \ldots, \alpha_T, \sigma_{11}, \ldots, \sigma_{TT}} \left\{ \sum_{r=1}^{T} \sum_{t=1}^{T} [s^{rt}]^2 \right\}, \tag{14}$$

where the T^2 slack variables s^{rt} are defined by

$$s^{rt} \equiv u^t - u^r - (\alpha_r^2 + 1) p^r \cdot (x^t - x^r) + \sigma_{rt}^2, \qquad r, t = 1, \ldots, T. \tag{15}$$

If we define $\lambda^r \equiv \alpha_r^2 + 1 \geq 1$ and $S^{rt} \equiv \sigma_{rt}^2 \geq 0$, it can be seen that eq. (15) corresponds to eq. (11).

Varian (1982, 1983) has developed extremely efficient algorithms for checking whether a body of data satisfied (3) and (5); however, his procedures do not seem to extend to the more complicated conditions that we are going to develop in sections 3 and 4 below. Until more efficient algorithms are invented, we can only suggest that the reader convert the problem of checking whether a solution exists to a certain system of inequalities into an unconstrained minimization problem in a manner analogous to our conversion of (3) and (5) into (14).

[8] If we are in the context of producer theory rather than consumer theory so that $f(x^t) \equiv u^t$ is output rather than utility, then we may want to add the non-negativity restrictions $u^t \geq 0$, $t = 1, \ldots, T$, to the linear program (10)–(13). Actually, the tests developed in this paper are efficient in the producer theory context only if output is unobserved.

It should be noted that the assumption of concavity is not required in order to derive conditions (3) and (5). Afriat's much stronger (but harder to prove) result is:

Theorem 3 [*Afriat* (*1967, 1976*), *Diewert* (*1973*), *Varian* (*1982*)]. *In order for the data* $\{(p^t, x^t)\colon\ t = 1,\ldots,T\}$, *where* $p^t \gg 0_N$ *and* $x^t \geq 0_N$,[9] *to be consistent with utility maximizing behaviour where the utility function* f *is continuous from above*[10] *and is subject to local non-station,*[11] *it is necessary that there exist* u^t *and* λ^t *such that* (*3*) *and* (*5*) *are satisfied.*

It should be noted that conditions (5) provide a generalization of Samuelson's (1938) weak axiom and Houthakker's (1950) strong axiom of revealed preference theory; see Afriat (1976). Furthermore, conditions (5) are also related to the integrability of demand functions literature; see Mas-Colell (1978).

There is one additional test for consistency that we wish to survey in this section. Frequently, one wishes to know whether a given data set is consistent with utility maximizing behaviour where the utility function f is restricted to be *homothetic*. Shephard (1953) defines a non-negative function $f(x)$ defined over $x \geq 0_N$ to be homothetic if there exists an increasing function of one variable g such that $g[f(x)]$ is positively, linearly homogeneous; i.e., for every $\lambda > 0$, $x \geq 0_N$, $g[f(\lambda x)] = \lambda g[f(x)]$. It can be shown [see Afriat (1972) or Diewert (1973, p. 424)] that a necessary and sufficient condition for the existence of a homothetic, continuous from above and locally non-satiated utility function f which is consistent with the data $\{(p^t, x^t)\colon\ t = 1,\ldots,T\}$ in the sense that x^t is a solution to the period t maximization problem in (1) for $t = 1,\ldots,T$ is that there exist numbers u^t and λ^t such that (3) and (5) hold and in addition:

$$u^t = \lambda^t p^t \cdot x^t, \qquad t = 1,\ldots,T. \tag{16}$$

The effect of the additional restrictions (16) is to make each of the linear functions f^t defined by (6) pass through the origin. Thus f defined by (7) will be the surface of a convex, polyhedral cone and so will be linearly homogeneous (and thus homothetic).

Thus, to test for the existence of a homothetic utility function f, we need only solve the linear programming problem (10)–(13) with the additional

[9] Note that we do not require that $x^t \gg 0_N$ as in Theorem 1.

[10] This means that, for each u, the set $\{x\colon\ f(x) \geq u\}$ is closed. This assumption is required to ensure that solutions to the utility maximization problems in (1) exist.

[11] This means that for every $x \geq 0_N$ and $\varepsilon > 0$, there exists $x^\varepsilon \geq 0_N$ such that $(x - x^\varepsilon)\cdot(x - x^\varepsilon) \leq \varepsilon^2$ and $f(x^\varepsilon) > f(x)$.

restrictions (16) and see whether the resulting optimal objective function is zero or not.[12]

For a geometrical interpretation of conditions (3), (5) and (16) for the case of two observations ($T=2$) and two goods ($N=2$), see Afriat (1977). For alternative formulations of (3), (5) and (16) in the general case plus an extremely efficient algorithm for checking whether a given data set satisfied (3), (5) and (16), see Varian (1982, 1983).

3. Tests for weak separability

Assume the decision-maker has preferences defined over $N^1 + N^2 + \cdots + N^H + M$ goods. We suppose that these preferences can be represented by a utility function $F(x_1, \ldots, x_H, y)$ where $x_h \geq 0_{N^h}$ is a non-negative vector of dimension N^h and $y \geq 0_M$ is a non-negative vector of dimension M. We wish to know whether the decision-maker's utility function F can be written as $F(x_1, \ldots, x_H, y) = f[g_1(x_1), \ldots, g_H(x_H), y]$, where f is a function of $H+M$ variables and g_h is a function of N^h variables for $h = 1, \ldots, H$; i.e., we wish to know if F is *weakly separable* with respect to its $x_1, \ldots, x_H$ arguments.[13] The function f is the macro function, while the functions g_h are called micro functions.[14] Assuming that the micro and macro functions are all concave leads to a simple set of necessary and sufficient conditions for the consistency of a given data set with the hypothesis of utility maximizing behaviour where the utility function is restricted to be weakly separable.

Theorem 4 [*Generalization of Afriat (1970) and Varian (1983)*].[15] *Suppose the macro function f is (i) concave, (ii) once differentiable, and (iii) increasing in its first H arguments and non-decreasing in its last M arguments where $H \geq 1$ and $M \geq 1$. Suppose the micro functions g_h, $h = 1, \ldots, H$, are (i) concave, (ii) once differentiable, and (iii) weakly increasing in their arguments. Suppose further that we are given T positive price vectors, $(p_1^t, \ldots, p_H^t, q^t) \gg (0_{N^1}, \ldots, 0_{N^H}, 0_M)$, and T* positive *quantity vectors, $(x_1^t, \ldots, x_H^t, y^t) \gg (0_{N^1}, \ldots, 0_{N^H}, 0_M)$, for $t = 1, \ldots, T$. Finally, we suppose that the given data are consistent with weakly separable utility maximizing behaviour*; *i.e., for $t = 1, \ldots, T$,*

[12]Alternatively, use eq. (16) to eliminate the u^t from (15) and solve the resulting unconstrained minimization problem (14).

[13]For alternative representations of the separability concept and extensive references to the literature, see Blackorby, Primont and Russell (1978).

[14]This terminology follows that of Diewert (1974, pp. 150–153).

[15]Afriat and Varian consider the case where $H = 1$. Afriat also considers the case where $H = 2$ and $M = 0$.

$(x_1^t, \ldots, x_H^t, y^t)$ *solves the following utility maximization problem*:

$$\max_{x_1,\ldots,x_H,y} \Big\{ f[g_1(x_1),\ldots,g_H(x_H),y]:$$

$$\sum_{h=1}^{H} p_h^t \cdot x_h + q^t \cdot y \le Y^t,\ x_1 \ge 0_{N^1},\ldots,x_H \ge 0_{N^H},\ y \ge 0_M \Big\}, \tag{17}$$

where period t 'income' Y^t *is defined by*

$$Y^t \equiv \sum_{h=1}^{H} p_h^t \cdot x_h^t + q^t \cdot y^t, \qquad t = 1,\ldots,T. \tag{18}$$

Then there exist $2HT$ *scalars* X_h^t, β_h^t, $h = 1,\ldots,H$, $t = 1,\ldots,T$, *such that the following inequalities hold*:

$$X_h^s \le X_h^t + \beta_h^t p_h^t \cdot (x_h^s - x_h^t), \tag{19}$$

$$\beta_h^t > 0, \qquad s,t = 1,\ldots,T, \quad h = 1,\ldots,H.$$

There also exist $2T$ *scalars* u^t, λ^t, $t = 1,\ldots,T$, *such that*

$$u^s \le u^t + \lambda^t \left[\sum_{h=1}^{H} (\beta_h^t)^{-1} (X_h^s - X_h^t) \right] + \lambda^t q^t \cdot (y^s - y^t), \tag{20}$$

$$\lambda^t > 0, \qquad s,t = 1,\ldots,T.$$

Proof. Since f is increasing in its first H arguments, by (17) x_h^t must maximize $g_h(x_h)$ subject to a period t expenditure constraint on the x_h goods; i.e., we must have

$$x_h^t \gg 0_{N^h} \quad \text{solves} \quad \max_{x_h} \{ g_h(x_h):\ p_h^t \cdot x_h \le p_h^t \cdot x_h^t,\ x_h \ge 0_{N^h} \}, \tag{21}$$

$$h = 1,\ldots,H, \quad t = 1,\ldots,T.$$

Now repeat the argument used in Theorem 1 applied to (21), and we obtain the existence of the X_h^t and β_h^t that satisfy (19), where

$$X_h^t \equiv g_h(x_h^t), \qquad h = 1,\ldots,H, \quad t = 1,\ldots,T. \tag{22}$$

The counterparts to the Kuhn–Tucker conditions (2) and (3) now are

$$\nabla_x g_h(x_h^t) = \beta_h^t p_h^t, \qquad \beta_h^t > 0, \qquad h = 1,\dots,H, \quad t = 1,\dots,T. \tag{23}$$

Define the level and first-order partial derivatives of f by

$$u^t \equiv f[X_1^t,\dots,X_H^t,y^t], \qquad t = 1,\dots,T, \tag{24}$$

$$\alpha_h^t \equiv \partial f[X_1^t,\dots,X_H^t,y^t]/\partial X_h > 0, \quad h = 1,\dots,H, \quad t = 1,\dots,T, \tag{25}$$

$$\gamma^t \equiv \nabla_y f[X_1^t,\dots,X_H^t,y^t] \geq 0_M, \qquad t = 1,\dots,T. \tag{26}$$

The inequalities in (25) and (26) follow from our monotonicity assumptions on f.

The concavity of f implies, using (4), (24), (25) and (26), that for each X_h in the range of g_h and $y \geq 0_M$,

$$f[X_1,\dots,X_H,y] \leq u^t + \sum_{h=1}^{H} \alpha_h^t (X_h - X_h^t) + \gamma^t \cdot (y - y^t), \tag{27}$$

$$t = 1,\dots,T.$$

Substitute $(X_1,\dots,X_H,y) = (X_1^s,\dots,X_H^s,y^s)$ for $s = 1,\dots,T$ into (27), and we obtain (using (24))

$$u^s \leq u^t + \sum_{h=1}^{H} \alpha_h^t (X_h^s - X_h^t) + \gamma^t \cdot (y^s - y^t), \qquad s,t = 1,\dots,T. \tag{28}$$

The Kuhn–Tucker conditions for the tth utility maximization problem in (21) and definitions (25) and (26) yield the existence of λ^t such that

$$\alpha_h^t \nabla_x g_h(x_h^t) = \lambda^t p_h^t, \qquad \lambda^t > 0, \qquad t = 1,\dots,T, \tag{29}$$

$$\gamma^t = \lambda^t q^t, \qquad t = 1,\dots,T. \tag{30}$$

Eqs. (23), (25) and (29) show that $\alpha_h^t = \lambda^t(\beta_h^t)^{-1}$ for $t = 1,\dots,T$, $h = 1,\dots,H$. Substitution of these equalities and the equalities in (30) into (28) yields (20). Q.E.D.

Somewhat surprisingly, we are unable to modify the above proof to cover the non-differentiable case (as was done in the case of Theorem 1).[16] However,

[16] We are unable to establish (29) in the non-differentiable case. In general, it is difficult to characterize the set of supergradients of a composite function like $f[g_1(x_1),\dots,g_H(x_H),y]$ in terms of the supergradients of $f, g_1,\dots,g_H$; see Rockafellar (1978) for a survey of the literature.

in Theorem 6 below, we indicate how a non-differentiable version of Theorem 4 can be obtained if we make use of the duality between utility and cost functions. Before proceeding to the non-differentiable case, we first show that conditions (19) and (20) are *sufficient* for the given data set to be consistent with weakly separable utility maximizing behaviour.

Theorem 5 [*Generalization of Afriat (1970) and Varian (1983)*]. *Suppose that we are given T positive price vectors,* $(p_1^t,\ldots,p_H^t,q^t) \gg (0_{N^1},\ldots,0_{N^H},0_M)$, *and t non-negative quantity vectors,* $(x_1^t,\ldots,x_H^t,y^t) \geq (0_{N^1},\ldots,0_{N^H},0_M)$, *for* $t=1,\ldots,T$. *Suppose that there exist* $2T(H+1)$ *numbers* $X_h^t, \beta_h^t, u^t, \lambda^t$, $h=1,\ldots,H$, $t=1,\ldots,T$, *such that these numbers and the given data satisfy the inequalities (19) and (20). Then there exists a concave, increasing macro function f of* $H+M$ *variables and there exist H concave, increasing micro functions* g_h, $h=1,\ldots,H$, *such that (17) and (21) holds for these functions.*

The proof is analogous to the proof of Theorem 2. The g_h are defined by

$$g_h(x_h) \equiv \min_t \{ g_h^t(x_h) : t=1,\ldots,T \}, \qquad h=1,\ldots,H,$$

where the TH linear functions g_h^t are defined by

$$g_h^t(x_h) \equiv X_h^t + \beta_h^t p_h^t \cdot (x_h - x_h^t).$$

The functions f and f^t are defined by

$$f^t(X_1,\ldots,X_H,y) \equiv u^t + \lambda^t \sum_{h=1}^{H} (\beta_h^t)^{-1} (X_h - X_h^t) + \lambda^t q^t \cdot (y - y^t),$$

$$f(X_1,\ldots,X_H,y) \equiv \min_t \{ f^t(X_1,\ldots,X_H,y) : t=1,\ldots,T \}.$$

The inequalities (19) and (20) play the same role in this section that the inequalities (3) and (5) played in the previous section. Unfortunately, the inequalities (19) and (20) are not linear in the 'unknowns', X_h^t, β_h^t, u^t and λ^t, so that linear programming techniques cannot be used to test whether a given body of price and quantity data is consistent with weakly separable utility maximizing behaviour. However, the unconstrained minimization technique associated with (14) in the previous section can be adapted to determine whether the inequalities (19) and (20) have a solution. The details are left to the reader.

Comparing Theorem 3 with Theorem 1, it seems evident that we should be able to weaken our regularity conditions on the macro and micro functions and establish a stronger version of Theorem 4. The following theorem is a step in this direction: the concavity assumption on the macro function f is replaced by a quasi-concavity[17] assumption.

The proof of Theorem 6 requires some knowledge about the duality between cost and utility functions. Define the cost function C_h that is dual to the micro function g_h for $h = 1, 2, \ldots, H$ by

$$C_h(X_h, p_h) \equiv \min_{x_h} \{ p_h \cdot x_h : g_h(x_h) \geq X_h,\ x \geq 0_{N^h} \}, \tag{31}$$

where $p_h \gg 0_{N^h}$ and X_h belongs to the range of g_h. If g_h is continuous, quasi-concave, and weakly increasing, then C_h will satisfy various regularity conditions, including continuity and increasingness in its X_h argument.[18] If in addition, g_h is concave, then C_h will be convex in its X_h argument.[19] In the following theorem, in order to simplify the proof, we shall assume that each $C_h(X_h, p_h)$ is differentiable with respect to its X_h argument.[20] The non-differentiable case is proven in the appendix.

Theorem 6 (*Generalization of Theorem 4*). *Suppose the macro function f is (i) continuous from above, (ii) subject to local non-satiation, and (iii) quasi-concave. Suppose the micro functions g_h, $h = 1, \ldots, H$, are (i) concave, (ii) weakly increasing, and (iii) have dual cost functions $C_h(X_h, p_h)$ that are differentiable with respect to their X_h arguments. Suppose further that we are given T positive price vectors, $(p_1^t, \ldots, p_H^t, q^t) \gg (0_{N^1}, \ldots, 0_{N^H}, 0_M)$; T non-negative quantity vectors, $y^t \geq 0_M$; HT non-negative but non-zero quantity vectors, $x_h^t > 0_{N^h}$, for $h = 1, \ldots, H$, $t = 1, \ldots, T$. Finally, suppose that the data are consistent with (weakly) separable utility maximizing behaviour; i.e., (17) holds. Then there exist numbers X_h^t, β_h^t, u^t and λ^t such that (19) and (20) hold.*

Proof. Define

$$X_h^t \equiv g_h(x^t), \qquad h = 1, \ldots, H, \quad t = 1, \ldots, T. \tag{32}$$

[17]A function f is quasi-concave iff the upper level sets $L(u) \equiv \{x : f(x) \geq u\}$ are convex for each level u in the range of f. A set S is convex iff $x' \in S$, $x'' \in S$, $0 < \lambda < 1$ implies $\lambda x' + (1 - \lambda)x'' \in S$.

[18]See Diewert (1982).

[19]See Diewert (1978, p. 33). A function f is convex iff $-f$ is concave.

[20]Blackorby and Diewert (1979) provide sufficient conditions on g_h which guarantee the differentiability of $C_h(X_h, p)$ with respect to X_h.

Using (31) and (32), the relations (17) may be rewritten as

$X_1^t, \dots, X_H^t, y^t$ solves

$$\max_{X_1,\dots,X_H,y}\left\{ f(X_1,\dots,X_H,y): \sum_{h=1}^{H} C_h(X_h, p_h^t) + q^t \cdot y \le Y^t, \right.$$

$$\left. y \ge 0_M,\ X_h \in \text{range } g_h,\ h = 1,\dots,H \right\}. \tag{33}$$

For $t = 1,\dots,T$, define the sets R^t and S^t by

$$R^t \equiv \left\{ (X_1,\dots,X_H,y): Y^t - \sum_{h=1}^{H} C_h(X_h, p_h^t) - q^t \cdot y \ge 0, \right.$$

$$\left. X_h \in \text{range } g_h,\ h = 1,\dots,H \right\}, \tag{34}$$

$$S^t \equiv \{ (X_1,\dots,X_H,y): f(X_1,\dots,X_H,y) \ge f(X_1^t,\dots,X_H^t,y^t),$$

$$y \ge 0_M,\ X_h \in \text{range } g_h,\ h = 1,\dots,H \}. \tag{35}$$

S^t is a convex set since f is quasi-concave. R^t is also a convex set, since the functions $-C_h(X_h, p_h^t)$ are concave in X_h.[21] The relations (33) show that S^t and R^t have no interior points in common, and hence by the Separating Hyperplane Theorem [Karlin (1959, p. 398)], there exists a hyperplane that separates the two sets; i.e., for $t = 1,\dots,T$, there exist vectors $A^t \equiv (A_1^t,\dots,A_H^t)$ and $a^t \equiv (a_1^t,\dots,a_M^t)$ (at least one of these two vectors is non-zero) and a scalar α^t such that

$$(X,y) \in R^t \quad \text{implies} \quad A^t \cdot X + a^t \cdot y \le \alpha^t, \tag{36}$$

$$(X,y) \in S^t \quad \text{implies} \quad A^t \cdot X + a^t \cdot y \ge \alpha^t. \tag{37}$$

Since (X^t, y^t) belongs to both R^t and S^t, we have

$$\alpha^t = A^t \cdot X^t + a^t \cdot y^t, \qquad t = 1,\dots,T. \tag{38}$$

[21] Since the g_h are concave, the C_h are convex in their X_h arguments and hence the functions $-C_h$ are concave.

Hence $(X_1^t,\dots,X_H^t,y^t)$ solves the concave programming problem (39) and the quasi-concave programming problem (40) below:

$$\max_{X_1,\dots,X_H,y}\left\{\sum_{h=1}^{H} A_h^t X_h + a^t\cdot y:\ Y^t - \sum_{h=1}^{H} C_h(X_h, p_h^t) + q^t\cdot y \geq 0,\right.$$

$$\left. X_h \in \text{range } g_h,\ h=1,\dots,H\right\}, \tag{39}$$

$$\min_{X_1,\dots,X_H,y}\left\{\sum_{h=1}^{H} A_h^t X_h + a^t\cdot y:\ f(X_1,\dots,X_H,y) \geq f(X_1^t,\dots,X_H^t,y^t),\right.$$

$$\left. y \geq 0_M,\ X_h \in \text{range } g_h,\ h=1,\dots,H\right\}. \tag{40}$$

Since $X_1^t,\dots,X_H^t, y^t$ solves (39) and since the constraints $X_h \in \text{range } g_h$ are not binding at this solution,[22] the Kuhn–Tucker conditions for (39) yield the existence of a Lagrange multiplier $\xi^t \geq 0$ such that the following first-order conditions hold:

$$A_h^t = \xi^t \partial C_h(X_h^t, p_h^t)/\partial X_h \equiv \xi^t P_h^t, \tag{41}$$

$$h=1,\dots,H,\quad t=1,\dots,T,$$

$$a^t = \xi^t q^t,\qquad t=1,\dots,T. \tag{42}$$

Since $(A^t, a^t) \neq 0_{H+M}$, we must have $\xi^t \neq 0$ and hence

$$\xi^t > 0,\qquad t=1,\dots,T. \tag{43}$$

The substitution of (41) and (42) into (40) and the use of (43) means that, for $t=1,\dots,T$,

$X_t^1,\dots,X_H^t, y^t$ solves

$$\min_{X_1,\dots,X_H,y}\left\{\sum_{h=1}^{H} P_h^t X_h + q^t\cdot y:\ f(X_1,\dots,X_H,y) \geq f(X_1^t,\dots,X_H^t,y^t),\right.$$

$$\left. y \geq 0_M,\ X_h \in \text{range } g_h,\ h=1,\dots,H\right\}. \tag{44}$$

[22] We need the weakly increasing property of the g_h and $x_h^t > 0_{N^h}$ to establish this. We can also establish that the Slater constraint qualification condition holds.

Since the problem of minimizing the cost of achieving a given utility level is dual to the problem of maximizing utility subject to an expenditure constraint (when the utility function is subject to local non-satiation), (44) implies that, for $t = 1,\dots,T$,

$$X_1^t,\dots, X_H^t, y^t \text{ solves}$$

$$\max_{X_1,\dots,X_H,y}\left\{ f(X_1,\dots,X_H,y): \sum_{h=1}^{H} P_h^t X_h + q^t\cdot y \le \sum_{h=1}^{H} P_h^t X_h^t + q^t\cdot y^t,\right.$$

$$\left. y \ge 0_M,\ X_h \in \text{range } g_h,\ h = 1,\dots,H\right\}. \tag{45}$$

The maximization problems that occur in (45) are exactly the kind of utility maximization problems that occurred in Theorem 3. Hence, applying Theorem 3, there exists λ^t, u^t such that

$$u^s \le u^t + \lambda^t \sum_{h=1}^{H} P_h^t(X_h^s - X_h^t) + \lambda^t q^t\cdot(y^s - y^t), \tag{46}$$

$$\lambda^t > 0, \qquad s,t = 1,\dots,T,$$

which is (20) if we define β_h^t by

$$(\beta_h^t)^{-1} \equiv P_h^t \equiv \partial C_h(X_h^t, p_h^t)/\partial X_h > 0, \tag{47}$$

$$h = 1,\dots,H, \quad t = 1,\dots,T.$$

We have yet to establish (19). Since the g_h are concave, the C_h are convex in their quantity arguments. Hence applying the negative of the inequality (4), we have, for $t = 1,\dots,T$ and $h = 1,\dots,H$,

$$C_h[g_h(x_h), p_h^t] - C_h[g_h(x_h^t), p_h^t]$$

$$\ge [\partial C_h[g_h(x_h^t, p_h^t]/\partial X_h][g_h(x_h) - g_h(x_h^t)]. \tag{48}$$

Let $x_h = x_h^s$ for $s = 1,\dots,T$ in (48) and use (32) and (47) to obtain

$$C_h[X_h^s, p_h^t] - C_h[X_h^t, p_h^t] \ge P_h^t(X_h^s - X_h^t), \tag{49}$$

$$h = 1,\dots,H, \quad s,t = 1,\dots,T.$$

We also have

$$C_h(X_h^t, p_h^t) = p_h^t \cdot x_h^t, \qquad h = 1, \ldots, H, \quad t = 1, \ldots, T, \tag{50}$$

$$\begin{aligned} C_h(X_h^s, p_h^t) &\equiv \min_x \{ p_h^t: g_h(x) \geq g_h(x_h^s) \equiv X_h^s,\ x \geq 0_{N^h} \} \\ &\leq p_h^t \cdot x_h^s, \qquad h = 1, \ldots, H, \quad s, t = 1, \ldots, T, \end{aligned} \tag{51}$$

where the last inequality follows from the feasibility of x_h^s for the cost minimization problem. Eqs. (49) to (51) yield

$$p_h^t \cdot (x_h^s - x_h^t) \geq P_h^t(X_h^s - X_h^t), \tag{52}$$

$$h = 1, \ldots, H, \quad s, t = 1, \ldots, T,$$

which is (19) using (47). Q.E.D.

Comparing the hypotheses of Theorem 6 with those of Theorem 4, we see that the hypotheses of the latter theorem are considerably weaker: (i) the concavity and monotonicity assumptions on the macro function f have been weakened to quasi-concavity and local non-satiation, (ii) the differentiability hypotheses on both the macro and micro functions have been dropped, and (iii) the positivity restrictions on the quantity data have been considerably weakened.

The hypotheses of Theorem 6 can be weakened and the result will still be true. Let $\tilde{g}_h$ denote the free disposal, quasi-concave hull of the micro function g_h for $h = 1, \ldots, H$.[23] Then all we require is that $\tilde{g}_h$ be concave and weakly increasing for $h = 1, \ldots, H$.[24] These hypotheses can be weakened even further: all we require is that the $\tilde{g}_h$ be transformable into concave functions.[25]

Note that even under our weakened hypotheses, we still seem to require some sort of curvature restriction on both macro and micro functions. However, the original Afriat result, Theorem 3, required no curvature restrictions at

[23] $\tilde{g}_h$ can be constructed from g_h as follows. Define the cost function C_h dual to g_h by (38). Define $\tilde{g}_h$ in terms of C_h for $x_h \geq 0_{N^h}$ by $\tilde{g}_h(x_h) \equiv \max_{X_h, p_h} \{ X_h: C_h(X_h, p_h) \leq p_h \cdot x_h$ for every $p_h \gg 0_{N^h} \}$.

[24] If x_h^* solves the competitive cost minimization problem (31), then x_h^* will also be a solution to $\min_{x_h} \{ p_h \cdot x_h: \tilde{g}_h(x_h) \geq X_h,\ x \geq 0_{N^h} \}$; see Diewert (1982, p. 554) for more details.

[25] Necessary and sufficient conditions for the existence of such concavifying transformations are surveyed and developed in Kannai (1981).

all.[26] This suggests to us that the hypotheses of Theorem 6 could be further weakened,[27] but we leave this task to other (more competent) researchers.

We turn now to tests for additive separability.

4. Tests for additive separability

Assume the same framework as in section 3, except that now we wish to derive necessary and sufficient conditions for a data set to be consistent with utility maximizing behaviour where the utility function F has the following additively separable form: $F(x_1,\ldots,x_H,y)=f[\sum_{h=1}^H g_h(x_h),y]$ where the macro function f is a function of $1+M$ variables and the micro function g_h is a function of N^h variables for $h=1,\ldots,H$.

Theorem 7 [*Generalization of Afriat (1970) and Varian (1983)*].[28] *Suppose the macro function f is (i) concave, (ii) once differentiable, and (iii) increasing in its first argument and non-decreasing in its last M arguments. Suppose $H\geq 2$ and the micro functions g_h, $h=1,\ldots,H$, are (i) concave, (ii) once differentiable, and (iii) weakly increasing in their arguments. Suppose further that we are given T positive price vectors, $(p_1^t,\ldots,p_H^t,q^t)$, and T positive quantity vectors, $(x_1^t,\ldots,x_H^t,y^t)$, for $t=1,\ldots,T$. Suppose the data are consistent with additively separable utility maximizing behaviour; i.e., for $t=1,\ldots,T$,*

$(x_1^t,\ldots,x_H^t,y^t)$ *solves*

$$\max_{x_1,\ldots,x_H,y}\left\{f\left[\sum_{h=1}^{H} g_h(x_h),y\right]:\ \sum_{h=1}^{H} p_h^t\cdot x_h+q^t\cdot y\leq Y^t,\right.$$

$$\left. x_1\geq 0_{N^1},\ldots,x_H\geq 0_{N^H},\ y\geq 0_M\right\}, \tag{53}$$

where Y^t is defined by (18). Then there exist HT scalars, X_h^t, $h=1,\ldots,H$, $t=1,\ldots,T$, and $3T$ scalars, β^t,λ^t,u^t, $t=1,\ldots,T$, such that the following

[26] However, we do require linear budget constraints in Theorem 3 and this is what allows us to dispense with curvature restrictions.

[27] One easy way of dispensing with the quasi-concavity assumption on f is to assume (45), instead of deducing it. However, we do not have a simple set of sufficient conditions that will imply this assumption.

[28] Afriat and Varian both consider the case where $H=2$, $M=0$ and $f(X)\equiv X$.

inequalities hold:

$$X_h^s \leq X_h^t + \beta^t p_h^t \cdot (x_h^s - x_h^t), \tag{54}$$

$$\beta^t > 0, \qquad h = 1, \ldots, H, \quad s, t = 1, \ldots, T,$$

$$u^s \leq u^t + \lambda^t (\beta^t)^{-1} \sum_{h=1}^{H} (X_h^s - X_h^t) + \lambda^t q^t \cdot (y^s - y^t), \tag{55}$$

$$\lambda^t > 0, \qquad s, t = 1, \ldots, T.$$

Proof. Repeat the proof of Theorem 4, except that (i) $f[\sum_{h=1}^{H} X_h^t, y^t]$ replaces $f[X_1^t, \ldots, X_H^t, y^t]$, (ii) α^t replaces α_h^t, and (iii) we deduce that $\beta_h^t = \lambda^t/\alpha^t \equiv \beta^t$ for $h = 1, \ldots, H$. Hence conditions (19) and (20) become (54) and (55). Q.E.D.

Corollary 7.1. Suppose $f[\sum_{h=1}^{H} g_h(x_h), y]$ *is replaced by the following* completely additive *structure*: $\sum_{h=1}^{H} g_h(x_h)$. *Then there exist HT scalars*, X_h^t, $h = 1, \ldots, H$, $t = 1, \ldots, T$, *and T scalars*, λ^t, $t = 1, \ldots, T$, *such that the following inequalities hold*:

$$X_h^s \leq X_h^t + \lambda^t p_h^t \cdot (x_h^s - x_h^t), \tag{56}$$

$$\lambda^t > 0, \qquad h = 1, \ldots, H, \quad s, t = 1, \ldots, T.$$

Proof. Under the present hypotheses, we find that $\alpha^t = \alpha_h^t = 1$ for $h = 1, \ldots, H$, $t = 1, \ldots, T$, and hence $\beta^t = \lambda^t/\alpha^t = \lambda^t$ for $t = 1, \ldots, T$. Suppressing the y variables and substituting $\beta^t = \lambda^t$ into (54) yields (56).[29] Q.E.D.

The interesting point to notice about the inequalities (56) is that they are linear in the 'unknowns' X_h^t and λ^t, and hence linear programming techniques may be used in order to check whether a given data set has a solution satisfying (56).

Theorem 8 below shows that (54) and (55) are sufficient for the given data set to be consistent with additively separable utility maximizing behaviour.

[29] We may also substitute $\beta^t = \lambda^t$ into (55) and deduce the inequalities $u^s \leq u^t + \sum_{h=1}^{H} (X_h^s - X_h^t)$ for $s, t = 1, \ldots, T$. However, if we define $u^t \equiv \sum_{h=1}^{H} X_h^t$ for $t = 1, \ldots, T$, we see that the above inequalities hold identically as equalities, and hence are not of any interest.

Theorem 8 [*Generalization of Afriat* (*1970*) *and Varian* (*1983*)]. *Suppose that we are given T positive price vectors,* $(p_1^t, \ldots, p_H^t, q^t)$, *and T non-negative quantity vectors,* $(x_t^1, \ldots, x_H^t, y^t)$, $t = 1, \ldots, T$. *Suppose that there exist* $(H+3)T$ *numbers,* $X_h^t, \beta^t, \lambda^t, u^t$, $h = 1, \ldots, H$, $t = 1, \ldots, T$, *such that these numbers and the given data satisfy the inequalities* (*54*) *and* (*55*). *Then there exists a concave, increasing macro function f of* $1 + M$ *variables and there exist H concave, increasing micro functions,* g_h, $h = 1, \ldots, H$, *such that* (*53*) *holds for these functions.*

The proof is analogous to the proof of Theorem 2.

Corollary 8.1. *Suppose that there exist* $(H+1)T$ *numbers,* X_h^t, λ^t, $h = 1, \ldots, H$, $t = 1, \ldots, T$, *such that these numbers and the given data satisfy the inequalities* (*56*). *Then there exist H concave, increasing functions* g_h, $h = 1, \ldots, H$, *such that* (*53*) *holds for these functions, except that* $f[\sum_{h=1}^H g_h(x_h), y]$ *in* (*53*) *is replaced by* $\sum_{h=1}^H g_h(x_h)$.

Recall how Theorem 6 generalized Theorem 4. We can similarly generalize Theorem 7 and its corollary: the differentiability assumptions on f and the g_h may be dropped, the concavity assumption on f may be replaced by the assumption of quasi-concavity, and the positivity restrictions on the quantity data may be relaxed. The proof of this generalization of Theorem 7 follows along the lines of Theorem 6, except that $f(X_1, \ldots, X_H, y)$ is replaced by $f(\sum_{h=1}^H X_h, y)$. The key to the proof is to look at the modified version of (40) and conclude that $X_1^t, \ldots, X_H^t$ solves

$$\min_{X_1, \ldots, X_H} \left\{ \sum_{h=1}^H A_h^t X_h : \sum_{h=1}^H X_h \geq \sum_{h=1}^H X_h^t \right\}, \tag{57}$$

and hence $A_h^t = A^t$ for $h = 1, \ldots, H$ and $t = 1, \ldots, T$. These equalities imply that $P_h^t = P^t \equiv (\beta^t)^{-1}$ for all h and t and the generalization of Theorem 7 follows.

5. Conclusion

We have derived generalizations of the Afriat–Varian necessary and sufficient conditions for a given body of data to be consistent with utility maximizing behaviour under the hypotheses that the utility function is either weakly separable or additively separable. Determining whether the resulting conditions are satisfied by the given data leads to *non-parametric tests for separability*. The tests are non-parametric because they do not depend on the underlying utility function having a particular parametric functional form, as is the case in the econometric literature on testing for separability. Blackorby, Primont and Russell (1978, ch. 8) have pointed out that this econometric literature is seriously deficient from a theoretical point of view, since the econometric tests tend to impose unwanted restrictions on the parametric functional form in addition to the particular separability hypothesis being tested. Thus the non-parametric tests developed here should serve as useful supplements to the usual econometric tests for separability.

Even if the tests developed in this paper fail, the tests may be used to construct utility functions (which satisfy the desired hypotheses) that are approximately consistent with the data. For example, even if the objective function (14) does not attain its lower bound of zero, the u^t and $\lambda^t \equiv (\alpha_t^2 + 1)$ which solve (14) may be used in definitions (6) and (7) in order to construct a utility function f that is approximately consistent with the data.[30]

The necessity of conditions (3) and (5), or (19) and (20), or (54) and (55), were very easy to derive, provided that we assumed positive data and that the relevant utility functions were both concave and differentiable. The resulting conditions turned out to be sufficient as well. Somewhat surprisingly, it proved to be difficult to relax the positivity and differentiability assumptions: we were forced to resort to rather complex arguments involving cost functions.

We have not derived all possible combinations of tests in this paper. For example, if we wish to impose linear homogeneity on the micro function g_h, then add the following restrictions to (19) and (54):

$$X_h^t = \beta_h^t p^t \cdot x^t, \qquad t = 1, \ldots, T. \tag{58}$$

If we wish to impose linear homogeneity on the macro function f, then add the following restrictions:

$$u^t = \lambda^t \sum_{h=1}^{H} \left(\beta_h^t\right)^{-1} X_h^t + \lambda^t q^t \cdot y^t, \qquad t = 1, \ldots, T, \tag{59}$$

to (20) or (55) [except that $\beta_h^t = \beta^t$ in (55)]. The restrictions (58) and (59) have the effect of forcing the linear functions g_h^t and f^t defined in Theorem 5 through the origin, and hence the g_h and f defined in Theorem 5 will be linearly homogeneous functions.

Finally, we note that Theorems 1–2, 4–5 and 7–8 may be adapted to yield theorems in the context of producer theory if we interpret utility as output. If output is *unobservable*, then the above theorems are applicable, except that we substitute the hypothesis of cost minimizing behaviour rather than utility maximizing behaviour. If in addition, output is *observable*, then the 'unknowns' u^t in (5), (20) and (54) become known output levels, and the above

[30] See Afriat (1973) for a further development of this approximate consistency idea.

theorems must be modified accordingly. Other tests for a separable production structure could be developed, but these developments are outside the scope of this consumer-oriented paper.

Appendix: Proofs of theorems in the non-differentiable case

Proof of Theorem 1. Apply the Uzawa (1958) and Karlin (1959, p. 201) Saddle Point Theorem to the concave programming problems in (1). Upon noting that the non-negativity constraints $x \geq 0_N$ are not binding since $x^t \gg 0_N$, we conclude that there exists $\lambda^t \geq 0$ such that x^t maximizes the concave function $f(x)+\lambda^t[p^t \cdot x^t - p^t \cdot x]$ for $t=1,\ldots,T$. By a result due to Rockafellar (1970, p. 270), $0_N \in [\partial f(x^t) - \lambda^t p^t]$ for $t=1,\ldots,T$, which may be rearranged to yield the following conditions:

$$z^t = \lambda^t p^t, \qquad \lambda^t \geq 0, \qquad z^t \in \partial f(x^t), \qquad t=1,\ldots,T, \tag{A.1}$$

where z^t is some supergradient to f around the point x^t. The weakly increasing hypothesis on f implies $z^t > 0_N$ and thus $\lambda^t > 0$ which is (3).

In the non-differentiable case, the inequality (4) is still valid except that $\nabla f(x^t)$ may be replaced by any member of $\partial f(x^t)$ [see Rockafellar (1970, p. 218)]; hence we replace $\nabla f(x^t)$ by the z^t which occurs in (A.1). The rest of the proof of Theorem 1 remains the same.

Proof of Theorem 6. Repeat the argument through (40). Now apply the Uzawa–Karlin Saddle Point Theorem to the concave programming problem (39). Thus there exists $\xi^t \geq 0$ such that $X_1^t,\ldots, X_H^t, y^t$ solves the unconstrained concave maximization problem:

$$\max_{X_1,\ldots,X_H,y} \left\{ \sum_{h=1}^{H} A_h^t X_h + a^t \cdot y + \xi^t \left[Y^t - \sum_{h=1}^{H} C_h(X_h, p_h^t) - q^t \cdot y \right] \right\}. \tag{A.2}$$

Applying Rockafellar's (1970, p. 218) optimality conditions to (A.2), we again obtain (42) but (41) becomes

$$A_h^t = \xi^t P_h^t, \qquad h=1,\ldots,H, \quad t=1,\ldots,T, \tag{A.3}$$

where $P_h^t \in \partial C_h^t(X_h^t)$, where $C_h^t(X_h^t) \equiv C_h(X_h^t, p_h^t)$ and $\partial C_h^t(X_h^t)$ is defined to be the set of subgradients to the convex function C_h^t at the point X_h^t. Our monotonicity assumptions on g_h imply that $P_h^t > 0$. The remainder of the proof goes through as before except that we replace the partial derivative

$\partial C_h(X_h^t, p_h^t)/\partial X_h$ whenever it occurs by the subgradient P_h^t that occurs in (A.3) above.

References

Afriat, S.N., 1967, The construction of utility functions from expenditure data, International Economic Review 8, 67–77.

Afriat, S.N., 1970, The construction of separable utility functions from expenditure data, Mimeo. (University of North Carolina, Chapel Hill, NC).

Afriat, S.N., 1972, The theory of international comparisons of real income and prices, in: D.J. Daly, ed., International comparisons of prices and output (National Bureau of Economic Research, New York) 13–129.

Afriat, S.N., 1973, On a system of inequalities in demand analysis: An extension of the classical method, International Economic Review 14, 460–472.

Afriat, S.N., 1976, Combinatorial theory of demand (Input–Output Publishing Co., London).

Afriat, S.N., 1977, The price index (Cambridge University Press, London).

Blackorby, C. and W.E. Diewert, 1979, Expenditure functions, local duality and second order approximations, Econometrica 47, 579–601.

Blackorby, C., D. Primont and R.R. Russell, 1978, Duality, separability and functional structure: Theory and economic applications (North-Holland, Amsterdam).

Diewert, W.E., 1973, Afriat and revealed preference theory, Review of Economic Studies 40, 419–426.

Diewert, W.E., 1974, Applications of duality theory, in: M.D. Intriligator and D.A. Kendrick, eds., Frontiers of quantitative economics, Vol. II (North-Holland, Amsterdam) 106–171.

Diewert, W.E., 1978, Hicks' aggregation theorem and the existence of a real value-added function, in: M. Fuss and D. McFadden, eds., Production economics: A dual approach to theory and applications, Vol. 2 (North-Holland, Amsterdam) 17–51.

Diewert, W.E., 1982, Duality approaches to microeconomic theory, in: K.J. Arrow and M.D. Intriligator, eds., Handbook of mathematical economics, Vol. II (North-Holland, Amsterdam) 535–599.

Diewert, W.E. and C. Parkan, 1978, Tests for the consistency of consumer data and nonparametric index numbers, Discussion paper no. 78-27 (Department of Economics, University of British Columbia, Vancouver).

Houthakker, H., 1950, Revealed preference and the utility function, Economica N.S. 17, 159–174.

Kannai, Y., 1981, Concave utility functions: Existence, constructions and cardinality, in: S. Schaible and W.T. Ziemba, eds., Generalized concavity in optimization and economics, (Academic Press, New York) 543–611.

Karlin, S., 1959, Mathematical methods and theory in games, programming and economics, Vol. I (Addison-Wesley, Palo Alto, CA).

Mas-Colell, A., 1978, On revealed preference analysis, Review of Economic Studies 45, 121–132.

Rockafellar, R.T., 1970, Convex analysis (Princeton University Press, Princeton, NJ).

Rockafellar, R.T., 1978, La theorie des sous-gradients et ses applications à l'optimisation, Collection de la Chaire Aisenstadt (Les Presses de l'Université de Montréal, Montréal).

Samuelson, P.A., 1938, A note on the pure theory of consumer's behaviour, Economica N.S. 5, 61–71.

Shephard, R.W., 1953, Cost and production functions (Princeton University Press, Princeton, NJ).

Uzawa, H., 1958, The Kuhn–Tucker theorem in concave programming, in: K.J. Arrow, L. Hurwicz and H. Uzawa, eds., Studies in linear and non-linear programming (Stanford University Press, Stanford, CA) 32–37.

Varian, H., 1982, The nonparametric approach to demand analysis, Econometrica 50, 945–973.

Varian, H., 1983, Nonparametric tests of consumer behaviour, Review of Economic Studies 50, 99–110.

NON-PARAMETRIC HYPOTHESIS TESTING PROCEDURES AND APPLICATIONS TO DEMAND ANALYSIS

Larry G. EPSTEIN and Adonis J. YATCHEW *

University of Toronto, Toronto, Canada M5S 1A1

This paper proposes a test of the hypothesis that a (possibly vector-valued) regression function g lies in a particular compact family of functions $\mathscr{F}$, where $\mathscr{F}$ is not necessarily a finite-dimensional parametric family. Under the assumption of a known covariance matrix of the errors, the test is shown to be consistent for a broad range of alternatives and an upper bound on the significance level is established. It is shown how the test may be used to test the utility maximization hypothesis and homotheticity, and the paper indicates how to apply the test to a broad range of other non-parametric hypotheses.

1. Introduction

This paper considers models of the following type:

$$\tilde{y}_t = g(\tilde{p}_t) + \tilde{\varepsilon}_t, \qquad t = 1, \ldots, T, \tag{1}$$

where the disturbances $\tilde{\varepsilon}_t$ are independently and identically distributed with mean 0 and known covariance matrix Σ. Realizations of the exogenous variables $\tilde{p}_t$ and of the endogenous variables $\tilde{y}_t$ are observed by the analyst, but the function g is unknown. In particular the values of $g(\tilde{p}_t)$ are not observed. Within this framework we describe consistent test procedures for null and alternative hypotheses of the form

$$\mathrm{H}_0 : g \in \mathscr{F}, \qquad \mathrm{H}_1 : g \in \mathscr{G} \backslash \mathscr{F}, \tag{2}$$

where $\mathscr{F} \subset \mathscr{G}$ are suitably defined classes of functions. The only restrictions that we require for $\mathscr{F}$ and $\mathscr{G}$ is that they be compact subsets of an appropriate topological space of continuous functions – one way of implementing these conditions is to require $\mathscr{F}$ and $\mathscr{G}$ to be closed, $\mathscr{G}$ to be totally bounded and elements of $\mathscr{G}$ to satisfy a common Lipschitz condition. The paper requires that these bounds be specified by the analyst and it is this a priori specification that replaces the assumption of a parametric family. Since $\mathscr{G}$ need not be

* We are indebted to Angelo Melino for many valuable discussions. We would also like to thank, but not implicate, Ron Gallant and Hal White for some extremely helpful comments and suggestions.

contained within some parametric class of functions that is defined by finitely many parameters, the procedure we describe can be applied to test a hypothesis of interest without the need to maintain a specific and generally ad hoc functional form for g. Moreover, we provide examples to show that common hypotheses can be put into the form (2), and that computation of the relevant test statistics involves only the solution of non-linear programming problems (in finitely many variables).

The general framework and results should be of use in a broad range of problems in empirical economics. The application upon which we focus in this paper is the non-parametric approach to demand and factor demand analysis. Thus, for example, our procedure may be applied to provide a test of the consistency of a set of price and quantity consumption data with the hypothesis of utility maximization, while maintaining only minimal and non-parametric assumptions.

Although adopting a different approach, the Fourier flexible form approach, Gallant's work (1981, 1982) [see also Elbadawi, Gallant and Souza (1983)] is directed at a similar goal – the estimation of economic models and testing of economic theory without augmenting the economic hypothesis with parametric assumptions. Gallant (1982) demonstrates how hypotheses like the maximization hypothesis, homotheticity, constant returns and so on can be tested by imposing restrictions on successively higher-order Fourier approximations. Gallant assumes a known covariance matrix Σ and obtains the (asymptotic) size of his procedure. In contrast, we adopt a revealed preference approach, and for a known covariance matrix Σ (in fact only the trace of Σ needs to be known) obtain consistent tests with an upper bound on the significance level.

Varian's paper in this volume that in part inspired our interest in the problem, also suggests a non-parametric test procedure which we generalize – indeed the results of this paper demonstrate that (a slightly modified version of) the Varian test procedure is consistent.

As a byproduct of the results below, it can be demonstrated that Σ (and higher-order moments) can be estimated consistently under the maintained hypothesis that $g \in \mathscr{G}$. However, the remaining task that is not resolved here is the demonstration of a consistent procedure (with approximate size) when Σ is unknown.

The paper proceeds as follows: Section 2 describes the test procedure for (2) in the most general setting. Consistency of the test procedure is established. The results of section 2 are applied in section 3 to demand and factor demand analysis. In particular, we describe asymptotically valid and consistent non-parametric tests of utility maximization and utility maximization with homothetic utility, and we indicate how corresponding tests may be constructed for numerous other common hypotheses. Section 4 concludes and suggests directions for future research. All proofs are collected in appendices.

The following notation is adopted: R^n is n-dimensional Euclidean space and R^n_+ (R^n_{++}) is the (open) non-negative orthant. All vectors are column vectors unless transposition is indicated by a superscripted prime. $|\cdot|$ denotes the Euclidean norm. A random variable is indicated by $\sim$ over the variable. A typical realization of $\tilde{x}$ is denoted x; e is the vector, of suitable dimension, all of whose components equal 1.

2. A non-parametric test

Model (1), which is the focus of this paper, is now specified more precisely. The following assumptions are used below:

Assumption 1. $(\tilde{p}_t, t=1,2,\dots)$ are independently and identically distributed on the probability space $(S, \mathscr{A}, \theta)$. For each t, $\tilde{p}_t: S \to P$, a compact subset of R^m, which is also the support of the distribution μ of each $\tilde{p}_t$, i.e., $P = \operatorname{supp}\mu$.

Assumption 2. $(\tilde{\varepsilon}_t, t=1,2,\dots)$ are independently and identically distributed on $(S, \mathscr{A}, \theta)$ with $\mathrm{E}(\tilde{\varepsilon}_t)=0$, $\operatorname{cov}(\tilde{\varepsilon}_t)=\Sigma$. For each $t, \tilde{\varepsilon}_t: S \to \Omega$, a subset of R^n, and $\tilde{\varepsilon}_t$ has distribution ν.

Assumption 3. For each t, $\tilde{p}_t$ and $\tilde{\varepsilon}_t$ are statistically independent.

Assumption 4. $\tilde{\varepsilon}_t$ possesses finite absolute moments up to fourth order.

These assumptions are self-explanatory. Some are needed only for a proper subset of the results that follow. However, for simplicity of exposition we maintain Assumptions 1–4 throughout and leave it to the interested reader to sort out where each assumption is used.

Consistency of the test of (2) described below requires further structure for $\mathscr{F}$ and $\mathscr{G}$. First, it is assumed that $\mathscr{F} \subset \mathscr{G} \subset C[P, R^n]$, the class of all continuous functions from P into R^n. Consistency results in parametric analyses often are proven by maintaining the compactness of the parameter space. By analogy we impose the compactness of the sets of functions $\mathscr{F}$ and $\mathscr{G}$ in a suitable topology. We choose the topology for $C[P, R^n]$ that is induced by the norm $\|\cdot\|_C$, $\|f\|_C \equiv \max\{|f(p)|: p \in P\}$. (There are other 'natural' topologies which could be adopted, such as those induced by various Sobolev norms; see Gallant's papers.) Thus the following assumption, which is also maintained throughout, is natural:

Assumption 5. $\mathscr{F}$ and $\mathscr{G}$ are compact subsets of $C[P, R^n]$, where the latter has the topology induced by the norm $\|\cdot\|_C$, and $\mathscr{F} \subset \mathscr{G}$.

The characterization of compact subsets of $C[P, R^n]$ is well-known. [See Kelley (1955, p. 233) and Royden (1963).] $\mathscr{F}$ is compact if and only if it satisfies all of the following conditions:

(i) $\mathscr{F}$ is closed.
(ii) $\mathscr{F}$ is bounded, i.e., $\exists B > 0$ such that $|f(p)| < B$, $\forall p \in P$, $\forall f \in \mathscr{F}$.

(iii) $\mathscr{F}$ is equicontinuous, i.e., $\forall p_0 \in P$, $\forall \varepsilon > 0$, $\exists \delta > 0$ such that $|p - p_0| < \delta$ and $p \in P \Rightarrow |f(p) - f(p_0)| < \varepsilon$, $\forall f \in \mathscr{F}$.

(Of course, similar remarks apply to $\mathscr{G}$.)

Now consider model (1) again. g is unknown and realizations of $g(\tilde{p}_t)$ are not observed. Realizations of $\tilde{p}_t$ and $\tilde{y}_t$ are observed. The latter include the 'true' function value $g(p_t)$ and an observation on measurement error corresponding to $\tilde{\varepsilon}_t$. (Alternative interpretations for $\tilde{\varepsilon}_t$ are possible as described in section 3.)

To construct a statistical test for (2) proceed as follows: For each $T > 0$ define the random variable

$$\tilde{V}_T \equiv \sum_{t=1}^{T} (\tilde{\varepsilon}_t' \tilde{\varepsilon}_t - \eta)/T^{1/2}\gamma, \tag{3}$$

where

$$\eta = \mathrm{E}(\tilde{\varepsilon}_t' \tilde{\varepsilon}_t) = \mathrm{trace}(\Sigma), \qquad \gamma^2 = \mathrm{var}(\tilde{\varepsilon}_t' \tilde{\varepsilon}_t).$$

By the Central Limit Theorem, $\tilde{V}_T$ is asymptotically distributed as N(0, 1). Though realizations of $\tilde{V}_T$ are not observed, we can compute realizations of the random variable $\tilde{W}_T$ defined by

$$\begin{aligned} \tilde{W}_T &\equiv \min_{f \in \mathscr{F}} \sum_{t=1}^{T} \{(\tilde{y}_t - f(\tilde{p}_t))'(\tilde{y}_t - f(\tilde{p}_t)) - \eta\}/T^{1/2}\gamma, \\ &= \min_{f \in \mathscr{F}} \sum_{t=1}^{T} (\tilde{y}_t - f(\tilde{p}_t))'(\tilde{y}_t - f(\tilde{p}_t))/T^{1/2}\gamma - \eta T^{1/2}/\gamma. \end{aligned} \tag{4}$$

(The intention is that the minimum be computed for each given set of realizations for the $\tilde{y}_t$'s and $\tilde{p}_t$'s. The minimum exists because of the compactness of $\mathscr{F}$.) In a sense $\tilde{W}_T + \eta T^{1/2}/\gamma$ gives the minimum 'distance' of the observed data from $\mathscr{F}$, where distance is defined by an appropriate metric. Note that the measurability of $\tilde{W}_T$ is established in appendix 2.

Under H_0, $\tilde{W}_T \leq \tilde{V}_T$. Given the significance level α, let b_α be the corresponding critical value in the standard normal distribution. Then $\mathrm{prob}(\tilde{W}_T \geq b_\alpha) \leq \mathrm{prob}(\tilde{V}_T \geq b_\alpha) = \alpha$. Thus if H_0 is rejected whenever a value of $\tilde{W}_T$ in excess of b_α is observed, then the probability of a type I error is no greater than α. [This bounding argument is due to Varian (1985).]

The consistency of the above test procedure follows from the following theorem:

Theorem 1. *Let g be in $\mathscr{G}$, but not necessarily in $\mathscr{F}$. Then there exists $A \subset S$,*

$A \in \mathscr{A}$ such that $\theta(A) = 0$ and, $\forall s \in S \backslash A$,

$$\lim_{T \to \infty} \min_{f \in \mathscr{F}} \frac{1}{T} \sum_{t=1}^{T} [\tilde{y}_t(s) - f(\tilde{p}_t(s))]'[\tilde{y}_t(s) - f(\tilde{p}_t(s))]$$
$$= \eta + \min_{f \in \mathscr{F}} \int_P [g(p) - f(p)]'[g(p) - f(p)] \, \mathrm{d}\mu(p). \tag{5}$$

Let the true function g lie outside $\mathscr{F}$. For any $f \in \mathscr{F}$, $\exists p_0 \in P$ such that $g(p_0) \neq f(p_0)$. By continuity $g(p) \neq f(p)$, $\forall p \in Q$, a (relatively) open subset of P. If $\mu(Q)$ were equal to zero, then p_0 would not lie in $\operatorname{supp}\mu = P$, a contradiction. Thus, $\mu(Q) > 0$ and $\int_P [g(p) - f(p)]'[g(p) - f(p)] \, \mathrm{d}\mu(p) > 0$. Moreover, this is true for all $f \in \mathscr{F}$. Since $\mathscr{F}$ is compact therefore, it follows that the minimum on the right side of (5) is positive. Denote it by d ($d > 0$).

The consistency of the test based on the $\tilde{W}_T$ statistic is now immediate: If $g \notin \mathscr{F}$, the probability of rejecting $\mathrm{H}_0 = \operatorname{prob}[\tilde{W}_T \geq b_\alpha] = \operatorname{prob}[\gamma \tilde{W}_T / T^{1/2} \geq \gamma b_\alpha / T^{1/2}]$. But $\gamma \tilde{W}_T / T^{1/2}$ converges almost surely to d [because of (5)] and $\gamma b_\alpha / T^{1/2}$ converges to 0. Almost sure convergence implies convergence in measure, thus $\lim_{T \to \infty} \operatorname{prob}[\gamma \tilde{W}_T / T^{1/2} \geq \gamma b_\alpha / T^{1/2}] = 1$, and we have shown that for any 'true' function $g \in \mathscr{G} \backslash \mathscr{F}$, the power of the test approaches 1 asymptotically as $T \to \infty$.

In the proof of Theorem 1, especially Lemma 2, the role played by Assumption 5, and in particular the boundedness and equicontinuity of $\mathscr{F}$, is apparent. These properties are used to strengthen a Law of Large Numbers proposition to an assertion of *uniform on* $\mathscr{F}$ convergence.

Finally, we note that in constructing the quadratic form in (4), we are implicitly using the identity matrix as a weighting matrix. But we could have used other positive definite weighting matrices – e.g., in finite-dimensional problems weighting by Σ^{-1} (or a consistent estimate) leads to more efficient estimation as well as more powerful tests. Discussion of these issues is beyond the scope of this paper.

For the case we have examined thus far, that is η and γ known, the test procedure is consistent for an even broader alternative than the compact $\mathscr{G}$ that we have assumed. However the compactness of $\mathscr{G}$ is required for the extension provided below where γ is consistently estimated.

Consider then eq. (3). The asymptotic normality of $\tilde{V}_T$ is not destroyed if we replace γ with a consistent estimate, nor is the inequality between $\tilde{W}_T$ and $\tilde{V}_T$ under the null hypothesis, so long as the estimate of γ is positive. The consistency of the test procedure also follows analogously. In appendix 2 we demonstrate that γ can be estimated consistently so long as $g \in \mathscr{G}$ where $\mathscr{G}$ is a compact set of functions. In fact, by a proof similar to that of Theorem 1, we may obtain consistent estimates of Σ or other moments of $\tilde{\varepsilon}_t$. Whereas the test procedure above still goes through if we replace γ with a consistent estimate, this is note necessarily the case if we replace η with a consistent estimate. Having noted this, for ease of exposition, we will, for the remainder of the paper, continue to assume that γ is known.

3. Hypothesis testing in consumer and producer theory

There have been numerous recent contributions to the non-parametric approach to demand and factor demand analysis. [In the consumer framework, see Diewert and Parkan (1978, 1982) and Varian (1982, 1983) which extend, refine and implement earlier work of Afriat (1967, 1972a, 1973). In the producer framework, see Afriat (1972b), Hanoch and Rothschild (1972), Diewert and Parkan (1979) and Varian (1984).] These papers describe non-parametric tests of the basic optimization models and also of various specializations of these models involving homotheticity or separability, for example. The papers by Varian also describe non-parametric approaches to other issues commonly addressed by the empirical demand analyst, such as the recovery of the underlying preferences or technology and the forecasting of behaviour in environments outside the given data sample. These procedures are free of arbitrary functional form specifications, which is their principal advantage over the more commonly adopted parametric approaches. However, a major deficiency of these procedures is that they are non-statistical. Thus they require that the data be measured without error and that any violation by the data of the test conditions, no matter how 'slight' that violation may appear to be, must result in the rejection of the model. This shortcoming has been noted with regret in several of the cited papers.

Recent work by Varian (1985) and by Gallant (1981, 1982) has attempted to extend the advantages of a non-parametric approach to a statistical framework. Here we describe how the results in the first part of this paper may be applied to provide a straightforward statistical procedure for testing hypotheses about consumer and producer behaviour.

The applications follow a pattern: Express the model of interest in the form (1) and consider null and alternative hypotheses that have the form (2). The null hypothesis is closely related to the existence of a solution to a set of inequalities. Diewert (1973) has pointed out that such inequalities can be checked numerically by solving an appropriate programming problem. The statistical test is based on the computed 'distance' of the observed data from the 'closest' point which admits a solution to the inequalities. This minimum distance problem takes the form of a non-linear programming problem. The null hypothesis is rejected if and only if the computed distance exceeds a prespecified critical value. The interpretation in that case is that the magnitude of the observed violations of the set of inequalities is a priori so unlikely given the size of the measurement error, that the null hypothesis can be rejected.

This argument is described in detail for two hypotheses: utility maximization and utility maximization with homothetic utility. The same pattern can be applied in a straightforward fashion to construct statistical tests of other hypotheses of interest; for example, weak or strong separability of utility, profit maximization or input cost minimization, constant returns to scale or forms of separability in production, the presence of rationing, or the consistency of asset demand data with expected utility maximization. The corresponding sets of inequalities are provided by the non-statistical non-parametric tests of these hypotheses described in the cited papers by Afriat, Diewert and Parkan, and Varian. [For a test of the asset demand model, see Varian (1981).]

Two further introductory comments are in order: First, recall that to prove consistency of our statistical tests (with γ unknown) it was necessary to adopt Assumption 5; i.e., that $\mathscr{F}$ and $\mathscr{G}$ are compact. As a result the test of utility maximization that we describe is in fact a test of utility maximization under the maintained hypothesis that the demand functions satisfy a suitable Lipschitz property. The latter condition is much weaker than the specification of a functional form as in the parametric approach.

Secondly, Varian (1982) reports that several aggregate consumption data sets which he examined are consistent with utility maximizing behaviour even without resorting to measurement error. For such data sets there is clearly no need for a statistical procedure. But there are many other data sets and hypotheses (separability, or homotheticity for example) that one might be interested in testing where a statistical approach could be important. For example, Diewert and Parkan (1979) and Varian (1985) report violations of the non-parametric conditions for various production models. The statistical procedure described in this paper could be used to determine whether these violations are statistically significant. The usefulness of a statistical procedure will undoubtedly become more evident as more data sets and hypotheses are investigated non-parametrically.

3.1. Utility maximization

A function $u\colon R^n_+ \to R^1$ is called a *utility function* if u is quasi-concave, increasing and continuous. Fix $P \subset R^{n+1}_{++}$ compact and for $p \in P$, write $p' = (M, q')$ where M is a positive scalar that is interpreted as income and $q \in R^n_{++}$ is a price vector. For any $f\colon P \to R^n$, say that f is *L-Lipschitzian* if $L > 0$ and $|f(p^1) - f(p^2)| \leq L|p^1 - p^2|$, $\forall p^1, p^2 \in P$. Call f a *demand function* if f is continuous and if there exists a utility function u such that, $\forall p \in P$ and $\forall x \in R^n_+$, $q'x \leq 1$ and $x \neq f(p) \Rightarrow u(f(p)) > u(x)$. Thus $f(p)$ gives the unique utility maximizing bundle given p and u. Call $g\colon P \to R^{n-1}$ a *share function* if there exists a demand function f such that, for all $p \in P$, $p' = (M, q')$,

$$f(M,q) = M\hat{q}^{-1}\begin{bmatrix} g(M,q) \\ 1 - e'g(M,q) \end{bmatrix}.$$

(Henceforth adopt the notation whereby $\hat{q}$ denotes the square diagonal matrix having the components of q as diagonal entries.) $g(p)$ represents the vector of budget shares of the first $(n-1)$ goods. One good (any choice is possible) is deleted because of the well-known dependence of error terms that occurs in systems of share equations. The dependence occurs also if the model is formulated with demands rather than shares as the dependent variable. We adopt the latter formulation because it is more common in parametric work and because it makes the constant-variance-assumption for the error term more plausible. Denote by $\mathbb{D}$ the set of all share functions.

Since $\mathbb{D}$ is a subset of $C[P, R^{n-1}]$, its closure with respect to the norm $\|\cdot\|_C$ is well-defined. The closure is $\overline{\mathbb{D}} \equiv \{f \in C[P, R^{n-1}]$: there exist functions $f^k \in \mathbb{D}$, $k = 1, 2, \ldots,$ such that $\max_{p \in P} |f^k(p) - f(p)| \to 0$ as $k \to \infty\}$. Thus $\overline{\mathbb{D}}$ consists of all functions that are limits of share functions in the sense of uniform convergence over P. Since any function in $\overline{\mathbb{D}}$ can be approximated arbitrarily well by a share function we cannot hope to distinguish empirically between elements of $\overline{\mathbb{D}} \setminus \mathbb{D}$ and those of $\mathbb{D}$. Consequently we take membership in $\overline{\mathbb{D}}$ as designating 'rational' behaviour.

Data are generated by model (1) where y_t represents the vector of budget shares in observation t. y_t, $g(p_t)$ and ε_t are all $(n-1)$-dimensional vectors, since it is understood that the last good has been deleted. Its budget share equals one minus the sum of the budget shares of all other goods, and this is true both for measured and true shares. The appropriate versions of Assumptions 1–4 are maintained. [In the statements of Assumptions 2 and 4 $(n-1)$ is substituted for n.] The 'true' function g is unknown.

As mentioned above, consistency of our test procedure requires that the set of functions $\mathscr{F}$ that defines the null hypothesis be compact, and thus that it be closed, bounded and equicontinuous. $\overline{\mathbb{D}}$ is closed and bounded, since $\|f\|_C \leq 1$, $\forall f \in \overline{\mathbb{D}}$. But it is not equicontinuous. Thus we define $\mathscr{F}$ to be the set[1]

$$\mathscr{F} \equiv \{f \in \overline{\mathbb{D}} : f \text{ is } L\text{-Lipschitz}\}. \tag{6}$$

Similarly, we take $\mathscr{G}$ to be the set

$$\mathscr{G} \equiv \Big\{ f \in C[P, R^{n-1}] : f \text{ is } L\text{-Lipschitz, and}$$

$$0 \leq f_i(p) \leq \sum_{j=1}^{n-1} f_j(p) \leq 1, \tag{7}$$

$$\text{for all } i = 1, \ldots, n-1 \text{ and all } p \in P,$$

$$\text{where } f_i \text{ is the } i\text{th component of } f \Big\}.$$

[1] By the mean value theorem, a common Lipschitz condition is implied if elements of $\mathscr{G}$ are continuously differentiable on P and if the norms of gradients share a common bound on P.

The latter defining constraints for $\mathscr{G}$ arise naturally because we are modelling budget shares.

Here L is a positive constant that is to be *chosen by the analyst*. The larger is L, the larger is the subset $\mathscr{F}$ of $\overline{\mathbb{D}}$, and the smaller the test statistic $\tilde{W}_T$ for any given sample. The analyst may have the prior belief that the true function g is L-Lipschitzian for some value of L. Then conditional on that prior, the test that $f \in \mathscr{F}$ amounts to a test that $g \in \overline{\mathbb{D}}$, which is the simple null hypothesis that is of concern.

For any choice of L, $\mathscr{F}$ and $\mathscr{G}$ are well-defined and compact. Thus the procedure based on the statistic $\tilde{W}_T$ (4), for example, provides a consistent test of the appropriate form of (2). (Recall that γ may be estimated consistently as described in appendix 2. For simplicity we assume below that it is known. Of course, η must be known.)

The only remaining difficulty is the computation of $\tilde{W}_T$ and in particular the minimization over elements of $\mathscr{F}$. The difficulty can be overcome with the help of Afriat's (1967) non-statistical test of utility maximizing behaviour.

Afriat's Theorem 1. Consider a data set $\{x_t, q_t\}_1^T$, *where* $x_t, q_t \in R^n_+$, $\forall t$, *and* x_t *denotes consumption,* q_t *is the corresponding (unnormalized) price vector. Then the following conditions are equivalent:*

(*a*) *There exist numbers* $u_t, \lambda_t > 0$, $t = 1, \ldots, T$, *that satisfy the Afriat inequalities* $u_t \le u_\tau + \lambda_\tau q'_\tau(x_t - x_\tau)$, $t, \tau = 1, \ldots, T$.

(*b*) *There exists a utility function* u *that rationalizes the data, i.e., for all* $t = 1, \ldots, T$, *and* $x \in R^n_+$, $q'_t x \le q'_t x_t \Rightarrow u(x) \le u(x_t)$.

Afriat's Theorem and the definition of $\mathscr{F}$ suggest that we define sets of functions of the form

$$\mathscr{F}_T(q_1, \ldots, q_T, M_1, \ldots, M_T) \equiv \Big\{ f \in C[P, R^{n-1}]: \{x_t, q_t\}_1^T \text{ satisfy the Afriat inequalities for some } \lambda_t, u_t > 0, t = 1, \ldots, T, \text{ where } x_t \equiv M_t \hat{q}_t^{-1} \begin{bmatrix} f(M_t, q_t) \\ 1 - e'f(M_t, q_t) \end{bmatrix} \text{ for all } t; \text{ and } |f(p_t) - f(p_\tau)| \le L \cdot |p_t - p_\tau| \text{ for } t, \tau = 1, \ldots, T, \text{ where } p'_t \equiv (M_t, q'_t) \text{ for all } t \Big\}.$$

$\mathscr{F}$ is a proper subset of $\mathscr{F}_T$. Roughly speaking, $\mathscr{F}_T$ differs from $\mathscr{F}$ in two respects: (a) $f \in \mathscr{F}_T$ need not be L-Lipschitzian over all of P though it satisfies the appropriate inequalities on $\{p_1, \ldots, p_T\}$. (b) The Afriat inequalities imply that price and quantity points $\left\{ M_t \hat{q}_t^{-1} \begin{bmatrix} f(M_t, q_t) \\ 1 - e'f(M_t, q_t) \end{bmatrix}, q_t \right\}_1^T$ can be rationalized by a utility function u. But $M_t \hat{q}_t^{-1} \begin{bmatrix} f(M_t, q_t) \\ 1 - e'f(M_t, q_t) \end{bmatrix}$ need not be the unique utility maximizing bundle for the given income M_t and price vector q_t, and $M\hat{q}^{-1} \begin{bmatrix} f(M, q) \\ 1 - e'f(M, q) \end{bmatrix}$ need not be the utility maximizing bundle for some vector p, $p' \equiv (M, q')$, lying outside the finite data set but lying in P. In short, f need not be a share function. On the other hand, the utility function u may be approximated arbitrarily closely by a strictly concave (and smooth) utility function and its demand and share correspondences may be approximated arbitrarily closely by demand and share functions respectively. [See Mas-Colell (1974, theorems 2, 3) for precise statements and proofs.] Thus, though f is not a share function, its values on $p_1, \ldots, p_T$ can be approximated by the values of a share function.

Speaking intuitively, both problems (a) and (b) disappear asymptotically if the infinite sequence $p_1, \ldots, p_t, \ldots$ is a 'large' subset of P. But that is the case with probability 1 by an appropriate Law of Large Numbers applied to the process $(\tilde{p}_t,\ t = 1, 2, \ldots)$. This provides the intuition underlying the use of the following statistic as a basis for testing $H_0: g \in \mathscr{F}$:

$$\tilde{\chi}_T \equiv \min \sum_{t=1}^{T} \{ [\tilde{y}_t - z_t]'[\tilde{y}_t - z_t] - \eta \} / \gamma T^{1/2}, \tag{8}$$

subject to

$$u_t \geq 0, \quad \lambda_t \geq 0, \quad z_t \in R_+^{n-1}, \quad e'z_t \leq 1, \qquad t = 1, \ldots, T, \tag{9}$$

$$u_t \leq u_\tau + \lambda_\tau \tilde{q}_\tau'(\tilde{x}_t - \tilde{x}_\tau), \qquad t, \tau = 1, \ldots, T, \tag{10}$$

where

$$\tilde{x}_t \equiv \tilde{M}_t \hat{\tilde{q}}_t^{-1} \begin{bmatrix} z_t \\ 1 - e'z_t \end{bmatrix}, \quad \text{for all } t,$$

$$\sum_1^T (u_t + \lambda_t) = 1, \tag{11}$$

$$|z_t - z_\tau| \leq L |\tilde{p}_t - \tilde{p}_\tau|, \qquad t, \tau = 1, \ldots, T. \tag{12}$$

The choice variables are $\lambda_t, u_t, z_t,\ t = 1, \ldots, T$.

The minimum in (8) is to be computed for any given set of realizations for the $\tilde{p}_t$'s and $\tilde{y}_t$'s. The optimization problem is a (finite-dimensional) non-linear programming problem. It admits a 'minimum distance' interpretation analogous to that provided for (4).

There are some minor innovations in the constraints. Strict inequalities for the u_t's and λ_t's have been replaced by weak inequalities, which substitution has no empirical significance; (11) is a harmless normalization which is necessary because of the homogeneity of the Afriat inequalities (10).

Theorem 2. Maintain Assumptions 1–4 and define $\mathcal{F}$ and $\mathcal{G}$ by (6) and (7) respectively, where L is an arbitrary positive constant. Let b_α be the $(1-\alpha)\%$ critical value from a standard normal distribution. Consider a test procedure for H_0: $g \in \mathcal{F}$ against H_1: $g \in \mathcal{G} \backslash \mathcal{F}$ in which H_0 is rejected if and only if the realized value of $\tilde{X}_T$ exceeds b_α. Then this test procedure is consistent for any $g \in \mathcal{G} \backslash \mathcal{F}$ and the size of the test is no larger than α.

An advantage of the above test procedure, pointed out by Varian (1985) for his related procedure, is that the solution of the minimization in (8) generates a perturbation of the data that satisfy the Afriat inequalities. These perturbed data could be used to calculate bounds on the underlying utility function or to forecast demand behaviour as described in Varian (1982). Investigation of the statistical properties of such exercises is beyond the scope of this paper.

This may be a suitable point at which to comment on the interpretation of the error term $\tilde{\varepsilon}_t$. If it represents measurement error, then the special form of model (1) considered in this section assumes that budget shares are measured with error, while prices and income are measured precisely. This unappealing asymmetry is removed if we assume that all data are measured precisely and if we reinterpret $\tilde{\varepsilon}_t$ as an optimization error. Alternatively, $\tilde{\varepsilon}_t$ could reflect the stochastic nature of underlying preferences. H_0 asserts that the expected values of budget shares can be rationalized by an appropriate (non-stochastic) utility function. This is analogous to the random preferences specification in parametric work.

3.2. Homothetic utility

Let $\mathbb{D}_h$ denote that subset of share functions in $\mathbb{D}$ that correspond to a homothetic utility function. If $\overline{\mathbb{D}}_h$ denotes its closure, let $\mathcal{F} \equiv \{ f \in \overline{\mathbb{D}}_h$: f is L-Lipschitz$\}$. Consider the null hypothesis $g \in \mathcal{F}$ and the alternative $g \in \mathcal{G} \backslash \mathcal{F}$ where $\mathcal{G}$ is given by (7).

A consistent test can be constructed by repeating the arguments in section 3.1. The only difference is that the Afriat inequalities are not sufficient for a data set to be rationalizable by a homothetic utility function. Necessary and sufficient conditions for such a utility function to exist are provided by the non-statistical tests of Afriat (1972) and Diewert (1973).

Afriat's Theorem 2. Consider a data set $\{x_t, q_t\}_1^T$ *as in the statement of Afriat's Theorem 1. Then the following conditions are equivalent*:

(a) *There exist numbers* $u_t > 0$, $t = 1, \ldots, T$, *such that* $u_t \leq u_\tau q_\tau' x_t$, $\tau, t = 1, \ldots, T$.

(b) *There exists a homothetic utility function u such that for all* $t = 1, \ldots, T$ *and* $x \in R_+^n$, $q_t' x \leq q_t' x_t \Rightarrow u(x) \leq u(x_t)$.

This theorem implies the obvious modification in the definition of the statistic $\tilde{X}_T$. Define $\tilde{X}_T$ as the minimum value in (8) subject to the constraints (9), (12), and

$$u_t \leq u_\tau \tilde{q}_t' \tilde{x}_t, \qquad \tau, t = 1, \ldots, T, \tag{10'}$$

where

$$\tilde{x}_t \equiv \tilde{M}_\tau \hat{\tilde{q}}_t^{-1} \begin{bmatrix} z_t \\ 1 - e'z_t \end{bmatrix}, \quad \text{for all } t, \qquad \sum_1^T u_t = 1. \tag{11'}$$

The choice variables are u_t, z_t, $t = 1, \ldots, T$.

A theorem analogous to Theorem 2 is readily proven.

4. Conclusions

There is a vast literature in statistics dealing with non-parametric estimation of regression functions. The problems range from estimation of a specific conditional density (and in particular the conditional mean, conditional variance, ...) given observations from a joint distribution [e.g. Stone (1977)] to more structured estimation problem such as estimation of a spline regression function with i.i.d. residuals [e.g. Wahba (1978), Wecker and Ansley (1983)]. Collomb (1981) provides a categorized bibliography. The comments on Burguete, Gallant and Souza (1981, pp. 198, 209), in particular, point out a disadvantage of these non-parametric regression methods – the difficulty of incorporating prior information, such as the null hypothesis $g \in \mathscr{F}$ from (2) or the integrability of a system of demand functions (section 3).

In the introduction we have already referred to the work of Gallant (1981, 1982). Some insight into the relationship between the Gallant approach to hypothesis testing and the procedure described in this paper may be derived from the following unifying view. (The representation of the Gallant approach that we offer is undoubtedly inaccurate and incomplete in numerous details, but we believe that it is nonetheless faithful in spirit.[2]) Adopt the general framework of section 2, assuming η and γ known. Then the statistic (4) defines a consistent test. But in order to apply the tests, the minimizations over $f \in \mathscr{F}$ must be carried out and this is obviously a difficult task if $\mathscr{F}$ is not a finite-dimensional parametric family. To proceed it is natural to seek approximating statistics that are asymptotically equivalent to $\tilde{W}_T$. It is the nature of the approximation procedure adopted that is the fundamental difference in the two approaches.

Consider this matter in the context of the demand theory model of section 3.1. The basis of the computationally practical test described in Theorem 2 is that the minimization is carried out over $\mathscr{F}_T$ (defined following Afriat's Theorem 1) instead of $\mathscr{F}$. For each $T > 0$, $\mathscr{F}_T \supset \mathscr{F}$ but the $\mathscr{F}_T$'s converge to $\mathscr{F}$ in the sense that if $h_T \in \mathscr{F}_T$ for all T, then some subsequence of $\{h_T\}_1^\infty$ converges to an element of $\mathscr{F}$. (Adapt the arguments in the proof of Theorem 2.)

But other approximations of $\mathscr{F}$ are conceivable. For example, take a class of subsets $\mathscr{F}_T$ of $\mathscr{F}$, $T = 1, 2, \ldots$, such that $\mathscr{F}$ equals the closure of $\bigcup_1^\infty \mathscr{F}_T$; i.e., such that any $f \in \mathscr{F}$ can be approximated arbitrarily well by an element of some $\mathscr{F}_T$. These $\mathscr{F}_t$'s provide an 'inner approximation' to $\mathscr{F}$. Define $\tilde{A}_T$ by (4) except that $\mathscr{F}$ is replaced by $\mathscr{F}_T$ as the constraint set. Then $(\tilde{A}_T - \tilde{W}_T)/T^{1/2} \to 0$ a.s. and so a test based on $\tilde{A}_T$ is consistent. Moreover, if $\mathscr{F}_T$ is a parametric family (corresponding to finitely many parameters) then the computation of $\tilde{A}_T$ is manageable. This is the case in Gallant's approach where $\mathscr{F}_T$ is defined as the class of suitably truncated Fourier expansions which are also share (or demand) functions. Alternative approximations are conceivable, e.g., if $\mathscr{F}_T$ is the class of suitably truncated Taylor expansions that are also share functions, though the details have not been worked out for other approximations.

In a personal communication, Gallant has indicated that, for example in the paper by Elbadawi, Gallant and Souza (1984), the proofs could accommodate infinite-dimensional parametrizations with a priori bounds to achieve compactness, in which case the two procedures would be quite similar.

The agenda for future research is extensive. Some problems appear to be solvable relatively easily – e.g. the extension to stationary ergodic processes for $\tilde{p}_t$ and $\tilde{\varepsilon}_t$. Others appear more difficult. For example the determination of the asymptotic distribution of $\tilde{W}_T$ and more importantly the development of consistent test procedures when Σ is unknown.

[2]For example, Gallant assumes more differentiability than we do and considers norms other than $\|\cdot\|_C$. Also, the tests he considers are not based on appropriate forms of (4). But his Fourier series approach could be applied to construct such tests and it is to this application of his approach that we refer.

Appendix 1

Lemma 1. *Let* $\{x_\alpha\}_{\alpha\in A}$ *and* $\{z_\alpha\}_{\alpha\in A}$ *be two subsets of* R^l_+, *where* A *is an arbitrary index set. Then* $\mathbf{x}\equiv\inf\{x_\alpha\colon\ \alpha\in A\}$ *and* $\mathbf{z}\equiv\inf\{z_\alpha\colon\ \alpha\in A\}$ *are both finite and, for all* $a>0$,

$$|x_\alpha - z_\alpha| < a,\quad \forall\alpha\in A \quad\Rightarrow\quad |\mathbf{x}-\mathbf{z}|\le a. \tag{A.1}$$

Proof. Clearly, $\mathbf{x}\ge 0$ and $\mathbf{z}\ge 0$. If (A.1) is false, then with no loss of generality $\mathbf{x}-\mathbf{z}=a+\delta$, $\delta>0$. There exists $\beta\in \text{A}$ such that $z_\beta<\mathbf{z}+\delta/2$. Thus $x_\beta - z_\beta \ge \mathbf{x}-z_\beta\ge \mathbf{x}-\mathbf{z}-\delta/2 = a+\delta/2>a$, which contradicts the hypothesis in (A.1). Q.E.D.

Lemma 2. *Let* $(\tilde{z}_t;\ t=1,2,\dots)$ *be a stationary ergodic process defined on* $(S,\mathscr{A},\theta)$. *For each* t, *let* $\tilde{z}_t\colon S\to\Omega$, *where* Ω *is a subset of* R^k. *Let each* $\tilde{z}_t$ *have distribution* δ, *where* δ *is a measure on* $(\Omega,\mathscr{B})$ *and* $\mathscr{B}$ *is the Borel* σ*-algebra restricted to* Ω. *Let* $b\colon\ \Omega\to R^l_+$ *be a continuous function that is* δ*-integrable, i.e.,* $\int_\Omega b\,\mathrm{d}\delta<\infty$. *Finally, let* $\mathscr{F}$ *be a family of continuous functions that map* Ω *into* R^l *such that (a)* $\mathscr{F}$ *is equicontinuous on* Ω, *and (b)* $|f(w)|\le b(w)$, $\forall w\in\Omega$ *and* $\forall f\in\mathscr{F}$.

Then there exists $A\in\mathscr{A}$ *such that* $\theta(A)=0$ *and,* $\forall s\notin A$,

$$\lim_{T\to\infty}\frac{1}{T}\sum_{t=1}^{T} f(\tilde{z}_t(s)) = \int_\Omega f(w)\,\mathrm{d}\delta(w),\qquad \forall f\in\mathscr{F}, \tag{A.2}$$

and the convergence is uniform over $\mathscr{F}$.

Proof. Apply the Law of Large Numbers and Rao (1962, theorem 6.2). Alternatively, the lemma is a special case of Burguete, Gallant and Souza (1982, theorem 1). Q.E.D.

Proof of Theorem 1. Expand the quadratic form on the left side of (5) and apply Lemma 2 to each term. Deduce that $\exists A\in\mathscr{A}$ such that $\theta(A)=0$ and, $\forall s\notin A$,

$$\frac{1}{T}\sum_{t=1}^{T}[g(\tilde{p}_t(s))+\tilde{\varepsilon}_t(s)-f(\tilde{p}_t(s))]'\cdot[g(\tilde{p}_t(s))+\tilde{\varepsilon}_t(s)-f(\tilde{p}_t(s))]$$

$$\to \eta + \int_P [g(p)-f(p)]'\cdot[g(p)-f(p)]\,\mathrm{d}\mu(p), \tag{A.3}$$

and the convergence is uniform over $f\in\mathscr{F}$. (Make use of the zero mean of $\tilde{\varepsilon}_t$

and the independence of $\tilde{\varepsilon}_t$ and $\tilde{p}_t$.) Thus, $\forall \varepsilon > 0$, $\exists T_0$ such that $s \notin A$ and $T \geq T_0 \Rightarrow$ the two expressions on the opposite sides of the arrow in (A.3) differ in absolute value by less than ε, and this is true $\forall f \in \mathscr{F}$. Now apply Lemma 1. Q.E.D.

Proof of Theorem 2. Suppose $g \notin \mathscr{F}$ and define $\tilde{W}_T$ as in (4). Theorem 1 and the ensuing discussion showed that $\gamma \tilde{W}_T / T^{1/2} \to d > 0$ almost surely. We show that

$$\gamma(\tilde{W}_T - \tilde{X}_T)/T^{1/2} \to 0 \quad \text{a.s.} \tag{A.4}$$

Consistency then follows precisely as in the discussion following Theorem 1.

Let Q be a Borel subset of R^m and denote by 1_Q its indicator function. By the Law of Large Numbers,

$$\frac{1}{T}\sum_1^T 1_Q(\tilde{p}_t) \to \mu(Q) \quad \text{and} \quad \frac{1}{T}\sum_1^T \tilde{\varepsilon}_t \to 0 \quad \text{a.s.}$$

Henceforth, consider fixed realizations $(p_1, \ldots, p_t, \ldots)$ and $(\varepsilon_1, \ldots, \varepsilon_t, \ldots)$ such that

$$\frac{1}{T}\sum_1^T 1_Q(p_t) \to \mu(Q), \tag{A.5}$$

for each Q in a countable basis of open sets, and

$$\frac{1}{T}\sum_1^T \varepsilon_t \to 0. \tag{A.6}$$

The set of such realizations has probability 1.

$D \equiv \{p_1, \ldots, p_t, \ldots\}$ is a dense subset of P: If not, then $\exists p \in P$ and an open set $Q \subset R^m$, such that $p \in Q$ and $p_t \notin Q$, $\forall t$. By (A.5) this implies $\mu(Q) = 0$. But then p cannot lie in $\operatorname{supp} \mu = P$, which is a contradiction.

Consider the computed value X_T of $\tilde{X}_T$. Let $z_1^T, \ldots, z_T^T$ be minimizing values in the appropriate version of (8). The price and share data $q_1, \ldots, q_T$, $z_1^T, \ldots, z_T^T$ can be rationalized by a utility function u_T by Afriat's Theorem 1. Let ϕ_T be the share correspondence for u_T.[3] By Mas-Colell (1974, theorem 3)

[3] By the share correspondence we mean the correspondence which assigns to each price–income vector the set of all budget share vectors implied by the demand correspondence.

there exists a share function $h_T \in \mathbb{D}$ which approximates ϕ_T in such a way that

$$|h_T(p_t) - z_t^T| < T^{-1}, \qquad t = 1, \dots, T, \tag{A.7}$$

$$|h_T(p_t) - h_T(p_\tau)| \le (L + T^{-1})|p_t - p_\tau|, \quad t, \tau = 1, \dots, T. \tag{A.8}$$

Since for any fixed t, $h_T(p_t)$ is bounded as T varies, we can choose a subsequence of functions, which we again denote by $\{h_T\}_1^\infty$, such that

$$\lim_{T\to\infty} h_T(p_t) \quad \text{exists for} \quad t = 1, 2, \dots . \tag{A.9}$$

[See Royden (1963, lemma 27).]

Condition (A.8) implies that for any subsequence $\{p_{t_k}\}_{k=1}^\infty$ of $\{p_t\}_1^\infty$,

$$h_T(p_{t_k}) \underset{k\to\infty}{\rightarrow} h_T(p) \quad \text{uniformly in } T, \quad \text{if} \quad p_{t_k} \to p. \tag{A.10}$$

To see this note that $\{h_T(p_{t_k})\}_{k=1}^\infty$ is a Cauchy sequence which is uniform in T in the sense that, $\forall \delta > 0$, $\exists K$ such that for all i, $j > K$ *and for all* T,

$$|h_T(p_{t_i}) - h_T(p_{t_j})| \le (L+1)|p_{t_i} - p_{t_j}| < \delta.$$

Next show that

$$\{h_T\colon T = 1, 2, \dots\} \quad \text{is equicontinuous on } P. \tag{A.11}$$

Let $\delta > 0$ be given. For $p, \bar{p} \in P$, let $\{p_{t_k}\}_1^\infty$ and $\{\bar{p}_{t_k}\}_1^\infty$ be subsequences of $\{p_t\}_1^\infty$ that converge to p and $\bar{p}$ respectively. They exist by the denseness of $\{p_t\}_1^\infty$ in P. Then $|h_T(p) - h_T(\bar{p})| \le |h_T(p) - h_T(p_{t_k})| + |h_T(\bar{p}) - h_T(\bar{p}_{t_k})| + |h_T(p_{t_k}) - h_T(\bar{p}_{t_k})|$. By (A.10), $\exists K > 0$ such that each of the first two terms on the right side is less than $\delta/3$ for $k > K$. The last term is less than $(L+1)|p_{t_k} - \bar{p}_{t_k}|$. Thus the entire sum can be made less than δ if $|p - \bar{p}|$ is chosen sufficiently small, e.g. less than $\delta/3(L+1)$, which is independent of T. This proves (A.11).

Since $\{h_T\colon T = 1, 2, \dots\}$ is an equicontinuous family that converges pointwise on a dense subset of P, it converges pointwise to a continuous function f on all of P [Royden (1963, lemma 28)]. Indeed by the Ascoli Theorem [Royden (1963, theorem 30)] the convergence is uniform on P, i.e.,

$$\sup_{p\in P} |h_T(p) - f(p)| \to 0 \quad \text{as} \quad T \to \infty. \tag{A.12}$$

Thus f is the limit (in the $\|\cdot\|_C$ topology) of elements of $\mathbb{D}$. Moreover, (A.8), (A.12) and the denseness of $\{p_t\}_1^\infty$ imply that f is L-Lipschitzian. Thus $f \in \mathscr{F}$.

Let $y_t \equiv g(p_t) + \varepsilon_t$. By the triangle inequality

$$\left| \frac{\gamma X_T}{T^{1/2}} - \frac{1}{T}\sum_1^T \left[(y_t - f(p_t))'(y_t - f(p_t)) - \eta \right] \right|$$

$$\leq \left| \frac{1}{T}\sum_1^T (y_t - z_t^T)'(y_t - z_t^T) - \frac{1}{T}\sum_1^T (y_t - h_T(p_t))'(y_t - h_T(p_t)) \right|$$

$$+ \left| \frac{1}{T}\sum_1^T (y_t - h_T(p_t))'(y_t - h_T(p_t)) - \frac{1}{T}\sum_1^T (y_t - f(p_t))'(y_t - f(p_t)) \right|.$$

The first expression on the right-hand side of the inequality becomes small as T grows because of (A.6) and (A.7). The second terms shrinks because of (A.6) and (A.12). Thus $\forall \delta > 0$, $\exists T_0$ such that

$$T > T_0 \Rightarrow \frac{\gamma X_T}{T^{1/2}} > \frac{1}{T}\sum_1^T (y_t - f(p_t))'(y_t - f(p_t)) - \eta - \delta \geq \frac{\gamma W_T}{T^{1/2}} - \delta.$$

On the other hand, $X_T \leq W_T$, since $\mathscr{F} \subset \mathscr{F}_T$, the set defined in the text. It follows that $\lim \gamma W_T / T^{1/2} \geq \lim \gamma X_T / T^{1/2} \geq \lim \gamma W_T / T^{1/2} - \delta$, $\forall \delta > 0$, which proves (A.4). [That $\lim \gamma W_T / T^{1/2}$ exists can be assumed with no loss of generality because of (5).]

Finally, note that $X_T \leq W_T \Rightarrow \text{prob}(\tilde{X}_T \geq b_\alpha) \leq \text{prob}(\tilde{W}_T \geq b_\alpha) \leq \alpha$, if $g \in \mathscr{F}$. Q.E.D.

Appendix 2

We show that γ from (3) can be estimated consistently if it is maintained that the true regression function g lies in $\mathscr{G}$. In that case the tests described in the text can be implemented if only $\eta = \mathrm{E}(\tilde{\varepsilon}_t' \tilde{\varepsilon}_t)$ is known by the analyst.

In fact, consistent estimators for both γ and η are provided by the following adaptation of Theorem 1:

Corollary. Let $g \in \mathscr{G}$. Then there exists $A \subset S$, $A \in \mathscr{A}$, such that $\theta(A) = 0$ and, $\forall s \in S \setminus A$,

$$\lim_{T \to \infty} \min_{f \in \mathscr{G}} \frac{1}{T} \sum_{t=1}^T [\tilde{y}_t(s) - f(\tilde{p}_t(s))]'[\tilde{y}_t(s) - f(\tilde{p}_t(s))] = \eta, \quad \text{(A.13)}$$

and

$$\lim_{T\to\infty}\min_{f\in\mathscr{G}}\frac{1}{T}\sum_{t=1}^{T}\left[[\tilde{y}_t(s)-f(\tilde{p}_t(s))]'[\tilde{y}_t(s)-f(\tilde{p}_t(s))]\right]^2=\gamma^2+\eta^2, \tag{A.14}$$

where

$$\eta=\mathrm{E}(\tilde{\varepsilon}_t'\tilde{\varepsilon}_t),\qquad \gamma^2=\mathrm{var}(\tilde{\varepsilon}_t'\tilde{\varepsilon}_t).$$

Note that the minimization problems in (A.13) and (A.14) are over the set $\mathscr{G}$, whereas the minimization problem in (5) is over the set $\mathscr{F}$.

Theorem 3. Redefine the statistic in (4) so that γ is replaced by the estimator contained in the corollary. Then the statistic is measurable and the corresponding test of (2) has size no greater than α and is consistent against any alternative $g\in\mathscr{G}\backslash\mathscr{F}$.

Proof. First prove that $\tilde{W}_T$ defined in (4) is measurable: Fix $T>0$ and define a real valued map ϕ that takes a vector $(y_1,\dots,y_T;\,p_1,\dots,p_T;\,b;\,c;\,f)$ into $\sum_{t=1}^{T}[(y_t-f(p_t))'(y_t-f(p_t))-b]/cT^{1/2}$. The domain is such that $(y_1,\dots,y_T)\in R^T$, $(p_1,\dots,p_T)\in P^T$, $b,c>0$, and f lies in $\mathscr{F}$. Topologizie the domain with the product topology. Then ϕ is continuous. Define β, on the obvious domain, by

$$\beta(y_1,\dots,y_T;\,p_1,\dots,p_T;\,b;\,c)$$
$$\equiv\min_{f\in\mathscr{F}}\phi(y_1,\dots,y_T;\,p_1,\dots,p_T;\,b;\,c;\,f).$$

By the Maximum Theorem [Berge (1963, theorems 1–2)] β is continuous. Thus $\tilde{W}_T=\beta(\tilde{y}_1,\dots,\tilde{y}_T;\,\tilde{p}_1,\dots,\tilde{p}_T;\,\eta;\,\gamma)$ is measurable. Similarly, we can show that the estimator of γ defined in (A.13) and (A.14) is measurable. Thus the statistic described in the statement of the theorem is also measurable.

Consistency of the test was demonstrated in the text. Q.E.D.

It remains to show that (A.13) and (A.14) can be replaced by appropriate finite-dimensional optimization problems without affecting the above results. This is accomplished for sets $\mathscr{G}$ that have the form

$$\mathscr{G}=\{f\in C[P,R^n]:\,|f(p)|\le B\text{ and }|f(p)-f(p_0)|\le L|p-p_0|$$
$$\text{for all }p\text{ and }p_0\text{ in }P\}, \tag{A.15}$$

for some positive constants B and L. Such sets are clearly compact, as the uniform Lipschitz property is stronger than equicontinuity.

Consider the following alternative estimators for η and γ:

$$\tilde{\eta}_T \equiv \min_{z_1,\ldots,z_T} \frac{1}{T}\sum_{t=1}^{T}(\tilde{y}_t - z_t)'(\tilde{y}_t - z_t), \tag{A.16}$$

subject to

$$z_t \in R^n \quad \text{and} \quad |z_t| \le B, t = 1,\ldots,T \tag{A.17}$$

$$|z_t - z_\tau| \le L|\tilde{p}_t - \tilde{p}_\tau|, \qquad t,\tau = 1,\ldots,T, \tag{A.18}$$

$$(\tilde{\gamma}_T)^2 \equiv \min_{z_1,\ldots,z_T}\left\{\frac{1}{T}\sum_{t=1}^{T}[(\tilde{y}_t - z_t)'(\tilde{y}_t - z_t)]^2 \right.$$

$$\left. \text{subject to} \quad (\text{A.17})\text{–}(\text{A.18})\} - (\tilde{\eta}_T)^2\right\}. \tag{A.19}$$

The usefulness of these estimators stems from their computational tractability (in principle) and from the following theorem which concludes this appendix.

Theorem 4. Suppose $\mathcal{G}$ satisfies (A.15) and that the true function $g \in \mathcal{G}$. Then the estimators $\tilde{\eta}_T$ and $\tilde{\gamma}_T$ are measurable and converge almost surely to η and γ respectively. Moreover, if $\tilde{\gamma}_T$ is substituted for γ in (4), then the appropriate form of Theorem 3 is valid.

Proof of Theorem 4. We prove the consistency of the estimator for η. Similar arguments may be provided for γ and the proof of the remaining assertions is straightforward.

Denote by $\tilde{\alpha}_T$ the minimum value in (A.13) for each fixed T. Consider fixed realizations $(p_1,\ldots,p_t,\ldots)$ and $(\varepsilon_1,\ldots,\varepsilon_t,\ldots)$ that satisfy the conditions described in the proof of Theorem 2. Denote by α_T and η_T the corresponding realizations of $\tilde{\alpha}_T$ and $\tilde{\eta}_T$ respectively, $T = 1,2,\ldots$, and let $z_1^T,\ldots,z_T^T$ be a set of minimizing values in (A.16). Then there exists $h_T \in C[P, R^n]$ such that

$$h_T(p_t) = z_t^T, \qquad t = 1,\ldots,T,$$

$$|h_T(p)| \le B, \qquad \forall p \in P.$$

Argue precisely as in the proof of Theorem 2, exploiting (A.18) heavily, that a subsequence of h_T converges in the $\|\cdot\|_C$ topology to an element of $\mathscr{G}$, and subsequently that

$$\overline{\lim}\, \eta_T \geq \overline{\lim}\, \alpha_T.$$

But for each $T, \alpha_T \geq \eta_T$ because $f \in \mathscr{G} \Rightarrow (f(p_1), \ldots, f(p_T))$ satisfies the constraints (A.17)–(A.18). Thus $\overline{\lim}\, \eta_T = \overline{\lim}\, \alpha_T = \eta$. Moreover, this argument can be repeated for any subsequence $(\eta_{T_k})_{k=1}^{\infty}$ of $(\eta_T)_1^{\infty}$. Thus $\lim \eta_T = \eta$. (Please see the proof of the related result in Theorem 2 for more detailed arguments.) Q.E.D.

References

Afriat, S., 1967, The construction of a utility function from expenditure data, International Economic Review 8, 67–77.

Afriat, S., 1972a, The theory of international comparison of real income and prices, in: D.J. Daly, ed., International comparisons of prices and output (National Bureau of Economic Research, New York).

Afriat, S., 1972b, Efficiency estimates of production functions, International Economic Review 13, 568–598.

Afriat, S., 1973, On a system of inequalities in demand analysis: An extension of the classical method, International Economic Review 14, 460–472.

Berge, C., 1963, Topological spaces (Oliver and Boyd, London).

Burguete, J., R. Gallant and G. Souza, 1982, On unification of the asymptotic theory of nonlinear econometric models, Econometric Reviews 1, 151–211 (including comments).

Collomb, G., 1981, Estimation non-parametrique de la regression: Revue bibliographique, International Statistical Review 49, 75–93.

Diewert, E.W., 1973, Afriat and revealed preference theory, Review of Economic Studies 40, 419–426.

Diewert, E.W. and C. Parkan, 1978, Tests for the consistency of consumer data and nonparametric index numbers, Discussion paper 78-27 (University of British Columbia, Vancouver).

Diewert, E.W. and C. Parkan, 1979, Linear programming tests of regularity conditions for production functions, Discussion paper 79-01 (University of British Columbia, Vancouver).

Diewert, E.W. and C. Parkan, 1982, Tests for the consistency of consumer data, IP-310 (University of California, Berkeley, CA).

Elbadawi, Ibrahim, A. Ronald Gallant and Geraldo Souza, 1983, An elasticity can be estimated consistently without a priori knowledge of functional form, Econometrica 51, 1731–1751.

Gallant, A.R., 1981, On the bias in flexible functional forms and an essentially unbiased form: The Fourier flexible form, Journal of Econometrics 15, 211–245.

Gallant, A.R., 1982, Unbiased determination of production technologies, Journal of Econometrics 20, 285–323.

Hanoch, G. and M. Rothschild, 1972, Testing the assumptions of production theory: A nonparametric approach, Journal of Political Economy 80, 256–275.

Kelley, J.L., 1955, General topology (Van Nostrand, Princeton, NJ).

Mas-Colell, A., 1974, Continuous and smooth consumers: Approximation theorems, Journal of Economic Theory 8, 305–336.

Rango Rao, R., 1962, Relations between weak and uniform convergence of measures with applications, Annals of Mathematical Statistics 33, 659–680.

Royden, H.L., 1963, Real analysis (Macmillan, New York).

Stone, C., 1977, Consistent nonparametric regression, Annals of Statistics 5, 595–645.

Varian, H., 1981, Nonparametric tests of models of investor behavior, CREST working paper C-33 (University of Michigan, Ann Arbor, MI).

Varian, H., 1982, The nonparametric approach to demand analysis, Econometrica 50, 945–973.

Varian, H., 1983, Nonparametric tests of consumer behavior, Review of Economic Studies 50, 99–110.
Varian, H., 1984, The nonparametric approach to production analysis, Econometrica 52, 579–598.
Varian, H., 1985, Non-parametric analysis of optimizing behaviour with measurement error, Journal of Econometrics, this volume.
Wahba, Grace, 1978, Improper priors, spline smoothing and the problem of guarding against model errors in regression, Journal of the Royal Statistical Society B 40, 364–372.
Wecker, William E. and Craig F. Ansley, 1983, The signal extraction approach to nonlinear regression and spline smoothing, Journal of the American Statistical Association 78, 81–89.

EXPLICITLY INFINITE-DIMENSIONAL BAYESIAN ANALYSIS OF PRODUCTION TECHNOLOGIES*

A. Ronald GALLANT and John F. MONAHAN

North Carolina State University, Raleigh, NC 27695-8203, USA

The firm's cost function is viewed as a point in a function space and data is viewed as following some probability law that has as its parameters various functionals evaluated at the firm's cost function. The Fourier flexible form is used to represent a cost function as an infinite-dimensional vector whose elements are the parameters of the Fourier form. This representation is used to assign a prior distribution to the function space. A procedure for numerical computation of the posterior distribution of an elasticity of substitution is set forth. The ideas are illustrated with an example.

1. Summary

In much empirical economic research the underlying economic theory is adequate to label one vector-valued variable y as endogenous, another x as exogenous, and to impose certain qualitative features such as linear homogeneity on a function $g(x)$ relating the two, but the theory is not adequate to assign a particular parametric form to the function $g(x)$. Viewed in the abstract, the theory asserts that the law $g(x)$ governing the behavior of y is a point in a function space $\mathscr{G}$ that is restricted to some extent. Taking into account the stochastic nature of observational data, such an assertion can be viewed as a statement that an observed y_t is distributed according to some probability law with density $p(y|\mu_t)$ whose parameter vector μ_t has components that can be viewed as functionals defined over $\mathscr{G}$, $\mu_t = \mathscr{E}y_t = g(x_t)$ for instance. Write, then, $\mu_t = \mu_t(g)$. Usually the study of data that follow the law $p(y|\mu_t)$ is undertaken to estimate the value σ of some functional $\sigma(g)$ defined over $\mathscr{G}$ or to test a hypothesis of the form H: $g \in \mathscr{G}^\circ$ against A: $g \in \mathscr{G} \sim \mathscr{G}^\circ$.

As an instance of this situation, the neoclassical theory of the firm asserts that the observed vector of log cost and factor cost shares y of a firm operating in competitive product and factor markets should follow a distribution with

*This research was supported in part by North Carolina Agricultural Experiment Station Project NC03641 and National Science Foundation Grant SES8207362. The paper has benefited from comments received from Christopher A. Sims, Peter E. Rossi, and participants of the 29th NBER-NSF Seminar on Bayesian Inference in Econometrics at Rutgers University.

location parameter

$$\mu_t = \begin{pmatrix} g(l_t, v_t) \\ (\partial/\partial l)g(l_t, v_t) \end{pmatrix} = \begin{pmatrix} g(x_t) \\ \nabla g(x_t) \end{pmatrix},$$

where $x' = (l', v)$, l is a vector containing logarithms of factor prices as elements, and v is the logarithm of output (Shepard's lemma). The focus of interest in an econometric analysis of data that can be expected to follow this probability law might be the estimation of an elasticity of substitution, an elasticity of substitution being an element $\sigma(g)$ of the matrix

$$\Sigma(g) = [\mathrm{diag}(\nabla g)]^{-1}[\nabla^2 g + \nabla g \nabla' g - \mathrm{diag}(\nabla g)][\mathrm{diag}(\nabla g)]^{-1}.$$

Alternatively, one may wish to test the claim that the production technology is homothetic, this being an assertion that $g(l, v)$ is of the form $h(v) + g(l)$.

To avoid vague generalities, we shall consider the specific problem just described although it is clear that the ideas have broader applicability. From the sampling theoretic point of view, dealing with the problem at the stated level of generality is extraordinarily difficult. One can construct consistent estimators of σ [Elbadawi, Gallant and Souza (1983)] and even construct asymptotically level α tests of, say, homotheticity [Gallant (1982)]. But finding a method for setting a sampling theoretic confidence interval on σ at the stated level of generality seems almost beyond reach.

In contrast, finding a confidence interval for an elasticity of substitution σ is straightforward from the Bayesian point of view. One simply sets a prior measure $P(g)$ on the function space $\mathscr{G}$, and computes the posterior distribution of σ given the data, viz.,

$$F(\sigma|y) = p^{-1}(y) \int_{\mathscr{G}} I_{(-\infty,\sigma]}[\sigma(g)]\, p[y|\mu(g)]\, \mathrm{d}P(g),$$

where

$$p[y|\mu(g)] = \prod_{t=1}^{n} p[y_t|\mu_t(g)] \quad \text{(likelihood)},$$

$$p(y) = \int_{\mathscr{G}} p[y|\mu(g)]\, \mathrm{d}P(g),$$

$$\begin{aligned} I_A(\sigma) &= 1, \qquad \sigma \in A, \\ &= 0, \qquad \sigma \notin A. \end{aligned}$$

One uses this posterior distribution in the standard way and computes the posterior probability that σ is between a and b using $F(b|y) - F(a|y)$.

Conceptually a Bayesian analysis is straightforward but there are two practical difficulties. The first is putting a reasonable prior distribution $P(g)$ on a function space $\mathscr{G}$, and the second is computing an integral such as $\int_{\mathscr{G}} p[y|\mu(g)]\,\mathrm{d}P(g)$. This paper is an exploration of these issues.

In order to put a prior measure on the class $\mathscr{G}$ of admissible cost functions we associate to each g in $\mathscr{G}$ an infinite-dimensional vector θ whose elements θ_j for $j = 0, 1, 2, \ldots$ are the coefficients of the Fourier flexible form as set forth in Gallant (1982). The natural norm for this setting associates to each coefficient θ_j a weight α_j for $j = 0, 1, 2, \ldots$, and we take the coefficients θ_j as independently distributed each having the double exponential (Laplace) distribution with density

$$p_j(\theta_j) = \tfrac{1}{2}\alpha_j^r \exp(-\alpha_j^r|\theta_j|),$$

for some $r \geqq m + (N+1)$, where N is the number of factor inputs and m is the largest order of partial derivative that g is presumed to possess *a priori*.

Sims (1971) shows that any Borel measure on a space such as that just described must put mass one on a meagre set; a meagre set is the countable union of nowhere-dense sets. He then argues that meagre sets should be regarded as small and their complement large, but this to some extent must be regarded as a matter of opinion for reasons that Sims himself sets forth. In the present context this means that we assign *a priori* mass one to a set $\mathscr{G}_r$ of functions $g(x)$ that possess all partial derivatives to the order $r-1$ but not higher orders. We can easily assign mass to the countable union of such $\mathscr{G}_r$, but we cannot assign mass to the collection $\mathscr{G}_\infty$ of functions $g(x)$ that are infinitely many times differentiable. $\mathscr{G}_\infty$ is the set of functions that we cannot reach according to Sims' theorem. In the paper we argue that this is not a serious difficulty with our approach because we are not interested in g itself but only in some functional $\sigma(g)$. We do assign positive *a priori* mass to the set $\{g: a < \sigma(g) \leqq b\}$ for any choice $a < b$ and we do obtain a consistent estimate of $\sigma(g)$.

The second issue is that of computing $F(\sigma|y)$ numerically. Our approach is to consider a related problem obtained by substituting a prior distribution that puts *a priori* mass one on those vectors θ having zeroes past some truncation point p_K and assigns mass to the leading components $\theta_0, \theta_1, \ldots, \theta_{p_K}$ of θ according to the double exponential prior just described; that is, prior mass is put on vectors of the form

$$\theta = (\theta_0, \theta_1, \ldots, \theta_{p_K}, 0, 0, \ldots).$$

This is a finite-dimensional problem and the posterior distribution $F_K(\sigma|y)$ for the finite-dimensional problem can be computed. We show that

$$\lim_{K\to\infty} \sup_{-\infty<\sigma<\infty} |F_K(\sigma|y) - F(\sigma|y)| = 0,$$

which justifies the use of $F_K(\sigma|y)$ to approximate $F(\sigma|y)$. It is important to realize that this is a numerical approximation, not a statistical approximation, and that we have in no way abandoned our goal of a formal Bayesian analysis on an infinite-dimensional parameter space.

We then apply these ideas to data on capital (K), labor (L), energy (E), and material (M) factor usage in U.S. manufacturing for the years 1947 to 1971 as reported by Berndt and Wood (1975) and Berndt and Khaled (1979). In the example we departed from the previous discussion somewhat in that we used an improper uniform prior on $(-\infty,\infty)$ for θ_j that correspond to constant or linear terms in the Fourier flexible form expansion of $g(x)$, and we used a double exponential prior of the form

$$p_j(\theta_j) = \tfrac{1}{2} s^r \alpha_j^r \exp(-s^r \alpha_j^r |\theta_j|),$$

for some positive scaling factor s on the remaining components of θ. $F_K(\sigma|y)$ was computed using straightforward Monte Carlo integration. We found that as the scaling factor s decreased, the results became more similar to the finite-dimensional sampling theoretic confidence statements reported in Gallant and Golub (1984) and thus more credible in our opinion. We also found that computational cost increased dramatically as s decreased. This was due to the fact that the probability of hitting a point g where the value of the likelihood $p[y|\mu(g)]$ is non-negligible with a random number generator decreases as the scale factor s decreases. We attempted to reduce computational costs by using importance sampling but the approach failed because we were unable to devise a scheme with sufficiently stable weights. But we continue to pursue this line of attack because integration using importance sampling has much theoretical support.

In summary, we feel that the notion of formal Bayesian analysis on an infinite-dimensional space has much appeal due to its conceptual simplicity but that the approach awaits faster, cheaper machines or an innovation in numerical analysis before the ideas can have widespread applicability.

2. Representation of the cost function

The idea behind our approach is to use the theory of the firm to describe the class of admissible cost functions and then put an *a priori* distribution on this class. The rest follows as a matter of course from the Bayesian methodology. To facilitate this process we shall derive a characterization of an admissible cost function as an infinite-dimensional vector θ with real-valued components. The components of the vector θ are interpretable which is an aid in formulating a prior distribution.

The producer's cost function $c(p,u)$ gives the minimum cost of producing output u during a given period of time using inputs $q=(q_1,q_2,\dots,q_N)'$ at prices $p=(p_1,p_2,\dots,p_N)'$. It is more convenient to work in terms of log cost as a function of log prices and log output. Accordingly, let

$$l_i = \ln p_i + \ln a_i, \qquad i=1,2,\dots,N,$$

$$v = \lambda_{N+1}(\ln u + \ln a_{N+1}),$$

and put

$$g(l,v) = \ln c\left[(1/a_1)\exp(l_1),\dots,(1/a_N)\exp(l_N),\right.$$
$$\left.(1/a_{N+1})\exp(v/\lambda_{N+1})\right],$$

where $l=(l_1,l_2,\dots,l_N)'$. At times we shall write $g(x)$ for $g(l,v)$ with $x'=(l',v)$.

The scaling factors $a_1,\dots,a_{N+1},\lambda_{N+1}$ are chosen for manipulative convenience as described in Gallant (1982). Their choice has no substantive impact since the choice of $a_i>0$, $i=1,2,\dots,N$, only amounts to a choice of units in which quantities are to be measured and such a choice is irrelevant as long as measured cost shares remain invariant; the choice of $\lambda_{N+1}>0$ and $a_{N+1}>0$ amounts to a choice of a scale of measurement for output and is also irrelevant to the substance of the discussion.

The cost function itself is assumed to possess the properties of linear homogeneity, monotonicity, and concavity. Letting $\boldsymbol{1}$ denote a vector whose entries are all ones, letting $\nabla g = (\partial/\partial l)g(l,v)$, and letting $\nabla^2 g = (\partial^2/\partial l\partial l')g(l,v)$, the equivalent conditions on the log cost function $g(l,v)$ are [Gallant (1982)]

Linear homogeneity: $g(l+\tau\boldsymbol{1},v)=\tau+g(l,v)$,

Monotonicity: $\nabla g>0,\quad \boldsymbol{1}'\nabla g=0,\quad (\partial/\partial v)g(l,v)>0$,

Concavity: $\nabla^2 g+\nabla g\nabla' g-\operatorname{diag}(\nabla g)$ is a negative semi-definite matrix of rank $N-1$ with $\boldsymbol{1}$ being the eigenvector of zero root.

Letting $s=(p_1q_1,p_2q_2,\dots,p_Nq_N)/(\sum_{i=1}^N p_iq_i)$ be the N-vector of input cost shares, the firms factor demand system is given by Shepard's lemma as

$$s = (\partial/\partial l)g(l, v),$$

elasticities of substitution σ_{ij} are elements of the matrix

$$\Sigma = [\mathrm{diag}(\nabla g)]^{-1}[\nabla^2 g + \nabla g \nabla' g - \mathrm{diag}(\nabla g)][\mathrm{diag}(\nabla g)]^{-1},$$

and price elasticities η_{ij} are elements of the matrix

$$\eta = \Sigma\, \mathrm{diag}(\nabla g),$$

where the rows of η correspond to inputs and the columns to prices [Gallant (1982)].

We seek a means to represent the function $g(l, v)$ as an infinite-dimensional vector θ with real-valued components. Notice that a series expansion,

$$g(l, v) = \sum_{i=0}^{\infty} \theta_i \varphi_i(l, v),$$

is not enough because of the need to recover the demand system and the price and substitution elasticity matrices from θ. If we had

$$\nabla g(l, v) = \sum_{i=0}^{\infty} \theta_i \nabla\varphi_i(l, v) \quad \text{and} \quad \nabla^2 g(l, v) = \sum_{i=0}^{\infty} \theta_i \nabla^2\varphi_i(l, v),$$

in addition to

$$g(l, v) = \sum_{i=0}^{\infty} \theta_i \varphi_i(l, v),$$

then the vector

$$\theta' = (\theta_1, \theta_2, \dots)$$

would suffice for our purpose. Knowing θ we could recover the cost function, the factor demand system, and the elasticity matrices. It would also be helpful if features of $g(l, v)$ such as linear homogeneity, monotonicity, concavity, homotheticity, constant returns, degree of differentiability, etc. corresponded to recognizable restrictions on θ.

Before going further, it is best to make the sense of the approximation of $g(l, v)$ by a series expansion precise. Recalling that $x' = (l', v)$, define

$$\mathrm{D}^{\lambda} g(x) = \frac{\partial^{|\lambda|}}{\partial x_1^{\lambda_1} \partial x_2^{\lambda_2} \cdots \partial x_{N+1}^{\lambda_{N+1}}} g(x),$$

where $\lambda = (\lambda_1, \lambda_2, \ldots, \lambda_{N+1})$ has non-negative integers as components and $|\lambda| = \sum_{i=1}^{N+1} |\lambda_i|$ is the order of the partial derivative; when λ is the zero vector take $\mathrm{D}^0 g(x) = g(x)$. We shall restrict attention to some rectangle $\mathscr{X}$ in $\mathbb{R}^{N+1}$ that contains the data; we shall not attempt to approximate $g(x)$ off $\mathscr{X}$. Let $\mu(x)$ be a continuous distribution function with bounded density function giving the relative frequency with which values of the independent variable x_t occur as sample size tends to infinity [Malinvaud (1970), Gallant and Holly (1980)]. With this notation we can define a norm:

Sobolev Norm. For p with $1 \leqq p < \infty$ the Sobolev norm of $g(x)$ with respect to the probability distribution μ is

$$\|g\|_{m,p,u} = \left[\sum_{|\lambda| \leqq m} \int_{\mathscr{X}} |\mathrm{D}^\lambda g(x)|^p \, \mathrm{d}\mu(x) \right]^{1/p}.$$

For $p = \infty$ the norm is

$$\|g\|_{m,\infty,\mu} = \sum_{|\lambda| \leqq m} \sup_{x \in \mathscr{X}} |\mathrm{D}^\lambda g(x)|. \quad \square$$

The sense of the representation of $g(x)$ by the series expansion θ is that

$$\lim_{I \to \infty} \|g(x) - \sum_{i=0}^{I} \theta_i \varphi_i(x)\|_{m,p,\mu} = 0,$$

where m, p, μ will be chosen as the occasion demands it, but we shall assume throughout that the representation holds at least for $m = 3$, $p = \infty$. By the Sobolev imbedding theorem, if the representation holds for $p = \infty$, then it holds for any p with $1 \leqq p < \infty$.

It remains to choose the basis functions $\phi_j(x)$. There are several choices of basis functions to use in a series expansion – splines, polynomials, trigonometric polynomials, etc. Of these the trigonometric polynomials (Fourier series) offer considerable manipulative advantages [Gallant (1982)] and there are a wealth of detailed results available on rates of convergence, rates of growth, etc. [Edmunds and Moscatelli (1977)]. A Fourier series with an appended linear and quadratic term to improve the accuracy of low-order expansions [Gallant (1984)] is written as

$$g_K(x|\theta) = u_0 + b'x + \tfrac{1}{2} x'Cx + 2 \sum_{|k| < K} u_k \cos(\lambda k'x) - v_k \sin(\lambda k'x),$$

where k is a multi-index (an $N+1$ vector whose elements are integers) and, recall, $|k| = \sum_{i=1}^{N+1} |k_i|$; λ is a scaling factor chosen so that the rectangle $\lambda\mathscr{X}$ has no edge longer than 2π [see Gallant (1982)]. To have a compact notation, write

$$g_K(x|\theta) = \sum_{j=0}^{p_K} \theta_j \phi_j(x)$$

for a truncated series of degree K, and write

$$g_\infty(x|\theta) = \sum_{j=0}^{\infty} \theta_j \phi_j(x)$$

for the infinite expansion. The parameters θ_j represent u_0, the b_i, the c_{ij}, the u_k, and the v_k written down in some order so that $|k|$ is increasing; exactly what order need not concern us save that $u_0, b_1, \ldots, b_{N+1}, c_{11}, \ldots, c_{N+1,N+1}$ are the leading elements of θ. The $\phi_j(x)$ represent the constant 1, the linear terms x_i, the quadratic terms $x_i x_j$ and the sine/cosine terms $2\cos(\lambda k'x)$ and $2\sin(\lambda k'x)$ written down in an order to correspond to the θ_j. We also associate to $\phi_j(x)$ a sequence $\{\alpha_j\}$ with $\alpha_j = \lambda$ for a constant, linear or quadratic term, and with

$$\alpha_j = \lambda|k|$$

for a term of the form $\cos(\lambda k'x)$ or $\sin(\lambda k'x)$. We shall make repeated use of the following facts regarding $\{\alpha_j\}$.

Let $a_j \approx b_j$ mean that there exist two positive constants c_1 and c_2, with $c_1 a_j \leqq b_j \leqq c_2 a_j$ for large enough j. We have from Edmunds and Moscatelli (1977, p. 11) that

$$p_K \approx K^{N+1},$$

and from Mood and Graybill (1963, p. 30) that

$$\sum_{j=0}^{p_K} (\alpha_j)^m \approx 2^{N+1}\lambda^m \sum_{i=0}^{K} \binom{N+i}{i} (i)^m.$$

Using Stirling's formula,

$$\sum_{j=0}^{p_K} (\alpha_j)^m \approx \lambda^m \sum_{i=0}^{K} (i)^{N+m}.$$

Observe that if $\sum_{j=0}^{\infty} |\theta_j| |\alpha_j|^m < \infty$ and $|\beta| \leqq m$, then

$$\limsup_{K\to\infty} \sup_{\mathscr{X}} \left| \sum_{j=0}^{p_K} \theta_j D^\beta \phi_j(x) \right| < \infty,$$

because

$$\left|\sum_{j=0}^{p_K}\theta_j \mathrm{D}^\beta\phi_j(x)\right| \leqq \text{const.} + 2\sum_{|k|\leqq K}|u_k\mathrm{D}^\beta\cos(\lambda k'x)| + |v_k\mathrm{D}^\beta\sin(\lambda k'x)|$$

$$\leqq \text{const.} + 2\sum_{|k|\leqq K}[\,|u_k| + |v_k|\,]\,|\lambda|^{|\beta|}\left[\sum_{i=1}^{N+1}k_i^{\beta_i}\right]$$

$$\leqq \text{const.} + 2\sum_{|k|\leqq K}[\,|u_k| + |v_k|\,]\,|\lambda|^{|\beta|}|k|^{|\beta|}$$

$$= \text{const.} + \sum_{j=\text{const.}}^{p_K}|\theta_j|\,|\alpha_j|^{|\beta|}$$

$$\leq \text{const.} + \sum_{j=\text{const.}}^{p_K}|\theta_j|\,|\alpha_j|^{m}.$$

Define

$$\|\theta\|_{m,\infty,\mu} = \sum_{j=0}^{\infty}|\theta_j|\,|\alpha_j|^m.$$

From the foregoing we have that

$$\lim_{r\to\infty}\|\theta - \theta_r\|_{m,\infty,\mu} = 0$$

implies

$$\lim_{r\to\infty}\|g_\infty(\cdot|\theta) - g_\infty(\cdot|\theta_r)\|_{m,\infty,\mu} = 0.$$

Restrictions on θ such that $g_K(x|\theta)$ or $g_\infty(x|\theta)$ exhibit linear homogeneity, constant returns, homotheticity, etc. are given in Gallant (1982). A discussion of curvature restrictions is found in Gallant and Golub (1984).

3. Bayesian methodology and a justification of the computational procedure

The observed dependent variable is y_t containing log cost as its first element and factor cost shares as the remaining elements. The independent variable is $x_t' = (l_t', v_t)$ containing log factor prices and log output as defined earlier. For $t = 1, 2, \ldots, n$ the observed y_t are assumed to be independently distributed, each with density $p(y_t|\mu_t, \Sigma)$. The location parameter μ_t is a vector of evaluation functionals which, according to the previous section, is given by

$$\mu_t = \mu_t(g) = \begin{pmatrix} g(x_t) \\ \nabla g(x_t) \end{pmatrix}.$$

Equivalently, we can write

$$\mu_t = \mu_t(\theta) = \sum_{j=0}^{\infty} \theta_j \begin{pmatrix} \phi(x_t) \\ \nabla \phi(x_t) \end{pmatrix},$$

which, observe, is linear in θ. Following Rossi (1983), the most plausible assumption is that factor shares follow the logistic normal distribution with location parameter $\nabla g(x_t)$, but to be able to compare our results with Gallant (1982) and to preserve the linearity in θ we shall take $p(y_t|\mu_t, \Sigma)$ to be the multivariate normal distribution with mean μ_t and variance–covariance matrix Σ. To avoid having a singular normal distribution, assume hereafter that y_t contains log cost as its first element and the first $N-1$ factor cost shares as the remaining elements. Thus y_t is an N-vector, μ_t is an N-vector, and Σ is N by N. Stack the y_t into a vector y and the μ_t into a vector μ, whence y is distributed as the multivariate normal with mean vector μ and variance–covariance matrix $I \otimes \Sigma$. Write $p(y|\mu, I \otimes \Sigma)$ for the density or, since μ can be computed from knowledge of θ alone, write $p(y|\theta, I \otimes \Sigma)$.

We shall take the prior distribution to be of the form

$$\mathrm{d}P(\Sigma) \times \mathrm{d}P(\theta),$$

where, recall, $P(\theta)$ is a distribution on $\mathbb{R}^\infty$. This is justified on the grounds that the prior information on the cost function is independent of the observational context, namely Σ. This form also avoids other difficulties for which see Zellner (1971, p. 238ff). Our specific choices are the inverted Wishart as the distribution $P(\Sigma)$ with density proportional to $|\Sigma|^{-\nu/2}\exp(-\frac{1}{2}\operatorname{tr}\Sigma^{-1}G)$ and, for $P(\theta)$, $\{\theta_j\}$ is taken as a sequence of independent, doubly exponentially distributed random variables with each coordinate having the density

$$p_j(\theta_j) = \tfrac{1}{2}\alpha_j^r \exp(-\alpha_j^r|\theta_j|);$$

the α_j are the weights defined earlier. Later we shall show that this prior puts probability one on

$$\Theta = \left\{ \theta\colon \sum_{j=0}^{\infty} |\theta_j| |\alpha_j|^{\beta} < \infty \right\},$$

for all $\beta < r-(N+1)$. We shall assume throughout that r is chosen large enough so that $m < r-(N+1)$.

Our objective is to find the posterior density of some evaluation functional $\sigma(g)$ such as a typical element of the substitution matrix

$$[\operatorname{diag}(\nabla g)]^{-1}[\nabla^2 g + \nabla g \nabla' g - \operatorname{diag}(\nabla g)][\operatorname{diag}(\nabla g)]^{-1},$$

evaluated at some price/output point x° in $\mathscr{X}$. Other choices of $\sigma(g)$ might be a predicted factor cost share at some price/output point or a price elasticity. Now $\sigma(g)$ can be computed from knowledge of θ alone so we can equally as well write $\sigma(\theta)$. Letting $I_A(z)=1$ if $z \in A$ and $I_A(z)=0$ if $z \notin A$, the posterior distribution function of σ given y is defined as

$$F(\sigma|y) = p^{-1}(y) \int_{\Theta} \int_{\mathscr{S}} I_{[-\infty,\sigma)}[\sigma(\theta)]\, p(y|\theta, I \otimes \Sigma)\, p(\Sigma)\, \mathrm{d}\Sigma\, \mathrm{d}P(\theta),$$

where

$$p^{-1}(y) = \int_{\Theta} \int_{\mathscr{S}} p(y|\theta, I \otimes \Sigma)\, p(\Sigma)\, \mathrm{d}\Sigma\, \mathrm{d}P(\theta).$$

Because the prior distribution of Σ is independent of θ and the functional $\sigma(\theta)$ does not involve Σ, we can write

$$p(y|\theta) = \int_{\mathscr{S}} p(y|\theta, I \otimes \Sigma)\, p(\Sigma)\, \mathrm{d}\Sigma$$

$$\propto \left(\det\left\{ G + \sum_{t=1}^{n} [y_t - \mu_t(\theta)][y_t - \mu_t(\theta)]' \right\} \right)^{-(\nu+n-N-1)/2}$$

and simplify the expression to read

$$F(\sigma|y) = p^{-1}(y) \int_{\Theta} I_{[-\infty,\sigma)}[\sigma(\theta)]\, p(y|\theta)\, \mathrm{d}P(\theta),$$

where

$$p(y) = \int_\Theta p(y|\theta)\,\mathrm{d}P(\theta).$$

The validity of these expressions is verified below.

Define

$$\theta_K = (\theta_0, \theta_1, \theta_2, \ldots, \theta_{p_K}, 0, 0, \ldots),$$

$$p_K(y|\theta) = p(y|\theta_K),$$

$$\sigma_K(\theta) = \sigma(\theta_K).$$

This is, $p_k(y|\theta)$ is the density $p(y|\theta)$ computed from the truncated series expansion $g_K(x|\theta) = \sum_{j=0}^{p_K} \theta_j \phi_j(x)$ rather than from $g_\infty(x|\theta)$ and similarly for $\sigma_K(\theta)$. We propose to approximate $F(\sigma|y)$ by

$$F_K(\sigma|y) = p_K^{-1}(y) \int_\Theta I_{(-\infty,\sigma]}[\sigma_K(\theta)]\, p_K(y|\theta)\,\mathrm{d}P(\theta),$$

where

$$p_K(y) = \int_\Theta p_K(y|\theta)\,\mathrm{d}P(\theta).$$

To justify this approximation, we shall show below that

$$\lim_{K\to\infty} \sup_{\sigma\in\mathbb{R}} |F_K(\sigma|y) - F(\sigma|y)| = 0.$$

Overall, our approach is intuitively obvious. We have chosen what seems to be a sensible expansion for the cost function

$$g_\infty(x|\theta) = \sum_{j=0}^{\infty} \theta_j \phi_j(x),$$

truncated the expansion to

$$g_K(x|\theta) = \sum_{j=0}^{p_K} \theta_j \phi_j(x),$$

and applied a straightforward Bayesian analysis to the truncated cost function

$g_K(x|\theta)$. It would seem that for a sensibly chosen prior distribution on θ, the choice of a sufficiently large truncation point K should have little affect on the computations. The remainder of this section is a verification of what is intuitively obvious. The reader who has no interest in detail can skip to the next section without loss of continuity. Before attending to the mathematical details we shall comment on an objection raised by Sims (1971) to formal Bayesian analysis on an infinite-dimensional space. First, we need to state the regularity conditions and describe the carrier of $P(\theta)$.

Regularity Conditions. The regularity conditions are

$p(y|\theta)$ is continuous on $\mathbb{R}^{nN} \times \Theta$ with respect to $\|(y,\theta)\| = \|y\| + \|\theta\|_{m,\infty,\mu}$,

$\sigma(\theta)$ is continuous on Θ with respect to $\|\theta\|_{m,\infty,\mu}$,

$p(y|\theta) > 0$ for every $y \in \mathbb{R}^{nN}$ and $\theta \in \Theta$,

$$\sup_{\mathbb{R}^{nN}} \sup_{\Theta} p(y|\theta) \leqq c < \infty,$$

$$\lim_{K \to \infty} p_K(y|\theta) = p(y|\theta) \text{ for every } (y,\theta) \text{ in } \mathbb{R}^{nM} \times \Theta,$$

$$\lim_{K \to \infty} \sigma_K(\theta) = \sigma(\theta) \text{ for every } \theta \in \Theta,$$

$$P\{\theta \in \Theta\colon \sigma(\theta) = \sigma\} = 0 \text{ for every } \sigma \in \mathbb{R}.$$

The choices of $p(y|\theta)$ and $\sigma(\theta)$ described above satisfy these restrictions as can be seen nearly at sight.

Carrier. If the random variables θ_j are independently distributed with density $p_j(\theta_j) = \frac{1}{2}\alpha_j^r \exp(-\alpha_j^r|\theta_j|)$, then we have

$$\sum_{j=0}^{p_K} \alpha_j^\beta \mathscr{E}|\theta_j| = \sum_{j=0}^{p_K} \alpha_j^{\beta - r} \approx \lambda^{\beta - r} \sum_{i=0}^{K} (i)^{N + \beta - r},$$

which converges if $N + \beta - r < -1$ or $\beta < r - (N+1)$. Similarly,

$$\sum_{j=0}^{p_K} \alpha_j^{2\beta} \operatorname{var}(|\theta_j|) = \sum_{j=0}^{p_K} \alpha_j^{2\beta - 2r} \approx \lambda^{2\beta - 2r} \sum_{i=0}^{K} (i)^{N + 2\beta - 2r},$$

which converges if $N+2\beta-2r<-1$ or $\beta<r-\frac{1}{2}(N+1)$. Thus, for $\beta<r-(N+1)$ we will have [Tucker (1967, sec. 5.1)] that

$$\mathrm{P}\left\{\theta\colon \sum_{j=0}^{\infty}|\theta_j||\alpha_j|^{\beta}<\infty\right\}=1.$$

We also have for any $c>0$ that

$$\sum_{j=0}^{p_K}\alpha_j^{\beta}\mathscr{E}|\theta_j I_{[-c,c]}(\theta_j)|=\sum_{j=0}^{p_K}\alpha_j^{\beta-r}-\sum_{j=0}^{p_K}\mathrm{e}^{-\alpha_j^r c}\left(c+\alpha_j^{-r}\right)\alpha_j^{\beta-r},$$

which diverges if $N+\beta-r=-1$ whence

$$\mathrm{P}\left\{\theta\colon \sum_{j=0}^{\infty}|\theta_j||\alpha_j|^{\beta}=\infty\right\}=1,$$

for $\beta=r-(N+1)$.

Sims' Objection. Sims (1971) shows that any Borel measure on a complete, separable metric space must put probability one on a meager set, a countable union of nowhere-dense sets. He then argues that meager sets should be regarded as small and their complement large, but this to some extent must be regarded as a matter of opinion as there is no analogue to Lebesgue measure in this setting. In our context, the natural parameter space is

$$\{\theta\colon \|\theta\|_{m,\infty,\mu}<\infty\}=\bigcup_{\beta=m}^{\infty}\{\theta\colon \|\theta\|_{\beta,\infty,\mu}<\infty, \|\theta\|_{\beta+1,\infty,\mu}=\infty\}$$

$$\cup\bigcap_{\beta=m}^{\infty}\{\theta\colon \|\theta\|_{\beta,\infty,\mu}<\infty\}.$$

As show above, we have put probability one on a set of the form

$$\{\theta\colon \|\theta\|_{\beta,\infty,\mu}<\infty, \|\theta\|_{\beta+1,\infty,\mu}=\infty\},$$

and while we could easily extend to the countable union of such sets we find ourselves unable to assign mass to $\bigcap_{\beta=m}^{\infty}\{\theta\colon \|\theta\|_{\beta,\infty,\mu}<\infty\}$ in any reasonable way. Indeed, Sims' result implies that we cannot. Stating this differently, while we can assign mass to all functions $g(x)$ that are exactly β times differentiable for some $\beta\geqq m$ in a reasonable way, we cannot assign mass to functions $g(x)$ that are infinitely many times differentiable in a reasonable way and so cannot assign mass to functions that are m times differentiable in a reasonable way.

We will now set forth an argument that we think mitigates against these considerations. Our interest is in some functional $\sigma(\theta)$, not in θ itself. Thus, as long as the prior puts positive probability on any set of the form $\{\theta\colon a < \sigma(\theta) \leqq b\}$, the set of admissible θ would be adequately weighted by the prior distribution in our opinion. One shows that $\mathrm{P}\{\theta\colon a < \sigma(\theta) \leqq b\} > 0$ as follows.

If $\sigma(\theta)$ is a share, substitution elasticity, or similar sort of evaluation functional involving low-order derivatives, then we can always find some θ_K° with zeroes past the p_K element with $a < \sigma(\theta_K^\circ) \leqq b$ because a solution to the linear system $\nabla g_K(x^\circ, \theta) = \nabla g(x^\circ)$, $\nabla^2 g_K(x^\circ, \theta) = \nabla^2 g(x^\circ)$, etc. must exist for large enough K. Let r be greater than $m+N+3$. There is a $\delta^\circ > 0$ such that $\|\theta - \theta^\circ\|_{m,\infty,\mu} < \delta^\circ \Rightarrow a < \sigma(\theta) < b$. Moreover, for some δ, $\{\theta\colon |\theta_i - \theta_i^\circ| < \delta\alpha_i^{-m-N-2}$ for $i = 0, \dots\} \subset \{\theta\colon \|\theta - \theta^\circ\|_{m,\infty,\mu} < \delta^\circ\}$.

Now

$$\mathrm{P}\{\theta\colon |\theta_i - \theta_i^\circ| < \delta\alpha_i^{-m-N-2} \text{ for } i = 0, \dots\}$$

$$= \prod_{i=0}^{p_K} \mathrm{P}\left[|\theta_i - \theta_i^\circ| < \delta\alpha_i^{-m-N-2}\right] \prod_{i=p_K+1}^{\infty} \mathrm{P}\left[|\theta_i| < \delta\alpha_i^{-m-N-2}\right]$$

$$< \prod_{i=0}^{p_K} \mathrm{P}\left[|\theta_i - \theta_i^\circ| < \delta\alpha_i^{-m-N-2}\right] \prod_{i=0}^{\infty} \mathrm{P}\left[|\theta_i| < \delta\alpha_i^{-m-N-2}\right],$$

and

$$\ln \prod_{i=0}^{\infty} \mathrm{P}\left[|\theta_i| < \delta\alpha_i^{-m-N-2}\right] = \sum_{i=0}^{\infty} \ln\left[1 - \mathrm{e}^{-\delta\alpha_i^{-m-N-2+r}}\right]$$

$$> \sum_{i=0}^{\infty} \ln\left[\left(\delta\alpha_i^{-m-N-2+r}\right) / \left(1 + \delta\alpha_i^{-m-N-2+r}\right)\right]$$

$$= -\sum_{i=0}^{\infty} \ln\left[1 + \frac{1}{\delta}\alpha_i^{m+N+2-r}\right]$$

$$> -\sum_{i=0}^{\infty} \frac{1}{\delta}\alpha_i^{m+N+2-r} > -\infty.$$

As pointed out to us by Sims, showing that the prior puts *a priori* mass on all sets of the form $\{\theta\colon a < \sigma(\theta) \leqq b\}$ does not imply that $\mathscr{E}(\sigma | y)$ is consistent for $\sigma(\theta)$ as sample size tends to infinity in either the sense of almost sure convergence with respect to the prior or almost sure convergence with respect to the likelihood. We are somewhat confused as to the relevance of consistency in an intrinsically finite sample setting, but nonetheless we can show that consistency obtains. This we do later after more notation is in hand.

Probability Spaces. The following proofs can be somewhat confusing if some care is not taken to describe the underlying probability spaces. The prior $\mathrm{d}P(\theta)$ is a measure on $(\mathbb{R}^\infty, \mathscr{B}^\infty)$ where $\mathscr{B}^\infty$ is the collection of Borel subsets of $\mathbb{R}^\infty$; see Tucker (1967, sec. 2.3) for details. Completing this space and intersecting with Θ we have a complete measure space $(\Theta, \mathscr{A}, \mathrm{d}P(\theta))$. Denote Lebesgue measure on $\mathbb{R}^{nN}$ by $(\mathbb{R}^{nN}, \mathscr{L}^{nN}, \mathrm{d}y)$. The underlying measure space is the product of these two denoted as $(\mathbb{R}^{nN}\times\Theta, \mathscr{L}^{nN}\times\mathscr{A}, \mathrm{d}y\,\mathrm{d}P(\theta))$; see Royden (1967, ch. 12, sec. 4) for details. By continuity, $p(y|\theta)$ is measurable with respect to $\mathscr{L}^{nN}\times\mathscr{A}$, whence $(\mathbb{R}^{nN}\times\Theta, \mathscr{L}^{nN}\times\mathscr{A}, \mathrm{d}\mu(y,\theta))$, with

$$\mu(B) = \int_\Theta\int_{\mathbb{R}^{nN}} I_B(y,\theta)\,p(y|\theta)\,\mathrm{d}y\,\mathrm{d}P(\theta),$$

is a probability space. Similarly, $\mathrm{d}\nu(y,\sigma)$ is a probability measure on the $(nN+1)$-dimensional real numbers if

$$\begin{aligned}\nu(A) &= \int_{\mathbb{R}^{nN}\times\Theta} I_A[y,\sigma(\theta)]\,\mathrm{d}\mu(y,\theta)\\ &= \int_\Theta\int_{\mathbb{R}^{nN}} I_A[y,\sigma(\theta)]\,p(y|\theta)\,\mathrm{d}y\,\mathrm{d}P(\theta).\end{aligned}$$

With reference to $(\mathbb{R}^{nN+1}, \mathscr{L}^{nN+1}, \mathrm{d}\nu(y,\sigma))$ we are trying to compute $F(\sigma|y)$, the conditional distribution of σ given y as defined in Lehmann (1959, ch. 2, sec. 5).

Verification of the Formula for $F(\sigma|y)$. What has to be shown is that

$$\mathrm{P}(A|y) = p^{-1}(y)\int_\Theta I_A[y,\sigma(\Theta)]\,p(y|\theta)\,\mathrm{d}P(\theta)$$

exists for every y in $\mathbb{R}^{nN}$ and is a conditional probability distribution on $\mathbb{R}^{nN+1}$, $\mathscr{L}^{nN+1}$, $\mathrm{d}\nu(y,\sigma)$). To see that this will suffice, let $f(\sigma)$ be a non-negative integrable function and let $\sum_{i=1}^I a_{i,I} I_{C_{i,I}}(\sigma)$ be a sequence of simple functions converging to $f(\sigma)$ from below as $I\to\infty$. Then

$$\begin{aligned}\mathscr{E}(f|y) &= \lim_{I\to\infty}\sum_{i=1}^I a_i P(\mathbb{R}^n\times C_i|y)\\ &= \lim_{I\to\infty}\sum_{i=1}^I a_i p^{-1}(y)\int_\Theta I_{\mathbb{R}^n\times C_i}[y,\sigma(\theta)]\,p(y|\theta)\,\mathrm{d}P(\theta)\\ &= \lim_{I\to\infty}\sum_{i=1}^I a_i p^{-1}(y)\int_\Theta I_{C_i}[\sigma(\theta)]\,p(y|\theta)\,\mathrm{d}P(\theta)\\ &= \lim_{I\to\infty}\sum_{i=1}^I a_i\int_\Theta I_{C_i}(\sigma)\,\mathrm{d}F(\sigma|y)\\ &= \int_\Theta f(\sigma)\,\mathrm{d}F(\sigma|y).\end{aligned}$$

To verify that $P(A|y)$ exists, note that $p(y) > 0$ because if not then $p(y|\theta) = 0$ a.e. P which is false by assumption. To show that $P(A|y)$ is a conditional probability distribution we must show that $P(A|y)$ is a probability measure on $\mathbb{R}^{nN+1}$ for each fixed y, which is obvious from the formula defining $P(A|y)$, and that $P(A|y)$ is a conditional expectation of $I_A(y, \sigma)$. Now $P(A|y)$ is measurable $(\mathbb{R}^{nN}, \mathscr{L}^{nN})$ by Fubini's theorem. Moreover, for any $B \in \mathscr{L}^{nN}$, we have

$$\int_\Theta \int_{\mathbb{R}^{nN}} I_B(y) P(A|y) p(y|\theta) \,\mathrm{d}y \,\mathrm{d}P(\theta)$$

$$= \int_\Theta \int_{\mathbb{R}^{nN}} p^{-1}(y) I_B(y) \int_\Theta I_A[\sigma(\theta'), y]\, p(y|\theta') \,\mathrm{d}P(\theta')$$

$$\times p(y|\theta) \,\mathrm{d}y \,\mathrm{d}P(\theta)$$

$$= \int_\Theta \int_{\mathbb{R}^{nN}} I_{\mathbb{R}\times B}[\sigma(\theta'), y]\, I_A[\sigma(\theta'), y]\, p(y|\theta') \,\mathrm{d}y \,\mathrm{d}P(\theta')$$

$$= \nu[(\mathbb{R} \times B) \cap A].$$

Verification of the Approximation Formula. By the assumption that $P\{\theta \in \Theta\colon \sigma(\theta) = \sigma\} = 0$ and the limit assumptions, we have that

$$\lim_{K\to\infty} p_K(y|\theta) = p(y|\theta) \quad \text{a.e. } P,$$

$$\lim_{K\to\infty} I_{(-\infty,\sigma]}[\sigma_K(\theta)]\, p_K(y|\theta) = I_{(-\infty,\sigma]}[\sigma(\theta)]\, p(y|\theta) \quad \text{a.e. } P,$$

whence, by the Dominated Convergence Theorem,

$$\lim_{K\to\infty} p_K(y) = \lim_{K\to\infty} \int_\Theta p_K(y|\theta) \,\mathrm{d}P(\theta) = \int_\Theta \lim_{K\to\infty} p_K(y|\theta) \,\mathrm{d}P(\theta)$$

$$= \int_\Theta p(y|\theta) \,\mathrm{d}P(\theta) = p(y).$$

Similarly for $\lim_{K\to\infty} \int_\Theta I_{(-\infty,\sigma]}[\sigma_K(\theta)]\, p_K(y|\theta) \,\mathrm{d}P(\theta)$. Thus, $\lim_{K\to\infty} F_K(\sigma|y) = F(\sigma|y)$. Since $F(\sigma|y)$ is a distribution function, pointwise convergence implies uniform convergence.

Restricting the Carrier. We may wish to restrict the carrier of the prior to $T = \{\theta \in \Theta\colon g(\theta) > 0\}$ and take $P'(A) = P(A \cap T)/P(T)$ to be the new prior.

Letting $g_K(\theta) = g(\theta_K)$, assuming that $\mathrm{P}\{\theta \in \Theta: g(\theta) = 0\} = 0$ and that $\lim_{K\to\infty} g_K(\theta) = g(\theta)$, we can approximate $P'(A)$ by $P'_K(A) = P(A \cap T_K) / P(T_K)$ where $T_K = \{\theta \in \Theta: g_K(\theta) > 0\}$. The argument is the same as before since, by the Dominated Convergence Theorem,

$$\lim_{K\to\infty} P(A \cap T_K) = \int_\Theta I_A(\theta) \lim_{K\to\infty} I_{(0,\infty)}[g_K(\theta)]\,\mathrm{d}P(\theta)$$

$$= \int_\Theta I_A(\theta) I_{(0,\infty)}[g(\theta)]\,\mathrm{d}P(\theta).$$

Consistency. We shall apply Theorem 3 of Sims (1971). For simplicity of notation reduce to the setting where costs are observed and cost shares are not; y_t becomes univariate in this setting. We have $\int_A p(y|\theta)\,\mathrm{d}y$ considered as a function of θ measurable with respect to $(\Theta, \mathscr{A})$ by Fubini's theorem which establishes condition (i) of Sims' Theorem 3. Let $f_\infty(y_\infty)$ defined on $\times_{t=1}^\infty \mathbb{R}$ be given by

$$f_\infty(y_\infty) = \underset{\Theta}{\arg\min} \lim_{n\to\infty} (1/n) \sum_{t=1}^n [y_t - g_\infty(x_t|\theta)]^2.$$

We have that

$$\lim_{n\to\infty} (1/n) \sum_{t=1}^n [y_t - g_\infty(x_t|\theta)]^2$$

$$= \int_{\mathscr{X}} [g_\infty(x|\theta^\circ) - g_\infty(x|\theta)]^2 \,\mathrm{d}\mu(x) + \sigma^2,$$

except for y_∞ in some null set $N_{\theta^\circ} \subset \times_{t=1}^\infty \mathbb{R}$. Thus, we have $f_\infty(y_\infty) = \theta$ except on N_θ. The last condition to be verified is that $f^{-1}(A)$ is measurable for every closed sphere A. This we are not able to do in as much generality as we would like. We must further restrict Θ to those θ with $\|\theta\|_{m+1,\infty,\mu} < B$ for some pre-chosen bound B. Under this condition we have that A is compact in the topology generated by $\|\theta\|_{m,\infty,\mu}$, whence the almost sure convergence is uniform on A and $\bigcup_{\theta\in A} N_\theta$ is a null set [Elbadawi, Gallant and Souza (1983)]. The pre-image of A is the whole space less this null set which is measurable. This establishes condition (ii) of Sims' Theorem 3 and consistency obtains.

4. Computational strategy

In the two previous sections we described an approach to Bayesian analysis on an infinite-dimensional parameter space Θ that has as its objective the determination of the posterior distribution $F(\sigma|y)$ of some functional $\sigma(\theta)$. We also showed that the posterior distribution $F_K(\sigma|y)$ of a related finite-dimensional Bayesian analysis can be regarded as an approximation to the infinite-dimensional analysis in the sense that

$$\lim_{K\to\infty} \sup_{-\infty<\sigma<\infty} |F(\sigma|y) - F_K(\sigma|y)| = 0.$$

(It is important to realize that this approximation is numerical not statistical.) In this section, various strategies for computing $F_K(\sigma|y)$ are considered.

The computational task is the numerical integration of

$$F_K^*(\sigma|y) = \int_\Theta I_{(-\infty,\sigma]}[\sigma_K(\theta)]\, p_K^*(y|\theta)\,\mathrm{d}P(\theta),$$

the posterior distribution function of σ given in unnormalized form, where $p_K^*(y|\theta)$ is the marginal likelihood in unnormalized form,

$$p_K^*(y|\theta) = \left(\det\left\{G + \sum_{i=1}^{n}[y_t - \mu_t(\theta_K)][y_t - \mu_t(\theta_K)]'\right\}\right)^{-(\nu+n-N-1)/2}$$

The normalized distribution is computed as

$$F_K(\sigma|y) = F_K^*(\sigma|y)/F_K^*(\infty|y).$$

Notice that for extreme values of θ, the determinant behaves like a polynomial in θ.

As indicated previously, the prior distribution on θ is taken to be that of a sequence of independent random variables with the double exponential (Laplace) distribution, centered at zero and with scale parameter α_j^r, so that

$$p_j(\theta_j) = \tfrac{1}{2}\alpha_j^r \exp\{-\alpha_j^r|\theta_j|\}.$$

For the example detailed in the next section, α_j is taken proportional to the length of the multi-index $|k_\alpha|$, except for the constant and linear components (u_0, b') whose prior was taken to be uniform over $(-\infty, \infty)$, $\alpha_j = 0$.

For numerical integration in many dimensions, the method of choice is Monte Carlo [Davis and Rabinowitz (1976)] for which we have two directions of attack. The first is straightforward. One generates vectors θ^i (of length p_K) independently according to the prior $P_K(\theta)$ and computes

$$\hat{F}_K^*(\sigma|y) = M^{-1}\sum_{i=1}^{M} I_{(-\infty,\sigma]}[\sigma_K(\theta^i)]\, p_K^*(y|\theta^i).$$

An estimate of $F_K(\sigma|y)$ is obtained by using

$$\hat{F}_K(\sigma|y) = \hat{F}_K^*(\sigma|y)/\hat{F}_K^*(\infty|y).$$

This is the simplest approach and the method used to obtain the results given in the next section. Notice that posterior means and variances of σ can be computed using

$$\hat{E}(\sigma|y) = M^{-1}\sum_{i=1}^{M}\sigma(\theta^i)p_K^*(y|\theta^i)/\hat{F}_K^*(\infty|y),$$

and

$$\hat{E}(\sigma^2|y) = M^{-1}\sum_{i=1}^{M}\sigma^2(\theta^i)p_K^*(y|\theta^i)/\hat{F}_K^*(\infty|y).$$

An alternative strategy, known as importance sampling, is to attempt to improve the accuracy by placing more points near the peak of the posterior of θ_K, that is at $p_K(\theta|y)(\mathrm{d}P(\theta_K)/\mathrm{d}\theta_K)$. Instead of generating vectors θ^i according to P_K, one generates random vectors θ^i independently from some distribution $Q_K(\theta)$ and uses weights

$$W_i = [\mathrm{d}P_K/\mathrm{d}Q_K](\theta^i)$$

to compute

$$\hat{F}_K^*(\sigma|y) = M^{-1}\sum_{i=1}^{M} I_{(-\infty,\sigma]}[\sigma_K(\theta^i)]\,W_i p_K^*(y|\theta^i).$$

The distribution Q_K is open to choice, the optimal choice being the posterior distribution of θ_K which would yield equally weighted values to be summed. However, since this is unavailable, we tried several alternative choices which we hoped would be close approximations to this choice:

(1) multivariate normal distribution using current estimates of the posterior mean vector and covariance matrix of θ_K,
(2) multivariate Student's t, chosen as in (1),
(3) uniform over an ellipsoid, chosen as in (1),
(4) independent Laplace, as in P_K, but moving the location to the current peak of the posterior of θ_K.

In each instance the method failed due to such extreme sampling variation in the weights W_i that a larger number of Monte Carlo trials would have been required with importance sampling than with a straightforward simulation using the prior. We are somewhat baffled by this experience because the method has desirable theoretical properties, a discussion of which is omitted for the obvious reason, and has worked well in other contexts, notably the simulation of nuclear reactor failure. We continue to experiment with this approach and will report in more detail if success obtains before patience has worn thin.

An alternative computational scheme suggested by Peter Rossi uses a normal prior on θ given Σ, reducing the dimension of integration to ten and yielding a conditional posterior on θ which is normal. The posterior on $\sigma(\theta)$, a non-linear (ratios and products) function of normal deviates, presents a difficult but surmountable obstacle, solved by applying mechanical quadrature to the transformation rule. However, all this is conditional on Σ and, in contrast to Rossi's experience, we found the marginal likelihood on Σ more poorly behaved and the computational situation worse.

As noted above, the computation of the usual numerical descriptors of $\hat{F}_K(\sigma|y)$ such as the mean and variance is straightforward. To obtain a graphical descriptor of $\hat{F}_K(\sigma|y)$ we plotted the derivative of a natural cubic spline interpolating points of $\hat{F}_K(\sigma|y)$. See Wahba (1975) for details.

5. An example: Fitting the log Fourier cost function to KLEM data

We shall illustrate using data on the U.S. manufacturing sector from 1947 to 1971 from Berndt and Wood (1975) and Berndt and Khaled (1979). Total input cost (C), input prices of capital (K), labor (L), energy (E), and materials (M) and the corresponding cost shares are taken from tables 1 and 2 of Berndt and Wood (1975). The output series (Y) is taken from table 1 of Berndt and Khaled (1979). Following the protocol set forth in Gallant (1982), these data are transformed as shown in table 1 of Gallant and Golub (1984).

In order to impose various restrictions (homogeneity, homotheticity, etc.) on a multivariate Fourier series expansion, it is more convenient to write it in terms of a double summation rather than in the form $\sum_{j=1}^{p_K} \theta_j \phi_j(x)$ used previously. Following Gallant (1982) write

$$g_K(x,\theta) = u_0 + b'x + \tfrac{1}{2}x'Cx + \sum_{\alpha=1}^{A}\left\{u_{0\alpha} + 2\sum_{j=1}^{J}\left[u_{j\alpha}\cos(j\lambda k_\alpha' x) - v_{j\alpha}\sin(j\lambda k_\alpha' x)\right]\right\},$$

$$\nabla g_k(x,\theta) = c - \lambda\sum_{\alpha=1}^{A}\left\{u_{0\alpha}\lambda k_\alpha' x + 2\sum_{j=1}^{J} j\left[u_{j\alpha}\sin(j\lambda k_\alpha' x) + v_{j\alpha}\cos(j\lambda k_\alpha' x)\right]\right\} r_\alpha,$$

$$\nabla^2 g_K(x,\theta) = -\lambda^2\sum_{\alpha=1}^{A}\left\{u_{0\alpha} + 2\sum_{j=1}^{J} j^2\left[u_{j\alpha}\cos(j\lambda k_\alpha' x) - v_{j\alpha}\sin(j\lambda k_\alpha' x)\right]\right\} r_\alpha r_\alpha',$$

where

$$\{k_\alpha\} = \text{a sequence of elementary multi-indexes (table 2)},$$

$$\theta_{(0)} = b' = (c', b_5),$$

$$\theta_{(\alpha)} = (u_{0\alpha}, u_{1\alpha}, v_{1\alpha}, \ldots, u_{J\alpha}, v_{J\alpha})',$$

$$\theta = (u_0, \theta'_{(0)}, \theta'_{(1)}, \ldots, \theta'_{(A)})',$$

$$C = -\sum_{\alpha=1}^{A} u_{0\alpha}\lambda^2 k_\alpha k'_\alpha.$$

The linear homogeneity restriction is

$$R'_0 \begin{cases} \sum_{i=1}^{4} b_i = 1, \\ u_{j\alpha} = v_{j\alpha} = 0 \quad \text{if} \quad \sum_{i=1}^{4} k_{i\alpha} \neq 0. \end{cases}$$

The set of elementary multi-indexes that satisfy $\sum_{i=1}^{4} k_{i\alpha} = 0$ and have norm $|k_\alpha| \leqq 3$ are displayed in table 2 of Gallant and Golub (1984). For this set $A = 19$, and we take $J = 1$, whence θ is a vector of nominal length 63. The effective number of parameters is 53 due to the following restrictions.

The non-homogeneous restriction $\sum_{i=1}^{4} b_i = 1$ reduces the number of effective parameters by one. The remaining restrictions are due to overparameterization of the matrix C. The matrix C is a 5×5 symmetric matrix which satisfies five linearly independent homogeneous restrictions $\sum_{j=1}^{4} c_{ij} = 0$ ($i = 1,2,3,4,5$). Thus C can have at most ten free parameters and in the parameterization $C = -\sum_{\alpha=1}^{19} u_{0\alpha}\lambda^2 k_\alpha k'_\alpha$, ten of the $u_{0\alpha}$ are free parameters and nine must be set to zero. These nine are $\alpha = 10, 11, 12, 14, 15, 16, 17, 18, 19$ and were identified numerically as described in Gallant (1982). To impose these restrictions, let

$$r = \begin{bmatrix} 0 \\ 0 \\ 0 \\ 0 \\ 1 \\ \hline \mathbf{0} \end{bmatrix}, \qquad R = \left[\begin{array}{cccc|c} 1 & 0 & 0 & 0 & \\ 0 & 1 & 0 & 0 & \\ 0 & 0 & 1 & 0 & \\ 0 & 0 & 0 & 1 & \mathbf{0} \\ 0 & -1 & -1 & -1 & \\ \hline & \mathbf{0} & & & R_{22} \end{array}\right],$$

where R_{22} is obtained by deleting columns 10, 11, 12, 14, 15, 16, 17, 18, 19 from the identity matrix of order 58; r is a 63 by 1 column vector and R is a 63 by 53 matrix. Then by writing

$$\theta = \phi(\rho) \quad \text{with} \quad \phi(\rho) = r + R\rho,$$

one can express the vector θ in terms of 53 independent parameters contained in ρ of length 53.

In order use the double exponential (Laplace) prior developed in section 3 to the parameters $\{\rho_i\}$ it is necessary to associate the vector of weights $\{\alpha_i\}$ to the sequence $\{\rho_i\}$. The association is as follows. If ρ_i corresponds to u_0 or one of the b_i, then $\alpha_i = 0$ which we take as meaning that ρ_i has an improper uniform prior on $(-\infty, \infty)$. If ρ_i corresponds to $u_{j\alpha}$ or $v_{j\alpha}$, then $\alpha_i = sj\lambda|k_\alpha|$. The addition of the scale factor s is to permit variation of the weight given the Fourier terms relative to the constant and linear terms. The prior distribution on ρ is obtained by taking the $\{\rho_i\}$ as a sequence of independently distributed random variables with each coordinate having the density

$$p_i(\rho_i) = \tfrac{1}{2}\alpha_i^r \exp(-\alpha_i^r|\rho_i|).$$

We took $r = 8$ and $s\lambda^r = 200$ and 400; from table 1, $\lambda = 5.9094$. To approximate the uniform on $\mathbb{R}^5$ we used the uniform over an ellipsoid in $\mathbb{R}^5$ that was large relative to the non-negligible support of likelihood.

Recall that the likelihood $p_K(y|\theta, I \otimes \Sigma)$ takes the data

$$y_t = \begin{pmatrix} s_{0t} \\ s_{1t} \\ s_{2t} \\ s_{3t} \end{pmatrix}, \qquad t = 1, \ldots, n = 25,$$

as independently and normally distributed with mean

$$\mu_t(\theta_K) = \begin{pmatrix} g_K(x_t|\theta) \\ (\partial/\partial l_1) g_K(x_t|\theta) \\ (\partial/\partial l_2) g_K(x_t|\theta) \\ (\partial/\partial l_3) g_K(x_t|\theta) \end{pmatrix},$$

and variance–covariance matrix Σ. The prior distribution $P(\Sigma)$ on Σ is the inverted Wishart which has density proportional to

$$p^*(\Sigma) = |\Sigma|^{-\nu/2} \exp(-\tfrac{1}{2} \operatorname{tr} \Sigma^{-1} G),$$

Table 1

Mean and standard deviation of the posterior distribution of elasticities of substitution; U.S. manufacturing; 1959.

	$s\lambda^8 = 400$				$s\lambda^8 = 200$				Sampling theoretic	
	$10^{-3}G^\circ$		$10^{-2}G^\circ$		$10^{-3}G^\circ$		$10^{-2}G^\circ$			
Elasticity	Mean	Std.dev.	Mean	Std.dev.	Mean	Std.dev.	Mean	Std.dev.	Est.	Std.err.
σ_{KK}	−17.232	0.681	−17.528	0.708	−16.428	1.341	−17.263	1.401	−6.532	9.922
σ_{KL}	0.968	0.071	0.987	0.073	0.923	0.137	0.945	0.164	0.329	1.896
σ_{LL}	−2.628	0.029	−2.636	0.029	−2.600	0.050	−2.607	0.051	−0.281	0.729
σ_{KE}	0.822	0.513	0.965	0.487	0.392	0.878	0.868	0.912	0.661	8.552
σ_{LE}	0.952	0.110	0.982	0.100	0.870	0.192	0.973	0.149	4.568	3.592
σ_{EE}	−20.682	1.062	−21.113	1.051	−19.567	1.872	−21.038	1.600	−28.513	36.271
σ_{KM}	0.989	0.032	0.993	0.032	0.978	0.056	0.994	0.057	0.455	1.476
σ_{LM}	1.000	0.006	1.000	0.006	0.996	0.011	0.993	0.012	−0.242	0.361
σ_{EM}	0.989	0.043	0.996	0.042	0.976	0.076	0.999	0.076	−0.016	3.500
σ_{MM}	−0.592	0.006	−0.593	0.006	−0.589	0.007	−0.592	0.010	0.064	0.358

whence

$$p_K(y|\theta) = \int_{\mathscr{S}} p_K(y|\theta, I \otimes \Sigma)\,\mathrm{d}P(\Sigma)$$

is proportional to

$$p_K^*(y|\theta) = \left(\det\left\{G + \sum_{t=1}^{n} [y_t - u_t(\theta_K)][y_t - u_t(\theta_K)]'\right\}\right)^{-(\nu+n-N-1)/2}$$

with $n = 25$ and $N = 4$. We took

$$G = a\begin{pmatrix} \frac{1}{5} & 0 & 0 & 0 & 0 \\ 0 & \frac{3}{8} & -\frac{1}{8} & -\frac{1}{8} & -\frac{1}{8} \\ 0 & -\frac{1}{8} & \frac{3}{8} & -\frac{1}{8} & -\frac{1}{8} \\ 0 & -\frac{1}{8} & -\frac{1}{8} & \frac{3}{8} & -\frac{1}{8} \\ 0 & -\frac{1}{8} & -\frac{1}{8} & -\frac{1}{8} & \frac{3}{8} \end{pmatrix} = aG^\circ,$$

for $a = 10^{-2}$ and 10^{-3}; $\nu = 2$.

Recall that an elasticity of substitution $\sigma_K(\theta)$ is a typical element of the 4 by 4 matrix

$$[\mathrm{diag}(\nabla g_K)]^{-1}[\nabla^2 g_K + \nabla g_K \nabla' g_K - \mathrm{diag}(\nabla g_K)][\mathrm{diag}(\nabla g_K)]^{-1}.$$

Following the computational methods discussed in the previous paragraph we report the mean and standard deviation of the posterior distribution $\hat{F}_K(\sigma|y)$ for our four choices of (a, s) pairs together with sampling theoretic estimates of σ taken from table 4 of Gallant and Golub (1984). For the case $(a, s\lambda^5) = (10^{-2}, 200)$, we display derivatives of spline interpolates of $\hat{F}_K(\sigma|y)$ as figs. 1 through 10.

The prior is in general looser as one moves from left to right in table 1, with variation in $s\lambda^8$ having the major effect and with variation in aG° having a minor effect. As $s\lambda^8$ increases the results become more similar to finite-dimensional sampling theoretic results and thus become more credible in our opinion. We also found that computational cost increased dramatically as s decreased beyond those values shown in table 1. This is due to the fact that the probability of randomly generating a point θ^i, where $p_K(y|\theta)$ is non-negligible decreases as the scale factor s decreases. It is interesting to note the lump of posterior probability on a Cobb–Douglas specification that is evident in figs. 1 through 10.

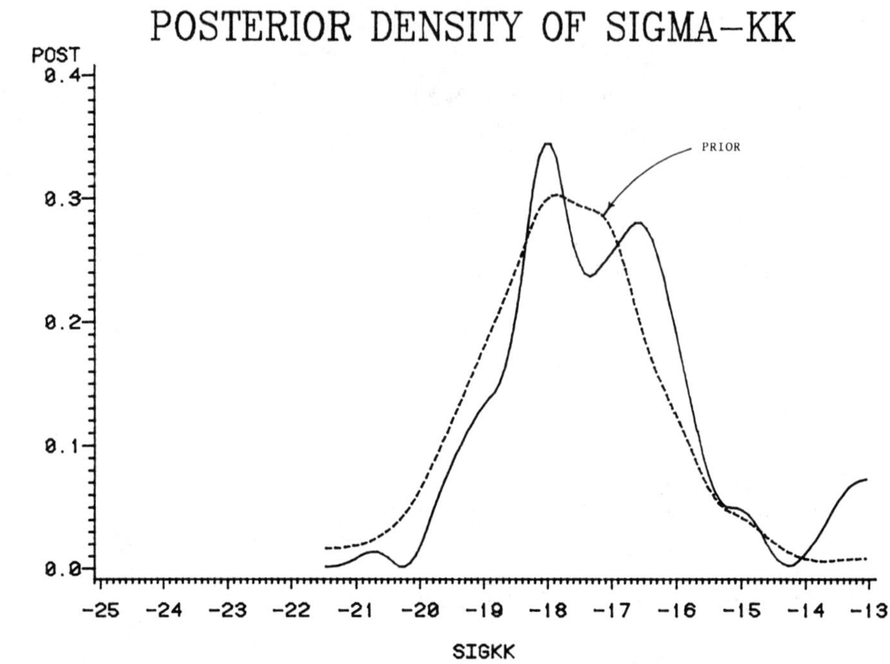
POSTERIOR DENSITY OF SIGMA-KK
POST
0.4
0.3
0.2
0.1
0.0
PRIOR
-25
-24
-23
-22
-21
-20
-19
-18
-17
-16
-15
-14
-13
SIGKK

Fig. 1

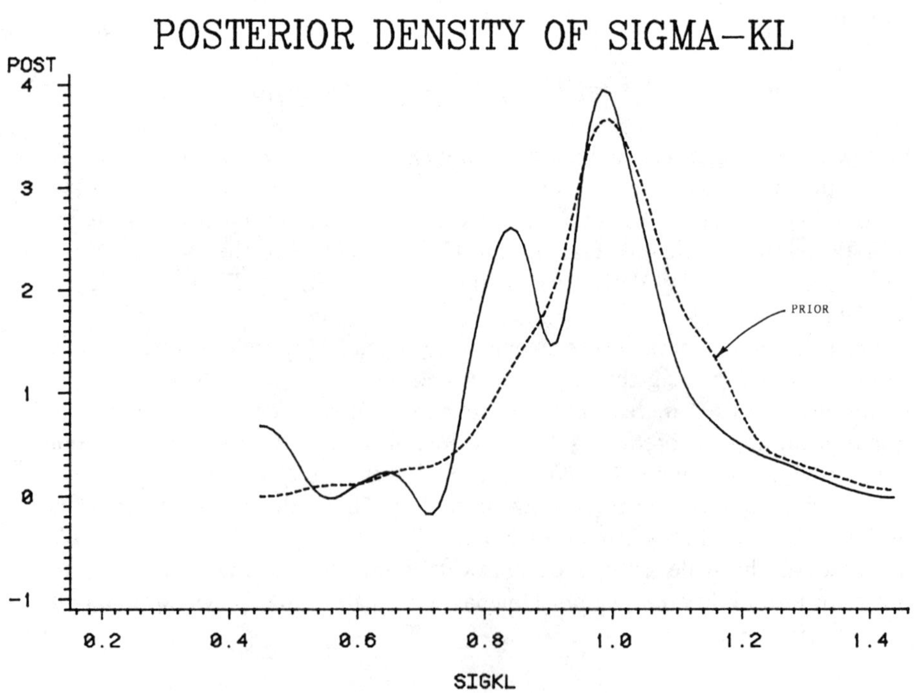
POSTERIOR DENSITY OF SIGMA-KL
POST
4
3
2
1
0
-1
PRIOR
0.2
0.4
0.6
0.8
1.0
1.2
1.4
SIGKL

Fig. 2

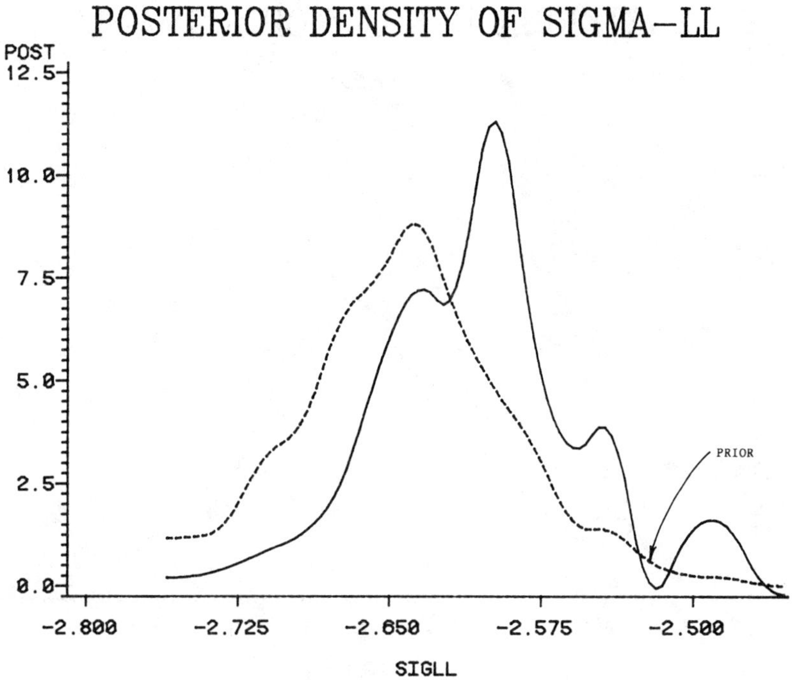
POSTERIOR DENSITY OF SIGMA-LL
POST
12.5
10.0
7.5
5.0
2.5
0.0
-2.800
-2.725
-2.650
-2.575
-2.500
SIGLL
PRIOR

Fig. 3

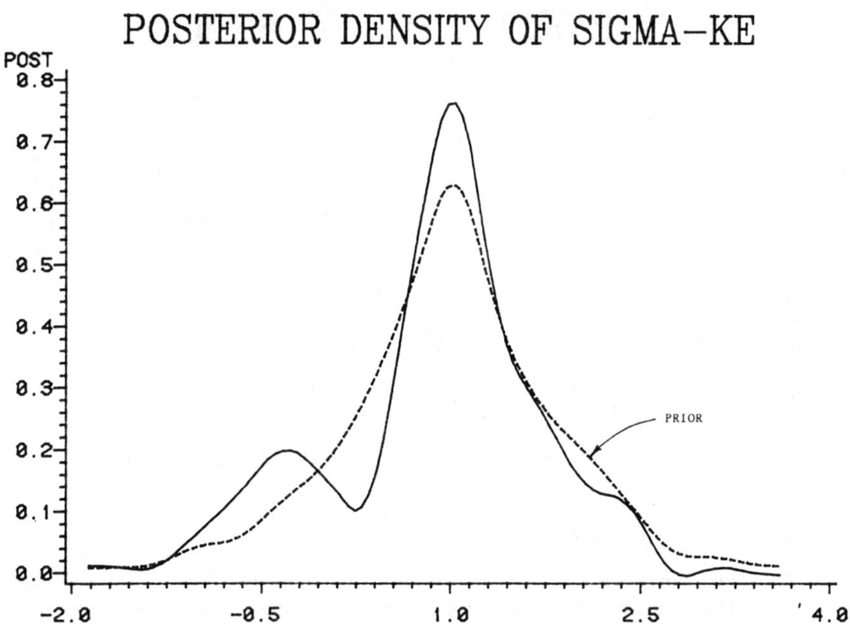
POSTERIOR DENSITY OF SIGMA-KE
POST
0.8
0.7
0.6
0.5
0.4
0.3
0.2
0.1
0.0
-2.0
-0.5
1.0
2.5
4.0
SIGKE
PRIOR

Fig. 4

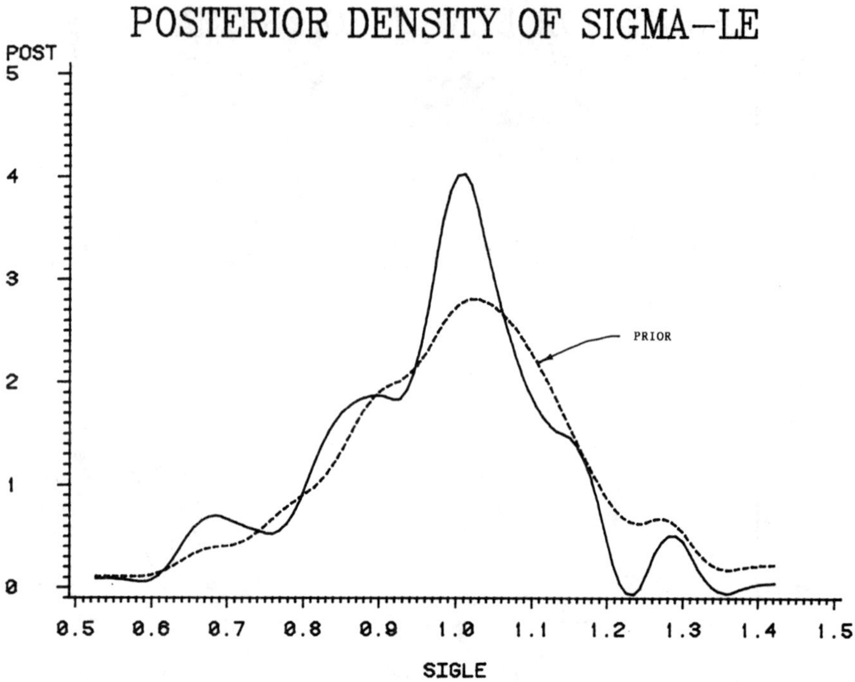
POSTERIOR DENSITY OF SIGMA-LE
POST
5
4
3
2
1
0
PRIOR
0.5
0.6
0.7
0.8
0.9
1.0
1.1
1.2
1.3
1.4
1.5
SIGLE

Fig. 5

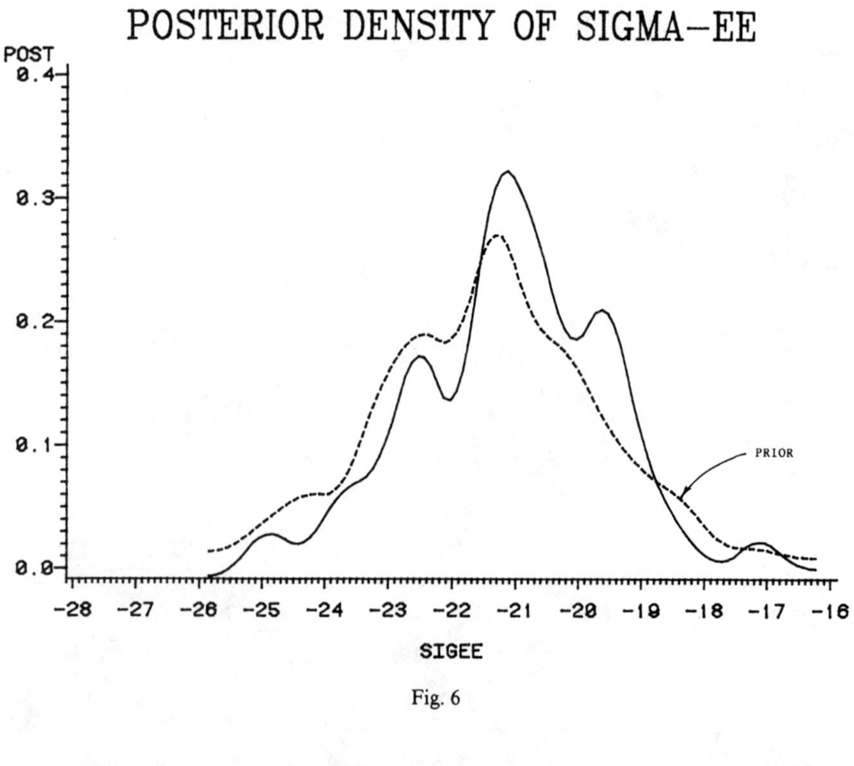
POSTERIOR DENSITY OF SIGMA-EE
POST
0.4
0.3
0.2
0.1
0.0
PRIOR
-28
-27
-26
-25
-24
-23
-22
-21
-20
-19
-18
-17
-16
SIGEE

Fig. 6

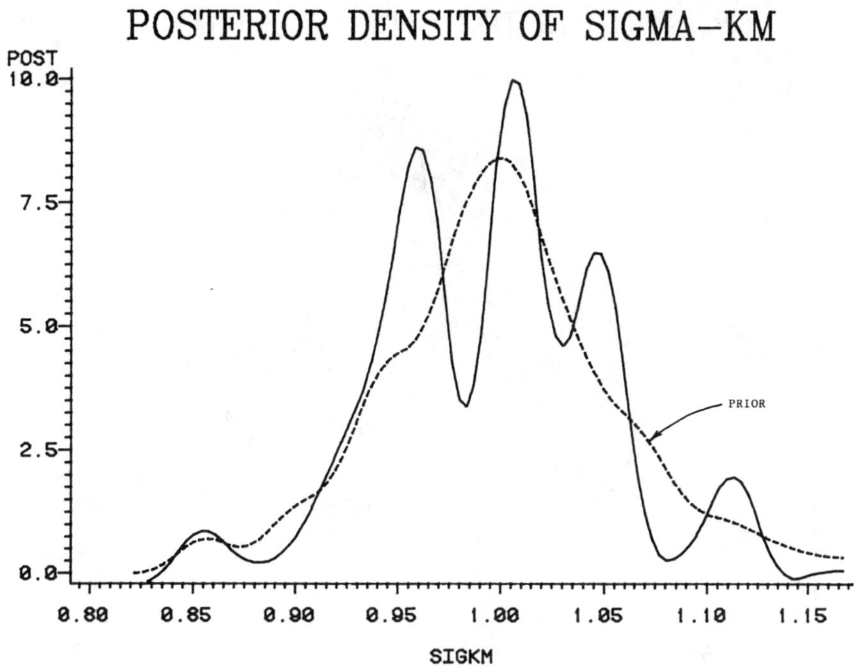
POSTERIOR DENSITY OF SIGMA-KM
POST
10.0
7.5
5.0
2.5
0.0
PRIOR
0.80
0.85
0.90
0.95
1.00
1.05
1.10
1.15
SIGKM

Fig. 7

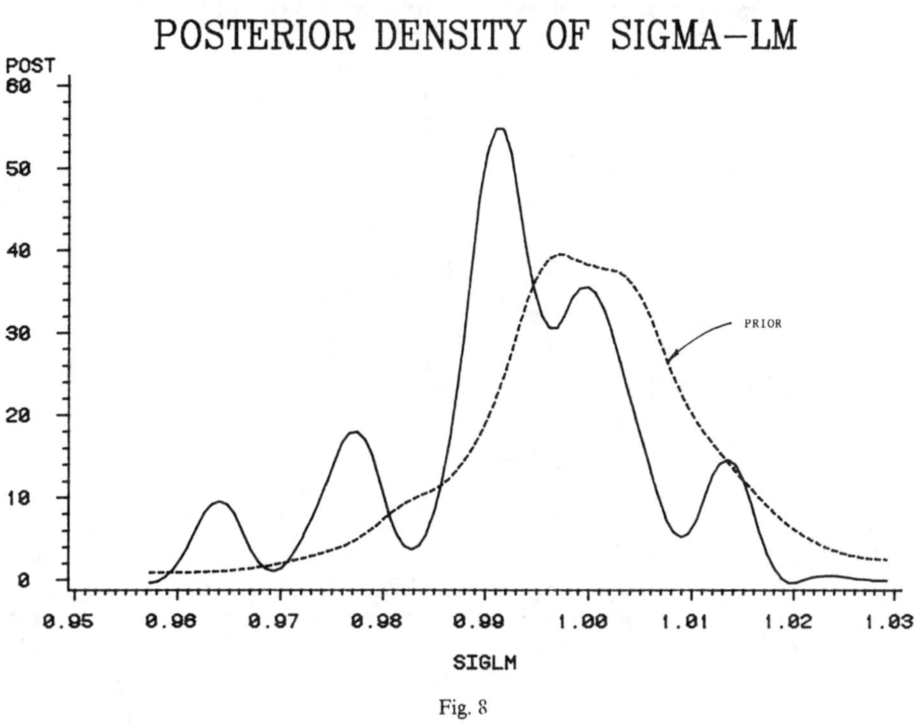
POSTERIOR DENSITY OF SIGMA-LM
POST
60
50
40
30
20
10
0
PRIOR
0.95
0.96
0.97
0.98
0.99
1.00
1.01
1.02
1.03
SIGLM

Fig. 8

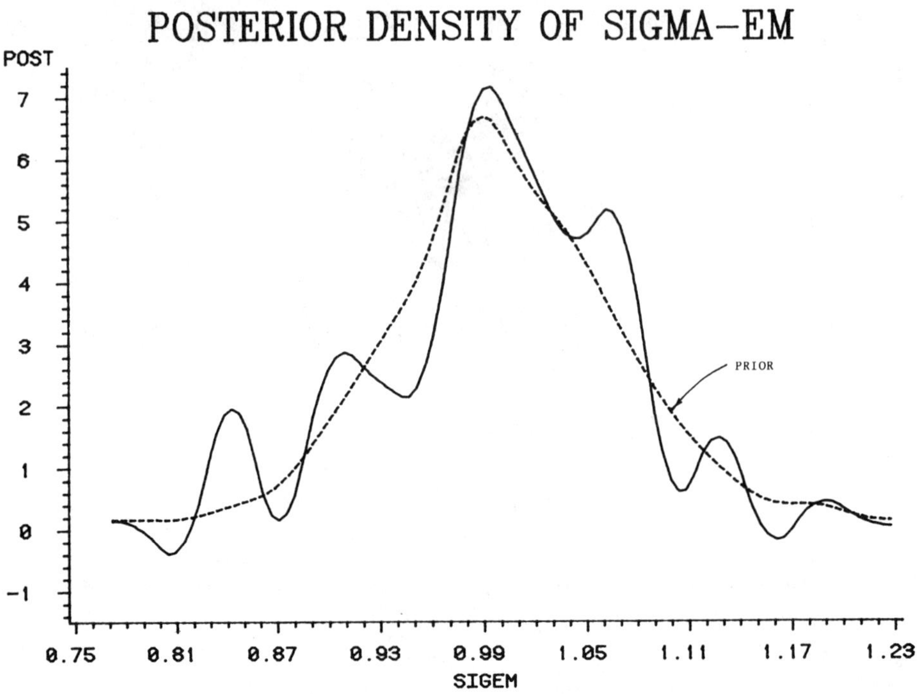
POSTERIOR DENSITY OF SIGMA-EM
POST
7
6
5
4
3
2
1
0
-1
PRIOR
0.75
0.81
0.87
0.93
0.99
1.05
1.11
1.17
1.23
SIGEM

Fig. 9

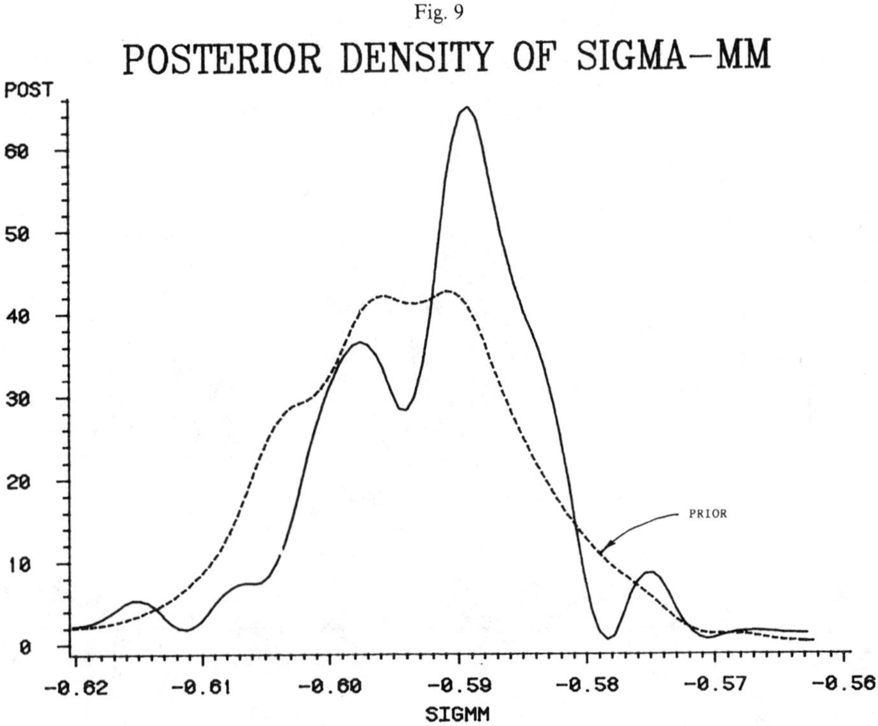
POSTERIOR DENSITY OF SIGMA-MM
POST
60
50
40
30
20
10
0
PRIOR
-0.62
-0.61
-0.60
-0.59
-0.58
-0.57
-0.56
SIGMM

Fig. 10

References

Berndt, Ernst R. and Mohammed S. Khaled, 1979, Parametric productivity measurement and choice among flexible functional forms, Journal of Political Economy 87, 1220–1245.

Berndt, Ernst R. and David O. Wood, 1975, Technology, prices and the derived demand for energy, Review of Economics and Statistics 57, 259–268.

Davis, Philip J. and Philip Rabinowitz, 1975, Methods of numerical integration (Academic Press, New York).

Edmonds, D.E. and V.B. Moscatelli, 1977, Fourier approximation and embeddings of Sobolev Spaces, Dissertationes Mathematyczne CXLV.

Elbadawi, Ibrahim, A. Ronald Gallant and Geraldo Souza, 1983, An elasticity can be estimated consistently without a priori knowledge of functional form, Econometrica 51, 1731–1751.

Gallant, A. Ronald, 1982, Unbiased determination of production technologies, Journal of Econometrics 20, 211–245.

Gallant, A. Ronald, 1984, The Fourier flexible form, American Journal of Agricultural Economics 66, 204–208.

Gallant, A. Ronald and Gene H. Golub, 1984, Imposing curvature restrictions on flexible functional forms, Journal of Econometrics 26, 295–321.

Gallant, A. Ronald and Alberto Holly, 1980, Statistical inference in an implicit, nonlinear, simultaneous equation model in the context of maximum likelihood estimation, Econometrica 48, 956–969.

Lehmann, E.L., 1959, Testing statistical hypotheses (Wiley, New York).

Malinvaud, E., 1970, The consistency of nonlinear regressions, Annals of Mathematical Statistics 41, 956–969.

Mood, Alexander M. and Franklin A. Graybill, 1963, Introduction to the theory of statistics, 2nd ed. (McGraw-Hill, New York).

Rossi, Peter E., 1983, Specification and analysis of production models with applications, Ph.D. dissertation (University of Chicago, Chicago, IL).

Royden, H.L., 1963, Real analysis (Macmillan, New York).

Sims, Christopher A., 1971, Distributed lag estimation when the parameter space is explicitly infinite-dimensional, Annals of Mathematical Statistics 42, 1622–1636.

Tucker, Howard G., 1967, A graduate course in probability (Academic Press, New York).

Wahba, Grace, 1975, Interpolating spline methods for density estimation I, Equispaced knots, Annals of Statistics 3, 30–48.

Zellner, Arnold, 1971, An introduction to Bayesian inference in econometrics (Wiley, New York).

A METHOD FOR CALCULATING BOUNDS ON THE ASYMPTOTIC COVARIANCE MATRICES OF GENERALIZED METHOD OF MOMENTS ESTIMATORS*

Lars Peter HANSEN

University of Chicago, Chicago, IL 60637, USA

For many time series estimation problems, there is an infinite-dimensional class of generalized method of moments estimators that are consistent and asymptotically normal. This paper suggests a procedure for calculating the greatest lower bound for the asymptotic covariance matrices of such estimators. The analysis focuses on estimation problems in which the data are generated by a stochastic process that is stationary and ergodic. The calculation of the bound uses martingale difference approximations as suggested by Gordin (1969) and a matrix version of Hilbert space methods.

1. Introduction

In many applications of instrumental variables estimation and more generally applications of generalized method of moments (GMM) estimation, there is a large set of candidates for instrumental variables and hence a large class of consistent, asymptotically normal GMM estimators. In fact the dimensionality of the set of instruments can be infinite for two reasons. First, in models in which the expectation of a disturbance vector is zero conditioned on a vector of random variables, virtually arbitrary functions of the random variables can be used as instrumental variables. Second, in many time series models when a particular variable is orthogonal to the disturbance vector, lagged values of that variable also are orthogonal to the disturbance vector. Hence, from the perspective of a large sample analysis, as the sample size grows the number of avaiiable instrumental variables grows as well. The purpose of this paper is to provide a general framework for calculating the greatest lower bound for the asymptotic covariance matrices of members of an infinite-dimensional class of GMM estimators.

We approach this problem from the perspective of an analyst with time series observations on a vector stochastic process that is stationary and ergodic. For such a process it is well-known that time series averages converge almost

*This research was supported in part by grants from the Sloan Foundation and the National Science Foundation. This research has benefited from conversations with Ricardo Barros, Bo Honore, and George Tauchen.

surely to averages taken over hypothetical states of the world (i.e., unconditional expectations). Additional assumptions are required to obtain a central limit theory. Gordin (1969) has suggested an approach in which time series averages of a stationary process are approximated in a certain sense by time series averages of a martingale difference sequence. By adopting his approach, the existing central limit results for martingale difference sequences can be applied to stationary processes as well. In this paper we use Gordin's approach in studying the asymptotic distribution of GMM estimators.

In section 2 of this paper, we specify the underlying estimation environment and give some results that exploit the martingale difference approximation suggested by Gordin (1969). The central limit results for stationary processes can be stated conveniently in terms of the approximating martingale difference sequences. For this reason, we use the approximating martingale difference sequences to define a matrix counterpart to an inner product between vector stochastic processes that are jointly stationary and ergodic.

In section 3 we define a large (infinite-dimensional) class of GMM estimators. Alternative estimators are indexed by alternative specifications of the instrumental variables used in constructing the estimators. Each choice of instrumental variables defines a stochastic process of products of instrumental variables and disturbances. The asymptotic distribution of the resulting GMM estimators can be expressed in terms of the asymptotic distribution of the stochastic processes of cross-products of instrumental variables and disturbances. Hence, the inner product defined in section 2 induces an inner product on the class of GMM estimators that is useful in representing asymptotic covariance matrices of these estimators.

In section 4 we pose the problem of determining the smallest asymptotic covariance matrix for the class of GMM estimators defined in section 3. This problem turns out to be the matrix counterpart to a minimum norm problem in a Hilbert space. We show that the solution to this problem can be obtained by solving the related problem of finding an inner product representation for a particular matrix linear functional. For many applications, it is convenient to calculate the smallest asymptotic covariance matrix by solving this related problem.

In section 5 we illustrate how to use this analysis to characterize the bound for two examples. In the first example the stochastic process for the disturbance vector is a conditionally homoscedastic martingale difference sequence so that the approximation described in section 2 is trivial. The bound we calculate can be viewed as a time series version of the bounds calculated by Basmann (1957), Sargan (1958), Jorgenson and Laffont (1974), and Amemiya (1977). Hence, the analysis of this example provides a link to previous literature on covariance matrix bounds for instrumental variables estimators. In the second example the disturbance vector is a finite linear combination of current and past values of a conditionally homoscedastic martingale difference sequence. We do not assume that variables used as instruments are strictly exogenous but only predetermined. The analysis of this second example illustrates the important role of the martingale approximation in calculating the bound. The two examples were chosen to illustrate the analysis in the previous sections. In Hansen (1985) bounds are calculated for several other examples with alternative restrictions imposed on the disturbance vector and the set of admissible instrumental variables.

There are two important limitations to the analysis in this paper. The first limitation is that we do not provide a decision-theoretic rationale for ranking estimators in terms of their asymptotic covariance matrices. In some circumstances particular GMM estimators are known to be locally minimax [e.g., see Chamberlain (1983)]; however, in our analysis we do not impose sufficient structure on the estimation problem and do not consider a sufficiently broad class of estimators to reach that conclusion. A second limitation is that we do not show how to construct estimators that attain the greatest lower bound. On the other hand, our method for calculating this lower bound often can be used to show how such a construction might take place. This second limitation will be addressed in a sequel to this paper.

2. Martingale difference approximation

In this section the probability structure underlying the generation of the time series data is specified, and the martingale difference approximation used for the central limit theory is defined. Following an approach suggested by Gordin (1969), a martingale difference approximation is used for obtaining central limit results. The approximating martingale difference sequences are then used to define a matrix counterpart to an inner product between two stochastic processes that are jointly stationary. This inner product will be used in subsequent sections to represent the asymptotic covariance matrices of GMM estimators and to calculate the greatest lower bound.

Let $(\Omega, A, Prob)$ denote the underlying probability space, and let S denote a measurable transformation mapping Ω onto itself that is measure-preserving and ergodic. The transformation S is used to specify how the time series data are generated. For instance, suppose h is a k-dimensional random vector. Then h and S together generate a time series via the relation

$$h_t(\omega) = h\left[S^t(\omega)\right] \quad \text{for all } \omega \text{ in } \Omega, \tag{2.1}$$

where S^t is interpreted as the transformation S applied t times. We assume that S is one-to-one and S^{-1} is measurable so that S^t is well-defined for both positive and negative values of t. A vector stochastic process $\{h_t\colon -\infty < t < +\infty\}$ generated in this fashion is stationary and ergodic. Under this construction h_0 and h are identical. Hence, we can index a k-dimensional vector stochastic process by a k-dimensional random vector corresponding to the time zero component of the process. Furthermore, any two index random vectors generate vector stochastic processes that are jointly stationary and ergodic. This indexation is used throughout our analysis.

Associated with this probability space is a sequential information structure. Let B denote a subsigma algebra of A, and let

$$B_t = \{ b_t \text{ in } A\colon b_t = \{\omega\colon S^t(\omega) \text{ is in } b\} \text{ for some } b \text{ in } B \}. \tag{2.2}$$

Under this specification, for any h that is measurable with respect to B, h_t is measurable with respect to B_t. We assume that the sequence of sigma algebras $\{B_t\colon -\infty < t < +\infty\}$ is non-decreasing. For many econometric examples, it is convenient to think of B as being the smallest sigma algebra with which a set of stochastic forcing variables with non-positive time subscripts are measurable.

A central limit theorem proved by Gordin (1969) can be applied to rich class of stochastic processes that are stationary and ergodic. Gordin's Theorem is used extensively in this section. In addition to the precise result stated in Gordin's Theorem, other results that are straightforward implications of his proof are required for our analysis. For this reason, we decompose the implications of Gordin's proof into three parts and make the appropriate extensions to each part.

To apply Gordin's Theorem, it is necessary to restrict the k-dimensional random vector h used in generating a stochastic process. This restriction uses the set

$$\begin{aligned} G = \{ g\colon & g \text{ is a } k\text{-dimensional random vector that is measurable} \\ & \text{with respect to } B, \text{ has a finite second moment,} \\ & \text{and } E(g|B_{-\tau}) = 0 \text{ for some non-negative } \tau \}, \end{aligned} \tag{2.3}$$

and the notation

$$P^T(h) = (1/\sqrt{T}) \sum_{t=1}^{T} h_t. \tag{2.4}$$

We then require that h satisfy:

Property 2.1. *h is measurable with respect to B, h has a finite second moment, and*

$$\inf_{g \text{ in } G} \limsup_{T\to\infty} \mathrm{E}[P^T(g-h)\cdot P^T(g-h)] = 0.$$

Since $\{h_t: -\infty < t < +\infty\}$ is stationary and ergodic, $\{(1/\sqrt{T})P^T(h): T \geq 1\}$ converges almost surely to $\mathrm{E}(h)$ as long as this expected value is finite. When h satisfies Property 2.1, $\mathrm{E}(h)$ is zero and h can be approximated arbitrarily well by elements in G, although the approximation is not a conventional mean-square (L^2) approximation.

There are two sets that are closely related to G. These sets are

$$H = \{h\text{: } h \text{ is a } k\text{-dimensional random vector that satisfies Property 2.1}\}, \tag{2.5}$$

and

$$F = \{f \text{ in } G\text{: } \mathrm{E}(f|B_{-1}) = 0\}. \tag{2.6}$$

The set H contains G which in turn contains F. All three sets, F, G, and H, satisfy the following linearity property:

Property 2.2. For any k-dimensional random vectors f and f^* in F (G or H) and any k by k matrices of real numbers c and c^*, $cf + c^*f^*$ is in F (G or H).

Lemma 2.1. F, G, and H satisfy Property 2.2.

Proofs of all lemmas in this section are provided in the appendix A.

The first implication of the proof of Gordin's Theorem is that elements in H and hence G can be approximated by elements in F. Our extended version of this first implication is given in the following lemma.

Lemma 2.2. There is a function M mapping H into F such that for any h in H, $\{P^T[h - M(h)]: T \geq 1\}$ converges in mean square (L^2) to zero. Furthermore, M satisfies the property that for any two elements h and h^* in H and any two k by k matrices of real numbers c and c^*, $M(ch + c^*h^*) = cM(h) + c^*M(h^*)$.

The first part of Lemma 2.2 is important because the stochastic process $\{M(h)_t: -\infty < t < +\infty\}$ is a stationary and ergodic martingale difference sequence. Billingsley (1961) proved a central limit theorem for martingale difference sequences that are stationary and ergodic. Hence, Billingsley's Theorem can be applied to $\{M(h)_t: -\infty < t < +\infty\}$. Taken together, Lemma 2.2 and Billingsley's Theorem imply the second implication of Gordin's Theorem.

Lemma 2.3. For any h in H, $\{P^T[M(h)]: T \geq 1\}$ and hence $\{P^T(h): T \geq 1\}$ converge in distribution to a normally distributed random vector with mean zero covariance matrix $\mathrm{E}[M(h)M(h)']$.

The second part of Lemma 2.2 establishes the linearity of the function M. This linearity makes

$$\langle h|h^*\rangle = \mathrm{E}[M(h)M(h^*)'] \tag{2.7}$$

a valid matrix counterpart to an inner product on H. Since h and h^* can be used in conjunction with S to generate stochastic processes that are stationary and ergodic, (2.7) can be used as an inner product of two such stochastic processes. Using this matrix inner product, the asymptotic covariance matrix of $\{P^T(h)\colon T \geq 1\}$ is $\langle h|h\rangle$. The third implication of Gordin's Theorem proof is an alternative representation of the inner product given in (2.7).

Lemma 2.4. *For any h and h^* in H, $\langle h|h^*\rangle = \lim_{T\to\infty} \mathrm{E}[P^T(h)P^T(h^*)']$.*

Taken together, Lemmas 2.2–2.4 show that for any h in H, $\{P^T(h)\colon T \geq 1\}$ is asymptotically normal with an asymptotic covariance matrix given by

$$\langle h|h\rangle = \lim_{T\to\infty} \mathrm{E}\left[P^T(h)P^T(h)'\right]. \tag{2.8}$$

This result is simply the vector counterpart to Gordin's Theorem. Since M is the identity transformation when restricted to F,

$$\langle h - M(h)|h - M(h)\rangle = 0 \quad \text{for all } h \text{ in } H. \tag{2.9}$$

Consequently, when viewing H as an inner product space with inner product (2.7) or equivalently (2.8), one can just as well restrict attention to the subspace F. For many econometric estimation problems, one is lead to examine subspaces of H when constructing econometric estimators. By applying the transformation M, the subspace of H can be mapped into a corresponding subspace of F. As we will see in the next two sections, the matrix inner product $\langle\cdot|\cdot\rangle$ defined using M is valuable in studying the large sample properties of infinite-dimensional classes of GMM estimators.

3. Econometric model and GMM estimators

In this section we specify a general econometric model, and we consider a class of GMM estimators of the parameter vector of that model. Let y denote a random vector observed by the econometrician that enters directly into the econometric model, let β_0 denote a k-dimensional parameter vector, and let m denote a function mapping y and β_0 into a K-dimensional disturbance vector e. Formally,

$$e = m(y, \beta_0), \tag{3.1}$$

where $m(\cdot,\beta)$ is Borel measurable for all β in a neighborhood of β_0. The function m is known a priori while the parameter vector β_0 is to be estimated. In addition, m is continuously differentiable in its second argument so that the K by k random matrix

$$\partial m(y,\beta_0)/\partial\beta' = d \tag{3.2}$$

is a well-defined matrix of random variables. The random vector y is assumed to be measurable with respect to B which guarantees that the elements in d and e are also measurable with respect to B.

To identify and estimate β_0, there is a set Z of k by K matrices of random variables that are measurable with respect to B. In addition Z satisfies the following five properties:

Property 3.1. *For any z in Z, ze is in H.*

Property 3.2. *For any z in Z, zd has a finite first moment and the random matrix function $z[\delta m(y,\cdot)/\delta\beta]$ is first-moment continuous at β_0.*[1]

Property 3.3. *There exists a z in Z for which Ezd is a non-singular matrix.*

Property 3.4. *For any z and z^* in Z and any k by k matrices of real numbers c and c^*, $cz + c^*z^*$ is in Z.*

Property 3.5. *For any sequence $\{z^j\colon j\geq 1\}$ in Z for which $\lim_{j\to\infty}\langle z^je|z^je\rangle = 0$, $\lim_{j\to\infty} \mathrm{E}(z^jd) = 0$.*

Among other things, Property 3.1 guarantees that elements of Z are valid instruments to be used in estimating β_0 in the sense that

$$\mathrm{E}(ze) = 0 \quad \text{for any } z \text{ in } Z. \tag{3.3}$$

Properties 3.2 and 3.3 are useful in verifying the asymptotic normality of GMM estimators that use elements of Z as instruments. Property 3.3 insures that β_0 is identified at least locally for one z in Z.[2] Property 3.4 can be

[1] Consider a function Fnc with domain that is Cartesian product of Ω and k-dimensional Euclidean space. For each β, $Fnc(\cdot,\beta)$ is assumed to be Borel measurable. Hansen (1982) defines Fnc to be jth-moment continuous if

$$\lim_{\delta\downarrow 0}\mathrm{E}\left[\mathrm{mod}(\cdot,\delta)^j\right] = 0,$$

where

$$\mathrm{mod}(\omega,\delta) = \sup\{\,|Fnc(\omega,\beta) - Fnc(\omega,\beta_0)|\colon |\beta-\beta_0| < \delta\,\}.$$

A matrix function is said to be jth-moment continuous if each row is jth-moment continuous.

[2] For β_0 to be locally identified using z as instruments we mean that there is a neighborhood of β_0 for which $|\mathrm{E}[zm(y,\cdot)]|$ has unique minimum at β_0.

interpreted as the matrix counterpart to the requirement that Z be a linear space. A matrix inner product $\langle\cdot|\cdot\rangle_*$ is induced on Z via

$$\langle z|z^*\rangle_* = \langle ze|z^*e\rangle. \tag{3.4}$$

Property 3.5 imposes a continuity requirement on the expected cross-product matrix functional defined by d. Among other things, this property implies that any two elements z and z^* in Z for which

$$\langle z - z^*|z - z^*\rangle_* = 0, \tag{3.5}$$

result in estimators with the same asymptotic covariance matrix.

The disturbance vector e may generate a serially correlated stochastic process $\{e_t\colon -\infty < t < +\infty\}$, and elements in Z are not restricted to be uncorrelated with e_t for all t. Therefore, this setup can accommodate models with serially correlated disturbances and instrumental variables that are predetermined but not strictly exogenous. Also, the set Z of matrices of instrumental variables can be infinite-dimensional. In section 5 we give illustrations of estimation problems for which Z is infinite-dimensional.

Alternative GMM estimators are indexed by alternative choices of z. For any given z we can think of estimating β_0 by minimizing

$$P^T[zm(y,\beta)]\cdot P^T[zm(y,\beta)], \tag{3.6}$$

by choice of β in some admissible parameter space that contains an open neighborhood of β_0. However, our analysis is not limited to estimators $\{\beta_T\colon T \geq 1\}$ that minimize objective functions of the form (3.6). For instance, many estimators solve minimization (or maximization) problems with first-order conditions which imply that $\{P^T[zm(y,\beta_T)]\colon T \geq 1\}$ converges in probability to zero for some choice of z. Such estimators have an instrumental variables interpretation and have an asymptotic distribution that is identical with the GMM estimator we associate with z.[3]

In this paper we do not establish the consistency and asymptotic normality of the estimators under consideration. Instead, we refer the interested reader to

[3] Many econometric estimators solve maximization or minimization problems with first-order conditions of the form

$$P^T[z^T m(y,\beta_T)] = 0, \tag{$*$}$$

where $\{P^T[(z^T - z)e]\colon T \geq 1\}$ converges in probability to zero. In $(*)$ z^T may depend on the estimator β_T or on any other estimated parameters as long as these estimators are consistent. Also, in time series problems in which elements of z depend on variables that are arbitrarily far back in the past, a z_t^T depending only on finite sample information can be found that approximates z_t in the sense that $\{P^T[(z^T - z)e]\colon T \geq 1\}$ converges in probability to zero.

Hansen (1982) for a formal study of these large sample properties.[4] From results in that paper, we know that the asymptotic covariance matrix for an estimator that uses the matrix z for instruments is given by

$$\mathrm{cov}(z) = [\mathrm{E}(zd)]^{-1}\langle z|z\rangle_*[\mathrm{E}(zd)']^{-1}. \tag{3.7}$$

If $\mathrm{E}(zd)$ is singular, the parameter vector β_0 ceases to be identified locally when z is used as the matrix of instruments, and we interpret (3.7) as being infinite.

4. Greatest lower bound calculation

A goal of this paper is to find the greatest lower bound for the asymptotic covariance matrices of GMM estimators for infinite-dimensional classes of estimators. In other words, the problem is to find a matrix $\inf(Z)$ for which

$$\inf(Z) \leq \mathrm{cov}(z) \quad \text{for all } z \text{ in } Z, \tag{4.1}$$

and for which there is a sequence $\{z^j: j \geq 1\}$ such that $\{\mathrm{cov}(z^j): j \geq 1\}$ converges to $\inf(Z)$. As is true in the Gauss–Markov Theorem, the matrix inequality $\leq$ is a partial ordering interpreted to mean that difference between the right-hand and left-hand matrices is positive semi-definite. The fact that the matrix inequality is only a partial ordering leaves open the possibility that the greatest lower bound is not well-defined. However, as is shown below, the restrictions placed on Z are sufficient for $\inf(Z)$ to exist. When $\mathrm{E}(zd)$ is singular implying that $\mathrm{cov}(z)$ is infinite, we interpret $\mathrm{cov}(z)$ as being greater than any finite positive semi-definite matrix.

Our strategy for solving this problem is to use minor modifications of standard Hilbert space methods. Assuming Z satisfies Property 3.1, it is convenient to transform the index set of the GMM estimators from Z to a vector linear subspace of F. Let

$$F^0 = \{f \text{ in } F: f = M(ze) \text{ for some } z \text{ in } Z\}. \tag{4.2}$$

For any elements z and z^* in Z for which $M(ze)$ and $M(z^*e)$ are equal,

$$\langle z - z^*|z - z^*\rangle_* = 0. \tag{4.3}$$

[4] The asymptotic distribution theory in Hansen (1982) imposes a more restrictive assumption than Property 3.1. However, given Lemma 2.3 it is straightforward to extend that analysis to situations in which Properties 3.1–3.5 are satisfied. The treatment of consistency given in Hansen requires additional assumptions; however, these assumptions are not always necessary. One set of assumptions used in Hansen is (i) the parameter space is compact; (ii) $\mathrm{E}[zm(y,\cdot)]$ exists and is finite at all points in the parameter space and has a unique zero at β_0; and (iii) $zm(y,\cdot)$ is first-moment continuous at all points in the parameter space. In order to have the parameter space be independent of the choice of z, it may be necessary to include some additional orthogonality conditions that are common for all GMM estimators under consideration.

When Z satisfies Properties 3.2 and 3.5, $\mathrm{E}[(z-z^*)d]$ is zero, or equivalently

$$\mathrm{E}(zd) = \mathrm{E}(z^*d). \tag{4.4}$$

Therefore, we can define a matrix function D on F^0 to be

$$D(f) = \mathrm{E}(zd) \quad \text{for any } f \text{ in } F^0. \tag{4.5}$$

Using the function D and transforming the index set of GMM estimators from Z to F^0, an alternative way to pose the general problem considered in this paper is to find the largest matrix $\inf(Z)$ for which

$$\inf(Z) \le D(f)^{-1}\mathrm{E}(ff')[D(f)']^{-1} \quad \text{for all } f \text{ in } F^0. \tag{4.6}$$

In general F^0 is not closed (in mean-square) which means that the greatest lower bound $\inf(Z)$ for the right-hand side of (4.6) may not be attained. To calculate $\inf(Z)$ it is convenient to add the closure points to F^0. The set of all closure points is given by

$$F^* = \left\{ f \text{ in } F\text{: } \lim_{j\to\infty} \mathrm{E}[(f-f^j)\cdot(f-f^j)] = 0 \right. \\ \left. \text{for some sequence } \{f^j\text{: } j \ge 1\} \text{ in } F^0 \right\}. \tag{4.7}$$

The linearity of M (Lemma 2.1) and Z (Property 3.4) induce linearity on F^0 and F^*, respectively.

Lemma 4.1. Suppose that Z satisfies Properties 3.1 and 3.4. Then F^0 and F^* satisfy Property 2.2.

Calculating $\inf(Z)$ is closely related to representing D using expected cross-products with an element of F^*. A matrix counterpart to the Riesz–Frechet Theorem can be applied to obtain such a representation.

Lemma 4.2. Suppose Z satisfies Properties 3.1–3.5. Then there exists a unique f^d in F^* such that

$$\mathrm{E}(ff^{d\prime}) = D(f) \quad \textit{for all } f \textit{ in } F^0. \tag{4.8}$$

Furthermore, $\mathrm{E}(f^d f^{d\prime})$ *is non-singular.*[5]

It turns out that f^d used to represent D can also be used to calculate $\inf(Z)$ in (4.1) and (4.6).

Lemma 4.3. Suppose Z satisfies Properties 3.1–3.5. Then $\inf(Z) = [\mathrm{E}(f^d f^{d\prime})]^{-1}$. *Furthermore, if f^d is in F^0, then* $\inf(Z) = (\langle z^d | z^d \rangle_*)^{-1}$ *for z^d such that $M(z^d e) = f^d$. Finally,* $\mathrm{cov}(z) = \inf(Z)$ *if and only if $M(ze) = M(cz^d e)$ for some k-dimensional non-singular matrix of real numbers c.*

Lemmas 4.2 and 4.3 show that the problem of finding an f^d in F^0 that attains $\inf(Z)$ is equivalent to the problem of finding an f^d in F^0 that satisfies (4.8). Since F^0 is not always closed, such an f^d may not exist, but it always can be approximated in the limit by a sequence $\{f^j : j \geq 1\}$ in F^0. There is a corresponding sequence $\{z^j : j \geq 1\}$ in Z for which $f^j = M(z^j e)$. Thus $\inf(Z)$ can always be approximated arbitrarily well by members of Z.

A problem that is equivalent to finding a f^d in F^0 that satisfies (4.8), is to find a z^d in Z that satisfies

$$\mathrm{E}(zd) = \langle z | z^d \rangle_* = \lim_{T \to \infty} \mathrm{E}\left[P^T(ze) P^T(z^d e)'\right]. \tag{4.9}$$

Relation (4.9) can be viewed as a set of first-order conditions that are sufficient for $\mathrm{cov}(z^d)$ to attain the greatest lower bound $\inf(Z)$. It is not surprising that this bound is attained by other elements in Z obtained by premultiplying z^d by a k-dimensional non-singular matrix of real numbers c since the equation system

$$P^T\left[z^d m(y, \beta)\right] = 0 \tag{4.10}$$

is equivalent to

$$P^T\left[c z^d m(y, \beta)\right] = 0. \tag{4.11}$$

Lemma 4.2 guarantees the existence of an f^d in F^* that satisfies (4.8) when, among other things, Z satisfies Property 3.5. For some examples, it turns out that the most convenient way of verifying that Z satisfies Property 3.5 is to find an f^d in F^* that satisfies

$$\mathrm{E}(zd) = \mathrm{E}\left[M(ze) f^{d\prime}\right] \quad \text{for all } z \text{ in } Z. \tag{4.12}$$

[5] Property 3.5 plays a crucial role in guaranteeing that $\mathrm{E}(f^d f^{d\prime})$ is non-singular. In some time series estimation problems in which Property 3.5 is violated, it is possible to construct a sequence of estimators with asymptotic covariance matrices that converge to a singular matrix.

Lemma 4.4. Suppose Z satisfies Properties 3.1–3.4 and there is an f^d in F^* satisfying (4.8). Then Z satisfies Property 3.5.[6]

Using the definition of D given in (4.5), it follows that the f^d that satisfies (4.12) also satisfies (4.8). Hence if we can find an f^d that satisfies (4.12), then we need not verify that Z satisfies Property 3.5.

In the remaining section of this paper, we provide a more explicit characterization of the function M and the matrix $\inf(Z)$ for two examples.

5. Illustrations

In this section we show how to apply the approach suggested in sections 2 through 4. We focus on two particular examples that were chosen for illustrative purposes. Hansen (1985) provides a more comprehensive set of applications of this approach. Some of the analysis underlying these two examples is common and will be presented first. For the first example we impose an additional restriction on the disturbance vector e, and for the second example we impose an additional restriction on the index set Z of instrumental variables.

Let w be an n-dimensional random vector that is measurable with respect to B and satisfies:

Assumption 5.1. $\mathrm{E}(w|B_{-1}) = 0$.

Assumption 5.1 guarantees that the stochastic process generated by w in conjunction with S is a martingale difference sequence. The disturbance vector e is assumed to satisfy:

Assumption 5.2. $e = \Gamma(L)w_0$ *and* $\Gamma(\sigma) = \sum_{j=0}^{s-1} \Gamma_j \sigma^j$,

where L is the lag operator, σ is a complex variable, and Γ_j is a K by n matrix of real numbers for $0 \leq j < s$. Taken together Assumptions 5.1 and 5.2 imply

$$\mathrm{E}(e|B_{-s}) = 0. \tag{5.1}$$

Many rational expectations models have the implication that the disturbance vector is an s-step ahead forecast error of some K-dimensional random vector

[6] Relation (4.12) can be modified to require that there exists an f^* in F such that

$$\mathrm{E}(zd) = \mathrm{E}[M(ze)f^{*\prime}] \quad \text{for all } z \text{ in } Z.$$

This is weaker than (4.12) since f^* is not required to be in F^*. This weaker condition is not particularly useful for our problem since we need to characterize f^d in order to characterize the $\inf(Z)$.

where s can be greater than one [e.g., see Hansen and Hodrick (1980, 1983)]. Assumptions 5.1 and 5.2 are consistent with those models.

Let J be a closed (in mean-square) linear space of random variables with finite second moments that are measurable with respect to B. One possibility is for J to contain all such random variables. A second possibility is for J to contain all linear combinations of a finite-dimensional random vector that is measurable with respect to B and has a finite second moment. A third possibility is for J to be the closed linear space generated by all finite linear combinations of current and past values of a random vector with a finite second moment. Flexibility in the specification of J is advantageous because it broadens the range of estimation problems to which the analysis applies. For instance, a researcher may wish to characterize the largest class of GMM estimators for which a particular estimator attains the greatest lower bound. In this way he can assess better the cost of obtaining further gains in asymptotic efficiency by expanding the class of estimators.

Let B^* be the sigma algebra generated by J, and let

$$Z = \{z : z \text{ is a } k \text{ by } K \text{ matrix of random variables that are in } J_{-s}\}. \tag{5.2}$$

We assume that:

Assumption 5.3. $\mathrm{E}(ww'|B^*_{-1}) = I$,

so that w is homoscedastic conditioned on B^*_{-1}.

Assumptions 5.1–5.3 and specification (5.2) of the index set Z imply that

$$\begin{aligned}\mathrm{E}(ze) &= \mathrm{E}[\mathrm{E}(ze|B^*_{-s})] \\ &= \mathrm{E}[z\mathrm{E}(e|B^*_{-s})] \\ &= 0 \qquad \text{for all } z \text{ in } Z.\end{aligned} \tag{5.3}$$

In this sense, members of Z are valid candidates for instrumental variables. However, in general

$$\mathrm{E}(z_t e) \neq 0 \quad \text{for positive values of } t, \tag{5.4}$$

so that members of Z may not be strictly exogenous. This feature of Z is central in the analysis of Example 2.

The following characterization of M is valid for these examples:

Lemma 5.1. Suppose Assumptions 5.1–5.3 are satisfied and Z is given by (5.2). Then Z satisfies Property 3.1 and

$$M(ze) = \left[z_0 \Gamma(L^{-1})\right] w. \tag{5.5}$$

The proofs of lemmas presented in this section are given in appendix C.

Next, we verify that $M(ze)$ as given by (5.5) is in F. Since z is measurable with respect to B_{-s} and Assumption 5.2 is satisfied, the elements of $[z_0 \Gamma(L^{-1})]$ are measurable with respect to B_{-1}. Consequently, (5.2) implies that

$$\mathrm{E}\{\left[z_0 \Gamma(L^{-1})\right] w | B_{-1}\} = \left[z_0 \Gamma(L^{-1})\right] \mathrm{E}(w | B_{-1}) = 0. \tag{5.6}$$

Therefore, $M(ze)$ as given by (5.5) is in F. Using (5.5) we can represent the matrix inner product $\langle \cdot | \cdot \rangle_*$ as

$$\begin{aligned} \langle z | z^* \rangle_* &= \mathrm{E}\{\left[z_0 \Gamma(L^{-1})\right] ww' \left[z_0^* \Gamma(L^{-1})\right]'\} \\ &= \mathrm{E}\{\mathrm{E}\{\left[z_0 \Gamma(L^{-1})\right] ww' \left[z_0^* \Gamma(L^{-1})\right]' | B_{-1}^*\}\} \qquad (5.7) \\ &= \mathrm{E}\{\left[z_0 \Gamma(L^{-1})\right]\left[z_0^* \Gamma(L^{-1})\right]'\} \quad \text{for any } z \text{ and } z^* \text{ in } Z. \end{aligned}$$

Let $\mathrm{proj}(\cdot | J_{-s})$ denote the linear least squares projection operator onto J_{-s} defined relative to the standard inner product on the L^2 space of random variables with finite second moments. To ensure that Z satisfies Properties 3.2 and 3.3, we assume:

Assumption 5.4. $\mathrm{E}[\mathrm{tr}(d'd)]$ *is finite and* $\partial m(y, \cdot)/\partial \beta$ *is second-moment continuous at* β_0.[7]

Assumption 5.5. $\mathrm{E}[\mathrm{proj}(d' | J_{-s}) \mathrm{proj}(d | J_{-s})]$ *is non-singular.*

Lemma 5.2. Suppose Assumptions 5.4 and 5.5 are satisfied and Z is given by (5.2). Then Z satisfies Properties 3.2 and 3.3.

Since J is a linear space of random variables, Z satisfies Property 3.4 (linearity) by construction. Finally, to guarantee that Z satisfies Property 3.5

[7]See note one for a definition of second moment continuity.

(continuity of D) we assume:

Assumption 5.6. $\det[\Gamma(\sigma)\Gamma(\sigma)'] \neq 0$ *for all* $|\sigma| = 1$,

where prime denotes transposition and complex conjugation.

Lemma 5.3. Suppose Assumptions 5.1–5.4 and 5.6 are satisfied and Z is given by (5.2). Then Z satisfies Property 3.5 and $F^0 = F^*$.

Taken together, Lemmas 5.1–5.3 show that the hypotheses of Lemmas 4.2 and 4.3 are satisfied. In the next two subsections we specialize our analysis in two distinct ways. In the first subsection, we restrict e by assuming s is one. In the second subsection we restrict Z by assuming J contains J_{-1}.

5.1. Example 1

In this example we assume that disturbance vector process is a martingale difference sequence ($s = 1$). By altering the specification of J, we can obtain time series counterparts to bounds calculated by Basmann (1957), Sargan (1958), Jorgenson and Laffont (1974), and Amemiya (1977). To obtain counterparts to the bounds calculated by Basmann and Sargan, J is taken to be finite-dimensional. To obtain the counterpart to the bounds calculated by Jorgenson and Laffont and Amemiya, J is taken to be the set of all random variables with finite second moments that are measurable with respect to B. In this case J will be infinite-dimensional in general. An additional case included in our analysis is where J is generated by all finite linear combinations of current and past values of a random vector with a finite second moment. Since the linear combinations can include arbitrary lags of the random vector, J will be infinite-dimensional for this case as well.

By applying Lemmas 4.2 and 4.3, inf(Z) is attained by a member z^d of Z that satisfies

$$\langle z|z^d\rangle_* = \mathrm{E}(zd). \tag{5.8}$$

Since the elements of z are in J_{-1}, it follows that

$$\mathrm{E}(zd) = \mathrm{E}[z\,\mathrm{proj}(d|J_{-1})] \quad \text{for all } z \text{ in } Z. \tag{5.9}$$

When s is one, (5.7) simplifies to

$$\langle z|z^d\rangle_* = \mathrm{E}(z\Gamma_0\Gamma_0' z^{d\prime}). \tag{5.10}$$

In this example $(\Gamma_0\Gamma_0')$ is the unconditional covariance matrix for e.

Substituting (5.9) and (5.10) into (5.8) gives

$$\mathrm{E}\left(z\Gamma_0\Gamma_0' z^{d\prime}\right) = \mathrm{E}\left[z \operatorname{proj}(d|J_{-1})\right] \quad \text{for all } z \text{ in } Z. \tag{5.11}$$

Members of Z have elements that are arbitrary elements of J_{-1}. Hence, relation (5.11) implies that

$$\Gamma_0\Gamma_0' z^{d\prime} = \operatorname{proj}(d|J_{-1}). \tag{5.12}$$

Since $\Gamma(\sigma)$ satisfies Assumption 5.6, $\Gamma_0\Gamma_0'$ is non-singular. Solving (5.12) for z^d gives the following result:

Lemma 5.4. Suppose Assumptions 5.1–5.6 are satisfied and Z is given by (5.2). If $s = 1$, then

$$z^d = \operatorname{proj}(d|J_{-1})'(\Gamma_0\Gamma_0')^{-1}, \tag{5.13}$$

and

$$\inf(Z) = \left\{\mathrm{E}\left[\operatorname{proj}(d|J_{-1})'(\Gamma_0\Gamma_0')^{-1}\operatorname{proj}(d|J_{-1})\right]\right\}^{-1}. \tag{5.14}$$

To derive characterization (5.14) of inf(Z), first apply Lemma 4.3 to obtain

$$\inf(Z) = \langle z^d | z^d \rangle_*^{-1} = \left[\mathrm{E}\left(z^d\Gamma_0\Gamma_0' z^{d\prime}\right)\right]^{-1}, \tag{5.15}$$

and then substitute for z^d from (5.13).

In this example the choice of instrumental variables that attains inf(Z) is obtained by calculating (or estimating) the least squares regression $\operatorname{proj}(d|J_{-1})$ and the unconditional covariance matrix $(\Gamma_0\Gamma_0')$.

5.2. *Example 2*

In this example, we allow s to be greater than one so that the disturbance vector can be serially correlated. However, we adopt a more restrictive specification of the space J. We assume that J is specified so that J_{-1} is a subspace of J. Consequently, for any variable in J, lagged values of that variable are also in J. This specification of J presumes that J is infinite-dimensional as long as there are elements in J that generate stochastic processes that are not perfectly forecastable. Among other things, the analysis in this section shows how to calculate the limiting asymptotic covariance matrix for the sequence of estimators suggested by Hayashi and Sims (1983).[8] Their sequence of estima-

[8] Hayashi and Sims (1983) do not impose the exact same assumptions that are imposed in this example although their analysis is entirely compatible with the assumptions maintained here.

tors is obtained by expanding the list of instrumental variables to include arbitrary lags of some underlying set of instrumental variables.

When s is greater than one, $[z_0\Gamma(L^{-1})]$ will not necessarily be in Z even though z is in Z. The operator $\Gamma(L^{-1})$ is a forward operator with terms in negative powers of L and z may not be strictly exogenous. For this reason we obtain an alternative to representation (5.7) of inner product $\langle \cdot|\cdot \rangle_*$. This alternative representation involves a backwards operator with a one-sided inverse. The existence of such an operator is guaranteed by the Wold Decomposition Theorem.

Lemma 5.5. *Suppose Assumptions 5.2 and 5.6 are satisfied. Then there exists an operator $\Gamma^*(L)$ such that*

$$\Gamma^*(\sigma) = \sum_{j=0}^{s-1} \Gamma_j^* \sigma^j, \tag{5.16}$$

where $\Gamma_0^*, \Gamma_1^*, \ldots, \Gamma_{s-1}^*$ are K by K matrices of real numbers;

$$\Gamma^*(\sigma)\Gamma^*(\sigma)' = \Gamma(\sigma')\Gamma(\sigma')', \tag{5.17}$$

for all complex numbers $|\sigma| = 1$; and

$$\det[\Gamma^*(\sigma)] \neq 0, \tag{5.18}$$

for all σ satisfying $|\sigma| \leq 1$.

Since Γ^* satisfies (5.17), $\langle \cdot|\cdot \rangle_*$ can be represented using Γ^*.

Lemma 5.6. *Suppose Assumptions 5.1–5.6 are satisfied and Z is given by (5.2). For any z and z^* in Z,*

$$\begin{aligned} \langle z|z^* \rangle_* &= \mathrm{E}\{ z[\Gamma^*(L^{-1})\Gamma^*(L)'z_0^{*\prime}]\} \\ &= \mathrm{E}\{[z_0\Gamma^*(L)][z_0^*\Gamma^*(L)]'\}. \end{aligned} \tag{5.19}$$

The following lemma characterizes z^d and $\inf(Z)$ for Example 2:

Lemma 5.7. *Suppose Assumptions 5.1–5.6 are satisfied and Z is given by (5.2). If J contains J_{-1}, then*

$$z^d = \mathrm{proj}\{[d_0'\Gamma^*(L^{-1})^{-1\prime}]|J_{-s}\}\Gamma^*(L)^{-1}, \tag{5.20}$$

and

$$\inf(Z) = \mathrm{E}\Big\{\mathrm{proj}\big\{\big[d_0'\Gamma^*(L^{-1})^{-1\prime}\big]|J_{-s}\big\} \times \mathrm{proj}\big\{\big[d_0'\Gamma^*(L^{-1})^{-1\prime}\big]|J_{-s}\big\}'\Big\}^{-1}. \tag{5.21}$$

Since Γ^* satisfies (5.16) and (5.18) of Lemma 5.5, it follows that Γ^* has a one-sided inverse on the space of stationary stochastic processes with finite second moments. In appendix C we use this fact to show that the right-hand side of (5.20) is a well-defined matrix of random variables in J_{-s}. Let z^* denote this matrix.

To prove (5.20) we must show that z^* equals z^d where z^d is the solution to

$$\mathrm{E}(zd) = \langle z|z^d\rangle_*. \tag{5.22}$$

Using the representation of $\langle\cdot|\cdot\rangle_*$ given in (5.19) of Lemma 5.6, it follows that

$$\langle z|z^d\rangle_* = \mathrm{E}\big\{z\big[\Gamma^*(L^{-1})\Gamma^*(L)'z_0^{d\prime}\big]\big\}. \tag{5.23}$$

Combining (5.22) and (5.23) gives

$$\mathrm{E}(zd) = \mathrm{E}\big\{z\big[\Gamma^*(L^{-1})\Gamma^*(L)'z_0^{d\prime}\big]\big\} \quad \text{for all } z \text{ in } Z. \tag{5.24}$$

For (5.24) to be satisfied, it is necessary and sufficient that

$$\mathrm{proj}(d|J_{-s}) = \mathrm{proj}\big\{\big[\Gamma^*(L^{-1})\Gamma^*(L)'z_0^{d\prime}\big]|J_{-s}\big\}. \tag{5.25}$$

To verify that z^* equals z^d, we substitute for z^* as given by the right-hand side of (5.20) for z^d in the right-hand side of (5.25). This gives

$$\begin{aligned} &\mathrm{proj}\big[\Gamma^*(L^{-1})\Gamma^*(L)'z_0^{*\prime}|J_{-s}\big] \\ &= \mathrm{proj}\big\{\Gamma^*(L^{-1})\mathrm{proj}\big[\Gamma^*(L^{-1})^{-1}d_0|J_{-s}\big]|J_{-s}\big\} \\ &= \mathrm{proj}\big\{\mathrm{proj}\big[\Gamma^*(L^{-1})\Gamma^*(L^{-1})^{-1}d_0|J_{-s}\big]|J_{-s}\big\} \\ &= \mathrm{proj}(d|J_{-s}), \end{aligned} \tag{5.26}$$

which verifies that z^* satisfies (5.25). Since z^* is in Z, z^* equals z^d and $\inf(Z)$

is attained by z^*. Lemmas 4.3 and 5.6 show that

$$\begin{aligned}\inf(Z) &= \langle z^d | z^d \rangle_*^{-1} \\ &= \mathrm{E}\{[z_0^d \Gamma^*(L)][z_0^d \Gamma^*(L)]'\}^{-1}.\end{aligned} \tag{5.27}$$

To prove (5.21) of Lemma 5.7, we substitute (5.20) into (5.27).

In this example the choice of instrumental variables that attains $\inf(Z)$ is obtained by calculating (or estimating) the operator $\Gamma^*(L)$ from the serial correlation properties of $\{e_t: -\infty < t < +\infty\}$ and calculating the least squares regression $\mathrm{proj}\{d_0'\Gamma^*(L^{-1})^{-1\prime}] | J_{-s}\}$.

6. Conclusions

In this paper we suggested and documented a method for calculating bounds on the asymptotic covariance matrices for estimators in an infinite-dimensional class of GMM estimators. The method we suggested uses the theory of stationary stochastic processes coupled with martingale difference decompositions as suggested by Gordin (1969). We illustrated how to use the method by calculating greatest lower bounds for GMM estimators under two different sets of auxiliary assumptions. These two sets of assumptions are by no means exhaustive. In Hansen (1985) this method is applied in calculating greatest lower bounds for many other sets of auxiliary assumptions corresponding to applications of GMM estimation in the literature. A crucial ingredient in these examples is the characterization of the approximating martingale difference sequence shown to exist in this paper.

Appendix A

In this appendix we prove the lemmas given in section 2. Throughout all of the appendices we let $\|h\| = \mathrm{E}(h \cdot h)^{1/2}$ where h is a k-dimensional random vector with a finite second moment. The norm $\|\cdot\|$ is the norm for the L^2 space induced by the product measure of *Prob* and the counting measure on the set $\{1, 2, \ldots, k\}$.

Proof of Lemma 2.1. This proof is divided into three parts. First, we establish the linearity of F, then of G, and finally of H.

(i) Linearity of F: Let f and f^* be in F and c and c^* be k by k matrices of real numbers. Since f and f^* are in F,

$$\mathrm{E}(f | B_{-1}) = \mathrm{E}(f^* | B_{-1}) = 0. \tag{A.1}$$

Hence,

$$\mathrm{E}(cf + c^*f^* | B_{-1}) = c\mathrm{E}(f | B_{-1}) + c^*\mathrm{E}(f^* | B_{-1}) = 0. \tag{A.2}$$

Also, the Triangle Inequality insures that $cf + c^*f^*$ has a finite second moment. Therefore, $cf + c^*f^*$ is in F.

(ii) Linearity of G: Let g and g^* be in G and c and c^* be k by k matrices of real numbers. Since g and g^* are in G, there exist non-negative integers τ and τ^* such that

$$\mathrm{E}(g|B_{-\tau}) = \mathrm{E}(g^*|B_{-\tau^*}) = 0. \tag{A.3}$$

Without loss of generality, let $\tau \geq \tau^*$. Then (A.3) and the Law of Iterated Expectations imply that

$$\mathrm{E}(cg + c^*g^*|B_{-\tau}) = c\mathrm{E}(g|B_{-\tau}) + c^*\mathrm{E}(g^*|B_{-\tau}) = 0. \tag{A.4}$$

Also, the Triangle Inequality insures that $cg + c^*g^*$ has a finite second moment. Therefore, $cg + c^*g^*$ is in G.

(iii) Linearity of H: Let h and h^* be in H and c and c^* be k by k matrices of real numbers. Define

$$h^+ = ch + c^*h^*. \tag{A.5}$$

Since h and h^* are in H, there are sequences $\{g^j\colon j \geq 1\}$ and $\{g^{*j}\colon j \geq 1\}$ in G such that

$$\limsup_{T\to\infty} \| p^T(h - g^j) \| < 1/j \quad \text{for} \quad j \geq 1, \tag{A.6}$$

and

$$\limsup_{T\to\infty} \| p^T(h^* - g^{*j}) \| < 1/j \quad \text{for} \quad j \geq 1. \tag{A.7}$$

Let $g^{+j} = cg^j + c^*g^{*j}$, and note that g^{+j} is in G for all $j \geq 1$. Also,

$$P^T(h^+ - g^{+j}) = cP^T(h - g^j) + c^*P^T(h^* - g^{*j}). \tag{A.8}$$

By the Triangle and Cauchy–Schwarz Inequalities

$$\begin{aligned} \| P^T(h^+ - g^{+j}) \| \leq{}& \mathrm{tr}(cc')^{1/2} \| P^T(h - g^j) \| \\ &+ \mathrm{tr}(c^*c^{*\prime})^{1/2} \| P^T(h^* - g^{*j}) \|, \end{aligned} \tag{A.9}$$

where $\mathrm{tr}(cc')$ denotes the trace of the matrix cc'. Hence,

$$\limsup_{T\to\infty} \| P^T(h^+ - g^{+j}) \| \leq \left[\mathrm{tr}(cc')^{1/2} + \mathrm{tr}(c^*c^{*\prime})^{1/2}\right]/j. \tag{A.10}$$

Taking limits as j goes to infinity, we obtain

$$\lim_{j\to\infty}\limsup_{T\to\infty}\left\| P^T\left(h^+ - g^{+j}\right)\right\| = 0. \tag{A.11}$$

Therefore, h^+ is in H. Q.E.D.

Proof of Lemma 2.2. This proof relies heavily on the proof of Gordin's (1969) Theorem. In proving this lemma, it is convenient to reproduce some of his steps. Let h be in H and let $\{g^j\colon\ j \geq 1\}$ be a sequence in G such that

$$\limsup_{T\to\infty}\left\| P^T\left(h - g^j\right)\right\| < 1/j. \tag{A.12}$$

Since g^j is in G, there is an integer $\tau(j)$ such that

$$\mathrm{E}\left[g^j | B_{-\tau(j)}\right] = 0 \quad \text{for} \quad j \geq 1. \tag{A.13}$$

The set F is a closed linear subspace of the L^2 space defined at the beginning of this appendix. Since g^j satisfies (A.13), it follows that

$$g^j = \sum_{t=1}^{\tau(j)} \operatorname{proj}\left(g^j | F_{1-t}\right), \tag{A.14}$$

where $\operatorname{proj}(\cdot|F)$ denotes the least squares projection operator onto F.

Following Gordin (1969), there is a sequence $\{f^j\colon\ j \geq 1\}$ in F that can be used to approximate the sequence $\{g^j\colon\ j \geq 1\}$. The approximating sequence is

$$f^j = \sum_{t=1}^{\tau(j)} \operatorname{proj}\left(g^j_{t-1} | F\right) \quad \text{for} \quad j \geq 1. \tag{A.15}$$

Then for each $j \geq 1$ and $T \geq [\tau(j) - 1]$,

$$P^T\left(g^j - f^j\right) = \left(g_0^{*j} - g_T^{*j}\right)/\sqrt{T}, \tag{A.16}$$

where

$$g^{*j} = \sum_{t=2}^{\tau(j)} \sum_{s=t}^{\tau(j)} \operatorname{proj}\left(g^j_{t-1} | F_{t-s}\right). \tag{A.17}$$

Notice that for each $j \geq 1$, g^{*j} is in L^2 so that

$$\limsup_{T\to\infty}\left\|\left(g_0^{*j} - g_T^{*j}\right)/\sqrt{T}\right\| \leq 2\lim_{T\to\infty}\|g^{*j}\|/\sqrt{T} = 0. \tag{A.18}$$

Taking norms and limits of (A.16) gives

$$\lim_{T\to\infty} \| P^T(g^j - f^j) \| = 0 \quad \text{for all} \quad j \geq 1. \tag{A.19}$$

Using (A.12), (A.19), and the Triangle Inequality, we obtain the following inequalities

$$\limsup_{T\to\infty} \| P^T(h - f^j) \| < 1/j \quad \text{for all} \quad j \geq 1, \tag{A.20}$$

and

$$\limsup_{T\to\infty} \| P^T(f^j - f^{j*}) \| < 2/j^* \quad \text{for all} \quad j \geq j^*. \tag{A.21}$$

Now for any f in F

$$\| P^T(f) \| = \|f\|, \tag{A.22}$$

so that (A.21) implies that

$$\|f^j - f^{j*}\| < 2/j^* \quad \text{for all} \quad j \geq j^*. \tag{A.23}$$

Consequently, $\{f^j\colon\ j \geq 1\}$ is a Cauchy sequence in L^2. Since F is closed, $\{f^j\colon\ j \geq 1\}$ converges in mean square (L^2) to some f^0 in F. Hence, (A.20), (A.22), and the Triangle Inequality imply that

$$\limsup_{T\to\infty} \| p^T(h - f^0) \| = 0. \tag{A.24}$$

We define $M(h) = f^0$.

Next, we show that (A.24) defines a unique f^0 in F. Let f^+ be any other element in F for which

$$\limsup_{T\to\infty} \| P^T(h - f^+) \| = 0. \tag{A.25}$$

Then, by the Triangle Inequality,

$$\limsup_{T\to\infty} \| P^T(f^+ - f^0) \| = 0. \tag{A.26}$$

Using relation (A.22) we conclude that

$$\|f^+ - f^0\| = 0, \tag{A.27}$$

so that $f^+ = f^0$. Therefore, (A.24) defines a unique value for $M(h)$.

Finally, we show that M is linear. This logic parallels closely the logic used in proving Lemma 2.1. Let h and h^* be in H and c and c^* be k by k matrices of real numbers. Define

$$h^+ = ch + c^*h^*. \tag{A.28}$$

Since F is linear, $cM(h) + c^*M(h^*)$ is in F. We must show that

$$\limsup_{T\to\infty} \| P^T[h^+ - cM(h) - c^*M(h^*)] \| = 0. \tag{A.29}$$

The Cauchy–Schwarz and Triangle Inequalities imply that

$$\begin{aligned} &\| P^T[h^+ - cM(h) - c^*M(h^*)] \| \\ &\leq \operatorname{tr}(cc')^{1/2} \| P^T[h - M(h)] \| \\ &\quad + \operatorname{tr}(c^*c^{*\prime})^{1/2} \| P^T[h^* - M(h^*)] \|. \end{aligned} \tag{A.30}$$

It follows that

$$\begin{aligned} &\limsup_{T\to\infty} \| P^T[h^+ - cM(h) - c^*M(h^*)] \| \\ &\leq \operatorname{tr}(cc')^{1/2} \limsup_{T\to\infty} \| P^T[h - M(h)] \| \\ &\quad + \operatorname{tr}(c^*c^{*\prime})^{1/2} \limsup_{T\to\infty} \| P^T[h^* - M(h^*)] \| \\ &= 0. \quad \text{Q.E.D.} \end{aligned} \tag{A.31}$$

Proof of Lemma 2.3. This Lemma is a simple application of Billingsley's (1961) Theorem extended to random vectors. Billingsley's Theorem implies that $\{\mu \cdot P^T[M(h)]: T \geq 1\}$ converges in distribution to a normally distributed random vector with mean zero and covariance matrix $\mu'\mathrm{E}[M(h)M(h)']\mu$ for any k-dimensional vector of real numbers μ. Consequently, it implies that $\{P^T[M(h)]: T \geq 1\}$ converges in distribution to a normally distributed random vector with mean zero and covariance matrix $\mathrm{E}[M(h)M(h)']$. Lemma 2.2 guarantees that $\{P^T[h - M(h)]: T \geq 1\}$ converges in mean square (L^2) to zero. Therefore, $\{P^T(h): T \geq 1\}$ converges in distribution to the same random vector as does $\{P^T[M(h)]: T \geq 1\}$. Q.E.D.

Proof of Lemma 2.4. The proof of this lemma relies heavily on Lemma 2.2. Lemma 2.2 implies that for any h and h^* in H, $\{P^T[h - M(h)]: T \geq 1\}$ and $\{P^T[h^* - M(h^*)]: T \geq 1\}$ converge in mean square to zero. However,

$$\begin{aligned} &\mathrm{E}[P^T(h)P^T(h^*)'] - \mathrm{E}[P^T[M(h)]P^T[M(h^*)]'] \\ &= \mathrm{E}\{P^T[h - M(h)]P^T[h^* - M(h^*)]'\} \\ &\quad + \mathrm{E}\{P^T[M(h)]P^T[h^* - M(h^*)]'\} \\ &\quad + \mathrm{E}\{P^T[h - M(h)]P^T[M(h^*)]'\}. \end{aligned} \tag{A.32}$$

Since $M(h)$ and $M(h^*)$ are in F,

$$\mathrm{E}[P^T[M(h)]P^T[M(h^*)]'] = \mathrm{E}[M(h)M(h^*)'], \tag{A.33}$$

$$\|P^T[M(h)]\| = \|M(h)\|, \tag{A.34}$$

$$\|P^T[M(h^*)]\| = \|M(h^*)\|. \tag{A.35}$$

Taking limits of (A.32) and applying the Cauchy–Schwarz Inequality gives

$$\lim_{T \to \infty} \{\mathrm{E}[P^T(h)P^T(h^*)'] - \mathrm{E}[M(h)M(h^*)']\} = 0. \tag{A.36}$$

Q.E.D.

Appendix B

In this appendix we prove the lemmas given in section 4.

Proof of Lemma 4.1. For any f and f^* in F^0 there is a z and a z^* in Z such that $f = M(ze)$ and $f^* = M(z^*e)$. Let c and c^* be any k by k matrices of real numbers. Since Z satisfies Property 2.6, $cz + c^*z^*$ is in Z. Hence, $M[(cz + c^*z^*)e]$ is in F^0. Lemma 2.2 guarantees that M is linear in the sense that

$$M[(cz + c^*z^*)e] = cM(ze) + c^*M(z^*e) = cf + c^*f^*, \tag{B.1}$$

which proves that F_0 satisfies Property 2.2.

Let f and f^* be in F^* and c and c^* be k by k matrices of real numbers. Then there are sequences $\{f^j\colon\ j \geq 1\}$ and $\{f^{j*}\colon\ j \geq 1\}$ in F^0 such that

$$\lim_{j \to \infty} \|f - f^j\| = 0, \tag{B.2}$$

and

$$\lim_{j \to \infty} \|f^* - f^{j*}\| = 0. \tag{B.3}$$

Since F^0 satisfies Property 2.2, $\{cf^j + c^* f^{j*}\colon\ j \geq 1\}$ is a sequence in F^0. By the Triangle and Cauchy–Schwarz Inequalities,

$$\begin{aligned} &\left\|(cf^j + c^* f^{j*}) - (cf + c^* f^*)\right\| \\ &\leq \left\|c(f^j - f)\right\| + \left\|c^*(f^{j*} - f^*)\right\| \\ &\leq \operatorname{tr}(cc')^{1/2}\|f^j - f\| + \operatorname{tr}(c^* c^{*\prime})^{1/2}\|f^{j*} - f^*\|. \end{aligned} \tag{B.4}$$

The limits in (B.2) and (B.3) imply that

$$\lim_{j \to \infty} \left\|(cf^j + c^* f^{j*}) - (cf + c^* f^*)\right\| = 0. \tag{B.5}$$

Therefore, $cf + c^* f^*$ is in F^* and F^* satisfies Property 2.2.

Proof of Lemma 4.2. This proof is divided into three steps. First we show that D is a bounded linear matrix functional on F^0. Then we extend this functional to F^*. Finally, we use the same logic as is used in the Riesz–Frechet Theorem to obtain a representation of D.

To show that D is a linear matrix functional, let f and f^* be in F^0, and let c and c^* be k by k matrices of real numbers. Then there exist a z and a z^* in Z such that $f = M(ze)$ and $f^* = M(z^* e)$. Hence,

$$D(f) = \mathrm{E}(zd), \tag{B.6}$$

and

$$D(f^*) = \mathrm{E}(z^* d). \tag{B.7}$$

Lemma 2.2 guarantees the linearity of M so that

$$cf + c^* f^* = M\left[(cz + c^* z^*)e\right]. \tag{B.8}$$

Consequently,

$$\begin{aligned} D(cf + c^*f^*) &= \mathrm{E}[(cz + c^*z^*)d] \\ &= c\mathrm{E}(zd) + c^*E(z^*d) \\ &= cD(f) + c^*D(f^*), \end{aligned} \tag{B.9}$$

which proves that D is a linear matrix functional.

To prove that D is bounded, let

$$\delta = \sup\{\mathrm{tr}[D(f)D(f)']^{1/2}: \|f\| = 1 \text{ and } f \text{ is in } F^0\}. \tag{B.10}$$

We must show that δ is finite. Suppose to the contrary that δ is infinite. Then there exists a sequence $\{f^j: j \geq 1\}$ in F^0 such that $\|f^j\| = 1$ and

$$\mathrm{tr}[D(f^j)D(f^j)']^{1/2} > j. \tag{B.11}$$

Now

$$f^{j*} = f^j/\mathrm{tr}[D(f^j)D(f^j)']^{1/2} \tag{B.12}$$

is in F^0,

$$\|f^{j*}\| \leq (1/j), \tag{B.13}$$

and

$$D(f^{j*}) = \left(1/\mathrm{tr}[D(f^j)D(f^j)']^{1/2}\right)D(f^j), \tag{B.14}$$

for $j \geq 1$. Hence

$$\lim_{j\to\infty} \|f^{j*}\| = 0, \tag{B.15}$$

and

$$\mathrm{tr}[D(f^{j*})D(f^{j*})']^{1/2} = 1 \quad \text{for all} \quad j \geq 1. \tag{B.16}$$

Since f^{j*} is in F^0, there exists a z^j in Z such that

$$f^{j*} = M(z^je) \quad \text{for all} \quad j \geq 1. \tag{B.17}$$

In light of (B.15)

$$\lim_{j\to\infty} \langle z^j | z^j \rangle_* = 0. \tag{B.18}$$

Since Z satisfies Property 3.5,

$$\lim_{j\to\infty} \mathrm{E}(z^j d) = \lim_{j\to\infty} D(f^{j*}) = 0. \tag{B.19}$$

This contradicts (B.16). Therefore, D is bounded.

Next, we prove that there is an extension of D to F^*. For any given f^* in F^*, let $\{f^j\colon\ j \geq 1\}$ be a sequence in F^0 for which

$$\lim_{j\to\infty} \|f^j - f^*\| = 0. \tag{B.20}$$

By the Triangle Inequality,

$$\lim_{j\to\infty} \|f^j\| = \|f^*\|. \tag{B.21}$$

Since D is bounded on F^0,

$$\delta^* = \sup\left\{\mathrm{tr}\left[D(f^j)D(f^j)'\right]^{1/2}\colon\ j \geq 1\right\} \tag{B.22}$$

is finite and there exists a subsequence $\{f^{j(\tau)}\colon\ \tau \geq 1\}$ for which

$$\lim_{\tau\to\infty} D\left[f^{j(\tau)}\right] = D(f^*) \tag{B.23}$$

exists and satisfies

$$\mathrm{tr}\left[D(f^*)D(f^*)'\right] \leq \delta^*. \tag{B.24}$$

Property 3.5 of Z then guarantees that

$$\lim_{j\to\infty} D(f^j) = D(f^*), \tag{B.25}$$

since

$$\lim_{\tau\to\infty} \|f^{j(\tau)} - f^\tau\| = 0. \tag{B.26}$$

Furthermore, Property 3.5 insures that any sequence in F^0 that converges to f^* gives rise to the same definition of $D(f^*)$ via (B.23). Hence, D is well-defined on F^*. Furthermore, the linearity and boundedness of D carry over from F^0 to its closure F^*.

The remainder of the proof of this lemma mimics the Riesz–Frechet Theorem. Let

$$F^+ = \{f \text{ in } F^*\colon\ D(f) = 0\}. \tag{B.27}$$

Then F^+ is a closed linear subspace of L^2. Since Z satisfies Properties 3.3 and 3.4, there exists an f^0 in F^0 such that

$$D(f^0) = I. \tag{B.28}$$

Let

$$f^* = f^0 - \text{proj}(f^0 | F^+). \tag{B.29}$$

Since D is a matrix linear functional,

$$D(f^*) = D(f^0) - D[\text{proj}(f^0 | F^+)] = I. \tag{B.30}$$

The random vector f^* is orthogonal to F^+ by construction, in other words,

$$\mathrm{E}(f^{*\prime} f) = 0 \quad \text{for all } f \text{ in } F^+. \tag{B.31}$$

Also, for any f in F^+ and any k by k matrix of real numbers c, cf is in F^+. Hence,

$$\mathrm{E}(f f^{*\prime}) = 0 \quad \text{for all } f \text{ in } F^+. \tag{B.32}$$

In addition, for any f in F^*, $f - D(f)f^*$ is in F^* since F^* satisfies Property 2.2 (see Lemma 4.1) and

$$D[f - D(f)f^*] = D(f) - D(f)D(f^*) = 0. \tag{B.33}$$

Hence, for any f in F^*, $f - D(f)f^*$ is in F^+. Consequently, relation (B.32) and the linearity of E imply that

$$\mathrm{E}(f f^{*\prime}) = D(f)\mathrm{E}(f^* f^{*\prime}) \quad \text{for all } f \text{ in } F^*. \tag{B.34}$$

If $\mathrm{E}(f^* f^{*\prime})$ is non-singular, then (B.34) can be expressed as

$$\mathrm{E}(f f^{d\prime}) = D(f), \tag{B.35}$$

where $f^d = \mathrm{E}(f^* f^{*\prime})^{-1} f^*$ which is the desired representation of D.

To show that $\mathrm{E}(f^* f^{*\prime})$ is non-singular, suppose to the contrary that $\mathrm{E}(f^* f^{*\prime})$ is singular. Then there exists a k by k matrix of real numbers c that has at least one non-zero element for which cf^* is zero. By the linearity of D, $D(cf^*) = c$ which is different from zero. However, since cf^* is zero (almost surely) and D is a matrix linear functional, $D(cf^*) = 0$ which implies that $c = 0$. This contradicts the fact that c has a non-zero element. Hence, $\mathrm{E}(f^* f^{*\prime})$ is non-singular as is $\mathrm{E}(f^d f^{d\prime})$.

Finally, we show that f^d is unique. Let f^{d*} be any element in F^* for which

$$\mathrm{E}(ff^{d*\prime}) = \mathrm{E}(ff^{d\prime}) = D(f) \quad \text{for all } f \text{ in } F^*. \tag{B.36}$$

Since $f^{d*} - f^d$ is in F^*,

$$\mathrm{E}[(f^{d*} - f^d)f^{d*\prime}] - \mathrm{E}[(f^{d*} - f^d)f^{d\prime}] = 0. \tag{B.37}$$

Hence,

$$\mathrm{E}[(f^{d*} - f^d)(f^{d*} - f^d)'] = 0, \tag{B.38}$$

which implies that $f^{d*} = f^d$. Q.E.D.

Proof of Lemma 4.3. The matrix linear functional D was defined over the entire domain F^* in the proof of Lemma 4.2. Furthermore, Lemma 4.2 implies that

$$D(f) = \mathrm{E}(ff^{d\prime}) \quad \text{for any } f \text{ in } F^*. \tag{B.39}$$

Hence, for any f in F^* for which $D(f)$ is non-singular

$$\mathrm{E}\{[D(f)^{-1}f - D(f^d)^{-1}f^d]f^{d\prime}\} = 0. \tag{B.40}$$

Consequently,

$$\mathrm{E}\{[D(f)^{-1}f - D(f^d)^{-1}f^d][D(f)^{-1}f - D(f^d)^{-1}f^d]'\}$$

$$= D(f)^{-1}\mathrm{E}(ff')[D(f)']^{-1} - D(f^d)^{-1}, \tag{B.41}$$

or

$$D(f^d)^{-1} \leq D(f)^{-1}\mathrm{E}(ff')[D(f)']^{-1}. \tag{B.42}$$

From (B.41) it follows that

$$D(f^d)^{-1} = D(f)^{-1}\mathrm{E}(ff')[D(f)']^{-1}, \tag{B.43}$$

if and only if

$$D(f)^{-1}f - D(f^d)^{-1}f^d = 0, \tag{B.44}$$

or

$$f = cf^d, \tag{B.45}$$

for some k-dimensional, non-singular matrix of real numbers c. Since there exists a sequence $\{f^j: j \geq 1\}$ in F^0 for which

$$\lim_{j \to \infty} \|f^j - f^d\| = 0, \tag{B.46}$$

$$\lim_{j \to \infty} D(f^j) = D(f^d), \tag{B.47}$$

and

$$\lim_{j \to \infty} \mathrm{E}(f^j f^{j\prime}) = \mathrm{E}(f^d f^{d\prime}). \tag{B.48}$$

Therefore,

$$\lim_{j \to \infty} D(f^j)^{-1} \mathrm{E}(f^j f^{j\prime})[D(f^j)']^{-1} = D(f^d)^{-1}, \tag{B.49}$$

and

$$\inf(Z) = D(f^d)^{-1} = \mathrm{E}(f^d f^{d\prime})^{-1}. \tag{B.50}$$

If f^d is in F^0, then there exists a z^d in Z such that

$$f^d = M(z^d e). \tag{B.51}$$

In this case it follows from (B.45) that $\mathrm{cov}(z) = \inf(Z)$ if, and only if, $M(ze) = M(cz^d e)$ for some k-dimensional non-singular matrix c. Finally,

$$\langle z^d | z^d \rangle_* = \langle z^d e | z^d e \rangle = \mathrm{E}(f^d f^{d\prime}) = [\inf(Z)]^{-1}. \quad \text{Q.E.D.} \tag{B.52}$$

Proof of Lemma 4.4. Let $\{z^j: j \geq 1\}$ be a sequence in Z that satisfies

$$\lim_{j \to \infty} \mathrm{E}[M(z^j e) M(z^j e)'] = 0, \tag{B.53}$$

and let f^d be an element of F^* that satisfies (4.12). Then for $j \geq 1$, $M(z^j e)$ is in F (Property 3.1) and

$$\mathrm{E}(z^j d) = \mathrm{E}[M(z^j e) f^{d\prime}]. \tag{B.54}$$

By the matrix version of the Cauchy–Schwarz Inequality,

$$\mathrm{tr}[\mathrm{E}(z^j d)\mathrm{E}(z^j d)']^{1/2} \leq \|M(z^j e)\| \|f^d\|. \tag{B.55}$$

Also, (B.53) implies that

$$\lim_{j\to\infty} \| M(z^j e) \| = 0. \tag{B.56}$$

Therefore, (B.55) and (B.56) imply that

$$\lim_{j\to\infty} \mathrm{E}(z^j d) = 0. \quad \text{Q.E.D.} \tag{B.57}$$

Appendix C

In this appendix we prove the lemmas given in section 5.

Proof of Lemma 5.1. First, we show that for any z in Z, ze is in G and hence H. Since the elements of Z have finite second moments and are measurable with respect to B^*_{-s}, it follows from Assumptions 5.1—5.3 that ze has a finite second moment and

$$\mathrm{E}(ze|B_{-s}) = z\mathrm{E}(e|B_{-s}) = 0. \tag{C.1}$$

Hence, ze is in G.

Next we show that M is given by (5.5). In the proof of Lemma 2.2, we established that for any g in G

$$\limsup_{T\to\infty} \| P^T(g - f^*) \| = 0, \tag{C.2}$$

where

$$\mathrm{E}(g|B_{-\tau}) = 0 \tag{C.3}$$

for some positive integer τ, and

$$f^* = \sum_{j=1}^{\tau} \left[\mathrm{E}(g_{j-1}|B) - \mathrm{E}(g_{j-1}|B_{-1})\right]. \tag{C.4}$$

Let $g = ze$ and $\tau = s$. Lemma 5.1 is proved once we show that $f^* = M(ze)$ as given by (5.5) or equivalently that

$$\sum_{j=1}^{s} \left[\mathrm{E}(z_{j-1}e_{j-1}|B) - \mathrm{E}(z_{j-1}e_{j-1}|B_{-1})\right] = \left[z_0 \Gamma(L^{-1})\right] w. \tag{C.5}$$

The matrix z_{j-1} is measurable with respect to B_{-1} for $j=1,2,\dots,s$, and

$$\begin{aligned} &E(z_{j-1}e_{j-1}|B) - E(z_{j-1}e_{j-1}|B_{-1}) \\ &= z_{j-1}E(e_{j-1}|B) - z_{j-1}E(e_{j-1}|B_{-1}) \\ &= z_{j-1}\Gamma_{j-1}w. \end{aligned} \tag{C.6}$$

Summing (C.6) gives

$$f^* = \sum_{j=1}^{s} z_{j-1}\Gamma_{j-1}w = [z_0\Gamma(L^{-1})]w. \quad \text{Q.E.D.} \tag{C.7}$$

Proof of Lemma 5.2. For any z in Z, the elements of z have finite second moments. Also, Assumption 5.4 implies that the elements of d have finite second moments. Hence, it follows from the matrix version of the Cauchy–Schwarz Inequality that the elements zd have finite first moments. Also,

$$\begin{aligned} &\operatorname{tr}\{z[\partial m(y,\beta)/\partial\beta - \partial m(y,\beta_0)/\partial\beta] \\ &\quad\times[\partial m(y,\beta)/\partial\beta - \partial m(y,\beta_0)/\partial\beta]'z'\}^{1/2} \\ &\le \operatorname{tr}(zz')^{1/2}\operatorname{tr}\{[\partial m(y,\beta)/\partial\beta - \partial m(y,\beta_0)/\partial\beta] \\ &\quad\times[\partial m(y,\beta)/\partial\beta - \partial m(y,\beta_0)/\partial\beta]'\}^{1/2}. \end{aligned} \tag{C.8}$$

Since $\partial m(y,\cdot)/\partial\beta$ is second-moment continuous at β_0, and $\operatorname{tr}(zz')$ has a finite first moment, $z\partial(y,\cdot)/\beta$ is first-moment continuous at β_0. Therefore, Z satisfies Property 3.2. Since $\operatorname{proj}(d'|J_{-s})$ is in Z, Property 3.3 is satisfied for $z=\operatorname{proj}(d'|J_{-s})$. Q.E.D.

Next we consider an intermediate result that will be used to prove Lemma 5.3.

Lemma C.1. Suppose Assumptions 5.2 and 5.6 are satisfied. Then there exist positive numbers δ^b and δ^a such that for any K-dimensional random vector h with a finite second moment,

$$\delta^b\|h\|^2 \le \|\Gamma(L^{-1})'h_0\|^2 \le \delta^a\|h\|^2. \tag{C.9}$$

Proof. Let R^h be the spectral measure of the process generated by h. The random vector $\Gamma(L^{-1})'h_0$ generates a stochastic process with spectral measure $C(\theta)'\mathrm{d}R^h(\theta)C(\theta)$ where $C(\theta)=\Gamma[\exp(-\mathrm{i}\theta)]$. By the Fourier inversion formula

$$\|\Gamma(L^{-1})'h_0\|^2=(1/2\pi)\int_{(-\pi,\pi]}\mathrm{tr}\big[C(\theta)'\mathrm{d}R^h(\theta)C(\theta)\big], \qquad \text{(C.10)}$$

and

$$\|h\|^2=(1/2\pi)\int_{(-\pi,\pi]}\mathrm{tr}\big[\mathrm{d}R^h(\theta)\big]. \qquad \text{(C.11)}$$

Since C is a continuous matrix function on the compact domain $[-\pi,\pi]$ and Assumption 5.5 is satisfied, there exist positive numbers δ^b and δ^a such that the eigenvalues of the product $C(\theta)C(\theta)'$ are in the interval $[\delta^b,\delta^a]$ for all θ in $[-\pi,\pi]$. Therefore,

$$\begin{aligned}\delta^b\int_{(-\pi,\pi]}\mathrm{tr}\big[\mathrm{d}R^h(\theta)\big] &\le \int_{(-\pi,\pi]}\mathrm{tr}\big[C(\theta)'\mathrm{d}R^h(\theta)C(\theta)\big]\\ &\le \delta^a\int_{(-\pi,\pi]}\mathrm{tr}\big[\mathrm{d}R^h(\theta)\big].\end{aligned} \qquad \text{(C.12)}$$

Relation (C.9) then follows from substituting (C.10) and (C.11) into (C.12). Q.E.D.

Proof of Lemma 5.3. First we show that Z satisfies Property 3.5. Then we show that $F^0=F^*$. Let $\{z^j\colon\ j\ge 1\}$ be sequence in Z that satisfies

$$\lim_{j\to\infty}\langle z^j|z^j\rangle_*=0. \qquad \text{(C.13)}$$

Given (5.7),

$$\langle z^j|z^j\rangle_*=\mathrm{E}\{[z_0^j\Gamma(L^{-1})][z_0^j\Gamma(L^{-1})]'\}\quad\text{for all}\quad j\ge 1. \qquad \text{(C.14)}$$

It then follows from Lemma C.1 that

$$\mathrm{E}\big[\mathrm{tr}(z^jz^{j\prime})\big]\le \mathrm{tr}\langle z^j|z^j\rangle_*/\delta^b. \qquad \text{(C.15)}$$

Thus, (C.13) implies that

$$\lim_{j\to\infty}\mathrm{E}\big[\mathrm{tr}(z^jz^{j\prime})\big]=0. \qquad \text{(C.16)}$$

Since the elements of d have finite second moments (Assumption 5.4), the matrix version of the Cauchy–Schwarz Inequality implies that

$$\lim_{j\to\infty} \mathrm{E}(z^j d) = 0. \tag{C.17}$$

Finally, we prove that $F^0 = F^*$. Let $\{f^j\colon\ j \geq 1\}$ be any sequence in F^0 that is mean-square Cauchy. Then there exists a sequence $\{z^j\colon\ j\geq 1\}$ in Z such that $M(z^j e) = f^j$ for $j \geq 1$. Thus

$$\mathrm{E}\big[(f^j - f^\tau)(f^j - f^\tau)'\big] = \langle z^j - z^\tau | z^j - z^\tau \rangle_*, \tag{C.18}$$

where $\langle\cdot|\cdot\rangle_*$ is given in (5.7). However, (C.18) and Lemma C.1 imply that

$$\mathrm{tr}(\langle z^j - z^\tau | z^j - z^\tau\rangle_*) \geq \delta^b \mathrm{tr}\{\mathrm{E}[(z^j - z^\tau)(z^j - z^\tau)']\}. \tag{C.19}$$

Hence, the elements of $[z^j\colon\ j\geq 1\}$ are mean-square Cauchy. Since J is closed in mean square, there exists a z^0 in Z such that

$$\lim_{j\to\infty} \mathrm{E}\{\mathrm{tr}[(z^j - z^0)(z^j - z^0)']\} = 0. \tag{C.20}$$

However,

$$\begin{aligned} \| f^j - M(z^0 e)\|^2 &= \mathrm{tr}(\langle z^j - z^0 | z^j - z^0\rangle_*) \\ &\leq \delta^a \mathrm{tr}\{\mathrm{E}[(z^j - z^0)(z^j - z^0)']\}. \end{aligned} \tag{C.21}$$

Consequently, the limit in (C.20) guarantees that $\{f^j\colon\ j\geq 1\}$ converges in mean-square to $M(z^0 e)$. Therefore, $F^0 = F^*$. Q.E.D.

Lemma 4.5 was proved in the text.

Proof of Lemma 5.5. Let R^w denote the spectral measure of the process generated by w. Then R^w is absolutely continuous with respect to Lebesgue measure and with density matrix I for almost all θ in $(-\pi, \pi]$. Furthermore, $\Gamma(L^{-1})w_0$ generates a stochastic process with a spectral measure that is absolutely continuous with respect to Lebesgue measure and has spectral density matrix given by

$$C(-\theta)C(-\theta)' \tag{C.22}$$

for almost all θ in $(-\pi, \pi]$ where $C(-\theta) = \Gamma[\exp(i\theta)]$. Since Assumption 5.5 is satisfied, the spectral density matrix given in (C.22) has constant rank K for all θ in $(-\pi,\pi]$ and the stochastic process $\{\Gamma(L^{-1})w_t\colon\ -\infty < t < +\infty\}$ is linearly regular. Hence, by the Wold Decomposition Theorem there exists a function Γ^* satisfying

$$\Gamma^*(\sigma) = \sum_{j=0}^{\infty} \Gamma_j^* \sigma^j \quad \text{where} \quad \sum_{j=0}^{\infty} \operatorname{tr}(\Gamma_j^* \Gamma_j^{*\prime}) < \infty, \tag{C.23}$$

$$C^*(\theta) = \lim_{r \uparrow 1} \Gamma^*[r\exp(-i\theta)] \quad \text{for almost all } \theta \text{ in } (-\pi, \pi], \tag{C.24}$$

$$C^*(\theta)C^*(\theta)' = C(-\theta)C(-\theta)', \tag{C.25}$$

$$\Gamma^*(\sigma) \neq 0 \quad \text{for} \quad |\sigma| < 1. \tag{C.26}$$

[See Rozanov (1967, pp. 56–63) for (C.23), (C.25) and (C.26), and see Zygmond (1959, p. 276) for (C.24).]

Let $h = \Gamma(L^{-1})w_0$. Since w defines a process that is a vector white noise, Assumption 5.2 implies that

$$\mathrm{E}(hh'_{-\tau}) = 0 \quad \text{for} \quad \tau \geq s. \tag{C.27}$$

Thus

$$\Gamma_j^* = 0 \quad \text{for} \quad j \geq s. \tag{C.28}$$

Taken together, (C.23) and (C.28) imply (5.16). Since Γ^* and Γ are polynomials that are well-defined for all complex values of σ, (C.24) and (C.25) imply (5.17). Finally, (C.26) and Assumption 5.6 imply (5.18). Q.E.D.

Proof of Lemma 5.6. Relation (5.7) states that

$$\langle z|z^*\rangle_* = \mathrm{E}\{[z_0\Gamma(L^{-1})][\Gamma(L^{-1})'z_0^{*\prime}]\} \quad \text{for all } z \text{ and } z^* \text{ in } Z. \tag{C.29}$$

Since $\{z_t\colon -\infty < t < +\infty\}$ and $\{z_t^*\colon -\infty < t < +\infty\}$ are jointly stationary processes,

$$\langle z|z^*\rangle_* = \mathrm{E}\{z[\Gamma(L)\Gamma(L^{-1})'z_0^{*\prime}]\}. \tag{C.30}$$

In light of (5.17) in Lemma 5.5, (C.30) can be written equivalently as

$$\langle z|z^*\rangle_* = \mathrm{E}\{z[\Gamma^*(L^{-1})\Gamma^*(L)'z_0^{*\prime}]\}, \tag{C.31}$$

which is the first equality in (5.19). Again, using the fact that $\{z_t\colon -\infty < t < +\infty\}$ and $\{z_t^*\colon -\infty < t < +\infty\}$ are jointly stationary, it follows that

$$\langle z|z^*\rangle = \mathrm{E}\{[z_0\Gamma^*(L)][z_0^*\Gamma^*(L)]'\}, \tag{C.32}$$

which is the second equality in (5.19). Q.E.D.

Proof of Lemma 5.7. Most of this theorem is proved in the text. The only missing step is to show that z^d as given by (5.20) is well-defined and in Z. In Lemma 5.5 it is shown that $\Gamma^*(\sigma)$ is a finite-order polynomial for which the zeroes of $\det[\Gamma^*(\sigma)]$ have absolute values that are greater than one. Hence, $\Gamma^*(\sigma)^{-1}$ is well-defined and has a power series expansion that is uniformly convergent in the closed unit disc of the complex plane. Since Assumption 5.4 is satisfied, $[d_0'\Gamma^*(L^{-1})^{-1\prime}]$ is a well-defined mean-square limit. Thus, $\text{proj}\{[d_0'\Gamma^*(L^{-1})^{-1\prime}]|J_{-s}\}$ is well-defined and has elements in J_{-s}. Similarly, $\text{proj}\{[d_0'\Gamma^*(L^{-1})^{-1\prime}]|J_{-s}\}\Gamma^*(L)^{-1}$ is a well-defined mean-square limit. Finally, since $\Gamma^*(\sigma)^{-1}$ has a power series expansion in a region containing the closed unit disc of the complex plane, $\Gamma^*(L)^{-1}$ is a one-sided operator. Also, J_{-1} is a closed linear subspace of J so that $\text{proj}\{[d_0'\Gamma^*(L^{-1})']|J_{-s}\}\Gamma^*(L)^{-1}$ has elements that are in J_{-s}. Therefore, z^d as given by (5.20) is in Z.

References

Amemiya, T., 1977, The maximum likelihood and the nonlinear three-stage least squares estimator in the general nonlinear simultaneous equation model, Econometrica 45, 955–968.

Basmann, R.L., 1957, A generalized classical method of linear estimation of coefficients in a structural equation, Econometrica 25, 77–83.

Billingsley, P., 1961, The Lindeberg–Levy theorem for martingales, American Mathematical Society 12, 788–792.

Chamberlain, G., 1983, Asymptotic efficiency in estimation with conditional moment restrictions, Social Systems Research Institute paper 8307 (University of Wisconsin, Madison, WI).

Gordin, M.I., 1969, The central limit theorem for stationary processes, Soviet Mathematics Doklady 10, 1174–1176.

Hansen, L.P., 1982, Large sample properties of generalized method of moments estimators, Econometrica 50, 1029–1054.

Hansen, L.P., 1985, Using martingale difference approximations to obtain covariance matrix bounds for generalized method of moments estimators, Manuscript.

Hansen, L.P. and R.J. Hodrick, 1980, Forward exchange rates as optimal predictors of future spot rates: An econometric analysis, Journal of Political Economy 88, 829–853.

Hansen, L.P. and R.J. Hodrick, 1983, Risk averse speculation in the forward foreign exchange market: An econometric analysis of linear models, in: J.A. Frenkel, ed., Exchange rates and international macroeconomics (University of Chicago Press, Chicago, IL).

Hayashi, F. and C. Sims, 1983, Nearly efficient estimation of time series models with predetermined, but not exogenous, instruments, Econometrica 51, 783–798.

Jorgenson, D.W. and J. Laffont, 1974, Efficient estimation of non-linear simultaneous equations with additive disturbances, Annals of Economic and Social Measurement 3, 615–640.

Rozanov, Y.A., 1967, Stationary random processes (Holden-Day, San Francisco, CA).

Sargan, J.D., 1958, The estimation of economic relationships using instrumental variables, Econometrica 26, 393–415.

White, H., 1982, Instrumental variables regression with independent observations, Econometrica 50, 483–499.

Zygmund, A., Trigonometric series, 2nd ed., Vol. 1 (Cambridge University Press, Cambridge).

ALTERNATIVE METHODS FOR EVALUATING THE IMPACT OF INTERVENTIONS
An Overview

James J. HECKMAN and Richard ROBB, Jr.*

University of Chicago, Chicago, IL 60637, USA

This paper presents methods for estimating the impact of training on earnings when non-random selection characterizes the enrollment of persons into training. We explore the benefits of cross-section, repeated cross-section and longitudinal data for addressing this problem by considering the assumptions required to use a variety of new and conventional estimators given access to various commonly encountered types of data. We investigate the plausibility of assumptions needed to justify econometric procedures when viewed in the light of prototypical decision rules determining enrollment into training. We examine the robustness of the estimators to choice-based sampling and contamination bias.

1. Introduction

This paper considers the problem of estimating the effect of training on earnings when enrollment into training is the outcome of a non-random selection process. The analysis of training presented here serves as a prototype for the analysis of the closely related problems of deriving selection bias free estimates of the impacts of unionism, migration, job turnover, unemployment and affirmative action programs on earnings.

Our previous study [Heckman and Robb (1985)] investigates the prior restrictions needed to be imposed to secure consistent estimators of the selection bias free impact of training on earnings when the analyst has access to different types of data. We consider the plausibility of these restrictions in the light of economic theory.

Here we report the key findings from our previous paper. Occasionally, the reader is referred to that paper for precise statements of technical conditions or proofs that do not provide essential insights for understanding the main points.

*We thank Ricardo Barros for helpful comments. This research was supported by NSF Grants SES-8107963 and SES-8411242 and NIH Grant R01-HD-19226 to the Quantitative Methods Center at NORC.

We present assumptions required to use three types of widely available data to solve the problem of estimating the impact of training on earnings free of selection bias: (1) a single cross-section of post-training earnings, (2) a temporal sequence of cross-sections of unrelated people (repeated cross-section data), and (3) longitudinal data in which the same individuals are followed over time. These three types of data are listed in order of their availability and in inverse order of their cost of acquisition. Assuming random sampling techniques are applied to collect all three types of data, the three sources form a hierarchy: longitudinal data can be used to generate a single cross-section or a set of temporal cross-sections in which the identities of individuals are ignored, and repeated cross-sections can be used as single cross-sections.

Our conclusions are rather startling. Although longitudinal data are widely regarded as a panacea for selection and simultaneity problems, there is no need to use longitudinal data to identify the impact of training on earnings if conventional fixed effect specifications of earnings functions are adopted. Estimators based on repeated cross-section data for unrelated persons identify the same parameter. An analogous statement holds for virtually all longitudinal estimators.

However, we question the plausibility of conventional specifications. They are not motivated by economic theory, and when examined in that light they seem implausible. We propose richer longitudinal specifications of the earnings process and enrollment decision derived from economic theory. In addition, we propose a variety of new estimators. A few of these estimators require longitudinal data, but for most, longitudinal data are not required. A major conclusion of our paper is that the relative benefits of longitudinal data have been overstated, because the potential benefits of cross-section and repeated cross-section data have been understated.

We also question recent claims that cross-section approaches to estimating the impact of training on earnings are strongly dependent on arbitrary assumptions about distributions of unobservables and about the nature of exclusion restrictions. While some widely-used cross-section estimators suffer from this defect, such commonly invoked assumptions are not an essential feature of the cross-sectional approach. However, we demonstrate that unless explicit distributional assumptions are invoked all cross-section estimators require the presence of at least one regressor variable in the decision rule determining training. This requirement may seem innocuous, but it rules out a completely non-parametric cross-section approach. Without prior information, it is not possible to cross-classify observations on the basis of values assumed by explanatory variables in the earnings function and do 'regressor free' estimation of the impact of training on earnings that is free of selection bias. A regressor is required in the enrollment rule. For most cross-section estimators this requires precise specification of the decision rule. Longitudinal and repeated cross-section estimators do not require this.

In analyzing the assumptions required to use various data sources to consistently estimate the impact of training on earnings free of selection bias, we discuss the following topics:

(1) How much prior information about the earnings function must be assumed?
(2) How much prior information about the decision rule governing participation must be assumed?
(3) How robust are the proposed methods to the following commonly encountered features of data on training:
    (a) non-randomness of available samples and especially oversampling of trainees (the choice based sample problem)?
    (b) time inhomogeneity in the environment ('non-stationarity')?
    (c) the absence of a control group of non-trainees or the contamination of the control group so that the training status of individuals is not known for the control sample?

Notably absent from this list of questions is any mention of the efficiency of estimators for cross-section, repeated cross-section and longitudinal data. A discussion of efficiency makes sense only within the context of a fully specified model. The focus in this paper is on the tradeoffs in assumptions that must be imposed in order to estimate a single coefficient when the analyst has access to different types of data. Since different assumptions about the underlying model are invoked in order to justify the validity of alternative estimators, an efficiency comparison is often meaningless. Under the assumptions about an underlying model that justify one estimator, properties of another estimator may not be defined. Only by postulating a common assumption set that is unnecessarily large for any single estimator is it possible to make efficiency comparisons. For the topic of this paper – model identification – the efficiency issue is a red herring.

Even if a common set of assumptions about the underlying model is invoked to justify efficiency comparisons for a class of estimators, for two reasons conventional efficiency comparisons are often meaningless. First, the frequently stated claim that longitudinal estimators are more efficient than cross-section estimators is superficial. It ignores the relative sizes of the *available* cross-section and longitudinal samples. Because of the substantially greater cost of collecting longitudinal data free of attrition bias, the number of persons followed in longitudinal studies rarely exceeds 500 in most economic analyses. In contrast, the *available* cross-section and repeated cross-section samples have thousands of observations. Given the relative sizes of the available cross-section and longitudinal samples, 'inefficient' cross-section and repeated cross-section estimators may have a much smaller sampling variance than 'efficient' longitudinal estimators fit on much smaller samples. In this sense, our proposed cross-section and repeated cross-section estimators may be *feasibly efficient* given the relative sizes of the samples for the two types of data sources.

Second, many of the cross-section and repeated cross-section estimators proposed in this paper require only sample means of variables. They are thus very simple to compute and are also robust to mean zero measurement error in all of the variables.

This paper is organized as follows. Section 2 describes the notation and an economic model for enrollment of individuals into training. Sections 3–9 each begin by listing a set of findings from our earlier paper. The findings are discussed and illustrated via simple examples. The paper concludes with a brief summary.

2. Notation and a model of program participation

2.1. Earnings functions

To focus on essential aspects of the problem, we assume that individuals experience only one opportunity to participate in training. This opportunity occurs in period k. Training takes a single period for participants to complete. During training, participants earn no labor income.

Denote earnings of individual i in period t by Y_{it}. Earnings depend on a vector of observed characteristics, X_{it}. Post-program earnings $(t > k)$ also depend on a dummy variable, d_i, which equals one if the ith individual participates and is zero if he does not. Let U_{it} represent the error term in the earnings equation and assume that $\mathrm{E}[U_{it}] = 0$. Adopting a linear specification,

$$\begin{aligned} Y_{it} &= X_{it}\beta + d_i\alpha + U_{it}, \qquad t > k, \\ &= X_{it}\beta + U_{it}, \qquad t \le k, \end{aligned} \tag{1}$$

where β and α are parameters.

Throughout this paper we assume that X_{it} is uncorrelated with U_{it}. When X_{it} contains lagged values of Y_{it}, we assume that (1) can be solved for a reduced form expression of exogenous variables, and we use that expression in place of (1). In some cases, independence between X_{it} and lagged, current or future values of U_{it} will be required as well.

Eq. (1) assumes that training has the same effect on everyone. In the next section we consider issues that arise when α varies among individuals. Throughout most of this paper we ignore effects of training which grow or decay over time. [See Heckman and Robb (1985) for a discussion of this topic.]

We now turn to the stochastic relationship between d_i and U_{it} in (1). For this purpose, we develop a more detailed notation which describes the enrollment rules that select individuals into training.

2.2. Enrollment rules

The decision to participate in training may be determined by a prospective trainee, by a program administrator or both. Whatever the specific content of the rule, it can be described in terms of an index function framework. Let IN_i be an index of benefits to the appropriate decision-makers from taking training. It is a function of observed (Z_i) and unobserved (V_i) variables. Thus

$$IN_i = Z_i\gamma + V_i. \tag{2}$$

In terms of this function,

$$\begin{aligned} d_i &= 1 \quad \text{iff} \quad IN_i > 0 \\ &= 0 \quad \text{otherwise.} \end{aligned}$$

The distribution function of V_i is denoted as $F(\mathrm{v}_i) = \Pr(V_i < \mathrm{v}_i)$. V_i is assumed to be independently and identically distributed across persons. Let $p = \mathrm{E}[d_i] = \Pr[d_i = 1]$ and assume $1 > p > 0$.

The central problem considered in this paper arises when the decision to take training is not random with respect to the disturbance in the earnings function. More precisely, the problem of selection bias arises when

$$\mathrm{E}[U_{it} d_i] \neq 0.$$

This may occur because of stochastic dependence between U_{it} and the unobservable V_i in (2) (selection on the unobservables) or because of stochastic dependence between U_{it} and Z_i in (2) (selection on the observables).

To interpret various specifications of eq. (2), we need to specify an economic model. A natural starting point is a model of trainee self-selection based on a comparison of the expected value of earnings with and without training. The earnings function is assumed to be (1). For simplicity, we assume that training programs accept all applicants. Our previous paper considers more general models.

All prospective trainees are assumed to discount earnings streams by a common discount factor $1/(1+r)$. From (1) training raises trainee earnings by α per period. While in training, individual i receives a subsidy S_i, which may be negative (so there may be direct costs of program participation). Trainees forego income in training period k. To simplify the expressions, we assume that people live forever.

As of period k, the present value of earnings for a person who does not receive training is

$$PV_i(0) = \mathrm{E}_{k-1}\left(\sum_{j=0}^{\infty}\left(\frac{1}{1+r}\right)^j Y_{i,k+j}\right).$$

E_{k-1} means that the expectation is taken with respect to information available to the prospective trainee in period $k-1$. The expected present value of earnings for a trainee is

$$PV_i(1) = \mathrm{E}_{k-1}\left(S_i + \sum_{j=1}^{\infty}\left(\frac{1}{1+r}\right)^j Y_{i,k+j} + \sum_{j=1}^{\infty}\frac{\alpha}{(1+r)^j}\right).$$

The risk-neutral wealth-maximizing decision rule is to enroll in the program if $PV_i(1) > PV_i(0)$ or, letting IN_i denote the index function in decision rule (2),

$$IN_i = PV_i(1) - PV_i(0) = \mathrm{E}_{k-1}[S_i - Y_{ik} + \alpha/r], \tag{3}$$

so the decision to train is characterized by the rule

$$\begin{aligned} d_i &= 1 \quad \text{iff} \quad \mathrm{E}_{k-1}[S_i - Y_{ik} + \alpha/r] > 0, \\ &= 0 \quad \text{otherwise.} \end{aligned} \tag{4}$$

Let W_i be the part of the subsidy which the econometrician observes (with associated coefficient ϕ) and let τ_i be the part which he does not observe:

$$S_i = W_i\phi + \tau_i.$$

A special case of this model arises when agents possess perfect foresight so that $\mathrm{E}_{k-1}[S_i] = S_i$, $\mathrm{E}_{k-1}[Y_{ik}] = Y_{ik}$ and $\mathrm{E}_{k-1}[\alpha/r] = \alpha/r$. Collecting terms,

$$\begin{aligned} d_i &= 1 \quad \text{iff} \quad S_i - Y_{ik} + \alpha/r = W_i\phi + \alpha/r - X_{ik}\beta + \tau_i - U_{ik} > 0, \\ &= 0 \quad \text{otherwise.} \end{aligned} \tag{5}$$

Then $(\tau_i - U_{ik}) = V_i$ in (2) and (W_i, X_{ik}) corresponds to Z_i in (2). Assuming that (W_i, X_{ik}) is distributed independently of V_i makes (5) a standard discrete choice model.

Suppose decision rule (5) determines enrollment. If the costs of program participation are independent of U_{it} for all t (so both W_i and τ_i are independent of U_{it}), then $\mathrm{E}[U_{it}d_i] = 0$ only if the unobservables in period t are (mean) independent of the unobservables in period k or

$$\mathrm{E}[U_{it}|U_{ik}]=0 \quad \text{for} \quad t>k.$$

Whether or not U_{it} and d_i are uncorrelated hinges on the serial dependence properties of U_{it}. If U_{it} is a moving average of order m so

$$U_{it}=\sum_{j=1}^{m} a_j \varepsilon_{i,t-j},$$

where the $\varepsilon_{i,t-j}$ are iid, then for $t-k>m$, $\mathrm{E}[U_{it}d_i]=0$. On the other hand, if U_{it} follows a first-order autoregressive scheme, then $\mathrm{E}[U_{it}|U_{ik}]\neq 0$ for all finite t and k.

3. Random coefficients and the structural parameter of interest

We identify two different definitions associated with the notion of a selection bias free estimate of the impact of training on earnings. The first notion defines the structural parameter of interest as the impact of training on earnings if people are randomly assigned to training programs. The second notion defines the structural parameter of interest in terms of the difference between the post-program earnings of the trained and what the earnings in post-program years for these same individuals would have been in the absence of training. The two notions come to the same thing only when training has an equal impact on everyone or else assignment to training is random and attention centers on estimating the mean response to training. The second notion is frequently the most useful one for forecasting future program impacts when the same enrollment rules that have been used in available samples characterize future enrollment.

In seeking to determine the impact of training on earnings in the presence of non-random assignment of persons to training, it is useful to distinguish two questions that are frequently confused in the literature:

Q1: 'What would be the mean impact of training on earnings if people were randomly assigned to training?'

Q2: 'How do the post-program mean earnings of the trained compare to what they would have been in the absence of training?'

The second question makes a hypothetical contrast between the post-program earnings of the trained in the presence and in the absence of training programs. This hypothetical contrast eliminates factors that would make the earnings of trainees different from those of non-trainees even in the absence of any training program. The two questions have the same answer if eq. (1) generates earnings so that training has the same impact on everyone. The two questions also have the same answer if there is random assignment to training and attention centers on estimating the *population* mean response to training.

In the presence of non-random assignment and variation in the impact of training among persons, the two questions have different answers. Question 2 is the appropriate one to ask if interest centers on forecasting the change in the mean of the post-training earnings of trainees when the same selection rule pertains to past and future trainees. It is important to note that the answer to this question is all that is required to estimate the future program impact if future selection criteria are like past criteria.

To clarify these issues, we consider a random coefficient version of (1) in which α varies in the population. In this model, the impact of training may differ across persons and may even be negative for some people. We write in place of (1)

$$Y_{it} = X_{it}\beta + d_i\alpha_i + U_{it}, \qquad t > k.$$

Define $E[\alpha_i] = \bar{\alpha}$ and $\varepsilon_i = \alpha_i - \bar{\alpha}$ where $E[\varepsilon_i] = 0$. With this notation, we can rewrite the equation above as

$$Y_{it} = X_{it}\beta + d_i\bar{\alpha} + \{U_{it} + d_i\varepsilon_i\}. \tag{6}$$

An alternative way to derive this equation is to express it as a two-sector switching model following Roy (1951), Heckman and Neumann (1977) and Lee (1978). Let

$$Y_{1it} = X_{it}\beta_1 + U_{1it}$$

be the wage of individual i in sector 1 in period t. Let

$$Y_{0it} = X_{it}\beta_0 + U_{0it}$$

be the wage of individual i in sector 0. Letting $d_i = 1$ if a person is in sector 1 and letting $d_i = 0$ otherwise, we may write the observed wage as

$$\begin{aligned} Y_{it} &= d_i Y_{1it} + (1 - d_i) Y_{0it} \\ &= X_{it}\beta_0 + E[X_{it}|d_i = 1](\beta_1 - \beta_0)\, d_i \\ &\quad + [(X_{it} - E[X_{it}|d_i = 1])(\beta_1 - \beta_0) + U_{1it} - U_{0it}]\, d_i + U_{0it}. \end{aligned}$$

Letting $\bar{\alpha} = E[X_{it}|d_i = 1](\beta_1 - \beta_0)$, $\varepsilon_i = (X_{it} - E[X_{it}|d_i = 1])(\beta_1 - \beta_0) + U_{1it} - U_{0it}$, $\beta_0 = \beta$ and $U_{0it} = U_{it}$, produces eq. (6).

In this model there is a fundamental non-identification result when no regressors appear in the decision rule (2). Without a regressor in (2) and in the absence of any further distributional assumptions it is not possible to identify $\bar{\alpha}$ unless $\mathrm{E}[\varepsilon_i|d_i=1, Z_i]=0$ or some other known constant.

To see this, note that

$$\mathrm{E}[Y_{it}|d_i=1, Z_i, X_{it}] = X_{it}\beta + \bar{\alpha} + \mathrm{E}[\varepsilon_i|d_i=1, Z_i, X_{it}] + \mathrm{E}[U_{it}|d_i=1, Z_i, X_{it}],$$

$$\mathrm{E}[Y_{it}|d_i=0, Z_i, X_{it}] = X_{it}\beta + E[U_{it}|d_i=0, Z_i, X_{it}].$$

Unless $\mathrm{E}[\varepsilon_i|d_i=1, Z_i, X_{it}]$ is known, without invoking distributional assumptions it is impossible to decompose $\bar{\alpha} + \mathrm{E}[\varepsilon_i|d_i=1, Z_i, X_{it}]$ into its constituent components unless there is independent variation in $\mathrm{E}[\varepsilon_i|d_i=1, Z_i, X_{it}]$ across observations [i.e., a regressor appears in (2)]. Without a regressor, $\mathrm{E}[\varepsilon_i|d_i=1, Z_i, X_{it}]$ is a constant which cannot be distinguished from $\bar{\alpha}$.

This means that in models without regressors in the decision rule we might as well work with the redefined model

$$Y_{it} = X_{it}\beta + d_i\alpha^* + \{U_{it} + d_i(\varepsilon_i - \mathrm{E}[\varepsilon_i|d_i=1])\}, \tag{7}$$

where

$$\alpha^* = \bar{\alpha} + \mathrm{E}[\varepsilon_i|d_i=1],$$

and content ourselves with the estimation of α^*. If everywhere we replace α with α^*, the fixed coefficient analysis of eq. (1) applies to (7).

The parameter α^* answers Q2. It addresses the question of determining the effect of training on the people selected as trainees. This parameter is useful in making forecasts when the same selection rule operates in the future as has operated in the past. In the presence of non-random selection into training it does not answer Q1. Indeed, without regressors in decision rule (2), this question cannot be answered unless specific distributional assumptions are invoked.

Random assignment of persons to training does not usually represent a relevant policy option. For this reason, we will focus attention on question two. Hence, if the training impact varies among individuals, we will seek to estimate α^* in (7). Since eq. (7) may be reparametrized in the form of eq. (1), we work exclusively with the fixed coefficient earnings function. Our earlier paper gives precise statements of conditions under which $\bar{\alpha}$ is identified in a random coefficient model.

4. Cross-sectional procedures

Standard cross-sectional procedures invoke unnecessarily strong assumptions. All that is required to identify α in a cross-section is access to a regressor in (2). In *the absence of a regressor, assumptions about the marginal distribution of U_{it} can produce consistent estimators of the training impact.*

4.1. Without distributional assumptions a regressor is needed

Let $\bar{Y}_t^{(1)}$ denote the sample mean of trainee earnings and let $\bar{Y}_t^{(0)}$ denote the sample mean of non-trainee earnings:

$$\bar{Y}_t^{(1)} = \sum d_i Y_{it} \Big/ \sum d_i, \qquad \bar{Y}_t^{(0)} = \sum (1 - d_i) Y_{it} \Big/ \sum (1 - d_i),$$

for $0 < \sum d_i < I$, where I is the number of observations. We retain the assumption that the data are generated by a random sampling scheme. If no regressors appear in (1) then $X_{it}\beta = \beta_t$ and

$$\operatorname{plim} \bar{Y}_t^{(1)} = \beta_t + \alpha + \mathrm{E}[U_{it} | d_i = 1],$$

$$\operatorname{plim} \bar{Y}_t^{(0)} = \beta_t + \mathrm{E}[U_{it} | d_i = 0].$$

Thus

$$\operatorname{plim}\left(\bar{Y}_t^{(1)} - \bar{Y}_t^{(0)}\right) = \alpha + \mathrm{E}[U_{it} | d_i = 1]/(1 - p),$$

since $p\mathrm{E}[U_{it}|d_i = 1] + (1 - p)\mathrm{E}[U_{it}|d_i = 0] = 0$. Even if p were known, α cannot be separated from $\mathrm{E}[U_{it}|d_i = 1]$ using cross-sectional data on sample means. Sample variances do not aid in securing identification unless $\mathrm{E}[U_{it}^2|d_i = 0]$ or $\mathrm{E}[U_{it}^2|d_i = 1]$ is known *a priori*. Similar remarks apply to the information from higher moments.

4.2. Overview of cross-sectional procedures which use regressors

If, however, $\mathrm{E}[U_{it}|d_i = 1, Z_i]$ is a non-constant function of Z_i, it is possible (with additional assumptions) to solve this identification problem. Securing identification in this fashion explicitly precludes a fully non-parametric strategy in which both the earnings function (1) and decision rule (2) are estimated in each (X_{it}, Z_i) stratum. For within each stratum, $\mathrm{E}[U_{it}|d_i = 1, Z_i]$ is a constant function of Z_i and α is not identified from cross-section data. Restrictions across strata are required.

If $\mathrm{E}[U_{it}|d_i = 1, Z_i]$ is a non-constant function of Z_i it is possible to exploit this information in a variety of ways depending on what else is assumed about the model. Here we simply sketch alternative strategies. In our earlier paper, we present a systematic discussion of each approach.

(a) Suppose Z_i or a subset of Z_i is exogenous with respect to U_{it}. Under conditions specified more fully below, the exogenous subset may be used to construct an instrumental variable for d_i in eq. (1), and α can be consistently estimated by instrumental variables methods. No distributional assumptions about U_{it} or V_i are required [Heckman (1978)].

(b) Suppose that Z_i is distributed independently of V_i and the functional form of the distribution of V_i is known. Under standard conditions, γ in (2) can be consistently estimated by conventional methods in discrete choice analysis [Amemiya (1981)]. If Z_i is distributed independently of U_{it}, $F(-Z_i\hat{\gamma})$ can be used as an instrument for d_i in eq. (1) [Heckman (1978)].

(c) Under the same conditions as specified in (b),

$$\mathrm{E}[Y_{it}|X_{it}, Z_i] = X_{it}\beta + \alpha(1 - F(-Z_i\gamma)).$$

γ and α can be consistently estimated using $F(-Z_i\hat{\gamma})$ in place of $F(-Z_i\gamma)$ in the preceding equation [Heckman (1976, 1978)] or else the preceding equation can be estimated by non-linear least squares, estimating β, α and γ jointly (given the functional form of F) [Barnow, Cain and Goldberger (1980)].

(d) If the functional forms of $\mathrm{E}[U_{it}|d_i = 1, Z_i]$ and $\mathrm{E}[U_{it}|d_i = 0, Z_i]$ as functions of Z_i are known up to a finite set of parameters, it is sometimes possible to consistently estimate β, α and the parameters of the conditional means from the (non-linear) regression function

$$\mathrm{E}[Y_{it}|d_i, Z_i] = X_{it}\beta + d_i\alpha + d_i\mathrm{E}[U_{it}|d_i = 1, Z_i] + (1 - d_i)\mathrm{E}[U_{it}|d_i = 0, Z_i]. \tag{8}$$

One way to acquire information about the functional form of $\mathrm{E}[U_{it}|d_i = 1, Z_i]$ is to assume knowledge of the functional form of the joint distribution of (U_{it}, V_i) (e.g., that it is bivariate normal), but this is not required. Note further that this procedure does not require that Z_i be distributed independently of V_i in (2) [Barnow, Cain and Goldberger (1980)].

(e) Instead of (d), it is possible to use a two-stage estimation procedure if the joint density of (U_{it}, V_i) is assumed known up to a finite set of parameters. In stage one $\mathrm{E}[U_{it}|d_i = 1, Z_i]$ and $\mathrm{E}[U_{it}|d_i = 0, Z_i]$ are determined up to some unknown parameters by conventional discrete choice analysis. Then regression (8) is run using estimated E values in place of population E values on the right-hand side of the equation.

(f) Under the assumptions of (e), use maximum likelihood to consistently estimate α [Heckman (1978)]. Note that a separate value of α may be estimated for each cross-section so that depending on the number of cross-sections it is possible to estimate growth and decay effects in training (e.g., α_t can be estimated for each cross-section).

Conventional selection bias approaches (d)–(f) as well as (b)–(c) rely on strong distributional assumptions but in fact these are not required. Given that a regressor appears in decision rule (2), if it is uncorrelated with U_{it}, the regressor is an instrumental variable for d_i. It is not necessary to invoke strong distributional assumptions, but if they are invoked, Z_i need not be uncorrelated with U_{it}. In practice, however, Z_i and U_{it} are usually assumed to be independent. We next discuss the instrumental variables procedure in greater detail.

4.3. The instrumental variable estimator

This estimator is the least demanding in the *a priori* conditions that must be satisfied for its use. It requires the following assumptions:

> There is at least one variable in Z_i, Z_i^e, with a non-zero γ coefficient in (2), such that for some known transformation of Z_i^e, $g(Z_i^e)$, $\mathrm{E}[U_{it}g(Z_i^e)] = 0$. (9a)
>
> Array X_{it} and d_i into a vector $J_{1it} = (X_{it}, d_i)$. Array X_{it} and $g(Z_i^e)$ into a vector $J_{2it} = (X_{it}, g(Z_i^e))$. In this notation, it is assumed that
>
> $$\mathrm{E}\left[\sum_{i=1}^{I_t} (J_{2it}' J_{1it}/I_t)\right]$$
>
> has full column rank uniformly in I_t for I_t sufficiently large, where I_t denotes the number of individuals in period t. (9b)

With these assumptions, the I.V. estimator,

$$\begin{pmatrix}\hat{\beta}\\ \hat{\alpha}\end{pmatrix}_{\mathrm{IV}} = \left(\sum_{i=1}^{I_t} (J_{2it}' J_{1it}/I_t)\right)^{-1} \sum_{i=1}^{I_t} (J_{2it}' Y_{it}/I_t),$$

is consistent for (β, α) regardless of any covariance between U_{it} and d_i.

It is important to notice how weak these conditions are. The functional form of the distribution of V_i need not be known. Z_i need not be distributed independently of V_i. Moreover, $g(Z_i^e)$ may be a non-linear function of variables appearing in X_{it} as long as (9) is satisfied.

The instrumental variable, $g(Z_i^e)$, may also be a lagged value of time-varying variables appearing in X_{it}, provided the analyst has access to longitudinal data. The rank condition (9b) will generally be satisfied in this case as long as X_{it} exhibits serial dependence. Thus longitudinal data (on exogenous characteristics) may provide a source of instrumental variables.

4.4. Identification through distributional assumptions about the marginal distribution of U_{it}

If no regressor appears in decision rule (2), the estimators presented so far in this section cannot be used to estimate α consistently unless additional restrictions are imposed. Heckman (1978) demonstrates that if (U_{it}, V_i) are jointly normally distributed, α is identified even if there is no regressor in enrollment rule (2). His conditions are overly strong.

If U_{it} has zero third and fifth central moments, α is identified even if no regressor appears in the enrollment rule. This assumption about U_{it} is implied by normality or symmetry of the density of U_{it} but it is weaker than either provided that the required moments are finite. The fact that α can be identified by invoking distributional assumptions about U_{it} illustrates the more general point that there is a tradeoff between assumptions about regressors and assumptions about the distribution of U_{it} that must be invoked to identify α.

We have established that under the following assumptions, α in (1) is identified:

$$\mathrm{E}\left[U_{it}^3\right] = 0, \tag{10a}$$

$$\mathrm{E}\left[U_{it}^5\right] = 0, \tag{10b}$$

$$\{U_{it}, V_i\} \text{ is iid.} \tag{10c}$$

A consistent method of moments estimator can be devised that exploits these assumptions. [See Heckman and Robb (1985).] Find $\hat{\alpha}$ that sets a weighted average of the sample analogues of $\mathrm{E}[U_{it}^3]$ and $\mathrm{E}[U_{it}^5]$ as close to zero as possible.

To simplify the exposition, suppose that there are no regressors in the earnings function (1), so $X_{it}\beta = \beta_t$. The proposed estimator finds the value of $\hat{\alpha}$ that sets

$$(1/I_t)\sum_{i=1}^{I_t}\left[(Y_{it} - \bar{Y}) - \hat{\alpha}(d_i - \bar{d})\right]^3 \tag{11a}$$

and

$$(1/I_t)\sum_{i=1}^{I_t}\left[(Y_{it} - \bar{Y}) - \hat{\alpha}(d_i - \bar{d})\right]^5 \tag{11b}$$

as close to zero as possible in a suitably chosen metric where, as before, the overbar denotes sample mean. In our earlier paper, we establish the existence of a unique consistent root that sets (11a) and (11b) to zero in large samples.

5. Repeated cross-section methods for the case when training identity of individuals is unknown

In a time homogeneous environment, estimates of the population mean earnings formed in two or more cross-sections of unrelated persons can be used to obtain selection bias free estimates of the training effect even if the training status of each person is unknown (but the population proportion of trainees is known or can be consistently estimated). With more data, the time homogeneity assumption can be partially relaxed.

Assuming a time homogeneous environment and access to repeated cross-section data and random sampling, it is possible to identify α (a) without any regressor in the decision rule, (b) without need to specify the joint distribution of U_{it} and V_i, and (c) without any need to know which individuals in the sample enrolled in training (but the proportion of trainees must be known or consistently estimable).

To see why this claim is true, suppose that no regressors appear in the earnings function.[1] In the notation of eq. (1), $X_{it}\beta = \beta_t$. Then, assuming a random sampling scheme generates the data,

$$\operatorname{plim} \bar{Y}_t = \operatorname{plim} \sum Y_{it}/I_t = \mathrm{E}[\beta_t + \alpha d_i + U_{it}] = \beta_t + \alpha p, \quad t > k,$$

$$\operatorname{plim} \bar{Y}_{t'} = \operatorname{plim} \sum Y_{it'}/I_{t'} = \mathrm{E}[\beta_{t'} + U_{it'}] = \beta_{t'}, \quad t' < k.$$

In a time homogeneous environment, $\beta_t = \beta_{t'}$ and

$$\operatorname{plim}(\bar{Y}_t - \bar{Y}_{t'})/\hat{p} = \alpha,$$

where $\hat{p}$ is a consistent estimator of $p = \mathrm{E}[d_i]$.

With more than two years of repeated cross-section data, one can apply the same principles to identify α while relaxing the time homogeneity assumption. For instance, suppose that population mean earnings lie on a polynomial of order $L-2$:

$$\beta_t = \pi_0 + \pi_1 t + \cdots + \pi_{L-2} t^{L-2}.$$

From L temporally distinct cross-sections, it is possible to estimate consistently the $L-1$ π-parameters and α provided that the number of observations in each cross-section becomes large, and there is at least one pre-program and one post-program cross-section.

If the effect of training differs across periods, it is still possible to identify α_t provided that the environment changes in a 'sufficiently regular' way. For

[1] If regressors appear in the earnings function, the following procedure can be used. Rewrite (1) as $Y_{it} = \beta_t + X_{it}\pi + d_i\alpha + U_{it}$. It is possible to estimate π from pre-program data. Replace Y_{it} by $Y_{it} - X_{it}\hat{\pi}$ and the analysis in the text goes through. Note that we are assuming that no X_{it} variables become non-constant after period k.

example, suppose

$$\beta_t = \pi_0 + \pi_1 t \quad \text{for} \quad t > k,$$

$$\alpha_t = \phi_0(\phi_1)^{t-k} \quad \text{for} \quad t > k.$$

In this case, $\pi_0, \pi_1, \phi_0, \phi_1$ are identified from the means of four cross-sections, so long as at least one of these means comes from a pre-program period.

In Heckman and Robb (1985) we rigorously state the conditions required to consistently estimate α using repeated cross-section data that does not record the training identity of individuals. Section 9 examines the sensitivity of this class of estimators to violations of the random sampling assumption.

6. Longitudinal procedures

Most longitudinal procedures require knowledge of certain moments of the joint distribution of unobservables in the earnings and enrollment equations. We present several illustrations of this claim, as well as a counterexample. The counterexample identifies α by assuming only that the error term in the earnings equation is covariance stationary.

We now consider three examples of estimators which use longitudinal data.

6.1. The fixed effects method

This method was developed by Mundlak (1961, 1978) and refined by Chamberlain (1982). It is based on the following assumption:

$$\mathrm{E}[U_{it} - U_{it'} | d_i, X_{it} - X_{it'}] = 0 \quad \text{for all } t, t', \quad t > k > t'. \tag{12}$$

As a consequence of this assumption, we may write a difference regression as

$$\mathrm{E}[Y_{it} - Y_{it'} | d_i, X_{it} - X_{it'}] = (X_{it} - X_{it'})\beta + d_i\alpha, \qquad t > k > t'.$$

Suppose that (12) holds and the analyst has access to one year of preprogram and one year of post-program earnings. Regressing the difference between post-program earnings in any year and earnings in any pre-program year on the change in regressors between those years and a dummy variable for training status produces a consistent estimator of α.

Some decision rules and error processes for earnings produce (12). For example, consider a certainty environment in which the earnings residual has a permanent-transitory structure:

$$U_{it} = \phi_i + \varepsilon_{it}, \tag{13}$$

where ε_{it} is a mean zero random variable independent of all other values of $\varepsilon_{it'}$

and is distributed independently of ϕ_i, a mean zero person-specific time-invariant random variable. Assuming that S_i in decision rule (5) is distributed independently of all ε_{it} except possibly for ε_{ik}, then (12) will be satisfied.

Eq. (12) may also be satisfied in an environment of uncertainty. Suppose eq. (13) governs the error structure in (1) and

$$E_{k-1}[\varepsilon_{ik}] = 0,$$

but

$$E_{k-1}[\phi_i] = \phi_i,$$

so that agents cannot forecast innovations in their earnings, but they know their own permanent component. Provided that S_i is distributed independently of all ε_{it} except possible for ε_{ik}, this model also produces (12).

We investigate the plausibility of (12) with respect to more general decision rules and error processes in section 8.

6.2. U_{it} follows a first-order autoregressive process

Suppose next that U_{it} follows a first-order autoregression:

$$U_{it} = \rho U_{i,t-1} + \nu_{it}, \tag{14}$$

where $E[\nu_{it}] = 0$ and the ν_{it} are mutually independently (not necessarily identically) distributed random variables with $\rho \neq 1$. Substitution using (1) and (14) to solve for $U_{it'}$ yields

$$Y_{it} = [X_{it} - X_{it'}\rho^{t-t'}]\beta + (1-\rho^{t-t'})d_i\alpha$$

$$+\rho^{t-t'}Y_{it'} + \left\{\sum_{j=0}^{t-(t'+1)} \rho^j \nu_{i,t-j}\right\}, \qquad t > t' > k. \tag{15}$$

Assume further that the perfect foresight rule (5) determines enrollment, and the ν_{ij} are distributed independently of S_i and X_{ik} in (5). Heckman and Wolpin (1976) invoke similar assumptions in their analysis of affirmative action programs. As a consequence of these assumptions,

$$E[Y_{it}|X_{it}, X_{it'}, d_i, Y_{it'}] = (X_{it} - X_{it'}\rho^{t-t'})\beta$$

$$+(1-\rho^{t-t'})d_i\alpha + \rho^{t-t'}Y_{it'}, \tag{16}$$

so that (linear or non-linear) least squares applied to (16) consistently estimates

α as the number of observations becomes large. (The appropriate non-linear regression increases efficiency by imposing the cross-coefficient restrictions.)

6.3. U_{it} is covariance-stationary

The next procedure invokes an assumption implicitly used in many papers on training [*e.g.*, Ashenfelter (1978), Bassi (1983), and others] but exploits the assumption in a novel way. We assume

U_{it} is covariance stationary so $\mathrm{E}[U_{it}U_{i,t-j}] = \mathrm{E}[U_{it'}U_{i,t'-j}] = \sigma_j$ for $j \geq 0$ for all t, t',

(17a)

Access to at least two observations on pre-program earnings in t' and $t'-j$ as well as one period of post-program earnings in t where $t-t'=j$,

(17b)

$$p\mathrm{E}[U_{it'}|d_i = 1] \neq 0. \tag{17c}$$

Unlike the two previous examples, we make no assumptions here about the appropriate enrollment rule or about the stochastic relationship between U_{it} and the cost of enrollment S_i.

By the argument of footnote 1, we lose no generality by suppressing the effect of regressors in (1). Thus let

$$Y_{it} = \beta_t + d_i\alpha + U_{it}, \qquad t > k,$$

$$Y_{it'} = \beta_{t'} + U_{it'}, \qquad t' < k,$$

where β_t and $\beta_{t'}$ are period-specific shifters.

From a random sample of pre-program earnings from periods t' and $t'-j$, σ_j can be consistently estimated from the sample covariances between $Y_{it'}$ and $Y_{i,t'-j}$:

$$m_1 = \left(\sum(Y_{it'} - \overline{Y}_{t'})(Y_{i,t'-j} - \overline{Y}_{t'-j})\right)/I, \qquad \operatorname{plim} m_1 = \sigma_j.$$

If $t > k$ and $t - t' = j$ so that the post-program earnings data are as far removed in time from t' as t' is removed from $t'-j$, form the sample covariance between Y_{it} and $Y_{it'}$:

$$m_2 = \left(\sum(Y_{it} - \overline{Y}_t)(Y_{it'} - \overline{Y}_{t'})\right)/I,$$

which has the probability limit

$$\operatorname{plim} m_2 = \sigma_j + \alpha p \mathrm{E}[U_{it'}|d_i = 1], \qquad t > k > t'.$$

Form the sample covariance between d_i and $Y_{it'}$,

$$m_3 = \left(\sum (Y_{it'} - \bar{Y}_{t'}) d_i\right)/I,$$

with probability limit

$$\operatorname{plim} m_3 = p\mathrm{E}[U_{it'}|d_i = 1], \qquad t' < k.$$

Combining this information and assuming $p\mathrm{E}[U_{it'}|d_i = 1] \neq 0$ for $t' < k$,

$$\operatorname{plim} \hat{\alpha} = \operatorname{plim}((m_2 - m_1)/m_3) = \alpha.$$

7. Repeated cross-section analogues of longitudinal procedures

Most longitudinal procedures can be fit on repeated cross-section data. Repeated cross-section data are cheaper to collect and they do not suffer from problems of non-random attrition which plague panel data.

The previous section presented longitudinal estimators of α. In each case, however, α can actually be identified with repeated cross-section data. Here we establish this claim. Our earlier paper gives additional examples of longitudinal estimators which can be implemented on repeated cross-section data.[2]

7.1. The fixed effect model

As in section 6.1, assume that (12) holds so

$$\mathrm{E}[U_{it}|d_i = 1] = \mathrm{E}[U_{it'}|d_i = 1],$$

$$\mathrm{E}[U_{it}|d_i = 0] = \mathrm{E}[U_{it'}|d_i = 0],$$

for all $t > k > t'$. Let $X_{it}\beta = \beta_t$ and define, in terms of the notation of section 4.1,

$$\hat{\alpha} = \left[\bar{Y}_t^{(1)} - \bar{Y}_t^{(0)}\right] - \left[\bar{Y}_{t'}^{(1)} - \bar{Y}_{t'}^{(0)}\right].$$

[2] We also produce one example of a longitudinal procedure which has no repeated cross-section analogue.

Assuming random sampling, consistency of $\hat{\alpha}$ follows immediately from (12):

$$\begin{aligned}\operatorname{plim}\hat{\alpha} &= [\alpha + \beta_t - \beta_t + \mathrm{E}[U_{it}|d_i = 1] - \mathrm{E}[U_{it}|d_i = 0]] \\ &\quad - [\beta_{t'} - \beta_{t'} + \mathrm{E}[U_{it'}|d_i = 1] - \mathrm{E}[U_{it'}|d_i = 0]] \\ &= \alpha.\end{aligned}$$

7.2. U_{it} *follows a first-order autoregressive process*

In one respect the preceding example is contrived. It assumes that in pre-program cross-sections we know the identity of future trainees. Such data might exist (*e.g.*, individuals in the training period k might be asked about their pre-period k earnings to see if they qualify for admission), but this seems unlikely. One advantage of longitudinal data for estimating α in the fixed effect model is that if the survey extends before period k, the identity of future trainees is known.

The need for pre-program earnings to identify α is, however, only an artifact of the fixed effect assumption (13). Suppose instead that U_{it} follows a first-order autoregressive process given by (14) and that

$$\mathrm{E}[\nu_{it}|d_i] = 0, \qquad t > k, \tag{18}$$

as in section 6.2. With three successive post-program cross-sections in which the identity of trainees is known, it is possible to identify α.

To establish this result, let the three post-program periods be t, $t+1$ and $t+2$. Assuming, as before, that no regressor appears in (1),

$$\operatorname{plim}\bar{Y}_j^{(1)} = \beta_j + \alpha + \mathrm{E}\left[U_{ij}|d_i = 1\right],$$

$$\operatorname{plim}\bar{Y}_j^{(0)} = \beta_j + \mathrm{E}\left[U_{ij}|d_i = 0\right].$$

From (18),

$$\mathrm{E}[U_{i,t+1}|d_i = 1] = \rho\mathrm{E}[U_{it}|d_i = 1],$$

$$\mathrm{E}[U_{i,t+1}|d_i = 0] = \rho\mathrm{E}[U_{it}|d_i = 0],$$

$$\mathrm{E}[U_{i,t+2}|d_i = 1] = \rho^2\mathrm{E}[U_{it}|d_i = 1],$$

$$\mathrm{E}[U_{i,t+2}|d_i = 0] = \rho^2\mathrm{E}[U_{it}|d_i = 0].$$

Using these formulae, it is straightforward to verify that $\hat{\rho}$, defined by

$$\hat{\rho} = \frac{\left(\bar{Y}_{t+2}^{(1)} - \bar{Y}_{t+2}^{(0)}\right) - \left(\bar{Y}_{t+1}^{(1)} - \bar{Y}_{t+1}^{(0)}\right)}{\left(\bar{Y}_{t+1}^{(1)} - \bar{Y}_{t+1}^{(0)}\right) - \left(\bar{Y}_{t}^{(1)} - \bar{Y}_{t}^{(0)}\right)},$$

is consistent for ρ, and that $\hat{\alpha}$ defined by

$$\hat{\alpha} = \frac{\left(\bar{Y}_{t+2}^{(1)} - \bar{Y}_{t+2}^{(0)}\right) - \hat{\rho}\left(\bar{Y}_{t+1}^{(1)} - \bar{Y}_{t+1}^{(0)}\right)}{1 - \hat{\rho}},$$

is consistent for α.

For this model, the advantage of longitudinal data is clear. Only two time periods of longitudinal data are required to identify α, but three periods of repeated cross-section data are required to estimate the same parameter. However, if Y_{it} is subject to measurement error, the apparent advantages of longitudinal data become less clear. Repeated cross-section estimators are robust to mean zero measurement error in the variables. The longitudinal regression estimator discussed in section 6.2 does not identify α unless the analyst observes earnings without error. Given three years of longitudinal data and assuming that measurement error is serially uncorrelated, one could instrument (15) using earnings in the earliest year as an instrument. Thus one advantage of the longitudinal estimator disappears in the presence of measurement error.

7.3. Covariance stationarity

For simplicity we suppress regressors in the earnings equation and let $X_{it}\beta = \beta_t$. Assume that conditions (17) are satisfied. Before presenting the repeated cross-section estimator, it is helpful to record the following facts:

$$\operatorname{var}(Y_{it}) = \alpha^2(1-p)p + 2\alpha \mathrm{E}[U_{it}|d_i = 1]\,p + \sigma_u^2, \qquad t > k, \tag{19a}$$

$$\operatorname{var}(Y_{it'}) = \sigma_u^2, \qquad t' < k, \tag{19b}$$

$$\operatorname{cov}(Y_{it}, d_i) = \alpha p(1-p) + p\mathrm{E}[U_{it}|d_i = 1]. \tag{19c}$$

Note that $E[U_{it}^2] = E[U_{it'}^2]$ by virtue of assumption (17a). Then

$$\hat{\alpha} = (p(1-p))^{-1}\left(\frac{\sum(Y_{it}-\bar{Y}_t)d_i}{I_t} - \sqrt{\left(\frac{\sum(Y_{it}-\bar{Y}_t)d_i}{I_t}\right)^2 - p(1-p)\left(\frac{\sum(Y_{it}-\bar{Y}_t)^2}{I_t} - \frac{\sum(Y_{it'}-\bar{Y}_{t'})^2}{I_{t'}}\right)}\right) \tag{20}$$

is consistent for α.

This expression arises by subtracting (19b) from (19a). Then use (19c) to get an expression for $E[U_{it}|d_i = 1]$ which can be substituted into the expression for the difference between (19a) and (19b). Replacing population moments by sample counterparts produces a quadratic equation in $\hat{\alpha}$, with the negative root given by (20). The positive root is inconsistent for α.

Notice that the estimators of sections 6.3 and 7.3 exploit different features of the covariance stationarity assumptions. The longitudinal procedure only requires that $E[U_{it}U_{i,t-j}] = E[U_{it'}U_{it'-j}]$ for $j > 0$; variances need not be equal across periods. The repeated cross-section analogue presented above only requires that $E[U_{it}U_{i,t-j}] = E[U_{it'}U_{i,t'-j}]$ for $j = 0$; covariances may differ among equispaced pairs of the U_{it}.

8. First difference methods

Plausible economic models do not justify first difference methods. Lessons drawn from these models are misleading.

8.1. Models which justify condition (12)

Whenever condition (12) holds, α can be estimated consistently from the difference regression method described in section 6.1. Section 6.1 presents a model which satisfies condition (12): the earnings residual has a permanent-transitory structure, decision rule (4) or (5) determines enrollment, and S_i is distributed independently of the transitory component of U_{it}.

However, this model is rather special. It is very easy to produce plausible models that do not satisfy (12). For example, even if (13) characterizes U_{it}, if S_i in (5) does not have same joint (bivariate) distribution with respect to all ε_{it}, except for ε_{ik}, (12) may be violated.

Even if S_i in (5) is distributed independently of U_{it} for all t, it is still not the case that (12) is satisfied in a general model. For example, suppose X_{it} is distributed independently of all U_{it} and let

$$U_{it} = \rho U_{i,t-1} + \nu_{it},$$

where ν_{it} is a mean-zero, iid random variable and $|\rho| < 1$. If $\rho \neq 0$ and the perfect foresight decision rule characterizes enrollment, (12) is not satisfied for $t > k > t'$ because

$$\begin{aligned}\mathrm{E}[U_{it}|d_i = 1] &= \mathrm{E}[U_{it}|U_{ik} + X_{ik}\beta - \alpha/r < S_i] = \rho^{t-k}\mathrm{E}[U_{ik}|d_i = 1]\\ &\neq \mathrm{E}[U_{it'}|d_i = 1] = \mathrm{E}[U_{it'}|U_{ik} + X_{ik}\beta - \alpha/r < S_i],\end{aligned}$$

unless the conditional expectations are linear (in U_{ik}) for all t and $k - t' = t - k$. In that case

$$\mathrm{E}[U_{it}|d_i = 1] = \rho^{k-t'}\mathrm{E}[U_{ik}|d_i = 1],$$

so $\mathrm{E}[U_{it} - U_{it'}|d_i = 1] = 0$ only for t, t' such that $k - t' = t - k$. Thus (12) is not satisfied for all $t > k > t'$.

For more general specifications of U_{it} and stochastic dependence between S_i and U_{it}, (12) will not be satisfied.

8.2. *More general first difference estimators*

Instead of (12), assume that

$$\begin{aligned}&\mathrm{E}[(U_{it} - U_{it'})(X_{it} - X_{it'})] = 0 \quad \text{for some} \quad t, t', \quad t > k > t',\\ &\mathrm{E}[(U_{it} - U_{it'})d_i] = 0 \quad \text{for some} \quad t > k > t'.\end{aligned} \tag{21}$$

Two new ideas are embodied in this assumption. In place of the assumption that $U_{it} - U_{it'}$ be conditionally independent of $X_{it} - X_{it'}$ and d_i, we only require uncorrelatedness. Also, rather than assume that $\mathrm{E}[U_{it} - U_{it'}|d_i, X_{it} - X_{it'}] = 0$ for all $t > k > t'$, the correlation needs to be zero only for some $t > k > t'$. For the appropriate values of t and t', least squares applied to the differenced data consistently estimates α.

Our earlier paper presents three examples of models that satisfy (21) but not (12). Here we discuss one of them. Suppose that

U_{it} is covariance stationary, (22a)

U_{it} has a linear regression on U_{ik} for all t
(i.e., $\mathrm{E}[U_{it}|U_{ik}] = \beta_{tk}U_{ik}$), (22b)

U_{it} is mutually independent of (X_{ik}, S_i) for all t, (22c)

α is common to all individuals (so the model is of the fixed coefficient form), (22d)

The environment is one of perfect foresight where decision rule (5) determines participation. (22e)

Under these assumptions, condition (21) characterizes the data.

To see this note that (22a) and (22b) imply there exists a δ such that

$$U_{it} = U_{i,k+j} = \delta U_{ik} + \omega_{it}, \quad j > 0, \quad t > k,$$

$$U_{it'} = U_{i,k-j} = \delta U_{ik} + \omega_{it'}, \quad j > 0,$$

and

$$\mathrm{E}[\omega_{it} | U_{ik}] = \mathrm{E}[\omega_{it'} | U_{ik}] = 0.$$

Now observe that

$$\mathrm{E}[U_{it} | d_i = 1] = \delta \mathrm{E}[U_{ik} | d_i = 1] + \mathrm{E}[\omega_{it} | d_i = 1].$$

But, as a consequence of (22c),

$$\mathrm{E}[\omega_{it} | d_i = 1] = 0,$$

since $\mathrm{E}[\omega_{it}] = 0$ and because (22c) guarantees that the mean of ω_{it} does not depend on X_{ik} and S_i. Similarly,

$$\mathrm{E}[\omega_{it'} | d_i = 1] = 0,$$

and thus (21) holds.

Linearity of the regression does not imply that the U_{it} are normally distributed (although if the U_{it} are joint normal the regression is linear). The multivariate t density is just one example of many examples of densities with linear regressions.

8.3. Anomalous features of first difference estimators

Nearly all of the estimators require a control group (i.e., a sample of non-trainees). The only exception is the fixed effect estimator in a time homogeneous environment. In this case, if condition (12) or (21) holds, if we let $X_{it}\beta = \beta_t$ to simplify the exposition, and if the environment is time homogeneous so $\beta_t = \beta_{t'}$, then

$$\hat{\alpha} = \bar{Y}_t^{(1)} - \bar{Y}_{t'}^{(1)}$$

consistently estimates α. The frequently stated claim that 'if the environment is stationary, you don't need a control group' [see, e.g., Bassi (1983)] is false except for the special conditions which justify use of the fixed effect estimator.

Most of the procedures considered here can be implemented using only post-program data. The covariance stationary estimators of sections 6.3 and

7.3, certain repeated cross-section estimators and first difference methods constitute an exception to this rule. In this sense, these estimators are anomalous.

Fixed effect estimators are also robust to departures from the random sampling assumption. For instance, suppose condition (12) or (21) is satisfied, but that the available data oversample or undersample trainees (i.e., the proportion of sample trainees does not converge to $p = \mathrm{E}[d_i]$). Suppose further that the analyst does not know the true value of p. Nevertheless, a first difference regression continues to identify α. Most other procedures do not share this property.

9. Non-random sampling plans

Virtually all methods can be readily adjusted to account for choice based sampling or measurement error in training status. Some methods require no modification at all.

The data available for analyzing the impact of training on earnings are often non-random samples. Frequently they consist of pooled data from two sources: (a) a sample of trainees selected from program records and (b) a sample of non-trainees selected from some national sample. Typically, such samples overrepresent trainees relative to their proportion in the population. This creates the problem of choice based sampling analyzed by Manski and Lerman (1977) and Manski and McFadden (1981).

A second problem, contamination bias, arises when the training status of certain individuals is recorded with error. Many control samples such as the Current Population Survey or Social Security Work History File do not reveal whether or not persons have received training.

Both of these sampling situations combine the following types of data:

(A) Earnings, earnings characteristics, and enrollment characteristics (Y_{it}, X_{it} and Z_i) for a sample of trainees ($d_i = 1$),
(B) Earnings, earnings characteristics, and enrollment characteristics for a sample of non-trainees ($d_i = 0$),
(C) Earnings, earnings characteristics, and enrollment characteristics for a national 'control' sample of the population (e.g., CPS or Social Security Records) where the training status of persons is not known.

If type (A) and (B) data are combined and the sample proportion of trainees does not converge to the population proportion of trainees, the combined sample is a choice based sample. If type (A) and (C) data are combined with or without type (B) data, there is contamination bias because the training status of some persons is not known.

Most procedures developed in the context of random sampling can be modified to consistently estimate α using choice based samples or contaminated control groups (i.e., groups in which training status is not known for individuals). In some cases, a consistent estimator of the population proportion of trainees is required. We illustrate these claims by showing how to modify the instrumental variables estimator to address both sampling schemes. Our earlier paper gives explicit case by case treatment of these issues for each estimator developed there.

9.1. The I.V. estimator: Choice-based sampling

If condition (9a) is strengthened to read

$$\mathrm{E}\left[X_{it}'U_{it}|d_i\right]=0, \qquad \mathrm{E}\left[g(Z_i^e)U_{it}|d_i\right]=0, \tag{23}$$

and (9b) is also met, the I.V. estimator is consistent for α in choice-based samples.

To see why this is so, write the normal equations for the I.V. estimator in the following form:

$$\begin{pmatrix} \dfrac{\sum X_{it}'X_{it}}{I_t} & \dfrac{\sum X_{it}'d_i}{I_t} \\ \dfrac{\sum g(Z_i^e)X_{it}}{I_t} & \dfrac{\sum g(Z_i^e)d_i}{I_t} \end{pmatrix} \begin{pmatrix} \hat{\beta} \\ \hat{\alpha} \end{pmatrix} = \begin{pmatrix} \dfrac{\sum X_{it}'Y_{it}}{I_t} \\ \dfrac{\sum g(Z_i^e)Y_{it}}{I_t} \end{pmatrix}$$

$$= \begin{pmatrix} \dfrac{\sum X_{it}'X_{it}}{I_t} & \dfrac{\sum X_{it}'d_i}{I_t} \\ \dfrac{\sum g(Z_i^e)X_{it}}{I_t} & \dfrac{\sum g(Z_i^e)d_i}{I_t} \end{pmatrix} \begin{pmatrix} \beta \\ \alpha \end{pmatrix} + \begin{pmatrix} \dfrac{\sum X_{it}'U_{it}}{I_t} \\ \dfrac{\sum g(Z_i^e)U_{it}}{I_t} \end{pmatrix}. \tag{24}$$

Since (23) guarantees that

$$\operatorname*{plim}_{I_t\to\infty} \frac{\sum X_{it}'U_{it}}{I_t}=0 \quad \text{and} \quad \operatorname*{plim}_{I_t\to\infty} \frac{\sum g(Z_i^e)U_{it}}{I_t}=0, \tag{25}$$

and the rank condition (9b) holds, the I.V. estimator is consistent.

In a choice based sample, let the probability that an individual has enrolled in training be p^*. Even if (9a) and (9b) are satisfied, there is no guarantee that condition (25) will be met without invoking (23). This is so because

$$\operatorname*{plim}_{I_t \to \infty} \frac{\sum X_{it}' U_{it}}{I_t} = \mathrm{E}[X_{it}' U_{it} | d_i = 1]\, p^* + \mathrm{E}[X_{it}' U_{it} | d_i = 0](1 - p^*),$$

$$\operatorname*{plim}_{I_t \to \infty} \frac{\sum g(Z_i^e) U_{it}}{I_t} = \mathrm{E}[g(Z_i^e) U_{it} | d_i = 1]\, p^*$$

$$+ \mathrm{E}[g(Z_i^e) U_{it} | d_i = 0](1 - p^*).$$

These expressions are not generally zero, so the I.V. estimator is generally inconsistent.

In the case of random sampling, $p^* = \Pr[d_i = 1] = p$ and the above expressions are identically zero. They are also zero if (23) is satisfied. However, it is not necessary to invoke (23). Provided p is known, it is possible to reweight the data to secure consistent estimators under the assumptions of section 4. Multiplying eq. (1) by the weight

$$\omega_i = d_i \frac{p}{p^*} + (1 - d_i)\left(\frac{1 - p}{1 - p^*}\right),$$

and applying I.V. to the transformed equation produces an estimator that satisfies (25). It is straightforward to check that weighting the sample at hand back to random sample proportions causes the I.V. method to consistently estimate α and β. [See Heckman and Robb (1985).]

9.2. The I.V. estimator: Contamination bias

For data of type (C), d_i is not observed. Applying the I.V. estimator to pooled samples (A) and (C), assuming that observations in (C) have $d_i = 0$, produces an inconsistent estimator.

In terms of the I.V. eq. (24), from sample (C) it is possible to generate the cross-products

$$\frac{\sum X_{it}' X_{it}}{I_C}, \quad \frac{\sum g(Z_i^e) X_{it}}{I_C}, \quad \frac{\sum X_{it}' Y_{it}}{I_C}, \quad \frac{\sum g(Z_i^e) Y_{it}}{I_C},$$

which converge to the desired population counterparts where I_C denotes the number of observations in sample (C). Missing is information on the cross-products

$$\frac{\sum X_{it}'d_i}{I_C}, \quad \frac{\sum g(Z_i^e)d_i}{I_C}.$$

Notice that if d_i were measured accurately in sample (C),

$$\operatorname*{plim}_{I_C\to\infty} \frac{\sum X_{it}'d_i}{I_C} = p\mathrm{E}[X_{it}'|d_i=1],$$

$$\operatorname*{plim}_{I_C\to\infty} \frac{\sum g(Z_i^e)d_i}{I_c} = p\mathrm{E}[g(Z_i^e)|d_i=1].$$

But the means of X_{it} and $g(Z_i^e)$ in sample (A) converge to

$$\mathrm{E}[X_{it}|d_i=1] \quad \text{and} \quad \mathrm{E}[g(Z_i^e)|d_i=1],$$

respectively. Hence, inserting the sample (A) means of X_{it} and $g(Z_i^e)$ multiplied by p in the second column of the matrix I.V. eq. (24) produces a consistent I.V. estimator provided that in the limit the size of samples (A) and (C) both approach infinity at the same rate.

9.3. Repeated cross-section methods with unknown training status and choice-based sampling

The repeated cross-section estimators discussed in section 5 are inconsistent when applied to choice-based samples unless additional conditions are assumed. For example, when the environment is time-homogeneous and (12) also holds, $(\overline{Y}_t - \overline{Y}_{t'})/p$ remains a consistent estimator of α in choice-based samples as long as the same proportion of trainees are sampled in periods t' and t. If a condition such as (12) is not met, it is necessary to know the identity of trainees in order to weight the sample back to the proportion of trainees that would be produced by a random sample in order to obtain consistent estimators. Hence the class of estimators that does not require knowledge of individual training status is not robust to choice-based sampling.

9.4. Control function estimators

A subset of cross-sectional and longitudinal procedures is robust to choice-based sampling. Those procedures construct a control function, K_{it}, with the following properties:

K_{it} depends on variables $\ldots, Y_{i,t+1}, Y_{it}, Y_{i,t-1}, \ldots, X_{i,t+1}, X_{it}, X_{i,t-1}, \ldots, d_i$ and parameters ψ, and

$$\mathrm{E}[U_{it} - K_{it} | d_i, X_{it}, K_{it}, \psi] = 0, \tag{26a}$$

$$\psi \text{ is identified.} \tag{26b}$$

When inserted into the earnings function (1), K_{it} purges the equation of dependence between U_{it} and d_i. Rewriting (1) to incorporate K_{it},

$$Y_{it} = X_{it}\beta + d_i\alpha + K_{it} + \{U_{it} - K_{it}\}. \tag{27}$$

The purged disturbance $\{U_{it} - K_{it}\}$ is orthogonal to the right-hand-side variables in the new equation. Thus (possibly non-linear) regression applied to (27) consistently estimates the parameters (α, β, ψ). Moreover, (26) implies that $\{U_{it} - K_{it}\}$ is orthogonal to the right-hand-side variables conditional on d_i, X_{it} and K_{it}:

$$\mathrm{E}[Y_{it} | X_{it}, d_i, K_{it}] = X_{it}\beta + d_i\alpha + K_{it}.$$

Thus if type (A) and (B) data are combined in *any* proportion, least squares performed on (27) produces consistent estimates of (α, β, ψ) provided the number of trainees and non-trainees in the sample both approach infinity. The class of control function estimators which satisfy (26) can be implemented without modification in choice-based samples.

We encountered a control function in section 6. For the model satisfying (14) and (18),

$$K_{it} = \rho(Y_{i,t-1} - X_{i,t-1}\beta - d_i\alpha), \qquad t > k+1,$$

so $\psi = (\rho, \beta, \alpha)$. The sample selection bias methods (d)-(e) described in section 4.2 exploit the control function principle. Our longer paper gives further examples of control function estimators.

10. Conclusion

This paper presents alternative methods for estimating the impact of training on earnings when non-random selection characterizes the enrollment of persons into training. We have explored the benefits of cross-section, repeated cross-section and longitudinal data for addressing this problem by considering the assumptions required to use a variety of new and conventional estimators given access to various commonly encountered types of data. We also investigate the plausibility of assumptions needed to justify econometric procedures when viewed in the light of prototypical decision rules determining enrollment into training. Because many of the available samples are choice-based samples and because the problem of measurement error in training status is pervasive in many available control samples, we examine the robustness of the estimators to choice-based sampling and contamination bias.

A key conclusion of our analysis is that the benefits of longitudinal data have been overstated in the recent econometric literature on training because a false comparison has been made. A cross-section selection bias estimator does not require the elaborate and unjustified assumptions about functional forms often invoked in cross-sectional studies. Repeated cross-section data can often be used to identify the same parameters as longitudinal data. The uniquely longitudinal estimators require assumptions that are different from and often no more plausible than the assumptions required for cross-section or repeated cross-section estimators.

References

Amemiya, T., 1981, Qualitative response models: A survey, Journal of Economic Literature 19, 1483–1536.

Ashenfelter, O., 1978, Estimating the effect of training programs on earnings, Review of Economics and Statistics 60, 47–57.

Barnow, B., G. Cain and A. Goldberger, 1980, Issues in the analysis of selectivity bias, in: E. Stromsdorfer and G. Farkas, eds., Evaluation studies, Vol. 5 (Sage Publications, Beverly Hills, CA).

Bassi, L., 1983, Estimating the effect of training programs with nonrandom selection, Ph.D. dissertation (Princeton University, Princeton, NJ).

Chamberlain, G., 1982, Multivariate regression models for panel data, Journal of Econometrics 18, 1–46.

Heckman, J., 1976, Simultaneous equations models with continuous and discrete endogenous variables and structural shifts, in: S. Goldfeld and R. Quandt, eds., Studies in nonlinear estimation (Ballinger, Cambridge, MA).

Heckman, J., 1978, Dummy endogenous variables in a simultaneous equations system. Econometrica 46, 931–961.

Heckman, J., 1979, Sample selection bias as a specification error, Econometrica 47, 153–161.

Heckman, J. and G. Neumann, 1977, Union wage differentials and the decision to join unions, Unpublished manuscript (University of Chicago, Chicago, IL).

Heckman, J. and R. Robb, 1985, Alternative methods for evaluating the impact of interventions, in: J. Heckman and B. Singer, eds., Longitudinal analysis of labor market data, Econometric Society monograph series (Cambridge University Press, New York).

Heckman, J. and K. Wolpin, 1976, Does the contract compliance program work? An analysis of Chicago data, Industrial and Labor Relations Review, 554–564.

Lee, L.F., 1978, Unionism and wage rates: A simultaneous equations model with qualitative and limited dependent variables, International Economic Review 19, 415–433.

Manski, C. and S. Lerman, 1977, The estimation of choice probabilities from choice-based samples, Econometrica 45, 1977–1988.

Manski, C. and D. McFadden, 1981, Alternative estimators and sample designs for discrete choice analysis, in: C. Manski and D. McFadden, eds., Structural analysis of discrete data with econometric applications (MIT Press, Cambridge, MA).

Mundlak, Y., 1961, Empirical production functions free of management bias, Journal of Farm Economics 43, 45–56.

Mundlak, Y., 1978, On the pooling of time series and cross section data, Econometrica 46, 69–85.

Roy, A., 1951, Some thoughts on the distribution of earnings, Oxford Economic Papers 3, 135–146.

IDENTIFICATION OF THE COEFFICIENTS IN A NON-LINEAR TIME SERIES OF THE QUADRATIC TYPE

Melvin J. HINICH

University of Texas, Austin, TX 78712, USA

Douglas M. PATTERSON

Virginia Polytechnic Institute and State University, Blacksburg, VA 24061, USA

This paper presents a method for identifying the structure of the quadratic model $x(t) = e(t) + \sum_{r=1}^{R} \sum_{s=0}^{S} a(r, s)e(t-s)e(t-r-s)$, where the $e(t)$ are independent, identically distributed zero mean random variables. This finite parameter model is a simplified second-order Volterra expansion of a stable non-linear filter. The standard deviation of $e(t)$ is not estimable from observations of the $x(t)$. It is shown that the $(m, m+n)$th third-order cumulant (called the bicovariance) of $\{x(t)\}$ is equal to $a(m, n)$ times the square of the variance of $e(t)$. The large sample distribution of the sample bicovariance is used to determine which quadratic coefficients are significantly different from zero. The method is illustrated using artificial and real data; daily stock price series for several securities.

1. Introduction

There is no compelling reason why time series found in the physical sciences and various social science applications should conform to linear time series models. Linear models, usually having a finite number of parameters, are employed for ease of statistical analysis, just as the assumption that variables are normally distributed is made for convenience and then is often accepted as a fact when data are interpreted. Indeed, a stationary *non-Gaussian* time series is usually the result of some non-linear operation on a Gaussian input process. The reason why time series analysis has historically relied so heavily on linear models is the dearth of non-linear statistical tools.

Recently, a few statistical methods designed to detect certain types of non-linearity in a time series have appeared in the literature. For the most part, these methods are based on the behavior of the third-order cumulant function of a non-linear time series. For example, Subba Rao and Gabr (1980) present a test for non-linearity using a sample estimate of the bispectrum of the time series. (The bispectrum is defined as the double Fourier transform of the third-order cumulant function.) Hinich (1982) presents a non-parametric test that also uses the sample bispectrum, but which takes advantage of the asymptotic properties of the bispectrum estimator. Maravall (1983) developed an easily applied test for detecting non-linearity in the estimated residuals of a time series which uses the autocorrelation function of the squared residuals. Also, Hinich and Patterson (1985) applied the Hinich test to realizations of daily stock returns for a sample of stocks covering the period July 1962 through December 1977. They rejected linearity for each of the fifteen series.

Although time series theorists have made considerable progress in developing the theoretical properties of non-linear models, an efficient statistical method for estimating these models in a parametric form from a finite set of observations remains elusive. A practical estimation method will, no doubt, consist of at least four iterative steps: (1) Detection of non-linearity in the data at hand. As pointed out in the previous paragraph, some progress has been made in this direction, at least for the case where the underlying process has a non-zero third-order cumulant function. (2) Identification, through use of the data, of candidate models to be tentatively considered. This step might also provide rough estimates of model parameters. (3) Estimation of candidate model parameters using appropriate statistical methods. This step may require that the candidate model be inverted; that is, to express the innovations as a function of past values of the non-linear process. In some situations inversion may not be necessary; see Haggan et al. (1984) for a concrete example of this approach. (4) Diagnostic checks. Here lack of fit of the data to the candidate model is discovered. Obviously, the tools employed in steps (1) and (2) can be profitably turned to the task of uncovering model inadequacy and suggesting model improvements.

In this article we present an applied method of model identification for that class of non-linear models featuring a non-zero third-order cumulant function. Specifically, the method presented below is designed to identify the coefficients in a non-linear time series of the quadratic type with a simple linear term. This class of non-linear models can be written as

$$x(t) = \varepsilon(t) + \sum_{m=1}^{R} \sum_{n=0}^{S} a_m(n)\varepsilon(t-n)\varepsilon(t-m-n),$$

where the $\varepsilon(t)$ are independent, identically distributed random deviates with zero mean. These models are characterized as having a 'simple linear term' because the linear component is uncorrelated; it consists of the innovation only, rather than a linear transformation of the innovation. The quadratic non-linear component for this model class restricts all of the non-linear variation to the third-order cumulant function.

The article is organized as follows. Section 2 provides a brief introduction to the general non-linear model. The reader will find a much more thorough presentation in the references. Section 3 presents our identification method, and briefly describes certain estimators and their sampling properties which we have developed for application to non-linear identification. In section 4 we demonstrate the identification method through the use of artificial data. The final section of the article applies the identification method to realizations of daily stock returns for a sample of fifteen randomly selected stocks, with some interesting results.

2. Non-linear stationary time series models

A general non-linear causal time series model can be regarded as the 'output' of a non-linear system whose 'input' is a stationary random process $\{\varepsilon(t)\}$. The output is of the form

$$x(t)=f[\varepsilon(t),\varepsilon(t-1),\ldots], \tag{2.1}$$

where f is a non-linear function that does not depend on t. Non-linear time series are analogous to ordinary non-linear differential equations in that they can exhibit limit cycles, clipping, hysteresis, and so on.

An important insight to the nature of the general non-linear model is provided by expressing (2.1) as a discrete time Volterra series expansion:

$$x(t)=\sum_{i=0}^{\infty}a(i)\varepsilon(t-i)+\sum_{i=0}^{\infty}\sum_{j=0}^{\infty}a(i,j)\varepsilon(t-i)\varepsilon(t-j)$$
$$+\sum_{i=0}^{\infty}\sum_{j=0}^{\infty}\sum_{k=0}^{\infty}a(i,j,k)\varepsilon(t-i)\varepsilon(t-j)\varepsilon(t-k)+\cdots. \tag{2.2}$$

The $a(i,j,k,\ldots)$ are the coefficients of the series and the $\varepsilon(t)$ input process is usually considered to be unobservable. Wiener (1958), in a classic study of non-linear systems, used the continuous time version of (2.2) to express the non-linear relationship between the input and output of a physical system. When $\{\varepsilon(t)\}$ is a purely random process with zero mean, the first term in (2.2) is a general linear model, and the successive terms are usually referred to as the 'quadratic', 'cubic',... components.

Consider the following example of the quadratic model:

$$x(t)=\varepsilon(t)+b\varepsilon(t-1)\varepsilon(t-2). \tag{2.3}$$

The parameter b can take on any non-zero value. Now, $\mathrm{E}[X(t)]=\mu_x=0$ since $\mathrm{E}[\varepsilon(t)]=0$, and the $\varepsilon(t)$ are independent variates. This model is also a white-noise series because its autocovariance function $c_x(m)=\mathrm{E}[x(t+m)\times x(t)]-\mu_x^2=0$ for all $m\neq 0$. Although the $x(t)$ variates are uncorrelated, there is a relationship between $x(t-2)$, $x(t-1)$, and $x(t)$ for all t, because

$E[x(t-2)x(t-1)x(t)] = b\sigma_\varepsilon^4$. This term is one element of the set of third-order cumulants of $\{x(t)\}$, which are defined for each (r, s) as

$$c_{xxx}(r,s) = E[x(t+r)x(t+s)x(t)], \tag{2.4}$$

when $E[x(t)] = 0$. From stationarity the following symmetries hold for all (r, s):

$$c_{xxx}(r,s) = c_{xxx}(s,r) = c_{xxx}(r-s,-s) = c_{xxx}(s-r,-r).$$

Note that for a zero-mean Gaussian time series, $c_{xxx}(r,s) \equiv 0$.

The quadratic time series shown in (2.3) above has six non-zero third-order cumulants, namely $c_{xxx}(1,2) = c_{xxx}(-1,-2) = c_{xxx}(1,-1)$, plus their three permutation symmetries. The general quadratic time series with a simple linear term

$$x(t) = \varepsilon(t) + \sum_{m=1}^{\infty} \sum_{n=0}^{\infty} a_m(n)\varepsilon(t-n)\varepsilon(t-m-n), \tag{2.5}$$

with parameters $a_1(0), a_1(1), \ldots, a_m(n), \ldots,$ has many non-zero cumulants and is white-noise if $a_m(n)a_m(n+r) = 0$. These processes are clearly non-Gaussian. From the Volterra series expansion of the general non-linear model in expression (2.2), we see how the general quadratic model can be regarded as an approximation to the general non-linear model when the linear component is simple. However, there are non-linear models where $c_{xxx}(r,s) = 0$ for all (r, s), and it is easy to construct linear models which just have a non-zero contemporaneous third-order cumulant. Hence, it is necessary to be able to distinguish between a linear non-Gaussian process (if the linear process has a non-zero third-order cumulant it is non-Gaussian) and a non-linear process. The test developed by Hinich (1982) accomplishes this task.

Because third-order cumulants are difficult to interpret, and their moment estimates even more difficult to comprehend, the Hinich test employs the statistical properties of the double Fourier transform of the third-order cumulant function (called the *bispectrum*).

The bispectrum, denoted by $B_x(f_1, f_2)$, is defined as follows: For frequencies f_1 and f_2,

$$B_x(f_1,f_2) = \sum_{r=-\infty}^{\infty} \sum_{s=-\infty}^{\infty} c_{xxx}(r,s)\exp[-i2\pi(f_1 r + f_2 s)], \tag{2.6}$$

assuming that $|c_{xxx}(r,s)|$ is summable. The symmetries of $c_{xxx}(r,s)$ translate into symmetries of $B_x(f_1, f_2)$ that produce a principal domain for the bispectrum, which is the triangular set $\Omega = \{0 < f_1 < \frac{1}{2}, 2f_1 + f_2 < 1\}$. The third-order cumulants are expressed in terms of the bispectrum by the inverse Fourier transform,

$$c_{xxx}(r, s) = \int\int_{\Omega} B_x(f_1, f_2) \exp[i2\pi(f_1 r + f_2 s)] \, df_1 \, df_2. \tag{2.7}$$

Eq. (2.7) implies that a consistent estimator of the bispectrum yields consistent estimators of the $c_{xxx}(r, s)$. See Brillinger and Rosenblatt (1967), Brillinger (1975), Subba Rao (1983), and Rosenblatt (1983) for a rigorous treatment of the bispectrum.

Suppose that a process $\{x(t)\}$ is generated by a linear model with $\{\varepsilon(t)\}$ a non-Gaussian purely random process. If $\sum_{i=0}^{\infty} |a(i)|$ is finite,

$$B_x(f_1, f_2) = \mu_3 A(f_1) A(f_2) A^*(f_1 + f_2), \tag{2.8}$$

where $\mu_3 = \mathrm{E}[\varepsilon^3(t)]$, the asterisk denotes complex conjugate, and $A(f) = \sum_{k=-\infty}^{\infty} b(k) \exp(-i2\pi fk)$. Since the spectrum of $x(t)$ is $S_x(f) = \sigma_\varepsilon^2 |A(f)|^2$, it follows from (2.8) that

$$(|B_x(f_1, f_2)|^2)/(S_x(f_1) S_x(f_2) S_x(f_1 + f_2)) = \mu_3^2/\sigma_\varepsilon^6, \tag{2.9}$$

for all (f_1, f_2) in the set Ω. If $\varepsilon(t)$ is Gaussian, $\mu_3 = 0$ and then $B(f_1, f_2) \equiv 0$. The square root of the left side of (2.9) is called the skewness of $\{x(t)\}$. The fact that the skewness of a linear time series is independent of frequency is used by Hinich to test the null hypothesis of linearity using the estimated bispectrum [the estimated bispectrum is used in a similar manner by Subba Rao and Gabr (1980) to test the linearity null hypothesis].

The upshot of this discussion is that if we apply the linearity test to an empirical time series, and if there is sufficient evidence to reject linearity, then we are justified in concluding that $c_{xxx}(r, s) \neq 0$ for some $r \neq 0$ and $s \neq 0$. Furthermore, we can now regard some unspecified form of the general quadratic model, (2.5), as an approximation to the underlying non-linear process.

We now turn to the problem of determining which of the $a_m(n)$ parameters in the general quadratic model are non-zero.

3. Identification of the quadratic parameters

Suppose a time series is adequately approximated by a quadratic time series model with a simple linear term:

$$x(t) = \varepsilon(t) + \sum_{m=1}^{\infty} \sum_{n=0}^{\infty} a_m(n) \varepsilon(t-n) \varepsilon(t-m-n), \tag{3.1}$$

where $\{\varepsilon(t)\}$ is an independent, identically distributed sequence of random variables with mean zero and variance denoted σ_ε^2. The $\{\varepsilon(t)\}$ process is unobservable. We want to determine those parameters $a_m(n)$ in (3.1) which are non-zero. Or, in other words, we want to identify a representational form of (3.1) which is worthy of serious consideration. Our technique for accomplishing this goal will be explained by stating and discussing four key theorems. The proofs of the theorems can be found in Hinich and Patterson (1984).

Theorem 1. The expected value of $x(t)$, *defined in* (3.1), *is zero, and the third-order cumulant* (*bicovariance*) *is*

$$\mathrm{E}[x(t)x(t+m)x(t+m+n)] = \sigma_\varepsilon^4 a_m(n), \tag{3.2}$$

for all $m \geq 1$ *and* $n \geq 1$. *For* $n = 0$, $\mathrm{E}[x(t)x^2(t+m)] = 2\sigma_\varepsilon^4 a_m(0)$.

Because $\varepsilon(t)$ is unobservable, we can not estimate σ_ε. As a consequence, we can only determine the coefficients up to the scale factor σ_ε^4, as shown in (3.2).

Suppose that we have a sample $x(1),\ldots,x(N)$ from the process. For each $m, n \geq 1$, the sample bicovariance $(N-m-n)^{-1}\sum_{t=1}^{N-m-n} x(t)x(t+m)x(t+m+n)$ is an unbiased estimator of $a_m(n)$ from Theorem 1. This unbiased estimator, as with the standard sample autocovariances, has a variance that increases with the size of the lags. As $m+n$ increases the number of products decreases in the above sum. The dependence of the variance of the sample bicovariance on $m+n$ is not its only problem. It is inefficient to compute all the sums of lagged products for a large number of m and n values. A more computationally convenient estimator uses the discrete Fourier transform of the data.

Using the convention that the first observation is taken at time zero, the discrete Fourier transform of the data is defined to be

$$X(\omega_j) = \sum_{t=0}^{N-1} x(t)\exp(-\mathrm{i}\omega_j t), \qquad j = 0,1,\ldots,N-1, \tag{3.3}$$

where $\omega_j = 2\pi j/N$ is the angular frequency with period N/j. Any one of the versions of the Fast Fourier transform is an efficient way to compute $X(\omega_j)$ for $j = 0,1,\ldots,N-1$. Since $x(t)$ is real, $X(\omega_{N-j}) = X^*(\omega_j)$ where again the asterisk denotes complex conjugate. The following estimator of $a_m(n)$ is biased, but it has the same variance for all m and $n \geq 1$ and it is computationally more efficient than the sample bicovariance approach for large N. Remember that from Theorem 1, $a_m(n)$ can be estimated only up to a scalar multiple since σ_ε is an unknown parameter.

Theorem 2. Define the estimator

$$\hat{a}_m(n) = N^{-3} \sum_{j=0}^{N-1} \sum_{k=0}^{N-1} X(\omega_j) X(\omega_{k-j}) X^*(\omega_k) \exp\left[i(\omega_j n + \omega_k m\right]. \tag{3.4}$$

The inverse discrete Fourier transform of $X(\omega_j)$ as defined in (3.4) gives $x(t) = N^{-1}\sum_{j=0}^{N-1} X(\omega_j)\exp(i\omega_j t)$, where $x(t+N) = x(t)$ for each $t = 0, \ldots, N-1$. Then, $\hat{a}_m(n) = N^{-1}\sum_{t=0}^{N-1} x(t)x(t+m)x(t+m+n)$.

The right-hand side of the expression for $\hat{a}_m(n)$ in (3.4) is the discrete double Fourier transform of the complex array $\{N^{-1}X(\omega_j)X(\omega_{k-j})X^*(\omega_k)\}$ for $j, k = 0, \ldots, N-1$. It can be computed by N Fast Fourier transforms of vectors of length N. The estimator is asymptotically normal.

The result in Theorem 2 can be used to efficiently compute the array of sample bicovariances by means of a simple trick to break the circularity in the $x(t)$'s. Suppose that N zeros are added to the end of the data array. The Fourier transform of this extended array of length $2N$ is $X(2\pi j/2N)$ for $j = 0, \ldots, 2N-1$. A double Fourier transform of the $(2N) \times (2N)$ array $\{N^{-1}X(\pi j/N)X(\pi(k-j)/N)X^*(\pi k/N)\}$ will yield the bicovariances since the $x(t)$'s are now periodic with period $2N$ with N consecutive zeros.

It can also be shown that in large samples the estimator $a_m(n)$ defined in Theorem 2 is correlated along both the m and n dimensions, and that the correlation falls off more slowly along the n dimension. In particular, the correlation along the n dimension rolls off at least as fast as the order of the difference in the n's.

The following results give the expected value and variance of $\hat{a}_m(n)$:

Theorem 3. For all $1 \le m < N$,

$$\sigma_\varepsilon^{-4} \mathrm{E}[\hat{a}_m(0)] = 2(1 - m/N) a_m(0), \tag{3.5}$$

and for $n \ge 1$,

$$\sigma_\varepsilon^{-4} \mathrm{E}[\hat{a}_m(n)] = [1 - (m+n)/N] a_m(n) + (n/N) a_{N-m-n}(m) + (m/N) a_n(N-m-n). \tag{3.6}$$

Corollary 3.1. If $m + n \le N/2$, then for $n \le 1$,

$$\sigma_\varepsilon^{-4} \mathrm{E}[\hat{a}_m(n)] = [1 - (m+n)/N] a_m(n). \tag{3.7}$$

Theorem 3 and its corollary show that the estimator of Theorem 2 is downward biased, with the bias following a ramp function. The variance of the estimator is given by Theorem 4.

Theorem 4. Assume that $\sum_{r=1}^{\infty}\sum_{s=0}^{\infty} a_r^2(s)$ *is finite, and let* $c_4 = \mathrm{E}[x^4(t)] - 3\sigma_x^4$ *denote the fourth cumulant of* $x(t)$. *Then,*

$$\operatorname{var}[\hat{a}_m(n)] = \sigma_x^6/N + \mathrm{O}(N^{-2}), \tag{3.8}$$

$$\operatorname{var}[\hat{a}_m(0)] = (c_4 + 3\sigma_x^4)\sigma_x^2/N + \mathrm{O}(N^{-2}). \tag{3.9}$$

We see from Theorem 4 that in testing the significance of an estimate, we must distinguish between the $n = 0$ cases and the $n \geq 1$ cases.

It can be shown that the signal to signal plus noise ratio (*SSPN*) of the quadratic process (3.1) is given by the sum of squares of the coefficients over the variance of the process cubed. That is,

$$SSPN = \frac{\sigma_\varepsilon^8 \sum_{m=1}^{\infty} \sum_{n=0}^{\infty} a_m^2(n)}{\sigma_\varepsilon^6 \left(1 + \sigma_\varepsilon^2 \sum_{m=1}^{\infty} \sum_{n=0}^{\infty} a_m^2(n)\right)^3} = \frac{\sigma_\varepsilon^2 \sum_{m=1}^{\infty} \sum_{n=0}^{\infty} a_m^2(n)}{\left(1 + \sigma_\varepsilon^2 \sum_{m=1}^{\infty} \sum_{n=0}^{\infty} a_m^2(n)\right)^3}. \tag{3.10}$$

The ratio has a maximum of (4/27), or -8.29 dB. The *SSPN* ratio measures the relative contribution of the quadratic terms to the variance of the process. The greater the ratio, the greater the quadratic non-linearity in a model.

In order to implement our identification method, we wrote a computer algorithm which can handle up to 1280 observations. The program breaks a time series into blocks of 256 observations, finds the coefficients for each block of 256, with 256 zeros added to the end of the array, and averages them together. This method was chosen because we wanted to limit the program size to less than 1 megabyte of core (storage requirements go up as $8N^2$). The $n = 0$ estimates are divided by 2 to adjust for part of the bias shown in Theorem 3. The program does not adjust for the ramp bias in calculating the coefficients.

With a sample size of 1280 this technique introduces additional correlation into the estimates beyond the large sample correlation mentioned above. This occurs because we are estimating $256 \times 256 = 65536$ coefficients from a total sample of 1280 observations. Obviously, the estimates are not independent. The correlation will not be particularly severe when the underlying quadratic model is sparse in non-zero coefficients. Coefficient sparseness is a reasonable assumption when considering real data, as will be shown in section 5.

Finally, the program compares the estimated coefficients to their standard error, for $n = 0, \ldots, 128$ and $m = 1, \ldots, 128$, and prints out those coefficients which exceed a user specified level of significance. Standard errors for the $n=0$ and $n \geq 1$ cases are calculated using the expressions in Theorem 4 with sample moments replacing population moments.

4. Artificial data experiments

In this section the non-linear identification technique is illustrated through the use of artificial data. Although the technique was tested using a variety of models, we will restrict our attention here to the following model:

$$x(t) = \varepsilon(t) + 31\varepsilon(t-9)\varepsilon(t-13) + 31\varepsilon(t)\varepsilon(t-95), \tag{4.1}$$

with $\sigma_\varepsilon^2 = 0.0003$ and $\sigma_x^2 = 0.0005$. The $\varepsilon(t)$ variates were generated by the GGNML pseudo-random number routine in the *IMSL* library.

A realization of (4.1) with 1280 observations is plotted in fig. 1. For this realization, $\hat{\mu}_x = -0.0001$, $\hat{\sigma}_x^2 = 0.00044$ and $\hat{\sigma}_\varepsilon^2 = 0.00030$. Note from fig. 1

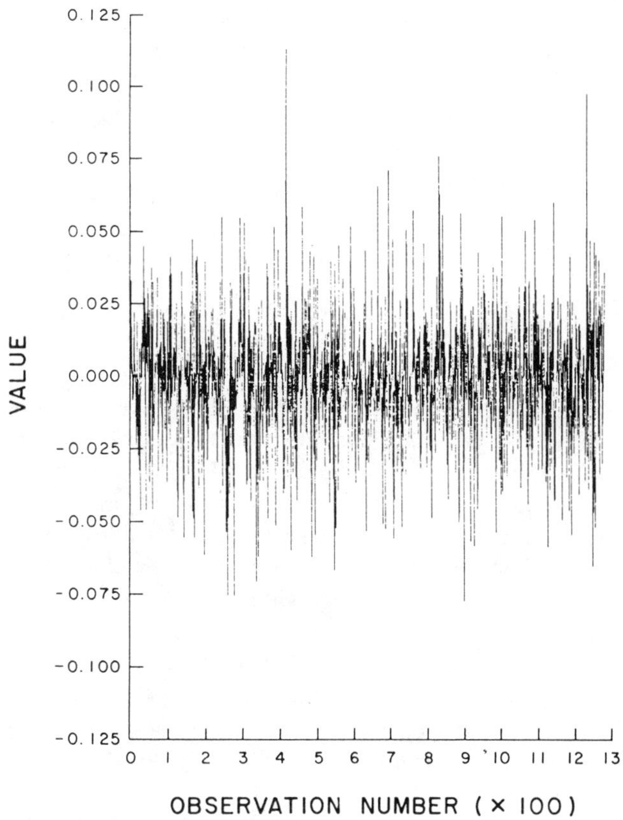

Fig. 1. Artificial data $m = 4.95$.

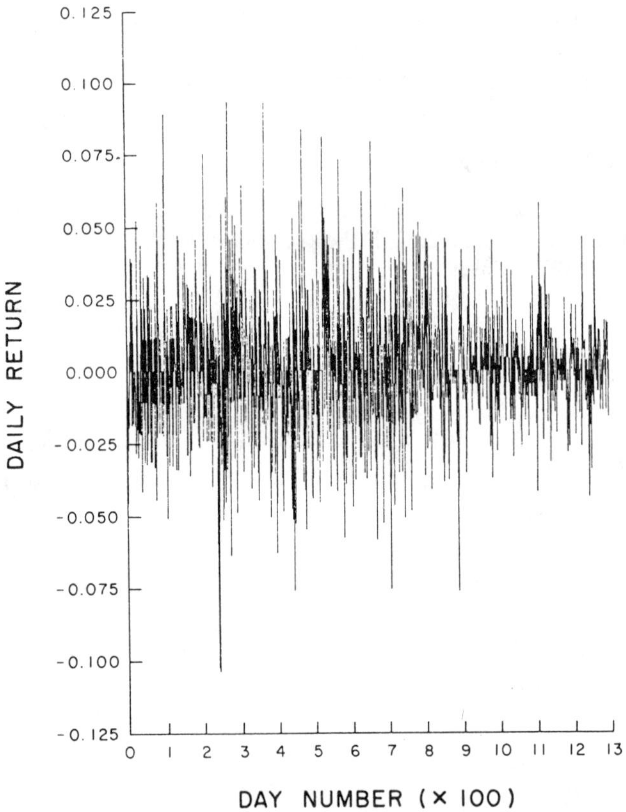

Fig. 2. American Standard 12/5/72–12/30/77.

that the model appears to be producing a large number of outliers vis-à-vis what we would expect from a Gaussian process; the sample kurtosis is 4.5, much larger than the reference value of 3 for a Gaussian process. In section 5 we will apply our identification technique to series of daily stock returns of length 1280, so it is worth mentioning that those series, and daily stock returns in general, exhibit leptokurtic behavior. For example, fig. 2 is a plot of the 1280 observations of American Standard, a series used in section 5. The sample kurtosis for this series is 4.74 with a sample variance of 0.0005, the same as the artificial data. For reference purposes, the reader's attention is directed to fig. 3, where we have plotted a purely random Gaussian process (it is linear) with a variance 0.0005. In comparing fig. 3 with figs. 1 and 2 we can easily see a difference between the behavior of the linear Gaussian process and the non-linear processes.

The coefficient estimates for the artificial data are $\hat{a}_4(9) = 0.236\text{E-}5$ and $\hat{a}_{95}(0) = 0.204\text{E-}5$. Because we know $\hat{\sigma}_\varepsilon^2 = 0.3\text{E-}3$, we can use Theorem 3 to

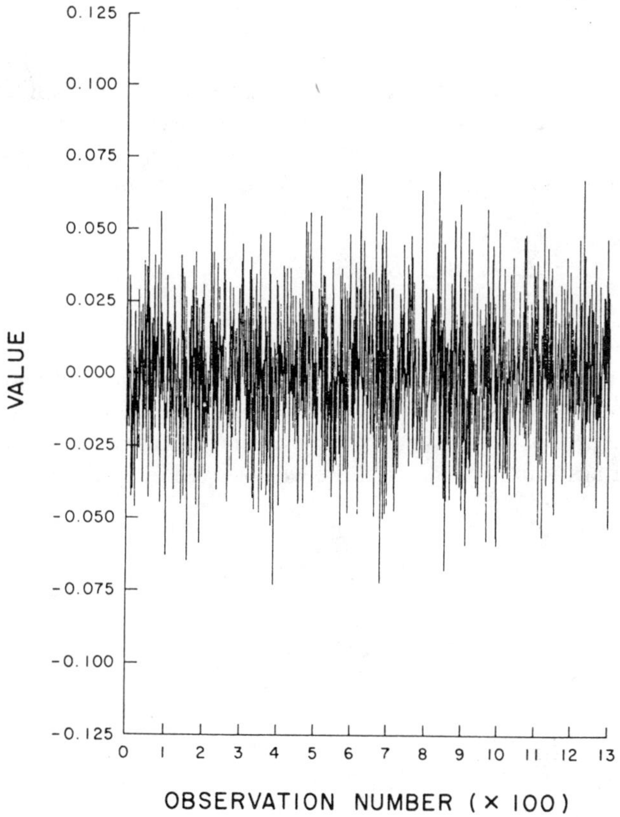

Fig. 3. Purely random Gaussian process.

calculate the implied $a_m(n)$'s: $\hat{a}_4(9) = 28$ and $\hat{a}_{95}(0) = 36$. Note that we use $N = 256$ in these calculations rather than the sample size of 1280, because the program uses blocks of size 256 to calculate the estimators. We can calculate a 95% confidence interval for the implied coefficients by adjusting the standard errors of the estimators in Theorem 4 by σ_ε^8. This gives 95% confidence intervals for the implied estimators of (22, 33) and (24, 48) for $a_4(9)$ and $a_{95}(0)$ respectively, which both cover the true coefficients.

The sample *SSPN* ratio for this particular realization of the process is 0.27, considerably greater than the true value of 0.15. What has happened is that sampling error has caused the program to identify 47 significant coefficients which exceed 2 standard errors in addition to the two 'correct' coefficients. In turn, this has inflated the numerator of the *SSPN* ratio, giving a value of 0.27. Using the result that the estimators are distributed normally, and assuming uncorrelatedness, we would expect to identify about 72 significant coefficients by chance at the 2 standard error level. As a consequence, we believe that the sample *SSPN* ratio is best used for making relative comparisons between sample series.

In our analysis of non-linear time series we have found the following method quite helpful in detecting the important differences, m. Compute for each $m = 1, 2, \ldots, 100$, the sum of squares of the 'significant' coefficients. Let $N(m)$ denote the number of significant $a_m(n)$ for difference m. Then,

$$L(m) = \sum_{j=1}^{N(m)} \hat{a}_m^2(n(j)), \tag{4.2}$$

where $n(j)$ is the lag n for the jth significant coefficient. We have found that a display of the $L(m)$ values, which we call the *Lagstrum*, provides a simple graphical method for detecting the differences of the quadratic model.

Fig. 4 is a plot of the Lagstrum for the artificial data generated by the model (4.1). This Lagstrum is typical of those we observed in other realizations of the

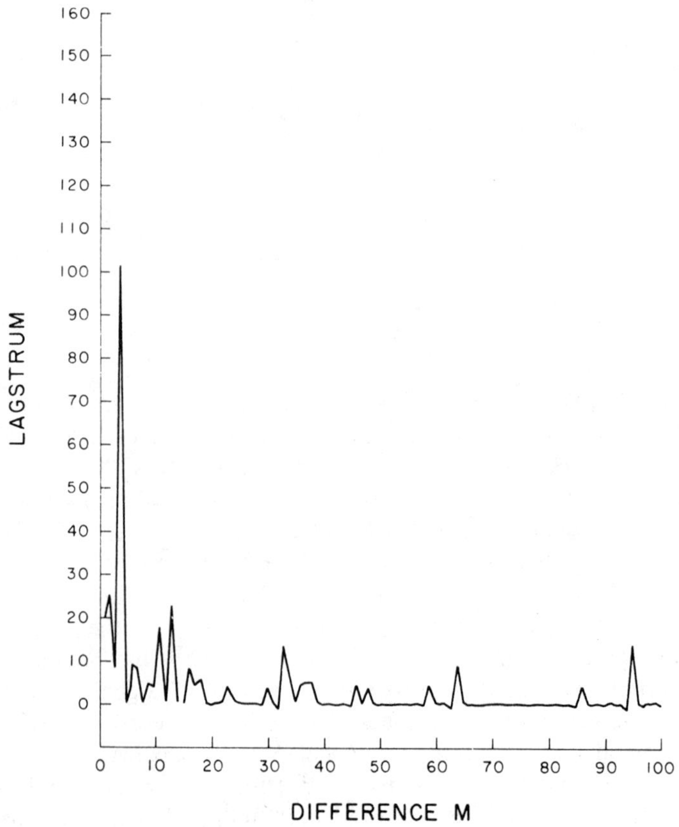

Fig. 4. Artificial data Lagstrum.

process. Note that the peaks at $m = 4$ and $m = 95$ are easily discerned. In calculating this Lagstrum we used a significance level of 2 standard errors. Although the coefficients in (4.1) are equal, the Lagstrum at $m = 95$ is smaller than the one at $m = 4$ because of the ramp bias in the estimator for $a_m(n)$.

5. Results with daily stock returns

Daily stock returns are a convenient source of real data which can be used to further illustrate our non-linear identification method. As mentioned in the Introduction, Hinich and Patterson (1985) tested fifteen randomly selected stock series for non-linearity with a test based on the sample bispectrum. Linearity was rejected for all fifteen series. The sample size for each series was 3881, covering the period July 1962 through December 1977. In this section we

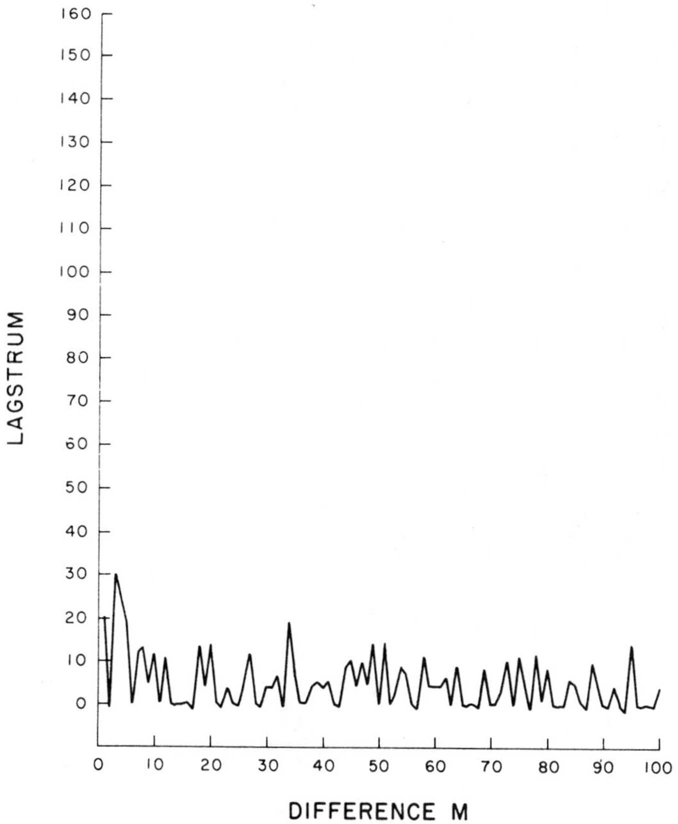

Fig. 5. American Standard.

report the results of non-linear identification for these same stocks, but with a sample size of 1280. The period spanned is December 5, 1972 through December 30, 1977, that is, approximately the last five years of the fifteen and one-half years covered in the earlier study. Because linearity has been rejected for this sample of stocks, our identification procedure becomes appropriate because, as argued above, the non-linear model generating returns can be approximated by a quadratic model.

Before we describe the results, some background information concerning daily stock returns is in order. In the opinion of most financial economists, daily stock returns closely follow a *martingale* or 'fair game'. This opinion is based on a large body of empirical work which suggests that the low levels of autocorrelation found in daily stock returns are not economically significant. To be more specific, daily stock returns tend to have low levels of marginally

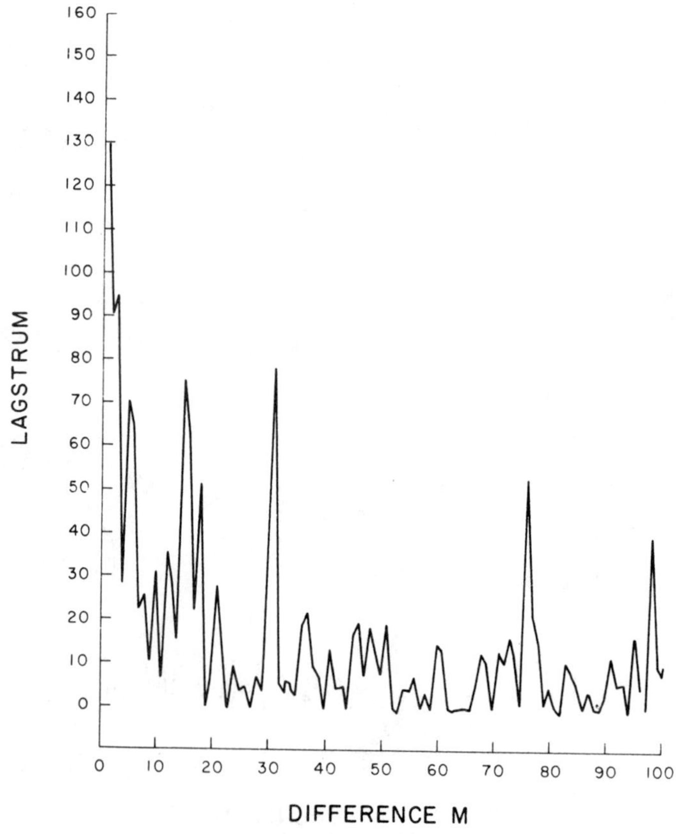

Fig. 6. Carolina Power & Light.

significant autocorrelation for lags varying between one and about ten days. As a consequence, the *martingale* model is not literally true, but writers in this area are quick to point out that the degree of linear dependence is not strong enough to form the basis of a profitable trading rule when transaction costs are included. Hence, the opinion that the stock market can be considered a fair game. Needless to say, we were quite surprised to find high levels of non-linearity in daily stock returns as most forms of non-linearity are inconsistent with the *martingale* hypothesis. It can be shown that the general quadratic model will generate a martingale when the linear term is simple and only $a_m(0)$ coefficients are allowed [see Hinich and Patterson (1984)]. However, as we will see shortly, the vast majority of identified coefficients for this sample of stocks have $n > 0$.

Table 1 lists the names of the fifteen common stocks as well as the sample variance, sample third cumulant, and sample signal to the signal plus noise

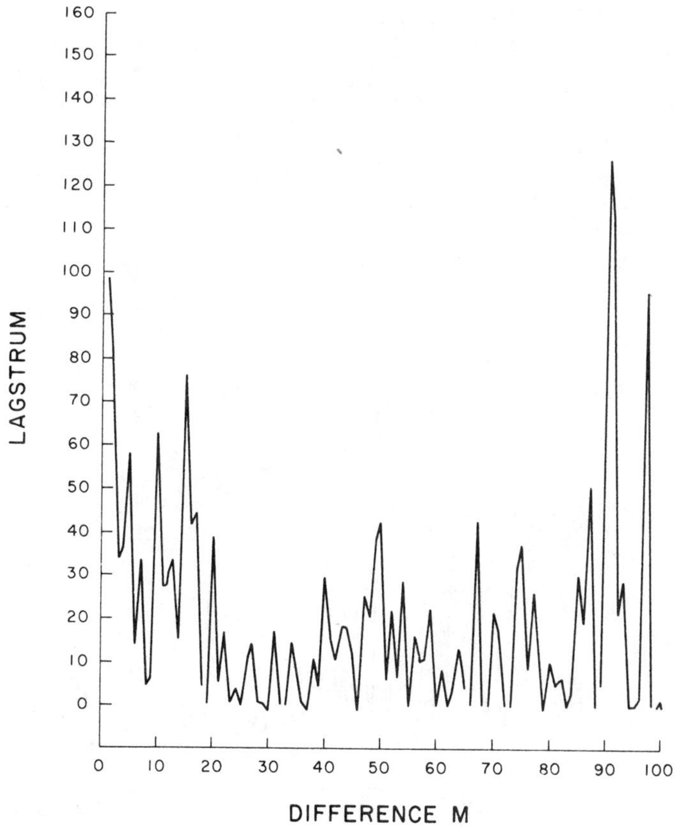

Fig. 7. General Public Utilities.

Table 1

Descriptive statistics.

Firm	Return variance	Third cumulant	Signal to signal plus noise
American Standard	5.0E-4	1.5E-6	0.486
Armstrong Rubber	4.4E-4	−4.9E-6	0.797
Brunswick Corp.	7.8E-4	7.2E-6	0.769
Carolina Power & Light	2.6E-4	3.7E-6	2.253
Chessie Systems, Inc.	5.7E-4	2.1E-6	0.580
Ex Cell 0	5.3E-4	7.5E-6	0.671
General Public Utilities	4.1E-4	5.6E-6	3.058
Holly Sugar	5.8E-4	3.8E-6	1.709
Kaiser Ind.	1.0E-3	1.6E-5	1.393
Liberty Fabrics	2.7E-3	1.4E-4	0.801
Pennzoil	5.2E-4	9.4E-7	1.566
Thiokol Chemical	6.5E-4	2.7E-6	0.794
Union Electric	1.6E-4	6.1E-7	2.473
United Park City Mines	3.0E-3	1.3E-4	0.448
Seagrave Corp	1.1E-3	2.2E-5	0.583

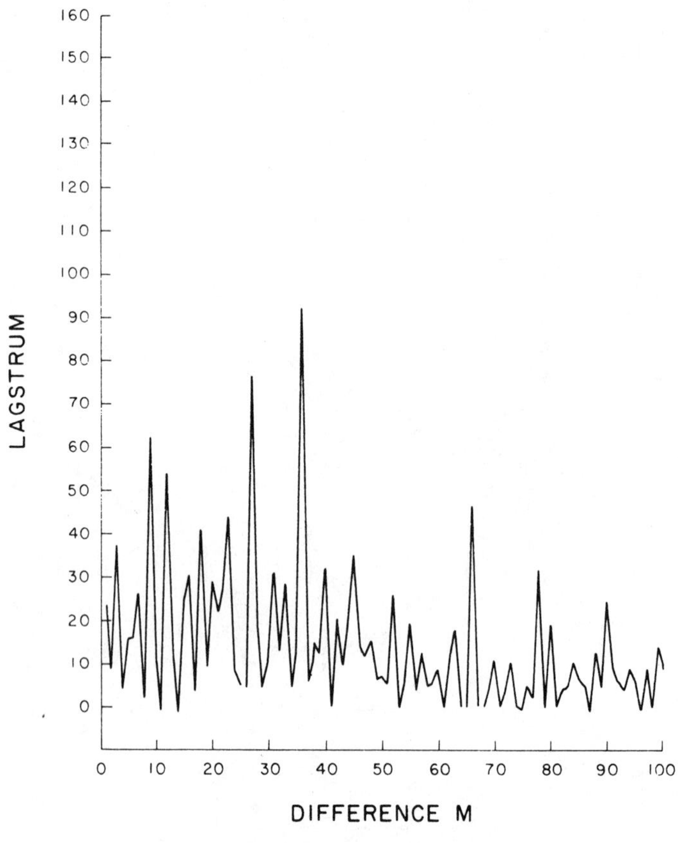

Fig. 8. Pennzoil.

ratio for each time series. Using the *SSPN* ratio for relative comparisons of quadratic non-linearity, we see that the series exhibiting the greatest degree of non-linearity is General Public Utilities.

The Lagstrums for five representative stock series are plotted in fig. 5 through 9. The Lagstrums were computed using those coefficients which were significant at 2 standard errors. In examining the Lagstrums, the first thing we noticed is that the stock Lagstrums tend to be much more cluttered than the artificial data Lagstrum. We were surprised to see that many of the Lagstrums have large peaks in the area of 75 to 100 days.

An example of the significant differences m and lags n is contained in table 2 for the General Public Utilities stock. In this table we display the number of significant coefficients within five- and six-day ranges for m and n. At the bottom of the table we show the total number of significant coefficients

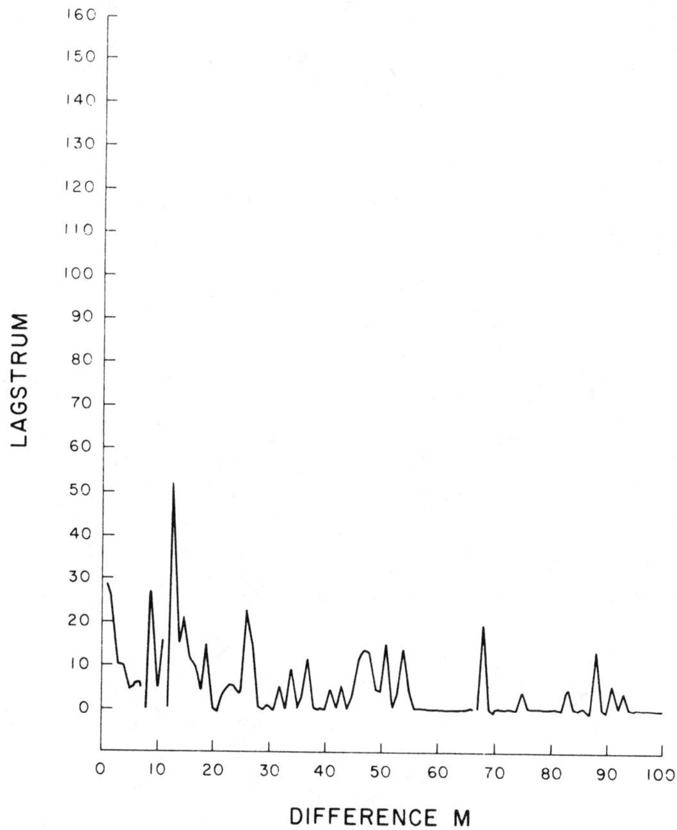

Fig. 9. United Park City Mines.

Table 2

General Public Utilities for differences m, 329 significant coefficients.

Lag n	1–5	6–10	11–15	16–20	21–25	26–30	31–35	36–40	41–45	46–50	51–55	56–60	61–65
0– 5	7	6	4	2		2		3	1	3		1	
6– 10	9	2	2	2		1	2		3	2	3	1	
11– 15	6		3	5	1		1	1	2	2			
16– 20	2	3	7	3	2	1		2	2	1		1	1
21– 25		3	2	1	1					2		1	2
26– 30	4		1	3					1	1			
31– 35	4		3	3			2				1	1	1
36– 40	3	1	1	1			1			1	2	1	1
41– 45	2	2	2							2	1	3	2
46– 50	4	1						1	2		2	3	
51– 55										4	1		
56– 60									1	1			
61– 65													
66– 70													
71– 75													
76– 80													
81– 85													
86– 90			1										
91– 95			1										
96–100													
101–105													
106–110													
111–115													
116–120													
121–126													

Table 2 (continued)

Lag n	66–70	71–75	76–80	81–85	86–90	91–95	96–100	101–105	106–110	111–115	116–120	121–126
0– 5		2			4	2	4	5	1	2	2	
6– 10		1		2	3	8	3	3	3		1	
11– 15		2	4		5	5	1	3	5			
16– 20	2	3	1	1	5	1	1	7	1	1		
21– 25	2	1	1	3	4	2	2	1	1			
26– 30	1	1	1		1	5	1	1	1			
31– 35	1		1	2	2			1	1			
36– 40	4					1		1				
41– 45	1				1	1						
46– 50						1						
51– 55						1						
56– 60												
61– 65												
66– 70												
71– 75												
76– 80												
81– 85												
86– 90												
91– 95												
96–100												
101–105												
106–110												
111–115												
116–120												
121–126												

identified at 2 standard errors. General Public Utilities has the greatest number of significant coefficients, 329, and American Standard and United Park City Mines the lowest, at 98. These results suggest that the non-linear models generating daily stock returns are rather complex. They also suggest that the process generating these returns is not a martingale.

6. Conclusions

When some of the coefficients in the quadratic term of the Volterra series expansion of the general non-linear model are non-zero, the bispectrum of the model will also be non-zero. This particular form of non-linearity can be detected through a statistical test based on the estimated bispectrum. We have shown that the non-linear model can then be approximated by a quadratic model with a simple linear term, and we have shown how the coefficients in the quadratic approximation can be identified. Given that the identified quadratic model can be inverted, it then becomes possible to estimate a parametric version of the model. At the estimation stage, any linear components will be swept into the estimated residuals, and at this point the methods for linear identification and estimation become applicable.

In conclusion, the methods presented here offer the data analyst a useful technique for identifying the significant coefficients in a non-linear quadratic model. The daily stock return series suggest the possibility of many interesting applications.

References

Brillinger, D.R., 1975, Time series: Data analysis and theory (Holt, Rinehart and Winston, New York).

Haggan, V., S.M. Heravi and M.B. Priestley, 1984, A study of the application of state-dependent models in non-linear time series analysis, Journal of Time Series Analysis 5, 69–102.

Hinich, M.J., 1982, Testing for Gaussianity and linearity of a stationary time series, Journal of Time Series Analysis 3, 169–176.

Hinich, M.J. and D.M. Patterson, 1984, A bispectrum based test of the martingale model, Unpublished working paper (Virginia Polytechnic Institute and State University, Blacksburg, VA).

Hinich, M.J. and D.M. Patterson, 1985, Evidence of nonlinearity in daily stock returns, Journal of Business and Economic Statistics 3, 69–77.

Maravall, A., 1983, An application of nonlinear time series forecasting, Journal of Business and Economic Statistics 1, 66–74.

Priestley, M.B., 1981, Spectral analysis and time series, Vol. 2 (Academic Press, New York).

Rosenblatt, M., 1983, Cumulants and cumulant spectra, in: D.R. Brillinger and P.R. Krishnaiah, eds., Handbook of statistics, Vol. 3 (North-Holland, Amsterdam) 369–382.

Subba Rao, T., 1983, The bispectral analysis of nonlinear time series with reference to bilinear time series models, in: D.R. Brillinger and P.R. Krishnaiah, eds., Handbook of statistics, Vol. 3 (North-Holland, Amsterdam) 293–319.

Subba Rao, T. and M. Gabr, 1980, A test for linearity of stationary time series, Journal of Time Series Analysis 1, 145–158.

Wiener, N., 1958, Non-linear problems in random theory (M.I.T. Press, Cambridge, MA).

ON NON-LINEAR SERIAL DEPENDENCIES IN STOCK RETURNS

Terry A. MARSH*

Sloan School of Management, M.I.T., Cambridge, MA 02139, USA

This paper considers the H&P tests of linearity and Gaussianity of daily stock returns, and their implications for non-linear models of those returns.

1. Introduction

In this paper, I discuss the work on non-linear time series models by Melvin Hinich and Douglas Patterson (H&P), particularly their use of these models to fit stock returns data. H&P (1983) examine the hypothesis that the time series of daily returns for fifteen randomly selected NYSE-listed stocks were generated by a linear Gaussian process over the period December 5, 1972 to December 30, 1977. They reject this hypothesis using a test based on the double Fourier transform of the third-order cumulant of the returns series. The hypothesis that this rejection occurs because the return generating process is linear, but non-Gaussian, is also rejected. In light of these results, H&P (1984) consider estimation of a non-linear moving average model which they apply to the daily returns of the fifteen-stock sample.

The other papers in this volume which are concerned with non-linear functional forms in econometrics amply demonstrate that techniques for dealing with non-linearity are advancing rapidly, and it is often contended that the time is ripe for similar developments in the time series area [e.g., Priestley (1981, p. 890)]. Progress on the latter score is not likely to outpace the problem, for the linear Gaussian model is, in general, not entirely at ease with time series data [e.g., Hampel (1973, p. 88)].[1]

In particular, daily stock returns tend to have tails that are 'fatter' (longer) than Gaussian, and they are often found to be autocorrelated. However, separate investigation of the fat tails and of the autocorrelation is hampered by possible incidence of the other. For example, Fama (1965, pp. 69–70) devotes considerable space to a discussion of the impact of fat tails in the marginal

*I am indebted to Richard Robb and Leonard Roseman for helpful comments, and to Douglas Patterson who patiently answered my questions concerning the H&P computer algorithm. Part of this paper was completed while I was a Batterymarch Fellow.

[1] Of course, a linear model might sometimes do reasonably well at fitting a given set of data generated by a non-linear model, but it is likely that the linear model would be far from parsimonious.

distribution of daily returns on tests for serial correlation in those returns. On the other hand, Mandelbrot (1963, pp. 406, 410) emphasizes that his estimates of the parameters of a stable Paretian model for (marginal) daily returns assume serial independence. H&P's tests, which pertain to the joint distribution of the return series, are not limited in this way.

The most popular method of testing for any serial dependence in stock returns which is not reflected in their autocorrelation, and which might provide some basis for the techniques used by chartists, has been to run filter strategies against buy-and-hold policies.[2] However, the statistical significance of excess of returns on a filter strategy over those on a buy-and-hold strategy is difficult to work out.[3] In contrast, to the extent that non-linear dependencies in stock returns are captured in H&P's bispectral analysis, their statistical properties can be systematically studied.

In the following, I discuss the evidence concerning non-linear dependencies in stock returns, and its implications for the type of stochastic process describing stock returns. I estimate the bispectrum for four daily stock return series, and discuss the sensitivity of those estimates to removal of calendar effects known to exist in stock returns, and to tapering of 'extreme' observations. I conclude with a discussion of some 'generic' problems which arise in fitting time series model to stock returns.

2. The non-linear model and its estimation

Wiener (1958) showed that a broad class of non-linear time series models may be obtained by 'Volterra series expansion' of a sufficiently regular non-linear relationship between the 'output' of a system $\{X_t\}$ and its 'input' $\{\varepsilon_t\}$:

$$X_t = \sum_{n=0}^{\infty} a_n \varepsilon_{t-n} + \sum_{n=0}^{\infty} \sum_{m=0}^{\infty} a_{m,n} \varepsilon_{t-m} \varepsilon_{t-n} + \sum_{n=0}^{\infty} \sum_{m=0}^{\infty} \sum_{p=0}^{\infty} a_{m,n,p} \varepsilon_{t-n} \varepsilon_{t-m} \varepsilon_{t-p} + \cdots, \tag{1}$$

where a_0 may be normalized to unity [Priestley (1981, p. 869)].[4]

[2] These filter strategies were originally proposed by Alexander (1961). The operation of an x percent filter is usually described as follows: If the daily closing price of a particular security moves up at least x percent, buy and hold the security until its price moves down at least x percent from a subsequent high, at which time simultaneously sell and go short. The short position is maintained until the daily price rises at least x percent above a subsequent low at which time one covers and buys. Moves less than x percent in either direction are ignored.

[3] Only if riskless arbitrage were possible would statistical significance of excess returns be irrelevant. This is not the case for comparisons between returns on filter and buy-and-hold strategies. In fact, these strategies are not even equally risky [e.g., Ball (1974)].

[4] The estimation of the non-linear model requires that higher-order moments exist for the i.i.d. series $\{\varepsilon_t\}$. That is, one needs to be confident that the stock returns data do not exhibit long tails in part because the underlying innovations are drawn from (say) a stable Paretian distribution.

If the ε_t in (1) are unobservable innovations, and the X_t – here, daily stock returns – are observed to be non-Gaussian, the most appropriate model could be a non-linear one like (1) which also contains Gaussian innovations, or it could be a model with non-Gaussian innovations but only the linear terms in (1), or it could be a model which contains both non-Gaussian innovations and non-linear terms.

To estimate models along the lines of the first and third alternatives which involve the non-linear terms, parameterization must somehow be reduced. One means of accomplishing this is to use some of the approximations considered elsewhere in this volume. A second approach is to search for a parsimonious representation of (1) such as the bilinear model. A third alternative, adopted by H&P, is to truncate the expansion in (1) at some point. Keeping only the quadratic lag terms, which can be described by the bispectrum if X_t is third-moment stationary, H&P estimate a non-linear moving average specialization of (1) of the form:

$$X_t = \varepsilon_t + \sum_{m=1}^{\infty} \sum_{n=1}^{\infty} a_{m,n}\varepsilon_{t-n}\varepsilon_{t-m-n}. \tag{2}$$

Clearly, the specification (2) will capture various irregularities in a time series [e.g., asymmetry in the responsiveness of X to the innovations, or a tendancy for large changes in X to be followed by large changes], while maintaining the hypothesis that the innovations $\{\varepsilon_t\}$ are 'well behaved'. If a lagged linear term is included in (2) to account for second-order serial dependence, the 'scale parameter' σ_ε^4 will be identified.[5]

The usefulness of H&P's estimation results for the non-linear moving average model (2) applied to daily stock returns depends crucially upon how closely the returns conform to that model. Once the assumption of linearity in the stochastic process generating daily stock returns is jettisoned, the 'identification step' must now include specification of both the type of non-linear model (second-order non-linear moving average in H&P's case) and the appropriate lags. H&P use a portmanteau test of lag length adequacy which is based on 'Lagstrum' values, and find an interaction between stock return lags of 1–5 days and 85–105 days.

In this respect, their results are roughly consistent with earlier studies which employ a methodology dubbed R/S analysis by Mandelbrot, and which seem to show the existence of some component in the generating process for stock returns which manifests itself as a 'long-run cycle' [e.g., Mandelbrot (1972),

[5] Robinson (1977) has investigated some properties of the method-of-moments estimators for the coefficients in a non-linear moving average model like (2) when a first-order linear autoregressive term is included.

Mandelbrot and Wallis (1969a, b, c)]. The letters 'R/S' stand for the rescaled range $R(t,s)/S(t,s)$ where $R(t,s)$ is the cumulated range of a process between times $t+1$ and $t+s$ after removal of the sample average, and $S^2(t,s)$ is the corresponding sample variance. For a given lag s, sample values of $R(t,s)$ as a function of t can be used to detect non-cyclic long-run dependencies in time series. Greene and Fielitz (1977) applied R/S analysis to daily stock returns and found considerable temporal dependence after accounting for simple serial correlation. The time period they examined, 12/23/63–11/29/68, is of roughly the same length as that covered by H&P.

On the other hand, there is little indication in these studies that the most appropriate specification of the process generating stock returns is a non-linear moving average. H&P test a null hypothesis of Gaussianity and linearity against a general alternative which encompasses the entire space of non-Gaussian non-linear models [of course, the bispectral test will not detect all types of non-linearity]. The corollary is that rejection of the null *per se* offers little insight into the robustness of that outcome, or into which alternative models might better fit the returns data. I interpret H&P's estimation of the special second-order moving average case of (1) to be in the spirit of a subsequent 'model identification' step,[6] and I hope the following comments might supplement this effort.

In the physical sciences, data analysts can often rely upon at least some knowledge of the probability laws generating time series of interest. Unfortunately, financial economists have little, if any, insight into the 'behavioral laws' governing stock price movements. It is true that the geometric Brownian motion–martingale model can be derived from particular assumptions about a firm's real investment returns [e.g., Samuelson (1973, pp. 372–373)], and that this model has served finance well in many respects – in fact, it has served so well that we sometimes forget that it constitutes only a special case. Merton (1971, 1973), LeRoy (1973) and Lucas (1978) have all rigorously demonstrated that stock returns need not follow a martingale process in an efficient market. Rosenberg (1972) and Merton (1980) show that neither variances nor expectations of stock returns are constant over time, and Brown, Kleidon and Marsh (1983) argue that 'anomalous' cross-sectional differences in expected returns on stocks are not constant over time either. There is some presumption that this instability of first- and second-order moments will create a model identification problem, since Priestley (1980) has shown that, at least in a state–space representation, non-linear models can resemble linear models with varying parameters. Of course, not all non-linear models will generate non-martingales [e.g., if $a_{m,n}=0$ unless $m=n=1$ in (2), stock returns behave as a martingale].

[6] Priestley (1981) suggests that one approach which could provide such model identification would be to nest a set of non-linear models in a state–space representation and then test the restrictions implied by different models. However, such tests have yet to be performed for stock returns data.

Calendar effects also seem to be present in stock returns. Keim (1983) reported that, since 1926, the average returns earned on stocks in January have been significantly higher than the average returns in other calender months, particularly for small firms.[7] Ariel (1984) showed that the mean return for stocks is positive only for days immediately before and during the first half of calender months, and indistinguishable from zero for days during the last half of the month. Gibbons and Hess (1981) and French (1980) reported that average returns on stocks from Friday's market close to Monday's close have been lower than those for other days of the week since 1962 – in fact, these Friday to Monday returns have, on average, been negative.

I estimated the bispectrum of daily returns,[8] over H&P's sample period, for two Dow-Jones stocks – American Can and Owens-Illinois – and for two stock market indices – the value-weighted and equally-weighted NYSE indices. I found some concentration of bispectral mass around five-day and twenty-day lags, but when I removed the calender effects using dummy variables,[9] the bispectral estimates changed only negligibly. A possible explanation for this insensitivity of results is that the calendar effects tend to be swamped by the substantial volatility of typical stock return series, and thus have a limited impact on the bispectral estimates. Over the sample period here [which includes only five Januaries for example], the standard deviation of daily returns was 1.145% and 1.65% for American Can and Owens-Illinois, respectively, while their sample period mean returns were 0.049% and 0.034%, respectively.

The high variability of daily stock returns relative to their mean, or to calendar-related shifts in their mean, suggests an alternative explanation for the bispectrum estimates. I find that the outcome of the linearity–Gaussianity tests is quite sensitive to slight downweighting of outliers, which I carried out using the Krasker and Welsch (1982) bounded-influence procedure implemented by TROLL. As is consistent with prior evidence [e.g., Fama (1965)], large changes in stock prices tend to be followed by large changes [of either sign], and thus the downweighted observations are not distributed randomly over the sample period. The sensitivity of the tests to outliers is less for the market indices than for the individual stocks. Of course, these results might just reflect the effects which a simplistic tapering of outliers has on estimates of the bispectrum of a model like (2), but if that is so, perhaps we'd want to

[7] Keim (1983) and Reinganum (1983) showed that, even more amazingly, the high average returns tend to occur in just the first few trading days of January (and the last trading day of December).

[8] H&P kindly provided me with a copy of their programs for testing Gaussianity and linearity of time series, and for estimating the non-linear moving average model (2).

[9] Most of the work heretofore in the finance literature has assumed the calendar effects to be deterministic. One notable exception is Morgan and Morgan (1984) who apply an ARCH model to the study of the January effect on stock returns.

scrutinize the choice of (2) more closely.[10] A possible counter-argument is that Godfrey (1965) found, in his early study applying bispectral analysis to the stock market, that he could not reject linearity of the process generating transaction-to-transaction price changes on ITT stock, yet jumps are most pronounced in transactions data [interestingly though, so are linear and non-linear dependencies induced by market making, e.g., Niederhoffer and Osborne (1966)].

An interesting alternative would be a model in which Poisson jumps of random, but serially dependent, amplitude are introduced to take account of occasional sequences of wide fluctuations in prices [e.g., along the lines of Merton (1976)]. A second would be a fractional noise process such as Mandelbrot has advocated for data containing semi-persistent fluctuations which he labelled 'Joseph Effects'. A third would be a conditional heteroscedasticity model like Engle's (1982). If one wants to fit non-linear models to time series of stock returns, there is probably no ultimate alternative to the derivation and comparison of the bispectra of these alternative models. To the extent that outliers are important, it may still be very difficult to discriminate among them, since extreme observations are, by definition, rare events.[11]

Sensitivity of test results and estimates to data trimming, etc. also brings up the issue of robustness of the higher-order moments of time series to which the double Fourier transform is applied. As far as I have been able to determine, little work has been done on the robustness of estimates of higher-order properties of time series. However, Mandelbrot and Wallis (1969c, p. 979) did argue that R/S tests for long-run dependence and estimation of an associated fractional differencing model are 'extremely robust with respect to changes in the marginal distribution'. Dufour (1981) has also presented some rank tests for serial dependence which do not require distributional assumptions, though they do require symmetry of the distribution and zero (or known) median. It is fairly easy to reject serial independence of daily stock returns using these non-parameteric methods.

In light of recent discussion in physics to the effect that simple (deterministic) non-linear models are capable of producing very 'chaotic behavior' in time series after a few iterations [e.g., May (1976), Kadanoff (1983)], one might conclude that temporal aggregation questions could be especially important

[10] Because the bispectral estimates are 'normalized' by power spectrum estimates (we don't want peaks in the bispectrum to be affected by peaks in the spectrum), it is important that peaks not be 'misplaced' in either set of estimates. It is possible that, when I trimmed the outliers, I did not change the window length to (say) maintain the probability of misplacement. Again, however, from a sampling point of view, this makes the bispectral (bicoherence) estimates somewhat fragile as a basis for fitting a particular non-linear model.

[11] Also, the discussion in Huber et al. (1971) suggests that various superimposed processes (e.g., those containing jumps) may be very difficult to distinguish using estimated bispectra or bicoherences.

here. Further, as Priestley (1980) discusses, most common non-linear models [e.g., the bilinear, threshold autoregressive, and exponential autoregressive models] can be cast, in a state–space framework, as state-dependent models which are locally *linear* ARMA models.

To sum up, I believe that the methodology developed by H&P provides a more rigorous means of testing for serial dependence in stock returns than that currently available. To determine how fruitful the bispectral-based estimation and tests will be in examining the behavior of stock returns, it will be necessary to derive the bispectra implied by alternative models, develop relative goodness-of-fit tests, and perhaps determine the robustness properties of the bispectral estimates.

References

Alexander, S.S., 1961, Price movements in speculative markets: Trends or random walks, Industrial Management Review 2, 7–26.

Ariel, R.A., 1983, A monthly effect in stock returns, Sloan School of Management working paper 1629 (Sloan School of Management, MIT, Cambridge, MA).

Ball, R., 1974, Filter rules: Interpretation of market efficiency, experimental problems and Australian evidence, in: R. Ball, P. Brown, F.J. Finn and R.R. Officer, eds., Share markets and portfolio theory (University of Queensland Press, Brisbane) ch. 10.

Black, F. and M.S. Scholes, 1973, The pricing of options and corporate liabilities, Journal of Political Economy 81, 637–659.

Brown, P., A.W. Kleidon and T.A. Marsh, 1983, New evidence on the nature of size related anomalies in stock prices, Journal of Financial Economics 12, 33–56.

Dufour, J.M., 1981, Rank tests for serial dependence, Journal of Time Series Analysis 2, 117–128.

Engle, R.F., 1982, Autoregressive conditional heteroscedasticity with estimates of the variance of United Kingdom inflation, Econometrica 50, 997–1007.

Fama, E.F., 1965, The behavior of stock-market prices, Journal of Business 38, 34–105.

French, K.R., 1980, Stock returns and the weekend effect, Journal of Financial Economics 8, 55–70.

Gennotte, G. and T.A. Marsh, 1984, Discrete-time estimates of variations in stock price volatilities and risk premiums, Unpublished working paper (Sloan School of Management, MIT, Cambridge, MA).

Gibbons, M.R. and P.J. Hess, 1981, Day of the week effects and asset returns, Journal of Business 54, 579–596.

Godfrey, M.D., 1965, An exploratory study of the bi-spectrum of economic time series, Applied Statistics 14, 48–69.

Greene, M.T. and B.D. Fielitz, 1977, Long-term dependence in common stock returns, Journal of Financial Economics 4, 339–349.

Hampel, F.R., 1973, Robust estimation: A condensed partial survey, Zeitschrift für Wahrscheinlichkeitstheorie und verwandte Gebiete 27, 87–104.

Hinich, M.J. and D.M. Patterson, 1983, Evidence of nonlinearity in daily stock returns, Journal of Business and Economic Statistics, forthcoming.

Hinich, M.J. and D.M. Patterson, 1985, Identification of the coefficients in a non-linear time series of the quadratic type, Journal of Econometrics, this issue.

Huber, P.J., B. Kleiner, T. Gasser and G. Dumermuth, 1971, Statistical methods for investigating phase relations in stationary stochastic processes, IEEE Transactions on Audio and Electroacoustics AV-19, 78–86.

Kadanoff, L.P., 1983, Roads to chaos, Physics Today, Dec., 46–53.

Keim, D.B., 1983, Size related anomalies and stock return seasonalities: Further empirical evidence, Journal of Financial Economics 12, 13–32.

Krasker, W.S. and R.E. Welsch, 1982, Efficient bounded-influence regression estimation, Journal of the American Statistical Association 77, 595–604.

LeRoy, S.F., 1973, Risk aversion and the martingale property of stock prices, International Economic Review 14, 436–446.

Lucas, R.E., Jr., 1978, Asset prices in an exchange economy, Econometrica 46, 1429–1445.

Mandelbrot, B., 1963, The variation of certain speculative prices, Journal of Business 36, 394–419.

Mandelbrot, B., 1971, When can price be arbitraged efficiently? A limit to the validity of the random walk and martingale models, Review of Economics and Statistics 53, 225–236.

Mandelbrot, B., 1972, Statistical methodology for nonperiodic cycles: From the covariance to R/S analysis, Annals of Economics and Social Measurements 1, 259–290.

Mandelbrot, B., 1975, Limit theorems on the self-normalized range for weakly and strongly dependent processes, Zeitschrift für Wahrscheinlichkeitstheorie und verwandte Gebiete 31, 271–285.

Mandelbrot, B. and J.W. Van Ness, 1968, Fractional Brownian motions, fractional noises, and applications, SIAM Review 10, 422–437.

Mandelbrot, B. and J.R. Wallis, 1969a, Computer experiments with fractional Gaussian noises, Parts I–III, Water Resources Research 5, 228–267.

Mandelbrot, B. and J.R. Wallis, 1969b, Some long-run properties of geophysical records, Water Resources Research 5, 321–340.

Mandelbrot, B. and J.R. Wallis, 1969c, Robustness of the rescaled range R/S in the measurement of noncyclic long run statistical dependence, Water Resources Research 5, 967–988.

May, R.M., 1976, Simple mathematical models with very complicated dynamics, Nature 261, 459–467.

Merton, R.C., 1971, Optimum consumption and portfolio rules in a continuous time model, Journal of Economic Theory 3, 373–413.

Merton, R.C., 1973, Theory of rational option pricing, Bell Journal of Economics and Management Science 4, 141–183.

Merton, R.C., 1976, Option pricing when underlying stock returns are discontinuous, Journal of Financial Economics 3, 125–144.

Merton, R.C., 1980, On estimating the expected return on the market, Journal of Financial Economics 8, 323–361.

Morgan, A. and I. Morgan, 1984, On measurement of abnormal returns of small firms, School of Business working paper 82-9 (Queens University, Kingston, Ont.).

Niederhoffer, V. and M.F.M. Osborne, 1966, Market making and reversal on the stock exchange, Journal of the American Statistical Association 61, 897–916.

Priestley, M.B., 1980, State-dependent models: A general approach to non-linear time series analysis, Journal of Time Series Analysis 1, 47–71.

Priestley, M.B., 1981, Spectral analysis and time series, Vols. I–II (Academic Press, New York).

Reinganum, M.R., 1983, The anomalous stock market behavior of small firms in January: Empirical tests for tax-loss effects, Journal of Financial Economics 12, 89–104.

Robinson, P.M., 1977, The estimation of a nonlinear moving average model, Stochastic Processes and Their Applications 5, 81–90.

Roll, R., 1983, Vas ist das? The turn-of-the-year effect and return premia of small firms, Journal of Portfolio Management, Winter, 18–28.

Rosenberg, B., 1972, The behavior of random variables with non-stationary variance and the distribution of security prices, Graduate School of Business Administration working paper 11 (University of California, Berkeley, CA).

Rosenfeld, E.R., 1982, Stochastic processes of common stock returns: An empirical examination, Graduate School of Business Administration working paper 82-34 (Harvard University, Boston, MA).

Samuelson, P.A., 1973, Proof that properly discounted present values of assets vibrate randomly, Bell Journal of Economics and Management Science 4, 369–374.

Wiener, N., 1958, Nonlinear problems in random theory (MIT Press, Cambridge, MA).

EFFICIENCY VERSUS EQUITY IN NATURAL GAS PRICE REGULATION*

Dale W. JORGENSON

Harvard University, Cambridge, MA 02139, USA

Daniel T. SLESNICK

University of Texas, Austin, TX 78712-1173, USA

The purpose of this paper is to present a new approach to the general equilibrium analysis of economic policy. Our objective is to provide an ordering of alternative economic policies. To this end, we specify measures of social welfare that satisfy the requirements of social choice. A social expenditure function is introduced to translate changes in social welfare based on a social welfare function into money metric social welfare. We decompose money metric social welfare into the sum of money metric equity and money metric efficiency. Finally, we present an evaluation of alternative regulatory policies for natural gas prices in the United States.

1. Introduction

The purpose of this paper is to present a new approach to the general equilibrium analysis of economic policy. Our objective is to provide an ordering of alternative economic policies. The most desirable economic policy is the policy yielding the highest level of social welfare. This principle can be used to evaluate a specific policy change or to select the optimal policy from a set of alternatives.

Dupuit (1969) originated the appraisal of alternative economic policies on the basis of their impact on consumer welfare. He proposed to measure individual welfare on the basis of preferences revealed by consumer behavior. The prices faced by the consumer and the corresponding quantities demanded were used to obtain estimates of consumer's surplus.[1] Hicks (1942) introduced measures of consumer's surplus based on compensating and equivalent variations in income or total expenditure.

*Dale W. Jorgenson is Frederic Eaton Abbe Professor of Economics at Harvard University. Daniel T. Slesnick is Assistant Professor of Economics, University of Texas, Austin. Research support by the National Science Foundation is gratefully acknowledged.

[1] Dupuit's approach to welfare economics has generated a voluminous literature. Key references include Harberger (1971), Hicks (1942), Hotelling (1938) and Marshall (1920).

Table 1

Test statistics using different bispectrum smoothing windows; spectra smoothed using $W = 199$ triangular window.

	Non-linear test statistics	Gaussian test statistics	Non-centrality parameters
$M = 44$ window			
Clean data	10.72	41.49	2.43
+/− 10% spikes	10.04	38.66	2.02
+/− 15% spikes	9.97	38.21	2.21
$M = 50$ window			
Clean data	11.28	37.12	2.36
+/− 10% spikes	10.33	34.49	2.20
+/− 15% spikes	10.49	34.39	2.07
$M = 64$ window			
Clean data	12.72	32.48	2.64
+/− 10% spikes	11.06	28.80	2.33
+/− 15% spikes	11.50	29.17	2.88

behavior of the test statistics to the presense of outliers we present the results summarized in table 1. We selected the 3880 daily rates of Armstrong Rubber Company that we used in our JBES paper. We randomly selected seventeen days during in the record, and changed the returns for those days to generate seventeen positive or negative spikes in the record. The signs of the spikes were chosen at random, and their magnitudes are the same, either 10% or 15%. A 10% daily return is nearly six standard deviations from the mean for the Armstrong returns data. The spikes reduce the non-linear test statistic as compared with the results obtained from the unaltered (good) data. The bispectra were computed using three smoothing windows: $M = 44$, 50 and 64. The power spectra were estimating using a triangular smoothing window whose base is $W = 199$. The standard deviation of the clean series is 1.68%. The standard deviations of the contaminated series are 1.80% for the 10% spike case, and 1.95% for the 15% case.

The seventeen contaminating spikes decrease the magnitudes of the test statistics as compared to the results obtained using the unaltered Armstrong Rubber data. The changes in the statistics are small, but are consistent with the following theoretical argument. The decreases will be greater for a higher percentage of spikes in the data.

Consider a time series $y(t) = x(t) + u(t)$, where $\{x(t)\}$ is the true series and $\{u(t)\}$ is a contaminating Poisson spike process which is assumed to be independent of the $x(t)$'s. Assume that there is only one spike of height d in a sample of the $y(t)$'s. Then the kth frequency term of the discrete Fourier transform of the $y(t)$, denoted $Y(k)$, is $X(k) + d\exp(-i2(\pi)kn^*)$, where $X(k)$

is the kth frequency term of the discrete Fourier transform of $\{x(t)\}$. With no loss of generality let the spike's time be $n^* = 0$. Thus $Y(k) = X(k) + d$ for all k. Setting the time n^* equal to zero eliminates the need to carry cosines and sines in the exposition of the magnitude of the spike's contamination of the estimated bispectral skewness. Finally let N denote the sample size. The estimated bispectrum of $\{y(t)\}$ at the (j, k)th frequency pair in the principle domain using our method is $\langle Y(j)Y(k)Y(-j-k)/N \rangle$, where bracket notation $\langle \cdot \rangle$ denotes an unweighted average of the triples in a square of $M \times M$ terms centered at (j, k). The reader can consult Hinich (1982) for details. It then follows from the model for $y(t)$ that the absolute value of the (j, k) frequency pair in the bispectrum estimate is equal to the absolute value of $\langle X(j)X(k)X(-j-k)/N \rangle + d \times d \times d/N$ plus a random error of order less than $d \times d/M + d \times N/(M \times M)$. This error is then negligible if $d \gg N/M$. If $d \times d \times d/N$ is larger than the absolute value of the bispectrum of $\{x(t)\}$, then the absolute value of the estimated bispectrum of the $y(t)$'s will be dominated by the $d \times d \times d/N$ term.

Now consider the effect of the spike on the estimated spectrum of the $y(t)$'s. By an argument similar to that used for the sample bispectrum of the contaminated process, the sample spectrum of the $y(t)$'s is the sample spectrum of the $x(t)$'s plus $d \times d/N$ since the spectrum estimate is a moving average of $Y(k)Y(-k)$ terms. If $d \times d/N$ is larger than spectrum of $\{x(t)\}$ at the kth frequency, then the estimated spectrum is dominated by $d \times d/N$. Thus the bispectral skewness measure is approximately root N for all frequency pairs when d is much larger than the scale of $x(t)$.

It is usually easy to detect large outliers in a data record. Thus a sensible downweighting or 'outliers' in a record of rates of return for a security should yield a time series that will exhibit a non-linear structure in the sample bispectral skewnesses. The Hinich test should be helped by eliminating gross outliers in the data.

REPLY TO MARSH'S NOTE

Melvin J. HINICH

University of Texas, Austin, TX 78712, USA

Douglas M. PATTERSON

Virginia Polytechnic Institute and State University, Blacksburg, VA 24061, USA

Professor Marsh's note suggests that the non-linear test statistic which we use in our 1985 JBES paper is inflated if the data contains outliers. Marsh transformed the returns data that he analyzed using the TROLL procedure and obtained non-linear test statistics which were smaller than the ones he obtained from the true returns data. We do not understand how he got the results he reports given our experience with the tests we apply in our JBES paper. Professor Marsh suggests that outliers were responsible for many of the significant non-linear test results which we report in our paper. Our experience with the Hinich test statistics on real and artificial data indicate that they are robust to modest outliers. Before presenting results which support our robustness claim, we wish the reader to consider the appropriateness of Marsh's transformation of rates of return data.

Daily rate of return data is not Gaussian. There are more large returns in the sample population than would be predicted from a Gaussian model. This is now well established in the finance literature. We present some results in our conference paper which suggest that the large returns are evidence of non-linear interactions in the market process which generates these returns. These large values should not be called outliers. Outliers in time series data are abnormally large deviations from the parent population which are due to gliches in data transcription or to data copying errors. The stock return data that we and Marsh analyze are unusually free from such errors as compared to typical economic or business time series data sets. Our data came from the Center for Research in Security Prices (CRSP) tapes and were screened for errors before they were used. There is no reason to believe that the large returns are gliches. They should be considered as part of the outcome set of the market return generating process, and they should be analyzed as is when testing for evidence of a non-linear time series generating mechanism.

Returning to the robustness issue, our experience with outliers in artificial data sets indicates that the tests are robust to modest outliers. To indicate the

Chipman and Moore (1980) have shown that a necessary and sufficient condition for Hicks' compensating variation to provide an appropriate ordering of economic policies is that individual preferences are homothetic. Homothetic preferences are inconsistent with well established regularities in the behavior of individual consumers, such as those reviewed by Houthakker (1957). Chipman and Moore recommend Hicks' equivalent variation.

The individual expenditure function introduced by McKenzie (1957) provides the simplest approach for implementing Hicks' measures of welfare. The expenditure function gives the minimum level of total expenditure required to attain a stipulated level of utility as a function of the prices faced by the consumer. This level of expenditure can be derived from the indirect utility function, which gives the maximum attainable utility level as a function of prices and total expenditure.[2]

In section 2 we present our approach to the measurement of individual welfare which is based on the indirect utility function and the individual expenditure function for each consuming unit. The indirect utility function can be used to generate measures of individual welfare. The individual expenditure function can then be employed to translate these measures of individual welfare into money metric individual welfare. Money metric individual welfare provides a monotone increasing transformation of individual welfare that is not fully comparable among consuming units. This measure can be used in evaluating economic policies by constructing partial orderings of these policies on the basis of the Pareto principle.[3] To obtain complete orderings we require the concept of a social welfare function originated by Bergson (1938) and discussed by Samuelson (1982, 1983).

A social welfare function gives the level of social welfare as a function of the distribution of individual welfare over the population of consumers. The social welfare function incorporates the effects of changes in economic policy on the welfare of individual consumers. A requirement often imposed on social welfare functions is that they must obey the Pareto principle. A social welfare function also includes the impacts of policy changes on horizontal and vertical equity among consumers.

Since the pioneering work of Atkinson (1970) and Kolm (1969), the measurement of social welfare has been based on explicit social welfare functions. However, the social welfare functions introduced by Atkinson and Kolm are defined on the distribution of income rather the distribution of individual welfare. Muellbauer (1974) and Roberts (1980b) have shown that measures of social welfare based on income coincide with measures based on individual

[2] Jorgenson, Lau and Stoker (1980, 1981, 1982) have developed methods for constructing indirect utility functions for a population of consumers. They introduce exact measures of compensating variations and equivalent variations.

[3] The approach to welfare measurement originated by Dupuit is limited to individual welfare. Under the Pareto principle a change in economic policy can be recommended if all consuming units are at least as well off under the policy change and at least one consuming unit is better off.

welfare if and only if preferences are identical and homothetic for all consumers.[4]

Muellbauer (1974) has defined social welfare functions on the distribution of Hicks' equivalent variation or money metric individual welfare. This approach has also been employed by Deaton and Muellbauer (1980), King (1983a, b) and McKenzie (1982). Roberts (1980b) has derived restrictions on preferences under which the measures of social welfare introduced by Muellbauer (1974) are independent of the prices faced by individual consuming units. In the absence of restrictions on social welfare functions, individuals must have identical homothetic preferences. Roberts (1980b) also derives possible restrictions on the class of social welfare functions. With no restrictions on individual preferences, the social welfare functions must be dictatorial in the sense of Arrow (1963).

Jorgenson and Slesnick (1983, 1984a, b) have introduced measures of social welfare that satisfy the requirements of the theory of social choice, but are not dictatorial.[5] For this purpose we define a social welfare function on the distribution of measures of individual welfare derived from indirect utility functions for a population of consumers. These measures are not independent of the prices faced by the population of consuming units and do not require identical homothetic preferences for all individuals. We present the resulting measures of social welfare in section 3.

In section 4 we present an evaluation of alternative regulatory policies for natural gas prices in the United States, based on projections of prices and the distribution of total expenditure from the Dynamic General Equilibrium Model (DGEM) of the U.S. economy constructed by Hudson and Jorgenson (1974). On the basis of these projections we first construct the distribution of measures of individual welfare for each policy. We then evaluate the corresponding level of social welfare and translate the differences in levels of social welfare among policies into money measures of changes in efficiency and changes in equity. Section 5 of the paper provides a summary and conclusion.

2. Individual welfare

To represent the preferences of individuals in a form suitable for measuring welfare, we take households as consuming units. We assume that expenditures on commodities are allocated so as to maximize a household welfare function. As a consequence, the household behaves in the same way as an individual maximizing a utility function, as demonstrated by Samuelson (1956) and Pollak (1981).

[4] Identical preferences are inconsistent with empirical findings on consumer behavior, such as those of Prais and Houthakker (1971), showing that expenditure patterns depend on the demographic characteristics of individual consuming units.

[5] The theory of social choice is discussed by Arrow (1963) and Sen (1970); Sen (1979b) and Roberts (1980a) provide surveys of recent developments.

The first step in measuring welfare for a single consuming unit is to represent preferences by means of an indirect utility function. For this purpose we introduce the following notation:

x_{nk} = quantity of the nth commodity group consumed by the kth consuming unit ($n=1,2,\dots,N$, $k=1,2,\dots,K$);
x = matrix with elements $\{x_{nk}\}$ describing the social state;
p_n = price of the nth commodity, assumed to be the same for all consuming units;
p = $(p_1, p_2, \dots, p_N)$ = vector of prices of all commodities;
$\ln p$ = $(\ln p_1, \ln p_2, \dots, \ln p_N)$ = vector of logarithms of prices of all commodities;
M_k = $\sum_{n=1}^{N} p_n x_{nk}$ = total expenditure of the kth consuming unit;
A_k = vector of attributes of the kth consuming unit.

We assume that individual welfare for the kth consuming unit, say W_k $(k=1,2,\dots,K)$, is a positive affine transformation of the logarithm of the translog indirect utility function:[6]

$$\begin{aligned} W_k &= \ln V_k \\ &= \ln p'\left(\alpha_p + \tfrac{1}{2}B_{pp}\ln p\right) - D(p)\ln\left[M_k/m_0(p, A_k)\right], \\ &\qquad k = 1,2,\dots,K, \end{aligned} \tag{1}$$

where $D(p) = -1 + i'B_{pp}\ln p$, and the function $m_0(p, A_k)$ is a general translog household equivalence scale.

Jorgenson, Lau and Stoker (1980, 1981, 1982) have shown how to recover indirect utility functions for a population of consuming units from an econometric model of aggregate consumer behavior. Individual expenditure functions and household equivalence scales can be constructed from the indirect utility functions. The general household equivalence scale m_0 is the ratio between total expenditures required by the kth household and by a reference household for the same level of utility, say V_k^0 $(k=1,2,\dots,K)$. This scale can be interpreted as the number of household equivalent members. It depends on the attributes A_k of the consuming unit and on the prices p, but is independent of the level of total expenditure M_k.

We can express total expenditure as a function of the level of individual welfare, prices and the number of household equivalent members:

$$\ln M_k = \frac{1}{D(p)}\left[\ln p'\left(\alpha_p + \tfrac{1}{2}B_{pp}\ln p\right) - \ln V_k\right] + \ln m_0(p, A_k), \qquad k = 1,2,\dots,K, \tag{2}$$

[6] This form of the translog indirect utility function is presented by Jorgenson and Slesnick (1983).

This is the translog individual expenditure function. The total expenditure M_k required to attain the level of individual welfare $\ln V_k$ is a function of prices p and the number of household equivalent members $m_0(p, A_k)$.

Suppose that after the change in policy has taken place the prices are p^1 and the expenditure for the kth household is M_k^1 $(k = 1, 2, \ldots, K)$. Let W_k^1 be the corresponding level of welfare of the kth household. To evaluate the impact of alternative economic policies we must compare the total expenditure required to attain the individual welfare resulting from each policy at prices prevailing before any change, say p^0. For this purpose we can define *money metric individual welfare* for the kth household, say N_k, as the difference between the total expenditure required to attain W_k^1 and the expenditure required to attain W_k^0, the level before the policy change. Both are evaluated at prices p^0:[7]

$$\begin{aligned} N_k &= M_k(p^0, W_k^1, A_k) - M_k(p^0, W_k^0, A_k), \\ &= M_k(p^0, W_k^1, A_k) - M_k^0, \qquad k = 1, 2, \ldots, K, \end{aligned} \tag{3}$$

where M_k^0 is total expenditure before the policy change. If money metric individual welfare is positive, the welfare of the consuming unit is increased; otherwise, the welfare of the consuming unit is decreased or left unaffected.[8]

Under the Pareto principle an economic policy can be recommended if all consuming units are at least as well off as under any alternative policy and at least one unit is better off. The Pareto principle provides a partial ordering of economic policies. This ordering is invariant with respect to monotone increasing transformations of individual welfare that differ among consuming units. Only welfare comparisons that are ordinal and not comparable among consuming units are required.

Money metric individual welfare (3) is a monotone increasing transformation of the measure of individual welfare (1). This transformation depends on the prices faced by all consuming units and on the attributes of the individual consuming unit. Considered as a measure of individual welfare in its own right, money metric individual welfare provides all the information about consumer preferences required for application of the Pareto principle. To obtain a complete ordering of economic policies we next introduce a social welfare function.

3. Social welfare

Arrow (1963) has shown that a complete social ordering based on measures of individual welfare that are ordinal and not comparable among consuming

[7] This concept of money metric individual welfare concides with the concept of net equivalent variation employed by Jorgenson, Lau and Stoker (1982).

[8] For an illustration of this approach to the measurement of individual welfare, see Jorgenson, Lau and Stoker (1981).

units must be dictatorial. A dictatorial social ordering reflects the preferences of a single individual, the dictator. To obtain a broader class of social orderings we must strengthen the assumptions on measures of individual welfare. For this purpose we employ the class of social welfare functions introduced by Roberts (1980a).

The measure of individual welfare (1) based on the indirect utility function is linear in the logarithm of total expenditure per household equivalent member. The coefficients of this function depend on the prices faced by the consuming unit, but are independent of the level of total expenditure for the attributes of the consuming unit. These properties are invariant with respect to positive affine transformations that are the same for all consuming units. The resulting measures of individual welfare are cardinal and fully comparable among consuming units.

The first step in measuring social welfare is to select a social welfare function capable of expressing a variety of ethical judgements. For this purpose we require the additional notation:

$$u = (W_1, W_2, \dots, W_K),$$

which is the vector of individual welfare functions. We assume that the social welfare, say W, is a function of the measures of individual welfare (1):

$$W(u, X) = \ln \bar{V} - \gamma(x) \left[\frac{\sum_{k=1}^{K} m_0(p, A_k) |\ln V_k - \ln \bar{V}|^{-\rho}}{\sum_{k=1}^{K} m_0(p, A_k)} \right]^{-1/\rho}, \tag{4}$$

where

$$\ln \bar{V} = \sum_{k=1}^{K} \frac{m_0(p, A_k) \ln V_k}{\sum_{k=1}^{K} m_0(p, A_k)}, \tag{5}$$

$$\gamma(x) = \left\{ \frac{\sum_{k \neq j}^{K} m_0(p, A_k)}{\sum_{k=1}^{K} m_0(p, A_k)} \left[1 + \left[\frac{\sum_{k \neq j}^{K} m_0(p, A_k)}{m_0(p, A_j)} \right]^{-(\rho+1)} \right] \right\}^{1/\rho},$$

$$m_0(p, A_j) = \min_k m_0(p, A_k).$$

The social welfare function (4) is the sum of two functions of the distribution of individual welfare. The first function $\ln \bar{V}$ is a weighted average of the measures of individual welfare $\{\ln V_k\}$ with weights that depend on the number of household equivalent members $\{m_0(p, A_k)\}$ of each consuming unit. The second function is a mean value function of order ρ of the deviations of measures of individual welfare from their average. We refer to the parameter ρ as the *degree of aversion to inequality*.

In assessing the impact of changes in economic policy on levels of individual welfare for each consuming unit, we have found it useful to express the change in welfare in terms of the change in total expenditure. Similarly, to provide a basis for comparisons among social states $\{x_{nk}\}$ we propose to formulate a money measure of social welfare.[9] Following Pollak (1981), we can define the *social expenditure function* as the minimum level of total expenditure $M = \sum_{k=1}^{K} M_k$ required to attain a given level of social welfare, say W, at a specified price system p. More formally, the social expenditure function $M(p, W)$ is defined by

$$M(p, W) = \min\left\{ M\colon W(u, X) \geqq W, M = \sum_{k=1}^{K} M_k \right\}. \tag{6}$$

The social expenditure function (6) is precisely analogous to the individual expenditure function (2). The individual expenditure function gives the minimum level of expenditure required to attain a stipulated level of individual welfare; the social expenditure function gives the minimum level of aggregate expenditure required to attain a stipulated level of social welfare. The individual expenditure function and the indirect utility function can be employed in assessing the impact of alternative economic policies on individual welfare. Similarly, the social expenditure function and the social welfare function can be employed in assessing the impacts of alternative policies on social welfare.

We can translate any level of social welfare into monetary terms by evaluating the social expenditure function at that level of welfare for a given price system p. Two different levels of social welfare can be compared with reference to a single price system by determining the minimum level of aggregate expenditure required to attain each level of social welfare for the reference prices. In addition, changes in social welfare can be decomposed into changes in efficiency and changes in equity. Money measures of both components of the change in social welfare can be defined in terms of the social expenditure function and the social welfare function.

In order to determine the form of the social expenditure function $M(p, W)$ in (6), we can maximize the social welfare function (4) for a fixed level of aggregate total expenditure by equalizing total expenditure per household equivalent member $\{M_k/m_0(p, A_k)\}$ for all consuming units. If aggregate total expenditure is distributed so as to equalize total expenditure per house-

[9]Alternative money measures of social welfare are discussed by Arrow and Kalt (1979), Bergson (1980), Deaton and Muellbauer (1980, pp. 214–239), Roberts (1980b) and Sen (1976). A survey of the literature is presented by Sen (1979a).

hold equivalent member, the level of individual welfare is the same for all consuming units. For this distribution of total expenditure the social welfare function reduces to the average level of individual welfare $\ln \bar{V}$.

For the translog indirect utility function the maximum value of social welfare for a given level of aggregate expenditure takes the form

$$W(x, u) = \ln \bar{V}$$
$$= \ln p'\left(\alpha_p + \tfrac{1}{2}B_{pp}\ln p\right) - D(p)\ln\left[M \Big/ \sum_{k=1}^{K} m_0(p, A_k)\right]. \tag{7}$$

This maximum value of social welfare reduces to average individual welfare. The average is obtained by evaluating the translog indirect utility function (1) at total expenditure per household equivalent member $M/\sum_{k=1}^{K} m_0(p, A_k)$ for the economy as a whole.

We can solve for aggregate expenditure as a function of the level of social welfare and prices:

$$\ln M(p, W) = \frac{1}{D(p)}\left[\ln p'\left(\alpha_p + \tfrac{1}{2}B_{pp}\ln p\right) - W\right]$$
$$+ \ln\left[\sum_{k=1}^{K} m_0(p, A_k)\right]. \tag{8}$$

We can refer to this function as the *translog social expenditure function*. The value of aggregate expenditure is obtained by evaluating the translog individual expenditure function (2) at the level of social welfare W and the number of household equivalent members $\sum_{k=1}^{K} m_0(p, A_k)$ for the economy as a whole.

To obtain a money measure of social welfare we first evaluate the social welfare function (4) at prices p^0 and distribution of total expenditure $\{M_k^0\}$ prevailing before any change in policy. We can express the level of social welfare before any change in policy, say W^0, in terms of the social expenditure function

$$\ln M(p^0, W^0) = \frac{1}{D(p^0)}\left[\ln p^{0\prime}\left(\alpha_p + \tfrac{1}{2}B_{pp}\ln p^0\right) - W^0\right]$$
$$+ \ln\left[\sum_{k=1}^{K} m_0(p^0, A_k)\right]. \tag{9}$$

Second, we can decompose our money measure of social welfare into money measures of efficiency and equity.[10] For this purpose we evaluate the social

[10]Alternative money measures of efficiency and equity are discussed by Arrow and Kalt (1979), Bergson (1980) and Sen (1976, 1979a).

welfare function at the maximum level, say W^2, that can be attained through lump-sum redistributions of aggregate expenditure $M^0 = \sum_{k=1}^{K} M_k^0$. Total expenditure per household equivalent member must be equalized for all consuming units, so that the social welfare function (4) reduces to average individual welfare (7). This is the maximum level of social welfare that is potentially available and can be taken as a measure of efficiency. Evaluating the social expenditure function at the potential level of welfare, say W^2, we obtain

$$M(p^0, W^2) = M^0, \tag{10}$$

so that aggregate total expenditure M^0 is the resulting money measure of efficiency.

Given a money measure of efficiency, we can define the corresponding money measure of equity as the difference between the money measure of actual social welfare $M(p^0, W^0)$ and the money measure of potential social welfare M^0. This measure of equity is non-positive and equal to zero only for perfect equality in the distribution of individual welfare. Under perfect equality total expenditure per household equivalent member is equalized among all consuming units. Using the social expenditure function, we can express our money measure of social welfare $M(p^0, W^0)$ as the sum of a money measure of efficiency M^0 and a money measure of equity $M(p^0, W^0) - M^0$:

$$M(p^0, W^0) = M^0 + \left[M(p^0, W^0) - M^0\right]. \tag{11}$$

The critical feature of this decomposition is that all three money measures are expressed in terms of the same set of prices p^0.

Finally, to analyze the impact of a change in economic policy on social welfare, we can evaluate the social welfare function (4) at prices p^1 and distribution of total expenditure $\{M_k^1\}$ after the change in policy has taken place. In order to evaluate the impact of a change in economic policy on social welfare, we must compare the levels of aggregate total expenditure required to attain the actual levels of social welfare before and after the policy change at prices prevailing before the change. For this purpose we define *money metric social welfare*, say M_A, as the difference between the total expenditure required to attain the actual level of welfare after the policy change, say W^1, and the expenditure required to attain the actual level of welfare before the policy change W^0 at prices prevailing before the policy change p^0:

$$M_A(p^0, W^0, W^1) = M(p^0, W^1) - M(p^0, W^0). \tag{12}$$

If money metric social welfare is positive, the level of social welfare is increased by the policy change; otherwise, social welfare is decreased or left unaffected.

We can decompose our money measure of social welfare after the change in economic policy into money measures of efficiency and equity. For this purpose we first determine the maximum level of welfare, say W^3, that can be attained through lump-sum redistributions of aggregate total expenditure $M^1 = \sum_{k=1}^{K} M_k^1$. As before, aggregate expenditure must be distributed so as to equalize individual expenditure per household equivalent member, so that the social welfare function (4) reduces to average individual welfare (7). This is the maximum level of social welfare that is potentially available after the change in economic policy and can be taken as a measure of efficiency.

Using (11) we can decompose money metric social welfare (12) into the sum of money metric efficiency and money metric equity. *Money metric efficiency*, say M_P, can be defined as the difference between the total expenditure required to attain the potential level of welfare after the policy change W^3 and the expenditure required to attain the potential level of welfare before the policy change W^2. Both are evaluated at prices prevailing before the policy change p^0:

$$M_P(p^0, W^2, W^3) = M(p^0, W^3) - M^0. \tag{13}$$

Similarly, *money metric equity*, say M_E, can be defined as the difference between money measures of equity before and after the policy change, evaluated at prices before the change p^0:

$$M_E(p^0, W^0, W^1, W^2, W^3) = \left[M(p^0, W^1) - M(p^0, W^3)\right] - \left[M(p^0, W^0) - M^0\right]. \tag{14}$$

Money metric social welfare is the sum of money metric efficiency and money metric equity:

$$M_A(p^0, W^0, W^1) = M_P(p^0, W^2, W^3) + M_E(p^0, W^0, W^1, W^2, W^3). \tag{15}$$

All three money measures of social welfare in this decomposition are expressed in terms of the same set of prices p^0.

4. Efficiency versus equity

To illustrate the measurement of social welfare we undertake a comparison of alternative policies for regulation of natural gas prices in the United States. These policies have been analyzed by the Office of Policy, Planning, and Analysis of the U.S. Department of Energy (DOE). Our reference case for policy analysis is the policy of natural gas price decontrol called for in the Natural Gas Policy Act (NGPA) of 1978. Under this policy price controls on natural gas remain until 1985, when prices on some types of natural gas are decontrolled. Our base case for policy analysis is the behavior of the U.S. economy under this policy.

Alternatives to current regulatory policy for natural gas prices considered by DOE are the following:

(1) *Continued controls.* Under this policy price controls on natural gas are continued beyond 1985, and an effort is made to shift consumption from domestic to imported natural gas. This policy was embodied in the Gephardt bill presented to Congress in 1983.

(2) *Immediate decontrol.* Under this policy price controls are maintained on some types of natural gas until 1985; at this time decontrol occurs for prices on most types of natural gas. This policy was embodied in a Senate–Adminstration bill presented to Congress in 1983.

The value of social welfare depends on prices for each of the five commodities included in our model of aggregate consumer behavior – energy, food, consumer goods, capital services, and consumer services. In addition, it depends on total expenditure for the U.S. economy as a whole. We make the simplifying assumption that total expenditure changes in the same proportion for all consuming units. To evaluate alternatives to current regulatory policy for natural gas prices considered by DOE, we require projections of prices and total expenditure under each policy. We obtain these projections from the Dynamic General Equilibrium Model (DGEM) of the U.S. economy constructed by Hudson and Jorgenson (1974).[11]

We can translate our evaluation of alternative policies for natural gas price regulation into money measures of social welfare by employing the social expenditure function introduced in section 3. In table 1 we present money metric social welfare for the two alternative policies described above. Although the magnitude of money metric social welfare depends on the degree of aversion to inequality, we find that the qualitative features of comparisons among alternative policies for different values of this parameter are almost identical. We present money metric social welfare for both alternatives to the base case for the degree of aversion to inequality ρ equal to minus one.

Under continued controls money metric social welfare is positive for the years 1983 to 1989, and becomes negative for the rest of the period. Money metric social welfare under immediate decontrol is positive throughout the

[11] This model is based on a breakdown of the U.S. economy into nine industrial sectors, including five energy sectors and four aggregates of the non-energy sectors. The price and total expenditure projections are based on projections of the U.S. economy under alternative regulatory policies for natural gas prices by Goettle, Hudson, Jorgenson and Slesnick (1983).

Table 1

Money metric social welfare (millions of constant dollars).

Year	Continued controls	Immediate decontrol
1983	1492.520	1717.654
1984	1799.619	1332.337
1985	2401.407	1650.275
1986	3117.486	1625.640
1987	2004.577	1636.300
1988	1221.106	1640.076
1989	452.995	1346.813
1990	−20.729	1114.807
1991	−239.067	695.305
1992	−467.214	579.660
1993	−519.304	532.518
1994	−681.827	276.191
1995	−740.451	160.032
1996	−759.793	768.837
1997	−786.539	569.036
1998	−816.259	429.719
1999	−789.273	349.180
2000	−796.057	280.520

period 1983 to 2000. Gains in social welfare under immediate decontrol exceed those under continued controls in 1983 and for all years after 1988. Our analysis of current regulatory policy for natural gas prices and the two alternative policies appears to justify immediate decontrol of natural gas prices. This policy is superior to current policy and to a policy of continued price controls.

Money metric social welfare is the sum of money metric efficiency and money metric equity. Money metric efficiency corresponds to the gain in potential social welfare associated with a change in regulatory policy and is independent of the degree of aversion to inequality ρ. We present money metric efficiency for both alternatives to the base case in table 2.

Under continued controls money metric efficiency is positive for 1983–1989 and negative for the rest of the period. Money metric efficiency under immediate decontrol is positive throughout the period. Money metric efficiency is higher for immediate decontrol than for continued controls for 1983 and 1988–2000. A common practice in welfare economics is to recommend the policy with the greatest efficiency. On these grounds the policy of immediate decontrol would be judged superior to current policy and to continued controls.

We next consider money measures of equity for both alternatives to current regulatory policy. Money metric equity is defined as the difference between actual and potential gains in social welfare resulting from a change in regulatory policy. Money metric equity, unlike money metric efficiency, depends on

Table 2

Money metric efficiency (millions of constant dollars).

Year	Continued controls	Immediate decontrol
1983	2162.315	2492.543
1984	2695.706	1963.536
1985	3483.171	2434.154
1986	4641.808	2405.515
1987	2978.186	2424.443
1988	1783.287	2437.363
1989	611.950	1998.672
1990	−114.416	1697.490
1991	−438.714	1012.105
1992	−808.774	843.876
1993	−872.335	790.947
1994	−1125.599	361.113
1995	−1219.799	180.499
1996	−1246.097	1099.865
1997	−1287.569	797.594
1998	1331.449	587.833
1999	−1291.577	464.389
2000	−1300.480	358.882

Table 3

Money metric equity (millions of constant dollars).

Year	Continued controls	Immediate decontrol
1983	−669.794	−774.890
1984	−896.087	−631.199
1985	−1081.765	−783.880
1986	−1524.322	−779.875
1987	−973.610	−788.143
1988	−562.181	−797.286
1989	−158.954	−651.859
1990	93.687	−552.683
1991	199.647	−316.800
1992	341.560	−264.216
1993	353.031	−258.429
1994	443.771	−84.922
1995	479.348	−20.467
1996	486.304	−331.028
1997	501.030	−228.557
1998	515.190	−158.114
1999	502.305	−115.209
2000	504.423	−78.363

the degree of aversion to inequality ρ. We have found, as before, that the qualitative features of comparisons among alternative policies are almost identical for different values of this parameter, so that we present money metric equity for the two alternatives to current regulatory policy in table 3 for degree of aversion to inequality ρ equal to minus one.

Money metric equity for a policy of continued natural gas price controls is negative for the period 1983–1989 and positive for the remainder of the period 1990–2000, reaching a level of $515.190 millions in 1998. By contrast a policy of immediate decontrol reduces equity throughout the period 1983–2000.

Finally, by comparing the results presented in tables 2 and 3 we can see that money metric efficiency and equity move in opposite directions. For example, a policy of immediate decontrol of natural gas prices is preferred to all other policies for the period 1988–2000. Throughout this period money metric efficiency under immediate decontrol is positive; however, money metric equity under this policy is lower than that for current policy. Under continued controls money metric efficiency is greater than under current policy through 1989 and less than under current policy for the period 1990–2000. By contrast money metric equity is lower than under current policy through 1989 and greater for the period 1990–2000.

5. Summary and conclusion

We can summarize our approach to welfare economics as follows: First we introduce a measure of individual welfare based on the indirect utility function for each consuming unit. The individual expenditure function can be used to translate changes in individual welfare into money metric individual welfare. Money metric individual welfare provides an ordinal measure of welfare that is not comparable among consuming units. This measure can be used in evaluating economic policies by constructing partial orderings of these policies based on the Pareto principle.

A complete ordering of economic policies requires a social welfare function. Jorgenson and Slesnick (1983, 1984a, b) have introduced a class of social welfare functions capable of expressing a variety of ethical judgements. This class is based on the distribution of individual welfare over the population of consuming units. In measuring social welfare we require cardinal measures of individual welfare that are fully comparable among units. For this purpose we employ indirect utility functions for all units. Jorgenson, Lau and Stoker (1980, 1981, 1982) have developed methods for recovering indirect utility functions for a population of consuming units from an econometric model of aggregate consumer behavior.

The social expenditure function can be used to translate changes in social welfare into money metric social welfare. The concept of money metric social welfare can be used in comparing alternative economic policies on the basis of the aggregate expenditure required for each policy. In addition, we introduce the maximum level of social welfare that can be attained by lump-sum redistributions of aggregate expenditure among consuming units as a measure of efficiency. Using this measure, we can decompose money metric social welfare into the sum of money metric equity and money metric efficiency.

Jorgenson and Slesnick (1983) have used the approach to welfare economics outlined in this paper to derive individual and social cost of living indexes. In a subsequent paper Jorgenson and Slesnick (1984a) have derived measures of inequality in the distribution of individual welfare. Finally, Jorgenson and Slesnick (1984b) have developed corresponding measures of inequality in the distribution of individual welfare for groups of consumers and have presented measures of inequality within and among groups.

While the approach to welfare economics we have presented has already been fruitful in generating interesting and useful applications, a great deal of important and worthwhile research remains to be done. For example, our methodology can be employed in constructing measures of the standard of living that incorporate distributional considerations. These measures can be used in place of real consumption per capita, which is best regarded as indicator of economic efficiency.

A second area for potential application of our new approach to welfare economics is to define measures of poverty on the distribution of individual welfare rather than the distribution of income. This approach can also be used in assessing gains to society from redistributional policies. Completion of this line of research promises to restore normative economics to its rightful place – as an equal partner of positive economics in designing and evaluating economic policies.

References

Arrow, K.J., 1963, Social choice and individual values, 2nd ed. (Yale University Press, New Haven, CT).

Arrow, K.J. and J.P. Kalt, 1979, Petroleum price regulation: Should we decontrol (American Enterprise Institute, Washington, DC).

Atkinson, A.B., 1970, On measurement of inequality, Journal of Economic Theory 2, 244–263.

Bergson, A., 1938, A reformulation of certain aspects of welfare economics, Quarterly Journal of Economics 52, 310–334.

Bergson, A., 1980, Consumer's surplus and income redistribution, Journal of Public Economics 14, 31–47.

Chipman, J.S. and J.C. Moore, 1980, Compensating variation, consumer's surplus, and welfare, American Economic Review 70, 933–949.

Deaton, A. and J. Muellbauer, 1980, Economics and consumer behavior (Cambridge University Press, Cambridge).

Dupuit, J., 1969, On the measurement of the utility of public works, in: K.J. Arrow and T. Scitovsky, eds., Readings in welfare economics (Richard D. Irwin, Homewood, IL) 255–283 (originally published in French in 1844).

Goettle, R.J., IV, E.A. Hudson, D.W. Jorgenson and D.T. Slesnick, 1983, The macroeconomic consequences of alternative natural gas policies (Dale W. Jorgenson Associates, Cambridge, MA).

Harberger, A.C., 1971, Three basic postulates for applied welfare economics: An interpretive essay, Journal of Economic Literature 9, 785–797.

Hicks, J.R., 1942, Consumers' surplus and index-numbers, Review of Economic Studies 9, 126–137.

Hotelling, H., 1938, The general welfare in relation to problems of taxation and of railway and utility rates, Econometrica 6, 242–269.

Houthakker, H.S., 1957, An international comparison of household expenditure patterns commemorating the centenary of Engel's law, Econometrica 25, 532–551.

Hudson, E.A. and D.W. Jorgenson, 1974, U.S. energy policy and economic growth, 1975–2000, Bell Journal of Economics and Management Science 5, 461–514.

Jorgenson, D.W., L.J. Lau and T.M. Stoker, 1980, Welfare comparison under exact aggregation, American Economic Review 70, 268–272.

Jorgenson, D.W., L.J. Lau and T.M. Stoker, 1981, Aggregate consumer behavior and individual welfare, in: D. Currie, R. Nobay and D. Peel, eds., Macroeconomic analysis (Croom-Helm, London) 35–61.

Jorgenson, D.W., L.J. Lau and T.M. Stoker, 1982, The transcendental logarithmic model of aggregate consumer behavior, in: R.L. Basmann and G.F. Rhodes, Jr., eds., Advances in econometrics, Vol. 1 (JAI Press, Greenwich, CT) 97–238.

Jorgenson, D.W. and D.T. Slesnick, 1983, Individual and social cost of living indexes, in: W.E. Diewert and C. Montmarquette, eds., Price level measurement (Statistics Canada, Ottawa) 241–323.

Jorgenson, D.W. and D.T. Slesnick, 1984a, Aggregate consumer behavior and the measurement of inequality, Review of Economic Studies 51, 369–392.

Jorgenson, D.W. and D.T. Slesnick, 1984b, Inequality in the distribution of individual welfare, in: R.L. Basmann and G.F. Rhodes, Jr., eds., Advances in econometrics, Vol. 3 (JAI Press, Greenwich, CT) 67–130.

King, M.A., 1983a, An index of inequality: With applications to horizontal equity and social mobility, Econometrica 51, 99–115.

King, M.A., 1983b, Welfare analysis of tax reforms using household data, Journal of Public Economics 21, 183–214.

Kolm, S.C., 1969, The optimal production of social justice, in: J. Margolis and H. Guitton, eds., Public economics (Macmillan, London) 145–200.

Marshall, Alfred, 1920, Principles of economics, 8th ed. (Macmillan, London).

McKenzie, G.W., 1982, Measuring economic welfare: New methods (Cambridge University Press, Cambridge).

McKenzie, L.W., 1957, Demand theory without a utility index, Review of Economic Studies 24, 185–189.

Muellbauer, J., 1974, Inequality measures, prices and household composition, Review of Economic Studies 41, 493–504.

Pollak, R.A., 1981, The social cost of living index, Journal of Public Economics 15, 311–336.

Prais, S.J. and H.S. Houthakker, 1971, The analysis of family budgets, 2nd ed. (Cambridge University Press, Cambridge).

Roberts, K.W.S., 1980a, Interpersonal comparability and social choice theory, Review of Economic Studies 47, 421–439.

Roberts, K.W.S., 1980b, Price-independent welfare prescriptions, Journal of Public Economics 13, 277–298.

Samuelson, P.A., 1956, Social indifference curves, Quarterly Journal of Economics 70, 1–22.

Samuelson, P.A., 1982, Bergsonian welfare economics, in: S. Rosefielde, ed., Economic welfare and the economics of Soviet socialism: Essays in honor of Abram Bergson (Cambridge University Press, Cambridge) 223–266.

Samuelson, P.A., 1983, Foundations of economic analysis, 2nd ed. (Harvard University Press, Cambridge, MA).

Sen, A.K., 1970, Collective choice and social welfare (Oliver and Boyd, Edinburgh).

Sen, A.K., 1976, Real national income, Review of Economic Studies 43, 19–40.

Sen, A.K., 1979a, The welfare basis of real income comparisons: A survey, Journal of Economic Literature 17, 1–45.

Sen, A.K., 1979b, Personal utilities and public judgements: Or what's wrong with welfare economics?, Economic Journal 89, 537–558.

THE ESTIMATION OF COMPLETE AGGREGATION STRUCTURES

James L. POWELL and Thomas M. STOKER*

M.I.T., Cambridge, MA 02139, USA

The object of this paper is to establish several results which permit efficient estimation of behavioral parameters in models of aggregate data. The approach follows the 'minimum chi-square' estimation strategy customarily applied to contingency tables; by treating aggregates as general functionals of empirical distribution functions for each 'cell' (i.e., aggregation unit), consistent and asymptotically normal estimates are obtained for a fixed number of aggregation units as the number of observations per unit increases. The paper also discusses conditions under which the proposed estimators are asymptotically efficient, and gives examples applying the approach to continuous and discrete demand models.

1. Introduction

The purpose of this paper is to establish several results which permit efficient estimation of behavioral parameters in models of aggregate data. The generic econometric situation of interest occurs when one observes data aggregates for a given number of groups, which for example could be separate time periods. The model for these data accounts for the problem of aggregation over individuals – it is constructed from a parameterized microeconometric model integrated over an assumed distribution form, in a way which permits identification of the micro behavioral parameters. The overall question addressed in this paper is how one can consistently and efficiently estimate the values of these behavioral parameters, using the observed aggregate data.

The issues involved in constructing models which account for the problem of aggregation over individuals are extensively covered in Stoker (1984). The empirical implications of individual heterogeneity and distribution shifts on aggregate data are formally modeled by an *aggregate function*, which is constructed from a microeconomic model integrated over an assumed distribution form. Completeness of the aggregation structure (or the absence of an aggregation problem) occurs when the parameters of micro behavior are identified by the aggregate function, which requires specific restrictions on the form of micro behavior and/or the form of the predictor variable distribution.

*The authors gratefully acknowledge support from the National Science Foundation for this research.

Stoker (1984) presents several examples of aggregate functions and characterizing results for complete aggregation structures, which include models with intrinsically non-linear microeconomic equations and specific restrictions on the predictor variable distribution.

In this paper we establish several foundational results which facilitate the use of complete aggregation structure modeling to study observed aggregate data. In particular, we advocate the estimation of behavioral parameters by weighted (non-linear) least squares (WLS) applied directly to the aggregate function evaluated using the observed data, and rigorously derive the properties of the estimator. Specifically, when all common factors are observed, we show the WLS estimators are consistent, and efficient within the class of minimum distance estimators (with the proper choice of weights). These results are based in part on an appropriate modification of the principal finding of the theory of minimum chi-square estimation; namely the first-order equivalence of minimum chi-square and other minimum distance estimators. As part of the exposition, we provide examples of estimation problems with aggregate data and connect the optimal selection of weights to the cross-section regression results of Stoker (1983). We also discuss the implications of our results to the estimation of models with random, unobserved factors; however, a rigorous treatment of this case is beyond the scope of this paper.

The major advantages of our results lie in their generality and computational simplicity. The results are applicable to a broad range of different empirical situations, being valid for: (i) many different types of aggregate data on both dependent and predictor variables – averages, medians, more general order statistics, etc., (ii) virtually arbitrary forms of micro behavior – linear or non-linear, continuous or discrete variables, and (iii) general specifications of the predictor variable distribution. The computational simplicity of the results lies in the first-order optimality of weighted least squares, which is now a standard (non-linear) estimation technique.

We begin by presenting the modeling framework in section 2. The rigorous treatment of WLS estimators – consistency, asymptotic normality and asymptotic efficiency – is given in section 3. Several related topics are addressed in section 4, namely the relation of the optimal weights to cross-section regression, estimation of the weights, and parameter estimation when there are unobserved, random common factors. Section 5 contains some concluding remarks.

2. General definitions, notation and discussion

2.1. The modeling framework

In this paper several results are established on the econometrics of properly specified models of aggregate data over T groups of individual agents, with groups indexed by $t=1,\ldots,T$. The framework presented below models the behavior of individual agents and distributions of individual differences for each group t, and the induced relationship among the aggregate data across groups.

We assume throughout that the object of statistical analysis is the estimation (with associated hypothesis tests) of an unknown parameter vector δ characterizing a single microeconomic behavioral equation,

$$y_{it}=f(x_{it},u_{it},\rho_t;\delta), \tag{2.1}$$

where y_{it} is a variable representing the behavioral response of an individual agent i in group t, x_{it} is k-vector of (potentially) observable characteristics of that individual, and u_{it} is a random disturbance embodying unobserved differences not captured by x_{it}. The components of ρ_t represent variables which are common to all agents in a particular group, which vary over groups, and may be observable or unobservable random variables.

The probability law generating a particular realization of y_{it} is therefore determined by the true value δ_0 of the unknown parameter δ and by the distribution of the characteristics (x_{it},u_{it},ρ_t) in the population. For the results of this paper, we consider the conditional distributions for each value of ρ_t; we assume that the distribution of (x_{it},u_{it}) within each group has conditional density $h_t(x,u|\rho_t)$ which is absolutely continuous with respect to a sigma-finite measure λ, invariant across groups. Further, we suppose that this density can be parameterized as

$$h_t(x,u|\rho_t)=g_t(u|x,\rho_t,\sigma_0)\,p_t(x|\rho_t,\theta_t), \tag{2.2}$$

where the forms of $g_t(\cdot)$ and $p_t(\cdot)$ are known up to the unknown parameters σ_0 and θ_t, which are assumed to be variation-free. We denote the behavioral parameters δ and the heterogeneity parameters σ collectively as $\gamma=(\delta,\sigma)$, with true value $\gamma_0=(\delta_0,\sigma_0)$.

Given (2.1) and (2.2), the distribution of y, x and u within group t are determined by ρ_t, θ_t and σ_0. The conditional density of unobserved differences u given x and ρ_t is known up to the parameter value σ_0, with a stable heterogeneity density over groups occurring when $g_t(u|x,\rho_t,\sigma_0)=g(u|x,\sigma_0)$ for all t. The density of (potentially) observable characteristics x is known up to the values of θ_t and ρ_t. When ρ_t is observable, θ_t completely characterizes the unknown aspects of differences in the x distribution across groups.

This setup, while not completely general in its treatment of individual and group heterogeneity, characterizes a broad class of economic models of interest. For macroeconomic applications, the groups denoted by t may represent populations observed over several time periods, with ρ_t representing common observed variables such as prices, general economic conditions and time trends, as well as common (unobserved) macroeconomic shocks. Alternatively, the groups may represent cross-section aggregation units; e.g. observations for particular states, countries or industries in a particular period of time.

The observed data formally consists of the observable components of ρ_t, and aggregates $\hat{Y}_t$ and $\hat{X}_t$ which represent 'typical' values of y_{it} and x_{it} for each group $t=1,\dots,T$. We assume that the aggregates $\hat{Y}_t$ and $\hat{X}_t$ have been constructed from a random sample of size N_t within each group t, namely (y_{it}, x_{it}) for $i=1,\dots,N_t$, and are 'democratic' to the extent that they depend only on the respective empirical distribution functions – i.e., $\hat{Y}_t$ and $\hat{X}_t$ are functionals of the form

$$\hat{Y}_t = Y(\hat{Q}_t), \qquad \hat{X}_t = X(\hat{P}_t) \tag{2.3}$$

where

$$\hat{Q}_t = \frac{1}{N_t}\sum_i 1(y_{it} \le y) \equiv \hat{Q}_t(y),$$

$$\hat{P}_t = \frac{1}{N_t}\sum_i 1(x_{it} \le x) \equiv \hat{P}_t(x), \tag{2.4}$$

with '1(A)' denoting the indicator function of the event 'A' and the inequality '$x_{it} \le x$' holding coordinate by coordinate. To the empirical aggregates $\hat{Y}_t$ and $\hat{X}_t$ correspond population aggregates $Y(Q_t)$ and $X(P_t)$, where Q_t is the (marginal) distribution of y_{it} given ρ_t in group t, and P_t is the (marginal) distribution of x_{it} given ρ_t in group t. The population aggregates are written explicitly as

$$Y(Q_t) = Y(Q_t(y|\theta_t, \rho_t, \gamma)) = \Lambda_t(\theta_t, \rho_t, \gamma),$$

$$X(P_t) = X(P_t(x|\theta_t, \rho_t)) = \Psi_t(\theta_t, \rho_t). \tag{2.5}$$

A key assumption is that for each value of ρ_t, $\Psi_t(\theta_t, \rho_t)$ is a known and invertible function of θ_t. This implies that we can reparameterize the distribution of x_{it} in group t by (μ_t, ρ_t) where $\mu_t \equiv \Psi_t(\theta_t, \rho_t)$, as in $\tilde{p}_t(x|\mu_t, \rho_t) = p_t(x|\Psi^{-1}(\mu_t, \rho_t), \rho_t)$, with inversion applying only to the elements of θ_t. Further, we assume that the functional $X(\cdot)$ is Fisher consistent – that is, $X(\hat{P}_t) \to X(P_t)$ as $\hat{P}_t \to P_t$ (where convergence is appropriately defined) – so that the empirical aggregate $\hat{X}_t$ consistently estimates $\mu_t = X(P_t)$.

The relation between the population aggregates $Y(Q_t)$ and $X(P_t)$ (the *aggregate function*) is defined directly from (2.5) using the (μ_t, ρ_t) parameterization as

$$Y(Q_t) = \Lambda_t(\Psi^{-1}(\mu_t, \rho_t), \rho_t, \gamma) \equiv \Phi_t(\mu_t, \rho_t, \gamma), \tag{2.6}$$

$$X(P_t) = \mu_t,$$

so that

$$Y(Q_t) = \Phi_t(X(P_t), \rho_t, \gamma). \tag{2.7}$$

The results of this paper apply to the estimation of γ from (2.7), where the empirical aggregates $\hat{Y}_t$ and $\hat{X}_t$ are used in place of the population aggregates $Y(P_t)$ and $X(P_t)$. We discuss the overall estimation issues in the next section, after discussing the applicability of the above framework to aggregate data.

The most natural special case of this framework occurs when $Y(\cdot)$ and $X(\cdot)$ are expectation operators, with $\hat{Y}_t$ and $\hat{X}_t$ the sample averages of y_{it} and x_{it}, as in

$$\hat{Y}_t = \int y \, \mathrm{d}\hat{Q}_t(y) \equiv \bar{Y}_t,$$
$$\hat{X}_t = \int x \, \mathrm{d}\hat{P}_t(x) \equiv \bar{X}_t. \tag{2.8}$$

The issues of parameter identification when $Y(P_t) \equiv \mathrm{E}_t(y)$ have been analyzed in Stoker (1984).

The framework applies to many other aggregates than sample averages, such as order statistic data. If $\hat{Y}_t$ is the pth quantile ($p \cdot 100$th percentile) of $\{y_{it}, i = 1, \dots, N\}$, then

$$\hat{Y}_t = Y(\hat{Q}_t) = \hat{Q}_t^{-1}(p). \tag{2.9}$$

The population aggregate associated with $\hat{Y}_t$ is

$$Y(Q_t) = Q_t^{-1}(p|\theta_t, \rho_t, \gamma).$$

Obviously, data on the medians of y and x in group t provides a special case of this example.

The assumption that $X(P_t) = \Psi_t(\theta_t, \rho_t)$ is invertible in θ_t is the major specification assumption of the framework. This implies that the observed data X_t captures all aspects of distribution change unrelated to ρ_t, which is essential for the identification of the parameters γ without severe (linearity) restrictions on the behavioral function (2.1). This assumption would fail if θ_t contained more components than $\hat{X}_t$, implying that there were distribution movements unaccounted for by $\hat{X}_t$.

2.2. Overall estimation issues

The overall issues addressed by this paper concern the implications of estimation of the parameters γ using the observed aggregate data $\hat{Y}_t$ and $\hat{X}_t$ when the true relation (2.7) is general, and possibly highly non-linear. Because our major interest is in the use of empirical aggregates, all of the results apply to modelling conditional on the value of ρ_t, the common factors affecting all agents within each group. This involves no loss of generality when ρ_t represents observed data. When components of ρ_t are random, unobserved factors, our results still characterize the implications of using empirical aggregates; however, we do not show results which formally utilize assumptions on stochastic properties of ρ_t. We discuss this extension, following the presentation of the basic results, in section 4.3. However, it should be kept in mind that the results on consistency and asymptotic normality of the estimators are strictly valid conditional on the value of ρ_t, with the extension to the case of random ρ_t left to future research.

With the extensive distribution modeling implicit in the above framework, a very natural approach for the estimation of γ is to employ maximum likelihood, based on the likelihood function for the observed data $\hat{Y}_t$, $\hat{X}_t$ (conditional on the value of ρ_t, $t=1,\dots,T$). Namely, given the form of the behavioral function (2.1), the density forms of (2.2) and the forms of the aggregation functionals of (2.5), the joint density function $d_t(Y, X|\gamma, \mu_t, \rho_t, N_t)$ of the induced probability law for $\hat{Y}_t$ and $\hat{X}_t$ can be derived. The unknown parameters γ and $\mu=(\mu_1,\dots,\mu'_T)'$ could then be estimated by

$$\begin{bmatrix}\hat{\gamma}\\ \hat{\mu}\end{bmatrix} = \arg\max_{\gamma,\mu} \sum_t \log d_t\big(\hat{Y}_t, \hat{X}_t|\gamma, \mu_t, \rho_t, N_t\big). \tag{2.10}$$

We do not explore this estimation strategy because of two important drawbacks. First, the calculation of the joint density function d_t is far from trivial in general; for example, if $\hat{Y}_t=\bar{Y}_t$, $\hat{X}_t=\bar{X}_t$ were sample averages, computation of $d_t(\cdot)$ involves an N_t-fold convolution of the joint density of (y_{it}, x_{it}), which is intractible unless f and h_t of (2.1) and (2.2) are of extremely simple form. A second, more fundamental issue is the applicability of the usual justification of the maximum likelihood estimator (2.10) – namely consistency, asymptotic normality and asymptotic efficiency – for studying the implications of using empirical aggregates. The usual asymptotic properties of the maximum likelihood estimator (2.10) can be demonstrated (under suitable regularity conditions) for T tending to infinity as each group size N_t is held constant. However, for typical problems involving aggregates, the group sizes N_t are large relative to T. An appropriate asymptotic theory for the maximum likelihood estimator (2.10) would let N_t tend to infinity for fixed T. In this case, the likelihood function is a fixed sum of log density functions, each of which varies as N_t increases, and so the standard asymptotic results for maximum likelihood do not apply.

A more attractive approach is to estimate the parameters γ directly using the aggregate function (2.7), where the empirical aggregates are used in place of the population aggregates. Put plainly, one could just insert the empirical aggregates into (2.7), and estimate γ by (non-linear) least squares regression. More generally, we consider estimating γ by weighted least squares as

$$\hat{\gamma}_w = \arg\min_{\gamma} \sum_t \hat{w}_t (\hat{Y}_t - \Phi_t(\hat{X}_t, \rho_t, \gamma))^2, \tag{2.11}$$

where $\{\hat{w}_t\}$ is some set of (possibly stochastic) weights. In this paper we derive the asymptotic properties of this estimator for large N_t and fixed T.

This approach is similar to minimum chi-square and related minimum distance estimation methods for multinomial models [see Rao (1973) and Bishop, Feinberg and Holland (1975), among others]. The major differences involve the generality of the aggregates considered, and the posture regarding the configuration of characteristics within each group. For the latter point, unlike the usual analysis of cell count data, it is not necessary to suppose that the characteristics within each group (as with dosage levels in bioassay) are fixed for all observations, or known with certainty – it suffices here that consistent estimates of the parameters governing distributional differences across groups are available.

Nevertheless, one of the principal findings of minimum chi-square estimation – namely, the first-order equivalence of minimum chi-square, maximum likelihood and other minimum distance estimators using cell proportions – carries over, with minor modification, to the aggregate estimation framework considered here. In section 3.2, we give the conditions under which $\hat{\gamma}_w$ will be first-order efficient (with proper weights $\{\hat{w}_t\}$) among minimum distance estimates, including the maximum likelihood estimator (2.10).

2.3. *Examples*

Before proceeding to introduce formal assumptions and results, it is useful to consider some concrete examples. In the examples, we take ρ_t to represent observable common variables.

Example 1: Continuous demand model

Suppose that y represents the expenditure on a given commodity, which is determined as

$$\begin{aligned} y_{it} &= f(x_{it}, u_{it}, \rho_t; \delta) \\ &= A(\rho_t, \delta) x_{it} + B(\rho_t, \delta) x_{it} \log x_{it} + u_{it}, \end{aligned}$$

where ρ_t is a vector of relative prices, presumed constant and observable for each group t, x_{it} is individual income (expenditures on all commodities), and u_{it} is a disturbance term, assume to have zero mean conditional on x_{it} and variance σ_0^2 (assumed fixed across individuals and groups for simplicity). This demand function is of the PIGLOG form of Muellbauer (1975) and includes the AIDS system of Deaton and Muellbauer (1980) and the translog model of Jorgenson, Lau and Stoker (1982) without attributes; δ represents individual preference parameters. We take $\delta = \gamma_0$.

Supposing

$$\hat{Y}_t = \bar{Y}_t = \frac{1}{N_t} \sum_{t=1}^{T} y_{it}$$

is the aggregate available for expenditure, and noting that

$$\mathrm{E}(y_{it}|x_{it}, \rho_t, \gamma) = A(\rho_t, \gamma) x_{it} + B(\rho_t, \gamma) x_{it} \log x_{it},$$

we obtain the population aggregate $Y_t(Q_t)$ by taking the expectation of this formula with respect to the distribution of x_{it}. Again for simplicity we suppose the income distribution is log-normal, i.e., the density of x_{it} (with respect to Lebesgue measure) is

$$p(x|\theta_t) = \frac{1(x>0)}{2\pi\theta_{2t} x} \exp\left(\frac{-(\ln x - \theta_{it})^2}{2\theta_{2t}^2} \right).$$

Since this distribution has two time-varying parameters, we require two aggregates for the characteristics to identify γ. If

$$\hat{X}_t = \left(\frac{1}{N_t} \sum_{i=1}^{N_t} x_{it}, \mathrm{median}\{x_{it}, i = 1, \ldots, N_t\} \right) \equiv (\bar{X}_t, \tilde{X}_t)$$

is available, the corresponding population aggregate characteristics for the tth group are

$$X_t(P_t) = \left(\mathrm{E}(x_{it}), P_t^{-1}(\tfrac{1}{2})\right) = \left(\exp(\theta_{1t} + \tfrac{1}{2}\theta_{2t}^2), \exp(\theta_t)\right)$$
$$= (\mu_{1t}, \mu_{2t}) \equiv \mu_t,$$

which is clearly an invertible function of $\theta_t = (\theta_{1t}, \theta_{2t})$.

For this distribution of characteristics,

$$Y_t(Q_t) = \mathrm{E}(y_{it})$$

$$= \exp\left(\theta_{1t} + \tfrac{1}{2}\theta_{2t}^2\right)\left(A(\rho_t,\gamma) + B(\rho_t,\gamma)\left(\theta_{1t} + \theta_{2t}^2\right)\right)$$

$$= \Lambda_t(\theta_t, \rho_t, \gamma),$$

or, in terms of μ_t,

$$Y_t(Q_t) = \mu_{1t}\left[A_\gamma(\rho_t) + B_\gamma(\rho_t)(2\log\mu_{1t} - \log\mu_{2t})\right].$$

$$= \Phi_t(\mu_t, \rho_t, \gamma).$$

With these calculations, computation of the weighted least squares estimator $\hat{\gamma}_w$ of (2.11) for given weights $\{w_t\}$ can be carried out with standard non-linear optimization techniques.

The behavioral equation in this example is intrinsically linear in functions of x_{it}, or an *exact aggregation* model, with $\hat{Y}_t = \overline{Y}_t = \sum y_{it}/N_t$ a linear function of $\overline{X}_t = \sum x_{it}/N_t$ and $\sum x_{it}\log x_{it}/N_t$. The latter statistic is not observed, and we include the example to point out the implications of using the median $\hat{X}_{2t}$ to represent distribution shifts. For later reference, we note that departures of $\hat{Y}_t$ from $\Phi_t(\hat{X}_t, \rho_t, \gamma)$ will depend not only on the average individual disturbance $\sum u_{it}/N_t$, but also on a term arising from the function of $\tilde{X}_t$ used in place of $\sum x_{it}\log x_{it}/N_t$.

The following example utilizes an intrinsically non-linear behavioral model.

Example 2: Discrete Choice Model

Suppose now that y is 1 or 0 according to whether a commodity (say a car) is purchased or not. In this setup, the behavioral model may be of the form

$$y_{it} = f(x_{it}, u_{it}, \rho_t; \delta)$$

$$= 1(u_{it} \leq \delta_1 + \delta_2 \log x_{it} + \delta_3\rho_t),$$

where x_{it} denotes income, ρ_t denotes the commodity price, and u_{it} represents individual heterogeneity, distributed normally with mean 0 and variance 1. Again supposing the aggregate $\hat{Y}_t = \overline{Y}_t$, the sample proportion of individuals in group t who purchase the commodity, and that x_{it} is lognormally distributed,

$$p(x|\theta_t) = \frac{1(x>0)}{2\pi\theta_{2t}x}\exp\left(\frac{-(\log x - \theta_{1t})^2}{2\theta_{2t}^2}\right),$$

the population aggregate $Y(Q_t)$ can be written as

$$Y(Q_t) = F\left[\frac{\delta_1 + \sigma_2\theta_t + \delta_3 \rho_t}{\sqrt{1+\delta_2^2\theta_{2t}^2}}\right] = \Lambda(\theta_t, \rho_t, \gamma),$$

where F is the standard normal cumulative, as shown by McFadden and Reid (1975). In terms of the previous characteristic aggregates,

$$\mu_t = \left(\mathrm{E}(x_{it}), P_t^{-1}(\tfrac{1}{2})\right) = \left(\mathrm{mean}(x_{it}), \mathrm{median}(x_{it})\right),$$

of Example 1, the function Φ_t relating $Y(Q_t)$ to $\gamma_0 \equiv (\delta_1, \delta_2, \delta_3)$ and μ_t is

$$Y(Q_t) = F\left[\frac{\delta_1 + \delta_2 \log \mu_{2t} + \delta_3 p_t}{\sqrt{1+\delta_2^2 2(\log \mu_{1t} - \log \mu_{2t})}}\right] = \Phi_t(\mu_t, \rho_t, \gamma).$$

Other examples of aggregated economic models with discrete, censored, or truncated data or other inherent nonlinearities can easily be devised. The examples above are informative in two respects: first, they demonstrate the feasibility of the estimation approach we propose [in particular, the calculation of the function $Y_t(Q_t) = \Phi_t(\mu_t, \rho_t, \gamma)$ for a population aggregate], and second, they show how this setup differs from the usual 'representative agent' methodology applied to aggregate data. The 'representative agent' assumption, applied to the demand example above, would suggest estimation of γ by

$$\tilde{\gamma}_w = \arg\min \sum_{t=1}^{T} w_t\left(\overline{Y}_t - F_t(\overline{X}_t, \gamma)\right)^2, \tag{2.12}$$

where $F_t(x_{it}, \gamma) = \mathrm{E}_t(y_{it}|x_{it}, \rho_t, \gamma)$, which was derived in the example above. It is clear from the example above that consistency of $\tilde{\gamma}_w$ would require either linearity of F_t in x_{it} or $x_{it} = \overline{X}_t$ in general, neither of which is true in the example above [for more detailed consideration of identification of γ in such circumstances, see Stoker (1984)].

3. Large sample properties of weighted least squares using empirical aggregates

This section presents the major assumptions and results of the paper, on consistency, asymptotic normality and asymptotic efficiency of the weighted least squares estimator (2.11). All results are conditional on the values $\{\rho_t, t = 1, \ldots, T\}$.

3.1. Consistency and asymptotic normality

For convenience, we summarize the discussion of the previous section in the following assumptions:

Assumption 1. For each group t $(t=1,\ldots,T)$, N_t underlying observations (y_{it}, x_{it}, u_{it}), $i=1,\ldots,N_t$, are generated from the behavioral relation

$$y_{it}=f(x_{it}, u_{it}, \rho_t; \delta_0)$$

and i.i.d. draws of (x'_{it}, u_{it}) according to the probability law

$$\Pr((x'_{it}, u_{it})\in A)=\int 1((x', u)\in A)\,g_t(u|x, \rho_t, \sigma_0)\,p_t(x|\rho_t, \theta_t)\,\mathrm{d}\lambda,$$

for λ-measurable $f(\cdot)$ and A, and for $\gamma_0\equiv(\delta_0', \sigma_0')'$ a fixed, finite-dimensional vector of unknown parameters.

Assumption 2. For each group $t=1,\ldots,T$, the individual observations are summarized by empirical aggregates $\hat{Y}_t=Y(\hat{Q}_t)$ and $\hat{X}_t=X(\hat{P}_t)$, where Y and X are functionals defined on the space of distribution functions of y_{it} and x_{it}, respectively, and $\hat{Q}_t$ and $\hat{P}_t$ are empirical distribution functions for $(y_{it}$, $i=1,\ldots,N_t)$ and $(x_{it}$, $i=1,\ldots,N_t)$, respectively.

Assumption 3. The population aggregates $Y_t(Q_t)$ and $X_t(P_t)$ satisfy the relation

$$Y_t(Q_t)=\Phi_t(\mu_t, \rho_t, \gamma_0), \qquad X_t(P_t)=\mu_t,$$

where the functional form of Φ_t is known for each t, and where Q_t and P_t are the marginal d.f.'s of y_{it} and x_{it} in group t.

To demonstrate strong consistency of the weighted least squares estimator $\hat{\gamma}_w$ of (2.11) as $N_t\to\infty$, we impose further regularity conditions on the unknown parameters, the aggregation functionals, and the group weights.

Assumption 4. The parameter vector γ_0 is an element of a compact parameter space Γ.

Assumption 5. The aggregation functionals Y and X are Fisher consistent at Q_t and P_t for each t; i.e., if $\hat{Q}_t$ and $\hat{P}_t$ converge weakly to Q_t and P_t, then $Y(\hat{Q}_t)\to Y(Q_t)$ and $X(\hat{P}_t)\to X(P_t)$.

Assumption 6. For each t, the function $\Phi_t(\mu, P_t, \gamma)$ is continuous in γ for any μ, and Φ is continuous at μ_t uniformly in $\gamma \in \Gamma$, i.e.,

$$\sup_{\gamma \in \Gamma} |\Phi_t(\mu, \rho_t, \gamma) - \Phi_t(\mu_t, \rho_t, \gamma)| \to 0 \quad \text{as} \quad \|\mu_t - \mu\| \to 0.$$

Assumption 7. The (possibly stochastic) weights $\{\hat{w}_t\}$ converge almost surely (as $N_t \to \infty$) to some non-negative constants $\{w_t\}$.

Assumption 8. If $\gamma \neq \gamma_0$, $\gamma \in \Gamma$, then

$$\sum_{t=1}^{T} w_t (\Phi_t(\mu_t, \rho_t, \gamma) - \Phi_t(\mu_t, \rho_t, \gamma_0))^2 > 0,$$

where the weights $\{w_t\}$ are given in Assumption 7.

Considering each of these conditions in turn, Assumption 4 is typically imposed in such non-linear estimation problems as considered here; with the continuity of Φ_t in γ (given in Assumption 6), it ensures the existence and measurability of γ_w, and is imposed in the lemma we use to show strong consistency. Assumption 5 and the uniform convergence (with probability one) of $\hat{Q}_t$ and $\hat{P}_t$ to Q_t and P_t imply the almost sure convergence of $\hat{Y}_t$ and $\hat{X}_t$ to their respective population aggregates, as noted by Rao (1973, p. 346). Assumptions 6 and 7 allow us to demonstrate the uniform almost-sure convergence of the WLS minimand to the sum given in Assumption 8.

Assumption 8 implies that γ is identified by the aggregate data, so that the unique values of the behavioral parameters can be estimated. The identification condition in Assumption 8 is a stronger version of the notion of a 'complete aggregation structure' introduced in Stoker (1984) [which, in this context, would require only that $\Phi_t(\mu, \rho_t, \gamma_1) - \Phi_t(\mu, \rho_t, \gamma_0)$ not be identically zero in μ for any $\gamma_1 \neq \gamma_0$].

With these preliminary conditions, strong consistency of $\hat{\gamma}_w$ is easily demonstrated.

Theorem 3.1. Under Assumptions 1–7, the estimator $\hat{\gamma}_w$ of γ_0 is strongly consistent, i.e., if

$$N \equiv \min\{N_t,\ t = 1, \ldots, T\},$$

and

$$\hat{\gamma}_w = \arg\min_{\gamma \in \Gamma} \sum_{t=1}^{T} \hat{w}_t (\hat{Y}_t - \Phi_t(\hat{X}_t, \rho_t, \gamma))^2 \equiv \arg\min_{\gamma \in \Gamma} S_N(\gamma),$$

then $\hat{\gamma}_w \to \gamma_0$ a.s. as $N \to \infty$.

Proof. As noted above, Assumptions 2 and 5 and the Glivenko–Cantelli lemma imply $\hat{X}_t \to \mu_t$ and $\hat{Y}_t \to \Phi_t(\mu_t, \rho_t, \gamma_0)$ a.s. as $N \to \infty$, and $\hat{w}_t \to w_t$ by Assumption 7. Writing

$$S(\gamma) = \sum_{t=1}^{T} w_t (\Phi_t(\mu_t, \rho_t, \gamma_0) - \Phi_t(\mu_t, \rho_t, \gamma))^2, \tag{3.1}$$

we clearly have

$$\sup_{\gamma \in \Gamma} |S_N(\gamma) - S(\gamma)| \to 0 \quad \text{a.s. as} \quad N \to \infty, \tag{3.2}$$

since, for example,

$$\sup_{\gamma \in \Gamma} \sum_{t=1}^{T} \hat{w}_t (\Phi_t(\hat{X}_t, \rho_t, \gamma) - \Phi_t(\mu_t, \rho_t, \gamma))^2 \to 0,$$

by Assumption 6 and the strong consistency of $\hat{X}_t$ and $\hat{w}_t$. Because γ_0 uniquely minimizes $S(\gamma)$ by Assumption 8, Lemma 2 of Amemiya (1973) yields the almost sure convergence of $\hat{\gamma}_w$ to γ_0.

Before turning to conditions for asymptotic normality of $\hat{\gamma}_w$, we should reiterate the essential difference between this approach and the usual demonstration of consistency of extremum estimators. By taking T fixed as $N \to \infty$, we can write the estimator $\hat{\gamma}_w$ as a fixed, continuous function of $\{(\hat{Y}_t, \hat{X}_t', \rho_t, \hat{w}_t)\}$ for suitably large N, so consistency of $\hat{\gamma}_w$ follows from consistency of these aggregates and the properties of the function defining $\hat{\gamma}_w$. In contrast, the usual approach would have the minimized S_N and the resulting estimator $\hat{\gamma}_w$ varying with the sample size T, requiring stronger conditions (such as bounded moments of the aggregates $\hat{Y}_t$ and $\hat{X}_t$) to establish strong convergence. Indeed, taking N_t fixed for all t and assuming $T \to \infty$, we would not expect $\hat{\gamma}_w$, as defined above, to be consistent if Φ_t is non-linear in $\hat{X}_t$. The appropriate regression function in the latter case would not be Φ_t but $\mathrm{E}_t(\hat{Y}_t | \hat{X}_t, \rho_t)$, which, in addition to the computational problems noted section 2, would in general involve the distribution parameters μ_t if the behavioral function f of Assumption 1 were non-linear in (x_{it}, u_{it}). Consistent estimation in this context would appear to require an instrumental variables approach or strong restrictions on the incidental parameters $\{\mu_t\}$.

To show asymptotic normality of the estimator $\hat{\gamma}_w$, we further restrict the model with the following conditions:

Assumption 9. The parameter vector γ_0 is an interior point of the parameter space Γ.

Assumption 10. The empirical aggregates $\hat{Y}_t$ and $\hat{X}_t$ are of the form

$$\hat{Y}_t = \Phi_t(\mu_t, \rho_t, \gamma_0) + \frac{1}{N_t}\sum_{i=1}^{N_t} \xi_t(y_{it}, \mu_t, \rho_t, \gamma_0) + o_p\left(1/\sqrt{N_t}\right)$$

$$\equiv \Phi_t(\mu_t, \rho_t, \gamma_0) + \frac{1}{N_t}\sum_{i=1}^{N_t} \xi_{it} + o_p\left(1/\sqrt{N_t}\right),$$

and

$$\hat{X}_t = \mu_t + \frac{1}{N_t}\sum_{i=1}^{N_t} \zeta_t(x_{it}, \rho_t, \mu_t) + o_p\left(1/\sqrt{N_t}\right)$$

$$\equiv \mu_t + \frac{1}{N_t}\sum_{i=1}^{N_t} \zeta_{it} + o_p\left(1/\sqrt{N_t}\right),$$

with

$$\mathrm{E}_t(\xi_{it}, \zeta_{it}') = 0,$$

$$\mathrm{E}_t\begin{bmatrix}\xi_{it}\\ \zeta_{it}\end{bmatrix}(\xi_{it}, \zeta_{it}') \equiv \Sigma_t \equiv \begin{bmatrix}\sigma_{yy} & \Sigma_{yx}\\ \Sigma_{xy} & \Sigma_{xx}\end{bmatrix}_t.$$

Assumption 11. The function $\Phi_t(\mu, \rho_t, \gamma)$ is continuously differentiable in μ and γ at $\mu = \mu_t$, $\gamma = \gamma_0$, for each t.

Assumption 12. For $N = \min\{N_t, t = 1, \ldots, T\}$,

$$\lim_{N\to\infty} (N/N_t) = \kappa_t \in (0, 1] \quad \text{for each } t.$$

Of these additional conditions, only Assumption 10 requires further elaboration. This assumption requires the aggregation functionals Y_t and X_t to be sufficiently regular to admit a Taylor's series expansion at Q_t and P_t; the functions $\xi_t(y, \mu_t, \rho_t, \gamma_0)$ and $\zeta_t(x, \rho_t, \mu_t)$ are then the influence curves associated with $\hat{Y}_t$ and $\hat{X}_t$ [see Huber (1981, ch. 1)]. When $Y(\cdot)$ and $X(\cdot)$ are expectation operators, the representation in Assumption 10 is trivial, while if $\hat{Y}_t = \text{median}\{y_{it}, i = 1, \ldots, N_t\}$, for example, it can be shown that

$$\hat{Y}_t = \Phi_t(\mu_t, \rho_t, \gamma_0) + \frac{1}{N_t}\sum_{i=1}^{N_t} [2\phi_t(\mu_t, \rho_t, \gamma_0)]^{-1}$$

$$\times \operatorname{sgn}(y_{it} - \Phi_t(\mu_t, \rho_t, \gamma_0)) + o_p\left(1/\sqrt{N_t}\right), \tag{3.3}$$

if y_{it} is continuously distributed with positive density at $\Phi_t(\mu_t, \rho_t, \gamma_0) = Q_t^{-1}(\frac{1}{2})$, where $\phi_t(\mu_t, \rho_t, \gamma_0)$ is the density value at Φ_t.

Theorem 3.2. Under Assumptions 1–12, the weighted least squares estimator $\hat{\gamma}_w$ *is asymptotically normal,*

$$\sqrt{N}(\hat{\gamma}_w - \gamma_0) \xrightarrow{d} \mathrm{N}(0, M^{-1}VM^{-1}) \quad \text{as} \quad N \to \infty,$$

where

$$M = \sum_{t=1}^{T} w_t \left[\frac{\partial \Phi_t}{\partial \gamma} \cdot \frac{\partial \Phi_t}{\partial \gamma'} \bigg|_{\mu_t, \rho_t, \gamma_0} \right],$$

$$V = \sum_{t=1}^{T} w_t^2 \kappa_t (v_t' \Sigma_t v_t) \left[\frac{\partial \Phi_t}{\partial \gamma} \cdot \frac{\partial \Phi_t}{\partial \gamma'} \bigg|_{\mu_t, \rho_t, \gamma_0} \right],$$

for w_t, κ_t *and* σ_t *defined above and*

$$v_t' \equiv \left(1, -\frac{\partial \Phi_t}{\partial \mu'} \bigg|_{\mu_t, \rho_t, \gamma_0} \right).$$

Proof. We first note that, for each t,

$$\sqrt{N} \begin{bmatrix} \hat{Y}_t - \Phi_t(\mu_t, \rho_t, \gamma_0) \\ \hat{X}_t - \mu_t \end{bmatrix} \xrightarrow{d} \mathrm{N}(0, \kappa_t \cdot \Sigma_t), \tag{3.4}$$

independently across t, by application of the Lindeberg–Levy central limit theorem. Since γ_0 is interior to Γ and $\hat{\gamma}_w \to \gamma_0$ a.s. by Theorem 1, the first-order condition,

$$0 = \sum_{t=1}^{T} \hat{w}_t (\hat{Y}_t - \Phi_t(\hat{X}_t, \rho_t, \gamma_w)) \frac{\partial \Phi_t}{\partial \gamma} \bigg|_{\hat{X}_t, \rho_t, \hat{\gamma}_w}, \tag{3.5}$$

must be satisfied for all N suitably large by the definition of $\hat{\gamma}_w$. Making a further mean-value expansion,

$$0 = \sum_{t=1}^{T} \hat{w}_t \left[\hat{Y}_t - \Phi(\mu_t, \rho_t, \gamma_0) - \frac{\partial \Phi_t}{\partial \mu_t'} \bigg|_{\mu_t^*, \rho_t, \gamma_t^*} (\hat{X}_t - \mu_t) \right.$$

$$\left. + \frac{\partial \Phi_t}{\partial \gamma'} \bigg|_{\mu_t^*, \rho_t, \gamma_t^*} (\hat{\gamma}_w - \gamma_0) \right] \left[\frac{\partial \Phi_t}{\partial \gamma} \bigg|_{\hat{X}_t, \rho_t, \hat{\gamma}_w} \right], \tag{3.6}$$

for μ_t^*, γ_t^* a convex combination of $\hat{X}_t, \hat{\gamma}_w$ and μ_t, γ_0. Since $\hat{w}_t$, $\hat{X}_t$ and $\hat{\gamma}_w$ converge a.s. to w_t, μ_t and γ_0, and the matrix M defined above is non-singular by Assumptions 8 and 11, the expression above implies

$$\sqrt{N}(\hat{\gamma}_w - \gamma_0) = M^{-1} \sum_{t=1}^{T} w_t \sqrt{N} \left[(\hat{Y}_t - \Phi_t(\mu_t, \rho_t, \gamma_0)) - \left.\frac{\partial \Phi_t}{\partial \mu'}\right|_{\mu_t, \rho_t, \gamma_0} (\hat{X}_t - \mu_t) \right] \left[\left.\frac{\partial \Phi_t}{\partial \gamma}\right|_{\mu_t, \rho_t, \gamma_0} \right] + o_p(1), \quad (3.7)$$

by the continuous differentiability of Φ_t. The result then follows by the usual properties of the multivariate normal distribution.

3.2. *First-order equivalence of weighted least squares and minimum distance estimation*

It is easy to see in general how the efficiency of the weighted least squares estimator $\hat{\gamma}_w$ can be maximized through judicious choice of weights $\{\hat{w}_t\}$ [see eq. (4.6)]. In this section we compare the large sample behavior of $\hat{\gamma}_w$ to a broader class of 'minimum distance' estimators, such as the maximum likelihood estimator $\hat{\gamma}_w$ of (2.10) above. Under appropriate conditions, it will be shown that such estimators will be first-order equivalent to a weighted least squares estimator, with weights depending upon the form of the minimand defining the estimator. An interesting result is that the corresponding estimators of μ_t need not be first-order equivalent to $\hat{X}_t$, even though the estimator of γ_0 is first-order equivalent to some $\hat{\gamma}_w$ which implicitly uses $\mu_t = \hat{X}_t$ in its construction.

Initially, we restrict attention to a narrower class of estimators than one which includes maximum likelihood, namely, estimators of γ_0 and $\mu_0 = (\mu_1, \dots, \mu_T)'$ defined by

$$\begin{bmatrix} \tilde{\gamma} \\ \tilde{\mu} \end{bmatrix} = \underset{\gamma, \mu}{\arg\min} \sum_{t=1}^{T} \nu_t(\hat{Y}_t, \hat{X}_t, \rho_t, \gamma, \mu), \quad (3.8)$$

where the $\{\nu_t(\cdot)\}$ are fixed 'distance functions' with properties to be specified below. The maximum likelihood estimator of (2.10) is not in this class, since its 'distance function' depends upon the group sample size N_t as well as the group index t; however, we will extend our results to include this case as well.

We impose the following conditions on the parameter vector μ_0 and the criterion functions $\{\nu_t\}$:

Assumption 13. The vector μ_0 of true characteristic aggregates is an interior point of a compact parameter space M.

Assumption 14. For each t and all $\gamma \in \operatorname{int} \Gamma$, $\mu \in \operatorname{int} M$,

$$\begin{aligned} \nu_t(y, x, \rho_t, \gamma, \mu) &= 0 \quad \text{if} \quad y = \Phi_t(\mu, \rho_t, \gamma) \quad \text{and} \quad x = \mu, \\ &> 0 \quad \text{otherwise.} \end{aligned}$$

Assumption 15. The $\{\nu_t\}$ are fixed functions which are twice continuously differentiable in their arguments.

Assumption 16. Under Assumptions 1 through 12, the minimum distance estimators $\tilde{\gamma}$ and $\tilde{\mu}$ are $\sqrt{N}$-consistent, i.e., $\sqrt{N}(\tilde{\gamma} - \gamma_0) = O_p(1)$ and $\sqrt{N}(\tilde{\mu} - \mu_0) = O_p(1)$.

The points $\{\mu_t\}$ are assumed to be interior points of M in Assumption 13 so that Taylor's series arguments are applicable; compactness of M is not used in the theorem which follows, but is needed to extend the results when the distance functions depend upon N_t. Assumption 14 makes more precise the sense in which $\nu_t(\cdot)$ reflects the 'distance' between the population aggregates $(Y(Q_t), X(P_t))$ and any arbitrary (y, x), while Assumption 15 permits criterion functions to be approximated by a quadratic form in a neighborhood of the true values $(y, x, \gamma, \mu) = (\Phi_t(\mu_t, \rho_t, \gamma_0), \mu_t, \gamma_0, \mu_t)$. Finally, Assumption 16 restricts attention to minimum distance estimators which are interesting alternatives to $\hat{\gamma}_w$, ruling out superefficient or inconsistent estimators; the condition is imposed in lieu of a list of assumptions which would imply it, since our objective is only to show that such estimators are of weighted least squares form asymptotically.

We note that $\hat{\gamma}_w$ and the $\{\hat{X}_t\}$ are not in the class of minimum distance estimators defined here unless the weights $\hat{w}_t$ are fixed and non-stochastic, and the functions $\Phi_t(\mu, \rho_t, \gamma)$ are twice differentiable, in which case

$$\nu_t(y, x, \rho_t, \gamma, \mu) = \hat{w}_t(y - \Phi_t(x, \rho_t, \gamma))^2 + \|x - \mu\|^2 \tag{3.9}$$

would generate $\tilde{\gamma} = \gamma_w$ and $\tilde{\mu}_t = \hat{X}_t$ in (4.1).

Theorem 3.3. Under Assumptions 1–16, the minimum distance estimator $\tilde{\gamma}$ of γ_0 given by (3.8) is first-order equivalent to a weighted least squares estimator,

$$\sqrt{N}(\tilde{\gamma} - \hat{\gamma}_w) = o_p(1),$$

where $\hat{\gamma}_w$ is of the form (2.11) with weights proportional to

$$w_t = \frac{\partial^2 \nu_t}{\partial y^2} + \frac{\partial^2 \nu_t}{\partial y\, \partial \mu'} \left[\frac{\partial^2 \nu_t}{\partial \mu\, \partial \mu'} \right]^{-1} \frac{\partial^2 \nu_t}{\partial \mu\, \partial y},$$

with the derivatives being evaluated by

$$(y, x, \rho_t, \gamma, \mu) = \left[\Phi_t(\mu_t, \rho_t, \gamma_0), \mu_t, \rho_t, \gamma_0, \mu_t \right].$$

Proof. Let H denote the matrix of second partials of $\nu_t(y, x, \rho_t, \gamma, \mu)$ with respect to y, x, γ and μ evaluated at $[\Phi_t(\mu_t, \rho_t, \gamma_0), \mu_t, \rho_t, \gamma_0, \mu_t]$. Since $\nu_t(\Phi_t(\mu, \rho_t, \gamma), \rho_t, \mu, \gamma, \mu) = 0$ identically in γ and μ, H must satisfy the restrictions

$$\begin{bmatrix} \partial \Phi_t / \partial \gamma & 0 & I_1 & 0 \\ \partial \Phi_t / \partial \mu & I_k & 0 & I_k \end{bmatrix} H = 0, \tag{3.10}$$

where the derivatives are evaluated at μ_t, ρ_t and γ_0, $k = \dim(\mu_t)$, $1 = \dim(\gamma)$, and I_m is the identity matrix of order m. We denote the various component submatrices of H by a double subscript, e.g.,

$$H_{\mu\gamma} = \left. \frac{\partial^2 \nu_t}{\partial \mu\, \partial \gamma'} \right|_{(\Phi_t(\mu_t, \rho_t, \gamma_0), \mu_t, \rho_t, \gamma_0, \mu_t)}, \quad \text{etc.}$$

With this notation, we observe that, with arbitrarily high probability, the minimum distance estimators must satisfy the first-order condition

$$0 = \sum_{t=1}^{T} \frac{\partial \nu_t}{\partial \gamma} (\hat{Y}_t, \hat{X}_t, \rho_t, \tilde{\gamma}, \tilde{\mu}_t), \tag{3.11}$$

for N suitably large. Making a mean-value expansion of the left-hand side of (3.11) at the limiting values, we have

$$0 = \sum_{t=1}^{T} \left[H_{\gamma y} \sqrt{N} (\hat{Y}_t - \Phi_t(\mu_t, \rho_t, \gamma_0)) + H_{\gamma x} \sqrt{N} (\hat{X}_t - \mu_t) \right.$$

$$\left. + H_{\gamma\gamma} \sqrt{N} (\tilde{\gamma} - \gamma_0) + H_{\gamma\mu} \sqrt{N} (\tilde{\mu}_t - \mu_t) \right] + o_p(1), \tag{3.12}$$

where the convergence of the remainder term to zero in probability follows from the continuity of the Hessian matrix and the $\sqrt{N}$-consistency of $\hat{Y}_t$, $\hat{X}_t$, $\tilde{\gamma}$

and $\tilde{\mu}_t$. Now, using the restrictions given in (3.10),

$$0=\sum_{t=1}^{T} H_{yy}\left[\frac{\partial\Phi_t}{\partial\gamma}\right]\left[\sqrt{N}\,(\hat{Y}_t-\Phi_t(\mu_t,\rho_t,\gamma_0)) - \frac{\partial\Phi_t}{\partial\mu'}\sqrt{N}\,(\hat{X}_t-\mu_t)-\frac{\partial\Phi_t}{\partial\gamma'}(\tilde{\gamma}-\gamma_0)\right] + \sum_{t=1}^{T}\frac{\partial\Phi_t}{\partial\gamma}H_{y\mu}\sqrt{N}\,(\hat{X}_y-\tilde{\mu}_t)+\mathrm{o}_p(1), \tag{3.13}$$

where, as always, all derivative are evaluated at the true values.

To obtain an expression for the term involving $(\hat{X}_t-\tilde{\mu}_t)$, we use the first-order conditions for $\tilde{\mu}_t$,

$$\begin{aligned}0&=\frac{\partial\nu_t}{\partial\mu}(\hat{Y}_t,\hat{X}_t,\rho_t,\tilde{\gamma},\tilde{\mu}_t),\\ &=H_{\mu y}\sqrt{N}\,(\hat{Y}_t-\Phi_t(\mu_t,\rho_t,\gamma_0))+H_{\mu x}\sqrt{N}\,(\hat{X}_t-\mu_t)\\ &\quad+H_{\mu\gamma}\sqrt{N}\,(\tilde{\gamma}-\gamma_0)+H_{\mu\mu}\sqrt{N}\,(\hat{X}_t-\tilde{\mu}_t)+\mathrm{o}_p(1),\end{aligned} \tag{3.14}$$

which also must hold in probability for large N by Assumptions 13 and 16. Again using the total-differential restrictions of (3.10), we can express the difference $\sqrt{N}\,(\hat{X}_t-\tilde{\mu}_t)$ as

$$\sqrt{N}\,(\hat{X}_t-\tilde{\mu}_t)=H_{\mu\mu}^{-1}H_{\mu y}\left[\sqrt{N}\,(\hat{Y}_t-\Phi_t(\mu_t,\rho_t,\gamma_0))+\frac{\partial\Phi_t}{\partial\mu'}\sqrt{N}\,(\hat{X}_t-\mu_t) + \frac{\partial\Phi_t}{\partial\gamma'}\sqrt{N}\,(\tilde{\gamma}-\gamma_0)\right]+\mathrm{o}_p(1), \tag{3.15}$$

where the non-singularity of $H_{\mu\mu}$ follows from the assumed $\sqrt{N}$-consistency of $\tilde{\mu}_t$. Combining (3.12) and (3.14) yields

$$0=\sum_{t=1}^{T}\left[H_{yy}+H_{y\mu}H_{\mu\mu}^{-1}H_{\mu y}\right]\left[\frac{\partial\Phi_t}{\partial\gamma}\right] \times\left[\sqrt{N}\,(\hat{Y}_t-\Phi_t(\mu_t,\rho_t,\gamma_0)) + \frac{\partial\Phi_t}{\partial\mu'}\sqrt{N}\,(\hat{X}_t-\mu_t)+\frac{\partial\Phi_t}{\partial\gamma'}\sqrt{N}\,(\tilde{\gamma}-\gamma_0)\right]+\mathrm{o}_p(1). \tag{3.16}$$

Hence $\sqrt{N}(\tilde{\gamma}-\gamma_0)$ can be written exactly in the form of eq. (3.7) above, with

$$w_t = \left[H_{yy} + H_{y\mu}H_{\mu\mu}^{-1}H_{\mu y}\right], \tag{3.17}$$

which is non-negative by Assumptions 14 and 15.

As noted above, Theorem 3.3 applies only to estimators with distance functions which do not vary with N_t; thus, both the maximum likelihood and weighted least squares estimators are excluded from this class (the latter due to its dependence on estimated weights $\hat{w}_t$). To extend the result of Theorem 3 to the case in which the distance functions $\hat{\nu}_t(y, x, \rho_t, \gamma, \mu)$ are (possibly stochastic) functions of N_t, we impose the following conditions:

Assumption 17. The functions $\{\hat{\nu}_t\}$ are twice continuously differentiable in y, x, γ and μ (with probability one) for all N_t.

Assumption 18. The minimum distance estimators based upon $\{\hat{\nu}_t\}$ are $\sqrt{N}$-consistent.

Assumption 19. The matrix of second partials of $\hat{\nu}_t$ converges to the corresponding Hessian of some function ν_t and satisfying Assumptions 14 and 15, uniformly in $\gamma \in \Gamma$, μ and $x \in M$, and $y \in \{\Phi_t(\mu, \rho_t, \gamma)\colon \mu \in M, \gamma \in \Gamma\}$, with probability one.

Corollary 3.4. Under Assumptions 1–19, the minimum distance estimator $\tilde{\gamma}$ based upon the distance function $\hat{\nu}_t$ satisfies the conclusion of Theorem 3.3.

Proof. The expressions (3.12) and (3.14) above for $\tilde{\gamma}$ and $\tilde{\mu}_t$ are still valid, since the Hessian of $\hat{\nu}_t$ evaluated at $(\hat{Y}_t, \hat{X}_t, \rho_t, \tilde{\gamma}, \tilde{\mu}_t)$ converges in probability to H by Lemma 4 of Amemiya (1973).

This corollary extends the result of Theorem 3.3 to a much broader class of estimators, including the WLS estimator $\hat{\gamma}_w$ (which trivially satisfied the conclusion of Theorem 3.3, and now satisfies Assumptions 17–19 as well) and the maximum likelihood estimator $\hat{\gamma}$ of (2.10). Strictly speaking, application of the corollary to maximum likelihood estimation requires that the log density, $\log d_t(\hat{Y}_t, \hat{X}_t | \gamma, \mu, \rho_t, N_t)$, can be transformed into a distance function $\nu_t(\hat{Y}_t, \hat{X}_t, \rho_t, \gamma, \mu)$ satisfying Assumptions 17–19 through proper normalization (e.g., multiplication by $-N^{-1/2}$); while we suspect such a transformation is feasible for most applied problems, it is beyond the scope of this paper to provide sufficient conditions for equivalence of maximum likelihood and minimum distance estimation because of the generality of the aggregates $\hat{Y}_t$ and $\hat{X}_t$ considered.

An interesting aspect of Theorem 3.3 is that the asymptotic distributions of $\tilde{\mu}_t$, the minimum distance estimators of the population aggregates, and $\hat{X}_t$, the empirical characteristic aggregate, need not coincide. Eq. (3.15) implies

$$\sqrt{N}\,(\hat{X}_t - \tilde{\mu}_t) = \sqrt{N}\,(\hat{Y}_t - \Phi_t(\hat{X}_t, \rho_t, \tilde{\gamma}))\,\alpha_t + o_p(1), \tag{3.18}$$

where

$$\alpha_t = \left[\partial^2 \nu_t / \partial\mu\, \partial\mu'\right]^{-1} \left[\partial^2 \nu_t / \partial\mu\, \partial y\right].$$

That is, the estimators $\tilde{\mu}_t$ may exploit the dependence of the distribution of $\hat{Y}_t$ (as well as $\hat{X}_t$) on the population characteristics μ_t in its estimation. For maximum likelihood estimates, it is clear that α_t will equal zero if $\hat{X}_t$ is a sufficient statistic for μ_t, as it will, for example, if $\hat{X}_t = \bar{X}_t$ and the distributions of the characteristics x_{it} are in the exponential family given in (4.5); the likelihood function will then factor into the sum of the conditional log likelihood of $\hat{Y}_t$ given $\hat{X}_t$ and γ (which will not depend on μ_t by sufficiency) and the marginal log density of $\hat{X}_t$ given μ_t. In general, though, when $\hat{X}_t$ is not (locally) sufficient for μ_t – that is, when the ζ_{it} are not the scores corresponding to maximum likelihood estimation of μ_t based upon cross-section data – we may expect the optimal α_t to differ from zero for estimation of the population characteristic vector.

Finally, we note that the results in this and the previous section do not depend upon the special form of the empirical aggregates $\hat{Y}_t = Y(\hat{Q}_t)$ and $\hat{X}_t = X(\hat{P}_t)$ assumed here; all that is required for Theorems 3.1, 3.2 and 3.3 are the consistency and asymptotic normality (or order $\sqrt{N}$) of the aggregates $\hat{Y}_t$ and $\hat{X}_t$ about $\Phi_t(\mu_t, \rho_t, \gamma_0)$ and μ_t respectively. Thus, for example, the results will still hold if $\hat{Y}_t$ is constructed from a stratified sample of the $\{y_{it}\}$, with stratification on the basis of the characteristics $\{x_{it}\}$. We have chosen to focus on the more restrictive forms of $\hat{Y}_t$ and $\hat{X}_t$ because they represent the most common type of aggregate available, that is, simple averages or percentiles from marginal tabulations of $\{y_{it}\}$ and $\{x_{it}\}$. It should be clear that more efficient aggregates could be computed given the original micro-data and knowledge of the micro model (Assumption 1); in such a case, though, no aggregation problem would be present, and the usual results on efficiency of maximum likelihood estimation of γ_0 would apply.

4. Related discussion

This section presents discussion on three topics related to the general estimation results of section 3. We begin by interpreting features of the asymptotic distribution of the weighted least squares estimator vis-a-vis cross-section (microeconomic) regression statistics. We then discuss practical issues associated with the consistent estimation of the variance–covariance matrix of the weighted least squares estimator. Finally, we raise the additional estimation issues inherent to models with random common factors ρ_t, indicating the import of our results to this case.

4.1. Relation to cross-section regression

It is clear from the development of section 3 that $v_t'\Sigma_t v_t$ (normalized by N_t^{-1}) is the relevant 'true' aggregate residual variance of departures of $\hat{Y}_t$ from $\Phi_t(\hat{X}_t, \rho_t, \gamma_0)$. In this section we point out how $v_t'\Sigma_t v_t$ can be regarded as the residual variance from cross-section linear regression, which indicates how non-linearities in micro behavior affect the size of the aggregate residual variance.

For the remainder of this section we focus attention on a single time period t. Consider the individual i.i.d. influence terms ξ_{it} and ζ_{it} of Assumption 10, for $i=1,\dots,N_t$ (or a smaller random sample), and define

$$s_{yy}=\sum_i \xi_{it}^{*2}/N_t,\quad S_{xy}=\sum_i \zeta_{it}^{*}\xi_{it}^{*}/N_t,\quad S_{xx}=\sum_i \zeta_{it}^{*}\zeta_{it}^{*\prime}/N_t$$

as the sample covariances, with

$$S=\begin{bmatrix} s_{yy} & S_{xy}' \\ S_{xy} & S_{xx}\end{bmatrix},$$

where $\xi_{it}^{*}=\xi_{it}-\bar{\xi}_{it}$ and $\zeta_{it}^{*}=\zeta_{it}-\bar{\zeta}_{it}$ are the deviations from sample averages. By a straightforward application of the (i.i.d.) Strong Law of Large Numbers, we have that $\lim S=\Sigma_t$ a.s. under Assumptions 1, 10 and 11.

We can obtain several interpretative results by considering cross-section linear equations of the form

$$\xi_{it}^{*}=b'\zeta_{it}^{*}+u_{it},\qquad i=1,\dots N_t, \tag{4.1}$$

where b could be considered as the slope coefficient of the regression of ξ_{it} on ζ_{it} which includes a constant term. We denote the OLS coefficient estimates as $\hat{\beta}_t=(S_{xx})^{-1}S_{xy}$, and $\beta_t=\lim\hat{\beta}_t=(\Sigma_{xx,t})^{-1}\Sigma_{xy,t}$. Of special interest is the large sample residual variance from (4.1), which we denote as the almost sure limit $\sigma(b)=\lim(\sum(\xi_{it}^{*}-b'\zeta_{it}^{*})^2/N_t)$. Clearly $\sigma(b)$ is minimized at $b=\beta_t$, and we denote the minimum as $\sigma(\beta_t)=\tilde{\sigma}$.

The first interpretative result is available by direct computation – namely, under Assumptions 1, 10 and 11,

$$\sigma\left[\left.\frac{\partial\Phi}{\partial\mu}\right|_{\mu_t,\rho_t,\gamma_0}\right]=v_t'\Sigma_t v_t.$$

Consequently, $v_t'\Sigma_t v_t$ can be viewed as the cross-section variance of the difference $\xi_{it}^* - \partial\Phi/\partial\mu|_{\mu_t,\rho_t,\gamma_0}\zeta_{it}^*$, or as the large sample residual variance of eq. (4.1) where b is set to $b = \partial\Phi/\partial\mu|_{\mu_t,\rho_t,\gamma_0}$, the macroeconomic effects.

Of more interest is the condition under which $v_t'\Sigma_t v_t = \tilde{\sigma}$, or that $v_t'\Sigma_t v_t$ represents the (least squares) cross-section residual variance of ξ_{it} regressed on ζ_{it}. In view of the above observation, an obvious sufficient condition occurs when $\lim \hat{\beta}_t = \beta_t = \partial\Phi/\partial\mu|_{\mu_t,\rho_t,\gamma_0}$, or when $\hat{\beta}_t$ consistently estimates the macroeconomic effects. This property is studied extensively by Stoker (1982, 1983). We state the following proposition, which easily follows from the development of Stoker (1983).

Theorem 4.1. Under Assumptions 1–6, 10 and 11, a sufficient condition for $v_t'\Sigma_t v_t = \tilde{\sigma}$ *occurs when the influence functions* $\zeta_t(x, \rho_t, \mu)$ *can be written as*

$$\zeta_t(x, \rho_t, \mu) = B(\mu, \rho_t) l(x, \rho_t, \mu), \tag{4.2}$$

for all x and for μ *in a neighborhood of* μ_0, *where* $B(\mu)$ *is a non-singular matrix and* $l(x, \rho_t, \mu)$ *is the score vector,*

$$l(x, \rho_t, \mu) = \frac{\partial \ln \tilde{p}(x|\mu_t, \rho_t)}{\partial\mu}. \tag{4.3}$$

Condition (3.12) is valid (locally) if and only if the aggregate $\hat{X}_t$ *is a (locally) efficient estimator of* μ_t.

Thus the true aggregate residual variance $v_t'\Sigma_t v_t$ coincides with the linear cross-section residual variance when $\zeta(x, \rho_t, \mu)$ is (locally) collinear with the score $l(x, \mu)$. In particular, when $B(\mu)$ is the inverse of the information matrix $I = \mathrm{E}(ll'|\mu)$, as in

$$\zeta(x, \rho_t, \mu) = (I_\mu)^{-1} l(x, \rho_t, \mu), \tag{4.4}$$

then we have $\lim \hat{\beta}_t = \beta_t = \partial\Phi/\partial\mu|_{\mu_t,\rho_t,\gamma_0}$. Moreover, the score condition is associated with the efficiency properties of the consistent aggregate $\hat{X}_t$, being globally valid when $\hat{X}_t$ is efficient (and hence a sufficient statistic) for μ. The condition holds locally if and only if $\hat{X}_t$ is locally sufficient and efficient in a neighborhood of $\mu = \mu_t$. While we do not provide proof here, it is easy to see that if $\hat{X}_t$ is consistent and locally efficient for μ, then the influence function can be written in the restricted form (4.4).

The sufficient conditions of Theorem 4.1 are of interest because they characterize the aggregate residual variance $v_t'\Sigma_t v_t$ as a cross-section OLS residual variance, regardless of the true form of the micro behavioral model $y_{it} = f(x_{it}, u_{it}, \rho_t)$. Thus, when the aggregates $\hat{X}_t$ are efficient estimators of the parameters μ_t, the aggregate residual variance $v_t'\Sigma_t v_t = \sigma(\beta_t)$ does not depend on whether the cross-section OLS residuals $\xi_{it}^* - \beta_t'\zeta_{it}^*$ arise from structural non-linearities of f_t in x_{it} or from random disturbances. While other sufficient conditions can be found, they will necessarily depend on restrictions on the functional form of micro behavior $y_{it} = f(x_{it}, u_{it}, \rho_t)$, such as conditions which would imply that ξ_{it} is a linear function of ζ_{it} plus an independent disturbance.

For motivation, it may be useful to consider these interpretations when the aggregates $\hat{X}_t$ and $\hat{Y}_t$ are simple averages of the respective micro variables. For $\hat{X}_t = \bar{X}_t = \sum x_{it}/N_t$, (4.2) is valid (locally) if and only if $p(x|\mu)$ is (locally) in exponential family form with driving variables x:

$$\tilde{p}(x|\mu, \rho_t) = c(\mu, \rho_t) h(x, \rho_t) \exp[\pi(\mu)'x]. \tag{4.5}$$

In this case $\zeta_{it} = x_{it} - \mu_t$ and $\hat{\beta}_t$ is the OLS slope coefficient vector of ξ_{it} regressed on x_{it}. When in addition, $\hat{Y}_t = \bar{Y}_t = \sum y_{it}/N_t$, we have $\xi_{it} = y_{it} - \Phi_t(\mu_t, \rho_t, \gamma_0)$, so that $\hat{\beta}_t$ is the OLS slope coefficient of y_{it} regressed on x_{it}, and $\tilde{\sigma} = v_t'\Sigma_t v_t$ is the large sample residual variance from the regression.

4.2. Estimation of the asymptotic covariance matrix

The proof of Theorem 3.2 shows that, for large N, the estimator $\hat{\gamma}_w$ behaves like γ_0 plus a weighted linear regression of the 'quasi-residuals' $\{\sqrt{N}[\hat{Y}_t - \Phi_t(\mu_t, \rho_t, \gamma_0) - (\hat{X}_t - \mu_t)'\partial\Phi_t(\mu_t, \rho_t, \gamma_0)/\partial\mu]\}$ on the vectors $\{\partial\Phi_t(\mu_t, \rho_t, \gamma_0)/\partial\gamma\}$. If κ_t and $v_t'\Sigma_t v_t$ were known (or could be consistently estimated as $N \to \infty$), an efficient choice of weights $\{\hat{w}_t\}$ (in the Gauss–Markov sense) would satisfy

$$\lim_{N\to\infty} \frac{\hat{w}_t}{\hat{w}_s} = \left[\frac{\kappa_s v_s'\Sigma_s v_s}{\kappa_t v_t'\Sigma_t v_t}\right]^{1/2}, \quad \text{a.s.} \tag{4.6}$$

In some circumstances, the matrices $\{\Sigma_t\}$ will be completely determined by the unknown behavioral parameters γ_0, the population characteristic aggregates $\{\mu_t\}$ (e.g. in Example 2 of section 2 above) and the common variables P_t. In this situation, when ρ_t is observed, construction of optimal weights $\hat{w}_t$ using $\Sigma_t = \Sigma_t(\hat{X}_t, \hat{\gamma}_w)$ is straightforward. In other cases, knowledge of the population aggregates $\{Y(Q_t)\}$ and $\{X(P_t)\}$ will be insufficient to determine the elements of $\{\Sigma_t\}$. In the continuous demand example of section 2, the covariance matrices $\{\Sigma_t\}$ involve the unknown variance σ_0^2 of the unobserved heterogeneity terms $\{u_{it}\}$; this parameter is clearly unidentified given only the location parameters of the data, i.e., given only the population means of $\{y_{it}\}$ and the population means and medians of $\{x_{it}\}$. In general, dependence of the distribution of y_{it} on unknown nuisance parameters not included in γ_0 inhibits not only construction of efficient weights but also consistent (for T fixed) estimation of the covariance matrix of $\hat{\gamma}_w$, which will depend upon these nuisance parameters (through Σ_t).

Consistent estimation of the covariance matrix of $\hat{\gamma}_w$ in this situation does appear feasible if T, the number of aggregation groups, also tends to infinity with N, the minimum group size. While we do not explore the details here, it seems reasonable to expect that the nuisance parameters in Σ_t can be consistently estimated using method-of-moments estimation applied to the 'between group' averages of squared values of the residuals $\sqrt{N}(\hat{Y}_t - \Phi_t(\hat{X}_t, \rho_t, \gamma_w)) \equiv \hat{e}_t$, whose limiting distributions have covariances involving Φ_t, μ_t, γ_0, and the nuisance parameters. Alternatively, following Eicker (1967) and White (1980), we could estimate V, the matrix given in the statement of Theorem 3.2, by

$$\hat{V} = \sum_{t=1}^{T} \hat{w}_t \left[\frac{N_t}{N}\right] \hat{e}_t^2 \left[\frac{\partial \Phi_t}{\partial \gamma} \cdot \frac{\partial \Phi_t}{\partial \gamma'}\bigg|_{\hat{X}_t, \rho_t, \hat{\gamma}_w}\right], \tag{4.7}$$

for $\hat{e}_t$ defined above and $\{\hat{w}_t\}$ a given (not necessarily optimal) set of weights. Because the proofs of Theorems 3.1 and 3.2 used the assumption of fixed T, the foregoing results cannot immediately be generalized to permit $T \to \infty$; still, the results seem very likely to hold in this case, with further regularity conditions, and we conjecture that, under such conditions,

$$\operatorname*{plim}_{T \to \infty} T^{-1}[\hat{V} - V] = 0, \tag{4.8}$$

provided $T/N \to 0$ as $T \to \infty$, so that large sample inference on γ_0 will be feasible if the number of groups is large.

4.3. Estimating models with unobserved common variables

As indicated in section 2, our results only strictly apply conditional on the value of the common factor ρ_t, or, from a practical standpoint, when ρ_t is observed. Here we discuss the implications for estimation when components of ρ_t are random and unobserved, although it is beyond the scope of this paper to introduce the additional formal assumptions required for a rigorous treatment. The asymptotic properties of the estimators using empirical aggregates and unobserved factors discussed below will require not only large populations ($N_t \to \infty$ for all t), but also a large number of groups ($T \to \infty$).

We begin by reinterpreting Theorems 3.1 and 3.2 in regression form as follows. The basic structural model is given by the aggregate function (2.7); here repeated as

$$Y(Q_t) = \Phi_t(X(Q_t), \rho_t, \gamma). \tag{4.9}$$

Theorems 3.1 and 3.2 can be reinterpreted to say that, for the purposes of estimation, the model for the empirical aggregates can be written as

$$\hat{Y}_t = \Phi_t(\hat{X}_t, \rho_t, \gamma) + \hat{\varepsilon}_t, \tag{4.10}$$

where the 'disturbance' $\hat{\varepsilon}_t$ has variance $v_t' \Sigma_t v_t / N_t$, with the efficient weighted least squares estimator just the standard non-linear regression estimator that accounts for the variance of $\hat{\varepsilon}_t$.

We confine the discussion of random common effects to the case where there is a single random component of ρ_t; namely $\rho_t = (\rho_t^{\mathrm{o}}, \omega_t)$, where ρ_t^{o} is observed and ω_t is distributed with mean 0 and finite variance. Suppose first that ω_t is an additive error in the individual behavioral eq. (2.1), so that

$$y_{it} = f(x_{it}, \mu_{it}, \rho_t; \delta) \equiv f^{\mathrm{o}}(x_{it}, \mu_{it}, \rho_t^{\mathrm{o}}; \delta) + \omega_t, \tag{4.11}$$

and further that ω_t does not effect the distribution of (x_{it}, μ_{it}) in group t. If the aggregation functional is a location measure for Q_t – that is, $Y(Q_t^*) = Y(Q_t) + a$ if $Q_t^*(\lambda) = Q_t(\lambda - a)$ – then the original aggregate function takes the form

$$Y(Q_t) = \Phi_t^{\mathrm{o}}(X(P_t), \rho_t^{\mathrm{o}}, \gamma) + \omega_t, \tag{4.12}$$

so that the estimation eq. (4.10) can be written as

$$\hat{Y}_t = \Phi_t^{\mathrm{o}}(\hat{X}_t, \rho_t^{\mathrm{o}}, \gamma) + \hat{\varepsilon}_t + \omega_t, \tag{4.13}$$

unconditional on the value of ρ_t, where equality is in the large population sense of (4.10), and $\hat{\varepsilon}_t$ and ω_t are uncorrelated in the same sense (since $\hat{\varepsilon}_t$ arises from within group variations). Thus, γ could be estimated by weighted least squares. When ω is uncorrelated over time, the proper weights (for efficiency) are proportional to $1/[(v_t' \Sigma_t v_t / N_t) + \operatorname{var}(\omega_t)]$. If ω_t represents a autocorrelated process over groups t, further efficiency gains are available from recognizing the induced correlations in $\hat{\varepsilon}_t + \omega_t$ in the weighting, as in generalized (non-linear) least squares.

In this case, our results imply that common additive unobserved factors can be incorporated into estimation by using standard techniques. The precise asymptotic distribution of the above estimator will depend on the relative rates of increase of N_t for all t and T, a complication which does not raise new conceptual issues but is beyond the scope of the paper.

It should be noted that we have not provided sufficient foundation to claim that weighted non-linear regression provides an overall first-order efficient estimator for large N_t and T in this case. To see the problem, note first that the likelihood function in (2.10) represents the conditional log density of $\hat{Y}_t$ and $\hat{X}_t$ given ρ_t for all t, and that we could combine this with a marginal density of ω_t

to obtain an overall likelihood function, say by assuming that ω_t is normally distributed; and obtain an overall first-order efficient estimation by maximum likelihood under standard conditions. To establish first-order efficiency for non-linear regression, it appears that one would need that the conditional density of $\hat{Y}_t$ and $\hat{X}_t$ in group t to converge to a normal density for large N_t. While the conditional distribution of $\hat{Y}_t$ and $\hat{X}_t$ in group t converges to a normal distribution, convergence of the density to normality is not necessary, and to assume it would be to assume away the interesting and subtle features of the estimation problem. Our introduction of arbitrary distance functions in section 3.3 is intended to establish general features of the estimation problem in lieu of results on the exact structure of the likelihood function for large group sizes N_t for all t.

An additional theoretical complication is introduced if ω_t appears nonadditively in the behavioral equation, so that the equation analogous to (4.13) is

$$\hat{Y}_t = \Phi_t^{\mathrm{o}}(\hat{X}_t, \rho_t^{\mathrm{o}}, \omega_t, \gamma) + \hat{\varepsilon}_t. \tag{4.14}$$

In this case, non-linear least squares can no longer be used to obtain consistent estimates of the γ parameters, since the Jacobian of the transformation from $(\hat{\omega}_t, \hat{\varepsilon}_t)$ to $(\hat{Y}_t, \hat{X}_t)$ is no longer unity. If $\hat{Y}_t = \bar{Y}_t$, the regression function for $\hat{Y}_t$ is the conditional expectation of $\hat{Y}_t$ given $\hat{X}_t$, ρ_t and γ; estimation in this context thus requires more explicit characterization of the distribution of the common characteristics ρ_t than we have heretofore assumed.

5. Conclusion

The theorems of this paper provide the theoretical basis for estimation and large sample inference on microeconomic behavioral parameters using observed aggregate data. Viewed in a broader context, the results imply that the most difficult step in constructing and implementing models of aggregate data (that properly account for individual heterogeneity) is the construction of the appropriate aggregate function, in that estimation is possible by straightforward non-linear regression techniques. In other words, the aggregate function will embody all appropriate heterogeneity influences, including stratified sample problems, and once specified, no additional concerns are raised for consistent estimation. Moreover, efficient minimum distance estimation is possible from the proper choice of weights.

A possible objection to this framework concerns the importance of the errors associated with using empirical aggregates relative to common unobserved factors, or in the notation of section 4.3, the size of $\hat{\varepsilon}_t$ relative to ω_t. Of course, this is an empirical issue in general; however, our results for ρ_t known are likely more appropriate for applications with cross-section aggregates (counties, states, industries, etc. as groups). For macroeconomic applications, where

N_t can be extremely large, $\hat{\varepsilon}_t$ may be dominated by the common factor ω_t, which can be used to naturally capture observed time series residual correlation. On this point, we mention two reservations. First, there is some evidence that much of the observed autocorrelation in aggregate data can be explained by properly accounting for individual heterogeneity (distributional) influences [Stoker (1984b)]. Second, many macroeconomic series are themselves constructed from random sampling – for example U.S. unemployment statistics arise from samples of 5,000–10,000 observations – so that the sample size N_t may not be nearly as large as the population size in the economy.

We have indicated the most natural extension of this work in section 4.3, namely to estimation with common unobserved factors. A second extension is to incorporate autocorrelated individual disturbances (u_{it}), as suggested by the interpretation that individual disturbances represent demographic attributes that do not vary dramatically over time. The issues here apply to efficiency, as the consistency of weighted least squares would not be affected. A third extension concerns how to incorporate endogeneity of predictor variables at the micro or macro level, which is natural in simultaneous equations modeling. Our results are currently applicable to estimating reduced form equations under such circumstances.

References

Amemiya, T., 1973, Regression analysis when the dependent variable is truncated normal, Econometrica 41, 997–1016.

Bishop, Y.M.M., S.E. Fienberg and P.W. Holland, 1975, Discrete multivariate analysis: Theory and practice (M.I.T. Press, Cambridge, MA).

Deaton, A. and J. Muellbauer, 1980, An almost ideal demand system, American Economic Review 70, 312–326.

Eicker, F., 1967, Limit theorems for regressions with unequal and dependent errors, Proceedings of the Fifth Berkeley Symposium 1, 59–82.

Huber, P.J., 1981, Robust statistics (Wiley, New York).

Jorgenson, D.W., L.J. Lau and T.M. Stoker, 1982, The transcendental logarithmic model of aggregate consumer behavior, in: R. Basmann and G. Rhodes, eds., Advances in econometrics (JAI Press, Greenwich, CT).

McFadden, D. and F. Reid, 1975, Aggregate travel demand forecasting from disaggregated behavioral models, Transportation Research Record, no. 534.

Muellbauer, J., 1975, Aggregation, income distribution and consumer demand, Review of Economic Studies 42, 525–543.

Rao, C.R., 1973, Linear statistical inference and its applications, 2nd ed. (Wiley, New York).

Stoker, T.M., 1982, The use of cross-section data to characterize macro functions, Journal of the American Statistical Association 77, 369–380.

Stoker, T.M., 1983, Aggregation, efficiency, and cross section regression, Econometrica, forthcoming.

Stoker, T.M., 1984a, Completeness, distribution restrictions and the form of aggregate functions, Econometrica 52, 887–908.

Stoker, T.M., 1984b, Simple tests of distributional effects on macroeconomic equations, Sloan School of Management paper no. 1529-84 (M.I.T., Cambridge, MA).

White, H., 1980, A heteroskedasticity-consistent covariance matrix estimator and a direct test for heteroskedasticity, Econometrica 48, 817–838.

COMPARISON OF ALTERNATIVE FUNCTIONAL FORMS IN PRODUCTION*

Peter E. ROSSI

Northwestern University, Evanston, IL 60201, USA

In this paper, a Bayesian approach to choosing between two non-nested multivariate regression systems is developed. The Bayesian approach involves the calculation of the posterior probabilities of alternative hypotheses and formation of a posterior odds ratio. Specific results are obtained for the comparison of a multivariate regression and seemingly unrelated regression model. These odds ratio results are applied to the choice between translog and Fourier flexible form cost share equation systems. When calculated for aggregate U.S. manufacturing cost data, the odds ratios favor the Fourier flexible form over the translog form. Even in small samples, the Fourier series expansion appears to be an effective approximation technique.

1. Introduction

In recent years, a wealth of different production models have been proposed by applied econometricians. Analysis of multi-input and multi-output firms has required more flexible functional forms than the traditional Cobb–Douglas and CES production functions. The process of obtaining a viable econometric specification of a system of factor demand equations has been considerably simplified by results in modern duality theory. In order to formulate an integrable demand system, a cost function is postulated and differentiated to obtain the associated system of conditional factor demand equations. The applied analyst is faced with a bewildering array of possible functional forms for cost relationships, each with its own set of advocates and 'desirable' approximation properties. The aim of this paper is to provide guidance in the choice of flexible functional forms by developing a statistical test of the relative flexibility and predictive accuracy of alternative functional forms.

By far the most popular flexible functional form used in applied demand analysis is the translog form proposed by Christensen, Jorgenson and Lau (1971). The translog form for a cost function, $c(\boldsymbol{p}, y)$ (here $\boldsymbol{p}$ is the vector of factor prices and y is output), is based on a second-order Taylor series expansion of the underlying log cost function in terms of the log of factor

*Financial support from the Alfred Sloan Foundation is gratefully acknowledged. The comments of Bruce Hill, David Hinckley, Arnold Zellner and an anonymous referee were extremely helpful in improving earlier drafts of this paper.

prices and log output. The associated system of conditional factor demands can be written as a system of cost share equations which are linear in the log of factor price. Closely related to the translog functional form are the generalized Leontief form proposed by Diewert (1972) and the miniflex Laurent functional form proposed by Barnett (1983). Both the miniflex Laurent and generalized Leontief functional forms should be viewed as second-order approximations to the underlying cost function.

Considerable effort has been devoted to examining the flexibility of functional forms based on second-order approximation methods. Caves and Christensen (1980) and Barnett and Lee (1984) have examined regular regions for the translog, generalized Leontief and miniflex Laurent forms of the indirect utility function. Guilkey and Lovell (1980) perform Monte Carlo simulation experiments to determine if the translog form is capable of approximating production technologies with both complementarity and substitutability of production factors. These studies of the theoretical properties of various functional forms reveal the limitations of local approximation methods; there is nothing to guarantee that these second-order forms will approximate the underlying cost function or its derivatives over a region of the price space. Moreover, there is no theoretical reason for restricting the approximation to second-order terms in a power series expansion. In fact, as more data is accumulated it might be desirable to increase the order of the series approximation to include third- or higher-order terms. Of course, the addition of higher-order terms would dramatically increase the number of unknown parameters which must be estimated. Thus, to provide guidance to the applied demand analyst we must determine which approximation methods provide the most flexibility at the least cost, as measured by the number of parameters. A purely theoretical exercise involving the tracing out of the regular region cannot determine which approximation method provides the best complexity–flexibility trade-off.

Gallant (1982) suggests that uniform methods of functional approximation may be the most appropriate for the approximation of cost functions. Gallant proves that a multivariate Fourier series approximation can uniformly approximate the true cost function and its derivatives. By increasing the length of the Fourier series expansions and the number of directions in which expansions are taken, the Fourier flexible form (hereafter, denoted FFF) proposed by Gallant can uniformly approximate the cost function and conditional factor demands over some cube in the price space. This method of approximation requires the number of parameters to increase with the sample size. Increased flexibility is achieved through a significant increase in the number of parameters and, therefore, it is not clear that the FFF provides a practical approximation method in the small samples encountered in most production work. Typically, investigators use econometric specifications in which there are some five to ten observations per parameter.

We will focus on the specification of cost functions and systems of cost share equations, restricting our attention to a comparison of the translog and FFF. Other flexible functional forms such as the miniflex Laurent form proposed by Barnett (1983) could easily be compared to the translog and FFF using the procedures developed here. Once a particular functional form has been postulated for the cost function, the associated system of cost share equations can be derived by applying Shephard's Lemma [see, for example, Varian (1978) for details]. In the case of the translog and Fourier flexible forms, the associated system of cost shares is linear in the parameters. Choice between translog and Fourier flexible forms is thus reduced to the choice between two non-nested multivariate regression systems of cost share equations. In this analysis, the cost function will not be appended to the system of cost share equations. Bayesian hypothesis-testing methods are developed for the choice between alternative functional forms. These Bayesian procedures do not involve large sample approximations and contain an explicit trade-off between the number of parameters and the goodness of fit.

2. The translog cost share system

A number of authors have used a translog cost function to analyze the properties of the aggregate U.S. production technology. In most studies [see Rossi (1984) for discussion and references], a three-input, non-homothetic cost function is postulated for U.S. aggregate manufacturing data. We use U.S. aggregate manufacturing data for the period 1947–1971 first collected and used by Berndt and Wood (1975).

$$\begin{aligned}\ln C = {} & \alpha_0 + \delta_0 \ln y + \alpha_L \ln P_L + \alpha_K \ln P_K + \alpha_M \ln P_M \\ & + \tfrac{1}{2}\gamma_{LL}(\ln P_L)^2 + \tfrac{1}{2}\gamma_{KK}(\ln P_K)^2 + \tfrac{1}{2}\gamma_{MM}(\ln P_M)^2 \\ & + \gamma_{ML} \ln P_M \ln P_L + \gamma_{KL} \ln P_K \ln P_L + \gamma_{MK} \ln P_M \ln P_K \\ & + \delta_L \ln y \ln P_L + \delta_K \ln y \ln P_K + \delta_M \ln y \ln P_M, \end{aligned} \tag{1}$$

where P_L = price of labor, P_K = price of capital, P_M = price of materials, C = total factor cost, and y = output. Differentiating (1) and applying Shephard's lemma, a system of translog cost share equations is obtained:

$$S_L = \alpha_L + \delta_L \ln y + \gamma_{LL} \ln P_L + \gamma_{KL} \ln P_K + \gamma_{ML} \ln P_M, \tag{2a}$$

$$S_K = \alpha_K + \delta_K \ln y + \gamma_{LK} \ln P_L + \gamma_{KK} \ln P_K + \gamma_{MK} \ln P_M, \tag{2b}$$

$$S_M = \alpha_M + \delta_M \ln y + \gamma_{LM} \ln P_L + \gamma_{KM} \ln P_K + \gamma_{MM} \ln P_M, \tag{2c}$$

where S_L = cost share of labor = $P_L L/C$, S_K = cost share of capital = $P_K K/C$, S_M = cost share of materials = $P_M M/C$. Since we are interested in the relative flexibility of functional forms, homogeneity and symmetry are not imposed as exact restrictions. Imposing homogeneity and symmetry would considerably complicate the computation of the test statistics for discriminating between alternative functional forms. One possibility not explored here is to impose these constraints in a stochastic sense through the prior specification. This approach has been taken by Ilmakunnas (1985).

In order to complete the stochastic specification of the system of cost shares, a multivariate normal disturbance is added to (2a)–(2c). Since cost shares are bounded between zero and one, the multivariate normal distribution can only serve as an approximation to the true distribution of cost shares. In Rossi (1984), an alternative logistic-normal stochastic specification for share equation systems is developed. In this study, we employ the additive normal specification. By definition, $S_L + S_K + S_M = 1$. This implies that the trivariate normal distribution of (S_L, S_K, S_M) is singular. For estimation purposes, one of the equations is dropped – S_M is arbitrarily chosen – to obtain a two-equation system.

Without imposing symmetry conditions, (2a) and (2b) can be rewritten as a system of regression equations:

$$y_1 = X\boldsymbol{\beta}_1 + \boldsymbol{\varepsilon}_1, \tag{3a}$$

$$y_2 = X\boldsymbol{\beta}_2 + \boldsymbol{\varepsilon}_2, \tag{3b}$$

$$\boldsymbol{\varepsilon}' = (\boldsymbol{\varepsilon}_1', \boldsymbol{\varepsilon}_2') \sim \mathrm{MVN}(\mathbf{0}, \Sigma \otimes I_T).$$

Here we have used the standard notation for multivariate regression in order to facilitate reference to the statistical literature. y_1 and y_2 are vectors of observations on the labor and capital shares, respectively. The X matrix contains observations on log factor prices. Writing (3a)–(3b) in matrix form,

$$Y = XB + U, \tag{4}$$

where

$$U = [\boldsymbol{\varepsilon}_1 \vdots \boldsymbol{\varepsilon}_2], \quad B = [\boldsymbol{\beta}_1 \vdots \boldsymbol{\beta}_2], \quad Y = [y_1 \vdots y_2].$$

The likelihood function for the multivariate regression model given in (4) can be written as

$$l(B, \Sigma^{-1}|Y, X)$$

$$= (2\pi)^{-T}|\Sigma^{-1}|^{T/2}\exp\{-\tfrac{1}{2}\mathrm{tr}(Y - XB)'(Y - XB)\Sigma^{-1}\}, \tag{5}$$

or, in stacked form,

$$l(\boldsymbol{\beta}, \Sigma | \boldsymbol{y}, Z)$$

$$= (2\pi)^{-T} |\Sigma^{-1}|^{T/2} \exp\{ -\tfrac{1}{2}(\boldsymbol{y} - Z\boldsymbol{\beta})'(\Sigma^{-1} \otimes I_T)(\boldsymbol{y} - Z\boldsymbol{\beta})\}, \tag{6}$$

with

$$\boldsymbol{y} = \text{vec}(Y), \quad \boldsymbol{\beta} = \text{vec}(B), \quad Z = [I_2 \otimes X].$$

3. Fourier flexible form share equation system

The Fourier flexible form can uniformly approximate the true cost function in the sense of Sobolov norm. By increasing the length of the Fourier series expansions and the number of directions in which the expansions are taken, the FFF can be made as close as possible to the true cost function as measured by Sobolov norm. The Sobolov norm measures how close the derivatives of a function as well as the function itself are approximated. This is especially important for the approximation of cost functions since the factor demand equations are obtained by computing the first derivatives of the cost function and the Allen–Uzawa elasticities of substitution involve second derivatives. The local series expansion methods which are used to derive the translog and other quasi-quadratic forms do not have these uniform approximation properties. However, the FFF cost function is parameterized by a large number of parameters even for low-dimensional systems. The sine–cosine representation of the FFF is

$$g(\boldsymbol{x}_t|\theta) = u_0 + \boldsymbol{b}'x_t + \tfrac{1}{2}\boldsymbol{x}_t'C\boldsymbol{x}_t$$

$$+ \sum_{\alpha=1}^{A} \{ u_{0\alpha} + 2[u_{1\alpha}\cos(\boldsymbol{k}_\alpha'\boldsymbol{x}_t) - v_{1\alpha}\sin(\boldsymbol{k}_\alpha'\boldsymbol{x}_t)]\}, \tag{7}$$

with

$$\boldsymbol{b}' = (\boldsymbol{c}', b_{M+1}), \quad \boldsymbol{k}_\alpha' = (\boldsymbol{r}_\alpha', k_{0\alpha}), \quad \boldsymbol{S}_t' = (S_{L,t}, S_{K,t}, S_{M,t}).$$

$\boldsymbol{x}_t$ is a scaled vector consisting of both the log input price vector and output at time t. $\boldsymbol{x}_t$ is scaled so that each element lies between 0 and 2π, $\boldsymbol{x}_t' = [(\ln \boldsymbol{p}_t - \boldsymbol{\delta})'/\lambda, (\ln y - \delta_0)/\lambda]$. The matrix of the quadratic form, C, can be written

$$C = \sum_{\alpha=1}^{A} u_{0\alpha}\boldsymbol{k}_\alpha\boldsymbol{k}_\alpha'.$$

Table 1

Multi-indices for the Fourier flexible cost function.[a]

L	1	0	0	0	1	1	0
K	0	1	0	0	−1	0	1
M	0	0	1	0	0	−1	−1
y	0	0	0	1	0	0	0
$\alpha =$	1	2	3	4	5	6	7

[a] $A = 7,\ K = \Sigma_i |k_{\alpha,i}| \le 2.$

The FFF can be viewed as a quadratic approximation with an appended set of univariate Fourier expansions along the directions, $\boldsymbol{k}_\alpha$. In this analysis, the length of the Fourier expansions in directions $\boldsymbol{k}_\alpha$, which Gallant denotes by J, is taken to be 1. Note that the matrix of the quadratic form is parameterized by A parameters instead of the usual $M(M+1)/2$ parameters. This parameterization reduces the number of parameters in the FFF and simplifies the expressions for the derivatives of the FFF. In addition, this method of parameterizing the matrix of the quadratic form prevents the nesting of the translog from within the FFF. The $\{\boldsymbol{k}_\alpha, \alpha = 1,2,\ldots, A\}$ are the set of multi-indices which determine the directions along which the Fourier expansions are taken. Table 1 presents the set of multi-indices used in this paper. Homogeneity restrictions are not imposed on the FFF cost function by ruling out multi-indices with $\boldsymbol{k}'_\alpha \boldsymbol{\iota}^* \neq 0\ [\boldsymbol{\iota}^{*\prime} = (\boldsymbol{\iota}', 0)]$.

Differentiation of g in (7) yields the system of FFF cost share equations

$$\boldsymbol{S}_t = \boldsymbol{c} - \sum_{\alpha=1}^{A} \{ u_{0\alpha} \boldsymbol{k}'_\alpha \boldsymbol{x}_t + 2[u_{1\alpha} \sin(\boldsymbol{k}'_\alpha \boldsymbol{x}_t) + v_{1\alpha} \cos(\boldsymbol{k}'_\alpha \boldsymbol{x}_t)] \} \boldsymbol{r}_\alpha. \tag{8}$$

Eq. (8) can be written as

$$\boldsymbol{S}_t = X_t \boldsymbol{\theta},$$

where $\boldsymbol{\theta}' = (\boldsymbol{c}', u_{01}, \ldots, u_{0A}, u_{11}, \ldots, u_{1A}, v_{21}, \ldots, v_{2A})$ is a $M + 3A = 3 + 21 = 24$ tuple (M is the number of inputs in the system).

Appending an additive multivariate normal error term to (8), a system of regression equations is obtained. Again, the standard statistical notation is employed where $\boldsymbol{y}_t$ is the vector of cost shares for each factor at time t and X_t is the matrix of transformed factor prices at time t:

$$\boldsymbol{y}_t = X_t \boldsymbol{\theta} + \boldsymbol{\varepsilon}_t, \qquad \boldsymbol{\varepsilon}_t \sim \text{MVN}(0, \Sigma). \tag{9}$$

Rearranging (9) and imposing the adding-up constraint, a system of seemingly unrelated regression equations is obtained. In our three-input case, the labor and capital cost share equations form a two-equation seemingly unrelated regression model:

$$y_1 = X_1\boldsymbol{\theta} + \varepsilon_1, \tag{10a}$$

$$y_2 = X_2\boldsymbol{\theta} + \boldsymbol{\varepsilon}_2. \tag{10b}$$

Note that the coefficient vector is constrained to be the same in both share equations. It is more convenient to write the system (10a)–(10b) in the stacked form

$$y = Z\boldsymbol{\theta} + \boldsymbol{\varepsilon}, \qquad \boldsymbol{\varepsilon} \sim \text{MNV}(\mathbf{0}, \Sigma \otimes I_T), \tag{11}$$

with

$$y' = (y_1', y_2'), \quad Z' = [X_1' \vdots X_2'], \quad \boldsymbol{\varepsilon}' = (\boldsymbol{\varepsilon}_1', \boldsymbol{\varepsilon}_2').$$

The likelihood function for (11) is

$$l(\boldsymbol{\theta}, \Sigma^{-1} | y, Z)$$
$$= (2\pi)^{-T} |\Sigma^{-1}|^{T/2} \exp\{\tfrac{1}{2}(y - Z\boldsymbol{\theta})'(\Sigma^{-1} \otimes I_T)(y - Z\boldsymbol{\theta})\}. \tag{12}$$

4. Methods of comparison of non-nested hypotheses

Comparison of the translog and FFF cost share systems involve a comparison of two non-nested multivariate regressions. Statistical procedures for comparing these two methods of approximation and the associated multivariate models should be designed to gauge which model provides a better approximation to some underlying cost function. Since both of these models should be regarded as approximations to an unknown cost function, we should not require that one of the models be the 'true' model which has generated the data. Further, these testing procedures should not be sensitive to the assignment of models to the maintained and alternative hypothesis and should not rely on tenuous asymptotic approximation methods.

Most of the work in econometrics on non-nested models can be traced to the seminal article of Cox (1961). Cox proposes three approaches to the problem of choice between alternative families of data densities: (1) the Bayesian approach which Cox regards as self-evident, (2) a generalized likelihood ratio testing approach, and (3) an exponential weighting method of nesting alternative distributions. Over the last decade, many workers in econometrics have been quick to take up Cox's second and third suggestions and apply these methods to a wide variety of testing problems see, for example, the special issue of the Journal of Econometrics, *Annals of Applied Econometrics 1983-1*, edited by Halbert White on non-nested models. Lagrange multiplier tests based on the exponential mixing model have been advocated by Pesaran and Deaton (1978). Hinckley and Runger (1984) analyze the 'mixing' Box–Cox model from a Bayesian perspective. Atkinson (1970) and Davidson and MacKinnon (1981) discuss the choice between alternative regression models. Aguirre-Torres and Gallant (1982) consider the distribution of the generalized likelihood ratio test for comparison of alternative multivariate regression models.

The central problem with classical approaches to non-nested hypothesis testing is the assumption that one of the models under scrutiny is the 'true' population model. In production modeling, the flexible forms are regarded as only approximations to the underlying technology. We are interested in which form provides a better approximation to the data distribution of cost shares. The Bayesian procedures developed here are specifically designed to address the approximation issue. The Bayesian approach is very much in the spirit of Efron's (1984) comparison of the mean squared errors for competing linear regression models.

Other key problems with the classical approach stem from the artificial designation of models as the maintained or 'null' and the alternative model. The assignment of models to the null and alternative hypothesis dramatically influences the outcomes of non-nested hypothesis-testing procedures. This sensitivity is due to the asymmetry of the Neyman–Pearson approach to hypothesis testing. Type I and type II errors should be regarded symmetrically in the comparison of non-nested hypotheses. The 'accept/reject' philosophy of classical testing procedures is also difficult to adapt to hypothesis-testing problems in economics. Very rarely do we have enough sample evidence to either conclusively affirm or reject a particular model or restriction. Instead, we accumulate a body of evidence from many different studies as to the adequacy of any particular model. Testing procedures should provide a method of aggregating information across many diverse studies.

Most classical procedures for testing non-nested hypotheses rely on asymptotic approximation methods to calculate the null distribution of proposed test statistics. The use of first-order asymptotic approximations to the null distribution of the likelihood ratio statistic may produce severe biases in favor of rejection of the null. Accounting for sampling error in the estimation of the share equation covariance matrix is a problem which is ignored in the use of first-order methods.

Few econometricians, however, have utilized Cox's first suggestion, the Bayesian approach. The Bayesian procedures outlined below do not suffer from the shortcomings associated with classical tests of non-nested hypotheses. Calculation of the Bayesian posterior odds ratios has only recently been made feasible by the introduction of a tractible prior specification and the availability of efficient procedures for the numerical evaluation of multiple integrals.

5. Posterior odds ratios

The two hypotheses under consideration are:

H_1: The cost share system is translog.
H_2: The cost share system is FFF.

In the Bayesian approach to hypothesis evaluation, the posterior probabilities of the hypotheses are compared. The posterior probabilities represent the weight of prior belief and sample evidence for a particular hypothesis. The posterior probabilities of hypotheses can be conveniently summarized in the posterior odds ratio:

$$K_{12}=\frac{p(H_1|D)}{p(H_2|D)}=\frac{p(D|H_1)}{p(D|H_2)}\cdot\frac{p(H_1)}{p(H_2)},$$

where D stands for the data. It should be noted that it is not necessary for the set of hypotheses to exhaust the possibilities. We do not require that $p(H_1)+p(H_2)=1$. The posterior odds ratio is designed to evaluate the relative merits of two models without assuming that these models are necessarily the only appropriate models. The quantity, $p(H_1)/p(H_2)=\Pi_{12}$, is called the prior odds ratio and is taken to be 1:1 in this study. The posterior odds ratio can be applied to non-nested hypotheses without modification, unlike the likelihood ratio testing procedure. In addition, the posterior odds ratio is completely symmetric and the decision outcomes are not dependent on which hypothesis is considered the 'maintained hypothesis'.

For parametric models, the posterior odds ratio can be expressed as the ratio of predictive densities of the data for each of the two models:

$$K_{12}=\frac{\int p_1(D,\phi_1)\,\mathrm{d}\phi_1}{\int p_2(D,\phi_2)\,\mathrm{d}\phi_2}\cdot\Pi_{12}=\frac{\int p_1(D|\phi_1)p_1(\phi_1)\,\mathrm{d}\phi_1}{\int p_2(D|\phi_2)p_2(\phi_2)\,\mathrm{d}\phi_2}\cdot\Pi_{12}.$$

$p_1(D|\phi_1)$ is the data density under H_1 and $p_2(D|\phi_2)$ is the data density under H_2. Π_{12} is the prior odds ratio. By integrating out the parameters from the joint distribution of the data and the parameters, we obtain the predictive density of the data for each of the two models. The posterior odds ratio is the ratio of the predictive densities evaluated at the observed data point. The predictive densities can be used as a diagnostic tool by comparing the properties of the predictive density with the data distribution. This predictive view of diagnostic checking is in the spirit of Johnson and Geisser (1983).

In the case of choice between share equation systems, the two parametric models for the translog (4) and FFF (12) can be compared using the following posterior odds ratio:

$$K_{12}=\frac{\int p_1(B,\Sigma^{-1},Y,X)\,\mathrm{d}\Sigma^{-1}\mathrm{d}B}{\int p_2(\boldsymbol{\theta},\Sigma^{-1},y,Z)\,\mathrm{d}\Sigma^{-1}\mathrm{d}\boldsymbol{\theta}}$$

$$=\frac{\int l_1(B,\Sigma^{-1}|Y,X)\,p_1(B,\Sigma^{-1})\,\mathrm{d}\Sigma^{-1}\mathrm{d}B}{\int l_2(\boldsymbol{\theta},\Sigma^{-1}|y,Z)\,p_2(\boldsymbol{\theta},\Sigma^{-1})\,\mathrm{d}\Sigma^{-1}\mathrm{d}\boldsymbol{\theta}}. \tag{13}$$

$p_1(B,\Sigma^{-1})$ and $p_2(\boldsymbol{\theta},\Sigma^{-1})$ are the prior distributions under each of the hypotheses. In order to evaluate (13), prior distributions for each set of parameters must first be specified. The key ingredients for the successful application of the posterior odds ratio is the formulation of a reasonable prior which does not unwittingly favor either of the models and a method for evaluating the integrals in (13).

5.1. Prior on (B,Σ^{-1})

We write

$$p_1(B,\Sigma^{-1})=p(B|\Sigma^{-1})\,p(\Sigma^{-1}),$$

and employ a diffuse prior on Σ^{-1} coupled with a conditional normal prior on B. Σ is the variance–covariance matrix of the cost shares. The flexible functional forms are introduced to give different specifications for the mean of cost shares. We assume that the variance–covariance matrix of cost shares has the same prior distribution under both cost share equation specifications. Since little prior information is available on Σ, the same diffuse prior is used in both the numerator and denominator of the odds ratios. Our odds ratio calculations are immune to the scaling problems sometimes encountered with the use of improper priors because any changes in the prior density of Σ under translog must also be made to the prior density of Σ under the FFF specification.

$$p(\Sigma^{-1})=|\Sigma^{-1}|^{-(2+1)/2}=|\Sigma^{-1}|^{-3/2}, \tag{14}$$

$$p(B|\Sigma^{-1})=(2\pi)^{-k}|\Sigma^{-1}|^{k/2}|A|^{1/2}\exp\{-\tfrac{1}{2}\mathrm{tr}(B-\bar{B})'A(B-\bar{B})\Sigma^{-1}\}, \tag{15}$$

where B is a $k\times 2$ matrix, Σ^{-1} is a 2×2 matrix.

The conditional normal prior on B given in (15) can also be expressed in stacked form as

$$p(\boldsymbol{\beta}|\Sigma^{-1}) = (2\pi)^{-k}|\Sigma^{-1}\otimes A|^{1/2}\exp\{-\tfrac{1}{2}(\boldsymbol{\beta}-\bar{\boldsymbol{\beta}})'(\Sigma^{-1}\otimes A)(\cdot)\},$$

with

$$\boldsymbol{\beta} = \mathrm{vec}(B) \quad \text{and} \quad \bar{\boldsymbol{\beta}} = \mathrm{vec}(\bar{B}).$$

The conditional prior mean of $\boldsymbol{\beta}$ and the elements of the A matrix must be specified.

$$\boldsymbol{\beta}' = (\alpha_L, \delta_L, \gamma_{LL}, \gamma_{KL}, \gamma_{ML}, \alpha_K, \delta_K, \gamma_{KL}, \gamma_{KK}, \gamma_{MK}).$$

We take the prior means of α_L and α_K to be the mean labor share and mean capital share, respectively. The prior mean of all other parameters are taken to be zero.

$$\bar{\boldsymbol{\beta}}' = (\bar{S}_L, \mathbf{0}', \bar{S}_K, \mathbf{0}').$$

This choice of prior mean centers the prior specification of the cost technology over the Cobb–Douglas specification with constant returns to scale.

The prior covariance of $\boldsymbol{\beta}$ is

$$\Sigma \otimes A^{-1} = \begin{bmatrix} \sigma_{11}A^{-1} & \sigma_{12}A^{-1} \\ \sigma_{21}A^{-1} & \sigma_{22}A^{-1} \end{bmatrix}.$$

The g-prior notion of Zellner (1980) can be generalized to the multivariate case by taking the A matrix to be of the form $gX'X$. We choose g small enough so that the prior standard deviation of $\boldsymbol{\beta}$ conditional on $\Sigma = I$ is 2.0. This results in a relatively non-informative or 'locally-uniform' prior. In a similar model selection problem, Klein and Brown (1984) utilize limiting arguments to construct odds ratios with 'un-informative' priors. Unfortunately, the odds ratios derived by Klein and Brown are sensitive to the way in which the limits are taken.

The g-prior introduced by Zellner has been received with some controversy. Some critics have argued that the g-prior is not appropriate because it appears to introduce a dependence of the prior on the data. The dependence of the g-prior on the data is a matter of interpretation. One can view the g-prior as coming from a previous set of observations taken with the same design matrix. One can also view the g-prior has the outcome of a prior assessment process in which the rows of the design matrix are presented to the investigator and the investigator is then asked to assess a conditional distribution of the vector of dependent variables. While this controversy over the g-prior is certain to continue for some time, the g-prior offers one of the few practical solutions to the assessment of non-diagonal prior covariance matrices. The exchangability notions of Lindley and Smith (1972) are not appropriate for cost share equation systems.

5.2. Prior on $(\boldsymbol{\theta}, \Sigma^{-1})$

For the FFF cost share system, it is specified that $(\boldsymbol{\theta}, \Sigma^{-1})$ are a priori independent. A diffuse prior on Σ^{-1} is coupled with a normal prior on $\boldsymbol{\theta}$.

$$p(\Sigma^{-1}) = |\Sigma^{-1}|^{-3/2}, \tag{16}$$

$$p(\boldsymbol{\theta}) = (2\pi)^{-l/2}|C|^{1/2}\exp\{-\tfrac{1}{2}(\boldsymbol{\theta}-\bar{\boldsymbol{\theta}})'C(\boldsymbol{\theta}-\bar{\boldsymbol{\theta}})\}, \tag{17}$$

where l is the length of the theta vector.

As in the translog prior specification, the prior mean of share equation intercepts is taken to be the mean cost shares and the prior mean of all other elements of $\boldsymbol{\theta}$ is zero. The prior precision matrix is specified in the g-prior form

$$C = fZ'Z.$$

f is chosen to keep all prior standard deviations at least 2.0. Again, a locally-uniform prior is specified.

6. Calculation of the numerator of posterior odds ratio

The numerator of the posterior odds ratio in (13) can be written as

$$\int l_1(B, \Sigma^{-1}|Y, X)\, p_1(B, \Sigma^{-1})\, \mathrm{d}\Sigma^{-1}\mathrm{d}B$$

$$= \int (2\pi)^{-2T/2}|\Sigma^{-1}|^{T/2}\exp\{-\tfrac{1}{2}\mathrm{tr}(Y-XB)'(Y-XB)\Sigma^{-1}\}$$

$$\times (2\pi)^{-k}|\Sigma^{-1}|^{(k-3)/2}|A|^{1/2}$$

$$\times \exp\{-\tfrac{1}{2}\mathrm{tr}(B-\bar{B})'A(B-\bar{B})\Sigma^{-1}\}\, \mathrm{d}\Sigma^{-1}\mathrm{d}B.$$

Combining common terms and completing the square in the exponent.

$$= \int (2\pi)^{-(T+k)}|\Sigma^{-1}|^{(T+k-3)/2}|A|^{1/2}$$

$$\times \exp\{-\tfrac{1}{2}\mathrm{tr}[S_1 + (B-\tilde{B})(X'X+A)(\cdot)]\Sigma^{-1}\}\, \mathrm{d}\Sigma^{-1}\mathrm{d}B,$$

where

$$S_1 = (Y - X\tilde{B})'(Y - X\tilde{B}) + (\bar{B} - \tilde{B})'A(\bar{B} - \tilde{B}),$$

and

$$\tilde{B} = (X'X + A)^{-1}(X'X\hat{B} + A\bar{B}), \quad \hat{B} = (X'X)^{-1}X'Y.$$

Properties of the Wishart distribution are needed to integrate out Σ^{-1}.

$$\int l_1(B, \Sigma^{-1}|Y, X)\, p_1(B, \Sigma^{-1})\,\mathrm{d}\Sigma^{-1}\,\mathrm{d}B$$

$$\propto \int |S_1 + (B - \tilde{B})'(X'X + A)(B - \tilde{B})|^{-(T+k)/2}\,\mathrm{d}B.$$

Using properties of the matrix-t distribution [see Dickey (1967) for details] integrate out over B,

$$\text{Numerator} = C_0'|S_1|^{-T/2}|X'X + A|^{-m/2}, \tag{18}$$

where C_0' is the appropriate constant of integration.

$$C_0 = \pi^{(m(m-1)/4 - mT/2)} \prod_{i=1}^{m} \Gamma[(T - i + 1)/2]\,|A|^{1/2}.$$

7. Calculation of the denominator of posterior odds ratio

The denominator of the posterior odds ratio can be written as

$$\int l_2(\boldsymbol{\theta}, \Sigma^{-1}|\, y, Z)\, p(\boldsymbol{\theta})\, p(\Sigma^{-1})\,\mathrm{d}\Sigma^{-1}\,\mathrm{d}\boldsymbol{\theta}$$

$$= \int (2\pi)^{-T}|\Sigma^{-1}|^{T/2}\exp\{-\tfrac{1}{2}(y - Z\boldsymbol{\theta})'(\Sigma^{-1} \otimes I_T)(y - Z\boldsymbol{\theta})\}$$

$$\times (2\pi)^{-l/2}|\Sigma^{-1}|^{-3/2}|C|^{1/2}\exp\{-\tfrac{1}{2}(\boldsymbol{\theta} - \bar{\boldsymbol{\theta}})'C(\boldsymbol{\theta} - \bar{\boldsymbol{\theta}})\}\,\mathrm{d}\Sigma^{-1}\,\mathrm{d}\boldsymbol{\theta}.$$

Completing the square and collecting terms,

$$= \int\int K_0 \exp\{-\tfrac{1}{2}(s_1 + (\boldsymbol{\theta} - \tilde{\boldsymbol{\theta}})'(Z'(\Sigma^{-1} \otimes I)Z + C)(\boldsymbol{\theta} - \tilde{\boldsymbol{\theta}})\}\,\mathrm{d}\boldsymbol{\theta}\,\mathrm{d}\Sigma^{-1},$$

where

$$\tilde{\boldsymbol{\theta}} = \left(Z'(\Sigma^{-1} \otimes I)Z + C\right)^{-1}\left(Z'(\Sigma^{-1} \otimes I)Z\hat{\boldsymbol{\theta}} + C\bar{\boldsymbol{\theta}}\right),$$

$$\hat{\boldsymbol{\theta}} = \left(Z'Z\right)^{-1}Z'\boldsymbol{y},$$

$$s_1 = (\boldsymbol{y} - Z\tilde{\boldsymbol{\theta}})'(\Sigma^{-1} \otimes I)(\boldsymbol{y} - Z\tilde{\boldsymbol{\theta}}) + (\bar{\boldsymbol{\theta}} - \tilde{\boldsymbol{\theta}})'C(\bar{\boldsymbol{\theta}} - \tilde{\boldsymbol{\theta}}).$$

Well-known properties of the normal distribution can be used to integrate out over $\boldsymbol{\theta}$. However, the integral with respect to Σ^{-1} above does not have an analytical solution. The integral can be approximated by conditioning on $\Sigma^{-1} = \hat{\Sigma}^{-1}$. Another alternative, which will be explored below, is to compute the integral over the three unique elements of Σ using numerical integration techniques.

$$\text{Denominator} \doteq \int K_0 \exp\left\{-\tfrac{1}{2}\left[\hat{s}_1 + (\boldsymbol{\theta} - \tilde{\tilde{\boldsymbol{\theta}}})'\right.\right.$$
$$\left.\left.\times\left(Z'(\hat{\Sigma}^{-1} \otimes I)Z + C\right)(\cdot)\right]\right\} \mathrm{d}\boldsymbol{\theta},$$

with

$$\hat{s}_1 = (\boldsymbol{y} - Z\tilde{\tilde{\boldsymbol{\theta}}})'(\hat{\Sigma}^{-1} \otimes I)(\boldsymbol{y} - Z\tilde{\tilde{\boldsymbol{\theta}}})' + (\bar{\boldsymbol{\theta}} - \tilde{\tilde{\boldsymbol{\theta}}})'C(\bar{\boldsymbol{\theta}} - \tilde{\tilde{\boldsymbol{\theta}}}),$$

$$\tilde{\tilde{\boldsymbol{\theta}}} = \left(Z'(\hat{\Sigma}^{-1} \otimes I)Z + C\right)^{-1}\left(Z'(\hat{\Sigma}^{-1} \otimes I)Z\hat{\boldsymbol{\theta}} + C\tilde{\boldsymbol{\theta}}\right),$$

and

$$\text{Denominator} \doteq K_0'|Z'(\hat{\Sigma}^{-1} \otimes I)Z + C|^{1/2}, \tag{19}$$

where

$$K_0 = (2\pi)^{-T}|\hat{\Sigma}^{-1}||C|^{1/2}\exp\left\{-\tfrac{1}{2}\hat{s}_1\right\}.$$

8. Results of posterior odds calculations

By combining the formula for the numerator, eq. (18), and the approximate result for the denominator in (19), odds ratios to compare the translog and FFF for aggregate U.S. manufacturing can be computed. These approximate expressions for the numerator and denominator contain two important terms – the determinant of the prior precision matrices and the determinant of the residual sum of squares matrices for each of the cost share specifications. The posterior odds ratio depends chiefly on three characteristics about each model: (1) the complexity of the model as measured by the number of parameters, (2) the goodness of fit as measured by the generalized variance of residuals, and (3) the amount of prior information available for each model.

In order to evaluate the adequacy of the approximate integral results for the denominator, numerical techniques are used to compute the three-dimensional integral over Σ^{-1}. The approximate integral, computed by conditioning on $\Sigma^{-1}=\hat{\Sigma}^{-1}$, may be sensitive to the choice of a conditioning matrix. The sensitivity of the odds ratios depends on the posterior distribution of Σ^{-1}. If the posterior distribution is tightly concentrated over $\hat{\Sigma}^{-1}$, then the error in the approximation of the integral in the denominator of the odds ratio will be small.

A variety of numerical integration techniques are available for multiple integrals. The univariate quadrature methods have been extended to multiple integrals with some limited success. Even for three-dimensional integrals, quadrature techniques may not be feasible due to the large number of functional evaluations required to achieve a desired level of accuracy.

Monte Carlo numerical integration techniques view the integral as taking the expected value of the integrand relative to some measure. Points in the region of integration are sampled according to some probability distribution and a simple sample average of the integrand evaluated at the sampled points is taken. Standard Monte Carlo integration techniques use an 'importance' function to sample points in the region of integration. Usually, the importance function is taken to be an elliptically symmetric density based on the asymptotic form of the integrand. For example, Zellner and Rossi (1984) use a multivariate Student t importance function. The integrand involved cannot be well approximated by an elliptically symmetric surface. To compute the integral over the elements of Σ non-standard Monte Carlo integration techniques due to Friedman and Wright (1982) are employed. The Friedman–Wright procedure breaks up the region of integration into hyper-rectangles within which the variation in the integrand is minimized. Points are sampled uniformly within each of the regions and then averaged [see Zellner and Rossi (1984) for a detailed comparison with other Monte Carlo techniques]. It should be emphasized that this problem has been made tractable by the use of analytical integration wherever possible. The dimension of the integral which must be computed numerically is very small relative to the dimension of the model parameter space.

Table 2 shows the odds ratios for H_1: translog vs. H_2: FFF as calculated for aggregate U.S. manufacturing data. The odds ratio calculations in parentheses are the result of using the approximate results in the text. The approximate and exact results agree quite closely. It appears that the integral in the denominator of the odds ratio is not very sensitive to choices of a conditioning value for Σ^{-1}. The FFF system is considered with a 'translog-like' quadratic term, $(\boldsymbol{x}_t'C\boldsymbol{x}_t)$, in the cost function and without the quadratic form. The FFF share system was found to be favored by slightly better than 3:2 odds with quadratic

Table 2

Posterior odds ratios; H_1: translog vs. H_2: Fourier flexible form.[a]

	H_1 vs.	
	H_2 with quadratic terms	H_2 without quadratic terms
K_{12}	0.69 (0.61)	0.98 (1.05)

[a]Estimated using U.S. aggregate manufacturing cost data, 1947–1971. Numbers in parentheses are odds ratios calculated using approximate integrals.

terms and by roughly 1:1 odds without quadratic terms. The conclusion is that the periodic terms resulting from the Fourier series expansion are important in providing a good approximation to the underlying cost structure.

9. Summary

In this paper, a Bayesian approach to choosing between two non-nested multivariate regression systems is developed. The Bayesian approach involves the calculation of the posterior probabilities of alternative hypotheses and formation of a posterior odds ratio. Specific results are obtained for the comparison of a multivariate regression and seemingly unrelated regression model. These odds ratio results are applied to the choice between translog and Fourier flexible form cost share equation systems. When calculated for aggregate U.S. manufacturing cost data, the odds ratios favor the Fourier flexible form over the translog form. Even in small samples, the Fourier series expansion appears to be an effective approximation technique.

References

Aquirre-Torres, V. and A.R. Gallant, 1982, The null and non-null asymptotic distribution of the Cox test for multivariate nonlinear regression alternatives and a new distribution free Cox test, Working paper (North Carolina State University, Raleigh, NC).

Atkinson, A., 1970, A method of discriminating between models, Journal of the Royal Statistical Society B 32, 323–353.

Barnett, W., 1983, New indices of the money supply and the flexible Laurent demand system, Journal of Business and Economic Statistics 1, 7–23.

Barnett, W. and Y. Lee, 1984, The regional properties of the miniflex Laurent, generalized Leontief and translog flexible functional forms, Working paper (University of Texas, Austin, TX).

Berndt, E. and D. Wood, 1975, Technology, prices, and the derived demand for energy, Review of Economics and Statistics 57, 259–268.

Caves, D. and L.R. Christensen, 1980, Global properties of flexible functional forms, American Economic Review 70, 422–432.

Cox, D.R., 1961, Tests of separate families of hypotheses, in: Proceedings of the fourth Berkeley symposium on mathematical statistics and probability, Vol. 1 (University of California Press, Berkeley, CA) 105–123.

Davidson, R. and J. MacKinnon, 1981, Several tests for model specification in the presence of alternative hypotheses, Econometrica 49, 781–793.

Dickey, J.M., 1967, Matricvariate generalizations of the multivariate t distribution and the inverted multivariate t distribution, Annals of Mathematical Statistics 42, 511–518.

Diewert, E., 1972, Applications of duality theory, in: M. Intriligator and D. Kendrik, eds., Frontiers of quantitative economics (North-Holland, Amsterdam).

Efron, B., 1984, Comparing non-nested models, Journal of the American Statistical Association 79, 791–803.

Friedman, J.H. and M. Wright, 1982, A nested partitioning procedure for numerical multiple integration, ACM Transactions on Mathematical Software 7, 76–92.

Gallant, A.R., 1982, Unbiased determination of production technologies, Journal of Econometrics 20, 285–324.

Guilkey, D. and C.A. Lovell, 1980, On the flexibility of the translog approximation, International Economic Review 21, 137–147.

Hinckley, D.V. and G. Runger, 1984, The analysis of transformed data, Journal of the American Statistical Association 79, 302–309.

Ilmakunnas, P., 1985, Bayesian estimation of cost functions with stochastic or exact constraints on parameters, International Economic Review, forthcoming.

Johnson, W. and S. Geisser, 1983, A predictive view of the detection and characterization of influential observations in regression analysis, Journal of the American Statistical Association 78, 137–144.

Klein, R. and S. Brown, 1984, Model selection when there is 'minimal' prior information, Econometrica 52, 1291–1312.

Lindley, D. and A.F.M. Smith, 1972, Bayes estimates for the linear model, Journal of the Royal Statistical Society B 34, 1–18.

Pesaran, M. and A. Deaton, 1978, Testing non-nested nonlinear regression models, Econometrica 46, 677–694.

Rossi, P.E., 1984, Specification and analysis of econometric production models, Unpublished dissertation (University of Chicago, Chicago IL).

Varian, H., 1978, Microeconomic analysis (W.W. Norton, New York).

Zellner, A., 1971, An introduction of Bayesian inference in econometrics (Wiley, New York).

Zellner, A., 1980, On Bayesian regression analysis with g-prior distributions, H.G.B. Alexander Research Foundation manuscript (University of Chicago, Chicago, IL).

Zellner, A. and P.E. Rossi, 1984, Bayesian analysis of dichotomous quantal response models, Journal of Econometrics 25, 365–393.

DISCUSSION OF ROSSI'S PAPER

David HINKLEY*

University of Texas, Austin, TX 78712, USA

Peter Rossi's paper makes a most interesting contribution to a difficult problem. In my brief remarks I should like to take a rather more general view of the statistical 'model-choice' problem, at the risk of seeming somewhat removed from the details of the paper.

Surprisingly, statisticians do not have agreed-upon methods for choosing among models, even when the models are nested. Of course different applications do have different objectives, so no single solution is possible. (One possible reason for difficulty may be the preponderance of anti-Bayesian statisticians.) Only fairly recently have the related methods of Akaike's AIC and cross-validation been explored systematically. For a new, unified theoretical account of several methods for nested models, see Li (1983).

Statistical theory has failed to incorporate data-based modelling into the formal structures of inference excepting possibly the subjective Bayesian treatment. There is confusion over whether or not inferences from a chosen model should make allowance for choice. Often the answer, apparent to applied statisticians, is 'no'. A case in point is the Box–Cox type of model, for example regression models

$$y^{\lambda} = \sum \beta_i X_i^{\lambda} + \text{gaussian noise},$$

where the data are used to choose λ. (This situation is similar in spirit to the mixture approach mentioned by Rossi.) An attempt to resolve this type of problem by Hinkley and Runger (1984) clearly shows the merit of a careful Bayesian approach.

In the particular context of non-nested models, the 'self-evident' aspect of the Bayesian approach is the formal mathematics. The ingredients, especially the priors on model parameters, need careful specification – the more so when complex models are fit to sparse data. We should ask questions like: would we expect less noise in the more complex model? Should the priors for regression

*Jane and Ronald Blumberg Centennial Professor of Mathematics.

coefficients be connected, for example to produce the same prior predictive density under each candidate model?

For the kind of situation described by Rossi, it would be worthwhile to discover which data vectors are most influential in the posterior odds. This would require (approximate) evaluation of $K_{12}(i)=p(H_1|D_{-i})/p(H_2|D_{-i})$, where D_{-i} is data set omitting the ith case. The very influential cases would be those where one model is greatly superior as a predictor, and the associated values of X might be especially important. Some initial work on assessment of influence in Bayesian predictive analysis has been published by Johnson and Geisser (1983). One small point: if one is interested in prediction, I think it unwise to choose a single model when the posterior odds are close to one.

Let me close by referring briefly to an entirely different approach to choice and assessment of models, the bootstrap approach. The assessment of prediction bias and random error in econometric models is discussed by Freedman and Peters (1983). One possible, untested version of the bootstrap is as follows: (1) fit $Y_t = \hat{Y}_t + \hat{e}_t$, $\hat{Y} = X\hat{\theta}$; (2) generate data $Y_t^* = \hat{Y}_t + e_t^*$, with e_t^* sampled randomly from $\{\hat{e}_\tau\}$; (3) refit $Y_t^* = \hat{Y}_t^* + \hat{e}_t^*$ to data (X, Y^*); (4) measure $Y_t - \hat{Y}_t^*$ as simulated prediction errors. When there are two or more candidate models, one can similarly investigate the consequences of using the wrong model. The more direct problem of choice, based on comparison of mean squared errors, for example, is addressed by Efron (1984).

References

Efron, B., 1984, Comparing non-nested linear models, Journal of the American Statistical Association 79, forthcoming.

Freedman, D.A. and S.C. Peters, 1983, Bootstrapping an econometric model: Some empirical results (Mathematical Science Research Institute, Berkeley, CA).

Hinkley, D.V. and G. Runger, 1984, The analysis of transformed data, Journal of the American Statistical Association 79, 302.

Johnson, W.O. and S. Geisser, 1983, A predictive view of the detection and characterization of influential observations in regression analysis, Journal of the American Statistical Association 78, 137.

Li, K., 1983, From Stein's unbiased risk estimates to the method of generalized cross-validation (Department of Statistics, Purdue University, Lafayette, IN).

THE INVARIANCE PRINCIPLE AND INCOME–WEALTH CONSERVATION LAWS
Application of Lie Groups and Related Transformations

Ryuzo SATO*

New York University, New York, NY 10006, USA
Harvard University, Cambridge, MA 02138, USA

The purpose of this paper is to uncover 'hidden' conservation laws in the models with heterogeneous capital goods. The first conservation law uncovered is a pseudo-net-productivity relation which implies that the rate of change in national income is equal to the discount rate multiplied by the utility-value-of-investment. Secondly, the 'modified income' conservation law is confirmed when the economy possesses taste change and/or technical change. From an empirical perspective, knowledge of conservation laws can assist in the econometric testing of optimal growth models. In addition to the capital–labor ratio and saving ratio the empirical validity of the models can be tested by the appropriate income–wealth ratios.

> Nature's ways are invariant.
>
> Hsün Tzu (ca. 305–235 B.C.)

> Just as simple harmonic motion... has motions which must conserve the sum of kinetic and potential energies,... so in a neoclassical von Neumann economy..., it will be true that there exists a conservation law.
>
> Paul A. Samuelson (1970a)

> When natural systems are idealized, unexpected symmetries (invariances) may be revealed that have far-reaching significance in the fields of physics, engineering and mathematics.
>
> Jurgen Moser (1979)

1. Introduction

In the early part of the 19th century William Rowan Hamilton discovered a principle which can be generalized to encompass many areas of physics, engineering and applied mathematics. Hamilton's principle roughly states that the evolution in time of a dynamic system takes place in such a manner that integral of the difference between the kinetic and potential energies for the system is stationary. If the 'action' integral is free of the time variable, the sum of the kinetic and potential energies, the Hamiltonian, is constant – the conservation law of the total energy.

*The author wishes to express his appreciation to Paul A. Samuelson, William A. Barnett, Hal R. Varian, Gilbert Suzawa, Takayuki Nono, Fumitake Mimura, and Shigeru Maeda and the referees of this Journal for their helpful comments on an earlier version of this paper.

In the early part of this century Emmy Noether (1918) discovered the fundamental invariance principle known as the *Noether Theorem*.[1] This principle not only extended the idea of Hamilton and the conservation law of total energy, but also provided the formal methodology to study the general 'invariance' problem of a dynamic system. Influenced by the work of Klein (1918) and of Lie (1891) on the transformation properties of differential equations under continuous (Lie) groups, Noether had the ingenious insight of combining the methods of the formal calculus of variation with those of Lie group theory. Since the first application of the Noether invariance principle to particle mechanics by Bessel-Hagan (1921), this new area of mathematics has exhibited remarkable development in the last fifty years.[2]

The study of economic conservation laws is still in its infancy compared with its counterparts in physics and engineering. Yet this is an area where rapid progress is being made. In economics the conservation law has its roots in Ramsey (1928). But it was Samuelson (1970) who first explicitly introduced conservation laws to theoretical economics. The recent work by Weitzman (1976), Sato (1981, 1982), Kemp and Long (1982), Samuelson (1982), Sato, Nôno and Mimura (1983) and Kataoka (1983) provide an indication of the rapid progress being made in this field and the great interest shown in the analysis of economic conservation laws. In Ramsey (1928), Samuelson (1970, 1982), Weitzman (1976) and Kemp and Long (1982), the authors used the standard invariance condition of the calculus of variation, which is a special case of the Noether invariance principle, while in Sato (1981, 1982) and Sato, Nôno and Mimura (1983) we employed the Noether invariance principle and, thus, were able to obtain the more general results of 'hidden' conservation laws.

The purpose of this paper is to extend the work on economic conservation laws in the direction of uncovering more 'hidden' conservation laws. We shall briefly discuss the application of the conservation laws to the econometric estimation of the optimal growth models. However, before we do so, we shall begin with a brief summary of the literature.

2. Brief summary of the literature

Ramsey's (1928, p. 547) famous rule of optimal saving is the first reference (implicit) to a conservation law in economics. His rule states that

$$\dot{c}=\frac{\mathrm{d}c}{\mathrm{d}t}=f(a,c)-x=\frac{B-(U(x)-V(a))}{u(x)}, \tag{2.1}$$

[1] Her paper has recently been translated into English by Tavel, who also supplies a brief motivation and historical sketch [see Noether 1918)].

[2] See Klein (1918), Lie (1891), Gelfand and Fomin (1963), Rund (1966), Logan (1977), Nôno (1968), Nôno and Mimura (1975,1976,1977,1978), Sagan (1969), Lovelock and Rund (1975), Whittaker (1937) and Moser (1979).

where f = production function, a = labor, c = capital, x = consumption, $U(x)$ = utility of consumption, $V(a)$ = disutility of labor, $u(x) = \partial U/\partial x$ = marginal utility of consumption. This rule is an *economic version of the law of conservation of energy*. Letting L (Lagrangian) $= -(U(x) - V(a))$ and Bliss $B = H$ (Hamiltonian), the Ramsey rule is derived from the conservation law,

$$H = B = u(x)\dot{c} + (U(x) - V(a)) = u(x)\dot{c} - L. \tag{2.2}$$

Samuelson (1970a) is the first economist to *explicitly* introduce conservation laws in theoretical economics. From the analogy of the law of conservation of (physical) energy, kinetic energy + potential energy = constant, Samuelson obtained the *conservation law of the aggregate capital–output ratio* in a neoclassical von Neumann economy, where all output is saved to provide capital formation for the system's growth.

A typical optimization model in modern economics deals with the problem of maximizing

$$\int_0^T L(t, k, \dot{k})\,\mathrm{d}t = \int_0^T D(t)U[f(t, k, \dot{k})]\,\mathrm{d}t, \tag{2.3}$$

where $D(t)$ = discount rate factor, U = utility function, f = consumption possibility function, k = capital–labor ratio and $\dot{k}$ = time derivative of k. Here, we also assume that U and f are neoclassical functions satisfying all the regularity conditions. In his recent work, Weitzman (1976) has derived the invariance condition of the income–wealth ratio in a neoclassical model (2.3) when the welfare of the society is discounted at a constant rate for $T = \infty$ and f is free of technical progress. A similar result is obtained by such authors as Kemp and Long (1982), Samuelson (1982) and Sato (1982).

The first derivation of economic conservation laws via the application of Noether's Theorem and Lie groups is contained in Sato (1981), where some of the existing known results are confirmed, and also several new hidden laws are uncovered. For instance, it is shown [Sato (1981, p. 279)] that Samuelson's (1970b) two conservation laws are the *only* laws globally operating for the von Neumann system of optimal growth. Also in studying the Ramsey and general neoclassical growth models, it was discovered that there exist several new conservation laws operating in the vicinity of the steady state. For example, in the Liviatan–Samuelson model (1969), *the discounted welfare measured in terms of the modified income, which is the sum of production income and rental income is constant* [Sato (1981, p. 264)]. The problem of how various types of technical progress will affect the conservation laws was studied by Sato, Nôno and Mimura (1983). By redefining income and supply price of capital, we were able to uncover several 'hidden' conservation laws.

In earlier works [e.g., Sato (1981)], an attempt was made to discover conservation laws which are *independent of the forms of production and utility functions*. In the present paper we intend to incorporate these functions in conservation laws, which will enable us to uncover more hidden invariances.

3. A model with heterogeneous capital goods

Let utility depend on consumption of many goods which in turn depend on a vector of capital goods, $k=(k^1,\dots,k^n)$, and a vector of investment, $\dot{k}=(\dot{k}^1,\dots,\dot{k}^n)$, so that

$$U=U(\dot{k},k). \tag{3.1}$$

Let $U(\dot{k},k)$ be a strictly concave function with existent partial derivatives, for which

$$\begin{aligned} &U(0,k)<U(0,\bar{k})=0, \qquad k\neq\bar{k},\\ &U_i(0,\bar{k})\neq 0, \qquad U_i=\partial U/\partial k^i, \qquad i=1,\dots,n. \end{aligned} \tag{3.2}$$

The society's problem is to maximize the welfare functional

$$J=\int_0^\infty \mathrm{e}^{-\rho t}U[\dot{k}(t),k(t)]\,\mathrm{d}t, \qquad \rho>0, \tag{3.3}$$

subject to the appropriate initial conditions. For simplicity we shall write

$$L(t,k,\dot{k})=\mathrm{e}^{-\rho t}U(\dot{k}(t),k(t)). \tag{3.4}$$

The necessary condition for the optimal solution is that the Euler–Lagrange equations vanish:

$$\begin{aligned} E_i&=\frac{\partial L}{\partial k^i}-\frac{\mathrm{d}}{\mathrm{d}t}\left(\frac{\partial L}{\partial \dot{k}^i}\right)=\mathrm{e}^{-\rho t}\frac{\partial U}{\partial k^i}-\frac{\mathrm{d}}{\mathrm{d}t}\left(\mathrm{e}^{-\rho t}\frac{\partial U}{\partial \dot{k}^i}\right)\\ &=\mathrm{e}^{-\rho t}\left[\frac{\partial U}{\partial k^i}+\rho\frac{\partial U}{\partial \dot{k}^i}-\frac{\mathrm{d}}{\mathrm{d}t}\left(\frac{\partial U}{\partial \dot{k}^i}\right)\right]=0, \end{aligned} \tag{3.5a}$$

which implies that

$$E_i=0\Leftrightarrow\frac{\partial U}{\partial k^i}+\rho\frac{\partial U}{\partial \dot{k}^i}-\frac{\mathrm{d}}{\mathrm{d}t}\left(\frac{\partial U}{\partial \dot{k}^i}\right)=0, \qquad i=1,\dots,n. \tag{3.5b}$$

If we define the supply price of the ith capital as $p^i=-\partial U/\partial \dot{k}^i$, (3.5) states that the time derivative of p^i is equal to

$$\dot{p}^i=-\partial U/\partial k^i+\rho p^i, \qquad i=1,\dots,n. \tag{3.5c}$$

4. Noether's theorem (invariance principle)[3]

Before we present the analysis of economic conservation laws (hidden or unhidden) associated with the above model, we briefly discuss the mathematical properties of Noether's theorem and invariance identities. As this theorem is relatively unknown to economists, we shall begin with the definitions of dynamic symmetry (or invariance).

Let us consider a Lagrange function L, which is twice continuously differentiable in each of its $2n+1$ arguments. We then have the variational integral

$$J(x)=\int_a^b L(t,x(t),\dot{x}(t))\,\mathrm{d}t, \tag{4.1}$$

where $x=$ the set of all vector functions $x(t)=(x^1(t),\ldots,x^n(t))$, $t\in[a,b]$. The type of invariance transformations that will be considered are (technical change) transformations of configuration space, i.e., $(t,x^1,\ldots,x^n)$ – space, which depend upon r real, independent (essential) parameters $\varepsilon^1,\ldots,\varepsilon^r$. To be more precise, we require here that the transformations are given by

$$\begin{aligned}\bar{t}&=\phi(t,x,\varepsilon), \qquad \varepsilon=(\varepsilon^1,\ldots,\varepsilon^r),\\ \bar{x}^i&=\psi^i(t,x,\varepsilon), \qquad i=1,\ldots,n.\end{aligned} \tag{4.2}$$

In economic terms, ϕ can be considered as 'subjective' time [Samuelson (1976)], while ψ^i represent 'technical' or 'taste' change. We assume that

$$\begin{aligned}&\phi(t,x,0)=t,\\ &\psi^i(t,x,0)=x^i, \qquad i=1,\ldots,n.\end{aligned} \tag{4.3}$$

Expanding the right-hand sides of (4.2) in a Taylor series around $\varepsilon=0$, we obtain

$$\begin{aligned}\bar{t}&=t+\tau_s(t,x)\varepsilon^s+\mathrm{O}(\varepsilon),\\ \bar{x}^i&=x^i+\xi^i_s(t,x)\varepsilon^s+\mathrm{O}(\varepsilon), \qquad i=1,\ldots,n,\end{aligned} \tag{4.4}$$

$s=1,\ldots,r$, summation convention in force.[4]

[3] A comprehensive treatment of Noether's theorem and invariance identities is given in Sato (1981, pp. 236–251). Those who are familiar with this aspect of the mathematics can skip this section.

[4] We adopt the so-called Einstein summation convention [Young (1978, pp. 333–334)]. When a lower case Latin index such as $j,h,k,\ldots$ appears twice in a term, summation over that index is implied, the range of summation being $1,\ldots,n$. For example, a^ix^i means $\Sigma_{i=1}^n a^ix^i$.

The principal linear parts τ_s and ξ_s^i are called the *infinitesimal generators* (or *transformations*) of the transformational (4.2) given by[5]

$$\tau_s(t,x)=\frac{\partial\phi}{\partial\varepsilon^s}(t,x,0),\qquad \xi_s^i(t,x)=\frac{\partial\psi^i}{\partial\varepsilon^s}(t,x,0). \tag{4.5a}$$

Using the customary symbol of the infinitesimal transformations, we write (4.5a) as

$$X_s=\tau_s(t,x)\frac{\partial}{\partial t}+\xi_s^i(t,x)\frac{\partial}{\partial x^i}+\left(\frac{\mathrm{d}\xi_s^i}{\mathrm{d}t}-\dot{x}^i\frac{\mathrm{d}\tau_s}{\mathrm{d}t}\right)\frac{\partial}{\partial\dot{x}^i}. \tag{4.5b}$$

Definition 1 *(Dynamic invariance or dynamic symmetry).* (a) The fundamental integral (4.1) is absolutely invariant under the r-parameter family of transformations (4.2) if and only if we have

$$\int_{\bar{t}_1}^{\bar{t}_2}L\left(\bar{t},\bar{x}(\bar{t}),\frac{\mathrm{d}\bar{x}(\bar{t})}{\mathrm{d}\bar{t}}\right)\mathrm{d}\bar{t}-\int_{t_1}^{t_2}L\left(t,x(t),\frac{\mathrm{d}x(t)}{\mathrm{d}t}\right)\mathrm{d}t=\mathrm{O}(\varepsilon). \tag{4.6}$$

(b) Alternatively, the fundamental integral is absolutely invariant if and only if

$$L\left(\bar{t},\bar{x}(\bar{t}),\frac{\mathrm{d}\bar{x}(\bar{t})}{\mathrm{d}\bar{t}}\right)\frac{\mathrm{d}\bar{t}}{\mathrm{d}t}-L\left(t,x(t),\frac{\mathrm{d}x(t)}{\mathrm{d}t}\right)=\mathrm{O}(\varepsilon). \tag{4.7a}$$

Definition 2 *(Divergence-invariance or invariance with nullity).* The fundamental integral is divergence-invariant or invariant up to a divergence term, if there exist r functions ϕ_s such that

$$L\left(\bar{t},\bar{x}(\bar{t}),\frac{\mathrm{d}\bar{x}(\bar{t})}{\mathrm{d}\bar{t}}\right)\frac{\mathrm{d}\bar{t}}{\mathrm{d}t}-L(t,x(t),x(t))$$

$$=\varepsilon^s\frac{\mathrm{d}\phi_s}{\mathrm{d}t}(t,x(t))+\mathrm{O}(\varepsilon),\quad\text{summation convention on } s, \tag{4.7b}$$

with the remaining conditions of Definition 1 holding true.

This definition is more general than Definition 1 in that the left-hand side of (4.7b) is equal to the sum of the exact differentials multiplied by the essential

[5] In many cases the transformations (4.2) may be Lie groups and, hence, (4.5) may be the infinitesimal transformations of a group. However, to study Noether's invariance principle the group property is *not* necessary. We simply assume the existence of the infinitesimal transformations.

parameters and to first-order terms in ε. Since the addition of the total exact differentials does *not* change the original Euler–Lagrange equations associated with L [see Sagan (1969)], we may call this case the *dynamic symmetry condition with nullity*, or simply the *dynamic invariance with nullity*. Alternatively Definition 2 is referred to as 'invariance up to an exact differential'. [See Rund (1966, p. 73).] Then the *fundamental invariance identities* are given by

$$X_s L + L\frac{\mathrm{d}\tau_s}{\mathrm{d}t} = \frac{\mathrm{d}\Phi_s}{\mathrm{d}t}, \tag{4.8a}$$

or

$$\frac{\partial L}{\partial t}\tau_s + \frac{\partial L}{\partial x^i}\xi_s^i + \frac{\partial L}{\partial \dot{x}^i}\left(\frac{\mathrm{d}\xi_s^i}{\mathrm{d}t} - \dot{x}^i\frac{\mathrm{d}\tau_s}{\mathrm{d}t}\right) + L\frac{\mathrm{d}\tau_s}{\mathrm{d}t} = \frac{\mathrm{d}\Phi_s}{\mathrm{d}t}, \tag{4.8b}$$

$$s = 1, \ldots, r, \quad \text{summation on } i.$$

[See Sato (1981, p. 244, eq. 17) for the derivation of (4.8).]

If the fundamental integral is invariant (either absolutely or up to an exact differential) under an r-parameter family (or group) of continuous transformations, the corresponding Lagrangian must satisfy certain conditions involving the Lagrangian, its derivatives and the infinitesimal generators of the continuous transformations. Using the Euler–Lagrange expressions the resulting transformation of these conditions is usually referred to as Noether's theorem. The importance of this theorem lies in the fact that it allows one to construct quantities which are constant along any extremal, that is, a curve which satisfies the Euler–Lagrange equations. Hence, it allows one to obtain relations which may be interpreted as 'conservation laws'.

We can now present [Sato (1981)]:

Noether's Invariance Theorem. If the fundamental integral of a problem in the calculus of variations is divergence-invariant under the r-parameter family of transformations, then r distinct quantities Ω_s $(s = 1, \ldots, r)$ are constant along any extremal.

In physical and economic applications, those quantities are thus interpreted as the 'conservation laws' of the system, where

$$\Omega_s = -H\tau_s + \frac{\partial L}{\partial \dot{x}^i}\xi_s^i - \Phi_s = \text{constant}, \qquad s = 1, \ldots, r, \tag{4.9a}$$

where H is the Hamiltonian defined by

$$H = -L + \dot{x}^i\frac{\partial L}{\partial \dot{x}^i}. \tag{4.9b}$$

[See Sato (1981, pp. 242–251) for proof.]

5. Income–wealth conservation laws

Using Noether's invariance principle we are now in a position to study the dynamic symmetry conditions in the heterogeneous capital model. Here we require that t and k^i are subjected to the transformations

$$\bar{t} = \phi(t, k, \varepsilon), \qquad \varepsilon = (\varepsilon^1, \dots, \varepsilon^r),$$
$$\bar{k}^i = \psi^i(t, k, \varepsilon), \qquad i = 1, \dots, n, \tag{5.1a}$$

and, hence, the infinitesimal transformations are given by

$$X_s = \tau_s(t,k)\frac{\partial}{\partial t} + \xi_s^i(t,k)\frac{\partial}{\partial k^i} + \left(\frac{\mathrm{d}\xi_s^i}{\mathrm{d}t} - \dot{k}^i\frac{\mathrm{d}\tau_s}{\mathrm{d}t}\right)\frac{\partial}{\partial \dot{k}^i}. \tag{5.1b}$$

We are interested in finding the dynamic symmetry conditions

$$\int_{\bar{t}_1}^{\bar{t}_2} \mathrm{e}^{-\rho\bar{t}} U\left[\bar{k}(\bar{t}), \frac{\mathrm{d}\bar{k}(\bar{t})}{\mathrm{d}\bar{t}}\right]\mathrm{d}\bar{t} - \int_{t_1}^{t_2} \mathrm{e}^{-\rho t} U\left[k(t), \frac{\mathrm{d}k(t)}{\mathrm{d}t}\right]\mathrm{d}t$$
$$= \varepsilon^s \Phi_s(t, k(t)) + \mathrm{O}(\varepsilon). \tag{5.2}$$

By applying the infinitesimal transformation (5.1b) on (3.4) and using the fundamental invariance identities (4.8), we obtain

$$\mathrm{e}^{-\rho t}\left[-\rho U\tau + \frac{\partial U}{\partial k^i}\xi^i + \frac{\partial U}{\partial \dot{k}^i}\left(\frac{\mathrm{d}\xi^i}{\mathrm{d}t} - \dot{k}^i\frac{\mathrm{d}\tau}{\mathrm{d}t}\right) + U\frac{\mathrm{d}\tau}{\mathrm{d}t}\right] = \frac{\mathrm{d}\Phi}{\mathrm{d}t}, \tag{5.3a}$$

or

$$\left(U - \dot{k}^i\frac{\partial U}{\partial \dot{k}^i}\right)\frac{\mathrm{d}\tau}{\mathrm{d}t} = \rho U\tau - \frac{\partial U}{\partial k^i}\xi^i - \frac{\partial U}{\partial \dot{k}^i}\frac{\mathrm{d}\xi^i}{\mathrm{d}t} + \mathrm{e}^{\rho t}\frac{\mathrm{d}\Phi}{\mathrm{d}t}. \tag{5.3b}$$

Since we assume that we are dealing with a one-parameter transformation group, i.e., $s = 1$, we omit the subscript 1 from τ_1, ξ_1^i, etc.

Warning:

$$\dot{k}^i\frac{\partial U}{\partial \dot{k}^i} \quad \text{means} \quad \sum_{i=1}^{n}\dot{k}^i\frac{\partial U}{\partial \dot{k}^i},$$

$$\frac{\partial U}{\partial k^i}\xi^i \quad \text{means} \quad \sum_{i=1}^{n}\frac{\partial U}{\partial k^i}\xi^i, \quad \text{etc.}$$

From the invariance principle (4.9a) the conservation law is now derived as

$$\Omega = \left(e^{-\rho t}U - e^{-\rho t}\dot{k}^i \frac{\partial U}{\partial \dot{k}^i}\right)\tau + e^{-\rho t}\frac{\partial U}{\partial \dot{k}^i}\xi^i - \Phi = \text{constant}, \tag{5.4a}$$

or

$$\frac{d\Omega}{dt} = -\rho e^{-\rho t}\left(U - \dot{k}^i \frac{\partial U}{\partial \dot{k}^i}\right)\tau + e^{-\rho t}\frac{d}{dt}\left(U - \dot{k}^i\frac{\partial U}{\partial \dot{k}^i}\right)\tau$$
$$+ e^{-\rho t}\left(U - \dot{k}^i\frac{\partial U}{\partial \dot{k}^i}\right)\frac{d\tau}{dt} - \rho e^{-\rho t}\frac{\partial U}{\partial \dot{k}^i}\xi^i$$
$$+ e^{-\rho t}\frac{d}{dt}\left(\frac{\partial U}{\partial \dot{k}^i}\xi^i\right) - \frac{d\Phi}{dt} = 0. \tag{5.4b}$$

Hence we have

$$\left[\frac{d}{dt}\left(U - \dot{k}^i\frac{\partial U}{\partial \dot{k}^i}\right) + \rho\dot{k}^i\frac{\partial U}{\partial \dot{k}^i}\right]\tau$$
$$= \rho U\tau - \frac{\partial U}{\partial \dot{k}^i}\xi^i - \frac{\partial U}{\partial \dot{k}^i}\frac{d\xi^i}{dt} - \left(U - \dot{k}^i\frac{\partial U}{\partial \dot{k}^i}\right)\frac{d\tau}{dt}$$
$$+ e^{\rho t}\frac{d\Phi}{dt} + \left[\frac{\partial U}{\partial k^i} + \rho\frac{\partial U}{\partial \dot{k}^i} - \frac{d}{dt}\left(\frac{\partial U}{\partial \dot{k}^i}\right)\right]\xi^i. \tag{5.4c}$$

The term inside the bracket of the last expression of the right-hand side is zero because of the vanishing condition placed on the Euler–Lagrange equations (3.5b). Eliminating $d\Phi/dt$ between (5.3b) and (5.4c) we obtain our first conservation law

$$\frac{d}{dt}\left(U - \dot{k}^i\frac{\partial U}{\partial \dot{k}^i}\right) = -\rho\dot{k}^i\frac{\partial U}{\partial \dot{k}^i}.$$

It is easy to identify $U - \dot{k}^i(\partial U/\partial \dot{k}^i)$ as income in utility terms – Marshall–Haig–Kuznets' definition, while

$$-\dot{k}^i\frac{\partial U}{\partial \dot{k}^i} \equiv -\sum_{i=1}^{n}\dot{k}^i\frac{\partial U}{\partial \dot{k}^i} \equiv \sum_{i=1}^{n} p^i\dot{k}^i$$

is the utility-value-of-investment. Hence, this conservation law states that along the optimal path

$$\frac{\mathrm{d}}{\mathrm{d}t}(\text{income at } t) = \rho \times (\text{utility-value-of-investment at } t), \tag{5.5b}$$

$$\begin{aligned}&(\text{rate of change in income at } t)\\ &= \rho \times (\text{utility-value-of-investment at } t).\end{aligned} \tag{5.5c}$$

For $\rho > 0$, we have along the optimal path

$$\frac{\frac{\mathrm{d}}{\mathrm{d}t}(\text{income at } t)}{(\text{utility-value-of-investment at } t)} = \rho = \text{constant}, \quad \text{for all } t. \tag{5.5d}$$

Our first conservation law is equivalent to what Samuelson (1982) calls a *pseudo-net productivity relation*. The *genuine net-productivity* relation for $i = 1$ can be obtained from

$$y(t) = c(t) + k(t) = f(k(t)), \tag{5.6a}$$

$$\frac{\mathrm{d}y(t)}{\mathrm{d}t} = f'(k(t))\dot{k}(t), \tag{5.6b}$$

$$\dot{y} = r(t)\dot{k}(t), \qquad \lim_{t \to \infty} r(t) = \rho. \tag{5.6c}$$

Hence, only in the limit, as $t \to \infty$, will the system settle down to stationary equilibrium at market rate equal to the ρ time-preference parameter.

It should be noted that the utility-value-of-net-capital formation is not equivalent to the time derivative of the utility-value-of-capital. The latter usually includes capital gains, or price changes, while the former does not. The ratio of the utility-value-of-income to the utility-value-of-capital-goods is to constant in the present model. We shall later discuss this aspect of the invariance conditions in a von Neumann model of economic growth (section 8).

Next we can derive the income–wealth conservation law. Let us assume that

$$\tau = 1, \tag{5.7a}$$

$$\xi^i = 0, \qquad i = 1, \dots, n. \tag{5.7b}$$

We then get, from (5.3a) and (3.5b), along the optimal path

$$\frac{\mathrm{d}\Phi}{\mathrm{d}t} = -\rho \mathrm{e}^{-\rho t} U. \tag{5.8a}$$

Also from (5.4b) we have

$$\frac{\mathrm{d}\Phi}{\mathrm{d}t} = -\rho \mathrm{e}^{-\rho t}\left(U - \dot{k}^i \frac{\partial U}{\partial \dot{k}^i}\right) + \mathrm{e}^{-\rho t}\frac{\mathrm{d}}{\mathrm{d}t}\left(U - \dot{k}^i \frac{\partial U}{\partial \dot{k}^i}\right)$$
$$= \frac{\mathrm{d}}{\mathrm{d}t}\left[\mathrm{e}^{-\rho t}\left(U - \dot{k}^i \frac{\partial U}{\partial \dot{k}^i}\right)\right]. \tag{5.8b}$$

Equating (5.8b) with (5.8a) we obtain

$$\frac{\mathrm{d}\Phi}{\mathrm{d}t} = \frac{\mathrm{d}}{\mathrm{d}t}\left[\mathrm{e}^{-\rho t}\left(U - \dot{k}^i \frac{\partial U}{\partial \dot{k}^i}\right)\right] = -\rho \mathrm{e}^{-\rho t}U, \qquad 0 \le t \le \infty. \tag{5.8c}$$

Note that the left-hand side of the above is equal to

$$\frac{\mathrm{d}}{\mathrm{d}t}\left[\mathrm{e}^{-\rho t}\left(U - \dot{k}^i \frac{\partial U}{\partial \dot{k}^i}\right)\right] = -\frac{\mathrm{d}H}{\mathrm{d}t}, \tag{5.8d}$$

while the right-hand side of (5.8c) is equal to

$$-\rho \mathrm{e}^{-\rho t}U = \frac{\partial L}{\partial t}. \tag{5.8e}$$

Hence (5.8) shows that

$$\frac{\mathrm{d}\Phi}{\mathrm{d}t} = \frac{\partial L}{\partial t} = -\frac{\mathrm{d}H}{\mathrm{d}t}. \tag{5.8f}$$

The null term Φ now turns out to be equal to the integral of the negative value of the Hamiltonian and to the integral of the Lagrangian function. Alternatively, we can say that the absolute value of the rate of change in the Hamiltonian must be equal to the rate of change in the null term for the entire planning period. Integrating (5.8c), we get the null term as

$$\Phi\Big|_t^{\infty} = \mathrm{e}^{-\rho s}\left[U(s) - \dot{k}^i(s)\frac{\partial U(s)}{\partial \dot{k}^i(s)}\right]\Bigg|_t^{\infty} = -\rho\int_t^{\infty} \mathrm{e}^{-\rho s}U(s)\,\mathrm{d}s, \tag{5.9a}$$

or

$$\Phi|_{\infty}^{t} = \rho\int_t^{\infty} \mathrm{e}^{-\rho s}U(s)\,\mathrm{d}s. \tag{5.9b}$$

By the concavity assumption on U and by the transversailty condition, we have

$$e^{-\rho s}\left[U(s)-\dot{k}^i(s)\frac{\partial U(s)}{\partial \dot{k}^i(s)}\right]\to 0 \quad \text{as} \quad s\to\infty. \tag{5.10}$$

Hence, (5.9a) becomes

$$-e^{-\rho s}\left[U(s)-\dot{k}^i(s)\frac{\partial U(s)}{\partial \dot{k}^i(s)}\right]_{s=t} = -\rho\int_t^\infty e^{-\rho s}U(s)\,ds, \tag{5.11a}$$

or

$$e^{-\rho t}\left[U(t)-\dot{k}^i(t)\frac{\partial U(t)}{\partial \dot{k}^i(t)}\right]=\rho\int_t^\infty e^{-\rho s}U(s)\,ds. \tag{5.11b}$$

Multiplying both sides of (5.11b) by $e^{\rho t}$, we get the conservation law

$$U(t)-\dot{k}^i(t)\frac{\partial U(t)}{\partial \dot{k}^i(t)}=\rho\int_t^\infty e^{-\rho(s-t)}U(s)\,ds. \tag{5.12a}$$

The left-hand side of the above is nothing but the utility measure of 'income', while the right-hand side is the utility measure of 'wealth'. Hence, we have

$$\text{income}(t)=\rho\ \text{wealth}(t), \qquad 0\le t\le\infty. \tag{5.12b}$$

For $\rho>0$, we have the income–wealth conservation law [see also Samuelson (1982), Sato (1982), Weitzman (1976) and Kemp and Long (1982)]

$$\text{income}(t)/\text{wealth}(t)=\rho=\text{constant}. \tag{5.12c}$$

We can give an alternative interpretation to (5.12b). Since $\int_t^\infty e^{-\rho(s-t)}U(s)\,ds$ is defined as wealth, the integral in the null term in eq. (5.9b) may be called 'discounted wealth', for we have

$$\Phi|_\infty^t=\rho\int_t^\infty e^{-\rho s}U(s)=\rho e^{-\rho t}\ \text{wealth}(t). \tag{5.13a}$$

This, then, becomes

$$\begin{aligned}\Phi(t)-\Phi(\infty)&=\rho\left[\int_t^0 e^{-\rho s}U(s)\,ds-\int_\infty^0 e^{-\rho s}U(s)\,ds\right]\\&=\rho\left[\int_0^\infty e^{-\rho s}U(s)\,ds-\int_0^t e^{-\rho s}U(s)\,ds\right],\end{aligned} \tag{5.13b}$$

$$\Phi|_\infty^t=\rho[S^*-S(t)]. \tag{5.13c}$$

Here S^* = discounted total (maximum) stock of consumption measured in terms of utility and $S(t)$ = discounted stock of consumption also measured in terms of utility up to time t. For short, we shall call S, the stock of consumption. Using (5.9b), (5.11b) and (5.13b), we can express the conservation law as

$$e^{-\rho t}\left[U(t)-\dot{k}^i\frac{\partial U(t)}{\partial \dot{k}^i(t)}\right]+\rho\int_0^t e^{-\rho s}U(s)\,ds=\rho\int_0^\infty e^{-\rho s}U(s)\,ds, \tag{5.14a}$$

or

discounted income$(t)+\rho\times$ discounted stock of consumption
$=\rho\times$ maximum discounted stock of consumption
= constant. (5.14b)

discounted income + discounted stock income
= modified income = constant. (5.14c)

This is an alternative formulation of the income–wealth conservation law in terms of the modified income [see Sato (1981)].

6. Special cases

It may be of interest to study special cases of the one capital good model of Ramsey (1928) and of Liviatan and Samuelson (1969). First, the Ramsey model corresponds to the case where $i=1$ and U takes the form

$$U=U[k,\dot{k}]=U[c(k,\dot{k})]=U[f(k(t))-\dot{k}(t)], \tag{6.1}$$

where c satisfies

$$U'(c)>0,\quad U''(c)<0 \quad \text{for} \quad 0<c<\infty, \tag{6.1a}$$

$$U'(0)=\infty, \tag{6.1b}$$

and f satisfies

$$f(k)>0,\quad f'(k)>0,\quad f''(k)<0 \quad \text{for} \quad 0<k<\bar{k}<\infty, \tag{6.2a}$$

$$f(k)<f(\bar{k})=\bar{c} \quad \text{for} \quad 0<k<\bar{k}, \tag{6.2b}$$

$$f(k)\le f(\bar{k}) \quad \text{for} \quad \bar{k}\le k, \tag{6.2c}$$

where $\bar{k}$ = golden rule capital and $\bar{c}$ = bliss consumption. Then the income–wealth conservation law (5.12b) reduces to

$$U(t)+\dot{k}(t)U'(t)=\rho\int_t^{\infty}\mathrm{e}^{-\rho(s-t)}U(s)\,\mathrm{d}s. \tag{6.3a}$$

$$\begin{aligned}\text{utility measure of consumption} + \text{utility measure of investment} &= \text{utility measure of income}\\ &= \rho\times\text{utility measure of wealth.}\end{aligned} \tag{6.3b}$$

This special case is extensively discussed by Samuelson (1982) and Sato (1982).

Secondly, the Liviatan–Samuelson model corresponds to the case where $i=1$ and U takes the general form

$$U=U[k,\dot{k}]=U(c)=U[c(k(t),\dot{k}(t))], \tag{6.4a}$$

$$\partial c/\partial k<0, \qquad \partial^2 c/\partial k^2<0, \tag{6.4b}$$

$$\max c(0,k) \quad \text{at} \quad k=\bar{k}, \tag{6.4c}$$

$$\partial c(0,k)/\partial k \gtreqless 0 \quad \text{as} \quad k \lesseqgtr \bar{k}. \tag{6.4d}$$

Here the conservation law (5.12b) holds for $i=1$ automatically.

7. Generalized income: Wealth conservation laws

We now consider the most general case of utility maximization where the society's purpose is to maximize

$$\int_0^{\infty} W[t,k(t),\dot{k}(t)]\,\mathrm{d}t, \qquad k(t)=(k^1(t),\dots,k^n(t)), \tag{7.1}$$

subject to the appropriate initial conditions. More specifically W may be expressed as

$$W[t,k(t),\dot{k}(t)]=\mathrm{e}^{-\rho(t)}U[t,k(t),\dot{k}(t)], \tag{7.2}$$

and W satisfies all the requirements of a social welfare function. In this general case the society may have: (1) variable discount rate $\rho(t)$, and (2) taste and technical change $\partial U/\partial t \neq 0$.

Noether's invariance condition for this case is now written as

$$\frac{\partial W}{\partial t}\tau + \frac{\partial W}{\partial k^i}\xi^i + \frac{\partial W}{\partial \dot{k}^i}\left(\frac{\mathrm{d}\xi^i}{\mathrm{d}t} - \dot{k}^i\frac{\mathrm{d}\tau}{\mathrm{d}t}\right) + W\frac{\mathrm{d}\tau}{\mathrm{d}t} = \frac{\mathrm{d}\Phi}{\mathrm{d}t}, \qquad \Phi = \Phi(t, k). \tag{7.3}$$

Then for the optimal path, we have the conservation law expressed in terms of the time derivative,

$$\frac{\mathrm{d}}{\mathrm{d}t}\left[\left(W - \dot{k}^i\frac{\partial W}{\partial \dot{k}^i}\right)\tau + \frac{\partial W}{\partial \dot{k}^i}\xi^i - \Phi\right] = 0. \tag{7.4}$$

Using (7.3) and (7.4) we obtain the null term as

$$\begin{aligned}\frac{\mathrm{d}\Phi}{\mathrm{d}t} &= \frac{\mathrm{d}}{\mathrm{d}t}\left[\left(W - \dot{k}^i\frac{\partial W}{\partial \dot{k}^i}\right)\tau + \frac{\partial W}{\partial \dot{k}^i}\xi^i\right] \\ &= \frac{\partial W}{\partial t}\tau + \frac{\partial W}{\partial k^i}\varepsilon^i + \frac{\partial W}{\partial \dot{k}^i}\left(\frac{\mathrm{d}\xi^i}{\mathrm{d}t} - \dot{k}^i\frac{\mathrm{d}\tau}{\mathrm{d}t}\right) + W\frac{\mathrm{d}\tau}{\mathrm{d}t}.\end{aligned} \tag{7.5}$$

This is the fundamental equation of the conservation law, which contains many special cases depending upon the forms of τ and ξ^i. Let $\xi^i = 0$ for $i = 1, \dots, n$. Then integrating (7.5) we have the *generalized income–wealth conservation law*

$$\frac{\mathrm{d}}{\mathrm{d}t}\left[\left(W - \dot{k}^i\frac{\partial W}{\partial \dot{k}^i}\right)\tau\right] = \frac{\partial W}{\partial t}\tau + \left(W - \dot{k}^i\frac{\partial L}{\partial \dot{k}^i}\right)\frac{\mathrm{d}\tau}{\mathrm{d}t}, \tag{7.6a}$$

$$\left[\left(W - \dot{k}^i\frac{\partial W}{\partial \dot{k}^i}\right)\tau\right]_{t=T}^{b} = \int_T^b\left[\frac{\partial W}{\partial t}\tau + \left(W - \dot{k}^i\frac{\partial W}{\partial \dot{k}^i}\right)\frac{\mathrm{d}\tau}{\mathrm{d}t}\right]\mathrm{d}t, \tag{7.6b}$$

$$\left[\left(W - \dot{k}^i\frac{\partial W}{\partial \dot{k}^i}\right)\tau\right]_{t=T} = -\int_T^\infty\left[\frac{\partial W}{\partial t}\tau + \left(W - \dot{k}^i\frac{\partial W}{\partial \dot{k}^i}\right)\frac{\mathrm{d}\tau}{\mathrm{d}t}\right]\mathrm{d}t, \tag{7.6c}$$

where we assumed, by the transversality condition, that

$$\left(W - \dot{k}^i\frac{\partial W}{\partial \dot{k}^i}\right)\tau \to 0, \quad \frac{\partial W}{\partial t}\tau + \left(W - \dot{k}^i\frac{\partial W}{\partial \dot{k}^i}\right)\frac{\mathrm{d}\tau}{\mathrm{d}t} \to 0 \quad \text{as} \quad t \to \infty.$$

The left-hand side of (7.6c) represents *generalized income* with the time transformation τ, while the right-hand side of (7.6c) represent *generalized wealth*. In particular, when

$$\tau = 1, \tag{7.7a}$$

we have

$$\left(W - \dot{k}^i \frac{\partial W}{\partial \dot{k}^i}\right) = \text{utility measure of generalized income,} \tag{7.7b}$$

and

$$-\int_t^\infty \frac{\partial W}{\partial t}\,\mathrm{d}s = \text{utility measure of generalized wealth.} \tag{7.7c}$$

The economic interpretation of (7.7c) as generalized wealth will become more apparent when we consider a special case of W in (7.2) as

$$W = \mathrm{e}^{-\rho(t)} U[k(t), \dot{k}(t)]. \tag{7.8a}$$

In this case $-\int_t^\infty (\partial W/\partial t)\,\mathrm{d}s$ is equal to

$$-\int_t^\infty \frac{\partial W}{\partial t}\,\mathrm{d}s = \int_t^\infty \rho'(s)\mathrm{e}^{-\rho(s)} U[k(s), \dot{k}(s)]\,\mathrm{d}s. \tag{7.8b}$$

The standard income–wealth conservation law (5.12a) can be derived when $\rho(t)$ takes a special form,

$$\rho(t) = \rho t, \tag{7.8c}$$

and

$$-\int_t^\infty \frac{\partial W}{\partial t}\,\mathrm{d}s = \rho \int_t^\infty \mathrm{e}^{-\rho s} U[k(s), \dot{k}(s)]\,\mathrm{d}s. \tag{7.8d}$$

Another special case of interest occurs when τ and W take the special forms

$$\tau = 1/\rho'(t), \tag{7.9a}$$

and

$$W = \mathrm{e}^{-\rho(t)} U[k(t), \dot{k}(t)]. \tag{7.9b}$$

After some somewhat complicated calculations, we obtain the generalized income–wealth conservation law as

$$\left[U-\dot{k}^i\frac{\partial U}{\partial \dot{k}^i}\right]=\rho_t\int_t^{\infty}\exp\left(-\int_t^s\rho_p\,\mathrm{d}p\right)\left[U-\dot{k}^i\frac{\partial U}{\partial \dot{k}^i}\frac{\mathrm{d}}{\mathrm{d}s}\left(\frac{1}{\rho_s}\right)\right]\mathrm{d}s, \quad (7.9c)$$

$$\text{income}=\rho_t\times\text{generalized wealth}, \qquad (7.9)$$

where

$$\rho_t=\mathrm{d}\rho/\mathrm{d}t=\rho'(t).$$

The generalized wealth expression now includes capital gains and losses, depending upon whether $-k^i(\partial U/\partial \dot{k}^i)(\mathrm{d}/\mathrm{d}s)(1/\rho_s)$ is positive or negative. This term depends on the supply price of investment, $-\partial U/\partial \dot{k}$, and the *variable* discount rate, $\rho_s(s)$. Needless to say that when $\mathrm{d}/\mathrm{d}s(\rho_s)\equiv 0$, i.e., the constant discount rate, (7.9c) reduces to the standard income–wealth conservation law (5.12a). Hence, when $\rho=$ constant, the time transformations $\tau=1$ and $\tau=1/\rho$ give the identical results.

Next we consider the effect of taste and technical change in the utility and production functions. The generalized income–wealth conservation law contains the case of the welfare function

$$W=\mathrm{e}^{-\rho t}U[t,k(t),\dot{k}(t)], \qquad (7.10a)$$

where U is subjected to taste and technical change so that

$$\partial U/\partial t\neq 0. \qquad (7.10b)$$

The null term in this case is simply equal to

$$\frac{\mathrm{d}\Phi}{\mathrm{d}t}=\mathrm{e}^{-\rho t}\left[-\rho U+\frac{\partial U}{\partial t}\right]. \qquad (7.10c)$$

Hence, the conservation law when $\tau=1$ and $\xi^i=0$ becomes

$$\left[U-\dot{k}^i\frac{\partial U}{\partial \dot{k}^i}\right]+\int_t^{\infty}\mathrm{e}^{-\rho(s-t)}\frac{\partial U}{\partial s}\,\mathrm{d}s=\rho\int_t^{\infty}\mathrm{e}^{-\rho(s-t)}U(s)\,\mathrm{d}s. \qquad (7.10d)$$

income + current worth of taste (technical) change
$= \rho\times$ wealth. (7.10e)

modified income $=\rho\times$ wealth. (7.10f)

The value of wealth can be expressed in the same form as in the case when $\partial U/\partial t = 0$, but income must be modified by the amount of taste (technical) change. Note that in deriving (7.10d), we used the transversality condition

$$e^{-\rho t}\left[U - \dot{k}^i \frac{\partial U}{\partial \dot{k}^i}\right] \to 0 \quad \text{as} \quad t \to \infty.$$

8. Income–capital (wealth) conservation law in the von Neumann model

As this problem has already been studied extensively by Samuelson (1970a, b) and Sato (1981), we shall briefly present the results. The von Neumann problem is to maximize

$$\int_0^T \dot{K}_1 \, dt \quad \text{subject to} \quad F[K_1, \ldots, K_n, \dot{K}_1, \ldots, \dot{K}_n] = 0, \tag{8.1a}$$

and subject to the appropriate initial conditions. Here K_i are the ith type of capital, $\dot{K}_i$ are the net capital formation of the ith type of capital $(i = 1, \ldots, n)$ and F is a smooth, neoclassical, concave first-degree-homogeneous transformation function.

The Lagrangian associated with (8.1a) is

$$L[t, \lambda, K_1, \ldots, K_n, \dot{K}_1, \ldots, \dot{K}_n, \dot{\lambda}]$$

$$= \dot{K}_1 + \lambda F[K_1, \ldots, K_n, \dot{K}_1, \ldots, \dot{K}_n] \tag{8.1b}$$

$$= \dot{K}_1 + \lambda F[K, \dot{K}], \tag{8.1c}$$

where

$$K = (K_1, \ldots, K_n).$$

The transformations under consideration are

$$\bar{t} = t + \varepsilon\tau(t, \lambda, K),$$

$$\bar{K}_i = K_i + \varepsilon\xi^i(t, \lambda, K), \quad i = 1, \ldots, n. \tag{8.2a}$$

$$\bar{\lambda} = \lambda + \varepsilon\omega(t, \lambda, K),$$

The Noether invariance principle requires that

$$\frac{d\Phi}{dt} = F\omega + \frac{d\xi^1}{dt} + \lambda\left(\frac{\partial F}{\partial K_i}\xi^i + \frac{\partial F}{\partial \dot{K}_i}\frac{d\xi^i}{dt} + K_i\frac{\partial F}{\partial K_i}\frac{d\tau}{dt}\right). \tag{8.3}$$

The conservation laws are derived from

$$\Omega=\lambda\left(F-\dot{K}_i\frac{\partial F}{\partial \dot{K}_i}\right)\tau+\xi^1+\lambda\frac{\partial F}{\partial \dot{K}_i}\xi^i-\Phi=\text{constant}. \tag{8.4}$$

Let $\tau=1$, $\omega=0$, $\xi^i=0$, and $\mathrm{d}\Phi/\mathrm{d}t=0$, i.e., $\Phi=\text{constant}\ =c$, we then have

$$\Omega=\lambda\left(F-\dot{K}_i\frac{\partial F}{\partial \dot{K}_i}\right)-c=\lambda K_i\frac{\partial F}{\partial \dot{K}_i}-c=\text{constant}, \tag{8.5a}$$

where

$$F=K_i\frac{\partial F}{\partial K_i}+\dot{K}_i\frac{\partial F}{\partial \dot{K}_i},$$

by homogeneity. Letting $Y=K_i(\partial F/\partial K_i)=$ national income, the above can be interpreted as

$$\Omega_1=\lambda Y=\text{constant}. \tag{8.5b}$$

Now let us assume that $\tau=0$ and $\xi^i=\alpha K_i$ and $\omega=-\alpha\lambda$. Then we have

$$\frac{\mathrm{d}\Phi}{\mathrm{d}t}=-\alpha\lambda F+\alpha K_1+\alpha\lambda\left(K_i\frac{\partial F}{\partial K_i}+K_i\frac{\partial F}{\partial \dot{K}_i}\right)=\alpha K_1. \tag{8.6a}$$

Hence, we have

$$\Phi=\alpha K_1+c,\qquad c=\text{constant}, \tag{8.6b}$$

which gives

$$\begin{aligned}\Omega_2&=\alpha K_1+\alpha\lambda K_i\frac{\partial F}{\partial \dot{K}_i}-(\alpha K_1+c)\\&=\alpha\lambda K_i\frac{\partial F}{\partial \dot{K}_i}-c=\text{constant},\end{aligned} \tag{8.6c}$$

or

$$\Omega_2=-\lambda K_i\frac{\partial F}{\partial \dot{K}_i}=\lambda W=\text{constant}, \tag{8.6d}$$

where

$$W=-K_i\frac{\partial F}{\partial \dot{K}_i}=K_iP^i=\text{national wealth}.$$

Using (8.5b) and (8.6d), we have the Samuelson conservation law

$$\frac{\Omega_1}{\Omega_2}=\frac{Y}{W}=\frac{\text{national income}}{\text{national wealth}}=\text{constant}. \tag{8.7}$$

The conservation law (8.7) is a global law independent of the form of technology. But if we allow for special forms, there may exist different types of conservation law in addition to (8.7). In my earlier work [Sato (1981, p. 289)] I posed an open question regarding the existence of any new conservation law for a special separable technology

$$F=Y(K)-I(\dot{K})=0, \tag{8.8a}$$

$$F=K_1^{a_1}K_2^{a_2}\cdots K_n^{a_n}-\left(\dot{K}_1^2+\dot{K}_2^2+\cdots+\dot{K}_n^2\right)^{1/2}=0, \tag{8.8b}$$

with

$$\sum_{i=1}^{n}a_i=1.$$

This form of technology has been used by many economists including Samuelson (1970b), Caton and Shell (1971). Kataoka (1983) has now shown that (8.7) is the only conservation law for this special case. Thus my question has been answered in the negative.

Let us briefly present Kataoka's arguments. To simplify the calculations, we set $i=1,2$. Then the invariance principle requires [Sato (1981, p. 289, eq. (109))] that

$$\frac{\partial\xi^1}{\partial K_1}=\frac{\partial\xi^2}{\partial K_2},\qquad \frac{\partial\xi^1}{\partial K_2}+\frac{\partial\xi^2}{\partial K_1}=0, \tag{8.9a}$$

$$K_1K_2\left(\alpha-\frac{\partial\xi^1}{\partial K_1}\right)+aK_2\xi^1+(1-a)K_1\xi^2=0, \tag{8.9b}$$

where $a=a_1$ in (8.8b) and α is the coefficient of the time transformation $\tau=\alpha t+\beta$. Rewriting the first part of (8.9a) as $\partial\xi^1/\partial K_1=\frac{1}{2}(\partial\xi^1/\partial K_1+\partial\xi^2/\partial K_2)$ and substituting it into (8.9b), we have

$$K_1K_2\left[\frac{1}{2}\alpha+\frac{1}{2}\alpha-\frac{1}{2}\left(\frac{\partial\xi^1}{\partial K_1}+\frac{\partial\xi^2}{\partial K_2}\right)\right]+aK_2\xi^1+(1-a)K_1\xi^2=0. \tag{8.9c}$$

This yields

$$\frac{\alpha}{2}-\frac{1}{2}\frac{\partial\xi^1}{\partial K_1}+\frac{a\xi^1}{K_1}=-\frac{\alpha}{2}+\frac{1}{2}\frac{\partial\xi^2}{\partial K_2}-(1-a)\frac{\xi^2}{K_2}. \tag{8.9d}$$

Assuming $\xi^1 = \xi^1(K_1)$ and $\xi^2 = \xi^2(K_2)$, (8.9d) yields two ordinary differential equations

$$\frac{\alpha}{2} - \frac{1}{2}\frac{\partial \xi^1}{\partial K_1} + a\frac{\xi^1}{K_1} = B = \text{constant},$$
$$-\frac{\alpha}{2} + \frac{1}{2}\frac{\partial \xi^2}{\partial K_2} - (1-a)\frac{\xi^2}{K_2} = B = \text{constant}. \tag{8.9e}$$

Among the solutions of (8.9e), the only relevant ones which satisfy (8.9a) and (8.9b) are

$$\alpha = 0, \qquad \xi^1 = \gamma K_1, \qquad \xi^2 = \gamma K_2, \tag{8.9f}$$

which proves that (8.7) is the only conservation law even for this special technology. Kataoka also shows that even if we specify $\xi^i(K_1, K_2)$ the final solution yields the same result.

9. A remark of econometric applications

The invariance principle and conservation laws may serve as useful devices for the purpose of empirically testing the validity of optimal growth models. Although much work has been done in recent years regarding the problem of optimal growth, little effort has been made to determine whether or not optimal growth models have any value as empirically explanatory tools–except the works of Lenard (1972), Sakakibara (1970) and a few others.

Both Lenard and Sakakibara tested the empirical validity of their optimal growth models by comparing the simulated optimal time paths for the capital–labor and saving ratios with the actual time paths of these ratios [e.g., see Lenard (1972, ch. 4)]. They used the sums of the deviation squared as the criterion for the test of their models.

The conservation laws discussed earlier can be used to indirectly check the validity of such models as Lenard and Sakakibara. For instance, by using reasonable utility functions, as in Lenard and Sakakibara, one can empirically construct the time series for the income–wealth ratio. If the series are relatively stable, this would be an indication that the models work and that the actual paths follow closely the optimal paths presented by the models. In the income–wealth equation,

$$\text{income/wealth} = f(t) = a + bt,$$

one may propose to test the hypothesis that the slope coefficient b is not statistically different from zero.

Of course, the actual paths will be affected by both technical and taste changes. Consequently, the test equation may be much more complicated than the one suggested above. Nevertheless, it should be apparent that knowledge of conservation laws could be of some assistance in the econometric testing of optimal growth models. This is an important and interesting area of research to which I plan to turn my attention in the future.

10. Summary

In this paper by using the Noether invariance theorem we have uncovered several 'hidden' conservation laws in the model with heterogeneous capital goods. Our first conservation law is a pseudo-net-productivity relation which implies that the rate of change in national income is equal to the discount rate multiplied by the utility-value-of-investment. The second conservation law is an integral version of the first law – the constancy of income–wealth ratio. It is shown that the second law can be interpreted as the law of variance of 'modified income'.

If we introduce taste change and/or technical change it can be proved that there exist several generalized income–wealth conservation laws. Income and wealth must now include the effects of taste and technical change. Also under a *variable* discount rate, income–wealth conservation laws contain terms related to capital gains.

The analysis is extended to the von Neumann model of capital accumulation. Here again we confirm the existence of the income–capital conservation law. Even if technology is limited to a specialized type, there exist no additional invariances, other than those discovered by Samuelson (1970) and Sato (1981).

From an empirical perspective, knowledge of conservation laws can assist in the econometric testing of optimal growth models. In addition to the capital–labor, and saving ratios, we can now examine the behavior of the appropriate income–wealth ratios. This additional dimension should be of some value in empirical research on optimal growth models.

Appendix

Consider the variational integral

$$J(x)=\int_a^b L(t,x(t),\dot{x}(t))\,\mathrm{d}t, \qquad \begin{aligned} x(t)&=(x^1(t),\ldots,x^n(t)).\\ \dot{x}(t)&=(\dot{x}^1(t),\ldots,\dot{x}^n(t)). \end{aligned} \tag{A.1}$$

Also consider *r*-parameter transformations

$$T:\quad \begin{aligned} \bar{t}\; &=\phi(t,x;\varepsilon), \quad \varepsilon=(\varepsilon^1,\ldots,\varepsilon^n),\\ \bar{x}^i&=\psi^i(t,x;\varepsilon), \quad i=1,\ldots,n, \end{aligned} \tag{A.2}$$

where

$$\phi(t, x; 0) = t,$$
$$\psi^i(t, x; 0) = x^i. \tag{A.3}$$

In addition, it is assumed that T does not change the end points (a, α) and (b, β) where

$$\phi(a, x(a); \varepsilon) = a, \qquad \phi(b, x(b); \varepsilon) = b,$$
$$\psi^i(a, x(a); \varepsilon) = \alpha^i, \qquad \psi^i(b, x(b); \varepsilon) = \beta^i. \tag{A.4}$$

Let X_s be the infinitesimal transformations for $s = 1, \ldots, r$, then we write X_s as

$$X_s = \tau_s(t, x)\frac{\partial}{\partial t} + \xi_s^i(t, x)\frac{\partial}{\partial x^i} + \eta_s^i(t, x, \dot{x})\frac{\partial}{\partial \dot{x}^i}, \tag{A.5}$$

where

$$\tau_s(t, x) = \frac{\partial \phi}{\partial \varepsilon^s}(t, x; 0), \qquad \xi_s^i(t, x) = \frac{\partial \psi^i}{\partial \varepsilon^s}(t, x; 0),$$
$$\eta_s^i(t, x, \dot{x}) = \frac{\mathrm{d}\xi_s^i}{\mathrm{d}t} - \dot{x}^i\frac{\mathrm{d}\tau_s}{\mathrm{d}t}, \tag{A.6}$$

and (A.4) obeys

$$\tau_s(a, x(a)) = \tau_s(b, x(b)) = 0,$$
$$\xi_s^i(a, x(a)) = \xi_s^i(b, x(b)) = 0. \tag{A.7}$$

If (A.1) is invariant under (A.2), we have

$$\int_a^b X_s(L\,\mathrm{d}t) = 0. \tag{A.8}$$

Lemma. *For any $\tau_s(t, x)$ and $\xi_s^i(t, x)$, we have*

$$N_s = \left(\xi_s^i - \dot{x}^i\tau_s\right)E_i + \frac{\mathrm{d}\Omega_s}{\mathrm{d}t}, \tag{A.9}$$

where

$$N_s = \frac{\partial L}{\partial t}\tau_s + \frac{\partial L}{\partial x^i}\xi_s^i + \frac{\partial L}{\partial \dot{x}^i}\left(\frac{\mathrm{d}\xi_s^i}{\mathrm{d}t} - \dot{x}^i\frac{\mathrm{d}\tau_s}{\mathrm{d}t}\right) + L\frac{\mathrm{d}\tau_s}{\mathrm{d}t},$$

$$E_i = \text{Euler–Lagrange equation} = \frac{\partial L}{\partial x^i} - \frac{\mathrm{d}}{\mathrm{d}t}\left(\frac{\partial L}{\partial \dot{x}^i}\right),$$

$$\frac{\mathrm{d}\Omega}{\mathrm{d}t} = \frac{\mathrm{d}}{\mathrm{d}t}\left[\left(L - \dot{x}^i\frac{\partial L}{\partial \dot{x}^i}\right)\tau_s + \frac{\partial L}{\partial \dot{x}^i}\xi_s^i\right].$$

Proof. By differentiating Ω_s with respect to t we have

$$\frac{\mathrm{d}\Omega_s}{\mathrm{d}t} = \frac{\mathrm{d}}{\mathrm{d}t}\left[\left(L - \dot{x}^i\frac{\partial L}{\partial \dot{x}^i}\right)\tau_s + \frac{\partial L}{\partial \dot{x}^i}\xi_s^i\right]$$

$$= \frac{\partial L}{\partial t}\tau_s + \frac{\partial L}{\partial \dot{x}^i}\left(\frac{\mathrm{d}\xi_s^i}{\mathrm{d}t} - \dot{x}^i\frac{\mathrm{d}\tau_s}{\mathrm{d}t}\right) + L\frac{\mathrm{d}\tau_s}{\mathrm{d}t}$$

$$+ x^i\tau_s\left[\frac{\partial L}{\partial x^i} - \frac{\mathrm{d}}{\mathrm{d}t}\left(\frac{\partial L}{\partial \dot{x}^i}\right)\right] + \frac{\mathrm{d}}{\mathrm{d}t}\left(\frac{\partial L}{\partial \dot{x}^i}\right)\xi_s^i$$

$$= N_s - (\xi_s^i - \dot{x}^i\tau_s)E_i. \quad \text{Q.E.D.}$$

When (A.1) is optimized, E_i vanishes and (A.9) reduces to

$$\mathrm{d}\Omega_s/\mathrm{d}t = N_s. \tag{A.10}$$

There are two cases: (1) when $N_s = 0$ and (2) $N_s \neq 0$. The conservation law when $N_s = 0$ is

$$\mathrm{d}\Omega_s/\mathrm{d}t = 0 \quad \text{or} \quad \Omega_s = \text{constant}. \tag{A.11a}$$

When $N_s \neq 0$ and $\mathrm{d}\Phi_s/\mathrm{d}t = N_s$, we have

$$\mathrm{d}(\Omega_s - \Phi_s)/\mathrm{d}t = 0 \quad \text{or} \quad \Omega_s - \Phi = \text{constant}. \tag{A.11b}$$

This is Noether's invariance up to divergence.

References

Bessel-Hagen, E., 1921, Über die Erhaltungssätze der Elektrodynamik, Math. Ann. 84, 258–276.
Caton, C. and K. Shell, 1971, An exercise in the theory of heterogeneous capital accumulation, Review of Economic Studies 32, 233–240.

Gelfand, I.M. and S.V. Fomin, 1963, Calculus of variations (Prentice-Hall, Englewood Cliffs, NJ), translated from the Russian by R.A. Silverman.
Kataoka, H., 1983, On the local conservation laws in the von Neumann model, in: R. Sato and M.J. Beckmann, eds., Technology, organization and economic structure, Lecture notes in economics and mathematical systems, Vol. 210, 253–260.
Klein, F., 1918, Über die Differentialgesetze für die Erhaltung von Impuls und Energie in der Einsteinschen Gravitationstheorie, Nachr. Akad. Wiss. Göttingen, Math-Phys. Kl. II, 171–189.
Kemp, M.C. and N.V. Long, 1982, On the evaluation of social income in a dynamic economy, in: G.R. Feiwel, ed., Samuelson and neoclassical economics (Kluwer-Nijhoff, Boston, MA).
Lenard, T.M., 1972, Aggregate policy controls and optimal growth: Theory and applications to the U.S. economy, Ph.D. dissertation (Brown University, Providence, RI).
Lie, S., 1891, Vorlesungen über Differentialgleichungen, mit bekannten infinitesimalen Transformationen, edited by G. Scheffers (Teubner, Leipzig), reprinted 1967 (Chelsea Publ. Co., New York).
Liviatan, N. and P.A. Samuelson, 1969, Notes on turnpikes: Stable and unstable, Journal of Economic Theory 1, 454–475.
Logan, J.D., 1977, Invariant variational principles, Mathematics in science and engineering, Vol. 138 (Academic Press, New York).
Lovelock, D. and H. Rund, 1975, Tensors, differential forms, and variational principles (Wiley, New York).
Moser, J., 1979, Hidden symmetries in dynamical systems, American Scientists 67, 689–695.
Noether, E., 1918, Invariante Variationsprobleme, Nachr. Akad. Wiss. Göttingen, Math.-Phys. Kl. II, 235–257, translated by M.A. Tavel, 1971, Invariant variation problems, Transport Theory and Statistical Physics 1, 186–207.
Nôno, T., 1968, On the symmetry groups of simple materials: Applications of the theory of Lie groups, J. Math. Anal. Appl. 24, 110–135.
Nôno, T. and F. Mimura, 1975/1976/1977/1978, Dynamic symmetries, I/III/IV/V, Bulletin of Fukuoka University of Education 25/26/27/28.
Ramsey, F., 1928, A mathematical theory of saving, Economic Journal 38, 543–559.
Rund, H., 1966, The Hamilton–Jacobi theory in the calculus of variations (Van Nostrand-Reinhold, Princeton, NJ).
Sagan, H., 1969, Introduction to the calculus of variations (McGraw-Hill, New York).
Sakakibara, E., 1970, Dynamic optimization and economic policy, American Economic Review 60, Dec.
Samuelson, P.A., 1970a, Law of conservation of the capital–output ratio, Proceedings of the National Academy of Sciences, Applied Mathematical Science 67, 1477–1479.
Samuelson, P.A., 1970b, Two conservation laws in theoretical economics, Mimeo., July (Department of Economics, M.I.T., Cambridge, MA).
Samuelson, P.A., 1972, The general saddlepoint property of optimal–control motions, Journal of Economic Theory 5, 102–120.
Samuelson, P.A., 1976, Speeding up of time with age in recognition of life as fleeting, in: A.M. Tang et al., eds., Evolution, welfare, and time in economics: Essays in honor of Nicholas Georgescu-Roegen (Lexington Books, Heath, Lexington, MA).
Samuelson, P.A., 1982, Variations on capital/output conservation laws, Mimeo., Jan. (M.I.T., Cambridge, MA).
Sato, R., 1981, Theory of technical change and economic invariance: Application of Lie groups (Academic Press, New York).
Sato, R., 1982, Invariant principle and capital/output conservation laws, Working paper no. 82-8 (Brown University, Providence, RI).
Sato, R., T. Nôno and F. Mimura, 1983, Hidden symmetries: Lie groups and economic conservation laws, Essay in honor of Martin Beckmann.
Weitzman, M.L., 1976, On the welfare significance of national product in a dynamic economy, Quarterly Journal of Economics 90, 156–162.
Whittaker, E.T., 1937, A treatise on the analytical dynamics of particles and rigid bodies, 4th ed. (Cambridge University Press, Cambridge), reprinted 1944 (Dover, New York).

TESTING SPECIFICATIONS OF ECONOMIC AGENTS' INTERTEMPORAL OPTIMUM PROBLEMS IN THE PRESENCE OF ALTERNATIVE MODELS*

Kenneth J. SINGLETON

Carnegie-Mellon University and NBER, Pittsburgh, PA 15213, USA

This paper develops statistics for testing the null specification of an economic agent's intertemporal optimum problem, that incorporate information about a specific non-nested alternative specification. The disturbances may be serially correlated and conditionally heteroskedastic. An optimal test is developed for a local alternative that reflects the specification of the alternative optimum problem through a term representing the 'best' approximation of the null model by the non-nested alternative model. Then, the procedures are implemented to study monetary and non-monetary models of consumption and portfolio decisions.

1. Introduction

Empirical investigations of dynamic rational expectations models have been conducted for a number of alternative specifications of agents' intertemporal optimum problems. For instance, consumption and investment decisions have been studied using specifications of consumers' preferences that are separable across decision variables and time and specifications that are non-separable across time and decision variables.[1] Similarly, rules governing firms' purchases of factors of production have been derived under various assumptions about production functions;[2] and under alternative assumptions about the inter-relations among industries or firms.[3] Although different specifications of agents' intertemporal optimum problems often have very different implications for behavior, little attention has been given to formally testing one specification against another. Perhaps the primary reason for this is that the empirical

*Helpful comments on an earlier draft were provided by an anonymous referee, Lars Hansen, Andrew Jonas, and members of the Econometrics Workshop at Carnegie-Mellon University. This research was supported by NSF grant SES-8121253.

[1]Examples of recent empirical studies of consumption decisions based explicitly on separable objective functions are Hall (1978), Grossman and Shiller (1981) and Hansen and Singleton (1983). Non-separable objective functions are considered by Bernanke (1983), Dunn and Singleton (1985) and Eichenbaum and Hansen (1985).

[2]See, for example, Abel (1980) and Kydland and Prescott (1982).

[3]Some implications of different industry structures are discussed in Sargent (1981) and Hansen, Epple and Roberds (1984).

relations deduced from alternative specifications (e.g. decision rules or Euler equations) are not 'nested' in the sense that neither relation is a special case of the other. The purposes of this paper are to develop procedures for testing over-identifying restrictions implied by the null specification of an agent's non-linear optimum problem in the presence of a competing specification; and to implement these procedures to study monetary and non-monetary models of consumption and portfolio decisions.

Test procedures that exploit information about a specific alternative hypothesis have been developed for certain estimation environments from 'centered' differences between the minimized values of the criterion functions used in estimation, and from artificial compound regression models. The statistical assumptions under which these procedures lead to valid tests do not apply to many of the estimation equations deduced from economic models in which agents maximize non-linear, intertemporal objective functions under uncertainty, however. For instance, in studying a consumer's or firm's problem separately, sufficient structure on the joint distribution of the variables may not be imposed a priori to determine the relevant log-likelihood functions and implement Cox's (1961) separate families test. Additionally, the estimation equations deduced from the optimum problems may be fundamentally non-linear relations with conditionally heteroskedastic and serially correlated disturbances.[4] In these circumstances, the tests proposed by Ericsson (1982), Godfrey (1983) and MacKinnon, White and Davidson (1983) based on the classical instrumental variables criterion function for linear models, and the generalized Cox-test proposed by Aguire-Torres and Gallant (1983) based on M-estimators for non-linear simultaneous equation models with i.i.d. disturbances, are not applicable.

These econometric considerations are illustrated in section 2 in the context of several specifications of a consumer's optimum problem. Consumers are assumed to have utility functions defined over the services provided by current and past acquisitions of durable and non-durable goods. Two non-nested specifications of preferences over services from goods are studied: a quadratic function [e.g. Bernanke (1983), Eichenbaum and Hansen (1984)] and a Cobb–Douglas type function raised to a power [Dunn and Singleton (1985), Eichenbaum and Hansen (1985)]. For the first example, consumers are assumed to have access to traded securities with payoffs denominated in terms of a numeraire good as in the non-monetary models of Lucas (1978) and Breeden

[4] Serial dependence of the errors may be a direct consequence of assumptions about shocks to objective functions [e.g. Hansen and Sargent (1980)] or a consequence of non-time-separable objective functions [e.g., Eichenbaum, Hansen and Singleton (1983)], in which cases the covariance structure of the disturbances may be dictated by the theories. On the other hand, under an 'omitted information' interpretation of the error term [Hansen and Sargent (1980)], the error will generally exhibit complicated and unknown forms of dependence even when the decision rules are linear relations.

(1979). The second example is a monetary economy in which consumers have the power objective function, but a different constraint set than in the non-monetary economy. Money is introduced into the model by imposing a Clower constraint on purchases of certain goods as in Lucas (1983) and Townsend (1984). With the imposition of this constraint, there is an explicit role for money and nominally denominated assets in individuals' portfolios. The corresponding monetary and non-monetary models imply different (non-nested) restrictions on the time series of consumptions and asset returns. Furthermore, the estimation equations deduced from these specifications are non-linear functions of the variables and parameters, and the disturbances in the equations all follow moving average processes.

Throughout this analysis it is assumed that the models are estimated using the generalized instrumental variables criterion function [Hansen (1982)]. This criterion function yields consistent estimators of the parameters of models with disturbances that exhibit the covariance properties described in the preceding paragraph. By judicious choice of the 'distance' matrix, this approach also yields a statistic – namely, the minimized value of the criterion function – for testing the over-identifying restrictions implied by the null specification [Hansen (1982)]. This test is not designed to incorporate explicitly information about a specific family of alternative specifications of the model, however. The development of tests that do incorporate such information is a primary objective of this paper.

The statistic based on the minimized value of the criterion function tests whether a certain linear combination of the sample orthogonality conditions used in estimation of the null model are zero. This is one among a large class of statistics for testing the null specification of an optimum problem that can be expressed as linear combinations of the sample orthogonality conditions for the null model. In section 3, the design of locally optimal tests of this form in the presence of non-nested alternatives is discussed. In particular, an optimal test is deduced for a local alternative that reflects the specification of the alternative optimum problem through a term representing the 'best' approximation of the null model by the non-nested alternative model.

Finally, in section 5 the tests are implemented for the examples discussed in section 2.

2. Monetary and non-monetary asset pricing models

Non-nested null and alternative models may arise in a number of different contexts. In this section, the nature of the inference problem for several competing representative consumer models of consumption and portfolio decisions is discussed. Let Φ denote a class of competing specifications of the intertemporal optimum problem for a representative consumer. Each $\phi \in \Phi$ represents a family of objective functions (concave utility functions), a set of decision and state variables that appear as arguments in the objective function, and a compatable set of constraints on choices of the consumer.[5] In general some, but not all, of the characteristics of two distinct elements of Φ may be the same; for instance, the constraint sets may be identical.

Suppose that under the null specification, H_0: $\phi = \phi_0$, preferences of a representative agent are of the power form considered in Dunn and Singleton (1985) and Eichenbaum and Hansen (1985):

$$\mathrm{E}_0 \sum_{n=0}^{\infty} \beta^n \{ c_n^{*\delta} d_n^{*(1-\delta)} \}^{\gamma} / \gamma, \qquad 0 < \delta < 1, \quad \gamma < 1, \tag{1}$$

where c_n^* and d_n^* are the service flows from non-durable and durable goods, respectively, $\beta \in (0,1)$ is a subjective discount factor, and E_0 denotes expectations conditioned on agents' information at date zero. Suppose further that under the alternative specification, H_1: $\phi = \phi_1$, utility is given by the quadratic function

$$\mathrm{E}_0 \sum_{n=0}^{\infty} \beta^n \left\{ \left[c_n^* - \frac{a_1}{2} c_n^{*2} \right] + \left[a_2 d_n^* - \frac{a_3}{2} d_n^{*2} \right] + a_4 c_n^* d_n^* \right\}, \tag{2}$$

which was also studied by Eichenbaum and Hansen (1985).

Service flows from goods are not observable and, therefore, in order to analyze these models empirically the service flows must be expressed in terms of measured acquisitions of goods. For the purpose of this analysis it is assumed that c_t^* and d_t^* are related to past acquisitions of goods according to the linear technologies:

$$c_n^* = c_n + \alpha c_{n-1} \equiv \alpha(L) c_n, \qquad \alpha \geq 0, \tag{3}$$

$$d_n^* = \theta \sum_{j=0}^{\infty} (1-\theta)^j d_{n-j}, \qquad 0 < \theta < 1, \tag{4}$$

where c_n and d_n denote purchases of non-durable and durable goods at date n, respectively.[6] Non-durable goods acquired at date n provide services for two periods, while the service flow from a durable good decays geometrically over time. Substituting (3) and (4) into (1) and (2) gives 'indirect' utility functions with the measured acquisitions of goods as arguments.

[5] A family of objective functions is a collection of parametrically given functions indexed by parameters in an admissible parameter space.

[6] Non-durable goods are allowed to provide services for more than one period, because non-durable goods as measured in the national income accounts may have a useful lifetime of more than one period (e.g., one month).

Initially, consumers are assumed to have access to a complete set of markets for contingent claims to goods under both specifications ϕ_0 and ϕ_1. Payoffs from all securities are denominated in terms of the numeraire good non-durables. For the purposes of the example, the period budget constraint is assumed to be[7]

$$c_n + p_n d_n + a_n' q_n \leq a_{n-1}' q_n^* + y_n, \tag{5}$$

where p_n is the price of durable goods in terms of the numeraire c, a_n denotes the vector of shares of securities purchased at date n at price q_n, q_n^* denotes the vector of payoffs from acquiring assets at date $n-1$, and y_n is labor income.[8] The constraint (5) allows for the payoffs at date n from assets acquired in previous periods to be used to acquire goods in period n.

To complete the specification of the consumer's optimum problem, a convention about when agents consume and invest in each time period must be adopted. Hansen and Singleton (1982), and most of the subsequent studies of intertemporal asset pricing models, assumed that agents consume at the end of each period. This convention represents a conservative assumption about agents' information. For, if instead, agents are assumed to make their decisions at the beginning of the period, then they are endowed with the recorded information about consumption for the entire period (one month) when making investment decisions.

The assumption that consumers solve the optimum problem ϕ_0 leads to a set of equilibrium conditions upon which estimation and inference can be based. Specifically, the maximization of (1) subject (5) implies the relations

$$\begin{aligned} &\mathrm{E}_n\{\delta\alpha(\beta L^{-1})c_n^{*\delta\gamma-1}d_n^{*(1-\delta)\gamma} \\ &-\beta\delta[\alpha(\beta L^{-1})c_{n+1}^{*\delta\gamma-1}d_{n+1}^{*(1-\delta)\gamma}]r_{n+1}\} = 0, \end{aligned} \tag{6}$$

$$\begin{aligned} &\mathrm{E}_n\{(1-\delta)\theta c_n^{*\delta\gamma}d_n^{*(1-\delta)\gamma-1} \\ &-(1-\theta\beta L^{-1})\delta p_n[\alpha(\beta L^{-1})c_n^{*\delta\gamma-1}d_n^{*(1-\delta)\gamma}]\} = 0. \end{aligned} \tag{7}$$

The intertemporal relation (6) links the marginal utilities with respect to c_n and c_{n+1} to the one-period real return r_{n+1} on a security that pays off units of the numeraire good. The intratemporal relation (7) is obtained from the equality between the marginal utility with respect to d_n^* and the product of the marginal utility of c_n and the price of a unit of services from durable goods in terms of the numeraire.

[7] Let w_t denote the value of the consumer's wealth at date t in terms of the numeraire good. I assume that the terminal wealth condition $\lim_{t\to\infty} w_t = 0$ is satisfied.

[8] Implicit in this analysis is the assumption that utility from leisure is separable from utility of non-durable and durable goods.

The corresponding relations for the utility function (2) and the budget constraint (5) are

$$\mathrm{E}_n\{\alpha(\beta L^{-1})(1 - a_1 c_n^* + a_4 d_n^*)$$
$$- \beta[\alpha(\beta L^{-1})(1 - a_1 c_{n+1}^* + a_4 d_{n+1}^*)] r_{n+1}\} = 0, \qquad (8)$$

$$\mathrm{E}_n\{\theta(a_2 - a_3 d_n^* + a_4 c_n^*)$$
$$- [1 - \theta\beta L^{-1}] p_n \alpha(\beta L^{-1})(1 - a_1 c_n^* + a_4 d_n^*)\} = 0. \qquad (9)$$

See Dunn and Singleton (1985) and Eichenbaum and Hansen (1985) for details.

Estimation and inference cannot in general be based directly on the conditional moment restrictions (6)–(9). Explicit expressions for these conditional means have been obtained only for certain specifications of preferences and fairly simple production technologies. However, following Hansen and Singleton (1982), estimators and test statistics can be constructed using implied unconditional moment conditions. Specifically, let d_{pn} denote the two-dimensional vector comprised of the expressions in brackets in (6) and (7), and let d_{qn} denote the corresponding vector for (8) and (9). Then an implication of (6) and (7) is that, under the null hypothesis of power utility, the vector of 'disturbances' d_{pn} satisfies the orthogonality conditions $\mathrm{E}\{d_{pn} \otimes w_n\} = 0$, for any vector w_n in agents' information set I_n. Similarly, under the null hypothesis of quadratic utility, d_{qn} satisfies $\mathrm{E}\{d_{qn} \otimes z_n\} = 0$, for any vector $z_n \in I_n$.

Whether two specifications of optimum problems are non-nested in this estimation environment depends on the choices of the estimation equations and the associated moment conditions. More precisely, suppose that ϕ_0 implies the relation

$$h(x_n, b) = u_n(b), \qquad b \in B, \qquad (10)$$

and that ϕ_1 implies the relation

$$g(y_n, \gamma) = v_n(\gamma), \qquad \gamma \in \Gamma, \qquad (11)$$

where the admissible parameter spaces $B \subset R^p$ and $\Gamma \subset R^q$ are compact, and u_n and v_n are r- and s-dimensional vectors of disturbances, respectively. Also, suppose that, under the specification ϕ_0, there is a unique $b_0 \in B$ such that the disturbance u_n and l-dimensional vector of instruments $w_n \in I_n$ satisfy

$$\mathrm{E}\{u_n(b_0) \otimes w_n\} = 0 \quad \text{under } \mathrm{H}_0; \qquad (12)$$

and similarly, suppose there is a unique $\gamma_1 \in \Gamma$ such that the k-dimensional vector $z_n \in I_n$ and the disturbance v_n satisfy

$$\mathrm{E}\{ v_n(\gamma_1) \otimes z_n \} = 0 \quad \text{under } \mathrm{H}_1. \tag{13}$$

For the means $\mathrm{E}\{u_n(b) \otimes w_n\}$ and $\mathrm{E}\{v_n(\gamma) \otimes z_n\}$ to be comparable, the dimension of $u_n \otimes w_n, r \cdot l$, must be equal to the dimension of $v_n \otimes z_n, s \cdot k$, a condition which is henceforth assumed to be satisfied.[9] Then, in terms of the unconditional moment restrictions (12) and (13), two elements ϕ_0 and ϕ_1 in Φ are non-nested if, for an arbitrary element $b \in B$, the expectation $\mathrm{E}\{u_n(b) \otimes w_n\}$ cannot be approximated arbitrarily well by a sequence of expectations $\mathrm{E}\{v_n(\gamma_j) \otimes z_n\}$, $\gamma_j \in \Gamma$, $j = 1, \ldots$.[10]

When ϕ_0 and ϕ_1 represent different specifications of the objective functions, then the associated estimation equations will typically be non-nested. For the example just presented, the functional forms of the marginal utilities associated with the power and quadratic utility functions (1) and (2) are non-nested in the sense that neither is a special case of the other. Notice, however, that for orthogonality conditions to be non-nested additional structure must be imposed implicitly on the joint distribution of the disturbances and the instruments.

Even if the utility functions under ϕ_0 and ϕ_1 are the same, non-nested Euler equations may be implied by alternative optimum problems if the budget constraints facing the consumers are different. For instance, Lucas (1983) and Townsend (1984) have introduced money into asset pricing models through a liquidity (Clower-type) constraint on consumption purchases. There are two goods in these models, one of which must be purchased with money. To illustrate how altering the constraint set may affect the Euler equations, suppose that non-durable goods must be purchased with money. Durable goods, on the other hand, may be acquired by issuing secured debt for the amount of the purchase. As in the models of Lucas (1983) and Townsend (1984), it is assumed that markets for contingent claims are not complete, so that there is a non-trivial monetary equilibrium. In particular, unsecured private debt is assumed not to circulate freely as a means of payment.

The timing of transactions in this model is different from the non-monetary model. During period n, consumers work and acquire goods and services. At the end of period n they consume and invest. In addition, they are paid for their work and receive interest and dividend payments on previous invest-

[9] If the null and alternative models have the same number of equations and a common set of instruments is used in estimation ($z_n = w_n$), as in Ericsson (1982), Godfrey (1982) and MacKinnon, White and Davidson (1983), then this order condition is automatically satisfied.

[10] Notice that the expectations in (12) and (13) are not indexed by ϕ. While different probability measures may be associated with ϕ_0 and ϕ_1, such differences cannot be detected based on the unconditional moment restrictions alone. Thus, to conserve on notation $\mathrm{E}\{\cdot\}$ will not be indexed.

ments. These payments can be used to acquire durable goods at the end of period n, or can be carried forward and used to acquire non-durable goods in period $(n+1)$ – they cannot be used to acquire non-durable goods at date n. For this timing convention, the budget constraints of the representative consumer are

$$P_{cn}c_n \leq M_{n-1}, \tag{14}$$

$$P_{cn}c_n + P_{dn}d_n + M_n + A_n \leq A_{n-1} + M_{n-1} + y_n, \tag{15}$$

where P_c and P_d are the prices of goods in terms of money and A_n denotes the nominal, net worth (excluding money holdings) at the end of period n. M_n denotes nominal cash balances held at the end of period n and used to acquire goods during period $n+1$.

The maximization of (1) subject to (14) and (15) leads to the first-order conditions

$$\mathrm{E}_n\{\beta^n\delta\alpha(\beta L^{-1})c_n^{*\delta\gamma-1}d_n^{*(1-\delta)\gamma}\} = P_{cn}\Lambda_n + P_{cn}\psi_n, \tag{16}$$

$$\mathrm{E}_n\{\beta^n(1-\delta)\theta[1-\theta\beta L^{-1}]^{-1}c_n^{*\delta\gamma}d_n^{*(1-\delta)\gamma-1}\} = P_{dn}\Lambda_n, \tag{17}$$

$$\Lambda_n - \mathrm{E}_n\psi_{n+1} - \mathrm{E}_n\Lambda_{n+1} = 0, \tag{18}$$

where ψ_n and Λ_n are the Lagrange multipliers associated with the constraints (17) and (18), respectively. Eq. (18) is the intertemporal relation among multipliers. Now, if R_n is the one-period nominal return on a security for period n, then the counterpart to (6) is

$$U_{1n} = \{\delta\alpha(\beta L^{-1})[c_n^{*\delta\gamma-1}d_n^{*(1-\delta)\gamma}]/P_{cn}$$
$$-\delta\beta\alpha(\beta L^{-1})[c_{n+1}^{*\delta\gamma-1}d_{n+1}^{*(1-\delta)\gamma}]R_n/P_{cn+1}\}, \tag{19}$$

with $\mathrm{E}_n\{U_{1n}\}=0$. Solving (18) for Λ_n and substituting this expression into (17), solving the version of (16) at date $n+1$ for $(\Lambda_{n+1}+\psi_{n+1})$ and substituting into (17), and filtering the associated disturbance by $[1-\theta\beta L^{-1}]$ leads to a second disturbance

$$U_{2n} = \Big\{(1-\delta)[c_n^{*\delta\gamma}d_n^{*(1-\delta)\gamma-1}]$$
$$-[1-\theta\beta L^{-1}]\frac{P_{dn}}{\theta}\delta[\beta\alpha(\beta L^{-1})c_{n+1}^{*\delta\gamma-1}d_{n+1}^{*(1-\delta)\gamma}]/P_{cn+1}\Big\}, \tag{20}$$

which satisfies $\mathrm{E}_n\{U_{2n}\}=0$.

The return in (19) is for period n, instead of $n+1$ as in (6), because the proceeds from asset holdings cannot be spent on goods during the period they are received. By acquiring a share of a security at the end of period $n-1$, an agent foregoes consumption at date n. The payoff from this security (principal plus distributions), which is received at the end of period n, can be used to acquire and consume goods during period $n+1$. For the corresponding non-monetary model with the end-of-period timing convention, assets pay off in terms of goods at the end of each period and these goods can be consumed immediately.

Eq. (20) also differs from the corresponding expression for the non-monetary model (7). The last term in (20) is dated one period in the future relative to its counterpart in (7). Intuitively, this is because durable goods must be sold at date n in order to acquire money for the purchase of non-durable goods, and the latter transaction is consummated during period $n+1$.

Notice that, for the first example involving power and quadratic utility functions, the corresponding functional forms for the estimation equations and admissible parameter spaces both differ across the specifications ϕ_0 and ϕ_1. Nevertheless, the autocovariance structures of the corresponding disturbances are the same. The disturbances d_{pn}^1 and d_{qn}^1 associated with (6) and (8), respectively, follow MA(1) processes, while d_{pn}^2 and d_{qn}^2 are serially uncorrelated. That d_{pn}^1 and d_{qn}^1 are serially correlated follows from the observation that they are both functions of c_{n+2} which is not known to consumers until date $(n+2)$. In contrast, the monetary and non-monetary models with power utility functions imply different functional forms for the estimation equations, but the parameter spaces are identical. Furthermore, in the latter example, the estimation equations associated with the disturbances d_{pn}^2 and U_{2n} [see (7) and (20)] have different autocovariance structures [U_{2n} follows an MA(1) process]. Finally, the conditional variances of all of the disturbances may be complicated functions of agents' information set. The tests developed in section 3 are designed to accommodate all of these econometric difficulties.

3. A locally optimal test in the presence of an alternative specification

In this section, the local properties of a family of tests of H_0 based on linear combinations of the sample orthogonality conditions for the null specification are discussed. Locally optimal tests of H_0: $\phi = \phi_0$ are derived for particular local alternative hypotheses that incorporate information about the specification $\phi = \phi_1$. Two cases are considered. Initially, a test is derived for specifications that admit an economically meaningful comprehensive model with ϕ_0 and ϕ_1 as special cases. Then the properties of this test in environments for which comprehensive economic models cannot be constructed are discussed.

The large-sample properties of the proposed test are intimately connected to the properties of the estimators of the parameters of the null and competing specifications. Throughout this analysis it is assumed that estimates are obtained using the generalized instrumental variables criterion function discussed in Hansen (1982), Hansen and Sargent (1982) and Hansen and Singleton (1982). Specifically, for $b \in R^p$ and $\gamma \in R^q$, let

$$H_N(b) = \frac{1}{N}\sum_{n=1}^{N} h(x_n, b) \otimes w_n,$$

$$G_N(\gamma) = \frac{1}{N}\sum_{n=1}^{N} g(y_n, \gamma) \otimes z_n$$

denote the sample counterparts of the population orthogonality conditions in (12) and (13), where N is the sample size. Then the estimators b_N of b_0 and γ_N of γ_0 are chosen from B and Γ, respectively, to minimize

$$H_N(b)' S_{uN}^{-1} H_N(b), \tag{21}$$

$$G_N(\gamma)' S_{\upsilon N}^{-1} G_N(\gamma), \tag{22}$$

where the distance matrices S_{uN}^{-1} and $S_{\upsilon N}^{-1}$, which have dimensions $r \cdot l$ by $r \cdot l$ and $s \cdot k$ by $s \cdot k$, are chosen to yield the smallest asymptotic covariance matrix for b_N and γ_N, respectively, given the choices of instrument vectors w_n and z_n. [See Hansen (1982) and eq. (25).]

Sufficient conditions for the strong consistency and asymptotic normality of $\{b_N\colon N \geq 1\}$ and $\{\gamma_N\colon N \geq 1\}$ under H_0 and H_1, respectively, are given in Hansen (1982), and these conditions are henceforth maintained in this paper. Several additional assumptions about the behavior of γ_N and $S_{\upsilon N}^{-1}$ under H_0 are required subsequently. It is assumed that under H_0 the matrices S_{uN}^{-1} and $S_{\upsilon N}^{-1}$ converge almost surely to positive definite matrices denoted by S_u^{-1} and S_υ^{-1}. Further, the population criterion function,

$$\mathrm{E}\{\upsilon_n(\gamma) \otimes z_n\}' S_\upsilon^{-1} \mathrm{E}\{\upsilon_n(\gamma) \otimes z_n\},$$

is assumed to have a unique minimum at the (non-zero) point $\gamma^* \in \Gamma$ when H_0 is true. [When H_1 is true, γ_1 is the unique minimizer, since $\mathrm{E}\{\upsilon_n(\gamma_1) \otimes z_n\} = 0$.] Under these conditions and certain continuity conditions that are maintained as well under H_1, Hansen's (1982) Theorem 2.1 implies that $\{\gamma_N\colon N \geq 1\}$ converges almost surely to γ^*.

Previous studies of intertemporal optimum problems have typically used N times the minimized value of the criterion function (21), $CS \equiv N H_N(b_N)' S_{uN}^{-1} H_N(b_N)$, to test H_0: $\phi = \phi_0$. To interpret this test, note that the p linear combinations $[\partial H_N(b_N)/\partial b]' S_{uN}^{-1} H_N(b_N)$ of $H_N(b_N)$ are set to zero in estimating b_0. Thus, there are $(rl-p)$ additional linear combinations of $H_N(b_N)$ that are not set to zero in estimation, but that should be close to zero if the null hypothesis is true. The statistic CS, which is asymptotically distributed as a chi-square with $(rl-p)$ degrees of freedom under H_0 [Hansen (1982)], provides a test of these $(rl-p)$ restrictions.

While the CS statistic is convenient to use, it is not designed to incorporate information about a specific alternative specification of the model, $\phi=\phi_1$. Additional tests of H_0 can be based on any linear combination of $H_N(b_N)$ that has a non-degenerate distribution under H_0, since the probability limit of $H_N(b_N)$ under H_0 is zero. This observation leads naturally to an inquiry into the design of tests that 'efficiently' incorporate information about an alternative model. Of particular interest here is the linear combination of $H_N(b_N)$ that yields a test with maximal power against a local alternative that incorporates information about the specification $\phi=\phi_1$.

Let A_N be an $r\cdot l$-dimensional vector such that $A'_N H_N(b_N)$ is not set to zero in the estimation of b_0, and A_N converges in probability under H_0 to a constant, non-zero vector A_0. Then Lemma 4.1 in Hansen (1982) implies that $A'_N\sqrt{N}\,H_N(b_N)$ converges in distribution to a normal variate with mean zero and covariance matrix $A'_0\Sigma_0 A_0$, where Σ_0 is given by

$$\Sigma_0=S_u-D_0\left(D'_0S_u^{-1}D_0\right)^{-1}D'_0, \tag{23}$$

with

$$D_0=\mathrm{E}\left[\frac{\partial h}{\partial b}(x_n,b_0)\otimes w_n\right]. \tag{24}$$

The probability limit of the inverse of the distance matrix in (21) is given by

$$S_u=\sum_{j=-\infty}^{\infty}\mathrm{E}\{u_0u'_{-j}\otimes w_0w'_{-j}\}. \tag{25}$$

A consistent estimator of the variance matrix Σ_0, Σ_N, is obtained under H_0 by replacing D_0 with $D_N=N^{-1}\Sigma[\partial h(x_n,b_N)/\partial b]\otimes w_n$ and S_u with a consistent estimator of the spectral density matrix of $\{u_n(b_0)\otimes w_n\colon n\geq 1\}$ at frequency zero.[11] It follows that, under H_0,

$$\lambda_N\equiv NH_N(b_N)'A_N(A'_N\Sigma_NA_N)^{-1}A'_NH_N(b_N) \tag{26}$$

[11] In many applications the expression (25) for S_u simplifies under the assumptions of the null model – see Hansen (1982). Consistent estimation of S_u under various assumptions about the autocovariance structure of $\{u_n(b_0)\otimes w_n\}$ is discussed more extensively in Eichenbaum, Hansen and Singleton (1983).

converges in distribution to a chi-square variate with one degree of freedom. Under a local alternative, λ_N has a non-central chi-square distribution. Accordingly, a locally optimal test for such an alternative (i.e., a test with maximal power) is obtained by choosing A_N to maximize the non-centrality parameter.

Defining the sense in which an alternative model gets close to the null model is complicated by the fact that the models are non-nested. The null specification is, by definition, not a special case of the alternative model, so the usual approach to local analyses does not apply. However, when a comprehensive model that embodies ϕ_0 and ϕ_1 as special cases can be constructed, then A_N can be chosen so that the test based on λ_N has maximal local power in the direction of ϕ_1 from ϕ_0 within this comprehensive model. The optimality of such a test will, of course, be conditional on the comprehensive model chosen, as well as on the particular member of the family of models ϕ_1 that enters the comprehensive model.

Consider first the case where an economically meaningful comprehensive model can be constructed. The construction of such a model will often be possible when the intertemporal optimum problems under investigation differ only in the forms of the objective functions of the agents. To be concrete, consider the first example discussed in section 2. A natural comprehensive disturbance is obtained for these models by forming a convex combination of the individual disturbances. Let γ represent the parameter vector characterizing the member of the alternative family of specifications against which maximal local power is desired. Then the comprehensive disturbance is given by

$$\varepsilon_n^i(b_0, \gamma_1, \S) = \omega(\S) d_{pn}^i(b_0) + (1 - \omega(\S)) d_{qn}^i(\gamma), \qquad i = 1,2, \tag{27}$$

where $0 \le \omega(\S) \le 1$ and $\S \in \psi$ indexes alternative specifications in Φ, with ψ being an open interval in R. If $\S_0$ and $\S_1$ index H_0 and H_1, respectively, and $E[\varepsilon_n^i(b_0 \cdot \gamma_1, \S) \otimes z_n] = 0$ with z_n in agents' information set I_n in both models, then $\omega(\S_0) = 1$ and $\omega(\S_1) = 0$ yield the orthogonality conditions for H_0 and H_1, respectively. That the disturbances $\varepsilon_n^i(b_0, \gamma_1, \S)$ are associated with a well-defined optimum problem follows from the observation that a convex combination of concave utility functions is a concave function.

Proceeding more generally, suppose that the null and alternative models are represented by the disturbances u_n and v_n, respectively. Then, for a given value of γ, a local alternative that has the true model ranging between $\phi = \phi_1$ and $\phi = \phi_0$ is given by

$$H_{1N}: \quad \omega(\S_N) E\{u_n(b_0) \otimes z_n | \S_N\} + (1 - \omega(\S_N)) E\{v_n(\gamma) \otimes z_n | \S_N\} = 0, \tag{28}$$

where $0 \leq \omega(\S_N) \leq 1$, $\omega(\S_0) = 1$, and a typical element of the sequence $\{\S_N\}$ is given by $\S_N = \S_0 + \eta/\sqrt{N}$; η a scalar constant. The function $\omega(\cdot)$ is assumed to satisfy the condition $\omega(\S_N) > 0$ for large enough N. For such N, (28) can be expressed equivalently as

$$\mathrm{H}_{1N}: \quad \mathrm{E}\{u_n(b_0) \otimes z_n | \S_N\} = \nu(\S_N)\mathrm{E}\{v_n(\gamma) \otimes z_n | \S_N\}, \tag{29}$$

where $\nu(\S_N) = -(1 - \omega(\S_N))/\omega(\S_N)$. The expectations are calculated using the joint distribution function of the underlying sources of uncertainty in the economy under the specification $\S_N$. Different specifications $\S_N$ may correspond to different assumptions about the distribution of the exogenous disturbances and, therefore, the expectations in (28) and (29) are indexed by $\S_N$.

It remains to select the value of γ at which the expectation $\mathrm{E}\{v_n(\gamma) \otimes z_n | \S_N\}$ is evaluated. As noted previously, different values for γ lead to different local alternatives in (29) and, hence, to different tests which are optimal for these alternatives. In other words, there is no single test statistic that is locally optimal against all members of the family of specifications ϕ_1. Accordingly, it seems reasonable to select the value of γ in (29) to be the value for which the alternative family gets 'closest' to the null specification $u_n(b_0)$. For then the optimal test has maximal power against the member of ϕ_1 that most resembles the null specification, when the alternative specification is correct.

More precisely, let $\tilde{\gamma}_N$ be chosen to minimize the function

$$[\mathrm{E}\{u_n(b_0) \otimes z_n | \S_N\} - \mathrm{E}\{v_n(\gamma) \otimes z_n | \S_N\}]' S_v^{-1}$$
$$\times [\mathrm{E}\{u_n(b_0) \otimes z_n | \S_N\} - \mathrm{E}\{v_n(\gamma) \otimes z_n | \S_N\}];$$

that is, $\tilde{\gamma}_N$ is chosen to make the orthogonality condition under ϕ_1 as close as possible to the orthogonality condition under ϕ_0, where distance is measured by S_v^{-1}.[12] The first-order conditions for this minimization problem are

$$\mathrm{E}\left\{\frac{\partial v_n}{\partial \gamma}(\tilde{\gamma}_N) \otimes z_n | \S_N\right\}' S_v^{-1}$$
$$\times [\mathrm{E}\{u_n(b_0) \otimes z_n | \S_N\} - \mathrm{E}\{v_n(\tilde{\gamma}_N) \otimes z_n | \S_N\}] = 0. \tag{30}$$

Under H_{1N}, the solution to these equations has the same limit as the solution, γ^*, to

$$\mathrm{E}\left\{-\frac{\partial v_n}{\partial \gamma}(\gamma^*) \otimes z_n | \S_0\right\}' S_v^{-1} \mathrm{E}\{v_n(\gamma^*) \otimes z_n | \S_0\} = 0. \tag{31}$$

[12] The estimator $\tilde{\gamma}_N$ is the counterpart to the estimator obtained from the regression of $\hat{f}$ on g in Davidson and MacKinnon's (1982) equation (10). The latter auxiliary regression is used by Pesaran and Deaton (1978) in their construction of a Cox test.

The latter equations are simply the first-order conditions to the population counterpart of the minimization problem (22). Thus, with $\gamma = \gamma^*$, the local alternative (29) represents a sequence of 'comprehensive' orthogonality conditions that ranges between the member of the alternative family $\{E[v_n(\gamma) \otimes z_n]: \gamma \in \Gamma\}$ that best approximates $E\{u_n(b_0) \otimes z_n\} = 0$, and zero.

Suppose that, under H_{1N}, $\sqrt{N}[H_N(b_0) - E\{u_n(b_0) \otimes z_n | \S_N\}]$ converges in distribution to a normal random variate with mean zero and covariance matrix S_u. Also, suppose that b_N is weakly consistent for b_0 under local misspecification of the form (29). Then Theorem 2.6 in Newey (1983) implies that λ_N converges weakly to a non-central chi-square variate with non-centrality parameter

$$\alpha'\Omega_0' A(\S_0)[A(\S_0)'\Sigma_0 A(\S_0)']^{-1} A(\S_0)\Omega_0\alpha, \tag{32}$$

where $\alpha = \eta\nu'(\S_0)E\{v_n(\gamma^*) \otimes z_n | \S_0\}$, $\Omega_0 = I - D_0(D_0'S_u^{-1}D_0)^{-1}D_0'S_u^{-1}$, and $A(\S_0)$ is the probability limit under H_{1N} of A_N. Minimizing this expression by choice of $A(\S_0)$ gives the optimal choice of weights $A_0^* = S_u^{-1}E\{v_n(\gamma^*) \otimes z_n | \S_0\}$. Locally equivalent tests are obtained by substituting consistent estimators of A_0^* (under H_{1N}) into (26). One consistent estimator of A_0^* is given by $S_{uN}^{-1}[H_N(b_N) - G_N(\gamma_N)]$, since $H_N(b_N)$ converges in probability to zero under H_{1N} and $G_N(\gamma_N)$ converges in probability to $E\{v_n(\gamma^*) \otimes z_n\}$. Using this set of weights, the optimal test statistic can be expressed as

$$\lambda_N^* = N\{[H_N(b_N) - G_N(\gamma_N)]'S_{uN}^{-1}H_N(b_N)\}^2/\hat{\sigma}_{\lambda N}^2, \tag{33}$$

where

$$\hat{\sigma}_{\lambda N}^2 = [H_N(b_N) - G_N(\gamma_N)]'S_{uN}^{-1}\Sigma_N S_{uN}^{-1}[H_N(b_N) - G_N(\gamma_N)].$$

A test of H_0: $\phi = \phi_1$ is conducted by comparing λ_N^* to the desired critical value for a chi-square with one degree of freedom.[13] Note that if H_1 is in fact the true model, then $[H_N(b_N) - G_N(\gamma_N)]'S_{uN}^{-1}H_N(b_N)$ will tend to be large and positive, since the probability limit of this statistic is a positive number under H_1. The use of a two-tailed test also allows for the possibility of rejecting H_0 in a 'direction' away from H_1 in the case where a third specification in Φ is the true model.

The λ^* statistic has the same basic form as the J test proposed by Davidson and MacKinnon (1982) and MacKinnon, White and Davidson (1983) for testing in the context of a compound regression model. The tests developed by Davidson and MacKinnon (1982) and Aguire-Torres and Gallant (1983) for

[13] In principle H_0 can also be tested by estimating the parameters of both models, together with $\S$, and testing the null hypothesis that $\S = \S_0$. However, this approach requires that a large number of parameters be estimated simultaneously.

regression models amount to tests of whether the difference between the residuals from H_0 to H_1 are orthogonal to the residuals from H_0. For the estimation environment studied in this paper, sample cross-products of the residuals and the instruments appear instead of the residuals themselves, but otherwise the optimal tests have essentially the same form. The primary difference between (33) and the statistic considered by MacKinnon, White and Davidson (1983) is that they calculated a t-statistic instead of an F-statistic.

This discussion has been premised on the assumption that the non-centrality parameter (32) is strictly positive. It follows that implicit null and alternative families of specifications of optimum problems are being tested, since the non-centrality parameter may be zero for members of the nominal null and alternative families ϕ_0 and ϕ_1, respectively. The non-centrality parameter will be zero when

$$\left(I - D_0\left(D_0' S_u^{-1} D_0\right) D_0' S_u^{-1}\right)\left[\mathrm{E}\{u_n(b_0) \otimes z_n\} - \mathrm{E}\{v_n(\gamma^*) \otimes z_n\}\right] = 0,$$

which is equivalent to

$$\left[\mathrm{E}\{u_n(b_0) \otimes z_n\} - \mathrm{E}\{v_n(\gamma^*) \otimes z_n\}\right] = D_0 \xi, \tag{34}$$

for some p-dimensional vector ξ. Recall that the vector $\mathrm{E}\{v_n(\gamma^*) \otimes z_n\}$ can be interpreted as the best approximation in $\{\mathrm{E}[v_n(\gamma) \otimes z_n]\colon \gamma \in \Gamma\}$ to $\mathrm{E}\{u_n(b_0) \otimes z_n\}$. Thus, for the λ^* test to have power against the local alternative (29) it must be the case that this approximation cannot be given exactly as a first-order Taylor's expansion of $\mathrm{E}\{u_n(b) \otimes z_n\}$ about the point $b = b_0$. This condition is the counterpart to the condition that assures a non-zero variance of the test statistic constructed by Aguire-Torres and Gallant (1983, eq. (4.2)) for non-linear regression models. The assumption that (34) does not hold with equality also assures that the asymptotic variance of $A_N^* \sqrt{N} H_N(b_N)$ is strictly positive.

In many circumstances, it may not be possible to construct a comprehensive disturbance like (27) that is associated with an economically meaningful model. For instance, the monetary and non-monetary models discussed in section 2 involve different budget constraints, because of the assumed differences in the structure of markets for contingent claims. Consequently, there appears to be no way of parameterizing a continuum of alternative models that includes ϕ_0 and ϕ_1 as special cases. Indeed, it seems to be the case more generally that when non-nested models arise because of differences in the structures of markets, comprehensive estimation equations may not be available.

When a comprehensive economic model is not available, there is no natural 'benchmark' alternative for evaluating the relative local powers of tests based on alternative choices of A_N. Furthermore, there may not be natural orderings for the disturbances u_n and v_n, or the instrument vectors when they differ

$(z_n \neq w_n)$. Different orderings of either the disturbance or instrument vectors will in general lead to tests with different large and small sample properties. Moreover, there may be no generally accepted criteria for selecting among these tests. Nevertheless, a valid test of H_0: $\phi = \phi_0$ can be conducted using a modified version of the statistic λ_N^*, calculated with $H_N(b_N) = N^{-1}\sum u_n(b_n) \otimes w_n$ and $G_N(\gamma_N) = N^{-1}\sum v_n(\gamma_n) \otimes z_n$.

For the monetary and non-monetary asset pricing models discussed in section 2, certain orderings do suggest themselves as being most appropriate. The fact that the nominal interest rate was positive over the sample period implies that the constraint (14) was always binding (assuming the monetary model was the true model). Thus, in estimating the models, it seems reasonable to use a common set of instruments, which are functions of the acquisitions of goods, the relative price of durable goods, and the asset return. Furthermore, the corresponding elements of the vectors $[d_{pn}^1, d_{pn}^2]$ and $[U_{1n}, U_{2n}]$ represent the analogous first-order conditions from the two models and they are similar functions of the data. Therefore, the statistic λ_N^* will be used to test the restrictions implied by these models.

Another consideration, that may be relevant in small samples, is that the relative scale of $u_n(b_0) \otimes w_n$ and $v_n(\gamma^*) \otimes z_n$ may be very different, even if $w_n = z_n$. The minimized values of (21) and (22) are unaffected by rescaling $u_n(b_N) \otimes w_n$ and $v_n(\gamma_N) \otimes z_n$, since the changes in scale will be offset through the optimal choices of S_{uN} and S_{vN}. However, $G_N(\gamma_N)'S_{uN}^{-1}H_N(b_N)$ is not insensitive to such changes in scale. If, for instance, $H_N(b_N)'S_{uN}^{-1}H_N(b_N) \gg G_N(\gamma_N)'S_{uN}^{-1}H_N(b_N)$, then λ_N^* may be approximately equal to the corresponding *CS* statistic, but will have fewer degrees of freedom. In this case, the λ_N^* statistic may tend to overstate the evidence against the null specification in small samples. One way of correcting for differences in scale is to premultiply the vectors $H_N(b_N)$ and $G_N(\gamma_N)$ by $U_N^{-1/2} = [\mathrm{diag}(S_{uN})]^{-1/2}$ and $V_N^{-1/2} = [\mathrm{diag}(S_{vN})]^{-1/2}$, where $U_N^{-1/2}$ and $V_N^{-1/2}$ are diagonal matrices with the ith diagonal elements being one over the square root of the ith diagonal element of S_{uN} and S_{vN}, respectively. Then (21) and (22) can be interpreted as quadratic forms with the distance matrices being correlation matrices. The resulting version of λ_N^* is given by

$$\lambda_N^*[\text{scaled}] = \frac{N\{[H_N^*(b_N) - G_N^*(\gamma_N)]'S_{uN}^{*-1}H_N^*(b_N)\}^2}{[H_N^*(b_N) - G_N^*(\gamma_N)]'U_N^{1/2}S_{uN}^{-1}\Sigma_N S_{uN}^{-1}U_N^{1/2}[H_N^*(b_N) - G_N^*(\gamma_N)]}, \tag{35}$$

where

$$H_N^*(b_N) = U_N^{-1/2} H_N(b_N), \quad G_N^*(\gamma_N) = V_N^{-1/2} G_N(\gamma_N),$$

$$S_{uN}^* = U_N^{-1/2} S_{uN} U_N^{-1/2}.$$

This statistic is optimal for the local alternative

$$\begin{aligned} \mathrm{H}_{1N}: \quad & \omega(\S_N) U_0^{-1/2} \mathrm{E}\{ u_n(b_0) \otimes w_n | \S_N \} \\ & + (1 - \omega(\S_N)) V_0^{-1/2} \mathrm{E}\{ v_n(\gamma^*) \otimes z_n | \S_N \} = 0, \end{aligned} \tag{36}$$

where $\omega(\S_0) = 1$ and the matrices U_0 and V_0 are the probability limits of the matrices U_N and V_N, respectively. The statistic λ_N^*[scaled] can be interpreted as the optimal test in the direction from H_0 in which the mean of the standardized cross-product $V_0^{-1/2}[v_n(\gamma^*) \otimes z_n]$ gets closest to the mean of the standardized cross-product $U_0^{-1/2}[u_n(b_0) \otimes w_n]$.

Both the λ^* and λ^*[scaled] statistics yield valid large-sample tests of H_0, whether or not a meaningful comprehensive model can be constructed. [The alternative (36) is not in general associated with a meaningful comprehensive economic model.] In constructing tests of H_0, there seems to be no widely accepted criterion for selecting among λ^* or λ^*[scaled] or, more generally, among tests that are optimal for any other rescalings of the disturbances in (36). Even when a meaningful comprehensive model can be constructed, there may be several such models available which are associated with correspondingly different optimal tests of H_0. Thus, the optimality results deduced here for the test based on λ^*, and the similar optimality results for the J test deduced by Davidson and MacKinnon (1982) for regression models, are quite limited in scope.

5. Empirical examples

This section reports the results frcm implementing the λ^* and λ^*[scaled] tests for the examples presented in section 2. The sample period for this analysis is January 1959 through December 1978. Monthly data on real purchases of non-durable goods plus services and real purchases of durable goods were obtained from the CITIBASE data tape. These series were deflated by the monthly population series published by the Bureau of Census in order to obtain per capita real series $\{c_t\}$ and $\{d_t\}$. The service flow series $\{c_t^*\}$ was then calculated using eq. (3). Eq. (4) was used to compute $\{d_t^*\}$ as a function of an initial stock of durable goods and subsequent purchases of goods. The initial value of the stock was set at the net value in December 1958 of the stock of durables computed by Musgrave (1979). The price of d_t relative to c_t was computed by dividing the implicit price deflator for durables by the deflator for non-durables plus services.

The large-sample properties of the proposed tests have been established under the assumption that the disturbances in the estimation equations are strictly stationary stochastic processes. In practice, it is often necessary to transform the disturbances obtained from the Euler equations or decision rules to induce stationarity. How these transformation impinge on the construction of the test statistics depends on whether or not it is desired to base the test procedure on a meaningful comprehensive model. To maintain a comprehensive model after detrending, the disturbances associated with ϕ_0 and ϕ_1 must be detrended using the same procedures. Whether simple transformations of the disturbances induce stationarity, or the series comprising the models must be detrended individually, depends on the models.

Following Dunn and Singleton (1985) and Eichenbaum and Hansen (1985), the levels of acquisitions of goods, c_n and d_n, are assumed to exhibit exponential growth (i.e., $\ln c_n$ and $\ln d_n$ have linear trends). Additionally, the real returns and $c_n^*/(p_n d_n^*)$ are assumed to be stationary stochastic processes.[14] Under these assumptions, the trends can be removed from the non-monetary models with power utility (Model I) by dividing the disturbance d_{pn}, constructed from (6) and (7), by $s_n = \{c_n^{*\delta\gamma-1} d_n^{*(1-\delta)\gamma}\}$. A similar transformation cannot be applied to the disturbances d_{qn} to induce stationarity, because of the additive form of the marginal utility for the non-monetary model with quadratic utility (Model II). Therefore, in the latter case, the series were individually detrended before estimation.[15] Finally, to preserve the comprehensive model, the disturbance d_{qn}, constructed from (8) and (9) with detrended series, was also divided by s_n calculated using the parameter estimates from Model I. Let $\tilde{d}_{pn}$ and $\tilde{d}_{qn}$ denote the resulting, scaled disturbances.

Initially, the vector of instruments used in the estimation of both models is

$$w_n' = \{1,\ c_n/c_{n-1} - 1,\ d_n/d_{n-1} - 1,\ p_n/p_{n-1} - 1,\ r_{n-1} - 1\}.$$

The return series appearing in d_{pn}^1, d_{qn}^1 and w_n is the one-month, value-weighted return on the New York Stock Exchange published by CRSP at the University

[14] The assumption that $c_n^*/(p_n d_n^*)$ is stationary implicitly restricts the exponential trend in c_n^* to equal the product of the trends in p_n and d_n^*.

[15] Eichenbaum and Hansen (1985) discuss the properties of the non-monetary models with trends in detail. Since this paper was completed, they also developed econometric procedures for estimating the parameters of intertemporal objective functions and the trend coefficients simultaneously. The large-sample distributions of all of the statistics except one in this paper are unaffected by the detrending procedures adopted here. The statistic for testing the null hypothesis of quadratic utility against the alternative of power utility is premised on the assumption that the trend coefficients are known, since the limiting covariance matrix of $H_N(b_N)$ is not adjusted for the two-step estimation procedure.

Table 1

Test results for the non-monetary models with power and quadratic utility functions.[a]

H_0	H_1	Inst.[b]	CS[d.f.][c]	λ^*	λ^*[scaled]
Model I	Model II	(w, w)	6.005 [5] (0.306)	0.1792[+] (0.672)	3.956[+] (0.047)
Model II	Model I	(w, w)	3.378 [3] (0.337)	3.382[+] (0.066)	1.788[+] (0.181)
Model I	Model II	(w, z)	6.005 [5] (0.306)	1.314[−] (0.252)	3.082[+] (0.079)
Model II	Model I	(z, w)	12.422 [3] (0.006)	1.927[+] (0.165)	12.134[+] (0.001)

[a] Probability values (levels of significance) of the test statistics are given in parentheses. The sign of λ_N^* is indicated in square brackets adjacent to the test statistic.

[b] This column indicates the set of instruments used to estimate the null and alternative models. For instance, (w, z) indicates that w was used for the null model and z was used for the alternative model.

[c] The degrees of freedom of the CS statistics are displayed in the square brackets.

of Chicago. Real returns were calculated by dividing the numerator and denominator of the nominal returns by the corresponding values of the price deflator for non-durables plus services (the numeraire).

When Model I is the null specification the distance matrix S_u is given by

$$S_u = \sum_{j=-1}^{1} \mathrm{E}\left[\tilde{d}_{pn}\tilde{d}'_{pn-j} \otimes w_n w'_{n-j}\right]. \tag{37}$$

The sample distance matrix S_{uN}^{-1} is calculated using the estimator of S_u described by Hansen and Singleton (1982), which replaces the population moments in (37) by their sample counterparts. Similarly, when Model II is the alternative specification, S_v is given by (37) with $\tilde{d}_{qn}$ in the place of $\tilde{d}_{pn}$ and estimation proceeds analogously.

The test statistics for Models I and II are displayed in table 1. The value of the CS statistic for testing Model I is 6.005. Since the CS statistic is distributed as a chi-square with five degrees of freedom under H_0, this finding does not provide much evidence against the specification (1)–(4) of a representative consumer's utility function. The values of the λ^* statistic calculated from $\tilde{d}_{pn}$ and $\tilde{d}_{qn}$ is 0.1792 (see column 5 of table 1). The probability value of this statistic is somewhat larger than the corresponding value for the CS statistic.

When Model II with quadratic utility is taken to be the null specification, the value of the CS statistic is 3.378, so again there is little evidence against H_0 from this test. The λ^* test based on $(\tilde{d}_{pn}, \tilde{d}_{pn})$ provides considerably more evidence against the model with quadratic utility, although H_0 would not be rejected at the five percent significance level.

The estimates for Models I and II are calculated using the distance matrices that yield the most efficient estimates of the parameters, given the choice of instrument vector, w_n. There is a sense in which w_n is not the most natural choice of instrument vector for the quadratic model, however. The optimal instruments for estimating non-linear time series models are functions of $\mathrm{E}[\partial u_n(b_0)/\partial b | I_n]$ [see Hansen (1985)]. For the quadratic case, the marginal utilities are linear in the consumptions and parameters, which suggest using the instrument vector

$$z'_n = (1, \tilde{c}_n, \tilde{d}_n, \tilde{p}_n, r_{n-1} - 1),$$

where $\tilde{c}_n$ is detrended c_n, etc. Of course, when w_n is used to estimate Model I and z_n is used to estimate Model II, there is no longer a meaningful comprehensive orthogonality condition. The results reported in rows 3 and 4 of table 1 were obtained for the disturbances $\tilde{d}_{pn}$ and d_{qn}, with the latter disturbance calculated using detrended variables, but not divided by s_n.

The λ^* test of Model I now provides more evidence against this specification than when Model II is estimated using the instrument vector w_n. At the same time, λ^*_N is negative, contrary to what would be expected if Model II is the true specification. Turning to the test of Model II, the probability value of the CS statistic has decreased substantially to 0.006. The probability value for the λ^* test is correspondingly small, so together the tests are not favorable to Model II.

As noted in section 4, these tests may be sensitive in small samples to the relative scale of the products of the instruments and disturbances for the two specifications. For comparison, the scaled versions of the λ^* test [given by (35)] are displayed in column 6 of table 1. Interestingly, the λ^*[scaled] test now provides relatively more evidence against Model I than Model II for the instrument set (w, w). Indeed, Model II would not be rejected at the five percent level, while Model I would be rejected at this level. Thus, even in the case of a meaningful comprehensive model, the conclusions one might draw about the validity of Model I or Model II are evidently sensitive to the scale of the orthogonality conditions. Equivalently, they are sensitive to the choice of local alternative for which the λ^* statistic is locally optimal.

Next, consider the non-monetary and monetary models with power utility functions. The asset return used in the intertemporal Euler equation (19) is the three-month return on a three-month Treasury bill, since at issue is whether the two models are consistent with the pricing of money market securities. The disturbances for the monetary model (Model III) are

$$d^1_{mn} = \{\alpha(\beta L^{-1}) c_n^{*\delta\gamma-1} d_n^{*(1-\delta)\gamma}$$

$$- \beta\alpha(\beta L^{-1}) c_{n+3}^{*\delta\gamma-1} d_{n+3}^{*(1-\delta)\gamma} R^3_{n+2} P_{cn}/P_{cn+3}\}/s_n,$$

Table 2

Test results for the monetary and non-monetary models with power utility functions.[a]

H_0	H_1	CS[d.f.][b]	λ^*	λ^*[scaled]
Model I	Model III	7.301 [5] (0.199)	1.525[+] (0.217)	2.425[+] (0.120)
Model III	Model I	7.541 [5] (0.183)	4.793[+] (0.029)	3.292[+] (0.070)

[a] Probability values (levels of significance) of the test statistics are given in parentheses. The sign of the statistic λ_N^* is indicated in square brackets adjacent to the test statistic.

[b] The degrees of freedom of the CS statistic are displayed in the square brackets.

where R_{n+2}^3 is the real return on a three-month Treasury bill issued at date $n-1$ that matures at date $n+2$; and $d_{mn}^2 = U_{2n}/s_n$. The disturbances d_{pn}^1 and d_{mn}^1 in this case follow MA(3) processes, because of the three-period maturity of the asset [see Dunn and Singleton (1985)]. Therefore, when the monetary model is the null specification, S_u is set equal to

$$S_u = \sum_{j=-3}^{3} \mathrm{E}\left[d_{mn} d'_{mn-j} \otimes w_n w'_{n-j}\right],$$

with all of the elements in the moment matrices for $|j| = 3$ set to zero except for the upper five by five block. The latter restriction is implied by the fact that U_{2n} follows an MA(2) process. On the other hand, for the non-monetary model, all of the elements of the moment matrices for $|j| = 2$ and $|j| = 3$ are zero except for the upper five by five block, since d_{pn}^2 follows an MA(1) process. These restrictions on the distance matrices are imposed in the estimation of S_u and S_v. Both models are estimated using w_n as the instrument vector, with $(R_n^3 P_{cn-3}/P_{cn} - 1)$ in the place of $r_{n-1} - 1$.

The results for Models I and III are displayed in table 2. The CS statistics for the non-monetary and monetary models are 7.301 and 7.541, respectively, so neither model is rejected at conventional significance levels based on this test. In contrast, the λ^* test for Model III has a probability value smaller than 0.05. The corresponding scaled versions of the λ^* test are also displayed in the last column of table 2. Although these tests provide somewhat less evidence against Model III, it would still be rejected at the seven percent level. The reason for this pattern, compared to the differences between the corresponding λ^* and λ^*[scaled] statistics in table 1, is that the disturbances in the monetary and non-monetary models are of comparable scale since the models differ only in the dating of the variables.

At least three patterns of results emerge from this analysis. First, when the probability value of the CS statistic is smaller than 0.1, then the probability value for the λ^* statistic is correspondingly small. Thus, in this case, the conclusions drawn from the *CS* test (which does not incorporate explicitly information about the alternative) and the λ^* test (which does incorporate information about ϕ_1) agree. Second, for any pair of models, the λ^* test typically provides substantial evidence against one of the models, even when the *CS* statistics are not unfavorable to either model. [See, e.g., Models I and II in table 1 with instruments (w, w) and Models I and III in table 2.]

Third, the conclusions drawn from an analysis may be sensitive in small samples to the scaling of the disturbances or choices of instruments for the null and alternative specifications. Different scalings or instrument choices are associated implicitly with different local alternatives for which the λ^* test is optimal. The potential for different tests to lead to different qualitative conclusions about the validity of the models is illustrated by the results in table 1.

References

Abel, A., 1980, Empirical investment equations, in: Karl Brunner and Allan Meltzer, eds., On the state of macroeconomics, Carnegie-Rochester conference series (North-Holland, Amsterdam).

Aguire-Torres, V. and R. Gallant, 1983, The null and non-null asymptotic distribution of the Cox test for multivariate nonlinear regression, Journal of Econometrics 21, 5–33.

Bernanke, B., 1983, Adjustment costs, durables, and aggregate consumption, Manuscript (Stanford University, Stanford, CA).

Breeden, D.T., 1979, An intertemporal asset pricing model with stochastic consumption and investment opportunities. Journal of Financial Economics 7, 265–296.

Cox, D.R., 1961, Tests of separate families of hypotheses, in: Proceedings of the fourth Berkeley symposium in mathematical statistics and probability (University of California Press, Berkeley, CA) 105–123.

Davidson, R. and J.G. MacKinnon, 1982, Some non-nested hypothesis tests and the relations among them, Review of Economic Studies 49, 551–565.

Dunn, K. and K.J. Singleton, 1985, Modeling the term structure of interest rates under nonseparable utility and durability of goods, Journal of Financial Economics, forthcoming.

Eichenbaum, M. and L.P. Hansen, 1985, Uncertainty, aggregation, and the dynamic demand for consumption goods, Manuscript (Carnegie-Mellon University, Pittsburgh, PA).

Eichenbaum, M., L.P. Hansen and K.J. Singleton, 1983, A time series analysis of representative agent models of consumption and leisure choices under uncertainty, Manuscript (Carnegie-Mellon University, Pittsburgh, PA).

Ericsson, N.R., 1982, Asymptotic properties of instrumental variables statistics for testing non-nested hypotheses, Review of Economic Studies 50, 287–304.

Godfrey, L.G., 1983, Testing non-nested models after estimation by instrumental variables or least squares, Econometrica 51, 355–366.

Grossman, S. and R.J. Shiller, 1981, The determinants of the variability of stock market prices, American Economic Review 71, 222–227.

Hall, R.E., 1978, Stochastic implications of the life-cycle-permanent income hypothesis: Theory and evidence, Journal of Political Economy 86, 971–987.

Hansen, L.P., 1982, Large sample properties of generalized method of moments estimators, Econometrica 50, 1029–1054.

Hansen, L.P., 1985, Asymptotic covariance matrix bounds for instrumental variables estimators, Manuscript (University of Chicago, Chicago, IL).

Hansen, L.P. and T.J. Sargent, 1980, Formulating and estimating dynamic linear rational expectations models, Journal of Economic Dynamics and Control 2.

Hansen, L.P. and T.J. Sargent, 1982, Instrumental variables estimation of linear rational expectations models, Journal of Monetary Economics.
Hansen, L.P. and K.J. Singleton, 1982, Generalized instrumental variables estimation of nonlinear rational expectations models, Econometrica 50, 1269–1286.
Hansen L.P. and K.J. Singleton, 1983, Stochastic consumption, risk aversion, and the temporal behavior of asset returns, Journal of Political Economy 91, 249–265.
Hansen, L.P., D. Epple and W. Roberds, 1984, Linear quadratic games of resource depletion, Manuscript (University of Chicago, Chicago, IL).
Kydland, F. and E. Prescott, 1982, Time to build and aggregate fluctuations, Econometrica 50.
Lucas, R.E., Jr., 1978, Asset prices in an exchange economy, Econometrica 46, 1429–1445.
Lucas, R.E., Jr., 1983, Money in a theory of finance, Manuscript (University of Chicago, Chicago, IL).
MacKinnon, J.G., H. White and R. Davidson, 1983, Tests of model specification in the presence of alternative hypothesis, Journal of Econometrics 21, 53–70.
Musgrave, J.C., 1979, Durable goods owned by consumers in the United States, 1925–1977, Survey of Current Business.
Newey, W.K., 1983, Generalized method of moments specification testing, Manuscript (Princeton University, Princeton, NJ).
Pesaran, M.H. and A.S. Deaton, 1978, Testing non-nested nonlinear regression models, Econometrica 46, 677–694.
Sargent, T.J., 1981, Interpreting economic time series, Journal of Political Economy 86.
Townsend, R., 1984, Asset prices in a monetary economy, Manuscript (Carnegie-Mellon University, Pittsburgh, PA).

DIAGNOSTIC TESTING AND EVALUATION OF MAXIMUM LIKELIHOOD MODELS*

George TAUCHEN

Duke University, Durham, NC 27706, USA

The paper develops a unified theory of maximum likelihood specification testing based on M-estimators of auxiliary parameters. The theory is sufficiently general to encompass a wide class of specification tests including moment-based tests, Pearson-type goodness of fit tests, the information matrix test, and the Cox test. The paper also presents a framework based on Frechet differentiation for determining the effects of misspecification on the almost sure limits of parameter estimates and specification test statistics.

1. Introduction

This paper develops the asymptotic distribution theory for a class of specification tests for the non-linear maximum likelihood model. The ideas that motivate consideration of this class of specification tests have their origins in Hausman's (1978) paper. Hausman suggested that in general, i.e., not only for the ML model, a useful specification test can be based upon the difference between two estimates of the vector of parameters of interest. This idea, however, is somewhat difficult to apply in a multivariate context when the likelihood function depends upon the parameters in a highly non-linear fashion. The difficulty lies in finding a computationally tractable form for the second 'specification-robust' estimate of the parameter vector that is required to implement Hausman's test. White (1982) suggests a different but related approach. Specifically, White derives a test that is based not upon difference between two estimates of the parameters of direct interest, but instead is based upon the difference between the two natural estimates of the expected information matrix. This paper extends White's work further by deriving the asymptotic properties of an entire class of specification tests that includes as a special case the information matrix test, and other specification tests, e.g., the Cox test [Aguirre-Torres and Gallant (1983)] and the Lagrange multiplier test [Engle

*Helpful comments were obtained from Ronald Gallant, James Heckman, James Mackinnon, Richard Robb, Robin Sickles, Donald Waldman, Dudley Wallace, Adonis Yatchew, and two referees. Earlier versions of this paper were presented at seminars at the University of Chicago, the University of Pennsylvania, Queen's University, the University of Toronto, the Triangle Area Econometrics Seminar, and the 1984 Austin Conference on Model Selection.

(1982)]. The asymptotic theory developed here is sufficiently general to include in the class of allowable tests those that are based upon non-differentiable and even discontinuous functions of the data and the parameter vector. In particular, the class of tests includes Pearson-type goodness of fit tests with random cell boundaries [Moore and Spruill (1975)].

This paper also develops a framework based on Frechet differentiation for characterizing the non-null behavior of these various specification tests. Within this framework, 'directions' of misspecification are identified against which the various specification tests can be expected to have maximum or minimum power.

Before describing the class of specification tests in more detail, it is helpful to review briefly the asymptotic distribution theory of the quasi-maximum likelihood estimator (the ML estimator with an incorrect likelihood function). Assume the observed data $Y_1, Y_2, \ldots, Y_n$ are mutually independent and identically distributed $m \times 1$ random vectors with common unknown distribution function G and density function g, both defined on R^m. Let $\{F(y,\theta): y \in R^m, \theta \in \Theta \subset R^p\}$ be a family of distribution functions on R^m that is the basis for the estimation. For each fixed parameter vector θ the function $F(y,\theta)$ is a probability distribution on R^m with density function denoted by $f(y,\theta)$. Together the elements of the family of distribution functions $\{F(y,\theta)\}$, or equivalently the family of density functions $\{f(y,\theta)\}$, comprise a probability model for the observed data. The quasi-maximum likelihood estimator $\hat{\theta}_n$ is the value of the parameter that maximizes the sample quasi-loglikelihood function

$$L_n(\theta) = \frac{1}{n}\sum_{1}^{n} l(Y_i,\theta), \tag{1}$$

where $l(y,\theta) = \log(f(y,\theta))$ is the log-density function. Burguette, Gallant and Souza (1982), Huber (1967) and White (1982) have shown that under a variety of regularity conditions the QML estimator $\hat{\theta}_n$ converges almost surely to the value $\bar{\theta}$ at which the expected log-density function,

$$L(\theta) = \mathrm{E}[l(Y_i,\theta)] = \int l(y,\theta)\,\mathrm{d}G(y), \tag{2}$$

achieves its maximum. Now, if the underlying model is correctly specified, then there exists a θ_0 such that the density $f(y,\theta_0)$ is a version of the true density $g(y)$. In this case the maximizing $\bar{\theta}$ for L in (2) equals θ_0 and $\sqrt{n}(\hat{\theta}_n - \theta_0)$ is asymptotically normally distributed with mean zero and variance–covariance matrix equal to the inverse of the information matrix. On the other hand, if the model is misspecified, then of course no such θ_0 exists; but the maximizing $\bar{\theta}$ for the expected quasi-loglikelihood function still exists and $\sqrt{n}(\hat{\theta}_n - \bar{\theta})$ has a well-defined asymptotic distribution. One interpretation for $\bar{\theta}$ is that it is the 'true' parameter value that is induced directly by the estimation procedure itself.

The class of specification tests considered in this paper consists of those tests based on the magnitude of the statistic

$$\hat{\tau}_n = \frac{1}{n}\sum_1^n c(Y_i, \hat{\theta}_n), \tag{3}$$

where $\hat{\theta}_n$ is the QML estimator and where the vector-valued function c satisfies

$$\int c(y,\theta)\,\mathrm{d}F(y,\theta) = 0, \tag{4}$$

for all θ. The condition (4) says that the function $c(y,\theta)$ has mean zero with respect to each distribution function in the probability model. A function that satisfies this condition will be called an *auxiliary criterion function*. As will become clearer below, for any given family of distribution functions $\{F(y,\theta)\}$ there are many auxiliary criterion functions. In practice, the better auxiliary criterion functions will be those for which the magnitude of the elements of the vector $\hat{\tau}_n$ in (3) provide useful diagnostic information about the specification of the model. A strategy for getting an informative $\hat{\tau}_n$ is to construct the auxiliary criterion function in such a way that the components of $\hat{\tau}_n$ equal the differences between two estimates of some statistical quantities of interest.

The statistic $\hat{\tau}_n$ is useful for specification testing because it converges almost surely to zero when the model is correctly specified and it converges to a non-zero quantity when the model is incorrectly specified. This result is proved in section 2, but it is intuitively clear from inspection of the expressions (3) and (4). In the former case when θ_0 exists,

$$\hat{\tau}_n \overset{\text{a.s.}}{\to} \mathrm{E}[c(Y_i,\theta_0)] = \int c(y,\theta_0)\,\mathrm{d}F(y,\theta_0),$$

which is zero by construction of the auxiliary criterion function. In the latter case,

$$\hat{\tau}_n \overset{\text{a.s.}}{\to} \bar{\tau} = \mathrm{E}[c(Y_i,\bar{\theta})] = \int c(y,\bar{\theta})\,\mathrm{d}G(y),$$

which in general is non-zero. As shown in section 3, the statistic $\hat{\tau}_n$ also has a well defined asymptotic distribution in either case. Its asymptotic variance–covariance matrix can be expressed as the sum of two parts, one of which corresponds to the variability in $(1/n)\sum_1^n c(Y_i,\bar{\theta})$ about $\bar{\tau}$ and the other to the variability in $\hat{\theta}_n$ about $\bar{\theta}$.

The following three examples help to illustrate the practical applications of the general results in this paper:

Example 1 (low-order moments)

For simplicity in exposition take y as scaler though θ may be multi-dimensional. Define

$$\mu_j(\theta) = \int y^j \mathrm{d}F(y,\theta),$$

for integer j. Thus $\mu_j(\hat{\theta}_n)$ is the predicted jth non-central moment from the estimated probability model. Let j be fixed at some integer and define

$$c(y,\theta) = y^j - \mu_j(\theta).$$

This function is a legitimate auxiliary criterion function since it satisfies the condition (4). Moreover, the statistic

$$\hat{\tau}_n = \frac{1}{n}\sum_1^n c(Y_i, \hat{\theta}_n)$$

is simply the difference between sample jth non-central moment and the predicted moment from the probability model. A large value for $|\hat{\tau}_n|$ would tend to indicate that the probability model does a poor job of 'matching' the jth moment of the distribution of the data. As shown in section 5 of this paper, there is a regression-based procedure for testing for whether the magnitude $|\hat{\tau}_n|$ is too large to be accounted for by sampling fluctuations: One regresses the values $\hat{c}_i = c(Y_i, \hat{\theta}_n)$ on the scores $\hat{h}_i = \partial l(Y_i, \hat{\theta}_n)/\partial\theta$ and performs a t test for a non-zero intercept. If the t statistic is large from a statistical point of view the model may need to be reformulated or else an explanation given as to why the difference in moments is too small to be of practical importance. Of course in some cases the estimation procedure may force some of the sample and predicted moments to be equal and no such test is possible. For instance, if the underlying model is the univariate normal distribution, then the first two sample and predicted moments must be equal. Diagnostic tests in this case would then have to be based on moments higher than the second. For the asymptotic theory to provide a good approximation to distribution of $\hat{\tau}_n$, the order of the moments above two should be kept reasonably small.

The extension of this to other unconditional moments is straightforward. For central moments in the scaler case let the auxiliary criterion function be $[y - \mu_1(\theta)]^j$ minus the expected value of this quantity with respect to $F(y,\theta)$. For central moments in the multivariate case, the auxiliary criterion function would be the distinct elements of the j-fold Kronecker product of the vector $y - \mu_1(\theta)$ with itself minus the expectation with respect to $F(y, \theta)$.

As noted by Newey (1984) in an independent paper, moment conditions can be used to form useful auxiliary criterion functions when the data vector is partitioned as $y' = (w', x')$ and the probability model is $f_1(w|x, \theta)$. Here w is a vector of jointly dependent variables and x is a vector of exogenous variables. The marginal density $f_2(x)$ for x is not specified by the model. A function of the form

$$c(w, x, \theta) = \left(\frac{\partial}{\partial\theta}\log f_1(w|x, \theta)\right) a(x, \theta),$$

where $a(x, \theta)$ depends only on x and θ, satisfies (4). A test based on this auxiliary criterion function is an 'instrumented score test'. Newey examines in detail the statistical properties of such tests and presents useful applications for regression models and limited dependent variable models.

Example 2 (tail areas)

In some applied work it is important to have information on how well the probability model predicts tail areas. An auxiliary criterion function that provides such information can be constructed along the following lines. Assume for simplicity in exposition that y is scalar though θ may be multi-dimensional. Let $\mu(\theta)$ and $\sigma(\theta)$ denote the mean and standard deviation of the distribution $F(y, \theta)$. Fix α as a small probability and let z_α satisfy

$$\text{prob}_F[y - \mu(\theta) \geq \sigma(\theta) z_\alpha] = \alpha,$$

where the subscript F is self-explanatory. Now put

$$c(y, \theta) = I[y - \mu(\theta) \geq \sigma(\theta) z_\alpha] - \alpha,$$

where $I[\cdot]$ is the 0–1 indicator function. Then the statistic

$$\hat{\tau}_n = \frac{1}{n}\sum_1^n c(Y_i, \hat{\theta}_n)$$

is the difference between the observed and the predicted frequency with which right-hand extreme values occur.

As illustrated in section 5, an asymptotically valid test for no difference in the frequencies can be computed by regressing the values $\hat{c}_i = (Y_i, \hat{\theta}_n)$ on the 'scores', i.e., the gradients $\partial l(Y_i, \hat{\theta}_n)/\partial\theta$ of the log-density function, and then performing the usual t test for no intercept. Interestingly, the square of this t

statistic is asymptotically a chi-square variate with one degree of freedom, but the t^2 does not equal the classical Pearson statistic. The reason is that this t^2 statistic properly accounts for the randomness in $\hat{\theta}_n$, where the classical statistic does not. The classical Pearson procedure implicitly assumes that the asymptotic variance is $\alpha(1-\alpha)$ which exceeds the true variance. [When the model is $\phi(y-\mu)$, where ϕ is the standard normal pdf, then the variance is $\alpha(1-\alpha)-\phi(z_\alpha)^2$.] Put another way, the classical procedure ignores the randomness in $\hat{\theta}_n$ and treats $(1/n)\sum_1^n c(Y_i, \hat{\theta}_n)$ as if it has the same asymptotic distribution as $(1/n)\sum_1^n c(Y_i, \theta_0)$, which is a 'Durbin' problem that leads to the incorrect expression for the asymptotic variance.

A more general chi-square goodness of fit test is as follows. Suppose the data vector is of the form $y' = (w', x')$ where, in a notation consistent with that used at the end of Example 1, the vector w contains the jointly dependent variables and x the exogenous variables. The probability model is the conditional density $f_1(w|x, \theta)$ of the dependent variables given x, with the marginal density $f_2(x)$ not specified. Let the components of the $K \times 1$ auxiliary criterion function be

$$c_k(y, \theta) = c_k(w, x, \theta) = I[w \in R_k(x, \theta)] - \pi_{0k}, \qquad k = 1, 2, \ldots, K,$$

where $I[\ ]$ is the 0–1 indicator function, the π_{0k} are fixed probabilities such that $\sum_{k=1}^K \pi_{0k} = 1$, and the regions $R_k(x, \theta)$ are chosen so that

$$\int I[w \in R_k(x, \theta)] f_1(w|x, \theta)\, \mathrm{d}w = \pi_{0k},$$

for each $k = 1, 2, \ldots, K$. Then the $K \times 1$ vector

$$\hat{\tau}_n = \frac{1}{n} \sum_{i=1}^{n} c(w_i, x_i, \hat{\theta}_n)$$

contains the differences between the observed and expected frequencies. The regression-based method described in section 5 can be used to construct an asymptotically valid chi-square statistic based on $\hat{\tau}_n$. This test is based on random cell boundaries [Moore and Spruill (1975)] and it accounts for covariates x. It differs from Heckman's (1984) test because here the regions $R(x, \theta)$ depend not only on x but also on θ. More specifically, here the probabilities are viewed as fixed and the regions then determined, whereas Heckman views the regions $R(x)$ as given independently of θ, and then the probabilities $\pi_k(x, \theta) = \int I[w \in R(x)] f(x, \theta)\, \mathrm{d}w$ are determined. The asymptotic theory of this paper is general enough to cover the case when the test is set up in Heckman's manner, but there may be advantages to setting it up the other way. First, with a priori fixed probabilities the test outcome could be easier to interpret and provide better diagnostic information. Second, with this setup the user can choose the probabilities so that $\pi_{0k} = 1/K$, i.e., so that the regions are equiprobable, which is a method that has been shown to have optimum properties [Kendall and Stewart (1973, ch. 30)] in the case with no covariates.

Example 3 (White's information matrix test)

To include White's test in this setup, take as the auxiliary criterion function $c(y,\theta)$ the vector function comprised of the distinct elements of the symmetric matrix function

$$h(y,\theta)h(y,\theta)' + \frac{\partial h}{\partial \theta'}(y,\theta),$$

where $h(y,\theta) = \partial l(y,\theta)/\partial\theta$ is the gradient of the log-density function. With the function c defined in this fashion the vector

$$\hat{\tau}_n = \frac{1}{n}\sum_1^n c(Y_i,\hat{\theta}_n)$$

contains all of the differences between the distinct elements of the two natural estimates of the information matrix. White derives an estimator for the asymptotic variance–covariance matrix of this $\hat{\tau}_n$ that requires the user to calculate analytical third-order partial derivatives of the log-density function. In section 3 it is shown that there is an extension of the classical information equality which, as also noted by Chesher (1983) and Lancaster (1984), eliminates the need for third partials and leads to regression based procedures for conducting White's test.

The remainder of this paper is organized as follows. Sections 2 and 3 present the consistency and asymptotic normality results. Section 4 examines some measures of the performance of the specification tests. Section 5 presents the regression-based procedure for conducting the specification tests discussed here. Section 6 contains some concluding remarks.

For the sake of completeness, the various assumptions which were either implicit or explicit in this introduction are now listed in one place.

Assumption 1

(i) The observed data $Y_1, Y_2, \ldots, Y_n$ are iid $m \times 1$ random vectors with distribution function G on R^m.
(ii) The probability model is the family of distribution functions $\{F(y,\theta)$: $y \in R^m$, $\theta \in \Theta \subset R^p\}$, where the parameter space Θ is a compact convex subset of R^p with a non-empty interior.

(iii) Both $G(y)$ and $F(y,\theta)$ are absolutely continuous with respect to some measure $\mu(y)$ on R^m with generalized (Radon–Nikodym) densities denoted by $g(y)=\mathrm{d}G(y)/\mathrm{d}\mu(y)$ and $f(y,\theta)=\mathrm{d}F(y,\theta)/\mathrm{d}\mu(y)$.
(iv) The auxiliary criterion function satisfies $\int c(y,\theta)\,\mathrm{d}F(y,\theta)=0$ for each $\theta\in\Theta$.

2. Consistency

As in the introduction let l: $R^m\times\Theta\to R^1$ be the log-density function and let c: $R^m\times\Theta\to R^s$ be the auxiliary criterion function. The QML estimator $\hat{\theta}_n$ and the statistic $\hat{\tau}_n$ are defined by

$$L_n(\hat{\theta}_n)=\max_{\theta\in\Theta}L_n(\theta), \tag{5}$$

$$\hat{\tau}_n=\psi_n(\hat{\theta}_n), \tag{6}$$

where ψ_n and L_n are the functions

$$L_n(\theta)=\frac{1}{n}\sum_1^n l(Y_i,\theta), \qquad \psi_n(\theta)=\frac{1}{n}\sum_1^n c(Y_i,\theta).$$

The key step in proving the consistency results is to establish the almost sure convergence of $L_n(\theta)$ and $\psi_n(\theta)$ to their expectations uniformly in the parameter θ. The almost sure convergence of $\hat{\theta}_n$ and $\hat{\tau}_n$ to well defined limits will then follow from assumptions guaranteeing that the almost sure limit of the function L_n has a unique maximum.

It proves useful to identify a large class of vector-valued functions on $R^m\times\Theta$ for which uniform almost sure convergence will hold.

Definition 1. A function ϕ: $R^m\times\Theta\to R^k$ is said to be *regular* if

(i) $\phi(y,\theta)$ is measurable in y for each $\theta\in\Theta$,
(ii) ϕ is separable [see Huber (1967, p. 222)],
(iii) ϕ is dominated, $|\phi(y,\theta)|\le b(y)$, where the function b is integrable with respect to G,
(iv) ϕ is almost surely continuous in the sense that for each fixed θ the set $\{y$: $\lim_{\gamma\to\theta}\phi(y,\gamma)=\phi(y,\theta)\}$ has probability 1(dG). The null set may depend on θ.

The measurability and separability conditions (i) and (ii) are weak and essentially non-restrictive side conditions. The domination assumption (iii) ensures that the expectation

$$\lambda(\theta)=\int\phi(y,\theta)\,\mathrm{d}G(y) \tag{7}$$

exists, while the almost sure continuity condition (iv) implies by dominated convergence that λ is a continuous function of θ. As the following lemma indicates, sample averages of $\phi(Y_i, \theta)$ have the requisite convergence properties if ϕ is regular.

Lemma 1. If ϕ is regular, then the function

$$\lambda_n(\theta) = \frac{1}{n}\sum_1^n \phi(Y_i, \theta)$$

converges uniformly almost surely to function λ in (7). (Proof: Appendix.)

The next two assumptions contain the conditions for consistency of $\hat{\theta}_n$ and $\hat{\tau}_n$:

Assumption 2. The auxiliary criterion function c is regular and the log-density function l satisfies (i)–(iii) of Definition 1 and a stronger version of (iv), namely, $l(y, \theta)$ is continuous in θ for all y.

The stronger continuity assumption is needed for the log-density function in order to ensure that the maximizing $\hat{\theta}_n$ for L_n in (5) exists for all n. The weaker continuity condition for the auxiliary criterion function c suffices because the existence of $\hat{\tau}_n$ in (6) is guaranteed once the existence of $\hat{\theta}_n$ is established.

Define the functions

$$L(\theta) = \mathrm{E}[l(Y_i, \theta)] = \int l(y, \theta)\,\mathrm{d}G(y), \tag{8a}$$

$$\psi(\theta) = \mathrm{E}[c(Y_i, \theta)] = \int c(y, \theta)\,\mathrm{d}G(y), \tag{8b}$$

both of which exist and are continuous by Assumption 2. From Lemma 1 it is known that $L_n(\theta) \overset{\text{a.s.}}{\to} L(\theta)$ and $\psi_n(\theta) = (1/n)\sum_1^n c(Y_i, \theta) \overset{\text{a.s.}}{\to} \psi(\theta)$ uniformly in θ. By continuity and compactness the limiting function L achieves its maximum at least once in the parameter space Θ. For the limit of the estimator $\hat{\theta}_n$ to be well defined, it is necessary to assume that there is only one such maximum.

Assumption 3. The limiting quasi-loglikelihood function L achieves its maximum uniquely at $\bar{\theta}$ in the interior of the parameter space.

The basic consistency result is:

Theorem 1. $\hat{\theta}_n \overset{\text{a.s.}}{\to} \bar{\theta}$ *and* $\hat{\tau}_n \overset{\text{a.s.}}{\to} \bar{\tau}$, *where*

$$\bar{\tau} = \psi(\bar{\theta}) = \int c(y, \bar{\theta})\, \mathrm{d}G(y). \tag{9}$$

Proof. The convergence of $\hat{\theta}_n \overset{\text{a.s.}}{\to} \bar{\theta}$ follows from arguments similar to those in Burguette, Gallant and Souza (1982). Since $\psi_n(\theta) \overset{\text{a.s.}}{\to} \psi(\theta)$ uniformly in θ and since ψ is continuous, then by standard arguments $\psi_n(\hat{\theta}_n) \overset{\text{a.s.}}{\to} \psi(\bar{\theta}) = \bar{\tau}$ as given in (9).

Note that this theorem covers both the null case in which the model is correctly specified and there exists $\theta_0 \in \Theta$ such that $f(y, \theta_0)$ is a version of $g(y)$, and it covers the non-null case in which no such θ_0 exist. In the null case, $\bar{\theta} = \theta_0$ and the almost sure limit of $\hat{\tau}_n$ is

$$\psi(\theta_0) = \int c(y, \theta_0)\, \mathrm{d}F(y, \theta_0) = 0,$$

by the construction of the auxiliary criterion function. In the non-null case the almost sure limit of $\hat{\tau}_n$ is $\psi(\bar{\theta})$, which is in general non-zero.

3. Asymptotic normality

3.1. *The joint asymptotic distribution of $\hat{\theta}_n$ and $\hat{\tau}_n$*

In order to allow for a large class of auxiliary criterion functions – in particular, those based on frequency counts or absolute moments – the conditions for asymptotic normality that are placed on the auxiliary criterion function $c(y, \theta)$ do not require differentiability with respect to θ. Instead, the conditions only require c to satisfy certain Huber-type Lipshitz conditions and $\psi(\theta) = \int c(y, \theta)\, \mathrm{d}G(y)$ to be a continuously differentiable function of θ. One of the costs, however, of not imposing differentiability on c is that a strategy for proving asymptotic normality that is based on Taylor approximations does not work. Specifically, it is not possible to adopt methods of proof similar to those commonly used in non-linear econometrics, because the difference $\sqrt{n}(\hat{\tau}_n - \psi_n(\bar{\theta}))$ cannot be approximated by $(\partial\psi_n/\partial\theta')(\bar{\theta})\sqrt{n}(\hat{\theta}_n - \bar{\theta})$ and then the asymptotic normality of $\sqrt{n}(\hat{\theta}_n - \bar{\theta})$ exploited. The alternative strategy adopted here is to embed the determination of $\hat{\theta}_n$ and $\hat{\tau}_n$ into a larger M-estimation problem which gives the joint asymptotic distribution of $\hat{\theta}_n$ and $\hat{\tau}_n$.

Joint asymptotic normality of $\hat{\theta}_n$ and $\hat{\tau}_n$ will be proved under the following conditions for l and c. In the statement of the conditions, the vector-valued function ϕ is

$$\phi(y,\theta)=\begin{bmatrix} h(y,\theta) \\ c(y,\theta) \end{bmatrix},$$

where h is the gradient of the log-density function and c is the auxiliary criterion function; the function u in (iii) below is

$$u(y,\theta,d)=\sup_{|\gamma-\theta|\le d}|\phi(y,\gamma)-\phi(y,\theta)|.$$

Assumption 4

(i) $l(y,\theta)$ is continuously differentiable in θ for all y with gradient denoted by

$$h(y,\theta)=\frac{\partial}{\partial\theta}l(y,\theta).$$

(ii) $|\phi(y,\theta)|\le b(y)$, where the function b is square integrable with respect to G.

(iii) There exist positive constants β_1 and β_2 such that for all θ

$$\limsup_{d\downarrow 0}\frac{\mathrm{E}[u(Y_i,\theta,d)]}{d}\le\beta_1,\qquad \limsup_{d\downarrow 0}\frac{\mathrm{E}[u(Y_i,\theta,d)^2]}{d}\le\beta_2.$$

(iv) The components of $\lambda(\theta)=\mathrm{E}[\phi(Y_i,\theta)]$ are continuously differentiable in θ and the matrix $\partial\mathrm{E}[h(Y_i,\theta)]/\partial\theta'|_{\bar{\theta}}$, which is the upper left $p\times p$ submatrix of $\partial\lambda(\bar{\theta})/\partial\theta'$, is non-singular.

A sketch of the asymptotic normality proof is as follows. The almost sure convergence of $\hat{\theta}_n$ and $\hat{\tau}_n$ to $\bar{\theta}$ and $\bar{\tau}$ was established in the previous section. By assumption, the limit $\bar{\theta}$ lies in the interior of the parameter space, and so ultimately the maximizing $\hat{\theta}_n$ must remain in the interior of the parameter space. Thus, ultimately the first-order condition

$$\frac{1}{n}\sum_1^n h(Y_i,\theta)=0$$

must be satisfied at $\theta=\hat{\theta}_n$. Now let T be a non-trivial closed ball about $\bar{\tau}$, and define the vector-valued function η on $R^m \times \Theta \times T$ by

$$\eta(y,\theta,\tau)=\begin{bmatrix} h(y,\theta) \\ c(y,\theta)-\tau \end{bmatrix}. \tag{10}$$

It is seen immediately that $\hat{\theta}_n$ and $\hat{\tau}_n$ will ultimately solve the expanded system of equations

$$\frac{1}{n}\sum_1^n \eta(Y_i,\theta,\tau)=0. \tag{11}$$

Therefore Huber's (1967, p. 231; 1981, p. 133) results for M-estimators determined by solving a system of implicit equations can thus be applied to $\hat{\theta}_n$ and $\hat{\tau}_n$.

The main asymptotic normality result is:

Theorem 2. The random vector

$$\sqrt{n}\begin{bmatrix} \hat{\theta}_n-\bar{\theta} \\ \hat{\tau}_n-\bar{\tau} \end{bmatrix}$$

converges in distribution to a multivariate normal with mean zero and with the variance–covariance matrix given by

$$\begin{bmatrix} \Sigma_\theta & \Sigma_{\theta\tau} \\ \Sigma_{\tau\theta} & \Sigma_\tau \end{bmatrix}=\begin{bmatrix} K_h & 0 \\ K_c & -I \end{bmatrix}^{-1}\begin{bmatrix} J_{hh} & J_{hc} \\ J_{ch} & J_{cc} \end{bmatrix}\begin{bmatrix} K_h & K_c' \\ 0 & -I \end{bmatrix}^{-1}, \tag{12}$$

where the submatrices on the right-hand side are

$$K_h=\frac{\partial}{\partial\theta'}\mathrm{E}[h(Y_i,\theta)] \quad at \quad \theta=\bar{\theta}, \tag{13a}$$

$$K_c=\frac{\partial}{\partial\theta'}\mathrm{E}[c(Y_i,\theta)] \quad at \quad \theta=\bar{\theta}, \tag{13b}$$

$$J_{hh}=\mathrm{E}[h(Y_i,\bar{\theta})h(Y_i,\bar{\theta})'], \tag{14a}$$

$$J_{hc}=\mathrm{E}[h(Y_i,\bar{\theta})(c(Y_i,\bar{\theta})-\bar{\tau})'], \tag{14b}$$

$$J_{ch}=J_{hc}', \tag{14c}$$

$$J_{cc}=\mathrm{E}[(c(Y_i,\bar{\theta})-\bar{\tau})(c(Y_i,\bar{\theta})-\bar{\tau})']. \tag{14d}$$

Proof. The main argument was given in remarks preceding the statement of the theorem. The expression for the joint asymptotic variance–covariance matrix of $\hat{\theta}_n$ and $\hat{\tau}_n$ follows from applying Huber's (1967, p. 231) corollary to his Theorem 3.

By way of interpretation, note that the rows of the matrices K_h and K_c are the gradients with respect to θ' of the components of $\mathrm{E}[h(Y_i,\theta)]$ and $\mathrm{E}[C(Y_i,\theta)]$, while the matrices J_{hh}, J_{hc} and J_{cc} are simply the variance–covariance matrices of the random variables $\tilde{h}_i = h(Y_i,\bar{\theta})$ and $\tilde{c}_i = c(Y_i,\bar{\theta})$. Note also that Theorem 2 gives

$$\Sigma_\theta = K_h^{-1} J_{hh} K_h^{-1}.$$

For the marginal asymptotic distribution of $\bar{\theta}$ which is the familiar form for the asymptotic variance–covariance matrix of the QML estimator.

For the purposes of formal testing and calculating confidence intervals, estimates are needed of the various K's and J's that appear in (12) through (14). The J's can be consistently estimated in the natural way by forming the corresponding sample product moment matrices:

Theorem 3. The estimates

$$\hat{J}_{hh} = \frac{1}{n}\sum_1^n h(Y_i,\hat{\theta}_n)h(Y_i,\hat{\theta}_n)',$$

$$\hat{J}_{hc} = \frac{1}{n}\sum_1^n h(Y_i,\hat{\theta}_n)(c(Y_i,\hat{\theta}_n) - \hat{\tau}_n)',$$

$$\hat{J}_{cc} = \frac{1}{n}\sum_1^n (c(Y_i,\hat{\theta}_n) - \hat{\tau}_n)(c(Y_i,\hat{\theta}_n) - \hat{\tau}_n)',$$

of the matrices J_{hh}, J_{hc} and J_{cc} in (14) are consistent in the sense of element-wise almost sure convergence.

Proof. By Assumption 2 and items (i) and (ii) of Assumption 4 each of the columns of the matrix $\phi(y,\theta)\phi(y,\theta)'$, where $\phi(y,\theta)' = [h(y,\theta)'c(y,\theta)']$, is a regular function in the sense of Definition 1; apply Lemma 1 to each column. This, plus the result $\hat{\tau}_n \xrightarrow{\text{a.s.}} \bar{\tau}$ from Theorem 1, establishes the conclusion.

These estimates of the J's are 'specification-robust' in the sense that they are valid even if the underlying probability model is misspecified. If the components of the gradient of the log-density function $h(y,\theta)$ and the auxiliary criterion function $c(y,\theta)$ are continuously differentiable in θ, then there are similar natural specification-robust estimates of the K's.

Theorem 4. Assume that the components of $h(y,\theta)$ *and* $c(y,\theta)$ *are continuously differentiable in* θ *for all* y *and put* $\tilde{K}_h(y,\theta)=\partial h(y,\theta)/\partial\theta'$ *and* $\tilde{K}_c(y,\theta)=\partial c(y,\theta)/\partial\theta'$. *If the columns of the matrix functions* $\tilde{K}_h$ *and* $\tilde{K}_c$ *are regular as defined in Definition 1 (note that continuity of the columns in* θ *is presupposed in the hypotheses of this theorem), then the random matrices*

$$\hat{K}_h=\frac{1}{n}\sum_1^n\tilde{K}_h(Y_i,\hat{\theta}_n), \tag{15a}$$

$$\hat{K}_c=\frac{1}{n}\sum_1^n\tilde{K}_c(Y_i,\hat{\theta}_n), \tag{15b}$$

are consistent estimates of K_h *and* K_c *in the sense of element-wise almost sure convergence.*

Proof. The proof is entirely analogous to that for Theorem 3.

In most applied work the log-density function $l(y,\theta)$ satisfies the differentiability condition in the hypotheses of Theorem 4, and so the natural estimate $\hat{K}_h$ in (15a) is nearly always available. If the auxiliary criterion is reasonably smooth – as would usually be the case if the model evaluation is based on the difference between predicted and sample moments – then the estimate $\hat{K}_c$ in (15b) is also available. In these cases, then, Theorems 3 and 4 lead to a specification-robust estimate $\hat{\Sigma}_\tau$.

3.2. *The generalized information equality and the estimation of* Σ_τ *under correct specification*

An estimate of Σ_τ that is valid under the maintained hypothesis that the probability model is correctly specified turns out to be very easy to compute, even if the auxiliary criterion function is not differentiable in θ. The reduction in computational burden is brought about by the availability of an extension of the classical information equality. This equality says that under suitable regularity conditions the expected information matrix equals minus the expected Hessian matrix. In the notation of Theorem 4, the information equality can be expressed as

$$K_h^o+J_{hh}^o=0, \tag{16}$$

where the superscript o means that these are the J_{hh} and K_h matrices in (13a) and (13b) when the model is correctly specified and θ_0 exists.

To motivate the generalization of the information equality, consider

$$\int c(y,\theta)f(y,\theta)\,\mathrm{d}\mu = 0,$$

and note that the equality holds identically in θ. Now, if differentiation could be brought freely in and out of the integration, then the usual Cramer calculus gives

$$\int c_{\theta'}(y,\theta_0)f(y,\theta_0)\,\mathrm{d}\mu + \int c(y,\theta_0)f_{\theta'}(y,\theta_0)\,\mathrm{d}\mu = 0,$$

or

$$\frac{\partial}{\partial\theta'}\int c(y,\theta)f(y,\theta_0)\,\mathrm{d}\mu\bigg|_{\theta_0} + \int c(y,\theta_0)h(y,\theta_0)'f(y,\theta_0)\,\mathrm{d}\mu = 0,$$

where the subscript θ' on c and f in the first equality denotes partial differentiation. The last equality is more compactly written

$$K_c^o + J_{ch}^o = 0, \tag{17}$$

where as in (16) the superscript o means that these are the corresponding K_h and J_{ch} matrices whenever θ_0 exists. The next theorem states that both the basic information equality and its generalization in (17) are valid even if $c(y,\theta)$ is not differentiable in θ and the differentiation cannot in general be brought inside the integration.

Theorem 5 (generalized information equality). Assume (i): θ_0 exists such that $f(y,\theta_0)$ is a version of $g(y)$, and (ii): the function

$$q(y,\theta) = f(y,\theta)/f(y,\theta_0) \tag{18}$$

satisfies $|\partial q(y,\theta)/\partial\theta| \leq b(y)$, where b is square integrable with respect to $F(y,\theta_0)$. Then both equalities (16) and (17) hold. (Proof: Appendix.)

The following corollary gives a simple method for getting null-consistent estimates of the asymptotic variance–covariance matrix of $\hat{\tau}_n$.

Corollary 5.1. If the hypotheses of Theorem 5 hold, then

$$\Sigma_\tau^o = J_{cc}^o - J_{ch}^o\left(J_{hh}^o\right)^{-1}J_{hc}^o \tag{19}$$

is the asymptotic variance–covariance matrix of $\sqrt{n}\,\hat{\tau}_n$. *Moreover, the natural estimator*

$$\hat{\Sigma}^o_\tau = \hat{J}_{cc} - \hat{J}_{ch}\hat{J}_{hh}^{-1}\hat{J}_{hc}, \tag{20}$$

with the $\hat{J}$*'s as in Theorem 3, is consistent in the sense of element-wise almost sure convergence.*

Proof. Apply the two equalities (16) and (17) to the expression (12) and then select off the lower right-hand corner of the joint variance–covariance matrix that corresponds to $\hat{\tau}_n$; the convergence of (20) follows from Theorem 3.

Interestingly, the estimate $\hat{\Sigma}^o_\tau$ in (20) is simply the usual estimate of the residual variance–covariance matrix from a seemingly unrelated regression of the components of $\hat{c}_i = c(Y_i, \hat{\theta}_n)$ on the 'scores' $\hat{h}_i = h(Y_i, \hat{\theta}_n)$.

4. The local behavior of $\bar{\tau}$ under misspecification

In the previous sections it was established that the estimator $\hat{\theta}_n$ and the statistic $\hat{\tau}_n$ converge almost surely to

$$\bar{\theta} = \arg\min_\theta \left\{ \int l(y,\theta)\,\mathrm{d}G(y) \right\}, \tag{21}$$

$$\bar{\tau} = \int c(y,\bar{\theta})\,\mathrm{d}G(y), \tag{22}$$

and that $\sqrt{n}\,(\hat{\theta}_n - \bar{\theta})$ and $\sqrt{n}\,(\hat{\tau}_n - \bar{\tau})$ have a joint asymptotic normal distribution with variance and covariance matrices Σ_θ, Σ_τ, $\Sigma_{\theta\tau}$, as given in Theorem 2 above. When the model is correctly specified and $G(y) = F(y, \theta_0)$ for some θ_0, then $\bar{\theta} = \theta_0$ and $\bar{\tau} = 0$. Under misspecification however, $\bar{\theta}$ need not equal θ_0, and likewise $\bar{\tau}$ will be non-zero, which is where the specification tests gets its power.

In this section we will investigate the ability of the test to detect misspecification by examining the local behavior of the $\bar{\tau}$ for small deviations of the idealized model from the true model. These deviations are generated in the following manner. Consider alternative true distributions G_v given by

$$\mathrm{d}G_v(y) = [1 + v(y)]\,\mathrm{d}F_0(y), \tag{23}$$

where v is a function on R^m and $\mathrm{d}F_0(y) = \mathrm{d}F(y, \theta_0)$. The parameter value θ_0 is fixed throughout, while v will vary over a class of functions on R^m, with each v giving rise to an alternative true model or distribution of the data. The particular class of functions are the elements of the following space.

Notation. Let V denote the set of functions v: $R^m \to R^1$ such that

(i) $1+v(y) \geq 0, \quad \text{for all } y,$

(ii) $\int v(y)\,\mathrm{d}F_0(y) = 0,$

(iii) $\int v(y)^2\,\mathrm{d}F_0(y) < \infty.$

The first two of these conditions simply ensure that G_v is a bona fide distribution function. The third condition ensures that a random variable of the form $v(Y)$, with $Y \sim F_0$, has finite variance, which proves to be convenient below. The norm of the space V is taken to be the natural $L_2(F_0)$ norm, $\|v\|_2 = (\int v(y)^2 \mathrm{d}F_0(y))^{1/2}$.

In this setup, then, for each $v \in V$ there is a true distribution G_v given by (23). For any non-zero v in V the probability model is misspecified since there will in general be no θ in Θ such that $G_v(y) = F(y,\theta)$. However, at $v=0$ the model is correctly specified with $G_v(y) = F_0(y) = F(y,\theta_0)$, by construction. Although this setup does restrict the true distribution to be absolutely continuous with respect to the distribution F_0, it does nonetheless generate a very wide class of alternative models. Furthermore one might argue that absolute continuity is no restriction at all, since any region in R^m over which the true distribution puts positive probability mass will ultimately be discovered in large samples anyways.

Under suitable regularly conditions both $\hat{\theta}_n$ and $\hat{\tau}_n$ will, for each G_v with v fixed, have almost sure limits

$$\hat{\theta}_n \overset{\text{a.s.}}{\to} \bar{\theta}(v) = \arg\min_{\theta} \left\{ \int l(y,\theta)\,\mathrm{d}G_v(y) \right\}, \tag{24}$$

$$\bar{\tau}_n \overset{\text{a.s.}}{\to} \bar{\tau}(v) = \int c(y,\bar{\theta}(v))\,\mathrm{d}G_v(y). \tag{25}$$

The almost surely here means with probability one with respect to the joint distribution of $\{Y_i\}$, where the Y_i are independent and have common distribution function G_v.

Both $\bar{\theta}(v)$ and $\bar{\tau}(v)$ are functionals on V that are highly non-linear in v, which makes a complete analysis of them difficult to obtain. However, an analysis of their local behavior near $v=0$, i.e., near a correctly specified model, is tractable and gives several interesting insights into the characteristics of the estimator and the specification test under misspecification. The analysis proceeds by examining the Frechet derivatives [Wouk (1979, ch. 12)] of $\bar{\theta}(v)$ and $\bar{\tau}(v)$ at $v=0$. These derivatives are by definition linear functionals, $\mathrm{D}\bar{\theta}$ and $\mathrm{D}\bar{\tau}$, on V such that

$$\bar{\theta}(v)=\theta_0+\mathrm{D}\bar{\theta}[v]+\mathrm{o}(\|v\|_2), \quad \bar{\tau}(v)=\mathrm{D}\bar{\tau}[v]+\mathrm{o}(\|v\|_2).$$

In other words, $\bar{\theta}(v)$ and $\bar{\tau}(v)$ can each be approximated by a linear function of v up to an approximation error that is $\mathrm{o}(\|v\|_2)$; the analogy is that a first-term Taylor approximation to an ordinary function. Strictly speaking, V itself is not a linear space for the domains of the linear operators $\mathrm{D}\bar{\theta}$ and $\mathrm{D}\bar{\tau}$. But this is not a problem because the derivatives are actually defined for all $v\in L_2(F_0)$, while here we are only restricting their domains to those values of v for which the G_v is a genuine distribution function.

Three recent papers that have also undertaken local specification analysis are Kiefer and Skoog (1984), Newey (1984) and Davidson and Mackinnon (1984a). The Kiefer–Skoog paper analyzes the effects of misspecification on the limiting parameter value $\bar{\theta}$ for a set of finite-dimensional 'directions' of misspecification generated by incorrect parametric restrictions. Here we study the effects of misspecification on both $\bar{\theta}$ and $\bar{\tau}$ for the more extensive infinite-dimensional set of directions generated by incorrect distributional assumptions. The Newey and Davidson–Mackinnon papers also use an infinite-dimensional set of directions, but the emphasis in these papers is more of studying the behavior of the limiting chi-square non-centrality parameter, while here we focus more on $\bar{\theta}$ and $\bar{\tau}$. Also, the mathematical methods of these other two papers are different than those used here. These papers use concepts of differentiation similar to the Gateaux derivative, whereas here we use the Frechet derivative [see Wouk (1979, ch. 12)]. The requirements for the existence of the Frechet derivative are more stringent than those for the Gateaux derivative – e.g., a Cobb–Douglas production function has Gateaux derivatives at the origin in all directions in the positive orthant but does not have a Frechet derivative there – and establishing the existence of the Frechet derivative entails more detailed arguments. However, because the Frechet derivative, or more precisely the corresponding linear functional, is independent of the direction at which it is evaluated, the qualitative predictions based on it are stronger. For instance, suppose it is found that a specification test locally has zero power in two different directions. Then, if the appropriate Frechet derivatives exist, the test will also be guaranteed to have zero power locally in all directions that are linear combinations of these two directions. A similar guarantee is not available if only the Gateaux derivatives exist and thus conclusions based on the weaker concept of differentiation could potentially be misleading in some cases.

The main results for the Frechet derivatives are in Theorem 6 below, which is proceeded by a technical lemma:

Lemma 2. Let Assumptions 1–4 hold for each G_v *of the form* $\mathrm{d}G_v = [1+v(y)]\,\mathrm{d}F_0(y)$ *and put*

$$\alpha(\theta,\tau,v) = \begin{bmatrix} \lambda_1(\theta,v) \\ \lambda_2(\theta,v)-\tau \end{bmatrix},$$

where

$$\lambda_1(\theta,v) = \int h(y,\theta)\,\mathrm{d}G_v(y), \qquad \lambda_2(\theta,v) = \int c(y,\theta)\,\mathrm{d}G_v(y).$$

Then the Frechet derivative of α *at* $(\theta,\tau,0)\in\Theta\times T\times V$ *exists and is given by*

$$\mathrm{D}\alpha[\Delta\theta,\Delta\tau,v] = \begin{bmatrix} \dfrac{\partial\lambda_1}{\partial\theta'}(\theta,0) & 0 \\ \dfrac{\partial\lambda_2}{\partial\theta'}(\theta,0) & -I \end{bmatrix}\begin{bmatrix}\Delta\theta \\ \Delta\tau\end{bmatrix} + \begin{bmatrix} \int h(y,\theta)v(y)\,\mathrm{d}F_0(y) \\ \int c(y,\theta)v(y)\,\mathrm{d}F_0(y)\end{bmatrix},$$

where $(\Delta\theta,\Delta\tau,v)\in\Theta\times T\times V$, *with the norm on* $\Theta\times T\times V$ *being* $|\Delta\theta|+|\Delta\tau| + \|v\|_2$. *In addition,* $\mathrm{D}\alpha$ *is continuous in* (θ,τ). (Proof: Appendix.)

Theorem 6. Let Assumptions 1–4 hold for each G_v; *let condition (ii) of Theorem 5 hold at* θ_0, *and let* $\bar\theta(v)$ *and* $\bar\tau(v)$ *be the implied almost sure limits of* $\hat\theta_n$ *and* $\hat\tau_n$. *Then* $\bar\theta(v)$ *and* $\bar\tau(v)$ *are Frechet differentiable in* v *at* $v=0$, *with the derivatives given by*

$$\mathrm{D}\bar\theta[v] = (J^o_{hh})^{-1}\int h(y,\theta_0)v(y)\,\mathrm{d}F_0(y),$$

$$\mathrm{D}\bar\tau[v] = \int c(y,\theta_0)v(y)\,\mathrm{d}F_0(y) - J^o_{ch}\,\mathrm{D}\bar\theta[v],$$

where, in the notation of the previous section,

$$J^o_{hh} = \int h(y,\theta_0)h(y,\theta_0)'\,\mathrm{d}F_0(y), \quad J^o_{ch} = \int c(y,\theta_0)h(y,\theta_0)'\,\mathrm{d}F_0(y).$$

Proof. Use Lemma 2 to apply the implicit function theorems for Frechet derivatives [Wouk (1979, Theorem 12,4.1, p. 294; Corollary 1, p. 296)] and the extended information equalities (16) and (17).

Note that implicit in the hypotheses of this theorem are the assumed existence and uniqueness of $\bar{\theta}(v)$ and $\bar{\tau}(v)$. Clarke (1983) provides a set of regularity conditions, albeit stronger than those assumed here, that guarantee existence and uniqueness.

An interesting way to express these derivatives is to put $\bar{\theta}_v = \mathrm{D}\bar{\theta}[v]$ and $\bar{\tau}_v = \mathrm{D}\bar{\theta}[v]$, and write them as

$$\bar{\theta}_v = (J^o_{hh})^{-1} J^o_{hv}, \tag{26}$$

$$\bar{\tau}_v = J^o_{cv} - J^o_{ch}\bar{\theta}_v, \tag{27}$$

where

$$J^o_{hv} = \int h(y,\theta_0)v(y)\,\mathrm{d}F_0(y), \quad J^o_{cv} = \int c(y,\theta_0)v(y)\,\mathrm{d}F_0(y).$$

By analogy with least squares, the derivative $\bar{\theta}_v$ is the vector of regression coefficients in a regression of a random variable $v = v(Y)$ on a random variable $h = h(Y,\theta_0)$, with $Y \sim F(y,\theta_0)$. Thus, misspecification of the model leads to an inconsistent estimate of θ_0, except when the misspecification is in a direction v that is orthogonal to the gradient of the log-density function in the sense that $\mathrm{cov}(v(Y), h(Y,\theta_0)) = 0$ under $F(y,\theta_0)$. The special set of directions in which orthogonality holds corresponds to estimation situations in which the distributional assumptions implicit in the hypothesized model for the data are incorrect but the estimator $\hat{\theta}_n$ is still consistent (i.e., its genuine quasi-maximum likelihood). One well-known example of this in econometrics is FIML applied to a linear simultaneous equations system under the assumption of normally distributed errors when in fact the errors are not normal. Another is Phillips's (1982) example consisting of a two-equation non-linear simultaneous system and a family of non-normal error distributions. Phillips shows that FIML estimation of his system under a normality assumption gives consistent estimates of the parameters despite the failure of the distributional assumptions. The essential feature of Phillips's example is that each true model generated by an error distribution in the family of allowable distributions lies in a direction v that is uncorrelated with h under a normality assumption. Such an example, however, is clearly special and misspecification in general can lie in directions that are not orthogonal to h, so that the limiting value $\bar{\theta}$ is directly affected by misspecification. An example of this more serious type of misspecification would be an omitted variable from a simultaneous equations system.

Considering the derivative $\bar{\tau}_v$ in (27), we see that under misspecification the limit $\bar{\tau}$ is perturbed away from zero in ways. The first is through J^o_{cv}, which is the covariance under F_0 between $c(Y,\theta_0)$ and $v(Y)$; the second is through $\bar{\theta}_v$, i.e., through the effect that the misspecification has on the limit of the estimated parameters. In the special case when the model is wrong but the derivative v is uncorrelated with h under F_0 and $\bar{\theta}_v = 0$, the specification test will detect the failure of the distributional assumptions so long as the auxiliary criterion function has some covariance with v. An example of this use would be applying White's information matrix test under the maintained model $Y \sim \mathrm{N}(\mu, \sigma^2)$ when the true distribution is symmetric about μ but with tails 'thicker' than those of the normal. In this example the ML estimators $\hat{\mu}$ and $\hat{\sigma}^2$ are consistent, but White's test would detect the departure from normality via the failure of the fourther moment about the mean to equal three times the square of the second moment. Again, though, this type of example is clearly special and in general misspecification will perturb $\bar{\theta}$ away from θ_0 and the second term in (27) will be non-zero.

The derivative $\bar{\tau}_v$ also has interesting interpretations based on a least squares analogy. Substitution of (26) into (27) gives

$$\bar{\tau}_v = J^o_{cv} - J^o_{ch}\left(J^o_{hh}\right)^{-1} J^o_{hv} \quad \text{or} \quad \bar{\tau}_v = \int [c - B_{ch}h]\, v \,\mathrm{d}F_0, \tag{28}$$

where $B_{ch} = J^o_{ch}(J^o_{hh})^{-1}$. The matrix B_{ch} is simply the matrix of regression coefficients in a regression of the random vector $c = c(Y,\theta_0)$ on the vector $h = h(Y,\theta_0)$, with $Y \sim F_0(y)$. That is, $B_{ch} = \mathrm{E}_0[ch'](\mathrm{E}_0[hh'])^{-1}$, where the expectation $\mathrm{E}_0[\cdot]$ is under $\mathrm{d}F_0$. Thus $\bar{\tau}_v$ is the covariance between v and the auxiliary criterion function c, after the linear effects of h have been removed from c. Intuitively, the reason that the direction h is 'parsed out' of c, so to speak, is that the condition $\mathrm{E}_0[h(Y,\theta_0)] = 0$ was imposed directly in the estimation, and thus no specification test can be based on this direction.

5. Procedures for application

5.1. Outline

The following three-step algorithm for diagnostic testing and model evaluation summarizes the method for applying Theorems 1–5:

Step 1: Calculate $\hat{\theta}$ by maximum likelihood and retain for subsequent use the 'scores' $\hat{h}_i = h(Y_i, \hat{\theta})$, which are the gradients of the log-density function evaluated at the ML estimate.

Step 2: Choose a set of k auxiliarv criterion functions, $c_k(y,\theta)$, for $k = 1, 2, \ldots, K$. Each of the $c_k(y,\theta)$ should have the property that a large absolute value for $\hat{\tau}_k = (1/n)\sum_1^n c_k(Y_i, \hat{\theta})$ would tend to cast some doubt on the assumptions underlying the likelihood model.

Step 3: Form $\hat{c}_{ki} = c_k(Y_i, \hat{\theta})$ and regress the $\hat{c}$'s on the scores. Specifically, estimate for each k the parameters of the equation

$$\hat{c}_{ki} = \beta_{k0} + \hat{h}_i'\beta_k + u_i, \qquad i = 1, 2, \ldots, n, \tag{29}$$

where u_i represents the error, and β_{k0} and β_k are the constant and the slope coefficients. The estimates $\hat{\beta}_{0k}$ of the intercepts in the regression equations will be the $\hat{\tau}_k$. Furthermore, individual t tests for non-zero intercepts in the regressions using the printed standard errors will be asymptotically valid tests for whether or not the corresponding $\hat{\tau}_k$ are significantly different from zero. Finally, the statistic $\hat{\tau}'(\hat{\Omega}/n)^{-1}\hat{\tau}$, where $\hat{\tau}$ is the vector of $\hat{\tau}_k$ and $\hat{\Omega}$ is the $K \times K$ cross-equation residual covariance matrix, is an appropriate chi-square statistic for testing whether or not all of the intercepts are jointly statistically significantly different from zero.

This regression-based procedure is the multivariate extension of a method proposed by Cox (1962, p. 411) for calculating the test statistic for his test for separate families. The procedure differs somewhat from that proposed by White (1982), Chesher (1983), Davidson and Mackinnon (1984b) and others for specification tests that are special cases of those considered here. In the other procedure the user calculates a single chi-square statistic equal to nR^2 (uncentered) for a regression of an $n \times 1$ column of ones on the $n \times (K+p)$ matrix whose ith row is $(\hat{c}_i', \hat{h}_i')$, where $\hat{c}_i' = (\hat{c}_{1i}, \hat{c}_{2i}, \ldots, \hat{c}_{ki})$ and $\hat{h}_i'$ is the transposed score vector. A major advantage of the procedure outlined above is that the individual t tests on the intercepts provide the user with detailed information on the statistical significance of each of the components $\hat{\tau}_k$. Using the other procedure the user obtains information only on the joint significance of all components taken together. A disadvantage, however, is that to get the chi-square statistic $\hat{\tau}'(\hat{\Omega}/n)^{-1}\hat{\tau}$ for joint significance the user must calculate a quadratic form in the residual covariance matrix for K separate regressions, while for the other procedure the user only calculates nR^2 for a single regression. Interestingly, the two chi-square statistics from the procedures are only asymptotically equivalent but not computationally equivalent in finite samples. If no degree of adjustment is used in calculating $\hat{\Omega}$, then least squares algebra shows that the statistics satisfy $\hat{\tau}'(\hat{\Omega}/n)^{-1}\hat{\tau} \geq nR^2$. With a degree of freedom adjustment, however, the inequality can go in either direction for finite n. Clearly, further work on the small sample properties of the chi-square statistics would be useful.

5.2. Empirical example

The potential uses of the type of specification tests considered in this paper can be illustrated with an application from the study of price behavior on speculative markets. One of the major stylized facts that has emerged from extensive research into the characteristics of short-term price movements on futures and equity markets is that the price changes generally have mean zero and are independent of one another, but their probability distribution is not a normal distribution. In particular, the pdf of the price changes has thick tails or is leptokurtic relative to the normal pdf. It is interesting, then, to see if the types of specification tests discussed here do in fact detect departure from normality in speculative price changes.

Suppose that the maintained model for the daily price change is $\Delta P_i \sim \mathrm{N}(0, \sigma^2)$. Given n observations on ΔP_i, the ML estimate of σ^2 is

$$\hat{\sigma}^2 = \frac{1}{n}\sum_1^n \Delta P_i^2.$$

Under weak conditions that do not require normality the estimater $\hat{\sigma}^2$ is consistent. However, the model $\Delta P_i \sim \mathrm{N}(0, \sigma^2)$ when viewed as a probability model for the data is misspecified if the ΔP_i are not normally distributed, and may give biased and misleading predictions. Consider the following four auxiliary criterion functions for detecting misspecification of the probability model:

$$\begin{aligned}
c_1(\Delta P, \sigma) &= \Delta P^4 - 3\sigma^4, \\
c_2(\Delta P, \sigma) &= |\Delta P| - \sqrt{2/\pi}\,\sigma, \\
c_3(\Delta P, \sigma) &= I[|\Delta P/\sigma| \geq z_{0.40}] - 0.80, \\
c_4(\Delta P, \sigma) &= I[|\Delta P/\sigma| \geq z_{0.005}] - 0.01,
\end{aligned}$$

where $I[\cdot]$ denotes the 0–1 indicator function, and where $z_{0.40}$ and $z_{0.005}$ are upper critical points of the normal distribution. Elementary calculations show that each of the $c_k(\Delta P, \sigma)$ integrates to zero under $\Delta P \sim \mathrm{N}(0, \sigma^2)$. Now put

$$\begin{aligned}
\hat{c}_{ki} &= c_k(\Delta P_i, \hat{\sigma}), \qquad & i = 1, \ldots, n, \\
\hat{\tau}_k &= \frac{1}{n}\sum_{i=1}^n \hat{c}_{ki}, \qquad & k = 1, \ldots, 4.
\end{aligned}$$

The random variable $\hat{\tau}_1$ is the difference between the observed and predicted fourth moments; $\hat{\tau}_2$ is the difference between the observed and predicted absolute first moments; $\hat{\tau}_3$ is the difference between the observed and the predicted fraction of the observations for which the magnitude $|\Delta P_i|$ lies more than $z_{0.40}$ standard deviations above zero; and $\hat{\tau}_4$ is analogously defined for $z_{0.005}$.

These quantities were evaluated using 876 observations on the daily price change for the T-bills futures markets, 1976–79, from a data set described more fully in Tauchen and Pitts (1983). The results are as follows:

		Observed	Predicted	Difference ($\hat{\tau}_k$)
(1)	Fourth moment	0.0124	0.0063	0.0061
(2)	Abs. first moment	0.153	0.171	−0.017
(3)	Outer 80%	0.728	0.800	−0.072
(4)	Outer 1%	0.027	0.010	0.017

The first two rows of this display suggest that the actual fourth moment is somewhat larger than what is predicted by the probability model, while the absolute first moment is somewhat smaller. The last two rows indicate that there are too few observations above $\hat{\sigma} z_{0.40}$ in magnitude and too many above $\hat{\sigma} z_{0.005}$ than would be expected on the basis of the normal distribution.

To determine the statistical significance of each of the four $\hat{\tau}_k$, we simply test for a non-zero intercept in the appropriate auxiliary regression

$$\hat{c}_{ik} = \beta_{0k} + \beta_{1k}\hat{h}_i + \text{error}, \qquad i = 1, 2, \dots, n,$$

where $\hat{h}_i = \partial l(\Delta P_i, \hat{\sigma}^2)/\partial\sigma^2$ is the gradient of the log-density function. Specifically,

$$\hat{h}_i = -\tfrac{1}{2}(\hat{\sigma}^{-2} - \Delta P_i^2 \hat{\sigma}^{-4}), \qquad i = 1, 2, \dots, 876,$$

with $\hat{\sigma} = 0.214$. The results are:

		$\hat{\beta}_{0k}$(s.d.)	$\hat{\beta}_{1k}$(s.d)
(1)	Fourth moment	0.0061 (0.0011)	0.0026 (0.000047)
(2)	Abs. first moment	−0.0170 (0.0020)	0.0056 (0.000089)
(3)	Outer 80%	−0.0717 (0.0145)	0.0050 (0.00060)
(4)	Outer 1%	0.0174 (0.0033)	0.0055 (0.00014)

The magnitudes of each of the four estimated intercepts exceeds twice their standard errors, which suggests that the four $\hat{\tau}_k$ are statistically significantly different from zero. The normal distribution thus appears to be inadequate as an approximation of the pdf of the ΔP_i.

6. Conclusions: suggestions for future research

This paper has developed the general asymptotic distribution theory for specification tests that are based on M-estimates of auxiliary parameters. Though this class of specification tests is quite large, there are some tests not included within it. For instance, the Kolmogorov–Smirnov test cannot be interpreted as being based on an M-estimator of some auxiliary statistic. Of course the large-sample theory for the K–S test statistic is well known, even for the case in which the distribution function being tested involves an estimated parameter. However, by embedding the K–S test statistic and others like it into the general theory of L- or U-estimates, one should be able to develop a new and very wide class of specification tests that is analogous to the class of tests developed here. This work is deferred to another paper.

Appendix

Proof of Lemma 1 (based on the ideas in Huber (1967, pp. 224–226)). Let $\varepsilon > 0$ be given. Define

$$u(y,\theta,d) = \sup_{|\gamma-\theta|\le d} |\phi(y,\gamma) - \phi(y,\theta)|.$$

By almost sure continuity, $\lim u(y,\theta,d) = 0$ as $d \to 0$, with θ fixed, almost surely $\mathrm{d}G$. Thus by dominated convergence, $\mathrm{E}[u(Y,\theta,d)] \le \varepsilon$ whenever $d \le \bar{d}(\theta)$. Let $B(\theta)$ denote an open ball of radius $\bar{d}(\theta)$ about θ. Together the $B(\theta)$ cover Θ. By compactness the $B(\theta)$ can be reduced to a finite open covering $B_k = B(\theta_k)$, $k = 1,\dots,K$. Put $d_k = \bar{d}(\theta_k)$ and $\mu_k = \mathrm{E}[u(Y,\theta_k,d_k)]$, and note that if $\theta \in B_k$, then $\mu_k \le \varepsilon$, and $|\lambda(\theta) - \lambda(\theta_k)| \le \varepsilon$. Now let $\theta \in B_k$ and consider

$$\left|\frac{1}{n}\sum_1^n \phi(Y_i,\theta) - \lambda(\theta)\right|$$

$$\le \frac{1}{n}\sum_1^n |\phi(Y_i,\theta) - \phi(Y_i,\theta_k)| + \left|\frac{1}{n}\sum_1^n \phi(Y_i,\theta_k) - \lambda(\theta_k)\right|$$

$$+ |\lambda(\theta_k) - \lambda(\theta)|$$

$$\le \left(\frac{1}{n}\sum_1^n u(Y_i,\theta_k,d_k) - \mu_k\right) + \mu_k + \left|\frac{1}{n}\sum_1^n \phi(Y_i,\theta_k) - \lambda(\theta_k)\right| + \varepsilon$$

$$\le 4\varepsilon,$$

whenever $n \geq N_k(\varepsilon)$ almost surely, by applying twice the strong law of large numbers and using $\mu_k \leq \varepsilon$. Thus

$$\sup_{\theta \in \Theta} \left| \frac{1}{n} \sum_1^n \phi(Y_i, \theta) - \lambda(\theta) \right| \leq 4\varepsilon,$$

whenever $n \geq \max_k N_k(\varepsilon)$ almost surely, which proves the result.

Proof of Theorem 5. Let Δ by any non-zero vector in R^p such that $|\Delta|$ is small enough that $\gamma = \theta_0 + \Delta \in \Theta$, and consider

$$|(J^o_{ch} + K^o_c)(\Delta/|\Delta|)|. \tag{A.1}$$

Since $\int c(y,\theta) f(y,\theta)\,\mathrm{d}\mu = 0$ for all θ in Θ, then (A.1) can be written as

$$\left| (1/|\Delta|) \int [c(y,\gamma) f(y,\gamma) - c(y,\theta_0) f(y,\theta_0)]\,\mathrm{d}\mu \right.$$

$$\left. - (J^o_{ch} + K^o_c)(\Delta/|\Delta|) \right|,$$

which is dominated by

$$(1/|\Delta|) \left| \int [c(y,\gamma) - c(y,\theta_0)]\, f(y,\theta_0)\,\mathrm{d}\mu - K^o_c \Delta \right|$$

$$+ \left| (1/|\Delta|) \int c(y,\gamma)[f(y,\gamma) - f(y,\theta_0)]\,\mathrm{d}\mu - J^o_{ch}(\Delta/|\Delta|) \right|. \tag{A.2}$$

The first of the two terms in (A.2) tends to zero as $|\Delta| \to 0$ since K^o_c is, by definition, the matrix of partial derivatives with respect to θ' of $\int c(y,\theta) f(y,\theta_0)\,\mathrm{d}\mu$ evaluated at $\theta = \theta_0$. Now write

$$f(y,\gamma) - f(y,\theta_0) = f(y,\dot{\theta}) h(y,\dot{\theta})'\Delta,$$

where $\dot{\theta}$ (which depends upon y and Δ) is on the line segment between θ_0 and γ. By definition $J^o_{ch} = \int c(y,\theta_0) h(y,\theta_0)' f(y,\theta_0)\,\mathrm{d}\mu$ and so the second term in (A.2) is dominated by the sum of

$$\left| \int c(y,\gamma) \left[\frac{f(y,\dot{\theta})}{f(y,\theta_0)} h(y,\dot{\theta}) - h(y,\theta_0) \right]' \frac{\Delta}{|\Delta|} f(y,\theta_0)\,\mathrm{d}\mu \right|, \tag{A.3}$$

and

$$\left|\int[c(y,\gamma)-c(y,\theta_0)]h(y,\theta_0)'\frac{\Delta}{|\Delta|}f(y,\theta_0)\,\mathrm{d}\mu\right|. \tag{A.4}$$

From (ii) of Assumption 4 the expected value of $|c(y,\gamma)|^2$ with respect to $f(y,\theta_0)$ is uniformly bounded in γ, and so by the Schwarz inequality the square of the term (A.3) is dominated by a constant times

$$\int\left|\frac{f(y,\dot\theta)}{f(y,\theta_0)}h(y,\dot\theta)-h(y,\theta_0)\right|^2 f(y,\theta_0)\,\mathrm{d}\mu.$$

The second hypothesis of the theorem and (ii) of Assumption 4 imply that the squared term in this integral is dominated by a function integrable with respect to $f(y,\theta_0)\,\mathrm{d}\mu$. Thus by dominated convergence this integral, and hence (A.3), tends to zero as $|\Delta|\to 0$. Finally, since c satisfies the Lipshitz conditions in Assumption 4 and $|h|^2$ is dominated, the term (A.4) is $\mathrm{O}(|\Delta|^{1/2})$.

In summary, the matrix $J^o_{ch}+K^o_c$ satisfies for any non-zero $\Delta\in R^p$

$$\lim_{|\Delta|\to 0}|(J^o_{ch}+K^o_c)(\Delta/|\Delta|)|=0,$$

irrespective of how $|\Delta|\to 0$; hence it equals zero because it maps every vector of unit length into zero.

Proof of Lemma 2. Put $\delta=|\Delta\theta|+|\Delta\tau|+\|v\|_2$, and consider

$$\begin{aligned}
&\delta^{-1}|\alpha(\theta+\Delta\theta,\tau+\Delta\tau,v)-\alpha(\theta,\tau,0)-\mathrm{D}\alpha[\Delta\theta,\Delta\tau,v]|\\
&\le\delta^{-1}\Big|\lambda_1(\theta+\Delta\theta,v)-\lambda_1(\theta,0)-(\partial\lambda_1/\partial\theta')(\theta,0)\Delta\theta\\
&\quad-\int h(y,\theta)v(y)\,\mathrm{d}F_0(y)\Big|\\
&\quad+\delta^{-1}\Big|\lambda_2(\theta+\Delta\theta,v)-\lambda_2(\theta,0)-(\partial\lambda_2/\partial\theta')(\theta,0)\,\Delta\theta\\
&\quad-\int c(y,\theta)v(y)\,\mathrm{d}F_0(y)\Big|.
\end{aligned}\tag{A.5}$$

We must show that the right-hand side of this inequality tends to zero as $\delta\to 0$. Now the first term on the right-hand side of the inequality (A.5) cannot exceed the sum of

$$\delta^{-1}|\lambda_1(\theta+\Delta\theta,0)-\lambda_1(\theta,0)-(\partial\lambda_1/\partial\theta')(\theta,0)\,\Delta\theta| \tag{A.6}$$

and

$$\delta^{-1}\left|\int[h(y,\theta+\Delta\theta)-h(y,\theta)]\,v(y)\,\mathrm{d}F_0(y)\right|. \tag{A.7}$$

From the definition of $\partial\lambda_1/\partial\theta'$, the expression (A.6) must tend to zero with δ. On the other hand, the expression (A.7) is dominated by

$$\delta^{-1}\|v\|_2\left[\int|h(y,\theta+\Delta\theta)-h(y,\theta)|^2\,\mathrm{d}F_0(y)\right]^{1/2}, \tag{A.8}$$

and by the second Lipshitz condition (iii) in Assumption 4 there is a constant β such that (A.8) is of the form

$$\delta^{-1}\|v\|_2\beta|\Delta\theta|^{1/2}\leq\beta|\Delta\theta|^{1/2},$$

which tends to zero with δ. In an exactly analogous manner the second term on the right-hand side of the initial inequality (A.5) (the term corresponding to λ_2) tends to zero with δ, and so the existence of the Frechet derivative of α with respect to θ,τ,v at $(\theta,\tau,0)$ has been established. The continuity of the derivative in (θ,τ) is presupposed in (iv) of Assumption 4.

References

Aguirre-Torres, V. and A.R. Gallant, 1983, The null and non-null asymptotic distribution of the Cox test for multivariate nonlinear regression, Journal of Econometrics 21, 1–33.

Burguette, J.F., A.R. Gallant and G. Souza, 1982, On unification of the asymptotic theory of nonlinear econometric models, Econometric Review 1, 151–190.

Chesher, Andrew, 1983, The information matrix test: Simplified calculation via a score interpretation, Economics Letters 13, 45–48.

Clarke, Brenton R., 1983, Uniqueness and Frechet differentiability of functional solutions to maximum likelihood type equations, Annals of Statistics 11, 1196–1205.

Cox, D.R., 1962, Further results on tests of separate families of hypotheses, Journal of the Royal Statistical Society B 24, 406–424.

Davidson, R. and J. Mackinnon, 1984a, Implicit alternatives and the local power of test statistics, Queen's University discussion paper no. 556.

Davidson, R. and J. Mackinnon, 1984b, Model specification tests based on artificial linear regressions, International Economic Review 25, 485–502.

Engle, Robert F., 1982, A general approach to Lagrange multiplier model diagnostics, Journal of Econometrics 20, 83–104.

Hausman, J., 1978, Specification tests in econometrics, Econometrica 46, 1251–1271.

Heckman, J., 1984, The χ^2 goodness of fit for models with parameters estimated from microdata, Econometrica 52, 1543–1548.

Huber, Peter J., 1967, The behavior of maximum likelihood estimates under nonstandard conditions, in: Lucien M. LeCam and Jerzy Neyman, eds., Proceedings of the fifth Berkeley symposium on mathematical statistics and probability, Vol. 1 (University of California Press, Berkeley, CA) 221–234.

Huber, Peter J., 1981, Robust statistics (Wiley, New York).

Kendall, M.G. and A. Stuart, 1973, The advanced theory of statistics, 3rd ed. (Griffin, London).

Kiefer, N. and G. Skoog, Local asymptotic specification error analysis, Econometrica 52, 873–886.

Lancaster, T., 1984, The covariance matrix of the information matrix text, Econometrica 52, 1051–1054.

Moore, D.S. and M.C. Spruill, 1975, Unified large-sample of general chi-squared statistics for tests of fit, Annals of Statistics 3, 599–616.

Newey, W.K., 1984, Maximum likelihood specification testing and instrumented score tests, Princeton University mimeo.

Phillips, P.C.B., 1982, On the consistency of FIML, Econometrica 50, 1307–1324.

Tauchen, George and M. Pitts, 1983, The price variability–volume relationship on speculative markets, Econometrica 51, 485–505.

White, H., 1982, Maximum likelihood estimation of misspecified models, Econometrica 50, 1–26.

Wouk, A., 1979, A course of applied functional analysis (Wiley, New York).

NON-PARAMETRIC ANALYSIS OF OPTIMIZING BEHAVIOR WITH MEASUREMENT ERROR*

Hal R. VARIAN

University of Michigan, Ann Arbor, MI 48109, USA

We consider how one might test observed choice data for consistency with optimizing models in the presence of measurement error. We derive an appropriate test statistic and conduct case study involving cost minimization behavior by electric utility plants.

1. Introduction

In several earlier papers listed in the references I have described methods for testing observed economic behavior for consistency with optimizing models. These tests have built on the work of Afriat (1967, 1972, 1976), Diewert (1973), Diewert and Parkan (1978, 1980) and Hanoch and Rothschild (1972). A defect of the methods proposed in these works is that there it seems difficult to incorporate measurement error into the analysis. The data are assumed to be observed without error, so that the tests are 'all or nothing': either the data satisfy the optimization hypothesis or they don't.

Despite this stringent nature of the tests, they may well be worth doing. Indeed, if some data pass such a test *without* resorting to any specification of measurement error one might feel more confident than usual about the veracity of the null hypothesis. (Or perhaps feel more dubious than usual about the power of the data to reveal violations of the null hypothesis.)

However, it seems that if some data fail the tests, but only by a small amount, we might well be tempted to attribute this failure to measurement error, left out variables, or other sorts of stochastic influences rather than to reject the hypothesis outright. The problem here of course is to give formal content to the phrase 'only a small amount'.

That is the goal of this paper. In the following sections I offer a general method that is, in principle, capable of measuring the magnitude of departure from the underlying model of optimizing behavior. I am able to interpret this procedure in terms of the classical statistical framework of hypothesis testing, and I provide a case study to illustrate the feasibility of the method.

* This research was supported by the National Science Foundation. I received helpful comments on earlier drafts from Bruce Hill, Peter Schmidt, and Adonis Yatchew.

2. Stochastic considerations in non-parametric analysis

The non-parametric tests mentioned above usually take the form of asking whether there exists a solution to a certain set of linear inequalities. For example, suppose that we have n observations on the output (y_i), the factor prices (w_i) and the factor demands (x_i) for a particular firm. It is shown in Varian (1984) that the following 'Weak Axiom of Cost Minimization' (WACM) is a necessary and sufficient condition for the observed behavior of the firm to be compatible with cost minimizing behavior:

$$w_i x_i \leq w_i x_j \quad \text{for all} \quad y_i \leq y_j.$$

The interpretation of this condition is that the cost at the observed operating positions should be no greater than the cost of using any other factors capable of producing at least as much output. If there are n observations, this gives rise to n^2 inequalities that must be satisfied by the observed choices if they are to be consistent with cost minimizing behavior.

This sort of condition is easy to test, but it may be a bit more difficult to interpret. If the data do not satisfy WACM, what are we to do? The answer seems to depend on the *magnitude* of the violation. If the data fail to satisfy WACM by only a small amount, then we might well be tempted to attribute this violation to measurement error and accept the hypothesis of cost minimization.

The problem here is to give specific content to the words 'magnitude of the violation' and if possible to phrase the discussion in the formal language of statistical hypothesis testing. I will describe my progress towards achieving these goals.

Let us suppose that the observed demand for factor k in observation i, x_{ik}, is related to the 'true' factor demand z_{ik} in the following way:

$$x_{ik} = z_{ik} + \varepsilon_{ik}, \qquad i = 1, \dots, n, \quad k = 1, \dots, m,$$

where ε_{ik} is a random error term. We will suppose that this error term ε_{ik} is iid $N(0, \sigma^2)$. Of course other stochastic specifications are possible; but this choice is a convenient one for discussion.[1]

The null hypothesis that I wish to consider can be stated as

$$H_0: \quad \text{the data } (w_i, z_i, y_i) \text{ satisfy WACM.}$$

It is convenient to think of the matrix of observations (x_{ik}) as a vector with mn components which we will denote by X. Thus the non-negative orthant of

[1] In most applications, an assumption of proportional measurement error is often more appropriate. This is in fact the specification that we use in the empirical work presented below.

R^{mn} is the set of all possible data. The set of data consistent with the null hypothesis is then that subset H of R^{mn} that satisfies WACM. The observed choices, X, is not an element of this set, but under the null hypothesis, the true choices, Z, is an element of H. The situation is depicted in fig. 1.

How can we conveniently test this null hypothesis? There are several approaches that one might consider. The first approach is somewhat Bayesian in flavor. Since $z_{ik} = x_{ik} - \varepsilon_{ik}$ we might regard z_{ik} as a Normal random variable with mean x_{ik} and variance σ^2. The vector Z can then be thought of as being multivariate Normal with a probability density $f(Z)$. We can integrate the density over the region H to compute the probability that the null hypothesis actually holds.

There are three sorts of problems with this approach that I can see. First, this procedure is not in the spirit of classical statistical hypothesis testing, since we generally want to consider the distribution of the observed data given that the null hypothesis is true, not the distribution of the true data given the observations. Secondly, the test may be computationally quite demanding, especially since it may need to be performed for several different values of σ^2. Thirdly, it does not generalize in a convenient way to other sorts of non-parametric tests.

For example, if we are given observations on a consumer's choices (x_i) when facing prices (p_i), a necessary and sufficient condition for the data to be consistent with maximizing behavior is that there exist positive numbers (U_i, λ_i) that satisfy the following system of inequalities:

$$U_i \leq U_j + \lambda_j p_j (x_i - x_j), \qquad i, j = 1, \ldots, n.$$

Thus in the case of consumer maximization, the region H will be all data sets for which these inequalities have a positive solution. This may be rather difficult to calculate, much less to integrate over.

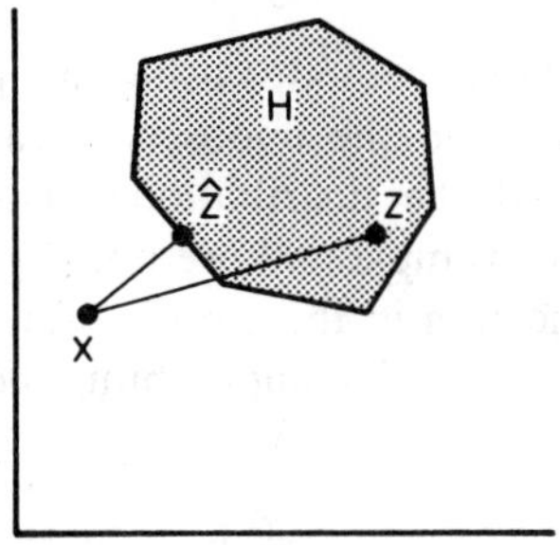

Fig. 1. Non-parametric test.

For these reasons I have adopted a different approach. There are two arguments that lead to the same test procedure, which we will examine in the following two sections.

3. A chi-squared test

Suppose that we could somehow observe the true data (z_{ik}). Then since $\varepsilon_{ik} = z_{ik} - x_{ik}$, we could compute the 'test statistic':

$$T = \sum_{i=1}^{n} \sum_{k=1}^{m} (z_{ik} - x_{ik})^2/\sigma^2.$$

Under the null hypothesis H_0, this 'statistic' has a chi-squared distribution. Thus we can find a critical value C_α for any desired level of significance, α. If $T > C_\alpha$ we would reject the null hypothesis.

The problem is of course that the 'statistic' T is not observable. However, it turns out that we can calculate an observable *lower bound* on T that will still allow us to apply the above testing method. Consider the following quadratic programming problem:

$$S = \min \sum_{i=1}^{n} \sum_{k=1}^{m} (\zeta_{ik} - x_{ik})^2/\sigma^2,$$

subject to

$$w_i \zeta_i \leq w_i \zeta_j \quad \text{for} \quad y_i \leq y_i.$$

Under the null hypothesis, the 'true data' (w_i, z_i, y_i) satisfy the constraint. Hence the minimum of the sum of squares S must be no larger than the 'test statistic' T.

Thus if we reject H_0 whenever $S > C_\alpha$, we are certain that in fact $T > C_\alpha$, and thus we have *at least* the desired level of significance. That is, the probability of rejecting H_0 when it is true will be less than α. In this sense, the test is very conservative.

The basic trick in the above method is using the mathematical programming problem to derive a bound on the unobserved random variable. The exact stochastic specification and the distributional assumptions were chosen in order to present a specific example and are not critical to the structure of the test. The choice of specification in these non-parametric methods rests on the trade-off between generality and computability here just as it does in all statistical work.[2]

[2] This idea has been used before in the statistics literature. The classic upper and lower bounds on the Durbin–Watson statistic were calculated by using a similar bounding argument.

Although I believe the hypothesis test described above is in the spirit of classical hypothesis testing, it is comforting to note that it is also quite sensible. We are simply asking for the minimal perturbation of the data that satisfies WACM. If the minimal perturbation is small relative to the amount of noise thought to be present in the data then it seems reasonable to accept the null hypothesis.

One particularly nice feature of the test outlined above is that it can handle 'nuisance parameters' quite easily. For example, in the case of the utility maximization problem described above the programming problem becomes

$$S = \min \sum_{i=1}^{n} \sum_{k=1}^{m} (\zeta_{ik} - x_{ik})^2/\sigma^2,$$

subject to

$$A_i \leq A_j + b_j p_j(\zeta_i - \zeta_j), \qquad i, j = 1, \ldots, n.$$

This time the minimization takes place over the variables (ξ_{ik}, A_i, b_i). Under the null hypothesis, there is a set of variables (z_i, U_i, λ_i) that satisfies the constraints, so the answer to this minimization problem will be an appropriate bound to the desired test statistic. It appears that it would be quite difficult, if not impossible, to analyze this problem by the integration technique mentioned earlier.

A further advantage of the method is that it actually constructs the perturbation of the data that satisfies cost minimization. If we want to go on to calculate bounds on the underlying technology or to forecast demand behavior as described in Varian (1984), we can use this constructed technology. The integration approach described above lacks this feature.

There is a nice geometric interpretation of the proposed test that is depicted in fig. 1. Here the Euclidean distance between X and Z is a sum of squared residuals, and this distance in obviously bounded by the minimal distance from X to H.

However, despite these observations, there are some unpleasant features of the proposed test. The major difficulty is the fact that one needs to specify a known variance.[3] However, the fact that one must postulate a value for this parameter does not make the undertaking entirely arbitrary. For example, one could use estimates of the error variance derived from parametric fits or from knowledge about how the variables were actually measured. In any event, it seems that postulating one parameter, an indication of how noisy the investigator believes the data to be, is much less objectionable than the common practice of postulating an entire functional form. It must be remembered that

[3] If there are several observed choices at each price it may be possible to actually estimate the variance. However, this type of data is rather rare.

the usual estimates of error variances are correct only under the maintained hypothesis of the specified functional form; and this maintained hypothesis is often arbitrary.

Even if we are not able to estimate the error variance as in parametric models, we can still derive bounds on the error variance that is necessary in order to reject the maintained hypothesis of maximizing behavior. Let us consider this point in more detail.

As above, let C_α be the critical value for our proposed test, and let S be the value of our objective function. Then by inspection of the objective function, $S = R/\sigma^2$, where σ^2 is the 'true' variance of the error term and R is the sum of squared residuals. We are proposing to reject the null hypothesis when $S > C_\alpha$ which means when $\sigma^2 < R/C_\alpha$. Let us refer to the $\bar{\sigma}^2 = R/C_\alpha$ as the *critical value* of σ^2, and let $\bar{\sigma}$ be its square root. Note that $\bar{\sigma}$ is easily computable once we have solved the quadratic programming problem.

The critical value, $\bar{\sigma}$, measures what the standard error of the data would have to be for us to consider the rejection of the maximization hypothesis to be a statistically significant rejection. If $\bar{\sigma}$ is much smaller than our prior opinions concerning the precision with which these data have been measured, we may well want to accept the maximization hypothesis.

4. A constrained maximum likelihood approach

Another approach to the sort of test described above is through the method of constrained maximum likelihood. Given some observations (x_{ik}) and the specification of a normal error term we can write the log-likelihood function

$$\log L = mn \log(2\pi)/2 - mn \log \sigma - \sum_{i=1}^{n} \sum_{k=1}^{m} (z_{ik} - x_{ik})^2/2\sigma^2.$$

We think of (z_{ik}) and σ^2 as unknown parameters to be estimated. Under the null hypothesis, $Z = (z_{ik})$ is an element of the set H, so we can consider the *constrained* maximum likelihood estimates derived by maximizing the likelihood over the set H. It is easy to see that this gives us as our estimator for (z_{ik}) the values that solve the quadratic programming problem described above. Let these values be denoted by $(\hat{z}_{ik})$. The associated estimator for σ^2 is

$$\hat{\sigma}^2 = \sum_{i=1}^{n} \sum_{k=1}^{m} (\hat{z}_{ik} - x_{ik})^2 \Big/ mn.$$

Thus the 'fitted values' $(\hat{z}_{ik})$ are a (constrained) maximum likelihood estimate of the true unknown values. However, I am unsure whether it is possible to establish any useful statistical properties for these estimates. After all, we are estimating one more parameter that we have observations. The only thing that allows our estimates to be identified at all is the constraint.

However, the statistic $\hat{\sigma}^2$ can be used for hypothesis testing purposes. As before we simply note that

$$mn\hat{\sigma}^2/\sigma^2 = R$$

is no larger than a chi-squared variable with mn degrees of freedom. Hence if we reject the null hypothesis that Z is in H whenever $R > C_\alpha$, we are guaranteed a test of *at least* the desired level of significance.

Rearranging the test condition, we have

$$\sigma^2 < mn\hat{\sigma}^2/C_\alpha = R/C_\alpha,$$

which is exactly the condition given earlier. If our prior beliefs suggest that σ^2 is less than R/C_α, we should reject the optimization hypothesis. Otherwise, it should not be rejected.

5. A comparison with parametric methods

The diagram in fig. 1 can be used to establish a nice link with standard parametric estimation techniques in models with optimizing behavior. Suppose that we have some parametric form for the underlying technology which we can use to derive functional forms for the factor demand for factor k at observation i as a function of the factor prices, output levels, and an unknown vector of parameters β. We denote this factor demand by $g_k(w_i, y_i, \beta)$.

Then under the null hypothesis of optimizing behavior and known parametric form, the true data, (z_{ik}), will satisfy the parametric relationship:

$$z_{ik} = g_k(w_i, y_k, \beta), \qquad i = 1, \ldots, n, \quad k = 1, \ldots, m.$$

If there are b unknown parameters, the set of all Z that satisfy this relationship will generically be a b-dimensional manifold in R^{mn} which we denote by M. Since Z satisfies the optimization conditions by construction, the manifold M must be a subset of the set H. This relationship is depicted in fig 2.

The usual approach to constrained parametric estimation involves maximizing the likelihood function over the manifold M. This simply means that we find some fitted values (z_{ik}) in M that maximize the likelihood function. The associated values of β are the maximum likelihood estimates of the unknown parameters. The maximum likelihood estimate for σ^2 is just the sum of squared residuals divided by mn.

These estimates are entirely analogous to the non-parametric estimates given above. The only difference is that we are maximizing the likelihood over the mn-dimensional set H rather than the b-dimensional manifold M. Despite this

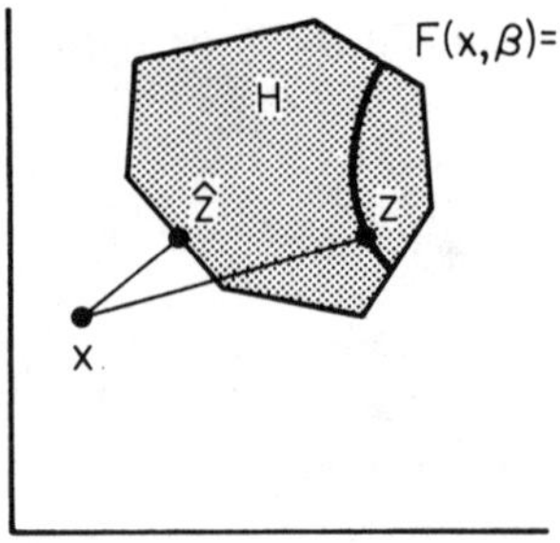

Fig. 2. Parametric test.

resemblance in method, the statistical properties of the estimators may be quite different. I suspect that the major differences arise because the dimension of the manifold M stays fixed as the number of observations increases while the dimension of H keeps growing.

Let us use R_p to denote the minimal sum of squared residuals for the parametric estimate and R_n the minimal sum of squared residuals for the non-parametric estimate. The ratio R_n/R_p is, in some sense, a measure of the 'goodness of fit' of the parametric model, conditional on the optimization hypothesis. If the perturbation of the data necessary to satisfy the optimization hypothesis in the presence of a specific parametric form is very large relative to the perturbation necessary to satisfy optimization alone, we might not find the parametric hypothesis very convincing.

Of course again we need to ask 'large relative to what?' I have not yet come up with a satisfactory answer to that question, and until someone does we will simply have to make do with an intuitive notion of what magnitudes are plausible.

6. A case study

In order to examine the feasibility of the methods described above I undertook a case study involving data on California electric power generation. The data in question were obtained from Woo (1982) and are discussed in detail in his Chapter 4. The data consist of eighteen time series observations from 1960–1979 on the factor inputs and output of two electric power generation plants.[4] The factors used in this study are labor, fuel and capital.

We first checked the plants for consistency with the cost minimization hypothesis. We found that the observed behavior *violated* the WACM inequalities. The natural question is: by how much were the inequalities violated?

[4]Woo's original data set contained two observations in which the cost of capital variable was negative. These observations were discarded.

To answer this question we solved up the quadratic programming problem described above. Each program involved fifty-four variables (three factors, eighteen observations) and around two hundred constraints. The actual program solved was different from that described above in that we postulated a proportional measurement error rather than an additive one. Since the factor demands were measured in very different units this seemed like a much more plausible specification.

Specifically, we assumed that the true demand was related to the observed demand in the following way:

$$z_{ik} = x_{ik}(1 + \varepsilon_{ik}),$$

where ε_{ik} is an iid Normal disturbance with mean zero and constant variance. This leads to an objective function of the form

$$\sum_{i=1}^{m} \sum_{k=1}^{n} (z_{ik}/x_{ik} - 1)^2.$$

The quadratic programming problem was solved by a quadratic programming package called MINOS by Murtagh and Saunders (1977). We found the cost of each quadratic programming problem was around \$2.00 during normal priority on the University of Michigan computer system, an Amdahl 5860 running MTS. The result of these calculations are presented in tables 1 and 2.

We will describe the data in table 1 since the story in table 2 is much the same. Columns 2–4 give the observed output and input levels, while columns 5–7 give the percent 'residuals' that would make the observed firm choices consistent with WACM and minimize the sum of squared deviations. The value *SSR*, the sum of squared residuals, is given for each factor and overall, as well as the square root of the overall *SSR* divided by the number of observations. The latter variable may be thought of as something like a standard error so we have denoted it by *SE*.

There are several interesting things about the 'fit' described in table 1. Note for example the size of the perturbations for the different factors. One would imagine that the labor cost component of these electric power plants would be the easiest to measure, with the fuel costs a close second. The most difficult factor to measure is certainly the capital stock. Indeed, when we look at the sum of squared residuals for each factor we find that they conform to this expected pattern.[5]

[5] Of course if the analyst thought that there were extreme differences in the degree of measurement error across the factors of production he would presumably modify the null hypothesis of equal percentage error variance. This seems to me to be analogous to the problem of heteroskedasticity in ordinary regression analysis. Just as in the case of ordinary least squares, we can minimize a *weighted* sum of squares if this problem is felt to be a serious one. In most cases, I doubt that it is.

Table 1

Alamitos.[a]

Year	Actual fuel	Actual labor	Actual capital	Residual ×100	Residual ×100	Residual ×100
1	24150	55.00	33.27	0.01	0.00	0.00
2	26624	67.00	63.24	0.00	0.00	0.00
3	50010	81.00	95.12	0.00	0.00	0.00
4	48608	67.00	90.39	0.00	0.00	0.00
5	56676	98.00	86.48	4.37	−0.15	1.94
6	52526	126.00	119.28	−4.00	−0.20	−2.68
7	88855	132.00	141.67	−1.03	−0.03	−0.53
8	97145	139.00	137.03	−6.32	−0.55	−4.42
9	95378	141.00	130.55	−3.23	−0.10	−2.74
10	98783	161.00	135.12	3.29	−0.12	−1.65
11	91613	158.00	128.72	0.49	0.24	−1.82
12	92427	156.00	122.53	−0.36	0.13	3.20
13	83392	154.00	116.54	0.00	0.00	0.00
14	90072	149.00	111.56	0.00	0.00	0.00
17	77048	140.00	99.49	0.00	0.00	0.00
18	101445	143.00	94.59	2.63	0.30	3.81
19	88150	147.00	90.22	0.00	0.00	0.00
20	111575	148.00	86.13	5.58	0.18	1.47
SSR				0.0136	0.0001	0.0710
SE				0.0275	0.0018	0.0199

[a] Overall $SSR = 0.0208$, overall $SE = 0.00196$, critical value $\bar{\sigma} = 0.0005$.

Secondly note how small the perturbations are. The largest perturbation is in the period 8 fuel usage, and this is only about 6.3 per cent. These perturbations seem to be quite small relative to my beliefs about the likely magnitude of the measurement error associated with these data.

We can be more precise about this statement. Following the discussion in section 2, I have computed the critical value of σ outlined there. The 95% critical value of a chi-squared variable with 54 degrees of freedom is about 44. This implies that $\bar{\sigma}$ is 0.0005. This means that one would have to believe the data were measured with a standard error of *less than* 0.05 percent in order to reject the null hypothesis of cost minimization. This seems a substantially smaller measurement error than anyone would be likely to attribute to these data. On these grounds I am willing to accept the hypothesis of cost minimization.

How do these data fare when confronted with standard sorts of parametric methods? To answer this question I found the minimal perturbation of the data to satisfy factor demands derived from Cobb–Douglas and CES production functions. The fit is described in table 3. Note that in the Cobb–Douglas case the sum of squared residuals is over 500 times as large as the perturbation needed to satisfy minimization alone! The CES case fares somewhat better,

Table 2

Pittsburg.[a]

Year	Actual fuel	Actual labor	Actual capital	Residual ×100	Residual ×100	Residual ×100
1	52336	100.00	110.22	0.57	0.01	0.40
2	76601	135.00	138.15	0.00	0.00	0.00
3	70065	135.00	131.62	−4.80	−0.12	−2.92
4	63000	129.00	125.07	0.00	0.00	0.00
5	69602	129.00	116.44	0.96	0.03	0.52
6	55398	134.00	110.25	2.32	−1.62	−4.75
7	70906	127.00	104.78	3.86	0.09	1.85
8	52797	132.00	99.67	3.41	1.62	3.77
9	61286	133.00	94.15	0.00	0.00	0.00
10	37792	139.00	89.42	0.00	0.00	0.00
11	44233	152.00	85.16	0.00	0.00	0.00
12	47155	157.00	81.08	0.00	0.00	0.00
13	108952	163.00	146.41	−1.01	−0.03	−0.21
14	84772	170.00	145.69	0.00	0.00	0.00
17	105566	185.00	150.17	0.67	0.47	2.51
18	105935	199.00	155.81	0.37	−0.47	−2.39
19	82745	204.00	150.76	0.00	0.00	0.00
20	86842	209.00	142.48	0.00	−0.00	0.00
SSR				0.0058	0.0006	0.0061
SE				0.0179	0.0056	0.0184

[a] Overall $SSR = 0.0125$, overall $SE = 0.0152$, critical value $\bar{\sigma} = 0.0002$,

Table 3

Comparison with parametric method.

Plant	*SSR*		
	Cobb–Douglas	CES	Non-parametric
Alamitos	12.359	1.0697	0.0208
Pittsburg	6.444	0.8704	0.0125

with a *SSR* only 50 times as large as that needed in the non-parametric case. Even so this perturbation seems quite large. The conclusion seems to be that the data are consistent with cost minimization – but not Cobb–Douglas or CES cost minimization.

7. Objections and replies

After describing the above method, I have often encountered various objections to it. In this section I will describe several of the most common objections and my replies.

(1) *You have specified error terms only on the quantity terms; the price terms may also be measured with error.*

I agree. It would be desirable to incorporate error terms on the prices as well. However, note that the resulting programming problem would then have non-linear constraints and thus be considerably more difficult to solve. Furthermore, note that standard regression methods typically specify that regressors are non-stochastic. If one is estimating conditional factor demand equations, this means that price and output variables are hypothesized to be measured without error, and only factor demands themselves are assumed to be measured with error – exactly as specified here.

(2) *Simply because you fail to reject the null hypothesis doesn't mean that the data were generated by optimization.*

Of course not. If we fail to reject the null hypothesis then we have simply stated that the observed departures from the model are not extremely unlikely given the null hypothesis. That is exactly what is done in ordinary statistical hypothesis testing.

(3) *It would be useful to have a measure of the power of this test.*

Absolutely. But of course the power of a test *depends* on the specific alternative hypothesis. Given some reasonable alternative and the distribution of the errors it would be possible to compute the probability that the proposed test would be satisfied. This would almost certainly have to be done by Monte Carlo methods, since I see little hope of an analytic solution. However, by way of comparison, let me note that it is quite rare that one sees power reported in parametric econometric studies.

(4) *The fact that one needs to specify the error variance effectively renders this approach worthless.*

I think not. Rather than speculate idly on this point, it is worth considering the particular example presented above. Does anyone really believe that the factor demand data described in table 1 were measured with a standard error of less than 0.05 percent? If not, the procedures outlined above indicate that the departures from cost minimizing behavior depicted in that table are not statistically significant. This seems to me to be a perfectly satisfactory statement. Furthermore, specifying the likely magnitude of the measurement error seems to me to be much *less difficult* a task than specifying a plausible functional form for a production function, as is required in the conventional approach.

And of course, one may be able to construct plausible estimates or bounds on the error variance by other means. One obvious choice is to use the standard errors that are generated by parametric methods. Moreover, Epstein and Yatchew (1984) have suggested a method of estimating σ that is consistent under certain hypotheses about the family of functional forms that could have generated the data. If the Epstein–Yatchew method works well in small samples, it may eliminate this objection entirely.

(5) *It is difficult to argue that we know enough to specify the way disturbances enter the demand equations and can specify a parametric form of the distribution while at the same time arguing that we do not know enough to specify the form for the demand system.*

I find the specification of a Normal error term much less difficult than the specification of a particular parametric form for technology or demand. In any event parametric studies usually require a specification of *both* the functional form of the demand relationship and the parametric form of the distribution.

(6) *What is the relationship of this approach to the literature on frontier estimation?*[6]

In this paper I have specified the error term as a measurement error associated with the factor demands, since in my opinion these are the variables that are the most poorly measured in this sort of study. However, one could consider alternative approaches in a non-parametric context as well.

For example, suppose that we thought that the output levels (y_i) were underestimates of the 'true' output frontier levels (y_i^*). That is,

$$y_i = y_i^* + \varepsilon_i, \qquad i = 1, \ldots, n,$$

where $\varepsilon_i \leq 0$. In this case we might find a minimal perturbation of the observations that would satisfy WACM, while respecting the sign restriction on the perturbations implied by the non-positivity of the error term. Under the null hypothesis this would be a lower bound on the actual perturbation and all the analysis of this paper applies. The only difficulty with this approach is that the minimization problem does not take a standard form.

8. Summary

I have shown how one can extend the non-parametric methods described in the introduction to cases involving measurement error. The logic of the approach involves asking for the minimal perturbation of the data that satisfies the inequality relations implied by the underlying theory. This sort of test can be given an interpretation consistent with the classical theory of statistical hypothesis testing. Furthermore, the methods are practical from the computational perspective and can be applied in a wide variety of stochastic specifications.

[6] For a survey of frontier estimation, see Aigner and Schmidt (1980).

References

Afriat, S.N., 1967, The construction of a utility function from expenditure data, International Economic Review 8, 67–77.

Afriat, S.N., 1972, Efficiency estimation of production functions, International Economic Review 13, 568–598.

Afriat, S.N., 1976, The combinatorial theory of demand (Input–Output Publ. Co., London).

Aigner, Dennis and Peter Schmidt, 1980, Specification and estimation of frontier production functions, profit and cost functions, Journal of Econometrics 13.

Diewert, Erwin, 1973, Afriat and revealed preference theory, Review of Economic Studies 40, 419–426.

Diewert, Erwin and Celik Parkan, 1978, Tests for consistency of consumer data and nonparametric index numbers, Working paper 78-27 (University of British Columbia, Vancouver).

Diewert, Erwin and Celik Parkan, 1980, Linear programming tests of regularity conditions for production functions, in: W. Eichorn, K. Henn, K. Neumann, R. Shepherd, eds. Quantitative studies on production and prices (Physica-Verlag) forthcoming.

Epstein, Lawrence and Adonnis Yatchew, 1984, Nonparametric hypothesis testing procedures and applications to demand analysis, this issue.

Hanoch, Giore and Michael Rothschild, 1972, Testing the assumptions of production theory, Journal of Political Economy 80, 256–275.

Murtagh, Bruce and Michael Saunders, 1967, MINOS: large scale nonlinear programming system (for problems with linear constraints), Department of Operations Research technical report SOL 77-9 (Stanford University, Stanford, CA).

Varian, Hal, 1982a, Nonparametric methods in demand analysis, Economics Letters 9, 23–29.

Varian, Hal, 1982b, The nonparametric approach to demand analysis, Econometrica 50, 945–973.

Varian, Hal, 1982c, Trois evaluations de l'impact 'social' d'un changement de prix, Cahiers du Seminar d'Econométrie 24, 13–30.

Varian, Hal, 1983a, Nonparametric tests of consumer behavior, Review of Economic Studies 50, 99–110.

Varian, Hal, 1983b, Nonparametric tests of models of investor behavior, Journal of Financial and Quantitative Analysis 18, 269–278.

Varian, Hal, 1984, The nonparametric approach to production analysis, Econometrica 52, 579–597.

Woo, Chi-Keung, 1982, The nonparametric approach to production analysis: A case study on a regulated electric utility, Ph.D. thesis (University of California, Davis, CA).

ENTRY AND EMPIRICAL DEMAND AND SUPPLY ANALYSIS FOR COMPETITIVE INDUSTRIES*

William VELOCE

Brock University, St. Catharines, Ont., Canada L2S 3A1

Arnold ZELLNER

University of Chicago, Chicago, IL 60637, USA

Since many theoretical and empirical models of competitive industries do not take appropriate account of entry, several deterministic demand, supply and entry (DSE) models are formulated and analyzed. The supply equation in these models is derived assuming profit maximization, identical production functions and competitive conditions for producer. Models are solved to yield equilibrium price, output, and number of producers and properties of solutions are analyzed. Annual data for the Canadian household furniture industry are employed to investigate and estimate various forms of supply and entry equations.

1. Introduction

In this paper we consider the problem of analyzing a competitive industry with entry. We formulate several variants of simple demand, supply and entry (DSE) models and analyze their properties. The emphasis will be placed on simple models based on identical firms with Cobb–Douglas production functions since even this simple case does not appear to have been analyzed explicitly in the literature. Future work will deal with analysis of broader models drawing on our experience in analyzing the 'simple' cases considered in this paper.

It is generally recognized that entry and exit of firms play an important role in Marshallian models of competitive industries. Attempts to formulate and estimate entry equations have been reported in Mansfield (1962), Peltzman (1965) and Telser et al. (1975), but these workers have not analyzed the dynamics of an industry DSE model. Brock (1972) presents an interesting perfect foresight model with entry. In addition, Prescott and Townsend (1980) in their ingenious multi-agent decision-theoretic model of a competitive in-

*A preliminary version of this paper was presented at the Conference on New Approaches to Modeling, Specification Selection, and Econometric Inference, University of Texas at Austin, May 10–11, 1984. We thank the participants and the Journal's referees for several helpful comments. Research financed in part by the National Science Foundation and by income from the H.G.B. Alexander Endowment Fund, Graduate School of Business, University of Chicago.

dustry allow for changes in total industry capital but do not explicitly model entry or exit. The fishery economics literature on entry has been reviewed in Berck and Perloff (1984) who provide interesting models of fishery industries with entry and biological population equations included. In Veloce and Zellner (1984), a simple three-equation DSE model is analyzed and some results relevant for applied econometric modeling of a competitive industry are noted. In this last paper, it was pointed out that many, including Muth (1961), have modeled a competitive industry with the number of firms assumed constant, an appropriate assumption for short-run analysis but not for intermediate or long-run analysis. On the other hand, in most empirical, econometric models of competitive industries, the number of firms in operation does not appear as a variable and no explicit allowance is made for entry and exit.

In the present paper, the analysis in Veloce and Zellner (1984) is extended. In particular, several formulations of three-equation DSE models are given and attention is directed toward establishing some of their dynamic properties. Also, some estimates of supply and entry relations for the Canadian household furniture industry are presented and discussed.

2. Deterministic demand, supply and entry (DSE) models

In this section, building on our previous work, we develop deterministic, continuous time DSE models for a competitive industry with identical, single-plant firms having two inputs – labor, L, and capital services, K – and Cobb – Douglas production functions for homogeneous output. That is output q for the individual firm is given by

$$q = AL^{\alpha}K^{\beta}, \qquad A > 0, \quad 0 < \alpha, \beta < 1, \quad 0 < \alpha + \beta < 1, \tag{1}$$

and firm profits by

$$\pi = pq - wL - rK, \tag{2}$$

where p, w and r are the real per-unit prices of output, labor and capital, respectively. The necessary conditions for profit maximization lead to $wL = \alpha pq$ and $rK = \beta pq$ and thus (2) can be expressed as

$$\pi = (1 - \alpha - \beta)s, \tag{3}$$

where $s = pq$ is sales. Also, since $L = \alpha pq/w$ and $K = \beta pq/r$, from (1) the firm's supply function is

$$q = A_1 p^{(\alpha+\beta)/\theta} w^{-\alpha/\theta} r^{-\beta/\theta}, \tag{4a}$$

or

$$s = pq = A_1 p^{1/\theta} w^{-\alpha/\theta} r^{-\beta/\theta}, \tag{4b}$$

where $A_1 \equiv (A\alpha^{\alpha}\beta^{\beta})^{1/\theta}$ and $\theta \equiv 1 - \alpha - \beta$. Then industry supply, expressed in terms of industry sales, S, where $S = Npq$, with N = number firms, is

$$S = NA_1 p^{1/\theta} w^{-\alpha/\theta} r^{-\beta/\theta}. \tag{5}$$

On taking the logarithms of both sides of (5) and differentiating with respect to time, (5) becomes

$$\dot{S}/S = \dot{N}/N + (1/\theta)\dot{p}/p - (\alpha/\theta)\dot{w}/w - (\beta/\theta)\dot{r}/r, \tag{6}$$

where $\dot{x} \equiv \mathrm{d}x/\mathrm{d}t$. Eq. (6) is the industry supply function expressed in terms of industry sales, $S = Npq$.

As regards the industry demand function, we assume

$$Q = Bp^{-\eta} x_1^{\eta_1} x_2^{\eta_2} \dots x_k^{\eta_k}, \qquad \eta, B > 0, \tag{7}$$

where Q is aggregate demand, $-\eta$ is the price elasticity of demand, the x_i's represent income and other variables and the η_i's their respective elasticities. We express (7) in terms of industry sales, $S = pQ$ as follows:

$$S = Bp^{1-\eta} x_1^{\eta_1} x_2^{\eta_2} \dots x_k^{\eta_k}, \tag{8}$$

or

$$\dot{S}/S = (1-\eta)\dot{p}/p + \sum_{i=1}^{k} \eta_i \dot{x}_i/x_i. \tag{9}$$

As regards entry, since as Friedman (1976, p. 103) states, '...a thoroughly satisfactory theory explaining the determinants of the number or structure of firms does not exist', we initially posit a net entry equation in the following form:

$$\dot{N}/N = \gamma(F_e - \Pi), \qquad \gamma > 0, \tag{10}$$

where Π is aggregate profits and $F_e = F_e(t)$ represents aggregate long-run equilibrium profits taking account of the costs of entry. If $\Pi < F_e$ entry occurs, while if $\Pi > F_e$ exit (negative entry) occurs. From (3) $\Pi = N\pi = (1\text{-}\alpha - \beta)Ns = \theta S$ and thus (10) can be written as

$$\dot{N}/N = \gamma(F_e - \theta S). \tag{11}$$

From above, the three-equation DSE model is given by eqs. (6), (9) and (11), that is:

Demand

$$\dot{S}/S = (1-\eta)\dot{p}/p + \sum_{i=1}^{k} \eta_i \dot{x}_i/x_i,$$

Supply

$$\dot{S}/S = \dot{N}/N + (1/\theta)\dot{p}p - (\alpha/\theta)\dot{w}/w - (\beta/\theta)\dot{r}/r,$$

Entry

$$\dot{N}/N = \gamma(F_e - \theta S),$$

with $0 < \theta < 1$.

From these three equations, we obtain the following non-linear differential equation for S:

$$\dot{S}/S = a(1 - S/F) + g, \tag{12}$$

where

$$a = -\gamma\theta^2 F(1-\eta)/[1-\theta(1-\eta)],$$

$$F = F_e/\theta,$$

$$g = \left[(1-\eta)(\alpha\dot{w}/w + \beta\dot{r}/r) + \sum_{i=1}^{k}\eta_i\dot{x}_i/x_i\right] \Big/ [1-\theta(1-\eta)].$$

If $g = 0$ and F is assumed constant, (12) becomes $\dot{S} = aS(1 - S/F)$ and $\dot{S} = 0$ for $S = 0$ and $S = F$, two stationary solutions. If $a > 0$, the stationary solution $S = F$ is stable since for $S > F$, $\dot{S} < 0$, and for $S < F$, $\dot{S} > 0$. Also, $S = 0$ is an unstable, stationary solution. For $a < 0$, $S = F$ is an unstable, stationary solution, and $S = 0$ is a stable, stationary solution. The condition $a > 0$ will obtain if and only if $\eta > 1$, that is the demand function in (7) is price-elastic. This surprising and unexpected result can be understood as follows. Suppose that N_0 is the initial number of firms and that $F_e - \theta S > 0$ in (11). As the number of firms grows from N_0 to N_1, the supply curve $S(N_0)$ shifts to $S(N_1)$ producing a fall in price from p_0 to p_1. If, for example, demand is of unitary elasticity ($\eta = 1$), sales revenue will remain unchanged as price falls. Thus there will be no change in $F_e - \theta S$ and there will be continued growth in the number of firms, an unstable result. If demand is inelastic $(0 < \eta < 1)$, as price falls from p_0 to p_1, S decreases and $F - \theta S_0$ will increase in value, another unstable result. Finally, if demand is elastic $(\eta > 1)$, then S rises as price falls and $F_e - \theta S$ diminishes in value which slows the rate of change of the number of firms. Thus the value of the price elasticity parameter η in (7) plays a key role in determining stability characteristics of solutions. Below an alternative formulation of the demand function will be considered which is not as restrictive as (7).

With $a > 0$, the solution to the homogeneous differential equation for industry sales, $\dot{S} = aS(1 - S/F)$, with F assumed constant, is

$$S(t) = F/(1 - [1 - F/S(0)]\mathrm{e}^{-at}), \qquad a, F > 0, \tag{13}$$

a form of the logistic function where $S(0)$ is industry sales at $t = 0$. Note that as $t \to \infty$, $S(T) \to F$ – the stationary, stable limiting solution. Also, if $F/S(0) > 1$, $S(t)$ approaches F from below, while if $F/S(0) < 1$, $S(t)$ approaches F from above.

The solution for S in (13) can be substituted in (11) to obtain a solution for $\dot{N}/N$, the rate of change of the number of firms. Also from (9) with all the $\dot{x}_i = 0$, $\dot{p}/p = 1/(1 - \eta)]\dot{S}/S = [a/(1 - \eta)](1 - S/F)$ provides the path for $\dot{p}/p$ on substituting the solution for S in (13).

If in (12), $g = g_c$, a non-zero constant, then $\dot{S} = aS(1 - S/F) + g_c S = a_c S(1 - S/F_c)$, where $a_c = a + g_c$ and $F_c = (1 + g_c/a)F$. Provided that $a_c > 0$, the limiting stationary solution $S = F_c = (1 + g_c/a)F$ is a stable solution. Given $g_c > 0$, $a_c = a + g_c > 0$ can hold for demand being elastic or inelastic, a relaxation of the condition on the elasticity of demand for stability of the solution of (12) with $g = 0$.

When g in (12) is a function of time, say $g = g(t)$, we rewrite (12) as

$$\dot{S} = aS(1 - S/F) + Sg = qS(1 - aS/qF), \tag{14}$$

where $q = q(t) = a + g(t)$. This differential equation is a special form of Bernoulli's differential equation – see, e.g. Rektorys (1969, p. 746). On making a change of variable, $Z = 1/S$, (14) becomes $\dot{Z} = -qZ + a/F$, and it solution, obtained by methods described in Rektorys (1969, pp. 743–746), is

$$Z(t) = (a/F)\int \exp\left\{\int q(t)\,\mathrm{d}t\right\}\mathrm{d}t \times \exp\left\{-\int q(t)\,\mathrm{d}t\right\}$$

$$+ c\exp\left\{-\int q\,\mathrm{d}t\right\}, \tag{15}$$

where c is a constant of integration and the solution to (14) is $S(t) = 1/Z(t)$. This result permits solution of (14) for many choices of the function $g(t)$. If

$g(t) = 0$, this procedure yields the logistic function, shown in (13) as the solution.

As an example illustrating this solution procedure, assume that $q(t) = a + 1/(t+b)$, $b > 0$. Then

$$\int q(t)\,\mathrm{d}t = at + \ln(t+b),$$

$$\int \exp\left\{\int q(t)\,\mathrm{d}t\right\}\mathrm{d}t = \int (t+b)\mathrm{e}^{at}\mathrm{d}t = \mathrm{e}^{at}\left[(at-1)/a^2 + b/a\right],$$

$$Z(t) = 1/F\left[1 - 1/a(t+b)\right] + c/(t+b)\mathrm{e}^{-at},$$

and $S(t) = 1/Z(t)$ is the solution. As $t \to \infty$, $S(t) \to F$, the limiting solution for $g = 0$ which is reasonable since $g(t) = 1/(t+b) \to 0$ as $t \to \infty$.

While we do not analyze cases in which $g(t)$ is an oscillatory function, it is clear that oscillations in $g(t)$, produced by oscillations in the rates of change of income and factor prices, which are components of $g(t)$, will induce oscillations in the solution. However, this is not the only way in which solutions can be oscillatory. As is well known – see, e.g., Cunningham (1958, pp. 250–253) – if we formulated our DSE model as a mixed difference-differential equation model, then solutions can have oscillatory features even when g does not. Also, if we used discounted future profits $\int_t^\infty \Pi(t)\mathrm{e}^{-\rho t}\mathrm{d}t$, with $\rho > 0$, in our entry equation, the dynamic properties of the model will be altered.

As remarked above, use of the log-log demand equation in (7) results in a stringent condition on the price elasticity of demand for reasonable solutions to be stable when $g = 0$. Of course the constant elasticity demand function (7) is rather special. Thus we consider the following variable elasticity demand function:

$$\log Q = \delta_0 + \delta_1/p, \qquad \delta_0, \delta_1 > 0, \tag{16}$$

for which the price elasticity is given by $-\delta_1/p$. Thus with (16), as price falls demand becomes more elastic. From (16) with $S = pQ$ and $z = 1/p$, $\log S = -\log z + \delta_0 + \delta_1 z$ or

$$\dot{S}/S = (\delta_1 z - 1)\dot{z}/z. \tag{17}$$

On combining (17) with eq. (6), with $\dot{w}/w = \dot{r}/r = 0$, and eq. (11), the following differential equation is obtained:

$$\dot{z} = \gamma\theta^2\left(F_z - \delta_2\mathrm{e}^{\delta_1 z}\right)/(1 - \theta + \theta\delta_1 z), \tag{18}$$

where $\delta_2 \equiv \mathrm{e}^{\delta_0}$. Since $0 < \theta < 1$ and $\delta_1 > 0$, the denominator on the right of

(18) is positive for $z = 1/p > 0$. Stationary solutions, if they exist, are given by solutions to $Fz - \delta_2 e^{\delta_1 z} = 0$. If F is assumed constant, there will usually be two stationary solutions z_1 and z_2 with $0 < z_1 < z_2 < \infty$. Phase diagram considerations indicate that z_1 is unstable, while z_2 is stable. Thus with the demand function in (16), a reasonable stationary, stable solution for $z = 1/p$ emerges without the need for a rigid condition on the price elasticity of demand. Of course, it would be of great interest to pursue this type of analysis with other assumed forms for the demand function.

To this point all analyses have been based on a particular form of the entry equation, namely that shown in (11). As remarked above, economic theory unfortunately does not provide very much guidance in formulating an entry equation. However, it is of interest to consider the following alternative formulations. Let Q^* and q^* be the equilibrium total quantity of output and equilibrium firm output, respectively. Then the equilibrium number of firms in the industry, N^*, is $N^* = Q^*/q^*$. Now assume that the entry relation takes the following form:

$$\dot{N}/N = b(N^* - N), \qquad b > 0. \tag{19}$$

With N^* assumed constant, (19) yields

$$\dot{N} = b_1 N(1 - N/N^*), \tag{20}$$

where $b_1 = bN^*$. It is seen that there are two stationary solutions $N_1 = 0$ and $N_2 = N^*$, with the latter being a stable solution. The solution to (20) is in the logistic form which can be inserted in the industry supply and demand equations to determine equilibrium price and output. Further, as noted in connection with (14), non-homogeneous forms of (20) can be considered.

Another simple discrete form of the entry equation is

$$r_{Nt} = \phi(r_{N^*t} - r_{Nt-1}), \qquad 0 < \phi < 1, \tag{21}$$

where $r_{Nt} = (1 - L)\log N_t$ and $r_{N^*t} = (1 - L)\log N_t^*$, where L is the lag operator and $N_t^* = Q_t^*/q_t^*$. A more general form of (21) involves replacing the scalar parameter ϕ with a polynomial lag operator, say $\phi(L) = w(L)/\delta(L)$, where $w(L)$ and $\delta(L)$ are finite polynomials in L, that is

$$r_{Nt} = \frac{w(L)}{\delta(L)}(r_{N^*t} - r_{Nt-1}). \tag{22}$$

By relating r_{N^*t} to observable variables, various forms of (22) can be investigated empirically.

In summary, it is the case that a variety of possible DSE models can be formulated. Indeed, the range of possibilities is rather broad including different forms for the production, demand and entry equations. Also, a variety of lagged responses may be plausible. In addition, it is possible to utilize future discounted profits in the entry equation (11) rather than current profits. In view of these many possible variants of our model, we have decided to formulate relatively simple models in approaching our data and to try to learn about possible inadequacies of these formulations in the sequential iterative process described in Zellner (1975, 1979). In the next section such formulations are described and analyzed with annual data relating to the Canadian household furniture industry.

3. Empirical analyses and results

In our empirical analyses, we shall estimate variants of supply and entry equations for the Canadian household furniture industry. One main objective is to provide evidence for the need to include the number of firms in operation in the industry supply function and to demonstrate the effects of omitting this variable as has been done in many previous analyses of industry supply functions. A second objective is to provide estimates of entry relations for the Canadian household furniture industry. In the course of our analyses, we shall utilize several alternative estimation procedures for structural econometric equations.

The variables which we employ in our analyses are defined below, with subscript t denoting a variable's value in year t, and referring to the Canadian household furniture industry:[1]

Q_t = real value of industry shipments (nominal values deflated by a household furniture price index),
P_t = real price of household furniture,
w_t = real wage rate per hour for the industry's production workers,
N_t = number of establishments in the industry at mid-year (average of beginning and end of year values),
r_t = real rate of interest measured by the difference between the nominal rate on ten-year Canadian industrial bonds and the rate of change of the Canadian CPI,
S_t = total industry real sales ($= P_t Q_t$).

In table 1 are shown estimates of the industry supply function which relate $\ln Q_t$, the natural logarithm of real industry shipments to other variables, including and excluding the number of firms variable, $\ln N_t$, based on annual data, 1957–81, 25 observations. For each of the three methods of estimation employed, ordinary least squares (OLS), Bayesian minimum expected loss

[1] The industry data for SIC 2611 and 2619 from statistics Canada, catalogue 35-211 were combined to yield our household furniture industry data.

Table 1

Estimates of the Canadian household furniture industry's supply function including and excluding the number of establishments, annual data, 1957–81 ($n = 25$).

Variable and associated statistics[a]	OLS[b]		MELO[b]		2SLS[b]	
	(1)	(2)	(3)	(4)	(5)	(6)
1	−10.1	6.29	−8.69	11.41	−9.21	10.75
	(5.93)	(5.71)	(6.13)	(6.03)	(8.28)	(8.11)
$\ln P_t$	3.42	1.30	3.10	0.15	3.22	0.30
	(1.33)	(1.29)	(1.38)	(0.14)	(1.86)	(1.83)
t	0.058	0.035	0.056	0.029	0.056	0.030
	(0.012)	(0.012)	(0.012)	(0.012)	(0.014)	(0.014)
$\ln W_t$	−0.13	0.49	−0.05	0.76	−0.078	−0.73
	(0.40)	(0.38)	(0.41)	(0.40)	(0.50)	(0.49)
$\ln r_t$	−0.35	−0.11	−0.35	−0.81	−0.35	−0.084
	(0.17)	(0.16)	(0.17)	(0.17)	(0.17)	(0.17)
$\ln N_t$	1.0	—	1.0	—	1.0	—
$\hat{\rho}_1$[c]	0.47	0.58	0.49	0.57	0.21	0.54
	(0.20)	(0.20)	(0.20)	(0.20)	(0.20)	(0.20)
$\hat{\rho}_2$	−0.13	−0.13	−0.10	−0.13	0.14	0.28
	(0.20)	(0.20)	(0.20)	(0.20)	(0.20)	(0.20)
$\hat{\rho}_3$	−0.30	−0.56	−0.28	−0.62	0.06	−0.08
	(0.20)	(0.20)	(0.20)	(0.20)	(0.20)	(0.20)
$\hat{\sigma}$[d]	0.077	0.075	0.078	0.076	0.078	0.076

[a] See text for definitions of variables. The supply variable is $\ln O_t$, the natural logarithm of annual real value of shipments.

[b] OLS ≡ ordinary least squares, MELO ≡ Bayesian minimum expected loss, 2SLS ≡ two-stage least squares. Figures in parentheses are standard errors. For MELO and 2SLS estimates, the instrumental variables used were 1, t, $\ln W_t$, $\ln r_t$, $\ln N_{t-1}$, $\ln N_{t-2}$, and $\ln r_{t-1}$.

[c] ρ_i, $i = 1, 2, 3$, are sample residual autocorrelations.

[d] $\hat{\sigma}$ = estimate of disturbance standard deviation.

(MELO), and two-stage least squares (2SLS), there are striking differences in the estimation results when the number of firms variable is included or excluded. Viewing the OLS estimates in columns (1) and (2), it is seen that including the variable $\ln N_t$ with a coefficient equal to 1.0, as suggested by eq. (5) above, the estimates of the coefficients of $\ln w_t$ and $\ln r_t$ are negative, as expected on the basis of theoretical considerations. When the variable $\ln N_t$ is left out, the results in column (2) include a positive estimate, 0.49, for the coefficient of $\ln w_t$, contrary to theoretical expectations. Also on comparing the OLS results in columns (1) and (2), it is seen that the point estimates of the intercepts, price and time trend coefficients differ considerably. The disturbance terms' sample autocorrelations, $\hat{\rho}_1$, $\hat{\rho}_2$ and $\hat{\rho}_3$, are somewhat different, with those in column (2) being larger for $\hat{\rho}_1$ and $\hat{\rho}_3$. While these conclusions must be tempered in view of the large standard errors and the fact that OLS produces inconsistent coefficient estimates and standard errors, the differences in estimation results in columns (1) and (2) are very striking.

To obtain consistent estimation results, two methods were employed – the MELO estimation procedure [Zellner (1978), Zellner and Park (1979) and Park (1982)] and the well known 2SLS procedure with results reported in columns (3)–(6) of table 1. Comparisons of the results in columns (3) and (4) and (5) and (6) show that leaving out the variable $\ln N_t$ produces major differences in the estimation results. For example, when $\ln N_t$ is left out, both the MELO and 2SLS estimates indicate large positive estimates of the coefficient of $\ln w_t$, contrary to theoretical expectations. Also, there are large differences in the estimates of other parameters. Again though, the precision of estimation is not very high, probably because of the small sample of 25 observations and of highly correlated exogenous variables. However, there is a strong indication that including the variable $\ln N_t$ leads to some improvement of the estimation results.

In the results reported in table 1, no allowance was made for inventory considerations. The supply variable used in the calculations underlying table 1 is real industry shipments, Q_t, which is related to output, X_t, by $X_t = Q_t + \Delta H_t$, where $\Delta H_t = H_t - H_{t-1}$ is the annual change in inventory stocks. In the theoretical section, the analysis was in terms of output, X_t. If $\Delta H_t = 0$, $X_t = Q_t$, but if $\Delta H_t \neq 0$, there is a divergence between X_t and Q_t. In view of these considerations, we write $X_t/N_t = Q_t/N_t + \Delta H_t/N_t$ and $y_t = \ln(X_t/N_t) = \ln(Q_t/N_t) + \ln(1 + \Delta H_t/Q_t)$. With data on ΔH_t, Q_t and N_t, observations on y_t were constructed and used to obtain the following estimates:

OLS

$$\underset{}{\hat{y}_t} = \underset{(5.99)}{-10.60} \underset{(1.35)}{+3.53} \ln P_t \underset{(0.012)}{+0.058}t \underset{(0.40)}{-0.17} \ln w_t \underset{(0.17)}{-0.35} \ln r_t,$$

$$\underset{(0.20)}{\hat{\rho}_1 = 0.45}, \quad \underset{(0.20)}{\hat{\rho}_2 = -0.16}, \quad \underset{(0.20)}{\hat{\rho}_3 = -0.30}, \quad \hat{\sigma} = 0.078,$$

MELO

$$\hat{y}_t = \underset{(6.26)}{-8.77} \underset{(1.41)}{+3.11} \ln P_t \underset{(0.012)}{+0.056}t \underset{(0.41)}{-0.072} \ln w_t \underset{(0.17)}{-0.34} \ln r_t,$$

$$\underset{(0.20)}{\hat{\rho}_1 = 0.47}, \quad \underset{(0.20)}{\hat{\rho}_2 = -0.13}, \quad \underset{(0.20)}{\hat{\rho}_3 = 0.28}, \quad \hat{\sigma} = 0.078.$$

These OLS and MELO estimates are not far different from those in columns (1) and (3) of table 1, probably reflecting the high correlation, 0.99, between y_t and $\ln(Q_t/N_t)$. Further work in progress to incorporate inventory considerations more explicitly indicates that lagged price may enter the industry supply equation, an effect which may help to reduce the high first-order disturbance autocorrelation. However, because the explanatory variables are highly correlated, coefficient estimates are not very precise and results are sensitive to changes in the model. Use of informative prior distributions and joint estimation of supply and factor demand equations, as in Zellner and Richard (1973), may be worthwhile.

We now turn to consider estimates of variants of the net entry relation shown in table 2. For the three variants shown, the dependent variable is $\Delta \ln N_t = \ln N_t - \ln N_{t-1}$, the proportionate rate of change of N_t, and least

Table 2

Least squares estimates of net entry equations for the Canadian household furniture industry, annual data, 1957–81.

Variable[a]	Coefficient estimates and associated statistics[b]		
	(1)	(2)	(3)
1	0.0019 (0.008)	0.29 (0.14)	0.37 (0.13)
$\Delta \ln N_{t-1}$	0.95 (0.17)	0.89 (0.16)	0.85 (0.14)
$\Delta \ln N_{t-2}$	−0.65 (0.17)	−0.52 (0.17)	−0.53 (0.15)
t	—	0.009 (0.004)	0.16 (0.005)
$\ln r_{t-1}$	—	−0.205 (0.095)	−0.20 (0.08)
S_{t-1}	—	—	-0.43×10^{-8} (0.18×10^{-8})
$\hat{\sigma}$	0.0378	0.0352	0.0309
$\bar{R}^2$	0.6115	0.6626	0.7389

[a] The dependent variable is $\Delta \ln N_t$, where N_t is the number of establishments in year t and $\Delta = 1 - L$ is the first difference operator. r_{t-1} and S_{t-1} are the lagged real rate of interest and lagged real sales, respectively. Standard errors are shown in parentheses.

[b] The first three sample residual autocorrelation coefficients are (with a large sample standard error of 0.23 in each case):

	Eq. (1)	Eq. (2)	Eq. (3)
$\hat{\rho}_1$	0.20	0.17	−0.05
$\hat{\rho}_2$	−0.23	−0.26	−0.49
$\hat{\rho}_3$	0.02	0.10	0.08

squares coefficient estimates and associated statistics are presented. In column (1) of table 2, a simple second-order autoregression for $\Delta \ln N_t$ was fitted. Additional variables, t, $\ln r_{t-1}$ and S_{t-1}, were added to the relation with results shown in columns (2) and (3). The results in column (3) indicate a positive trend effect, and negative effects of $\ln r_{t-1}$ and S_{t-1} on the rate of entry. Heuristically, high r_{t-1}, the lagged real rate of interest may discourage entry. Also, past real sales, S_{t-1}, in a discrete form of eq. (11), would be expected to exert a negative influence on $\Delta \ln N_t$, a discrete approximation to $\dot{N}/N$ in (11). Further work is in progress to appraise alternative formulations of the entry relation. However, the present analysis does indicate that the considerable variation in N_t can in part be explained by variables suggested by economic considerations.

4. Summary and concluding remarks

In this paper we have explored several variants of an industry demand, supply and entry (DSE) model and found that it is important to take account of variation in the number of firms in formulating industry supply functions. Consideration of deterministic, dynamic DSE models led to interesting non-linear differential equations that were solved. The stability of stationary solutions was examined and in one special case involved an unusual condition on the price elasticity on demand, namely that demand be price elastic. While these analyses treated a range of models, there is room for considerable more mathematical work to explore other formulations, involving other than Cobb–Douglas technology, different forms for the entry relation, expectational effects, etc. It is our view that this work can yield very useful results.

As regards our empirical results, it was found that including the number of firms in the industry supply function produced more reasonable estimation results than were obtained when it was excluded. Further work is in progress to take better account of inventory behavior and its effects on supply as well as use of other production functions and rational expectations. However, we believe that our present results imply that it is wise to include the number of firms as a variable in a competitive industry's supply equation. Our estimation results for the industry's entry equation indicate that a second-order autoregression for $\Delta \ln N_t$, augmented to include several other variables, provides a relatively good fit to the data. Further work is needed to explore alternative variants of the entry relation and their theoretical interpretations.

In closing, it is concluded that intermediate and long-run econometric industry models which fail to take account of entry and exit of firms and the resulting impact on industry supply are in general misspecified. In the present paper, we have demonstrated that supply relations which are responsive to entry and exit of firms and entry relations can be estimated without undue difficulty and lead to better explanations of industry supply.

References

Berck, P. and J.M. Perloff, 1984, An open-access fishery with rational expectations, Econometrica 52, 489–506.

Brock, W., 1972, On models of expectations that arise from maximizing behavior of economic agents over time, Journal of Economic Theory 5, 348–376.

Cunningham, W.J., 1958, Introduction to non-linear analysis (McGraw-Hill, New York).

Friedman, M., 1976, Price theory (Aldine, Chicago, IL).

Mansfield, E., 1962, Entry, Gibrat's law, innovation, and the growth of firms, American Economic Review 52, 1023–1051.

Muth, J.F., 1961, Rational expectations and the theory of price movements, Econometrica 29, 315–355.

Park, S.B., 1982, Some sampling properties of minimum expected loss (MELO) estimators of structural coefficients, Journal of Econometrics 18, 295–311.

Peltzman, S., 1965, Entry in commercial banking, Journal of Law and Economics 8, 11–50.

Prescott, E.C. and R.M. Townsend, 1980, Equilibrium under uncertainty: Multiagent statistical decision theory, in: A. Zellner, ed., Bayesian analysis in econometrics and statistics: Essays in honor of Harold Jeffreys (North-Holland, Amsterdam) 169–194.

Rektorys, K., ed., 1969, Survey of applicable mathematics (M.I.T. Press, Cambridge, MA).

Telser, L.G., W. Best, H. Egan and H. Higginbotham, 1975, The theory of supply with applications to the ethical pharmaceutical industry, Journal of Law and Economics 18, 449–478.

Veloce, W. and A. Zellner, 1984, Modeling a competitive industry with entry: Implications for demand and supply analysis, Economics Letters 16, 71–75.

Zellner, A., 1975, Time series analysis and econometric model construction, in: R.P. Gupta, ed., Applied statistics (North-Holland, Amsterdam) 373–398.

Zellner, A., 1978, Estimation of functions of population means and regression coefficients including structural coefficients: A minimum expected loss (MELO) approach, Journal of Econometrics 8, 127–158.

Zellner, A., 1979, Statistical analysis of econometric models, Journal of the American Statistical Association, 74, 628–651.

Zellner, A. and S.B. Park, 1979, Minimum expected loss (MELO) estimators for functions of parameters and structural coefficients of econometric models, Journal of the American Statistical Association 74, 185–193.

Zellner, A. and J.F. Richard 1973, Use of prior information in the analysis and estimation of Cobb–Douglas production function models, International Economic Review 14, 107–19.

INDEX